Understanding Social Psychology Across Cultures

Understanding Social Psychology Across Cultures

Engaging With Others in a Changing World

2ND EDITION

Peter B. Smith, Ronald Fischer, Vivian L. Vignoles
and Michael Harris Bond

Los Angeles | London | New Delhi
Singapore | Washington DC

Los Angeles | London | New Delhi
Singapore | Washington DC

SAGE Publications Ltd
1 Oliver's Yard
55 City Road
London EC1Y 1SP

SAGE Publications Inc.
2455 Teller Road
Thousand Oaks, California 91320

SAGE Publications India Pvt Ltd
B 1/I 1 Mohan Cooperative Industrial Area
Mathura Road
New Delhi 110 044

SAGE Publications Asia-Pacific Pte Ltd
3 Church Street
#10-04 Samsung Hub
Singapore 049483

Editor: Michael Carmichael
Assistant editor: Keri Dickens
Production editor: Imogen Roome
Copyeditor: Audrey Scriven
Proofreader: Kate Harrison
Marketing manager: Alison Borg
Cover design: Wendy Scott
Typeset by C&M Digitals (P) Ltd, Chennai, India
Printed in India at Replika Press Pvt Ltd

Library of Congress Control Number: 2012954630

British Library Cataloguing in Publication data

A catalogue record for this book is available from
the British Library

ISBN 978-1-4462-6710-3
ISBN 978-1-4462-6711-0

Table of Contents

Authors

Peter B. Smith was born near Colchester, UK, in 1937, and obtained his PhD from Cambridge University in 1962. After working at Leeds University, he joined the University of Sussex in 1966 and never found a good reason to leave. He is currently Emeritus Professor of Social Psychology. He has studied cross-cultural aspects of leadership, conformity and informal influence processes, as well as cultural differences in styles of communication. He is the author of eight books and more than 180 other publications. He is former president of the International Association for Cross-Cultural Psychology, and has served as Editor of the *Journal of Cross-Cultural Psychology*.

Ronald Fischer was born near Leipzig in the former East Germany in 1976, and completed his doctorate in cross-cultural psychology at the University of Sussex in 2002. He is currently Reader in Psychology at the Victoria University of Wellington, New Zealand. He has spent much of his adult life exploring remote corners of the world, carrying a laptop and camera. He has broad interests concerning the interplay between culture and human functioning in diverse ecological settings, tackling these big questions by applying multivariate statistics and multilevel models. He has published more than 100 papers and book chapters, and is an Associate Editor of the *Journal of Cross-Cultural Psychology*.

Vivian L. Vignoles was born near Rochester, UK, in 1973, and obtained his PhD in social psychology at the University of Surrey in 2000. He is currently Reader in Social Psychology at the University of Sussex. His principal research interests are in self and identity processes and cross-cultural psychology, especially understanding the interplay of cultural, contextual, and motivational influences on identity construction, and he is principal investigator of the *Culture and Identity Research Network*. He has published more than 30 journal articles and book chapters and one edited book, and is an Associate Editor of the *European Journal of Social Psychology*.

Michael Harris Bond was born in Toronto, Canada, in 1944, obtaining his PhD in social psychology from Stanford University in 1970. Working first at Kwansei Gakuin University in Japan, he next joined the Chinese University of Hong Kong, where he was Professor of Social Psychology for many years. He has contributed to many aspects of cross-cultural psychology, focusing particularly on Chinese social behaviour, comparative studies of belief systems, and improvements in cross-cultural research methods. He has published more than 270 papers and books in the field. In 2009, he was appointed Chair Professor at Hong Kong Polytechnic University.

Acknowledgements

This is in essence a fourth edition of *Social Psychology Across Cultures*, first published way back in 1993, at a time when there were very few books that addressed the cultural aspects of any area of psychological investigation. Cultural change proceeds apace and we, the new range of contributing authors to this edition, have sought to keep abreast of it. With Sage, our third publisher, for the second time and again with a slightly modified title, we intend to sustain the prime intent of earlier editions. That can perhaps be best expressed as a wish to highlight and debate contemporary research-based explanations for cultural variations in social behaviour. We have made substantial changes to all chapters and have introduced much expanded coverage of the origins of culture, of methods of cross-cultural investigation, and of processes of acculturation.

We are also grateful to John Berry, Rupert Brown, Sabina Cehajic-Clancy, Peter Dorfman, Don Dutton, Matt Easterbrook, Miriam Erez, Johnny Fontaine, Nina Hansen, Çigdem Kâgitçibaşi, David Matsumoto, Ellinor Owe, Floyd Rudmin, Mary Sully de Luque, Evert van de Vliert, Nathalie van Meurs and Colleen Ward for their various helpful comments, contributions and suggestions in the preparation of this edition.

The photographs of key researchers are reproduced by permission of those portrayed. Box 1-3 is reproduced by permission of Sylvette Cormeraie and John Harper. The epigraph to Chapter 2 is reproduced by permission of Princeton University Press. Figure 2.3 is reproduced by permission of Shalom Schwartz. Figure 2.4 is reproduced by permission of Cambridge University Press and Shalom Schwartz. Figure 2.5 is reproduced by permission of Taylor-Francis LLC from Schwartz (2009); permission conveyed through Copyright Clearance Centre, Inc. Figure 3.2 is reproduced by permission of John Berry and Cambridge University Press. Figure 3.3 is reproduced by permission of Michele Gelfand and the American Association for the Advancement of Science. Figure 5.2 is reproduced by permission of Juri Allik. Figure 6.7 is reproduced by permission of David Matsumoto and Bob Willlingham. Box 7.2 is reproduced by permission of John Wiley and sons. Everyday Life Box 9.1 is reproduced by permission of Nannette Ripmeester. The information in Table 10.1 is reproduced by permission of Peter Dorfman. The items from the cultural intelligence scale quoted in Chapter 11 are reproduced by permission of Linn van Dyne. Boxes 11.1 and 11.2 are reproduced by permission of Richard Brislin. Figure 12.4 is reproduced by permission of Malcolm Evans. Figure 13.4 is reproduced by permission of U-T SanDiego. Figure 13.6 is reproduced by permission of Veronica Benet-Martinez. Table 14.1 and Figure 14.2 are reproduced by permission of Princeton University Press.

The masks shown on the cover of this book illustrate cultural variations in the ways in which humans have sometimes chosen to represent themselves to others. From top left are: Russian mask; Chinese opera mask; Japanese Noh mask; West African Ashanti mask; Native

American mask; Indonesian mask; Hindu mask of Vishnu; Mayan mask; Maori mask; Greek theatre mask; East African Masai mask; Venetian mask. Reproduced by arrangement with Shutterstock.

Peter B. Smith
Ronald Fischer
Vivian L. Vignoles
Michael Harris Bond
November 2012

SECTION 1

Establishing the Framework

1

Why Does Social Psychology Need a Cross-Cultural Perspective?

'The only true exploration, the only true fountain of delight, would not be to visit foreign lands, but to possess others' eyes, to look at the world through the eyes of others.'

(Marcel Proust, *The Prisoner and the Fugitive*, 1905)

Two English-speaking acquaintances meet on a street corner. 'How are you?', says one. 'Terrific', replies the other, 'how about you?' 'Not too bad', says the other. From this conventional interchange, we can infer that the first speaker is probably US American and the second is probably from one of the other Anglo cultures around the world, such as the UK, Australia or New Zealand. They both speak the same language, but the norms guiding opening self-presentations will differ even between these two relatively similar cultural groups. A distinctive aspect of US culture is the value placed on expressing oneself positively, which is not found to the same extent in all other parts of the world. For instance, Kitayama, Markus, Matsumoto, and Norasakkunkit (1997) found that American students reported being more often in situations that led to feeling positive about themselves, whereas Japanese students reported being more often in situations where they felt critical of themselves. Furthermore the Americans were more likely to feel positive even in situations where the Japanese did not.

Of course we cannot be sure about the nationality of either party in our imaginary exchange of greetings, because there is tremendous individual variability within any large cultural grouping, and there is also some variability in how a given person chooses to present him- or herself on any specific day. Nonetheless, there are reliable cultural differences around the world in how people do relate to one another, and these differences pose challenges that are increasingly important in a globalising world. If we as social psychologists are to understand these challenges, and provide effective help in facing them, we need to do so in terms of theories and findings that are based on an adequate understanding of cultural variability.

In this book we will outline a social psychology that can help us to understand and cope with the unparalleled processes of social change that are occurring in the world at the present time. This book has three sections. In the first, we lay the conceptual groundwork. In the second, we address major areas of social psychological study. In the third, we consider some major contemporary issues where culturally informed social psychologists can make a contribution. We conclude each chapter with a summary, suggestions for further reading and some study questions. We have also provided a glossary at the end of the book, in which you will find definitions of the technical terms that have proven useful for cross-cultural social psychologists. Terms that are included in the glossary appear in **bold** when they are first mentioned.

Formulating a social psychology that can address a changing world will not be an easy task, as it requires us to focus equally on two important issues that are most often kept quite separate: whom we should be studying, and how we should make sense of social change.

WHOM SHOULD WE BE STUDYING?

Firstly, we need to show how social psychologists can address the diversity of the world's population. Social psychology has most frequently been conducted by focusing on standardised and simplified settings. This type of focus can yield a sharply delineated understanding of what occurs within the few types of setting that are mostly sampled, but it raises problems if we wish to apply those understandings to more everyday settings, especially those that are located in different cultural contexts.

Arnett (2008) reported that in recent issues of six top US psychology journals 68% of samples were from the US and a further 28% were from other Western, industrialised nations. The final 4% were drawn from the rest of the world, whose population makes up 88% of the total world population. As Henrich, Heine, and Norenzayan (2010) neatly summarised the situation, social psychology is WEIRD – in other words, it has mostly been based on studies of people from the relatively few nations that are Western, Educated, Industrialised, Rich, and Democratic. Even within those nations its research findings have mostly been based on studies of relatively young persons who are attending university, and especially on those who are also unusual because they are studying psychology.

Studies on this basis would only be a reliable guide to social behaviour in the rest of the world if people and the ways that they relate to others were much the same everywhere. So where do you, the reader, fit into this pattern? Are you from one of the WEIRD nations, or are you from what Kağıtçıbaşı (2007) calls the Majority World, namely the much larger portion of humankind that is not WEIRD? And how does your situation affect how you think about cultural differences in social behaviour?

Later in this chapter, we examine the evidence showing that studies conducted in different parts of the world often yield different results. In Chapter 2, we then look at how this variability can be systematically described and explained. In Chapter 3, we examine ways in which different cultures have arisen and sustained themselves over the centuries, while also accommodating increasing globalisation. These early discussions raise questions as to how cross-cultural studies can be done in valid ways, and Chapter 4 provides guidelines on how to identify and conduct studies that can best meet these challenges.

UNDERSTANDING SOCIAL CHANGE

Our second major issue is that in the modern world we need to focus on change as much as on stability. Research methods that sample events at a single point in time, as most do, can give us an illusion of social stability, even though our individual experiences tell us that things are in flux. In the central section of this book, we go along with the convenient assumption that we are studying a stable world, in order to provide a cross-cultural perspective on some of the major topics of social psychology. In the third section, we then focus on the ways in which social psychological perspectives can be applied to contemporary issues that are being triggered by increasing cross-national contact through the travel, education, migration, electronic media and trade that have been unleashed by globalisation.

Our focus can be introduced in a few paragraphs. Over the past 10,000 years, human evolution has differentiated a series of relatively small and relatively separate groups that we can describe as societies or cultures. These cultures were adapted to sustaining life in a wide variety of differing and often hostile environments. Depending on how we might choose to define 'culture', several thousand cultures may be considered to have evolved. In the early part of the twentieth century, social anthropologists made detailed ethnographic studies of many of these groups. Their observations have been documented and summarised in the 'Human Relations Area Files' at Yale University, which contain information on 863 cultural groups (Murdock, 1967).

Some of the earliest of these anthropological investigations also involved psychologists. Over 100 years ago, a group of social scientists visited the islands in the Torres Straits which separate Australia and New Guinea. One member of the team, the psychologist William Rivers, focused his studies upon the islanders' perceptual processes. You can see an account of some of his experiences in Everyday Life Box 1.1. Look also at the results that he obtained, which are described in Key Research Study Box 1.1.

Some of the early anthropologists also employed psychological terms to describe the whole cultures that they studied and explain the social processes that characterised them. This approach became known as the 'culture and personality' school of thought (Benedict, 1932). For instance, drawing on this perspective, Benedict (1946) asserted that the national character of the Japanese was based on shame, in contrast to that of Western nations that was based more on guilt. She acknowledged that some individuals might not fit the overall pattern, but was primarily concerned with understanding the overall profile of a given society. As is often the case in cultural work, there was a powerful motivation for providing such an understanding – in this case Japan, an unknown foe, had just entered the Second World War against the United States, and the US War Office was eager to know how to deal with its enemy.

This perspective subsequently fell out of favour, partly because it assumed that most members of a culture shared the same personality and partly because there were no established personality measures at the time (Piker, 1998). As we shall see in Chapter 5, there is now some evidence of cultural variability in the distribution of personality traits, but there is also much

Everyday Life Box 1.1   The Torres Straits Expedition

In 1898, a team from Cambridge University visited a set of islands in the Torres Straits, which lie between Australia and New Guinea. The team included three psychologists, of whom the leader was W.H.R. Rivers. Their purpose was to test the hypothesis that, while 'savages' were lacking in higher mental functions, they had superior visual skills. Their studies were impeded by the failure in this very different climatic context of many of the types of psychological apparatus that they had taken with them. Rather than working in a controlled laboratory setting, studies took place in the open with an appreciative audience of spectators. The way in which they explained their studies conveyed strong demand characteristics:

> The natives were told that some people had said that the black man could see and hear better than the white man, and that we had come to find out how clever they were and their performances would all be described in a big book, so that everyone would read about them. This appealed to the vanity of the people and put them on their mettle...
> (Rivers, 1901, cited by Richards, 2010)

One research assistant further encouraged participation by telling islanders that if they did not respond truthfully, Queen Victoria would send a gunboat. The 'control' samples from which data were collected in the UK were poorly matched with the islanders, so that many of the findings must be considered inconclusive (Richards, 2010). Nonetheless, this very first cross-cultural study illustrates many of the difficulties that more recent cross-cultural comparisons must overcome if they are to yield valid conclusions.

As was normal at the time, the research team collected many cultural artefacts, which were then deposited in museums in Cambridge, UK. In 1998, a group of Torres Islanders were invited to Cambridge. The leader of this group expressed pleasure that these artifacts had been preserved, as they had great symbolic meaning, and were no longer found in the Torres Straits islands. Discussions ensued as to where the artifacts should now be located.

variability between individuals. To explain social behaviour, we will need to understand both types of variation.

The fact that anthropologists were able to visit and document all these cultural groups was itself a symptom of an evolutionary process that commenced long before the industrial revolution and has been accelerating ever since. The development of modern technology has steadily increased the speed and ease with which we can travel the world and has virtually eliminated the time within which messages can pass between two points located anywhere on the globe. New technologies and the economic developments that these have engendered have increasingly unleashed a new 'anthropocene'

Ethnicity/Ethnic Group Ethnicity is a problematic concept widely used in some parts of the world to identify sub-cultural groups on the basis of criteria such as ancestry, skin colour and other attributes. A person's self-identified ethnic identity does not always coincide with his or her ethnicity as identified by others.

Key Research Study Box 1.1   Visual Illusions

Despite whatever preconceptions the researchers of the Torres Straits Expedition may have held, they obtained some rather striking results. In particular, they reported that the susceptibility to visual illusions varied, depending on the perceiver's **ethnicity**. The islanders were less susceptible than British respondents to the Müller-Lyer illusion, namely the false perception that the vertical lines with outward and inward facing arrow heads in Figure 1.1 differed in length. However, they were more susceptible than Caucasians to the illusion that the vertical line in Figure 1.1 was longer than the horizontal line.

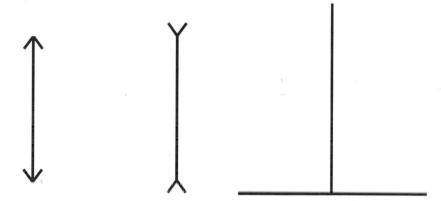

Figure 1.1   Visual Illusions

Susceptibility to various types of visual illusions has been studied extensively by cross-cultural psychologists in more recent times (Segall, Dasen, Berry, & Poortinga, 1999). The Müller-Lyer illusion is found in societies in which people live in houses with upright walls and square corners. The results are not wholly consistent, but it appears that differential sensitivity to illusions is a product of the particular type of environment in which one lives. The presence or absence of particular types of routine visual stimuli in the environment is thought to give differential encouragement to the development of relevant types of perceptual discrimination.

Rivers and his colleagues used a great variety of tests, not just those that have been mentioned here. He was perhaps lucky, in that they chose to include two different tests of visual illusion. Had they used only one, they might have been led toward a false and possibly racist conclusion about the greater susceptibility of one group to illusions.

stage in earth's history (Ruddiman, 2003). This encompasses the period during which human activity has started to affect the global environment. Ruddiman argues that this began with the invention of agriculture, but its effects have become particularly marked over the past two centuries.

Many of the several thousand languages that have evolved out of distinct cultural niches and traditions are in the process of being lost. In parallel with this reduction in linguistic diversity, a few languages are becoming more and more widely spoken. Most of the cultural groups studied earlier by anthropologists are no longer insulated from external influences and many have disappeared in the form first described by anthropologists. Mass media ensure that the cultural products of a few industrialised nations are beamed into all corners of the world. Very large numbers of persons visit other parts of the world, as tourists, as workers for either non-governmental organisations or foreign governments, as students or for business purposes. Large numbers of persons migrate to other parts of the world, some as foreign workers, some as economic migrants, and some as refugees or as victims of political or religious persecution. Even larger numbers of people are moving from the countryside to ever growing cities, with the proportions of humans living in cities rising from 29% in 1950 to 50% today, and expected to reach 69% by 2050 (United Nations, 2010).

So how can we best understand these processes of social and cultural change and stability? The world is now organised as a system not of thousands of cultural groups, but of slightly more than 200 nation states. The geographical locations and human histories of these nation states vary greatly, leading each toward their current circumstances. Nations are politically defined entities, containing a broad range of persons most of whom will share a single nationality, but who may well choose to describe themselves in terms of differing genders, occupations, ethnic origins, religious affiliations and skin colours. In some cases, one's nationality defines one's ethnicity, but skin colour, prior migration history and regional loyalties are frequently involved as well. Whether a nation can be best understood as a society, as a culture or as an amalgam of ethnicities is a question that we shall discuss in the next chapter. Until we reach that point we shall be referring simply to nations, not cultures.

CHOOSING WHAT TO STUDY AND HOW TO STUDY IT

In order to examine the world as it now is, we first need to consider how best to study and describe the existing similarities and differences between groups and between nations. Social scientists have devised many useful ways to do this, each of which can illuminate specific aspects of how people respond to current stability and change. Our perspective stems from **cross-cultural psychology**. Cross-cultural psychologists resemble researchers in most other fields of psychology in that they usually favour research methods that entail quantitative forms of measurement, but they are distinctive in their emphasis on the need to test theories across a broad range of geographical locations in order to test their universality. What is fundamental and basic about human nature, and what is malleable and likely to emerge in a different form, depending on the ways in which particular individuals are socialised in changing nation states? As we shall see, cross-cultural psychologists have developed measures that enable the existing differences between nation states to be dimensionalised and hence compared. But will these differences persist, or will contemporary developments gradually create a global monoculture?

Socialisation is most typically studied as a process occurring during childhood, and in Chapter 8 we will consider the ways in which childhood socialisation processes vary across nations. However, as individuals move through the lifespan with its various stages and occasionally also from one nation to another, further socialisation processes become equally salient. Multinational businesses seek to socialise their employees to operate within a global organisational culture. Governments

Cross-Cultural Psychology An approach to the study of culture that focuses on comparisons between different groups and testing theories as to why they do or do not differ from one another.

adopt a variety of practices concerning the provision of schooling within multiethnic contexts, and these schools in turn function as agents of socialisation. Political alliances and conflicts create pressures for particular kinds of relationships and social change. Tourists make particular kinds of demands on local residents. People form relationships with, and sometimes marry, partners from nations other than their own. In doing so, they must confront the differences in the assumptions and values to which their prior lives have socialised them. Everyday Life Box 1.2 identifies one such pattern.

Everyday Life Box 1.2   Jan meets Maria

Jan grew up in a Dutch Protestant family. By the time he completed his *doctorandus* degree at a university in the Netherlands, he, like his classmates, was a fluent speaker of Dutch, English, German, and French. He was keen to find a way to express his internationalist values and obtained a scholarship to study at a university in the UK for a doctorate concerning development issues in Brazil. Maria grew up in a Catholic family in Sao Paulo, Brazil. She learned English in school, and after completing a top-graded psychology degree in Sao Paulo, she was delighted to be awarded a Brazilian government scholarship to study for a doctorate in the UK.

The students in the doctoral programme at the UK university were drawn from all over the world. They soon found themselves in a friendship group that included British, American, German, Swedish, and Japanese students. In conversations among friends, they told one another that their different backgrounds were unimportant: they felt a sense of personal freedom. Jan was attracted to Maria's warmth and spontaneity. He said that he could respond to it much more freely when speaking English than he could have in Dutch. Maria was first attracted to Jan because of his evident concern and knowledge about Brazil. They became romantic partners, or as their friends put it, 'an item'.

As their studies progressed, they decided to marry, and to live in Brazil. Jan had done fieldwork for his dissertation in Brazil, and when their doctorates were completed, they married and set up home in Sao Paulo. Maria's mother immediately started to press her to start a family. Jan had initially found Maria's family delightfully welcoming. However, he soon began to feel that their demands on Maria and their all-encompassing sociability were smothering his individuality and interfering with their time together. He expressed his discontents to Maria in the open manner to which he had been socialised, but it did not seem to have any effect. She sighed and said in Portuguese, 'That's the way it is'. He began to realise that he had not only married Maria, but had also chosen to live in a context that challenged his whole sense of who he was. If his relationship was to survive, he would need to talk and interact with Maria in ways that had not seemed necessary in their student days.

Psychologists mostly treat individuals as the focus of their studies. Their research methods are better adapted to doing so than those that are mostly employed by sociologists, anthropologists or economists. However, it has been apparent from the early days of psychological research that social context is also very important in determining how people behave. An early pioneer in this field was Vygotsky (1934/1962). Vygotsky studied peasant communities in Central Asia, focusing upon the development of thought and language. He emphasised the manner in which learning derives from the socio-cultural context within which the child develops. For instance, the child acquires language skills from the more competent practitioners with whom he or she interacts. These models provide illustrations of ways of speaking and thinking that are slightly more complex than those the child has yet mastered, but still within its 'zone of proximal development'. The child first learns to speak in the new ways observed from his or her socialisation models, and then internalises these skills. This focus on cultural transmission within the cognitive development of children has been an important precursor to contemporary **cultural psychology** (Rogoff, 1990; Cole, 1996; Heine, 2007; see also the recommended Further Reading by Valsiner, 2003).

Vygotskyan cultural psychology is no longer distinctively focused upon children, but highlights the reciprocal process by which everyday interactions between individuals transmit and reformulate our sense of what goes on around us and how to behave within that field of sense. This interplay between individual and context will be important throughout this book. Cross-cultural psychologists differ from cultural psychologists in their somewhat stronger preference for obtaining measures both of the individual and of the broader contexts such as nation that they inhabit, but there is an increasing convergence between the two perspectives (Markus & Hamedani, 2007).

Cultural Psychology An approach to the study of culture that emphasises the interrelatedness of persons and their specific contexts. This requires culturally appropriate research methods and makes no assumption that results will be cumulative or will lead to the identification of causal relationships.

Various critiques of the research methods favoured by mainstream psychologists have been formulated. In some nations, researchers have argued in favour of the development of **'indigenous'** psychologies, abandoning experimental methods and using instead those that are more compatible with local cultural norms (Sinha, 1996). Table 1.1 summarises these three approaches, as well as some more specific approaches to the study of culture that we shall also be examining.

So what happens when I from my nation meet you from yours? Will some aspects of the cultural milieu within which you and I have been socialised make it difficult for us to relate effectively with one another? Will we make adjustments to our interpretations of one another, our language use and our actions

Indigenous Psychology An approach, whose goal is to achieve an understanding of a particular national or cultural group, using concepts that are developed locally rather than drawing on those provided from mainstream psychology.

Table 1.1   Psychological Approaches to the Study of Culture

Name	Goal	Focus	Example	Coverage in this Book
Cross-Cultural Psychology	Show how the culture affects behaviour	Values, beliefs, self-conceptions	Comparisons between national groups	This is the major focus of this book
Cultural Psychology	Show how the self and the social system are interdependent	Qualitative and quantitative studies	A very wide variety of approaches under this heading	Some coverage in most chapters
Indigenous Psychology	Identify psychological processes without starting from US concepts	Single-nation qualitative and quantitative studies	Taiwanese indigenous psychology movement	Chapters 4 and 10
Cognitive Toolkit Approach	Show the consequences of different cognitive processes	Analytic versus holistic cognition	Attention and perception	Chapter 6
Eco-cultural Approach	Show how the environment can shape cultural differences	Ecological factors that precede human influence	Hunter-gatherer societies versus agricultural societies	Chapter 3
Dynamic Constructivism	Show how a changed context elicits different cultural orientations	Experimental studies	Studies of biculturals	Chapters 6 and 13
Intercultural Psychology	Understand the interactions between different cultures	Intergroup relations	Acculturation of migrants	Chapters 11–14

towards one another? Whether or not this comes about will contribute to the success or failure of that particular interaction. Whether failures or successes are typical of the interactions of you and me as individuals will determine the quality of our individual life experiences and the success of our joint enterprise.

Everyday Life Box 1.3 illustrates some of the intercultural issues than can arise. In one respect, this box is unusual in that the English speaker in the episode described was able to speak the language of the other party. Native English speakers frequently underestimate the extent to which mastery of language is a prime contributor to failed cross-cultural interactions. Whether successes or failures are more typical of the millions of interactions that occur between members of two nations will contribute to the further evolution of those nations' cultures. Will they merge, polarise or remain as they are? What level of contact between nations can be expected to leave them as separate, self-sustaining entities and what will facilitate their integration? Which groups within nations will carry the challenge of interacting across national cultural borders?

Everyday Life Box 1.3 *'C'est Trop Anglais, Monsieur'*

Paul was a British senior manager, negotiating to sell machinery to a large French organisation. A series of meetings took place in Paris, with Paul often being the sole representative of the British firm, meeting a group from the French side. Paul felt the negotiations were going well, and commented that he was 'getting a feel for the French' and was taking the chance to improve his French language skills. He worked hard at anticipating the possible problems that might arise in reaching an agreement and was confident that there were none. Preparing for the next stage in the negotiation, Paul arranged for a standard legal contract to be prepared, founded on the points agreed in previous meetings. There was no difficulty in the French partner translating the document into French. At the next and decisive meeting, Paul was shocked when the French team rejected his draft contract: *'C'est trop Anglais, Monsieur'* ['It's too English'], they said. Paul was astonished.

After some time, Paul made contact with a French business consultant, trying to find a way forward. Taking account of the points that emerged from their discussion, he was able to reopen negotiations with the French company and agree a contract without further difficulty. The consultant highlighted six issues that had contributed to the initial failure to secure a contract:

1 Paul had neglected the importance of hierarchy in France and had not ascertained whether those with whom he was dealing had been given the appropriate authority to reach an agreement.
2 Paul had assumed that the contract terms were not affected by cultural differences and simply required a literal translation from English to French.
3 The draft contract was written in a way that reflected the English preference for indirectness and flexibility. It contained non-specific phrases indicating, for instance, that possible future events would be handled by such procedures 'as may be agreed from time to time'. To the French, this undermined the basis for the creation of trust.
4 Paul had not arranged for the British and French lawyers who were involved to meet and discuss the much greater need for precision that existed in the French legal code.
5 The contract was lengthy, specifying many unlikely eventualities, but was also so vague that the French would not be able to find specific codified elements within it that they could contest.
6 Paul had taken responsibility for the project overall, whereas it was important for the French to have representatives for the various specialisations involved. Consequently, Paul appeared to the French as more of an amateur, compared to their specialist strengths. While Paul had seen his solo trips to France as an effective way to cut costs, to the French it had appeared that by not sending a full team, the British were not giving them respect and investing sufficient resources in the collaboration to guarantee their sincerity and ensure its success.

Source: Harper & Cormeraie (1992)

The main concern of the later sections of this book is with the social psychological consequences of contemporary modes of transport and communication. These consequences are most evident (and have been most studied) among those who travel both between nations and from the countryside to the cities, as well as among those who communicate globally. In reviewing what is happening among this section of humanity, we must also remember that these processes may barely touch those persons within all nations who continue to live in great poverty. Indeed, aspects of modernity, such as the spread of HIV/AIDS, the long distance transportation of basic commodities such as food, minerals or timber, and the global arms, sex, and drug trades, may well be accelerating the growth of poverty and the gap between rich and poor, along with environmental degradation. A full understanding of what is universal about human nature requires that we focus not just on how humans cope with the context of modernity, but also on how they cope within a context of poverty and disparities in the distribution of a cultural group's wealth (Wilkinson, 1996). If these are the agendas that define our future, we can start by mapping how social psychologists have begun to develop the expertise to make a useful contribution.

THE DEVELOPMENT OF MODERN CROSS-CULTURAL SOCIAL PSYCHOLOGY

Although the fieldwork of pioneers such as Rivers, Vygotsky, and the social anthropologists contributed substantially to the early stages of cross-cultural psychology's evolution, the most distinctive approach characterising mainstream psychological research has long been an emphasis on some form of experimental method. Psychologists have favoured the experimental method because it offers the best chance for determining causal relationships between variables. Simplified settings are required if one is to set up an adequately controlled experiment, but this simplification has mostly been seen as a price worth paying for the development of a truly scientific psychology, one that can establish causal relationships.

Many of the key figures in the foundation of modern social psychology favoured experimentation, particularly those who practised in the USA. The political turbulence of the 1930s in Europe led to prominent researchers such as Kurt Lewin and Muzafer Sherif seeking refuge in the United States. Other key figures including Fritz Heider and Solomon Asch had migrated there a little earlier. Furthermore, although the origins of social psychology were European, as a consequence of the widespread destruction and dislocation surrounding the Second World War, the practice of social psychology was for a time largely confined to the USA (Farr, 1996).

Lewin, Sherif, and Asch all espoused theories that emphasised the effect of the immediate social context on social behaviour. The generation of US researchers that succeeded them sought ways to illustrate these effects of context experimentally. In order to do so, they created simplified and often dramatic settings in which experimental participants were exposed to various kinds of social pressures. Over the years, these procedures and the theories that they had been designed to test have become more sophisticated, but they all seek to explore the variable impact of the surrounding social field on those persons interacting in that setting.

A series of stages can be identified through which North American social psychologists and those from other parts of the world have sought an understanding of the similarities and differences between the outcomes of their studies. Table 1.2 summarises these stages in the way that Bond (2009) has described them. Initially, US researchers initiated collaborative work with researchers from other parts of the world, attempting to replicate the results that they had obtained back home.

Table 1.2 Stages in the Development of Cross-Cultural Psychology

Stage	Aristotelian	Linnaean	Newtonian
Activity	Replicate US studies in other nations	Mapping the world in terms of psychological variables	'Unpackaging' reasons for the differences that are found
Focus	Comparing against existing US results	Major variables such as values, beliefs, self-concept and aspects of personality	Theories that have arisen from results of earlier cross-cultural studies
Methods used	US measures unchanged	Measures based on major variables, but increasingly tested for local validity	Measures based on theories of cultural difference
Coverage in this book	Chapter 1	Chapters 2 and 5	Throughout later chapters

As we shall see, these studies often yielded problematic results. As social psychology was practised more widely around the world, a second stage became apparent. Large-scale studies sampling many nations became available, as a basis for classifying the ways in which national groups might differ from one another in terms of major psychological attributes such as values, beliefs and personality. The first of these studies (Hofstede, 1980) classified nations along four dimensions, the best-known of which was individualism-collectivism. The third, 'Newtonian', stage in this process is one where social psychologists from different nations are increasingly collaborating on an equal basis, and drawing on theories and methods that are explicitly formulated to explain the cultural differences identified. We shall consider these second and third stages in later chapters.

Key Researcher Box 1.1 Solomon Asch

Solomon Asch was born in Poland in 1907, but moved to the USA when his parents migrated there in 1920. He received his PhD from Columbia University in 1932. He was an early pioneer of the use of experimental method in social psychology. In his most famous study he sought to show that individuals can stand out against pressures to conform. In the late 1940s, the intellectual community in the USA was under threat from a witch hunt led by Senator McCarthy, who targeted and pilloried those believed to have espoused communism in the 1930s. Ironically, Asch's experiment has subsequently almost always been interpreted as a study of conformity rather than of independence, even though 62% of participants did successfully resist group pressure to yield to the majority.

Replications

Replicating research studies is a crucial element in the establishment of their validity. Even within a single nation, it is not always the case that the results of a study would prove replicable, since there are many ways in which one sample of participants in a study might differ from another. Perhaps the most widely replicated experimental study in social psychology has been Asch's (1956) conformity study. Asch showed that when a group of experimental accomplices repeatedly gave unanimously incorrect judgments as to which of several lines matched another line, naïve experimental participants rather often also gave incorrect responses.

R. Bond and Smith (1996) have reported a **meta-analysis** of 134 published Asch conformity effects. Of these effects, 97 had been obtained with US respondents, while the remainder were drawn from 16 other nations. Bond and Smith used the US data to estimate the effect of variations in the types of experimental procedures that were used, the type of respondents, and the date of the study. They were then able to discount these sources of variance when examining the amount of influence that occurred within the studies done outside North America. As Figure 1.2 shows, the degree of group influence on conformity responses was less within Europe than it had been in the United States, but it was greater in the rest of the world than it had been in the United States.

> **Meta-Analysis** A statistical technique for summarising the results of a large group of related studies. Even though the studies may have used different measurement scales, each can be analysed to yield an 'effect size', which is an estimate of the extent of change reported on whatever measure was used, minus the change found on any control or comparison group.

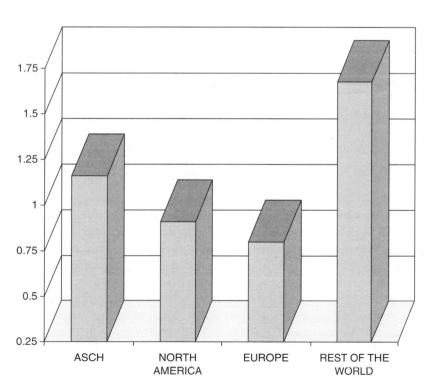

Figure 1.2   Average Effect Sizes Found in Asch Replication Studies

The results of this extensive analysis pose two questions. Firstly, it appears that a standard experimental procedure produces different results in different parts of the world, even after all variations that could be detected within a great number of US replications have been discounted. We need a theory to explain why this change in effect size might occur. Cross-cultural psychologists have studied systematic variation in behaviours, beliefs, values and attitudes around the world and have discovered some major dimensions that can help us to understand how people think, feel and act in different parts of the world. Bond and Smith tested various relevant culture-based explanations and we shall return to this study after cultural dimensions have been introduced in Chapter 2.

Secondly, it is necessary to consider what to call the specific experimental effect that Asch obtained. The results are almost always referred to as conformity. However, in differing cultural contexts, it is possible that the same behaviour may have different meanings. One possible way to investigate the meanings of a behaviour is by asking those who engage in that behaviour why they are doing it. Asch did so and obtained a variety of answers from his US respondents. Some said that they thought their eyesight must be defective; others wanted to avoid embarrassment by giving 'wrong' answers publicly. We lack similar interview data from other nations. One possibility, supported by subsequent research (Singelis, Bond, Sharkey, & Lai, 1998) is that respondents may have given incorrect answers not to save themselves from embarrassment, but to save the others from embarrassment! Confronted with a group of people who were obviously giving wrong answers, someone who valued sensitivity and a concern for others might choose to reduce other people's humiliation by tactfully also giving wrong answers (Hodges & Geyer, 2006). We need to take care to ensure that the terms we use to describe social behaviours do not contain hidden assumptions that reflect our own cultural values.

These different interpretations of behaviour become an important issue in intercultural interactions in many modern multicultural societies. Imagine yourself having to interact with a woman who is dressed in a *burqa* (the clothing worn by many women in some Islamic nations that completely covers the body) and a *niqab* (the face veil that covers the face and only reveals the eyes). You may have your personal thoughts and opinions about this person, her reasons for wearing this type of dress, and her behaviour that may appear strange to you (e.g., her not wishing to shake hands, her expectation of being accompanied by her husband on all visits). Yet your interaction partner may have very different reasons for her behaviour. The interpretation of behaviour in intercultural interactions is a major source of misunderstandings and we shall return to this issue in Chapter 11.

Other very well-known US studies have also been quite often repeated outside the USA, and as with Asch's findings also demonstrate significant variability around the world. For instance, Milgram's (1961) study of obedience to a destructive authority figure has been repeated in 12 other countries (Blass, 1999), most recently as part of a television game show in France (Beauvois, Courbet & Oberlé, 2012). Although the compliance effect was obtained in all studies, the actual levels of obedience that were found have been varied. Many other well-known US studies have been repeated in new locations, and the results have sometimes been non-significant and on occasion even in the opposite direction from those obtained in the United States. One reason that may contribute to this is that the measures developed are assumed to be valid in other locations. Measures of this type are referred to as imposed-**etic**, because they assume universal applicability. Locally-developed measures are referred to as **emic**. The meaning and origin of these terms are discussed more fully in Chapter 4.

Amir and Sharon (1987) attempted to estimate the magnitude of the problem of non-replicability. Rather than focus on famous studies, they selected six studies that had been published in major US social psychology journals and attempted to replicate their results, using both high school and university students within Israel. They deliberately selected studies whose design and methods would be appropriate to Israeli respondents. The six original studies had yielded 37 significant effects. Amir and Sharon succeeded in replicating only 16 of these outcomes within both their Israeli samples, and nine more

> **Emic and Etic Studies** Emic studies are those that draw material from the immediate context being studied and make no assumption about the cultural generality of what is discovered. Etic studies are those that make a provisional assumption that the phenomena being studied are universal and attempt to establish their validity everywhere.

within just one of their samples. They also found 27 significant effects that had not been found in the original studies. Thus it appears that the replicability problem is very substantial, even when assessed in two cultural systems like those of Israel and the USA that many would regard as relatively similar.

A particularly striking instance comes from studies of the so-called social loafing effect. These have shown that, in the USA, individuals put less effort into a task when working with others than when working alone. Karau and Williams (1993) reported a meta-analysis of 147 social loafing effects obtained within the USA and 15 obtained in Pacific Asian nations. On simple tasks, such as clapping one's hands or shouting, social loafing effects were obtained equally in Pacific Asia and the United States. On more complex tasks, the Pacific Asian studies showed a complete reversal: people worked harder when they were in groups than when they were alone.

Subsequent studies by Earley (1993) provided further insight into these results. Earley studied managers working on tasks in the USA, China and Israel. Both the Israeli and the Chinese managers worked harder when they believed that their tasks were part of a group effort, whereas the Americans worked harder when they believed that they were working alone. In addition, some of those participants who thought that they were working in a group were led to believe that the group comprised others known to them, whereas other participants were told that they were working with strangers. The enhanced social effort expended by the Israelis and Chinese was found only when working with one's own group, not with strangers. This study begins to provide clues as to the nature of the cultural differences that may explain the reversal across nations of the social loafing effect, and will be explored further after we have considered the key concept of collectivism in Chapter 2. An key pioneer in developing and popularising this concept and the research methods required to investigate it validly has been Harry Triandis, as we note in Key Researcher Box 1.2.

Key Researcher Box 1.2   Harry Triandis

Figure 1.3   Harry Triandis

Harry C. Triandis (b. 1926) grew up on the Greek island of Corfu. During the Second World War the local schools were closed and he taught himself by reading the *Encyclopaedia Britannica*. He obtained a bachelor's degree in engineering in Canada, but transferred his interest to psychology, gaining a PhD in social psychology from Cornell University in 1958. Moving to the University of Illinois, he developed a cross-cultural perspective on the use of semantic differential questionnaires to map the meaning of concepts. His early understanding that cultural differences are best thought of as differences in assigned meanings was summarised in *The Analysis of Subjective Culture* (1972). He pioneered the development of a network of cross-cultural psychologists, was one of the first presidents of the International Association for Cross-Cultural Psychology, and was the chief editor of the *Handbook of Cross-Cultural Psychology* (1980). More recently, his many publications did much to popularise interest in individualism and collectivism. He also pioneered the development of questionnaire measures of self-construal, as well as the use of experimental priming in studying the consequences of self-construal and methods of training in cross-cultural skills. His publications have been cited more than 40,000 times. Many leading contemporary cross-cultural psychologists were his students at the University of Illinois.

One of the requirements of experimental method is that one needs a supply of participants who will present themselves at a psychology laboratory without too much difficulty and will understand the experimental instructions. This consideration provides one reason why experimental social psychologists have often based their sampling on students. Students differ from the general population in many important psychological respects, even within a single nation. However, there are additional hazards in basing cross-cultural comparisons on student populations: these populations of students will differ greatly across different countries. In Western nations, university education is undertaken by a relatively large percentage of the age cohort. However, in many nations, participating in a university education is achieved only by a small percentage of the age cohort, and is drawn disproportionately from elite families. Comparing such inequivalent student samples may give misleading results. Using other populations that are matched on key characteristics, as was done in Earley's studies, is preferable.

Thus far we have seen that studies conducted in different parts of the world quite often yield different results. Sometimes this is just a matter of the results of the experimental manipulation being stronger in one location than another, but in the instance of the visual illusions (see Key Research Study Box 1.1), effects found in one location were completely absent from another, and in the case of Earley's study, the effects found were actually in opposite directions. These types of results are not just a challenge to psychological theory, but also a threat to the application of psychological knowledge to practical problems. Some examples of difficulties that have arisen when research findings were incautiously applied in new cultural contexts are shown in Everyday Life Box 1.4.

Everyday Life Box 1.4

Real world problems can arise when techniques developed and tested in WEIRD nations are applied without adequate forethought in other parts of the world:

- A multinational company produced a research-based specification of the qualifications and achievements that validly predict performance at a given level of seniority. A consultant visiting Venezuela asked how the local implementation of this system was going. He was assured that when promotions were made, 'we know who would be best for the job, so we make up the listing of necessary qualifications and submit them to head office'.
- A company decided to implement '360 degree feedback'. This is a procedure when superiors, colleagues and subordinates all provide comments to an individual on his or her work performance. When such a session was scheduled in Hong Kong, almost all those concerned called in sick on the day scheduled for the workshop.
- A company decided to introduce group participation into a garment factory in Puerto Rico. The use of groups by managers was seen by workers as indicating that management did not know how to manage. Labour turnover increased, because people felt that the company would soon be out of business.

It is useful to know that the results of experimental studies often vary in different contexts. However, if we are to make sense of why this occurs, we need conceptual frameworks that help us to understand why this variation occurs. In the next chapter, we outline the conceptual frameworks that have guided the development of cross-cultural psychology over the past several decades.

SUMMARY

Our purpose in this book is to expose the benefits than can be achieved by extending the range of persons upon whom we base our understanding of social and psychological processes. By providing an up-to-date analysis of the achievements of cross-cultural psychologists, we demonstrate how understandings that are more broadly based can modify and strengthen contemporary social psychology. We also show how these achievements can be used to address the issues raised by the current impact of enhanced global interdependence, mobility and communications.

FURTHER READING

1 Replications in other nations of early US studies are discussed in much fuller detail in Smith and Bond (1998: Chapter 2).
2 Bond, R., & Smith, P.B. (1996). Culture and conformity: A meta-analysis of studies using Asch's (1952b, 1956) line judgment task. *Psychological Bulletin, 119*, 111–137.

3   Markus, H.R., & Hamedani, M.G. (2007). Sociocultural psychology: The dynamic interde-
    pendence among self systems and social systems. In S. Kitayama & D. Cohen (Eds), *Handbook
    of cultural psychology* (pp. 3–39). New York: Guilford.
4   There is an online website that contains short articles written by many of the leading contem-
    porary cross-cultural psychologists. The website was established by Dr Walter Lonner and
    his colleagues at Western Washington University, USA. The Online Readings in Psychology
    and Culture (ORPC) are now provided as a free resource by the International Association for
    Cross-Cultural Psychology and located at Grand Valley State University, USA. Lonner was
    also the founding editor of the *Journal of Cross-Cultural Psychology*, which is the premier journal
    in this field. The ORPC website can be freely accessed at http://scholarworks.gvsu.edu/*orpc*.
    Take a look at the introduction to the website. Specific suggestions for relevant readings taken
    from this website are indicated after most of the chapters in this book.
5   E-books containing a selection of peer-reviewed papers given at recent congresses of the
    International Association for Cross-Cultural Psychology are also available online, free of
    charge. These books can be found at http://www.iaccp.org
6   Valsiner, J. (2003). Culture and its transfer: Ways of creating general knowledge through the
    study of cultural particulars. *Online Readings in Psychology and Culture.* Available at http://
    scholarworks.gvsu.edu/*orpc*
7   Van Hemert, D.A. (2003). Cross-cultural meta-analyses. *Online Readings in Psychology and
    Culture.* Available at http://scholarworks.gvsu.edu/*orpc*

STUDY QUESTIONS

1   How would you describe yourself in terms of nationality and ethnicity? How important are
    these sources of identity to you, compared to thinking about yourself in alternative sources of
    identity, such as age, gender and role? How important are these aspects of your identity to the
    other people with whom you interact on a daily basis?
2   What issues arise for you when you interact with persons of a different nationality or ethnicity?
3   What contemporary problems can you identify where an understanding of culture may
    improve our capacity to improve the situation?

2

Clarifying the Way Forward with Culture: Theories and Frameworks

The trouble is that no one is quite sure what culture is. Not only is it an essentially contested concept, like democracy, religion, simplicity, or social justice, it is a multiply defined one, multiply employed, ineradicably imprecise. It is fugitive, unsteady, encyclopedic, and normatively charged, and there are those, especially those for whom only the really real is really real, who think it vacuous altogether, or even dangerous, and would ban it from the serious discourse of serious persons. An unlikely idea, it would seem, around which to try to build a science.

From Geertz, Clifford; Available Light. © 2000, Princeton University Press.
Reproduced by permission of Princeton University Press.

Thus far we have explored some of the reasons why cross-cultural studies might be needed, so now we need to address the questions that are most central to the field we are exploring. In this chapter we discuss how best to define the concepts that are needed to guide the work of cross-cultural researchers and then evaluate initial progress in understanding how these concepts can be measured, so that they can be used to explain both cultural similarities and cultural differences as well as culture's relationship with interpersonal processes.

There has been extensive debate over the past century about the most useful way in which to define the concept of **culture**. Psychologists have been relatively late entrants into this debate, drawing upon the earlier work of anthropologists. Anthropologists found particular value in the concept of culture as a way of encapsulating their understandings of the relatively small and relatively isolated groups of people upon whom many of their early studies had focused, but were not all agreed as to how best to define what a culture is conceptually. An influential early definition was provided by Tylor in 1871. He saw culture as '... that complex whole which includes knowledge, belief, art, morals, laws, customs and any other capabilities and habits acquired by man as

Culture A concept applicable to all levels in the analysis of social systems – nations, ethnicities, organisations, teams, families, dyadic relationships. The culture of a social system comprises similar ways of responding to context, similar ways of processing information, and shared interpretations of the meanings of events occurring within the system. In this book we avoid labelling nations as cultures, even though very many of the studies that we discuss do base their sampling on nations. Nations have many of the characteristics of cultures, but many nations are too diverse to fully satisfy their definition as having a unified culture. They are better thought of as political systems in which many types of other systems are embedded.

a member of society' (Tylor, 1871: Volume 1: 1). Herskovits (1948) provided an apt and concise summary of the early anthropological perspective, describing a culture as 'the man-made part of the human environment', where 'man-made' included both physical artifacts and social systems. So, for example, in studying the Trobriand Islanders in the Pacific Ocean, Malinowski (1927) was able to survey both the behaviours and the physical structures that the islanders had created, and which together defined and sustained a particular way of life. Trobriand Islanders comprised a distinctive culture, which could be contrasted and compared with those found elsewhere.

More recently, psychologists (and many anthropologists) have focused their attention on human behaviour within the more modernised world. For this rather different purpose, different approaches to the study of culture may be appropriate. Faulkner, Baldwin, Lindsley, and Hecht (2006) could identify as many as 300 definitions of culture, among which they discerned six themes, three of which are of greatest relevance to the issues that we discuss in this book. Different authors have examined culture in terms of structures, in terms of functions and in terms of processes.

Theories of culture that focus on structural features such as norms and roles and the phenomena such as beliefs, values and attitudes that underpin them have until recently been the most fully explored. Theorists in this tradition typically define a culture in terms of the existence of a system of meanings that is shared between its members. This perspective is examined in the present chapter and revisited in Chapter 8.

Theorists who define culture in terms of functions take an evolutionary perspective (Schaller, Norenzayan, Heine, Yamagishi, & Kameda, 2011). They note ways in which present-day behaviours are adaptive to the contexts in which humans have lived in the past and the information available to them that enables them to handle the challenges they continue to face. This approach is most fully explored in Chapter 3.

Theorists who define culture in terms of processes posit that the types of cognitive processes in which persons engage differ around the world (Nisbett, Choi, Peng, & Norenzayan, 2001). They see an individual's cognitive abilities in terms of a type of 'toolkit' whose tools can be drawn upon in different ways, depending on the momentary activities and longer-term processes of socialisation that one encounters. They focus in particular on the more analytic types of cognition favoured in Western cultures versus the more holistic types of cognition emphasised in East Asian cultures. This approach is explored in full in Chapter 6.

Each of these approaches involves a differing definition of the central elements constituting culture. Understanding culture is a complex undertaking and the three approaches differ from one another only in the emphasis that they give to relevant factors. All of them can be helpful in making sense of what is universal and what is variable about human nature and social behaviour.

CULTURE, NATIONS AND SOCIETIES

The modern world is currently organised politically into just over 200 nations, many of which are large and all of which enjoy substantial contact with one another. Is a nation the same as a society, and can it be said to have a culture? Rohner (1984) explored how best to answer these questions within a modern and changing world. He proposed that the essence of 'culture' lies in the shared way in which individuals interpret what goes on around them. These shared interpretations could cover both individual behaviours and the environment within which those behaviours occur. If you and I agree that a certain gesture indicates friendliness rather than aggression, or if we agree that that gesture is beautiful rather than ugly, we are interpreting the world around us in a similar manner. If those similarities are numerous, you and I can be said to share a culture.

Note that in principle this judgment could be applied at all levels of generality. We could identify the culture of a marriage, a nuclear family, a work team, an entire organisation, or a whole nation. In each case we should need to find a criterion against which to judge how much similarity was required before we could state that it was useful to say that a culture was present rather than absent. Given the various numbers of individuals involved, specifying a standard for consensus may be difficult. In deciding whether a family group had enough consensus to indicate that it had a shared culture, we would probably set the criterion higher than we would when deciding whether a nation has a culture.

The move over time from definitions that emphasise behaviour patterns to those that emphasise the sharing of the meanings that are attributed to behaviour parallels the evolution of behaviourist psychology into cognitive psychology. A similar evolution has occurred in anthropology. Thus Geertz, the influential anthropologist with whom we commenced this chapter, has written 'The study of culture, the accumulated totality of such patterns [of behaviour] is thus the study of the machinery individuals and groups of individuals employ to orient themselves in a world otherwise opaque' (Geertz, 1973: 363).

Culture defined in this way is a feature that persons inhabiting and interacting in that cultural setting have in relation to one another, not of the individuals that comprise that entity. Individuals are sometimes said to be cultured, but in the sense in which it is being used here culture can only be defined collectively – that is, it is shared. As Rohner put it, culture is 'the totality of equivalent and complementary learned meanings maintained by a human population, or by identifiable segments of a population, and transmitted from one generation to the next' (Rohner, 1984: 119–120).

In later chapters we shall rather frequently refer to individuals as having a particular '**cultural orientation**'. By this phrase we mean a propensity to interpret their surroundings in a way that is consistent with one or other of the dimensions of culture that we shall be exploring in this chapter. Speaking of individuals' 'cultural

Cultural Orientation A general term used in this book to refer to any one of the various measures that are currently used to characterise culturally relevant individual-level attributes, such as self-construal, values or beliefs.

orientation' acknowledges the continual interplay between a culture and the individuals who are socialised by it and in turn sustain it. This interplay is of particular interest to those who define themselves as cultural psychologists. Shweder (1991) for instance defines the goal of cultural psychology as the study of 'mentalities' and locates mentalities equally within individuals and within the larger population. His position is formulated in terms of two principles:

> The principle of existential uncertainty asserts that human beings starting at birth … are highly motivated to seize meanings and resources out of a socio-cultural environment that has been arranged to provide them with meanings and resources to seize and use. The principle of intentional (or constitutional) worlds asserts that subjects and objects, practitioners and practices cannot be analyzed into independent and interdependent variables. Their identities are interdependent; neither side of the supposed contrast can be defined without borrowing from the specifications of the other. (Shweder, 1991: 74)

Shweder's sharply formulated perspective helps to clarify the distinction between the approaches used by cultural psychologists and cross-cultural psychologists. While cultural psychologists emphasise the way that the individual and culture are inextricably interwoven, cross-cultural psychologists see benefits in using different terms to characterise the perspective of individuals (personality or cultural orientation) and the extent to which their understanding of events around them is shared by others (culture).

Rohner also emphasises that it is important to distinguish between a culture and a social system. A social system comprises 'the behavior of multiple individuals within a culturally-organized population, including their patterns of interaction and networks of social relationships' (Rohner, 1984: 126). Social systems can also be as small as a family or as large as a nation, but they are defined in terms of patterns of behaviour, not in terms of the meanings that are placed on those behaviours.

The distinction between behaviour and the meaning attached to the behaviour is vital, because the meanings of most behavioural actions are not by themselves self-evident. If I stand one metre away while talking to you, you may interpret my behaviour from one culture's perspective as friendly, from a second as aggressive, and perhaps even from a third as a form of sexual harassment (see, for example, Sussman & Rosenfeld, 1982). Even if I hit you, you may depend upon a variety of contextual cultural clues to interpret that physical contact as playful, accidental, or hostile (Bond, 2004). Social systems define the patterns of behaviour whose meaning is provided by their cultural context. Social systems *have* cultures. Cultures do not have social systems – they make social systems comprehensible, and thereby provide guidance for appropriate responses.

In exploring the perspective on culture exemplified by Rohner's definition, we shall need to consider carefully exactly what might be the process by which shared meanings are established in a culture. Atran, Medin, and Ross (2005) note that many theories of culture do not specify the type of consensus that one would expect to find within a culture. Are culturally shared meanings achieved because there is a system of shared values and beliefs, or is there some set of normative reference points in a culture that leads individuals to interpret what goes on around them in similar ways even though their values and beliefs differ from those around them? Not all persons in any cultural group agree, and the question of whether a person's social behaviour arises from personal dispositions or cultural guidelines is fundamentally important (Bond, 2013). Its answer may depend on the culture into which the person was initially socialised or the cultural group in which that person is currently functioning.

Contemporary cross-cultural psychologists frequently define their samples on the basis of respondents' nationality. It is evident that nations are social systems, because they comprise extensive interconnected networks of people, but can they be thought of as having cultures? A few nations, like Japan, are very homogeneous in the ethnicity of their population, while many others, like the United States, Germany, Brazil, and Singapore, have considerable and increasing ethnic diversity. China, for example, officially recognises 55 minority groups within its national borders. According to the definition advanced here, nations, as well as the ethnic, regional and socio-economic groups that may be present within them, can be defined as having cultures to the extent that there is evidence that their members interpret the events around them in relatively similar ways. We need to look next at the ways in which cross-cultural psychologists can test for such homogeneity of outlook within any particular social system.

VALUES, BELIEFS AND BEHAVIOURS

We discuss in the next chapter both how the world's national cultures have arisen and how they are sustained. For the moment, let us assume that a certain culture exists in a steady state at a given point in time. How do its members interpret the actions that occur around them? We argued above that a cross-cultural psychologist cannot assume that a particular behaviour has the same meaning in different cultural contexts. However, a member of a specific culture will frequently assign meanings to behaviours. The processes of socialisation, acting on both children and adults, teach one to interpret the most likely meanings of specific acts. One way for researchers to determine whether a nation could or could not be considered a culture would be to survey culture members and determine the extent to which there is consensus about the meanings of particular actions. This would be an example of the type of emic research design that we noted in the previous chapter. However, a difficulty with this approach would be to determine which of thousands of possible behaviours are the ones on which it would be best to focus. Most probably some would be found to have shared meanings and many others would not.

A more parsimonious way to address this problem is not to focus on the meanings of specific behaviours, but on the more organised conceptual frameworks 'held' by culture members, which are likely to guide their interpretations of specific events. As cross-cultural psychology has developed, the most popular choice has been to focus on the values that are held by members of a culture. A person's values provide guidelines as to favoured goals to pursue in living. They are abstract and general and therefore easier to measure. A second basis for prediction is provided by the types of belief endorsed by members of a culture. While values concern what is desirable, beliefs concern what is thought to be true. If a social system were to be characterised by particular sets of values and beliefs typically held by members of that system, then social scientists would have a basis for defining the existence of a culture.

We need to remind ourselves that social systems are not composed in the manner of a laboratory experiment. It is rarely the case that we can be sure that one variable causes another to change. The multiple elements of a culture will over time all be acting upon one another. Patterns of behaviour may arise that will cause values or beliefs to change, just as changing values or beliefs may cause behaviours to change. However, in order to get inside social systems and begin to understand this complex and dynamic interplay, we need defensible measures of the relevant elements in the system at any given time. As a first step in this direction, we will explore a sequence of key empirical studies that have emerged over the past three decades. These are studies in which researchers have sought to classify nations on the basis of their prevailing values, beliefs and practices.

THE HOFSTEDE PROJECT

The single work that has most influenced the development of research into cross-cultural psychology has been the seminal study that was carried out by the Dutch social psychologist, Geert Hofstede. During the late 1960s and early 1970s, Hofstede was one of a team of researchers employed by the US company IBM. The team was engaged in worldwide morale surveys of their employees in more than 70 nations and eventually accumulated a huge databank of some 116,000 responses. Hofstede conducted extensive analyses of these data, leading in 1980 to the publication of his classic study, entitled *Culture's Consequences*.

Key Researcher Box 2.1   Geert Hofstede

Figure 2.1   Geert Hofstede

Geert Hofstede (b. 1928) graduated as a mechanical engineer from Delft Technical University in the Netherlands and worked in industry for 10 years before completing his PhD in social psychology at the University of Groningen. He subsequently joined IBM Europe, where he founded and managed their personnel research department. After leaving the company, he worked in a series of management schools during the 1970s and prepared his classic work, *Culture's Consequences*, which was published in 1980. Based on the survey responses of 117,000 IBM employees worldwide, the book provided the first empirically-based classification of dimensions along which the nations of the world could be classified in terms of their values. More recently he held positions at Maastricht University and Tilburg University, where he established a programme of cross-cultural training based on his cultural dimensions. His later more popular work, *Cultures and Organizations*, has been published in 16 languages. His publications have also been cited by other authors more than 80,000 times, a figure surpassed by few psychologists and none from Europe.

Hofstede's conceptualisation of culture is similar to the position taken in this book. He defined culture as 'the collective programming of the mind that distinguishes the members of one group or category of people from another' (Hofstede, 2001: 9). His goal was to identify some dimensions of this programming that could be used to characterise the ways in which nations differed from one another. He

Individual-Level Studies Studies in which the data from each individual respondent are treated as a separate case.

was seeking to establish culturally for nations what latitude and longitude established for nations geographically, i.e., the axes for locating them in terms of useful coordinates. His study is described in Key Research Study Box 2.1 below.

Nation-Level Studies Studies in which all the data from each nation on each available variable are first averaged and then analysed, thereby treating each nation as a single case.

Key Research Study Box 2.1
Dimensions of National Culture

In conducting his study, Hofstede was constrained by the fact that the IBM surveys had been designed to provide the type of information that the company required, rather than for the purposes of cross-cultural research. Most items tapped values, others tapped descriptions of behaviours or intentions to behave in certain ways. Nonetheless, the size of the existing databank gave him some advantages. For instance, he was able to construct samples from each nation that were similar to one another demographically, so that he could be sure that whatever differences he found were attributable to national differences rather than to differences in, for instance, type of job or gender. Once comparable samples had been created, his data set was reduced to 72,215 respondents and the number of nations had declined to 40. However, he was unable to control the number of respondents from different nations, which varied between 11,384 from Germany and 58 from Singapore.

The next step that Hofstede took was crucial. He reasoned that if he was to characterise whole nations rather than individuals, he must analyse his data not at the **individual level** but at the **nation level** (or, as he termed it, the 'ecological' level). In other words, taking the answers for each specific question, he *averaged* the scores of all the respondents from each particular nation. Some of the items in the IBM survey required answers on Likert scales anchored by phrases such as 'agree' and 'disagree'. Hofstede was also aware of the problem of cultural differences in **acquiescent response style**, the general tendency to respond positively to questionnaire items, regardless of what the item is about. To address this, he standardised the averaged responses to the items on which he focused. To do this, each nation's mean across all items was subtracted from each separate item's mean and the resultant score was divided by the standard deviation of the item means. With this standardisation accomplished, he was ready to determine whether the average answers to each survey item in each nation varied in ways that could be classified along any particular dimension.

By comparing the correlations between specific item scores and conducting a factor analysis of some of the standardised nation averages for questionnaire items, he eventually identified four dimensions of national variation. He named these Power Distance, Uncertainty Avoidance, Individualism-Collectivism, and Masculinity-Femininity. Those who are familiar with **factor analysis** with individual-level data would argue that 40 cases are insufficient to conduct a valid factor analysis. However, within his nation-level analysis, most data points are the mean of hundreds and in some instances thousands of responses. Such numbers give these data points a much enhanced stability, reducing the error of measurement and basing the resulting analyses upon extremely reliable scores. Each dimension was defined by the answers to between three and six questions from within the original survey. The items that define each dimension are shown in Table 2.1.

Table 2.1   Defining the Hofstede Dimensions

Dimension	Items
Power Distance	1 Employees are afraid to disagree with their managers
	2 My manager is autocratic, OR persuasive/paternalistic
	3 I prefer managers who are autocratic OR participative, but not those who consult and then make their own decision
Uncertainty Avoidance	1 Company rules should not be broken, even when the employee thinks it is in the company's best interest
	2 I intend to stay with the company for at least five years
	3 I feel nervous and tense at work
Individualism (versus Collectivism)	It is important for me to have: personal time/freedom to use my approach/ challenging work
	It is less important for me to have: good physical conditions/training opportunities/use of all my skills
Masculinity (versus Femininity)	It is important for me to have: high earnings/recognition for good work/ advancement/challenges
	It is less important for me to have: good relations with my manager/ cooperation with others/a desirable living area/job security

Note: Item wordings have been modified for greater clarity

As with other factor analyses, there is some degree of subjectivity in deciding how to name the factors that emerge. Hofstede's choices have had a substantial impact on how others have later responded to each of the factors so named. The dimension that he first identified was labeled Power Distance, which he defined as '… the difference between the degree to which B can determine the behavior of S and the extent to which S can determine the behavior of B' (Hofstede, 2001: 83; B and S refer to Boss and Subordinate). Subsequent to his original analysis, Hofstede has provided additional scores for some additional countries. Drawing also on these data, the nations rated highest on Power Distance were Malaysia, Slovakia, Guatemala, Panama, the Philippines, and Russia, while those rated lowest were Austria, Israel, Denmark, New Zealand, and Ireland.

The second dimension was called Uncertainty Avoidance. This was defined as the shunning of ambiguity. Hofstede (2001: 148) notes that many writers have understood his concept as risk avoidance. However, he argues that this is a misinterpretation and that in high uncertainty avoidance national cultures risks may sometimes be taken simply as a way to escape from uncertainty. High Uncertainty Avoidance nations were found to be Greece, Portugal, Guatemala, Uruguay, and Malta, while those rated lowest were Singapore, Jamaica, Denmark, Sweden, and Hong Kong.

The third dimension was named **Individualism-Collectivism**. Individualist cultures are defined as those in which individuals see themselves as having a relatively separate identity, whereas collectivist cultures are those in which identity is more strongly defined by long-lasting group memberships. The manner in which this dimension is defined lends itself rather easily to application within individual-level studies, and these are discussed in Chapter 7.

However, for Hofstede individualism-collectivism is an attribute of nations rather than individuals. The most individualistic nations were shown to be the USA, Australia, the UK, the Netherlands, and Canada, while the most collectivistic nations were reported as Guatemala, Ecuador, Panama, Venezuela, and Colombia.

Hofstede's final dimension was named Masculinity/Femininity. This differentiates nations that value assertiveness from those that value nurturance. As with the other dimensions, Hofstede's concern is with nations, not with individuals, and he notes that his labels 'should not be taken to imply that men always actually behave in a more masculine manner than do women or that women behave in more feminine ways than do men' (Hofstede, 2001: 284). It is nations that are characterised as more masculine or more feminine, not the people within those nations. Despite Hofstede's disclaimer, many subsequent critics have had difficulty in accepting his labels for this dimension, as they appear to reify a gender distinction that has been much debated in recent times. 'Masculine' nations were found to be Slovakia, Hungary, Japan, Austria, and Venezuela, while the most 'feminine' nations were Sweden, Norway, the Netherlands, Denmark, and Costa Rica.

Evaluating Hofstede's Study

Nation scores for Hofstede's individualism-collectivism correlate strongly and positively with those for power distance. Indeed, both dimensions were loaded together on the same factor in his analysis. He argued that this was a consequence of the fact that they were both correlated with national wealth, and that they were unrelated when wealth was controlled for (Hofstede, 2001: 59). He concluded that it is conceptually useful to keep them separate and subsequent researchers have followed his proposal. Individualism-collectivism is the dimension of cultural variation that has generated the greatest interest among cross-cultural researchers and it provides the basis for many of the studies to be discussed in later chapters.

As Table 2.1 indicated, the actual survey items used by Hofstede to define individualism and collectivism concerned the relative preference for differing work motivations. In nations defined as individualist, 'personal' time, freedom and challenges were favoured more strongly, whereas in nations defined as more collectivist, the use of skills, good physical conditions and training opportunities were more strongly endorsed. Although the text of these items does not closely match the definitions of individualism and collectivism employed by Hofstede and by later researchers, the distinction between nations with individualist and collectivist cultures has proved robust.

Acquiescent Response Style The tendency to agree with rather than disagree with many or all of the statements that are provided by a researcher.

Factor Analysis A statistical technique indicating the extent to which different survey items have received similar responses and can therefore be grouped together as 'factors'.

Individualism-Collectivism Hofstede's description of a nation-level dimension, derived from earlier writing by Kluckhohn and Strodtbeck (1961), and defined by many authors in varying ways. The central element concerns the continuity of and commitment to group affiliations in collectivist cultures, compared with the negotiability of group affiliations and their rule-based operation in individualist cultures.

Overall, the study yielded four dimensions along which a substantial number of the world's nations could be located. Hofstede himself tested the predictive validity of these dimensions by exploring what he termed their 'consequences' through correlating them with other measures available in the 1970s that can be used to characterise nations. We shall examine some of these correlations later in this chapter.

For the moment, we need to explore some of the other key issues raised by his study. Obviously this was completed before the current focus of interest on cross-cultural psychology had developed. Indeed, it contributed to the triggering of that development by providing a rich conceptual structure for these studies (Bond, 2002). So how does it fare in terms of the criteria we might now set for a good study? On the positive side, we can note that the samples from different nations were well matched, the survey was translated into local languages, acquiescent response style was controlled, the appropriate level of analysis was correctly defined, and respondents were unaware that they were contributing to cross-national comparisons. On the negative side, the survey items had been selected to assess employee morale and could well have missed other important aspects of cultural difference. The items were also likely to reflect the preoccupations of the American-owned company. By drawing the items selectively from the much larger number of items in his original survey, Hofstede was in some instances also following a hunch as to what was important, rather than relying on factor analyses of a full range of his data. This therefore reduced the objectivity of his findings.

While this study does provide a provisional map of cultural differences, better and more recent measures are desirable, and we shall discuss some of these measures shortly. There are some further issues to consider first. Some critics argue that the scores are based on data obtained so long ago that they cannot any longer provide valid guidance as to the differences between nations in the twenty-first century. Hofstede, however, sees these differences as rather robust and unlikely to change fast. In the revised 2001 edition of his book, he notes numerous instances in which his country scores are found to be significant predictors of effects measured by other researchers as much as 30 years after the IBM data were collected.

In the intervening years, many researchers have undertaken studies in which samples from two or three nations were compared on some attribute, and the results were then interpreted on the basis of Hofstede's scores for those nations. This kind of interpretation can only be trusted if it is based on data showing that the actual samples surveyed within a study did differ in terms of individualism, collectivism, or whatever cultural dimension was used to formulate a hypothesis. It is risky to infer that because samples drawn from IBM employees 40 years ago differed in a certain way, contemporary samples of, for instance, students from those same nations will differ in the same ways at the present time.

Another issue that we need to consider has to do with diversity within nations. In undertaking his nation-level analysis, Hofstede controlled for the demographic variability of his samples. That does not mean that there is no variability to be found within his data. He reports additional analyses that showed variability in terms of gender and occupational role. Within nations we can expect there to be subcultures based on regions, on social class, on professional groupings, on ethnicity, and on gender. What we need to know is how much variation there is at each level of analysis. Using data from the World Values Survey (discussed later in this chapter), Minkov and Hofstede (2012) tested whether there was much variation in values between regions *within* nations, compared to the variation between nations. In East and South East Asia, they found that the value profiles of 73 out of 84 regions were close to the profiles of other regions *within* the same nation. A similar degree of intra-national homogeneity was found in South America and in Sub-Saharan Africa, although there was rather more over-lap across national boundaries for the value profiles of regions within their sample of Anglo nations. Of course, these results do not show that there is no variation between individuals within a nation, because the authors collapsed their data across individuals within each region to yield a single score for each region on each dimension. Minkov and Hofstede's results show that regional differences in values within nations tend to be smaller than the differences between nations.

Van Herk and Poortinga (2012) made a similar study within Europe comparing variation between nations with variation within the 195 much smaller territorial units specified by the European Union for analysis of statistical data. This study used measures of values developed by Schwartz, Melech, Lehmann, et al. (2001), to be discussed below. Van Herk and Poortinga reported that two-thirds of the variance in values across these territorial units was attributable to national differences.

The final aspect of the Hofstede project that needs more discussion is fundamental and brings us back to the discussion of definitions with which this chapter began. If cultures are defined by shared meanings, do the IBM survey data actually provide us with information on whether particular values were or were not shared in different nations? A social system with a certain national culture defined by average scores on a psychological measure cannot by itself be evidence of shared meanings. It is individuals who do or do not share meanings. If we could show that individuals within a particular nation do share particular sets of meanings, then we should be in a stronger position to make more valid *cultural* comparisons between larger systems such as nations.

How would the sharedness of meanings be established? The most obvious approach would be to compare the levels of agreement across a cultural unit's members to establish the consensus around the value or belief in question. We thus need to do individual-level analyses to prepare the way for more valid culture-level analyses, whether these be analyses of marriages, families, organisations, or nations.

STUDYING INDIVIDUALS AND STUDYING NATIONS

While Hofstede considered the best way into the study of cultural differences was to focus on value differences at the nation level, an alternative approach has been developed over the past 20 years by Shalom Schwartz in Israel. Schwartz (1992) emphasised that one cannot validly compare variations in nation-level endorsed values until one has first undertaken more basic research into the structure of values that are held by individuals. By checking how values are organised within the minds of individuals in many different parts of the world, we can check whether a values survey relies on the same psychological meanings in these different parts of the world. Since cross-national surveys necessarily involve translations into numerous different languages, the scope for variation in meaning is considerable. How can we be sure that when persons in different parts of the world endorse values such as 'honesty', 'freedom' or 'loyalty', they mean the same thing to each of these individuals?

Key Researcher Box 2.2   Shalom Schwartz

Figure 2.2   Shalom Schwartz

Shalom H. Schwartz (b. 1936) grew up in the United States and received his PhD in social psychology from the University of Michigan in 1967, subsequently teaching in the sociology department of the University of Wisconsin. In 1979, when many of Israel's leading researchers were moving to universities in the United States, Schwartz headed in the opposite direction to the Department of Psychology at the Hebrew University in Jerusalem. During the 1970s and 1980s, he was a pioneer of research on pro-social and altruistic behaviour. Subsequently, he has focused on investigating the fundamental structure of human values, testing his model in more than 70 countries. In an extensive set of studies, he has examined the antecedents and consequences of individual differences in value priorities and the relations of cultural dimensions of values to societal characteristics and policies. His publications have been cited more than 30,000 times. His value measures are now part of the ongoing, biannual European Social Survey and of the World Values Survey. In 2007, he was awarded the Israel Prize for psychology, the highest honour bestowed on Israeli citizens by their government.

The Schwartz Value Surveys

Schwartz proposed that one could test for uniformity of meaning by doing a parallel series of individual-level studies of a set of specific values within many different nations. His respondents were asked to rate the extent to which each of 56 values was a guiding principle in his or her life. Each value was stated as a single word or phrase, with a brief illustration or two provided in brackets, for instance: 'successful (achieving goals)' and 'social justice (correcting injustice, caring for the weak)'. Many of these items were drawn from earlier surveys conducted by Rokeach (1973) in the USA, but further values were added in an attempt to draw also from other cultural traditions. Separate samples of students as well as schoolteachers from 20 nations were surveyed initially, with many further later additions.

For each nation's data, Schwartz then undertook separate **smallest space analyses**. This is a technique similar in principle to factor analysis, which does not make parametric assumptions about the intervals between points on the rating scales. The output from smallest space analysis is a two-dimensional plot that portrays the proximity within the data of every value to every other value. Schwartz reasoned that if the endorsement of a given value falls close to the same set of other values in other nations' data sets, then the values must have relatively close meanings for the individuals within each of the nations represented. Figure 2.3 shows the results averaged across separate individual-level analyses from 20 national groups (Schwartz, 2011).

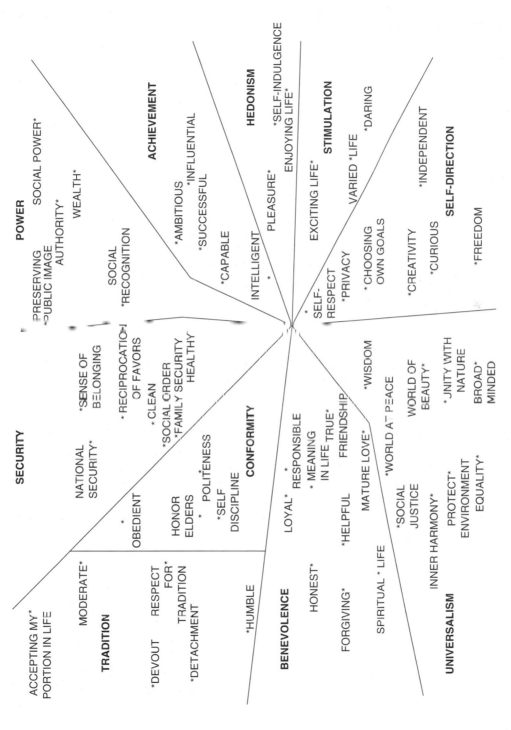

Figure 2.3 Schwartz's Mapping of the Individual-Level Structure of Values

Source: Schwartz & Sagiv (1995).

Smallest Space Analysis A statistical technique analogous to factor analysis, which does not make the same statistical assumptions that are made in factor analysis, since the technique rests on ordinal measurement rather than interval scale measurement.

As the figure shows, Schwartz interpreted his results by drawing lines that divide his 56 values into clusters of relatively similar values, defining each of these as a 'value type' or domain. This is a subjective procedure, equivalent to the subjectivity involved in deciding on the number of factors to extract from a data set and then assigning names to the factors that have emerged from the factor analysis. Schwartz identified ten separate value types and assigned a name to each. In assigning names, he was originally guided by a theoretical framework in which he reasoned that human values may be expected to reflect the three universal human requirements: biological needs, needs for social coordination, and needs for group welfare and maintenance. However, the value types that were identified do not clearly separate into these three types of need.

Since the structure of values is circular, it can be summarised in a variety of ways. Initially, Schwartz chose to summarise it as two bipolar dimensions, which are represented diagonally in Figure 2.3. The dimension of Openness to Change versus Conservation contrasts the endorsement of novelty and autonomy (bottom right in the figure) with the endorsement of tradition and conformity (top left). The dimension of Self-Enhancement versus Self-Transcendence contrasts striving for individual ends (top right) against cooperation with others for supra-individual ends (bottom left). More recently, Schwartz, Cieciuch, Vecchione et al. (2012) have suggested that it can be useful to contrast values with a personal focus (right in the figure) with those having a social focus (left), as well as values favouring growth (bottom) against those focusing on self-protection (top).

Schwartz found that 75% of the original 56 values fell consistently within the same value type or domain across his 20 national samples. Schwartz and Sagiv (1995) extended this analysis to 88 samples from 40 nations. Schwartz et al. (2001) reported that by using a new and simpler measure, the Portrait Value Questionnaire, they were also able to obtain a similar structure of values. These results make it clear that (at least after Schwartz's detailed attention to **back-translations** of his survey), most individual value items do have equivalent meanings in the majority of nations. He eventually concluded that 44 of his original 56 items had adequately similar meanings for persons across a wide sample of nations. The consistency in meaning of most values implies that measurements based upon these values do provide a useful way of comparing persons across nations and other cultural groups. This opened the way to the next stage in his project, which was to undertake nation-level analyses using average value scores that were more directly comparable than were those that had been conducted by Hofstede.

Back-Translation The translation of a survey into a second language, followed by its translation back into the original language by a different bilingual person, who has not seen the original version.

After adjusting the scores for possible differences in acquiescent response style and then averaging the responses for each separate value

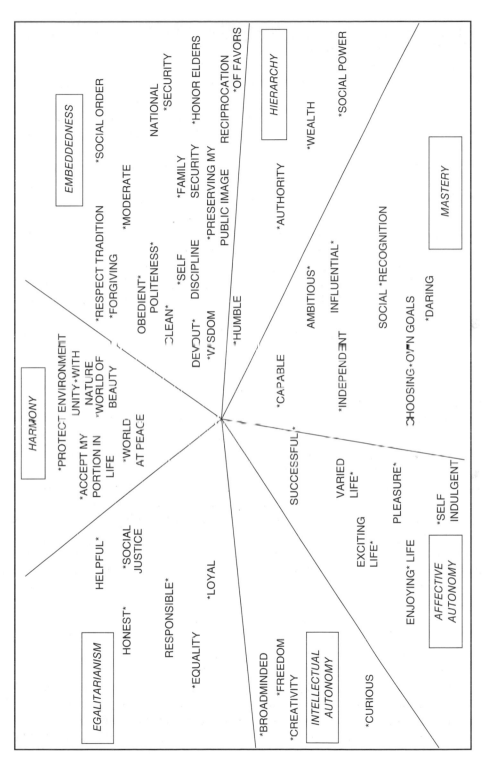

Figure 2.4 Schwartz's Mapping of the Nation-Level Structure of Values

Source: S.H. Schwartz (1994), 'Values: cultural and individual', in F. van de Vijver et al. (Eds.) (2010), *Fundamental questions in cross-cultural psychology.* Reproduced by permission of Cambridge University Press.

across individuals within each country, a nation-level smallest space analysis was conducted (Schwartz, 1994). As Figure 2.4 shows, the structure that emerged was not identical to that obtained in the individual-level analyses. Seven nation-level value types were identified, which could be summarised as three bipolar dimensions. These are named as Autonomy-Embeddedness, Hierarchy-Egalitarianism, and Mastery-Harmony. Schwartz chose to assign different labels to his nation-level dimensions of values than had earlier been assigned to his individual-level dimensions, because he wanted to emphasise the importance of distinguishing the separate levels semantically.

The availability of Schwartz's two separate analyses enables us to address one of the most central and vexing questions in contemporary cross-cultural psychology, and one that many people find difficult to comprehend. How can it be that when the same data are analysed at two different levels, the results are not the same? Look carefully at the results for endorsement of the values 'humble' and 'authority' in Figures 2.3 and 2.4. In Figure 2.3, 'humble' appears in the value type for tradition, whereas 'authority' appears in the value type for power. The two values are located on opposite sides of the plot, which indicates that the endorsement of them is negatively correlated. In other words, those who endorse authority as a guiding principle in their life are not at all likely to be the same as those who see being humble as a guiding principle in their life.

Contrast this finding with the results in Figure 2.4. At the nation level, both 'humble' and 'authority' appear in the same value type of hierarchy. Nations in which there is a strong average endorsement for authority tend to be the same as those in which there is a strong average endorsement of being humble.

Putting the results for both levels together, the picture is clear enough: in certain nations there is a relative preponderance of some individuals who endorse authority and of other individuals who endorse humility. These individuals are likely to relate to one another through a system of hierarchically ordered roles. These nations can be expected to be those whom Hofstede identified as high on power distance. Conversely, in some other nations there are lesser numbers of individuals who endorse authority and humility and these should be the nations in which power distance is relatively low. Within any given nation, however, individuals who endorse the value of authority do not endorse the value of humility, and vice versa. Nations are not individuals.

Fischer, Vauclair, Fontaine, and Schwartz (2010) showed that around 15 of the 56 values in the Schwartz survey held a changed position at the nation level compared to the individual level of analysis. Whether or not different values (or other attributes of cultures) go together at each level will depend upon the factors operative at each level. The logic governing their positioning is different (Leung & Bond, 2007). At the individual level, we may expect genetic dispositions and individual socialisation histories to be strong predictors of the way that different values go together. At the nation level, we may expect the success or failure of different types of social systems to predict the values that go together (Fischer, 2012).

To construct a valid cross-cultural psychology we need to draw on both perspectives. Above all, we need to ensure that our analysis is done at the level that matches the reasoning characterising our hypotheses. To infer that a relationship holds at the individual level because it has been found true at the nation level is illogical and has been termed the '**ecological fallacy**' by Hofstede and others: to infer that a relationship holds at the nation level because it has been found true at the individual level is likewise illogical and has been termed the 'reverse ecological fallacy'.

In discussing Schwartz's studies, we have so far only considered his analyses of the *structure* of values. While this is essential groundwork if

> **Ecological Fallacy** The false belief that the relationship between two variables must be the same at different levels of analysis. Usually used to refer to the invalid extrapolation from nation-level relationships to individual-level relationships.

values are to provide a conceptual framework for cross-cultural studies, the reward for establishing a reliable structure is that one may then proceed to make comparisons across different samples and surveys at any given level of analysis. The techniques used to plot the structure of values can, for example, be used to plot the distribution of each *nation's* scores. We have already noted the nations that scored high or low on each of Hofstede's dimensions. Figure 2.5 shows the location of 67 nations in relation to Schwartz's seven nation-level value types (Schwartz, 2004). Later in this chapter, we consider how much convergence there is between means from all of the published surveys that have included large numbers of nations with their data analysed at the level of nations.

Schwartz and Bardi (2001) have provided a different type of comparison, focusing upon which individual-level value types are most endorsed within each of the 123 samples of teachers and students for which data were available. A remarkable consensus was found across these samples. The two most favoured value types were benevolence and self-direction and the two least favoured value types were tradition and power. Since cross-cultural psychologists most frequently study and try to explain the *differences* between the samples they study, these results help to provide a necessary overall caution: there are differences, but there is also substantial global agreement on which values are most desired. While there is a global convergence on the most desirable values, each nation's data diverge from this global average in informative ways, and it is these variations upon which cross-cultural psychologists have mostly focused. So, for example, Singaporean teachers favour security, conformity and tradition much more than the global average, while American students endorse achievement, power and hedonism much more than the global average.

Fischer and Schwartz (2011) have examined the Schwartz data in yet another way, examining whether there is more disagreement on values between individuals than there is between nations. An **intra-class correlation** is a statistic comparing the percentage of variability within a sample at different levels of analysis. Across the 67 nations in Schwartz's database, nation-level intra-class correlation scores for individual value items ranged between an average of 6% and 26%. In other words, between 74% and 94% of the variability is between individuals rather than between nations. Thus, if specific nation-level values are to be used to explain differences between the results of studies done in different parts of the world, the values that show the greatest cross-national differences would be the most likely candidates. In Fischer and Schwartz's analyses these were the values identified in Figure 2.3 as the value types of conformity and tradition. Of course, the estimates of nation-level variation obtained by Fischer and Schwartz are averages for their overall sample. There might be larger variations between the values of specific pairs or groups of nations.

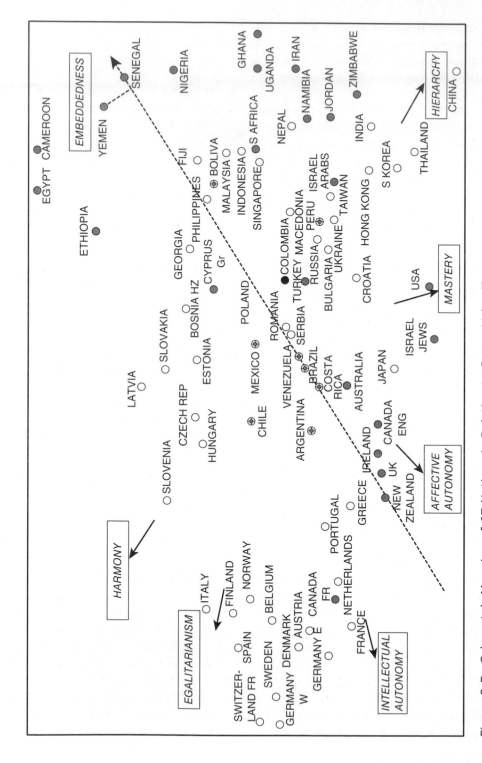

Figure 2.5 Schwartz's Mapping of 67 Nations in Relation to Seven Value-Types

Source: Schwartz (2009).

There are several possible perspectives on the finding that there is typically much more variation within nations than there is across nations on the Schwartz measure. One possibility is that his measure does not detect the key values underlying cultural difference. This is unlikely, given the comprehensiveness of his measure, but

Intra-Class Correlation An estimate of how much variability there is in subsamples within a dataset, compared to the variability in the dataset as a whole.

we can test the possibility by comparing his results with other recent value surveys. A second perspective would be to argue that cultural differences do not rest so much on objective differences in values, more on how you and I respond to what we perceive to be the prevailing values around us as a basis for our own behaviour. This is likely to be the case, given the finding that there is a substantial amount of individual-level variation in values within each nation. Finally, it could be that these rather abstractly stated value priorities are interpreted in different ways in different contexts. You and I may interpret the precise behavioural implications of 'freedom', 'obedience' or 'equality' in rather different ways. If this is so, we should look at studies of more specific indices of beliefs and reactions to behaviours as the basis of cultural differences. We shall discuss each of these perspectives in this as well as later chapters.

Other Value Surveys

Smith, Dugan, and Trompenaars (1996) analysed a databank comprising a survey of the values of organisational employees in 43 nations. Multidimensional analysis of all the individual-level data regardless of the respondent's nation revealed two principal dimensions of variation. The first contrasted individuals whose involvement in their organisation was based on loyalty and those whose involvement was more utilitarian. The second dimension contrasted conservatism values against more egalitarian values. Smith et al. computed the average scores for each nation along these dimensions.

Another large database that yields nation-level means for values is that derived from the World Values Survey (Inglehart, 1997). The World Values Survey comprises a coordinated set of opinion surveys that are repeated every few years and which draw on representative national populations. Commencing within Europe in the 1980s, the survey now spans more than 80 nations. Inglehart has analysed the changes in these values over time that are most relevant to political preferences. Factor analysing individual responses to 47 items, Inglehart identified two dimensions of variation across nations: focus on Well-Being versus on Survival and preference for Secular-Rational versus Traditional Authority. The items constituting each of these two factors are grouped in the same way by respondents within each of his nations, thereby meeting the requirement emphasised by Schwartz that national averages should only be compared for those value items whose meaning is the same across individual persons in all cultural groups. Fischer and Schwartz (2011) also computed intra-class correlations for relevant value items from 62 nations in the World Values Survey databank. Here too they found much more variance at the individual level than at the nation level.

In what is often referred to as the GLOBE (Global Leadership and Organizational Behavior Effectiveness) project, House, Hanges, Javidan, Dorfman, and Gupta (2004) surveyed business managers in 62 nations. Respondents were asked to describe their society 'as it is' and 'as it should be' on rating scales comprising nine dimensions of national culture. The 'should be' ratings could be considered as measures of values, but the 'as is' ratings comprise the most extensive survey to date that has focused upon description of behaviours. House et al. found marked differences between the 'should be' and 'as is' responses. Their choice of different types of measures provoked an important debate, which is discussed in Research Debate Box 2.1.

Research Debate Box 2.1   Which Measure of Values Best Summarises Cultural Differences?

House et al. (2004) created measures for nine separate dimensions of cultural variation, measuring each with four items. The formulation of these dimensions was much influenced by the definition of Hofstede's dimensions. House et al. asked business managers in 62 nations to complete these scales in two ways, firstly by describing 'how things are in this society', and secondly by describing 'how things in this society should be'. The first of these versions is clearly a measure of perceived norms; the second of these versions is clearly a measure of values.

Hofstede (2006) presented many criticisms of the House et al. project, but here we discuss only the issue of how best to measure values. Hofstede sees a difference between my expressing a view on how people in general should behave, in other words what is generally desirable, and me saying how I personally desire to behave. Thus, I might personally endorse ambition and success, while at the same time saying that other people should be more nurturant and less competitive. Hofstede sees personal values as a better basis for cultural comparisons, because he believes that they provide a more certain basis for predicting behaviour (but see Bond, 2013, as well as our discussion of intersubjective norms in Chapter 8).

Responding to this critique, Javidan, House et al. (2006) asserted that 'cultural dynamics go beyond mathematical averages of what is desirable to individual actors' (p. 900). In their view, asking respondents which practices are widely endorsed yields a more valid measure, spicing up their response by quoting text from Hofstede (2001), who wrote that 'we are better observers of others than of ourselves' (p. 9). Javidan et al. also pointed out that it is desirable to test whether there is a relationship between values and behaviour, rather than assuming as Hofstede did that the behaviours found in a culture are a direct expression of prevailing values.

Hofstede (2006) was unimpressed with these arguments, suggesting that respondents are not likely to be able to validly rate either the values or the behaviours that prevail generally in a society, because most respondents would not have had enough experience of other cultures. In his view, these types of ratings will generate stereotypes rather than valid information.

This debate has had a positive effect, encouraging researchers to move beyond a simple enumeration of values and to start considering and testing empirically the complex ways in which values, beliefs and behaviours are interwoven in the construction of cultures (Smith, 2006). These issues are examined more fully in Chapter 3.

The four large-scale values surveys described above each sampled a rather different range of nations. Inglehart's data were derived from nationally representative surveys, while all the others sampled distinctive sub-samples from within nations. They also used different measures, were conducted at different times, and analysed their data in different ways. This range of variation makes it difficult to identify the extent to which their results confirm or contradict one another.

It would certainly be remarkable if their results were to converge with one another. Surprisingly, as the correlations in Table 2.2 indicate, there is in fact considerable convergence, with the exception of some of House et al.'s dimensions:

Table 2.2   Are Hofstede's Dimensions Replicable? Correlations across Different Value Surveys

Newer Dimensions	Power Distance	Uncertainty Avoidance	Individualism (versus Collectivism)	Masculinity (versus Femininity)
Schwartz				
Autonomy (versus Embeddedness)	−.52***		.64***	
Hierarchy (versus Egalitarianism)	.41**	−.29*	−.50***	
Mastery (versus Harmony)	.29*			
Smith et al.				
Loyal Involvement	.67***		−.77***	.37*
Conservatism	.63***		−.74***	
Inglehart				
Well-being (versus Survival)	−72***	−55**	.74***	−39*
Rational Authority	−.56**		.49**	
House et al. (Values)				
Institutional Collectivism	.45*	.42*	−.57**	
Power Distance		−.37*		
Uncertainty Avoidance	.70**	.31*	−.75**	

Note: The direction of these correlations refers to the dimension names that are not placed in brackets. Results for in-group collectivism values are omitted because no correlations were significant.

As Hofstede's original analysis indicated, his dimensions of individualism-collectivism and power distance are significantly and negatively correlated with one another. Each of the more recent surveys has identified dimensions that are strongly associated with this basic polarity. Correlations of around +0.6 between two measures indicate that less than half of their variance is shared, but correlations of this magnitude are nonetheless encouraging, especially considering the very different samples used across these studies. As Hofstede also noted, nation scores for individualism-collectivism are strongly correlated with a nation's wealth. Thus it appears that the nation-level surveys of values that we have explored have succeeded primarily in identifying the values that predominate in rich nations in contrast to those that prevail in less rich nations. There is also some evidence for the replicability of Hofstede's other dimensions, but as we shall see, these dimensions have thus far exercised a lesser influence upon subsequent research.

Values and Morality. If we can now have some confidence in mapping the world in terms of endorsed values, we need to begin examining their consequences and correlates. Vauclair and Fischer (2011) have examined the links between Schwartz's values and measures of attitudes to morality that have been included in the World Values Survey. They have distinguished moral issues that concern relations between the individual and others (e.g., the moral acceptability of personal and sexual behaviours such as suicide, prostitution, abortion and divorce) from those that concern the common good (e.g., cheating and bribery). Across 56 nations, they predicted and found that because personal and sexual morality concerns relations between individuals, it will be more influenced by norms in different cultural contexts about appropriate relations with others. Moral leniency towards personal and sexual behaviours was higher in nations high on autonomy and low on embeddedness. However, for morality concerning the common good, they predicted and found that there would be no relation to nation-level differences in values, because this type of morality is of equal concern in all cultures. Thus, we can better understand some of the behavioural implications of value differences.

CULTURES AS SYSTEMS OF SHARED BELIEFS

Rather than focus on values, some researchers have looked at the extent to which nations can be characterised by sets of shared beliefs. Research in this field has paralleled developments in the study of values, progressing from simply using unmodified US measures to those that have greater emic content and which take account of the need to differentiate individual-level and nation-level data analysis. Within the USA, Rotter (1966) developed a measure of 'locus of control', that is to say a generalised belief in internal versus external control over events. Put more simply, to what extent did respondents expect that the events occurring around them were amenable to influence by themselves, rather than being due to external agencies, such as powerful others or fate? Smith, Trompenaars, and Dugan (1995) analysed locus of control data from 43 nations. After standardisation, individual-level multidimensional scaling revealed three dimensions of beliefs. The first dimension contrasted belief in personal efficacy with belief in the efficacy of politicians. Scores on this dimension correlated strongly with Schwartz's nation scores for mastery values. The second locus of control dimension contrasted belief in personal autonomy with belief in the need to depend on others. Scores on this dimension correlated strongly with Schwartz's nation scores for autonomy and Hofstede's scores for individualism. This provided a preliminary indication of links between the values and beliefs that prevail in nations.

   More recently, Leung, Bond, de Carrasquel et al. (2002) identified an extensive list of several hundred beliefs (described by them as **social axioms**) that were prevalent in Venezuela and Hong Kong, and added in others from established scales of beliefs such as Rotter's. After translation and pilot testing, responses to 60 of these axioms by students were then surveyed in Hong Kong, Venezuela, Japan, Germany, and the United States. Five comparable individual-level factors were identified within each of these nations. The survey was then

Social Axiom A widely shared belief as to what is true rather than false. It is distinct from values, which concern what is desirable versus what is undesirable.

repeated with further student respondents from 41 nations, and the same five factors were found (Leung & Bond, 2004). Thus, within nations, individuals differ in: Social Cynicism (a negative view of human nature), Social Complexity (belief in multiple solutions to problems), Reward for Application (belief that effort and knowledge will be rewarded), Religiosity (belief in positive functions of religious practices and institutions) and Fate Control (belief that events are predetermined but can be influenced).

Everyday Life Box 2.1   The Richness of Proverbs

In conducting their study of social axioms, Leung and Bond (2002) had to rewrite the traditional proverbs that they collected into simple language, so that respondents from all nations could understand their meaning clearly. However, this procedure loses much of the richness of the original imagery, as shown in the examples listed here:

From China

A nation's treasure is in its scholars.
A rat who gnaws at a cat's tail invites destruction.
Do not remove a fly from your friend's forehead with a hatchet.
Dig the well before you are thirsty.

From India

God made a match: one is blind, one is a leper.
Walk like an elephant.
The cat went to pray after eating 900 rats.
Monkey doesn't know the taste of ginger.

From Egypt

He who unties his belt will stay the night.
Dawn breaks without the crowing of the cock.
What the crazy wife eats, her blind husband will eat.

From Brazil

The trees with most leaves will not necessarily produce juicy fruit.
An old man with a torn sleeve never dishonoured anyone.
If it were ever to rain soup, the poor would only have forks.

The same data were next aggregated to the nation level, in order to determine the structure of beliefs at that level (Bond, Leung, Au et al., 2004). As had been the case with Schwartz's analyses of values, the nation-level structure of beliefs differs in some respects from the individual-level structure. At the nation level, four of the five individual-level factors merge into one strong factor, which Bond et al. label as Dynamic Externality. This cluster of beliefs is focused around religiosity and a belief that effort will ultimately lead to just outcomes. The second nation-level factor was named Societal Cynicism, and was constituted almost exclusively by items that defined the factor of social cynicism at the individual level. In relation to values, nations' scores on dynamic externality are highest where Schwartz's measure of embeddedness values is high. Endorsement of societal cynicism was significantly associated with Hofstede's measures of power distance and collectivism. Once again, some consistency is found between endorsements of values and beliefs at the nation level.

Since scores on Hofstede's collectivism and Schwartz's embeddedness are strongly correlated with one another, these results create an initial impression that the values and beliefs surveys all point toward a single dimension of cultural variation, distinguishing nations that are wealthy, individualistic, secular and taking a positive view of human nature, in contrast to nations that are less wealthy, more collectivistic, more traditional, more religious, and more cynical. However, this is reading a little too much into these results. Just because two measures correlate with one another at +0.5 or +0.6 does not mean that they are identical. The variance in common between two measures correlating at 0.6 is the square of 0.6, namely 0.36, or only 36%. So while these two measures have substantial elements in common, they are sufficiently distinct from one another to add predictive power to one another in explaining some nation-level outcome of interest, like homicide or suicide, for example.

How do we interpret the divergent structure of beliefs at the two levels of analysis, individual and national? The consistency across levels in the structure of societal cynicism indicates that in nations where social cynicism is high, there will be some individuals who endorse all of the cynical beliefs that comprise the overall factor and others who endorse none of these beliefs. In contrast, in nations where dynamic externality is high, we may expect to identify differentiated subcultures or sets of individuals where, for instance, those who endorse religiosity are not necessarily the same ones as those who believe more strongly in a reward for application.

CULTURE AS PATTERNS OF BEHAVIOUR

In exploring the use of values and beliefs as a basis for understanding cultures, we have noted that researchers have seen the need to ensure that their measures have equivalent meanings in different settings. Schwartz (1992) did this for values, and Leung et al. (2002) did it for beliefs. If culture is to be understood in terms of behaviour, a similar exercise is required. No one has made an analysis of this type on the required scale, although Triandis (1977) made initial studies in Greece and the USA. To be done effectively, behaviours would have to be described in very general terms. We have already discussed some examples of specific behaviours that have quite different meanings in different contexts.

As discussed earlier, respondents to the House et al. (2004) survey were also asked to rate how most other people in their society did behave. Their measures did use very general terms: for instance, one item in their survey was 'In this society people are generally assertive'. Respondents from different parts of the world might have very different behaviours in mind when agreeing or disagreeing with this statement. Their answers probably tell us more about the types of terms that are used to evaluate behaviours and behavioural norms than about specific actions. Perhaps because of this, significant correlations with values measures at or above +0.6 were found, particularly between House et al.'s behavioural scores for collectivism and power distance and Hofstede's scores with the same names.

Two further large-scale surveys have been reported, each of which yields measures that are more directly related to behaviour than those considered so far. Smith, Peterson, and Schwartz (2002) surveyed managers in 47 nations. Respondents were asked to what extent they had relied on various sources of guidance in handling different events that arose at work. Smith et al. computed an index of verticality, which reflected a reliance on one's superior and on formal rules, as opposed to a reliance on oneself or one's subordinates. Verticality was significantly higher for nations scoring higher on Hofstede's power distance and on Schwartz's measures of hierarchy, mastery and embeddedness. Again, there seems to be a meaningful convergence of results at the nation level.

Gelfand and 41 co-authors (2011) conducted a study to determine the extent to which behaviour in different societies is tightly constrained by rules and norms. In this study, participants from a range of occupations in 33 nations rated how strong were the norms in their society as to how people should behave and how much people would be punished if they deviated from those norms. (This study is discussed in detail in Chapter 3.) Tightness scores were found to correlate positively with Hofstede's scores for power distance and collectivism. The correlations between the Hofstede dimensions and all the nation-level indices of beliefs and behaviours that we have discussed are summarised in Table 2.3. As was the case with measures of values, there is a rather consistent pattern of correlations with the dimensions of individualism–collectivism and power distance. There is a sharp contradiction between the two available measures of uncertainty avoidance, and very few associations with the masculinity-femininity dimension.

Table 2.3   Correlations between Hofstede's Dimensions and Surveys of Beliefs and Behaviours

Beliefs and Behaviour Dimensions	Power Distance	Uncertainty Avoidance	Individualism (versus Collectivism)	Masculinity (versus Femininity)
Locus of Control (Smith et al.)				
Personal Autonomy	–.47**		.70**	
Social Axioms (Leung et al.)				
Dynamic Externality	.55**		–.63**	
Societal Cynicism			–.50*	
Sources of Guidance (Smith et al.)				
Vertical Sources	.60**		–.54**	.30*
Perceived Practices (House et al.)				
In-group Collectivism	.68**		–.79**	
Institutional Collectivism		–.52**		
Power Distance	.49**	.40**	–.52**	
Uncertainty Avoidance	–.46**	–.64**	.50**	
Gelfand et al.				
Tight-Loose	.41**		–.43**	

Note: The direction of these correlations refers to the dimension names that are not placed in brackets

All of the studies that have contributed to the map of the world that has been explored in this chapter have been based on responses to questionnaires. We can gain additional confidence in the usefulness of the map if evidence from other sources can confirm its validity. Morling and Lamoreaux (2008) made a meta-analysis of 40 studies, each of which had compared the content of cultural products (advertisements, newspaper articles, song lyrics etc.) in two or more nations. They found a greater emphasis on collectivist themes in nations that had higher Hofstede scores for collectivism than they did in the USA. In a further study, Lamoreaux and Morling (2012) found less evidence for matching between the content of cultural products and dimensions of cultural variation other than individualism-collectivism. However, there were few studies available for most comparisons, so further investigation of this important form of validity check will be required.

A second way of assessing the value of the dimensions of national culture is to examine their relationship with objective indices that are available to characterise nations as a whole, such as wealth, political systems, human development and so forth. In his ground-breaking study, Hofstede (1980) reported that his scores for individualism-collectivism correlated with national wealth at 0.84, with respect for human rights at 0.61, and with absence of corruption at 0.71. In a similar way, Schwartz (2009) has reported that across 75 nations, his dimension of autonomy minus embeddedness correlates 0.76 with wealth, 0.72 with democratisation, 0.72 with average family size and -.76 with average household size. His dimension of mastery versus harmony correlates -.79 with competitive types of capitalism. Thus national differences in values are associated with substantive behavioural differences. But what causes what? The title of Hofstede's (1980) book suggested that behaviours and other attributes of nations are *consequences* of culture. Correlation does not establish causation, so we should for the moment adopt the more moderate position that these various indices are interrelated with one another.

To test for causal relationships we would need to look at data over time, and we examine studies of this type in Chapter 14. The strong association found between wealth and individualism-collectivism is especially important. Great care is needed in ensuring that when we study individualism-collectivism, we are not simply examining wealthy nations versus less wealthy nations. If we consider wealth not to be an element in what we define as culture, then the contribution of wealth must be partialled out in testing for other correlates of cultural dimensions.

PUTTING THE PICTURE TOGETHER

So far in this chapter, we have argued for a particular way of defining culture and social system, and have then reviewed a series of studies that can lead us toward an application of these definitions. However, in the process, we have raised as many questions as we have resolved. In particular, we have opened up the crucial question of how to connect our understandings of individuals and of large cultural entities such as nations. Reflecting on the studies that we have reviewed, we can differentiate two ways of describing the data that arise from cross-cultural comparisons. Firstly, we can study a sample of individuals. The respondents may be drawn from a single nation, but within cross-cultural psychology, they are more typically drawn from at least two nations. Even if the data are drawn from two or more nations, this does not mean that the comparison between mean scores from nation A and nation B is a nation-level comparison. If the analysis treats *each individual respondent as a separate case*, this is an individual-level comparison. Many cross-national comparisons of this kind have been published and we shall be discussing relevant examples in later chapters.

Comparisons between different nations of this type are only likely to be valid if checks have been made that the measures that have been used have the same structure at the individual level in both nations, and account has

> **Citizen Mean** A score representing an attribute of the average member of a nation, computed using data that have been analysed at the individual level and then aggregated to the nation level.

been taken of possible differences in acquiescent response style. One popular procedure for checking the similarity of the structure of scales is factor analysis. We noted earlier that Schwartz (1994) prefers to use smallest space analysis. Whichever technique is used, analysis is first done within each nation's data separately. If convergence is found in the structure of the data across each of the groups, then the basis for nation-level comparisons of individuals is established. The next step is to *aggregate* the data from each sample before testing a hypothesis. Aggregation will yield a mean score, and if that mean score represents a national group, we will call that score a **citizen mean** for each national sample. If we use the citizen mean as a data point, we shall have *only one score for each nation that is sampled*. Consequently, when a researcher is using only citizen means, conclusions can only be compared statistically when large numbers of nations have been sampled, with each nation providing only a single score.

The alternative procedure, pioneered by Hofstede (1980) is to aggregate individuals' responses before the structure of the items has been established within each national group. The researcher computes the average score of each item within each national set of data, and then tests the nation-level structure of the items. We call means computed in this way nation-level means. When factor analysed, these means yield national-level factor scores. This is the procedure followed by Hofstede (1980) in his original work, and he called his procedure an 'ecological factor analysis'. One could also term it a nation-level factor analysis, as have Bond et al. (2004). The results of such procedures enable researchers to locate nations relative to one another; they do not enable researchers to compare individuals within nations. Many studies in the published literature do not make clear which type of analysis was undertaken, or else identify their method in a way that uses terms confusingly. In Chapter 4, we shall discuss these techniques and issues further.

Relating Individuals and Cultures

From the perspective of psychology, the meaning of nation-level scores is less immediately clear. Even though researchers in this tradition start with measures of psychological constructs like values, by averaging these responses before factor analysing them across individuals, they create non-psychological, higher-order groupings, in this case national groupings. These groupings bear no necessary logical or empirical relation to groupings developed at the individual level of analysis (Leung & Bond, 1989, 2007). Nation-level analysis has been adopted by many social scientists. These researchers often compound the potential for confusion by giving their nation-level constructs psychological-sounding names, like 'Assertiveness', and 'Loyal Involvement'. These labels suggest qualities of individuals, not nations, and mislabeling nation-level factors in these ways perpetuates the confusion. A major goal of cross-cultural social psychology is to understand how these nation-level constructs relate to individual-level constructs (Bond, 2002).

Addressing this crucial distinction, Schwartz (1994) has argued that:

> Individual-level value dimensions presumably reflect the psychological dynamics of conflict and compatibility that individuals experience in the course of pursuing their different values in everyday life ... In contrast, culture-level dimensions presumably reflect the different solutions that societies evolve to the problems of regulating human activities, the different ways that institutional emphases and investments are patterned and justified in one culture compared with another ... The culture-level values that characterize a society ... must be inferred from various cultural products [e.g., folktales] ... these cultural products reflect assumptions about the desirable that are built into the institutions of the society and are passed on through intentional and unintentional socialization ... The average of the value priorities of societal members reflects these commonalities of enculturation. Individual variation around this average reflects unique personality and experience. Thus, averaged values of societal members [and their factor groupings], no less than their folktales or textbooks can point to cultural values. (1994: 92)

It is these nation-level values that cross-cultural psychologists link to individuals' psychological processes and outcomes (Bond, 2002).

Evaluating Progress

The studies reviewed in this chapter have revealed a surprising consensus in the findings of the various surveys. Despite differences in methods, survey contents and samples, results often concur to a significant extent. In contrast to geographical maps of the world, this series of studies has provided a series of what we can think of as psychological maps of the world. Like the early maps of geographers, the maps may be wrong at certain points, but they have given us a starting point. Geographers deal in longitude and latitude, but these maps are defined in terms of dimensions of variation in values, beliefs, and behaviours. Among these dimensions, individualism-collectivism has proved the most influential in guiding the studies that we review in the following chapters.

Although this progress is encouraging, we need to consider several limitations to what has been achieved. Firstly, we do not know whether the dimensions of cultural variation that have been identified are the most important ones. They may be the easiest to identify and seem to have substance as social scientific constructs, especially where they prove to be correlated with such major attributes as the wealth of a nation. They also put together a range of different attributes that we may need to distinguish more precisely. For instance, Triandis (1995) proposed that the broad concept of individualism-collectivism comprises at least four different elements: different understandings of the self; different types of goals; a focus on relatedness or rationality; and behaviour guided by one's attitudes versus behaviour guided by social norms.

Secondly, we need to consider how accurate observers are in judging the qualities that go to make up our existing measures of culture. As Heine, Lehman, Peng, and Greenholz (2002) have pointed out, we can only make judgments that are relative to our own experience. Someone who has grown up in a hierarchical culture may perceive hierarchical behaviour as less autocratic than would someone who has grown up in a culture favouring equality. Our experiences in life give each of us different points of reference against which we are likely to make our comparisons. Cross-cultural researchers have attempted to eliminate these sources of bias in varying ways, for example by standardising scores within a national group (Bond, 1988a). It is better to seek out measures that are more firmly anchored to phenomena that can be judged objectively.

Thirdly, we need to take greater account of the varying contexts in which life is lived. We can show that one nation is more collectivist or hierarchical than another, but there may be equally strong sources of variation within nations. For instance, it may be that work organisations everywhere are more hierarchical than families are everywhere. The ways in which we act upon our values and our beliefs may be tempered by the differing contexts within which we operate and from which we receive feedback in the course of daily living.

Key Researcher Box 2.3   Steven Heine

Figure 2.6   Steven Heine

Steven J. Heine (b. 1966) obtained his Bachelor's degree at the University of Alberta, taking Japanese language as a minor. His subsequently went to Japan to teach English and his experiences strengthened his interest in becoming a cross-cultural psychologist. He obtained his PhD in that field from the University of British Columbia in 1996. After working with Shinobu Kitayama at Kyoto University in Japan for two years and subsequently holding a post at the University of Pennsylvania, he returned to the University of British Columbia, where he is now Professor of Social and Cultural Psychology. He received a distinguished early career award from the American Psychological Association in 2003. He has published more than 60 research papers, and a cultural psychology textbook. His discussions of aspects of research method are relevant to many chapters in this book, and his research into cultural differences in self-enhancement is particularly important in Chapter 7.

Fourthly, few of the studies reviewed in this chapter have taken account of diverse ethnicities within the nations sampled. Members of groups perceive greater diversity within their own group than they see in other groups (Linville, Fischer, & Yoon, 1996), and this effect is as typical of nations as it is of small groups. Despite this perceptual enhancement of differences, where comparisons have been made across ethnic groups within a single nation, they show surprisingly small differences. For instance, a mapping of Israel's profile of values using the Schwartz (1994) survey looks much the same using the Druze, Muslim, Christian Arab, or Jewish populations when locating Israel relative to other national groups (Bond, 1996: 217). In larger nations such as China greater regional variability is found (Bond, 1996).

Finally, we have noted that there is much greater variability between the values of individuals within nations than there is between nations. Consequently, there must be a limit to the usefulness of Rohner's (1984) definition of culture as based on shared meanings. If the individuals within a culture only partially share the meanings that are placed on events, there must be some additional factors that bind culture members together sufficiently to generate the distinctive attributes of nations. These factors may include awareness of the prevailing values and beliefs of those around one, as well as the direct impact of the practices and institutions that characterise particular social and ecological contexts. We explore the nature of these additional factors, particularly in Chapters 3, 6 and 8.

SUMMARY

Culture has been defined as the shared meanings found within a given social system. Psychologists have provided a conceptual framework for studies involving culture by surveying endorsements of values, beliefs, and the differential occurrence of behaviours. Progress has been dependent upon obtaining a clear conceptualisation of the different levels of analysis involved in doing cross-cultural psychology. Valid characterisations of nation-level differences in psychological processes and outcomes can only be achieved if prior individual-level studies show that measures are equivalent across samples; measures derived from individual-level rather than nation-level studies are required for predictions about individuals. Nation-level measures define the contexts within which individuals are socialised. The relation of these nation-level measures to objective indices derived from other social sciences is of major interest in ascertaining the nature of the national context within which its citizens are socialised and become 'cultured'.

FURTHER READING

1 Hofstede, G. (2009). Dimensionalising cultures: The Hofstede model in context. *Online readings in psychology and culture.* Available at http://scholarworks.gvsu.edu/*orpc*
2 Smith, P.B. (2002). Levels of analysis in cross-cultural psychology. *Online Readings in Psychology and Culture.* Available at http://scholarworks.gvsu.edu/*orpc*
3 Smith, P.B., & Schwartz, S.H. (1997). Values. In J.W. Berry, M.H. Segall, & C. Kağıtçıbaşı (Eds), *Handbook of cross-cultural psychology* (2nd edn, Vol. 3, pp. 77–108). Needham Heights, MA: Allyn & Bacon.
4 Schwartz, S.H. (2004). Mapping and interpreting cultural differences around the world. In H. Vinken, J. Soeters, & P. Ester (Eds), *Comparing cultures: Dimensions of culture in a comparative perspective* (pp. 43–73). Leiden, Netherlands: Brill.

STUDY QUESTIONS

1 What would you say are some of the salient values and beliefs held by the members of the nation within which you reside? How do these relate to the dimensions of cultural difference that researchers have identified?
2 What is a citizen score for a psychological measure and how can members of different cultural groups be compared in their psychological functioning?
3 What are the consequences of defining culture in terms of shared values, beliefs and meanings as opposed to behaviours?
4 Is it better for measures of culture to be derived from self-reports or from respondents' perceptions of their cultural context?
5 What value do nation-level dimensions have for psychologists, given that psychology tries to understand individuals?

3

The Origins and Dynamics of Culture

'The present is the funeral of the past and man the living sepulchre of life.'

(John Clare, 1845)

Over the past few billion years, life on earth has slowly evolved into a myriad of life forms, each of which is propagated through genetic inheritance, for just so long as that particular life form can prosper within its current environmental circumstances. Over the past few thousand years, humans have made much greater use than any other species of an additional form of evolution, which supplements rather than replaces genetic transmission. Through the processes of speech and writing, films and now digital media, it has become possible for discoveries made by one generation to be passed to later generations, whether this transmission is accomplished through parental training, schooling, media, or peer pressure.

Some indications are also found that chimpanzees are able to retain and transmit inventions to other members of their troop, and thus to create different chimpanzee cultures at different locations, which may well diverge over time if further inventions are made (Laland & Galef, 2009). However, these culture-building processes are far more extensive among humans (Tomasello, 2011). Combined with cooperativeness, transmissibility of culture may be a key defining quality of our species. Life for all of us is very different from that experienced by our forebears of 500 years ago, and no-one can say in what ways current social structures will differ from those that may exist 500 years ahead. In this chapter, we present different perspectives on the origins of cultural differences.

THAIPUSAM: AN INTERPRETIVE CHALLENGE

Let us consider for a moment a cultural ritual that observers from a Western perspective may find fascinating, extreme or disgusting. Every year around January and February, millions of Hindus will gather in parts of South East Asia and East Africa for the Thaipusam festival. Thousands of devotees in major centres will fast and pray for weeks, and on the day of the festival offerings are made to Lord Murugan in the fulfilment of vows for favours that were granted. Many people will carry pots of blessed milk to a central temple, often doing so while crawling on their knees. A smaller group of a few hundred will put metal rods or spears through their tongues or cheeks or skin while in a trance state and some will put hooks through their skin and drag *kavadis* (wooden altars , which sometimes now can take the form of carts or tractors) to the temple in order to increase their pain and suffering (Ward, 1984; Xygalatas et al., 2013).

Such striking and shocking cultural rituals highlight the variety of human experience. These events unfold once a year in honour of the god Murugan among Tamil communities. Dramatic events like this are more common in traditional societies and provide experiences that are often puzzling, revolting and shocking to outsiders, as ethnographic reports from missionaries, traders, travelers and early anthropologists confirm. In Chapter 2, we saw that contemporary nations around the world also vary in less dramatic ways, with different values, beliefs and practices being most prevalent in different nations. One of the questions that has fascinated and inspired scholars for centuries is how any cultural differences have emerged, whether they be in customs, traditions and religious practices, or in their members' way of thinking, feeling and interpreting the world. Why do cultural rituals arise in which individuals first starve themselves, then pierce metal rods through their cheeks, pull wooden carts attached to their body by hooks inserted in their skin, and parade down a street towards a colourful decorated stone building to the cheers and applause of thousands of onlookers? Why are such highly arousing and dramatic rituals more common in some cultural groups than others? Why is gender equality with few notable differences in the status of men or women in daily life emphasised in some societies, whereas in other societies men have a higher status than women in all domains of life?

Figure 3.1   Thaipusam Festival

Evolutionary anthropologists and biologists have studied the emergence and origins of these different behaviours, religions, and cultural customs and traditions. Social scientists, including sociologists and psychologists, have been more concerned with the mental world – in other words, the values, beliefs, cognitions and meaning systems that differentiate populations. Hence, the previous chapter examined *how* nations differ along some important psychological dimensions, whereas the current chapter examines *why* these differences have emerged.

FRAMEWORKS ADDRESSING THE ORIGINS OF CULTURAL DIFFERENCES

Brown, Dickins, Sear, and Laland (2011) reviewed the different models and theories that have been proposed, and concluded that most theories highlight either one of two influence mechanisms. They contrast the genetic inheritance system in which genes as blueprints for behaviour are passed from one generation to the next, with the cultural inheritance system, in which culture is seen as socially transmitted information that is passed on from one generation to the next. These two systems interact with the environment in which individuals and groups are situated. Different evolutionary models exist that give priority either to the genetic or to the cultural inheritance system, or to a combination of these two systems and the surrounding environment.

Some of these approaches have been very controversial when applied to social phenomena and have raised significant debates in the media, as can be seen for instance in Everyday Life Box 3.1. If we think of the Holocaust or the euthanasia programmes implemented in those nations that have used biological theories of racial superiority to kill allegedly inferior races and individuals, we can appreciate that these theories are not just ivory tower musings but have also brought significant suffering and death to millions of people. Variants of the approaches that emphasise the role of genes, social factors, or the environment can be seen in contemporary explanations for the origins of culture. We will take the classification by Brown et al. as a framework to introduce the major theoretical approaches.

GENETIC TRANSMISSION: RACIAL THEORIES OF INTELLIGENCE

Most researchers today agree that psychological differences *between individuals* are at least partially determined by genetics. A **genotype** is the unique genetic information that each one of us carries and which is expressed in the **phenotype**, that is the expressed and observable variability of each individual. Yet few psychologists would agree with the famous statement by Lumsden and Wilson (1981) that 'genes keep culture on a leash', meaning that genetic transmission is responsible for behavioural variability. The attribute that is most often discussed in terms of genetic differences between different ethnic and cultural groups is that of intelligence. While individuals certainly differ from one another for a variety of reasons, many researchers reject claims that differences in intelligence as measured by conventional IQ tests *between populations* or nations can be accounted for by genetic differences. Genetic theories of racial differences have had a lamentable history, culminating in the attempted extermination of supposedly genetically inferior Jews in Nazi Germany during the Third Reich and the slaughtering of Armenians during the First World War by Turkish forces. Critics of genetic explanations for 'racial' differences can point to the strong genetic similarities between people from different ethnic groups.

Everyday Life Box 3.1   Why Are There Regional Differences in Intelligence?

On 16 October 2007, the Nobel prize winner James Watson proclaimed the he was 'inherently gloomy about the prospect of Africa' because 'all our social policies are based on the fact that their intelligence is the same as ours [presumably he meant white people] – whereas all the testing says not really'. The implied genetic notions of superiority created a public uproar and ultimately cost him his job as the chancellor of Cold Spring Harbor Laboratory near New York City.

There are many debates about whether such differences are valid and where they come from. (We examine challenges about the validity of such claims in Chapter 4.) Here we present an example of a study that points to some very practical interventions, if these IQ differences are regarded as valid.

Eppig, Fincher, and Thornhill (2010) offered a new hypothesis that may explain why worldwide distributions of intelligence differ. The brain is the most complex and energy-consuming organ, with newborns requiring nearly all the energy they consume for brain development. Having sufficient energy for brain growth is essential, and there is good evidence that malnutrition affects mental development (Lynn, 1990).

However, parasite infections are also likely to play a role as they affect the energy balance within the human body. First, parasites such as flukes and some forms of bacteria often feed on host tissue which must be replaced, and this requires energy. Other parasites such as tapeworms, bacteria, giardia and amoebae infect the intestinal tract or cause diarrhoea, which limits the amount of energy that the body can absorb. Diarrhoea may be the single biggest threat, as it can prevent the body from absorbing any nutrients at all and is one of the top killers for children under five years of age. Viruses often hijack body mechanisms to reproduce themselves, which also takes energy. The body needs to fight these parasites by activating the immune system, again requiring energy. Therefore, parasites affect the energy balance in the body and this draining of energy has significant effects on the brain development of children.

Eppig et al. tested their hypothesis using a variety of intelligence scores and measures of parasite stress. They also controlled for a number of other variables that previous research and common sense indicated as significant predictors of intelligence, including distance from the equator, climate, average years of education, and wealth. Having controlled for all of these variables, they found a strong negative relationship between the prevalence of parasites and infectious diseases and levels of intelligence: the higher the prevalence of parasites and infectious disease, the lower the level of tested IQ scores in a population. These relationships also held when examined within continents (except in South America). Therefore, even within Western Europe and North America, regions with higher disease prevalence have populations with lower levels of IQ.

These findings have markedly different implications when compared to the views of Watson. They imply that levels of intelligence can be affected dramatically by reducing the number of parasites and infectious diseases to which pregnant mothers, toddlers and young children are exposed. Of course, receiving education is also important and has significant effects on reducing the differences in IQ (Nisbett et al., 2012), but this research suggests other, less obvious mechanisms that could have large and positive social benefits. Might expending money on parasite control in African countries pay off in higher levels of cognitive ability?

Genetic variability between populations around the world is no more than about 8% (Rosenberg et al., 2002), which is somewhat less than the variability in values (see Chapter 2). At the same time, small differences can matter, and we discuss in Chapter 5 the extent to which mean differences in personality across nations may have a genetic component. Recent epidemiological studies suggest that there are

> Your **Genotype** is the set of genes with which you are born. It is the complete hereditary information of an organism. **Phenotype** refers to the form in which these genes are expressed once environmental influences have taken effect.

genetic differences that leave some populations susceptible to certain diseases, while other populations are provided with protection against those diseases (Risch et al., 2002). A well-known example is the distribution of the sickle-cell gene in Africa, which overlaps almost completely with the distribution of malaria. This gene confers some immunity to malaria but also increases vulnerability to sickle-cell anaemia (Ashley-Koch et al., 2000). Pharmaceutical companies are very keen to explore these kinds of genetic difference, since people from different ethnic groups may respond differently to medications.

However, we have to be careful not to overextend these findings of genetic difference. First, these broad differences between regional populations span diverse cultural groups. Genetic information is easily disseminated, as a visiting individual may mate with a local and produce genetically mixed off-spring. This has often been the case with traders, sailors, soldiers, missionaries and other more recent foreign sojourners such as students and business persons who visit distant shores. In contrast, cultural traditions, norms and beliefs are more enduring and resistant. Studies in Papua New Guinea have shown that genetic mixing between cultural groups is much more extensive than the persistence of their distinctive cultural systems would lead one to expect (Friedlaender et al., 2008).

A second caution in interpreting genetic contrasts is that the phenomena on which we focus in this book (attitudes, beliefs, values, abilities, and socially relevant behaviours) are most likely determined by many factors within an individual's environment. Genetic differences between individuals undoubtedly contribute to explaining individual differences. Indeed some **polymorphisms** that encode neurotransmitters such as dopamine or serotonin have been found to correlate with differences in personality (Savitz & Ramesar, 2004). Yet these genetic variables produce only weak effects and to date we cannot point to single alleles or genes that uniquely and strongly encode information for complex psychological phenomena, such as personality traits, aggression or anxiety. These traits and characteristics are most likely determined by numerous genes in combination and by their interactions with environmental variables. The distribution of combinations of multiple genes within and across populations and their impact on the phenotypic expression of genetic information in observable behaviours is unknown. Nevertheless, studies of population genetics are rapidly expanding and can inform psychological theories, especially when considered in combination with the environmental variables that we discuss below.

> A **Polymorphism** is a situation where two or more phenotypes exist in the same population – that is, there is more than one form (morph). In biological studies of personality, it often refers to variations in the DNA sequence. Single nucleotides (A, T, C or G) are changed in the alleles and this leads to differences between paired chromosomes in an individual.

The one area of research where genetic theories of group differences linger in the public and the scientific arenas is for the explanation of 'racial' or population differences in cognitive abilities, or intelligence. Herrnstein and Murray (1994) argued in their book *The Bell Curve* that population differences are by and large determined by genetics. Reporting large IQ differences between white and black Americans, they claimed that these differences are also driven by genetic differences and that educational and other interventions have little effect in reducing these differences. Extending these ideas, Lynn and Vanhanen (2002) published *IQ and the Wealth of Nations.* In this book, they reported mean scores for intelligence in 81 nations, based on previous intelligence tests sampling various populations in each nation. Their central tenet was to show that these IQ estimates could predict the economic development of a nation. In short, they argued that genetic differences between nations make some nations smarter and some nations dumber, which then explains why some nations are highly developed and others are struggling economically.

This book and its tenets have rallied both vocal supporters (see Everyday Life Box 3.1) and strong critics. In an authoritative summary of research since the publication of *The Bell Curve*, Nisbett, Aronson, Blair, Dickens, Flynn, Halpern, and Turkheimer (2012) have shown that the genetic arguments used to explain differences between groups are flawed. The many studies reviewed in their paper show that genetic differences between individuals have the strongest effect among the well-off in the USA, whereas environmental factors can better explain IQ differences among the poor. This is the exact opposite of what would be expected if genetics drive mean IQ differences between the economically advantaged and disadvantaged. Furthermore, the IQ gap has been continuously reduced in the United States, and educational interventions do show long-lasting effects on academic achievement and life outcomes.

The correlation between mean IQ and economic wealth at the nation level has been shown repeatedly, but the causal direction of this link cannot be determined through correlational methods. As Hunt (2012) has noted, differences in national wealth are associated with differences in health, environmental quality and schooling, each of which can be expected to contribute to the ability to do well on IQ tests. We shall come back to the debate about IQ in the next chapter, when we will discuss cultural variations in the definition of intelligence. Some other promising approaches to accounting for population differences were discussed in Everyday Life Box 3.1.

CULTURAL TRANSMISSION

If genetics cannot directly explain differences between populations, we need to investigate alternatives. The other major candidate is the social inheritance system, namely the transmission of social information, including knowledge, routines, scripts, programmes and practices – in other words, culture. Evolutionary anthropologists and biologists have adopted slightly different definitions of culture from those favoured by the cross-cultural psychologists whose approach we discussed in Chapter 2. Working with archaeological records and observed rituals, practices and behaviours from field studies in exotic locations, evolutionary scholars have mostly been interested in the information about the local environment that is available in a cultural group, how this information is adaptive to the local context, and how it is passed from one generation to the next.

Culture is therefore often defined as the information acquired from other individuals through imitation or teaching that affects how individuals learn to behave (Boyd & Richerson, 1985, 2005). Having knowledge about computers drastically changes how we gather information about the world compared to the options of an individual who grows up in a village in a remote Papua New Guinean mountain valley. The definitions of culture as meaning systems discussed in Chapter 2 and this information perspective are compatible in that both types of definitions assume that the crucial element is shared and passed on from generation to generation, but they differ about whether it is meaning systems or information that is being passed on.

Cross-cultural psychologists have usually focused more on presumed consequences than on the origins of the cultural differences in values and beliefs that were discussed in Chapter 2. These authors see values and beliefs as relatively stable over generations, being passed on relatively unchanged from one generation to the next and probably being caused by more **distal** historical events. Hofstede (2001) claimed that value differences between Central and Southern Europeans can be traced back to the Roman Empire: in Southern Germany, which was occupied by the Romans, people are more conservative, whereas just north of the furthest extension of the Roman Empire, people are considerably more open and modern. Schwartz and Bardi (1997) analysed value patterns in Eastern Europe and found that people socialised into the former communist system showed a slightly different profile from those in Western Europe. They argued that these patterns are relatively stable and enduring.

A recent study examined these claims more closely. Van Herk and Poortinga (2012) analysed data from Schwartz's Portrait Value Questionnaire (see Chapter 2) that was included in the European Social Survey, focusing on regions within nations. This allows a better test of these historical claims, as regions within today's European nations were often part of other nations in previous times. They found that more **proximal**, recent events were stronger predictors of value importance ratings in these representative European samples than more distal legacies, such as belonging to the Roman Empire.

> **Proximal** causes are the immediate causes of behaviour. **Distal** causes are longer-term and further-removed causes which may exercise their effect through one or more proximal causes.

In summary, the cultural transmission of values, beliefs and information from one generation to the next is certainly an important process and is discussed in much more detail in Chapter 8. However, this perspective does not tell us much about the longer-term distal reasons for why it is that cultural groups and nations come to possess the cultural characteristics that they exhibit today. For this, we need to look more closely at the interaction between inheritance systems and the environment.

THE INFLUENCE OF THE ENVIRONMENT: ECO-CULTURAL THEORY

Humans have colonised nearly all the niches on Earth. They have overcome the challenges of eking out a living in freezing arctic conditions with darkness for a substantial part of the year, of inhabiting dry and hot deserts with no potable water and no chance to grow any plants for food, and of overcoming altitude sickness, domesticating fractious animals and cultivating hardy plants in the highest mountain ranges of South America and Asia. The fundamental tenet of eco-cultural theory is that humans can adapt their behaviour so that it maximises their reproductive success in a given environment. This is basically an aspect of Darwin's (1859) theory of natural selection and was first applied to humans by anthropologists in the 1930s (Forde, 1934).

Different strategies are required to deal with different environments, leading to different subsistence systems. These subsistence systems in turn then require different knowledge, skills and abilities, which are passed on through socialisation practices. The ecological and social context therefore interacts with the two inheritance systems (genetic and cultural transmission), leading to different behaviours, practices and psychological processes. The resulting behaviours and psychological processes obviously also maintain some specific aspects of the ecological and social context and change others, leading to feedback loops within the system. Figure 3.2 shows a recent summary of the basic model (Berry, 2011).

Berry (1967) provided one of the first tests of this model within the discipline of psychology. He studied the Inuit of Baffin Island in Canada and the Temne in Sierra Leone. The Inuit are a hunting and fishing society, typified by their relative leniency in child socialisation. This encourages individualism and self-reliance, as these traits are adaptive in the harsh environment where individuals forage alone or in small groups. In contrast, the Temne are mainly rice farmers who collectively grow and harvest one crop per year, a harvest that needs to be divided and shared among all members in a regulated and equitable fashion if people are to survive. Here, socialisation practices are much stricter, and individualistic self-assertion is not encouraged.

Berry administered a version of the Asch (1956) conformity study that was presented in Chapter 1. His prediction was that the more individualistic Inuit group members would reject the group norm, whereas the Temne would conform to the group. This was confirmed. One Temne offered this explanation: 'When Temne people choose a thing, we must all agree with the decision – this is what we call cooperation' (Berry, 1967: 417). Obviously, these samples differ along a number of other important dimensions, and these results may not be due to the particular socialisation differences rooted in their subsistence systems. More rigorous hypothesis tests that control many of the potentially confounding variables have supported the basic tenets of the eco-cultural model (Uskul, Kitayama, & Nisbett, 2008). With such support, the eco-cultural model has become one of the most influential models in cross-cultural psychology (Berry, Poortinga et al., 2011), providing the basis for several more specific theoretical frameworks. For an important recent application of this perspective, take a look at Key Research Study Box 3.1.

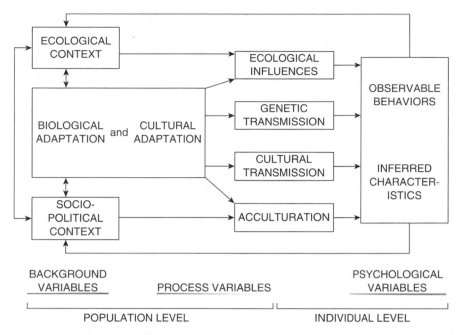

Figure 3.2 The Eco-cultural Framework

Source: J. W. Berry, 'The eco-cultural framework: A stocktaking', in F.van de Vijver et al. (Eds.) (2010), *Fundamental questions in cross-cultural psychology*. Reproduced by permission of Cambridge University Press.

Key Research Study Box 3.1   Tight and Loose Cultures

Gelfand et al. (2011) have developed and tested a multi level model of 'situational constraint', which illustrates the interplay between eco-cultural and historical factors, the structure of social situations, and psychological processes. Gelfand et al. drew on Mischel's (1977) notion of *strong versus weak* situations, arguing for the first time that nations can be differentiated in the degree to which situations are generally strong versus weak. They argued that strong situations will mostly be found in *tight* rather than *loose* cultures – a crucial distinction among social systems that had first been highlighted by Pelto (1968), whose anthropological explorations alerted him to groups whose members varied widely in terms of their level of compliance with norms. Gelfand et al. argued that certain eco-cultural and historical factors would create an increased need for predictability and coordinated social action within cultures. For example, factors such as high population density, a lack of natural resources, extreme temperatures, and/or a history of external threat would be associated with the need to create social structures to facilitate coordinated action within the social environment.

(Continued)

(Continued)

These 'distal' or background contextual factors conspire to influence the structure of situations that comprise the cultural context, producing a preponderance of strong or weak situations. Individual members of such cultural systems are socialised to develop social psychological characteristics that then enable them to function effectively within the typical situations that characterise their cultural setting. Individuals in cultural contexts with a generally high degree of situational constraint are predicted to have a greater need for structure, greater impulse control and conscientiousness, and a greater concern for the sanctioning of inappropriate behaviour as compared to individuals in societies with low situational constraint. Individuals in contexts with high situational constraint are predicted to have more readily accessible *ought* self-guides and a *prevention* regulatory focus, as compared to individuals in loose cultural systems, who will generally have more readily accessible *ideal* self-guides and a *promotion* regulatory focus (Higgins, 1987).

The model is represented graphically in Figure 3.3. In this model, the structure of social situations mediates between the distal level of ecological-historical influences and the proximal level

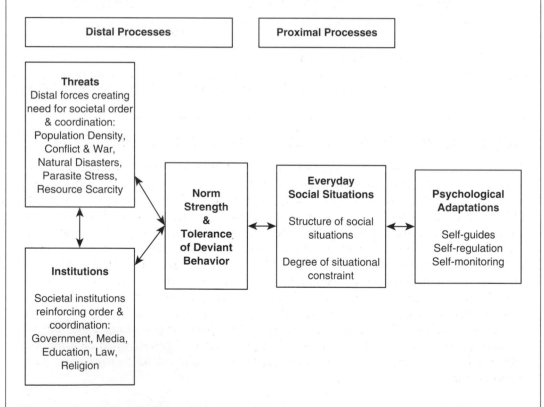

Figure 3.3   Gelfand's Eco-cultural Model

Source: M. J. Gelfand et al., (2011), Differences between tight and loose cultures: A 33 nation study', *Science*, 332, 1100–1104. Reprinted with permission from American Association for the Advancement of Science.

of adaptive individual-level processes. Note that this model, like Figure 3.2, specifies two-way causal influences between ecological factors and psychological processes. While causation may historically have operated from ecological factors to psychological processes, current research into global warming serves to remind us that human activity can and does affect even the most basic aspects of the environment to which we shall again need to adapt.

To test this theory, Gelfand et al. (2011) developed two measures and obtained responses from nearly 7,000 participants (around half of whom were students) in 33 nations. The first measure comprised the six items shown in Research Instrument Box 3.1, which asked respondents to describe the tightness or looseness of the nation in which they lived. The second measure listed 15 different social situations and asked respondents to rate how appropriate it would be for a person to behave in each of 12 ways in these various situations. For instance, should one eat, laugh, swear, cry, sing or flirt in a job interview, in an elevator, in a church, in a park, or in a bedroom? It was found that situations varied in the relative amount of situational constraint in almost exactly the same way in all the 33 nations sampled, with job interviews most tight and bedrooms least tight. However, the level of situational looseness-tightness differed across nations and this accorded with the nation-level ratings of general looseness-tightness. Pakistan, Malaysia and India were highest on tightness and the Ukraine, Estonia and Hungary were highest on looseness.

Research Instrument Box 3.1 Tightness-Looseness

How much do you agree with each of these statements? Gelfand et al. used a scale from 1 to 6 (1 = Strongly Disagree; 6 = Strongly Agree), but then made corrections for cultural variations in response style, so it is not easy to compare your responses with those obtained in the study.

1 There are many social norms that people are supposed to abide by in this country.
2 In this country there are very clear expectations as to how people should act in most situations.
3 People agree on what behaviours are appropriate versus inappropriate in most situations in this country.
4 People in this country have a great deal of freedom in deciding how they want to behave in most situations. (reverse coded)
5 In this country, if someone acts in an inappropriate way, others will strongly disapprove.
6 People in this country almost always comply with social norms.

Finally, Gelfand et al. correlated more than 80 indices of cultural difference with their scores for tightness-looseness. Cultural tightness was significantly associated with value measures of collectivism and power distance, as well as beliefs in fate control, spirituality and reward for application. More importantly, it was also significantly associated with contextual factors such as vulnerability to natural disasters, a lack of access to safe water, population density and food deprivation, again supporting eco-social theorising that psychological adaptations of populations are responsive to environmental factors constraining what is possible and permissible in different cultural contexts.

Key Researcher Box 3.1   Michele Gelfand

Figure 3.4   Michele Gelfand

Michele J. Gelfand (b. 1968) received her PhD in Social/Organisational Psychology from the University of Illinois in 1996, working with Harry Triandis. She taught at New York University before moving to her current position as Professor of Psychology and Distinguished University Scholar Teacher at the University of Maryland, College Park. She has published four books and over 90 book chapters and journal articles. She co-edited the *Handbook of Negotiation and Culture,* and is co-editor of the annual series *Advances in Culture and Psychology.* Her contributions to cross-cultural psychology are relevant to many of the chapters in this book including work on the origins of culture, self-construal, subjective culture, conflict, negotiation, organisational attachment, intergroup relations and globalisation. She designed and directed the study of tight versus loose cultures, a recent major innovation in the field.

Considering the emphasis on the dimension of individualism-collectivism that we stressed in Chapter 2, we briefly review here two further theoretical approaches that have used an eco-cultural model to predict the emergence of individualism-collectivism. Fincher, Thornhill, Murray, and Schaller (2008) focused on the prevalence of pathogens and disease in the environment and whether this has influenced the development of individualism-collectivism as measured by Hofstede (1980) and the GLOBE project (House et al., 2004). Widespread diseases pose a threat to humans and need to be contained and neutralised. Collectivism may have emerged as an effective strategy to defend against these threats, since socialising people to maintain close ties with their immediate in-group will reduce contact with outsiders carrying potentially contagious diseases. High conformity to cultural rituals and taboos that have often evolved as protection mechanisms would also reduce the risk of self-infection. Collectivism can thereby become an effective anti-pathogenic defence function. In line with Fincher et al.'s rationale, contemporary and historic pathogen levels were found to be associated with greater collectivism, in-group sociality and in-group bonding (Fincher et al., 2008; Fincher & Thornhill, 2012). Historic pathogen levels were derived from data from the mid-twentieth century. Using historic data helps to establish the plausibility of causal linkages in correlational analyses.

Van de Vliert (2009) has offered a different theory of culture, focusing on climato-economic predictors. The basic tenet of his theory is that humans have to adapt to climatic stress and use available income resources to counter the stressful effects of climate on human functioning. Individuals located in either very hot tropical or very cold climates have to use their income to secure sufficient edible food, and gain adequate clothing, housing and medical support. If the climatic demands of either hot summers or cold winters can be met by sufficient income, then these threats are perceived as challenges and allow opportunities to grow. As a consequence, a

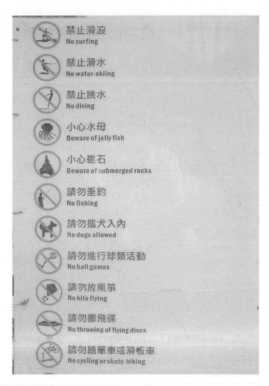

禁止滑浪
No surfing

禁止滑水
No water-skiing

禁止跳水
No diving

小心水母
Beware of jelly fish

小心礁石
Beware of submerged rocks

請勿垂釣
No fishing

請勿攜犬入內
No dogs allowed

請勿進行球類活動
No ball games

請勿放風箏
No kite flying

請勿擲飛碟
No throwing of flying discs

請勿踏單車或滑板車
No cycling or skate biking

Figure 3.5   Enjoy Your Day at the Beach in a Tight Culture

demanding climate combined with adequate resources provides stimulation which then results in greater individualism, more self-expression values and openness to new experiences.

By contrast, in demanding climates where individuals are struggling to meet these demands, individuals will be more concerned about the survival of their immediate in-group, which as a consequence leads to a greater focus on the immediate in-group, collectivism and protection values. In temperate climates, groups face lesser challenges and therefore resources are not so relevant for survival. At the same time, this type of climate does not provide many challenges for growth or incentives for individualisation. Hence, cultures in temperate climates are predicted to be moderately high on individualism and related dimensions. These hypotheses were supported when studying self-expression values (Van de Vliert, 2009), various measures of individualism-collectivism (Fischer & van de Vliert, 2011) and in-group favouritism (Van de Vliert, 2011), as well as the relative frequency of social behaviours such as altruism, bullying and leadership style, which we discuss in later chapters.

Pitching Fincher et al.'s parasite stress hypothesis against the climato-economic theory of culture, Van de Vliert and Postmes (2012) found that both can account for a significant amount of variability in a combined measure of collectivism when entered into regression equations separately, but once the climato-economic effects are controlled, pathogen prevalence is no longer a significant predictor. Hence, climatic effects in interaction with economic resources may be a more proximal factor affecting contemporary levels of collectivism values. Disease stress may affect societal collectivism values indirectly through other variables (see Everyday Life Box 3.1) or it may have an influence on other types of values.

Key Researcher Box 3.2   Evert van de Vliert

Figure 3.6   Evert van de Vliert

Evert van de Vliert (b. 1940) received his PhD in organisational psychology from the Free University of Amsterdam in 1973. He then held teacher and researcher positions at the same University, at the University of St Andrews in Scotland, and at the Royal Military Academy in the Netherlands. In 1987, he was appointed professor of organisational and applied social psychology at Groningen University in the Netherlands. He has published more than 200 journal articles, numerous book chapters, and seven books. His research interests were initially focused upon the study of conflict, but during the past 15 years he has developed and tested his theory of the origins of cultural differences that focus on a culture's resources and climate demandingness. He was appointed as Companion in the Order of Orange-Nassau in 2004, and received the Lifetime Achievement Award of the International Association for Conflict Management in 2005. At present, he is Professor Emeritus of Organisational and Applied Social Psychology at the University of Groningen in The Netherlands, and Research Professor of Work and Organisational Psychology at the University of Bergen in Norway.

In summary, these approaches focus on the role of the environment in eliciting the optimal, most adaptive, and therefore most frequently expressed responses over time. Proponents of these theories do not differentiate much between whether the adaptive processes are channelled through genes or through some other mechanism. What is important is that the cultural system is adaptive to the environmental context in which it is located. Of course, this does not imply that all practices, behaviours or psychological traits are adaptive, especially if the environmental context is changing. Current environmental changes are discussed in detail in Chapter 14.

ENVIRONMENT SHAPING GENETIC TRANSMISSION: EVOLUTIONARY PSYCHOLOGY

Evolutionary psychologists such as Tooby and Cosmides (1992) have questioned the widespread assumption that the human brain is a blank slate or *tabula rasa* which can quickly be formed, adjusted and moulded by experience derived from current cultural processes. Their critical point is that modern humans (*Homo sapiens*) emerged during the Pleistocene epoch probably around 195,000 years ago, and then spread in cumulative waves out of Africa, with the last and most important population wave probably occurring about 50,000 years ago. Modern humans thus developed in an environment in which small bands of individuals roamed bushy savannah areas in Africa. Evolutionary psychologists assume that the Darwinian processes of natural selection operative then and into the present are important for understanding human behaviour.

Evolution occurs through random variations in genetic make-up, some of which enhance survival and are therefore retained within the gene pool of succeeding generations. Selection processes of this type can radically affect human culture. Since the principal mode of selection is through reproduction, why for instance do women typically continue to live long after they are capable of childbearing? In savannah life, it is thought that there was survival value in grand-mothers' helping to tend infants (who are helpless for much longer than is the case in other apes), so there was selection pressure in favour of women with greater longevity.

Traditionally, it is assumed that the natural selection processes described by Darwin require a rather long timeframe. If this is true, our current genetic make-up is still shaped by the requirements of the Pleistocene natural environment. As a consequence, evolutionary psycho-logists assume that our evolved psychological mechanisms process incoming inputs from the environment and that these then activate certain states in the brain that trigger behavioural reactions. This can be likened to the metaphor of a jukebox, in which our brain is wired to respond to distinct stimuli with specific reactions, in the same way that pressing a certain key on the jukebox changes the tune. Differences in behaviours, both within and between cultures, are therefore seen as situationally invoked expressions of pre-existing adaptive programmes in the brain that have been retained through natural selection over the millennia of human evolution. According to this perspective, the cultural traditions and customs that have been acquired and passed on by human populations around the world since moving out of Africa (the material that we reviewed in Chapter 2) are seen as non-consequential and believed to have had little causal role in our evolution.

There are two different positions concerning evolutionary effects on culture. First, a number of anthropologists have argued that there is only one universal culture that describes all humans. Brown (1991) reviewed available ethnographic and anthropological work and argued that there is so much functional similarity in our customs, traditions and behaviours, despite sometimes differ-ent ways of expressing the same type of behaviour, that it is best to use the term 'universal culture'. Therefore, we humans are thought to all share the same human culture, that which makes us human (Baumeister, 2005). The propensity to have this particular culture is seen as being passed on through our genes.

This view has strong implications for responses to real-life problems such as the attempts to reduce intergroup prejudice and stereotyping that we discuss in Chapter 12. For example, Gil-White (2001) proposed that our evolutionary history of roaming in small groups hard-wired an out-group detection system into our brains that would automatically differentiate our in-group from the out-group. This is because our ancestors had to compete for food with other bands and therefore the detection of rivals and discrimination against them was essential for in-group survival in a resource-scarce environment.

A second perspective, the concept of 'evoked culture', has been proposed by Tooby and Cosmides (1992). They assume that contemporary environments are similar in some character-istics to those experienced by our Pleistocene ancestors. Consequently, a subset of cultural traits will be triggered by the local environment. This is similar to the jukebox metaphor, because the same trigger will evoke somewhat different reactions depending on the environment in which the trigger is situated. If the same key is pressed in France say, the jukebox will play one tune, whereas in Brazil it will play another. All humans have a propensity to believe in spirits (Bering, 2010). However, whether these are interpreted as evil ghosts, neutral jinns or caring angels will depend on local historical belief systems (Boyer, 1994).

A key aspect of the jukebox metaphor of evoked culture is that behaviours that are assumed to have been adaptive in Pleistocene environments may not be adaptive any more today: for example, in situations of food scarcity it would have been advantageous to seek out sweet foods, because they have a high caloric content, which would have enhanced the chance of survival (Rozin, 2007). In a similar way, gender differences in aggression can be understood in terms of male aggression toward other males, giving them improved chances of mating with more females. Archer (2009) showed that male physical aggression was greater than female aggression in 13 different sampled nations. However, when rates of physical aggression between male and female partners in 12 nations are compared, a different result is found (Archer, 2006). Within Western nations, physical aggression by women towards men is as frequent as physical aggression by men toward women, especially among student samples. However, physical aggression by men toward women still predominates in India, Jordan, Japan, Nigeria, South Korea, and especially in Papua New Guinea. Predominance of aggression by men was strongly and negatively correlated with an index of gender empowerment. These results suggest that gender roles, which are to a certain extent biologically mandated, can evolve and become modified in response to changes in social power. This favours the more complex gene-culture models that we discuss below. Many researchers using the evolutionary perspective have also looked at gender differences in mating preferences, and these are discussed in Chapter 9.

In summary, this perspective assumes that human behaviour is strongly shaped by natural selection processes that worked on our ancestors and created a set of automatic response systems in our brain that can be switched on by environmental input variables. The main mechanism for transmission of behavioural predispositions is therefore via the genetic system. Our modern environment differs dramatically from that of the Pleistocene savannah, but it contains triggers that switch on behavioural responses that were adaptive in this distant environment, though they may not be adaptive in today's environments. Hence, it is the environment that triggers which genetically transmitted behavioural responses will be activated.

ENVIRONMENT SHAPING CULTURE: THEORIES OF CULTURAL EVOLUTION

Proponents of cultural evolution theory can look back on a long and controversial history within the social sciences. Like evolutionary psychologists, they will look at the effects of the environment, but they will also examine how cultural systems change in reaction to environmental stimuli. Hence, cultures are thought to change and adapt to the environment, and traits and information found to be adaptive are then passed to the next generation through the *cultural* inheritance system. This can occur in exactly the same way as in natural selection, by the random occurrence of new behaviours or new ways of thinking about things and the selective retention of those that prove advantageous (Campbell, 1960). This process can be sped up by any of the influence processes that have been well studied by social psychologists, such as imitation, leadership and conformity (Mesoudi, 2009). Consequently this type of evolution can be much more rapid (Chentsova Dutton & Heath, 2008).

The grandfather of anthropology, E.B. Tylor (1871), attempted to rank cultures into a system that differentiated primitive from more advanced societies, which was intended to portray a universal stage process of cultural evolution. These ideas were widespread in the eighteenth and nineteenth century when rapidly developing Western European countries started to colonise traditional societies around the world and encountered what to the European mind appeared like primitive forms of society that had been successfully transformed and modernised in Europe hundreds of years previously. In a recent study, Currie et al. (2010) demonstrated that in the islands of South East Asia and the Pacific, political organization slowly developed in small incremental steps from non-hierarchical tribal bands, to simple chiefdoms, to complex chiefdoms, and finally to state-like structures. They found a natural progression from simpler to more complex organization over millenia. A reversal may also occur and here abrupt and dramatic changes are possible that result in the collapse of social structures when environmental and social conditions change (Diamond, 2005). These anthropological studies have focused on simpler societies, but related ideas concerning modernism and post-modernism remain popular within sociology and the political sciences, and we shall discuss these in Chapter 14.

Anthropologists in this tradition often focus on behaviours that are adaptive in specific environmental contexts. For example, Henrich and Henrich (2010) have conducted extensive field research on Yasawa Island in Fiji, a small state in the Pacific. The local population consists of fishing communities that largely depend on a variety of fish species. Henrich and Henrich examined the reasons for food taboos that are enforced on women during pregnancy and when lactating, as an example of culturally transmitted prohibitions. Using extensive observation, surveys, interviews and medical measurements, they found that marine toxins in fish pose an important threat to health in the islands and that food taboos target especially those species of fish that are most likely to carry marine toxins. Injunctions against eating such fish therefore protect foetuses and nursing infants. This information is crucial for survival and is passed on vertically to childbearing women by their mothers and grandmothers. It is also important to note that several safe foods were also tabooed, which shows that cultural adaptations are not always optimal, as important sources of nutrition become unavailable for consumption.

A more general example is provided by Rozin's (2007) account of our biologically mandated preference for sweetness. This preference has over time contributed toward the evolution of systems of agriculture that generate sweet produce and was a major impetus toward the colonisation of the Americas. In more recent times, it has led to the creation of industries that extract and market sweetness, which in turn has contributed to the contemporary obesity epidemic. This too is a cultural adaptation that is less than optimal, as diabetes exacts a heavy burden on medical services.

In summary, models of cultural evolution emphasise the linkage of cultural systems to the environment through adaptations in the cultural inheritance system. Learning and the imitation of behaviours that are effective are thought to give rise to changes in social systems, which are then passed on to the next generation. This emphasis on the system of cultural inheritance differentiates these models from the eco-cultural theory, which does not make strong predictions as to whether changes will occur within the system of cultural or genetic inheritance (that is, they are process-neutral). Modern models of cultural evolution have attracted considerable interest from policy-makers, as they present clear causal pathways that can be targeted and changed through planned interventions.

GENE-CULTURE CO-EVOLUTION

One of the implications of cultural evolution and of the feedback loops included in the eco-cultural theories discussed above is the possibility that, through social learning, novel behaviour emerges that allows a cultural group to modify the extent to which natural selection affects the genetic inheritance system. Social practices that are effective in addressing some selection pressures will then have effects on the selection of the genes.

The earliest and best-known example of this is gene-culture co-evolution between the spread of dairy farming and genes permitting the absorption of lactose in milk (Simoons, 1970). In mammals, the enzyme permitting lactose absorption disappears around the time of weaning. With the initiation and widespread adoption of cultivating cattle for milk consumption, genetic changes in both cattle and humans occurred, with cows producing more milk and humans preserving the needed enzyme. The important point here is that the cultural invention of milk consumption and herding altered the gene pool of those human populations that engaged in this practice.

Brown et al. (2011) suggest that gene-culture co-evolution is probably very common, even affecting basic brain processes. (See also Baumeister, 2005). A recent example has been reported by Chiao and Blizinsky (2010), who examined the distribution of mood disorders around the world. They noticed that, according to World Health Organisation (WHO) statistics, anxiety and mood disorders show a very imbalanced distribution around the world, with Asian countries having lower frequencies of clinical levels of anxiety and depression compared to Western nations. Genetic studies have previously shown that individuals with at least one short allele of the serotonin-encoding gene 5-HTT are more likely to develop anxiety and mood disorders than individuals who have two long alleles (Lesch et al., 1996). Serotonin is a neurotransmitter implicated in regulating mood and affect. Although there is substantial evidence that mood disorders are equally widespread in Asian nations, but are expressed more in terms of somatic symptoms (e.g., Kleinman, 2004), Chiao and Blizinsky's viewpoint remains relevant as an explanation of mood disorders as defined by Western criteria.

Chiao and Blizinsky (2010) conducted a meta-analysis of **population genetic studies** and found that Asian populations were *more* likely to have at least one short allele. This difference, however, would mean they should be *more* likely to experience anxiety and mood imbalance. So how did they reconcile these findings? Assuming that cultural values such as collectivism have an adaptive function and have evolved for specific purposes, they have argued that the greater prevalence of short alleles in Asian populations has been counterbalanced by the emergence of collectivism, as collectivism provides protection through increased social support, social harmony and structure in people's lives. Collectivism could reduce the risk of exposure to environmental and social stressors.

Population Genetics is the study of the frequency and interaction of alleles and genes in a population.

A second factor contributing to the growth of collectivism is the higher historical and contemporary level of pathogens in Asia compared to Europe and North America. As we have seen, this may have led to the emergence of collectivistic societies (Fincher et al., 2008). Higher rates of infectious diseases require some form of social response and collective systems are more likely to provide anti-pathogen defence functions, as we discussed above.

Putting these pieces together, higher pathogen levels may have resulted in the emergence of collectivistic values, which then acquired a second protective function by neutralising the higher frequency of anxiety-inducing alleles. This buffer mechanism would therefore result in lower rates of phenotypic anxiety and mood disorder than would be expected on the basis of the genetic evidence. Chiao and Blizinsky supported their analysis by computing a series of path models that linked pathogen levels to the genetic pre-disposition to experience anxiety and mood disorder (higher frequency of at least one short 5-HTT allele), which in turn was associated with greater collectivism as a buffer, and finally led to lower levels of anxiety and mood disorders as reported by the WHO.

With the advance of population genetics, we are becoming more aware of the subtle ways in which populations come to differ genetically. These genetic differences are likely to interact in complex ways with the ecological and social environments of the people who carry these genes and who have shaped these environments over generations. Fischer (2013a) provided an example of such gene-environment interactions for predicting variability in hierarchy beliefs and values. Drawing upon Social Dominance Theory (Sidanius & Pratto, 2001) which we discuss in more detail in Chapter 12, Fischer argued that hierarchically organised societies are more successful in securing resources and warding off threats. The benefits of hierarchy should be particularly pronounced if groups are situated in locations where there are more threats and fewer resources and group members have a greater biological vulnerability to react negatively to these stressors and threats. Using the same data as Chiao and Blizinsky (2010), Fischer was able to demonstrate that environmental stressors and genetic vulnerability (higher probability of carrying a short allele of the 5-HTT gene) interact and jointly predict higher levels of support for central authority and higher dominance values.

This broad area of research has much potential, especially as it can provide a theoretical integration of the various perspectives presented in this chapter. However, there are many unresolved issues. Most importantly, we do not have population estimates of the frequencies of the single genes that have been identified, because the current research has been based on small and often highly selected samples. Genes often interact with each other and most psychological constructs such as traits or cognitive abilities are influenced by more than one gene. Furthermore, it is unclear to what extent the effects obtained by Chiao and Blizinsky and by Fischer can considered to be co-evolutions, or whether they have just mapped **genetic drifts** that appeared randomly. Gene-environment interaction studies are more robust than gene-culture co-evolution studies, as they do not require the assumption of co-evolution, but genetic drift may still have some effect on the psychological functioning of specific populations.

> **Genetic Drift** refers to changes in the frequency of genes or alleles in a particular population that are due to random fluctuations.

> **Epigenetics** refers to a wide range of processes that involves changes in gene expression and modifications in the genome that are not caused by genetic mechanisms. This involves regulation of gene expression by environmental factors that does not change the underlying DNA sequence.

These studies belong to a rapidly expanding field of research called **epigenetics** that has potentially large but as yet unexplored consequences for cultural differences. Epigenetics refers to non-genetic factors that change the expression of genes without changing the actual gene. It is highly plausible that cultural or environmental variables can switch certain genes on or off, so that the genes then manifest themselves in different phenotypes in populations around the world. Fischer's (2013a) study is probably the first epigenetic study that has examined these processes in relation to the distribution of cultural values and beliefs. We know very little about the highly complex interactions between culture and biological processes, but epigenetic processes further complicate any simple analysis of genetic or social determinism. Future research may yield surprising and fascinating insights into how the genetic and cultural inheritance systems interact with each other and with the environment in the production of behaviours in today's environments.

CAUSES, CORRELATES OR CONSEQUENCES?

In Chapter 2, we reported large cross-national studies that examined the distribution of values and beliefs around the world and in this chapter we have been looking at some of the frameworks that may help us to understand why such differences emerge. However, we are equally concerned with the potential consequences of such cultural differences. When we discussed theories of eco-cultural adaptation and cultural evolution, we already alluded to sequences of events in which value differences were just part of a larger causal chain. For example, Welzel (in press; see also Inglehart, Welzel & Klingemann, 2003) has proposed that economic conditions have a unidirectional causal effect on values. In contrast, Schwartz (2006) argues for reciprocal relationships, with economic development leading to higher autonomy values, which in turn then provides a catalyst for further economic development. Because studies of this type mostly use cross-sectional data, any claims about causality in either direction will remain speculative. In Chapter 14, we examine studies that try to overcome this problem by using longitudinal data.

Among cross-cultural psychologists there is a widespread belief that nation-level value dimensions do have strong effects on a large number of social, institutional and psychological variables. Many correlations have indeed been reported between the frameworks discussed in Chapter 2 and a host of other variables. In disentangling the plausibility of different causal chains over both long time periods and short time periods, we shall need to draw in later chapters on the full range of available research methods, including both experimentation and longitudinal analyses.

Thaipusam: A Tentative Explanation

We can now return to our opening example and see what the various explanatory frameworks that we have described can offer us in understanding this particular ritual behaviour, which involves such extreme levels of voluntary pain and suffering. At the most abstract level, we could ask why people believe in supernatural beings such as Murugan. A number of evolutionary theories have been proposed to explain the emergence of religious beliefs. Most emphasise the predisposition of humans to assume agency in actions. In other words, we are seen as predisposed to detect agency in all kinds of innate objects and ambiguous signals. This tendency may have had evolutionary advantages for early humans because unexplained events – think of a strange sound at night – had important survival value. If the sound was a made by a lion or an enemy you had to react fast, which encourages false positives, leading to an adaptive overgeneralisation of this system.

As humans, we also develop a sense of our own individuality and mental states and assume that other humans also have their individuality and mental states. This so-called theory of mind is important for interacting with fellow human beings, as it helps us to predict both our own and others' behaviour. Both agency detection and theory of mind are involved when humans attempt to explain events. These processes can lead to a cognitive illusion of invisible agency on occasions when no obvious causal agent can be detected. Believing in higher spiritual beings can therefore be seen as an adaptive cognitive illusion (Bering, 2010).

Such a hyperactive agency detection mechanism and the associated beliefs in higher entities would have had significant survival benefits when shared and spread within a community. People would come together and worship their higher beings, thereby bonding an ever larger number of people beyond the extended family. Several theorists have argued that religion was one of the fundamental binding elements that allowed larger groups of unrelated individuals to live together. Religious practices differentiating one group of believers from another would also have had the advantage of distinguishing in-group from out-group members (see Chapter 12) and eliciting greater commitment from in-group members (Norenzayan & Shariff, 2008; Atran & Henrich, 2010).

One of the greatest problems in threatening environments is to judge whether individuals are really committed and can be trusted. Hence, the public display of actions that have no function apart from serving the higher spiritual beings of a community demonstrates commitment publicly. Similarly, observers of acts that are extremely costly to the individual will attribute greater commitment to that person. Following the maxim 'actions speak louder than words', observers are also more likely to believe and follow individuals who engage in extreme actions. Strong rituals such as those exemplified by Thaipusam will invoke commitment to the group, so that members on average will cooperate more with other in-group members. This in turn will increase success in competition with out-groups (Irons, 2001; Bulbulia & Sosis, 2011).

Atkinson and Whitehouse (2011) have shown that rituals high in intensity and arousal (similar to Thaipusam) are more common in traditional groups and societies. With increasing economic development, rituals become less extreme and involve lower arousal but are performed more often, for instance as Sunday Church services. The extreme ritualistic suffering during Thaipusam can be seen as a costly but advantageous display of commitment to the group in relatively traditional societies, which helps to bind the group of followers more strongly together. However, such effects may also have benefits for groups in modern societies, as extreme behaviours inducing pain and strong emotions can still bind non-blood related individuals together (Bulbulia & Sosis, 2011).

Directly testing these claims, Xygalatas et al. (2013) found that individuals who participated in a high ordeal Thaipusam ritual in Mauritius were more likely to donate money to their in-group but also to have a more inclusive social identity at the national level, compared to participants in a less arousing and painful ritual. Most importantly, they found that perceived and experienced pain explained both the increased prosociality and the more inclusive identity. Participating in a painful religious ritual like Thaipusam facilitates and increases group bonding and solidarity. Hence, such rituals can act as generalised mechanisms for social coordination, which have adaptive value for the groups that use them. In this way, evolutionary and cultural evolutionary theories can explain why rituals such as Thaipusam emerged and continue to be celebrated.

SUMMARY

This chapter has examined various theoretical approaches that can help us to understand how cultural differences have emerged. Research into the origins of culture is an interdisciplinary and expanding field and many questions remain to be answered. We distinguished between systems of genetic and cultural inheritance that interact with each other and the environment. Cultural traits are seen as adaptive inventions that have helped humans to survive in diverse ecological settings as they spread out of Africa and populated the most remote and often hostile parts of the planet. The variations in values and beliefs discussed in Chapter 2 most likely emerged as adaptations to the requirements of particular local environments.

FURTHER READING

1 Boyd, R., & Richerson, P. (2005). *The origin and evolution of cultures*. New York: Oxford University Press.
2 Chasiotis, A. (2011). Evolution and culture. *Online Readings in Psychology and Culture*. Available at http://scholarworks.gvsu.edu/*orpc*
3 Cohen, A. (2011). Religion and culture. *Online Readings in Psychology and Culture*. Available at http://scholarworks.gvsu.edu/*orpc*
4 Mesoudi, A. (2009). How cultural evolutionary theory can enhance social psychology and vice versa. *Psychological Review, 116*, 929–952.
5 Sternberg, R. (2002). Cultural explorations of human intelligence around the world. *Online Readings in Psychology and Culture*. Available at http://scholarworks.gvsu.edu/*orpc*

STUDY QUESTIONS

1 What variables may have played a role in the development of the dominant culture in your nation? Discuss possible candidates and how they may have interacted with each other.
2 Would you agree with the argument that genetics are more important than culture for understanding differences between people around the world?
3 Discuss whether contrasts between nations are the right basis for understanding genetic or cultural evolution. Do you think evolutionary processes are operating for nation states?
4 What are your predictions for culture change in the future? Which of your predictions could you derive from the models discussed in this chapter?
5 If you were a politician, how could you attempt to change the tightness-looseness scores of your society? Discuss the direction of the desired change, how you could achieve this and the possible behavioural consequences.

4

How to do Cross-Cultural Psychology

I cannot rest from travel …
For always roaming with a hungry heart
Much have I seen and known;
cities of men and manners, climates, councils, governments …
To follow knowledge like a sinking star,
Beyond the utmost bound of human thought…

(from *Ulysses*, by Alfred Lord Tennyson)

Thus far we have outlined some of the intellectual challenges and major insights into how cultures have emerged and how they differ today in their values and beliefs. Before we continue with our quest to chart the cultural side of social psychology, we need to pause and consider some of the practical issues involved in doing and interpreting cross-cultural research, and in researching the cultural diversities that exist on our planet. Take a look at Everyday Life Box 4.1 below.

Everyday Life Box 4.1 presents distressing events occurring among a tribe who had been displaced from their traditional land in a remote area of Eastern Africa. Imagine that you are a researcher and you are encountering a cultural group in which people routinely behave like the Ik. How could you make sense of these incidents as a psychologist? In this chapter we examine the question of how we can conduct research across cultures. What methods can you use and what are the particular challenges or obstacles that await you if you venture into the field? Throughout the chapter we will identify a series of guidelines which summarise how best to face up to these challenges.

Everyday Life Box 4.1

Anthropologists have sought to create detailed pictures of everyday life in a very wide range of social contexts. In a particularly vivid study, Turnbull (1972) documented the progressive effects of very severe famine among the Ik tribal group in the mountains of Uganda. After the oldest people had died, the children were next at risk. In the face of acute hunger, Turnbull noted the way that the other children turned against a child named Adupa, snatching whatever food she was able to obtain from her as she became weaker, and even teasing her by giving her food and then taking it away from her again. As days passed, Turnbull was unable to bear watching this process and compromised his observer status by starting to give her food, but this only prolonged her agony. When she turned to her parents they rebuffed her. Eventually her parents placed her in a hut and sealed it up until she had died, thus raising the survival chances of other children. Turnbull observed that the parents preserved good relations with their neighbours by taking Adupa's remains a good distance away and preventing wild animals from scattering body parts onto their land.

One issue in particular that will demand our attention is how to balance the typical emphasis on the individual in psychological research with the fact that cultural processes do not exist in isolation, but exist within collectives and are shared between individuals. This inter-individual nature of culture requires analyses at a collective level. In Chapter 2, we saw that the landmark studies in cross-cultural psychology have been made at the nation level. Now we must consider how we can use these insights to understand the experiences and behaviours of individuals. We will present core issues, the debates around these and their implications with examples drawn from real and illustrative research, returning to the plight of the Ik mountain people at several points in the chapter.

ETHNOGRAPHIC FIELDWORK

The first option available to cross-cultural researchers going into the field was to use ethnographic research. Travelers for millennia have recorded and reported the customs of the peoples they visited. Marco Polo's famous account of travels to what is today India and China is one of the first examples in the Western world. Marco Polo's near contemporary, the Muslim Ibn Batutta, provides an equally fascinating account from a non-Western viewpoint of a much longer and further journey. These explorers collected extensive but casual observations while working and living among alien cultural groups, often describing the exotic and bizarre events that accentuated the differences between the Venetian and Berber societies that they hailed from and the strange new worlds that they encountered.

The Polish anthropologist, Bronislaw Malinowski (1922), challenged this idiosyncratic method in his classic study *Argonauts of the Western Pacific*, in which he first outlined the scientific method of ethnographic fieldwork for the new discipline of anthropology. He emphasised that a researcher must have the scientific goal of comprehending the complete society rather than reporting selected facts of living that are salient to the foreign observer ('this goal is, briefly, to grasp the native's point of view, his relation to life, to realize *his* vision of *his* world', p. 25), to live and participate completely in the culture of interest (a process that we now call 'cultural immersion') and to apply scientific methods of collecting, reporting and interpreting evidence:

> In Ethnography, the writer is his own chronicler and the historian at the same time, while his sources are no doubt easily accessible, but also supremely elusive and complex; they are not embodied in fixed, material documents, but in the behavior and in the memory of living men. (1922: 3)

As you can imagine, living with the Ik while they struggled with a constant state of famine was a major physical and psychological struggle for Turnbull. Staying on location, remaining professional and maintaining his ethical sensibilities were major issues for him. His study has been lauded as showing humanity and objectivity even in the face of great suffering and societal collapse, while not offering judgments about the lives and culture of others, even if what they do seems inhumane and cruel to us. This is a reminder of the conclusions that we drew in Chapter 1, that researchers should carefully consider alternative cultural viewpoints when interpreting their research findings.

Guideline 1: Researchers should recognise the cultural contingencies of their own values and beliefs when conducting research and should guard against evaluating other cultures against the criteria of their own cultural understanding.

Ethnographic methods have been the hallmark of social anthropology, cultural psychology, and some approaches to indigenous psychology for nearly a century. The startling account of Ik society is based on exactly these ethnographic methods. Turnbull was an anthropologist, so he was more interested in kinship and living arrangements than in the traits and values that are commonly studied by psychologists. In psychology, similar methods have been described as 'participant observation', referring to the systematic observation of behaviour while living among the group of interest, but keeping a professional distance from the 'objects' of observation. Sometimes, the moral agonies can be too much for anthropologists to bear and they will leave their placement, as in the case of Laura Bohannan (1964), who was confronted with a smallpox epidemic during a year among the Tiv, a primitive bush tribe in West Africa.

Much ethnographic work has used informed insiders as a key source of interpretation and validation of observations. These are typically individuals who work more closely with the ethnographer and help with making sense of the tremendous amount of information that has been gathered. This use of informed insiders in the description of culture has been adopted recently by psychologists studying **intersubjective culture**, which we discuss in more detail in Chapter 8.

Intersubjective Culture refers to shared perceptions of the psychological characteristics that are widespread within and characteristic of a culture.

However, ethnographic methods have their problems. The famous study by Margaret Mead on the sexuality of young Samoan women (Mead, 1928) is widely cited as an example. Mead was said to have imposed her own feminist beliefs on her representation of Samoan society and sexual norms in ways that could not be sustained by the observed data. Other problems include the status of the ethnographer in the group being studied: can observers truly immerse themselves in a native culture without altering others' behaviour by their presence? Consider Turnbull's decision to feed Adupa. There is also an important distinction between observation and interpretation: to what extent is it possible for an observer ever to realise *a cultural member's* vision of *their* world, as Malinowski proposed?

Other forms of observation may not require participation or informed insiders. Levine and Norenzayan (1999) measured how fast people walked a distance of 60 feet in two downtown areas of major cities in 31 nations, how long it took a clerk to process a request for stamps on a written note at a post office, and how accurate clocks were in public areas. These indicators of 'pace-of-life' were found to be correlated with individualism, wealth and temperature. People in individualistic societies, in rich countries, and in cold climates walk and process economic transfers faster and clocks are more accurate. Since the outcomes of interest in these studies were objective measures of behaviour, they require no interpretation by a possibly biased observer. However, they can tell us little about the lived experience of cultural members.

INTERVIEWS AND FOCUS GROUPS

Interviews and **focus group discussions** are two other widely used methods in cross-cultural psychology that also require interaction between the researcher and cultural informants. Interviews are typically conducted on a one-to-one basis. They can be conducted in a more or less structured manner, ranging from casual interactions between an interviewer and an interviewee to highly structured interviews in which the questions and their order are predetermined. A looser approach allows for a more open exchange of perspectives between the interviewer and interviewee and the possibility of following up any leads provided by the interviewee. The downside of using unstructured interviews is that it can be difficult to compare information across interviews, raising issues of validity and reliability. Obviously, highly structured interviews provide more comparability, but they may be too rigid to explore fully the experiences and viewpoints of the interviewee on a specific topic. Interviews and group discussions are the prime research methods used by indigenous psychologists.

Structured interviews are more common in cross-cultural psychology. For example, Kärtner, Keller et al. (2007) used a highly standardised form of interview. They presented standardised photographs of child-mother interactions to mothers with 2-month old infants in Berlin and Los Angeles (representative of urban individualistic families), Delhi and various cities in Cameroon (representative of urban and most likely collectivistic families), as well as to

Interviews are used in qualitative research to capture the meaning and significance of particular themes, events, or experiences in the life of individuals by asking each respondent a series of relevant questions. **Focus Groups** are a form of qualitative research in which a group of individuals is asked to discuss their opinions, beliefs, attitudes or perceptions judgments about a particular object, construct, or topic of interest with each other and the researcher.

rural Nso mothers in Cameroon (representative of rural and collectivistic families), and asked them to pick and describe their favourite pictures of those presented. As predicted by the authors, mothers from urban (individualist or collectivist) locations referred more to themselves when describing the pictures, whereas mothers from collectivist (urban or rural) locations referred more to other people, to the social context within which the interactions were taking place, and to authorities. (The theory underlying this study is discussed in Chapter 8.)

Focus group research typically involves a researcher interviewing a group of individuals or leading a discussion on a particular topic. As with one-to-one interviews, focus groups can be conducted in a more or a less structured manner; however, because the group members are interacting with each other, the researcher typically has less control over a group discussion than they would over an interview. One advantage of focus group interviews or discussions is that they can reveal areas of contention or multiple interpretation emerging from the interactions among members of the same cultural group or between members of different cultural groups. A potential downside here is that the personality characteristics of the participants (e.g., dominating or shy individuals) may change the dynamics of the interview, and subtle or unrecognised status differences may strongly influence the outcome of discussions. For example, in many traditional societies there are norms and rules about who is allowed to talk first, as well as who may contradict others or provide different information. If there is an individual with higher status participating in a focus group, other members may not speak up and may concur with the views aired by the higher status individual. Nonetheless, focus group discussions are often used in projects focusing on practical issues such as ethnic diversity, discrimination, or mental health among minority employees.

The choice between structured or less structured methods is often linked to researchers' assumptions about reality and about the nature of knowledge. Some researchers prefer structured methods because they assume that there is a reality that can be studied relatively objectively. Where data collection is highly structured, analysis is more likely to involve quantifying the occurrence of particular themes or contents, which can then be subjected to statistical analyses. In contrast, unstructured approaches are typically associated with a greater emphasis on subjectivity and interpretation. Researchers who use these approaches are more likely to conduct purely qualitative analyses, aiming to identify important themes or novel insights through their engagement with what the participants have said, but without seeking to make statistical generalisations beyond the specific context of the study. Research Debate Box 4.1 surveys some of the differing assumptions that researchers can make about reality and about the nature of knowledge.

CULTURAL PRODUCTS AND MEDIA CONTENT

Other options for qualitative researchers are to examine published texts (archival or historical analyses) or cultural products. Such approaches have had a relatively long history in cross-cultural psychology. McClelland (1961) studied children's books from various societies and coded the extent to which a need for achievement was evident in these texts. In Chapter 2, we also discussed a qualitative study of cultural products by Morling and Lamoreaux (2008): these authors

Ontology is the philosophical discussion of being or reality. It is concerned with questions about what entities exist, how we know that an entity exists and what is its meaning, and how any entities may be grouped or related to each other.

Epistemology is a branch of philosophy that discusses the nature, limits and scope of knowledge. It addresses questions such as 'What is knowledge?', 'What is a truth?' or 'How do we acquire knowledge?'.

Positivism is a philosophy of science that is based on empirical observation and verification of data that can be derived from sensory experiences. It is assumed that general laws about the physical and social world can be formulated and that the researcher proceeds in an objective manner to draw conclusions from the collected data.

Postmodernism is a broad philosophical movement that rejects scientific or objective efforts to describe (in our context: psychological) processes. Reality is not independent of human understanding, but is socially constructed by humans. There is no absolute truth, and the way people perceive the world is subjective and shaped by language and power relations.

Post-positivism shares with positivism the meta-theoretical assumption that reality exists, but does not assume that reality can ever be known perfectly. Instead, it is recognised that the process of scientific research, like everyday understanding, is biased by the theoretical background, knowledge and values of the observer or researcher. Karl Popper, an influential proponent of this approach, argued that theories can only be falsified (that is, rejected based on empirical data), and never verified. One important implication is that theories need to be amenable to falsification for them to be assessed scientifically.

counted frequencies of collectivist themes in cultural products, and then related the observed differences to scores on the cultural dimensions identified by Hofstede (2001) and others.

Bardi, Calogero, and Mullen (2009) studied US newspaper content from 1900 to 2000 as a test of the validity of Schwartz's (1992) theory of values (which we discussed in Chapter 2). They developed lists of words that were thought to reflect the ten basic values in Schwartz's theory. They then examined whether newspaper articles across this time period mentioned these values and whether the frequency of mentioned values was correlated with observed behaviours over the same period. They found that values as indexed by newspaper content did indeed relate significantly to behavioural indicators, such as military participation (power), alcohol consumption (hedonism), number of movies released (stimulation), unwed births (conformity) and numbers of police and guards employed (conformity). Thus, they successfully used archival records to examine cultural change in one national culture over time.

The emergence of the internet and new technologies has created opportunities for conducting qualitative research in much broader ways. For example, Boer and Fischer (2012) placed questions about how individuals use music in their daily lives on various internet sites accessed by young people, sampling from New Zealand, the USA and Germany as examples of individualistic societies, and from Hong Kong, the Philippines, Brazil and Singapore as examples of more collectivistic societies. They were able to identify seven main themes of how young people used music on a daily basis, which differed somewhat between the samples. In individualistic cultural samples, respondents reported greater use of music for remembering good times (especially among Germans), whereas in collectivistic settings respondents reported greater use of music for emotion regulation and socialising with friends and family (especially among Brazilians).

Research Debate Box 4.1   Assumptions about Knowledge and Meaning

Research methods differ in the basis of the knowledge that researchers seek. Up to now, we have described some examples of qualitative research methods that can be used in cross-cultural psychology. These methods cover a diverse array, differing in their views of reality (**ontology**) and the nature of knowledge (**epistemology**).

Traditionally, scientists have typically based their research on **positivism**, which assumes that scientific methods are a valid way to describe empirical phenomena in a systematic, objective and logical fashion. Yet this focus on searching for objective descriptions of reality has been criticised. Amongst others, the French philosopher Michel Foucault and the American historian Thomas Kuhn were some of the influential thinkers who have challenged the positivist view, and their critique is now considered part of a broader paradigm of **postmodernism**. Postmodernism encompasses a diverse set of philosophical approaches that stress the subjectivity of experience and emphasise that our reality is socially constructed and therefore subject to change. 'Culture' has been a popular field of investigation among postmodern scholars: these scholars focus on the role of language and power relations in constructing and legitimising particular ideas, categories, or ways of being, rather than the broader patterns of similarity and difference that are more focal within cross-cultural psychology. Central to the postmodern view of reality as socially constructed is that concepts and ideas that are usually taken for granted can be reinterpreted as cultural inventions, and thus they are open to being questioned or 'de-constructed'.

The emergence of postmodern approaches has created many intellectual problems for ethnographers and anthropologists. Some core assumptions of positivist approaches to culture that have been questioned (see Greenfield, 2000, for a summary and response) include:

- that culture can be objectively described by an outsider without the intrusion of the observer's subjective stance on what s/he feels, believes or values;
- that cultures are homogeneous systems;
- that it is possible to describe culture in factual terms without subjective interpretation by a researcher;
- that knowledge is derived from a world that exists independent of the person (i.e., the researcher) knowing it.

Returning to our initial example, a postmodern view suggests that Turnbull's description of the Ik culture was undoubtedly shaped by his own values and beliefs, reflecting his own cultural origins in mid-twentieth century London; that his conclusions about the cultural group as a whole would have been narrowly based on his interactions with selected individuals in the various villages; and that his presence would have changed the actions of the individuals he was observing.

Partly in response to these critiques, philosophers of science have developed **post-positivist** epistemological perspectives (see, for example, Hwang, 2006). Like postmodernism, post-positivism

(Continued)

(Continued)

is not a unitary philosophy. Typically, post-positivists accept that knowledge is contingent on processes of social construction, and thus it is inevitably incomplete and imperfect: however, they do not deny the existence of an external reality, and they tend to view the scientific method as pragmatically useful for describing both objective and constructed realities. In particular, scientific method provides a means of falsification (rejecting incorrect beliefs about reality), and treats human knowledge as not unchallengeable or absolutely true, but open to modification based on further investigation.

Within psychology, postmodernism has been especially associated with a critique of quantitative methodologies. Postmodernist researchers argue that meanings are too fluid and subjective to be quantified or generalised, and thus they tend to adopt relatively unstructured research methods and qualitative analyses involving intensive interpretation. However, many of the quantitative methods we review recognise the impossibility of knowing another person's subjective experience. Grounded in post-positivist assumptions, these methods are based on understanding psychological constructs as 'latent variables' (constructs that cannot be observed directly, but that may be inferred from patterns of observable behaviour, for example responses to multiple items on a questionnaire).

Moreover, from a post-positivist perspective, ideas arising from postmodernism about the culturally contingent nature of beliefs, values, and other constructs can be viewed as theoretical propositions that are amenable to scientific testing. Cross-cultural psychology is ideally suited to test these ideas. For instance, in a study discussed in Chapter 12, Pehrson, Vignoles, and Brown (2009) drew inspiration from postmodern theories of identity in order to derive and test hypotheses about the cultural contingency of the relationship between national identity and prejudice against immigrants.

We strongly encourage research that uses mixed methods, and we would encourage the reader to pay attention to research from different epistemological and methodological perspectives. However, researchers interested in culture need to be aware of these broader philosophical debates and will have to take a position on these matters.

Golder and Macy (2011) examined Twitter posts from around the world and explored whether the way in which people express their mood varies systematically with diurnal and seasonal patterns. They found that, independent of nation of origin, people post more positive tweets in the morning with their mood declining over the course of the day, a finding which fits with biological patterns of sleep and circadian rhythms. People are generally happier at weekends, but are also affected by the relative day length over the course of the year.

One major advantage of these methods is that they tap data that individuals produce either for public consumption (e.g., books, internet web sites and advertisements) or in order to communicate with the outside world (e.g., Twitter or Facebook postings), and therefore they represent culture in the making. Of course, these methods also require carefully prepared coding schemes, highly trained coders and careful interpretation. Golder and Macy (2011) restricted their analysis to tweets in English, and sampling was based on the location from which tweeters (people who post messages on Twitter) had sent their messages. This sampling strategy could have obscured true cultural differences that would have been of interest to social psychologists and, as we shall see, the use of English may also have led to a convergence of responses.

When examining the use of such cultural products and media content, we need to pause and ask whether the use of English as a universal language of international communication changes the results of studies. Harzing (2005) investigated this problem by sampling students in 24 countries. In each of these, she administered questionnaires to half of the students in their local language whereas the other half received an English language version. Overall, she found that responses in English showed fewer cultural differences, supporting claims that individuals subconsciously accommodate their responses to the stereotypical cultural norms of the language to which they are responding. This effect has been confirmed subsequently (e.g., S.X. Chen & Bond, 2010, discussed in Chapter 5), and used in experimental priming studies, which we discuss below.

Harzing also differentiated between different types of questions. She found the largest effects of language on questions about cultural values and norms, and smaller but still significant effects on more culturally neutral questions, such as reasons for selecting course electives. Consequently, research that uses non-native languages is likely to underestimate cultural differences on more culturally sensitive topics.

> **Guideline 2: Researchers should study psychological processes in the native language of participants, as using English or other business or trading languages is likely to lead to cultural accommodation of responses to the perceived cultural stereotypes of the language being used, thereby underestimating cultural differences.**

PSYCHOMETRIC TESTS

Ethnographic and qualitative approaches have been popular methods for observers of cultural differences for centuries. Researchers looking for more objective ways of describing individuals and groups often rely on psychometric data, in other words the quantitative measurement of knowledge, abilities, attitudes, personality traits, and other such constructs. Rudimentary forms of psychometric testing were developed in ancient China about 4,000 years ago and formalised during the Han dynasty (Gregory, 1996). The most widely used current method for collecting cross-cultural psychological data is by way of paper-and-pencil surveys or questionnaires, as well as online surveys.

These methods are similar to interviews in that researchers seek a response from research participants on questions of interest about their inner feelings, states, personality, beliefs, attitudes, goals, values, or other psychological variables, which usually require some form of introspection. One major difference is that participants are asked to respond using fixed formats, typically with a **Likert-type** response scale requiring respondents to grade their responses along a scale of relative strength of endorsement (e.g., from strongly agree through neutral to strongly disagree). The studies discussed in Chapter 2 all used some form of such questionnaires, as did many other studies discussed in later chapters.

A **Likert Scale** is a rating scale used in questionnaires, named after an American psychologist, Rensis Likert. Respondents are asked to specify their level of agreement or disagreement with a specific statement on a symmetric agree-disagree rating scale (typically a 5- or 7-point graded scale). The response is taken as indicating the intensity of their reaction towards the stated topic.

Reliability refers to the consistency of a measure, both in terms of its component parts and its repeated use over time. A measure has high reliability if it produces consistent results under consistent conditions.

Validity in the statistical sense refers to whether a measure is fit for its intended purpose. Several subtypes can be distinguished. Predictive validity is concerned with whether the measure can predict some other construct of interest (sometimes called utility). Construct validity is the extent to which a measure accurately reflects the variability and relative position of test takers on the underlying construct that the measure is designed to measure.

Objectivity refers to the absence of bias in the measurement process. The measurement process should yield equivalent results independent of the researcher or the instrument used.

Psychometric researchers aim to produce valid, reliable, and objective information about underlying constructs that are not directly observable (e.g., a person's subjective beliefs, or their level of intelligence), by analysing patterns of observable behaviour across a series of tasks (e.g., responses to a series of items on a questionnaire). In single-culture studies, inferences are drawn about the **reliability** of a measure based on careful analyses of the patterns of correlation among individuals' responses to the separate items and/or the similarity of responses on multiple testing occasions. Inferences about **validity** require interpreting how well the contents of the measure match the theoretical construct that the researcher is aiming to measure: this interpretation may be aided by testing correlations of the measure with measures of other constructs that are expected to be related to it (convergent or predictive validity), or that are expected to be unrelated (discriminant validity).

In cross-cultural research, this becomes more complex. A measure that is reliable and valid in one cultural context when transposed to a new context may not yield comparable scores. Moreover, even when the measures are comparable, differences in the testing environment may affect the **objectivity** of measurements. We now consider some of the sources of bias in cross-cultural research, as well as some of the techniques that are available to researchers seeking to make cross-cultural comparisons that are as valid, reliable, and objective as possible.

Sources of Bias in Cross-Cultural Research

Construct bias

One important issue is the extent to which any psychological construct is understood and conceptualised in the same way across cultural groups. Construct bias refers to the cultural specificity of a psychological construct or process. If there is construct bias, the construct is defined differently in two or more cultural groups. For example, greeting procedures are functionally universal, but structurally non-equivalent (compare kisses to handshakes to bowing). An example of direct practical importance concerns cross-national comparisons of reading skills, as discussed in Box 4.1.

Box 4.1   When is a Difference a Cultural Difference?

National differences in scores of intelligence tests focus on abilities considered without referring to the context. What happens if we make comparisons that do include context? After one year of schooling, children in Finland, Germany, Italy, Spain and Greece all achieve accuracy levels of greater than 90% on reading of words and non-words constructed by the researcher. Children in Portugal and Denmark achieve around 70% accuracy. Children in the UK achieve an accuracy of just 40%. It takes them three or four years to achieve 90% accuracy.

Why is this very large difference found? Is it because children in the UK often start school between the ages of 4 and 5, while those in most other European countries start later? Is it because teachers in the UK are less well trained in the specific skills required to teach reading? Are UK teachers less motivated? The principal explanation for the difference is that English is a much more difficult language to read. It is relatively easy for a Spanish or Greek child to learn to read, because their language is phonetically consistent. In other words, a given combination of characters always has the same sound. In English, vowels are frequently pronounced in different ways depending upon the consonants with which they are paired. Consider for instance the sound of 'a' in 'cap', 'call' and 'car', or of 'o' in 'go' and 'do'.

Comparisons of rates of learning to read differ from comparisons of intelligence scores, because languages differ from one another, whereas intelligence testers attempt to make their tests 'culture-fair'. Should differences in learning to read be considered a cultural difference, or should differences only be attributed to culture when measures are used that are equivalent across cultures? Is language a part of culture?

Sources: Goswami, Porpodas & Wheelwright (1997); Seymour, Aro & Erskine (2003).

A related threat is **domain under-representation**, where a test or questionnaire may miss out important aspects of a construct in a specific cultural setting. The example of the wider definition of intelligence in African communities is one such instance. Qualitative studies where respondents are asked what attributes they associate with intelligence have repeatedly found that intelligence is more broadly defined in collectivist cultural groups (Sternberg, 2007). Intelligence is

> **Domain Under-Representation** is present in a measure if an aspect of the domain that is important to the function of a theoretical variable is missing from that measuring instrument in at least one of the sampled groups.

seen as including social competence in Taiwan, Japan and China. Studies in sub-Saharan Africa have frequently shown that the skills of maintaining harmonious and stable relations within and between groups are seen as key aspects of intelligence, in addition to the cognitive alacrity that is typically understood as intelligence in Western societies. These differences indicate the need for caution in cross-cultural comparisons of intelligence (see our previous discussion in Chapter 3). Box 4.2 provides a telling example of the problems of testing across cultures.

Box 4.2   The Challenges of Conducting Research Across Cultures

A researcher administered an intelligence test to an African child. However, the child sat there mute and did not respond to any of the questions asked by the tester. One of the tasks was to recount the story read out by the tester. As with all the other tasks, the child remained silent and avoided eye contact. Disappointed, the tester finally dismissed the child, convinced that the child had some serious developmental delays in her social and cognitive development. The child was picked up by her caregiver and walked a few hours back to her ancestral village. A few days later another child from that village came for testing. This child was much more forthcoming with answers and was very energetic and talkative. When the tester started reading out the story as for the first child, she interrupted the experimenter and said that she had already heard this story from her friend and started recalling the correct story with all the necessary details. The tester was baffled. The first child had not only remembered the story on the way back to her village, she had also correctly recounted it to other children, including this one now sitting in front of her who memorised it and retold it accurately. Therefore, the first child probably had normal or even outstanding intellectual capacities, but had interpreted the testing situation differently. In her culture it was socially intelligent not to talk back to the tester as an adult, and she had aimed to present herself as an intelligent and wise child that did not talk back to an older person, even if tempted repeatedly.

Source: Adapted from Harkness & Super (1977).

The dilemmas of construct bias can be considered in light of the useful distinction between etic and emic approaches, proposed by Pike (1967) and popularised by Berry (1969). In attempting to learn a Mexican Indian language, Pike found that the use of differing pitches and tones influenced the meaning of specific sounds in that language. In terms of the concepts used in linguistics, phonetic production affects the meaning of specific phonemes. Drawing on this distinction, Berry contrasted two approaches to cross-cultural study. Firstly, one could start from the assumption that there are universals and proceed in that manner until evidence is found for differences. He termed this the 'etic' approach, paralleling the universalist assumptions made in phonetics, the study of sounds. Alternatively, one can start by studying intensively the distinctive attributes of one specific cultural group. He termed this the 'emic' approach, because it focuses on local meanings, and draws most readily on information provided by persons within that cultural group. This orientation parallels linguists' focus on the phonemic attributes of a specific language.

The debate between emic versus etic methods somewhat resembles the debate between positivism and post-modernism that was discussed in Research Debate Box 4.1. Etic research is strongly associated with positivist and post-positivist epistemologies. Emic research focuses on culture-specific attributes that can only be understood within the local context. The approach used by most indigenous researchers falls under this heading, as summarised in Box 4.3.

Box 4.3   How to do Indigenous Psychology

In Chapter 1, we discussed indigenous psychology as one area of cross-cultural research. Indigenous researchers often prefer to use the less standardised methods that allow for more mutual and egalitarian exchanges between researcher and interviewee (Pe-Pua, 2006). Enriquez (1993) distinguished between two main types of indigenous research: 'indigenisation from within' and 'indigenisation from without'. The former refers to locals or insiders developing a psychology within and for their own culture. The latter describes attempts by foreigners to understand and describe a culture in its own terms, moving from an imposed-etic understanding to an emic understanding (in Berry's terminology). There are some guidelines that indigenous researchers have used for such endeavours.

Do tolerate ambiguous or vague states of understanding and suspend decisions as long as possible in dealing with theoretical, methodological and empirical problems, until something indigenous emerges in your mind during the research process.

Do be a typical native in the cultural sense when functioning as a researcher.

Do take the studied psychological or behavioural phenomenon and its sociocultural context into consideration.

Do give priority to the study of culturally unique phenomena.

Do base your research on the intellectual tradition of your own culture rather than on that of a Western culture.

Don't neglect Western psychologists' important experiences in developing their own indigenous psychologies, which may be usefully transferred to the development of non-Western indigenous psychologies.

Source: Excerpted from Yang (2000) (emphases added).

Emic studies are often equated with postmodernist concepts, but in fact they can also be conducted within a post-positivist framework. For example, if you develop a testable hypothesis about psychological processes within a specific culture (for instance, 'there will be relationship between the importance placed on children and the sharing of food'), then you are conducting an emic study within a positivist paradigm. Ferreira, Fischer, Porto, Pilati, and Milfont (2012) conducted such a study. They developed measures of *jeitinho brasileiro*, an indigenous social influence strategy in Brazil (see Chapter 10) and then examined how individual preferences and normative perceptions of *jeitinho brasiliero* related to other psychological variables.

Berry (1969) suggested that cross-cultural research often starts as 'imposed-etic', that is to say, it is based on applying Western concepts and measures in non-Western contexts. Imposed-etic research relies on the assumption that the concepts and measures will have the same meaning in new contexts. Rokeach's (1973) study of social values using a survey developed in the USA is a good example of emic US research that was subsequently 'imposed' in nine other nations (Ng et al., 1982, discussed in Chapter 14).

As a research field becomes more fully developed, an accumulation of emic studies can contribute to the development of improved 'derived-etic' measures, that have equal validity in a broad range of cultural contexts. Rokeach's work strongly influenced Schwartz's (1992) subsequent cross-cultural studies of values. His survey items were drawn in part from Rokeach, but he also consulted Muslim and Druze scholars and included values from previous instruments developed in China, Israel and Zimbabwe. Moreover, he allowed for the possibility that he might be missing further values, by asking his collaborators in each country to add culture-specific values of local relevance. However, the local items proved compatible with the universally identified dimensions, so his individual-level value dimensions can be considered the best current example of a derived-etic measure encompassing a broad range of cultural groups.

Instrument bias

Even if an underlying construct can be defined equivalently across cultures, it may not be measurable in the same way. Serpell's (1979) study of British and Zambian children provides a good example of instrument bias in the area of cognitive abilities. British students were much more familiar with using pencils (or pens) and paper in their daily lives, and when standard pencil-and-paper tests were used the British outperformed Zambian children. In contrast, if iron wire figures were used, Zambian children showed superior test performances, since making toys from iron wire was a common pastime in Zambia and children were familiar with performing these tasks. Importantly, the two groups did not differ on a task involving clay figures that was unfamiliar to both cultural groups.

Let us reconsider some of the studies discussed in Chapter 3, for example the study by Henrich et al. (2010) who sampled participants from 15 traditional cultures around the world and asked them to play a number of economic games. Imagine you are a Hadza forager who is roaming the Tanzanian savannah and is used to collecting and hunting for the food that is necessary for survival. You do not use money on a regular basis, although you are probably aware of its existence. Now you are interacting with some foreigners who play a game where you have to imagine that a person that you do not know is giving you a large amount of this money and you have to divide it between yourself and an anonymous person that you have never seen and indeed never will. In their study, Henrich et al. reported that the Hadza were among the least likely to offer any money to the anonymous player. They explained differences across communities by showing that integration into a market economy and believing in a monotheistic god are necessary for the emergence of fairness (operationalised as sharing in the so-called Dictator Game). This is an imposed-etic interpretation and we could equally argue that the results test instead for a familiarity with Western concepts such as money and abstract, non-personal notions of fairness that are not relevant in a Hadza community.

It is preferable to use locally meaningful and relevant objects for exchange games like this one. A good example is a study by Apicella, Marlowe et al. (2012) which also involved Hadza participants. They studied exchange networks in Hadza camps by giving participants three sticks of honey (a prized food source among the Hadza) and then asked them to distribute these three honey sticks in any way they liked among people in their camp. Of course, this was a study within a single cultural group. In a cross-cultural study, locally equivalent objects would need to be found so that the results could be compared across groups.

> **Translation-Back Translation** is the classic translation procedure. An instrument is first translated from the source language into the target language and then independently translated back into the source language. The original and the back-translated versions are then compared and changes are made so as to improve accuracy.
>
> **Decentering** involves replacing culturally specific expressions in the initial version of an instrument with alternative wordings that are more translatable but still preserve the underlying meaning.

The creation of measures that are understood equally well and in similar ways across different parts of the world is not simply a matter of using items that refer to issues or tasks that are familiar to respondents. There is also a need to ensure that translations from one language to another are done in a manner that yields items with equivalent meaning (Hambleton & Zenisky, 2011). The most widely accepted procedure for achieving linguistic equivalence is **back-translation** (Brislin, Lonner, & Thorndike, 1973): a translation is first made from the language in which the test was originally developed into the language of the society in which it is to be used. A second bilingual person is then asked to translate the items back into the original language, usually English, without having seen the original version. A comparison of the retranslated version and the original by a native speaker-writer of the first language can then be used to detect problematic translations and to create an improved version through discussion between the two translators.

Back-translation is cost-effective and fast, but can result in stilted and awkward sentences in the target language. It is therefore not the optimal solution. A 'committee' approach, where a group of bilinguals get together and discuss the meaning and appropriateness of each item, may overcome this problem. It is possible to combine back-translation and committee approaches to capitalise on the strengths of each method. However, such methods are very labour and time intensive (see Harkness, 2003, for more details).

Difficulties often focus on the relative merits of a literal translation versus linguistic '**decentering**'. A decentered translation does not necessarily use terms that have a precise linguistic equivalence, but may draw on the cultural knowledge of the translators to use phrases that have an equivalent meaning in the two languages. For instance, while English speakers discussing some misfortune might seek hope by claiming that 'every cloud has a silver lining', speakers of Mandarin Chinese would claim that 'every cloud has a pink edge'. A further step in decentering would be to drop the specific descriptors in the original version in favour of a similar, more general saying, like 'something good comes from any misfortune'. A good example of decentering was the development of the social axioms study discussed in Chapter 2; Leung, Bond et al. (2002) gathered proverbs, maxims and adages in Hong Kong and Venezuela, but then had to rewrite them to capture the underlying social beliefs in more general terms that would be understandable outside their cultures of origin.

Key Researcher Box 4.1   Kwok Leung

Kwok Leung (b. 1958) grew up in Hong Kong. After discovering cross-cultural psychology while taking an undergraduate course at the Chinese University of Hong Kong with Michael Bond, he obtained his PhD in social and organisational psychology from the University of Illinois, Urbana-Champaign, supervised by Alan Lind and inspired by Harry Triandis. He is currently chair professor of management at the City University of Hong Kong. He has collaborated with Michael Bond in pioneering cross-cultural studies of beliefs (social axioms) and has conducted many studies of justice. He has also co-authored key publications on cross-cultural research methods. Overall, he has published several books and more than 100 academic articles.

Figure 4.1   Kwok Leung

Administration bias

Administration bias refers to any aspect in the administration of a test or survey that affects results. This can include differences in physical conditions and social environments (e.g., the noise or temperature of the test setting, or the presence of other people in the test situation), instructions (e.g., the different experience of test administrators in different contexts or the use of vague language in instructions), the status of the test administrator (e.g., their ethnicity, profession, status, religion, or local versus foreign status) and communication problems (e.g., differences in the language used, the use of interpreters or the culture-specific interpretation of instructions). The goal in classic psychometrics is to standardise the test situation as much as possible, so as to rule out any variation in the results that could be interpreted as arising from differences in the administration of the scientific procedure.

However, from a cultural perspective this standardisation may introduce error variance if the required procedures result in a situation that is not compatible with local customs and cultural standards. Practitioners of ethnomethodologies such as *pagtatanong-tanong* (roughly translated as casual asking around) in the Philippines (Pe-Pua, 2006) have criticised Western psychologists for striving to standardise social situations and limit the interactions between participants and researchers. One of the key aspects of *pagtatanong-tanong* as an alternative to Western psychological procedures has been the concept of casual and non-directed conversations that are driven by the respondent rather than the researcher. It is through these conversations that the researcher can obtain valuable information once a certain level of trust has been established and the researcher is no longer treated as an outsider.

Nevertheless, these unstructured approaches have been heavily criticised as yielding unreliable and non-replicable results in cross-cultural psychology (Van de Vijver & Leung, 1997) and similar criticisms have also been raised within the Philippines. Pe-Pua argues that these problems can be overcome through a systematic documentation of findings, the replication of studies, and giving attention to ethical guidelines. Indigenous methodologists stress that the relationship takes priority and that interview procedures cannot be guided by the demands for standardisation required by positivist methodologies. According to this approach, any strict standardisation would feel alienating to participants in non-Western contexts.

Key Researcher Box 4.2   Fons van de Vijver

Figure 4.2   Fons van de Vijver

Fons van de Vijver (b. 1952) grew up in the Netherlands, and completed his PhD at the University of Tilburg. He is currently a professor at the same university and holds additional posts at North-West University, South Africa, and the University of Queensland, Australia. He has published 16 books and more than 350 papers and book chapters, mainly in the domain of cross-cultural psychology. His main research topics involve measurement bias and equivalence, psychological acculturation and multiculturalism, cognitive similarities and differences, survey response styles, and translations and adaptations of psychometric tests. He has co-authored key publications on cross-cultural research methods.

In the context of developmental psychology, Abubakar (2008) has suggested that tests that require strict standardisation can be administered last to overcome some of these limitations when testing children in African contexts. For example, the test administrator may start off by playing football with the child and her siblings, which allows for observations of balance, control and other aspects of motor function that are important for assessment. Once the child has developed some trust and feels comfortable with the test administrator, more standardised instructions to test cognitive abilities can be used. This graduated approach circumvents problems associated with strict standardisation that may alienate respondents.

Sampling bias

Finally, sampling bias refers to the characteristics of the sample that is used for comparisons. Reconsider the discussion of the Ik at the beginning of this chapter. What sample should be used against which to compare the values and moral inclinations of the Ik? The Ik groups studied by Turnbull varied in so many different ways from most other samples studied by psychologists that it would be hard to find a comparable group. Cross-cultural studies frequently compare student samples, but students are drawn from elite groups in some nations much more than in others. Enrolment in tertiary education varies between 73% in the USA and 7% in China. Even in the 'Western' nations of Europe it varies between 70% in Finland and 30% in the Czech Republic (www.nationmaster.com).

In many of the studies reviewed in this book, psychology students were the research participants. You may ask the question to what extent do psychology students differ across societies in ways that are additional to their cultural background? One important difference can be the status of psychology in a given society, and the educational requirements for studying psychology there. If you are a student residing in Germany, you probably went through a central allocation system before being admitted to a university that takes into account your grades from high school. In Germany, there is a high demand to obtain a degree in psychology, so entry to university is competitive and few students will get their choice of university. In the UK and the USA, psychology is similarly attractive to students, but few constraints exist on choosing to study psychology rather than another major. Psychology students therefore differ between these three nations on important cognitive and motivational variables. In many non-Western societies, psychology has much less prestige and there is no competition for places. Another difference is the socio-economic status of students in each society. These factors are likely to influence motivations, attitudes and beliefs in addition to any cultural variable that may influence survey responses.

As a general rule, the more culturally and economically diverse the samples, the more likely it is that one or more biases will affect the findings. This raises the probability of finding differences that cannot be explained by a single or limited set of variables. This awareness leads to a so-called 'interpretation paradox' (Van de Vijver & Leung, 2000). It is relatively easy to find differences between samples that differ along many different social, cultural and economic dimensions, but it is then more difficult to pinpoint why these differences exist and what factor or factors can explain them.

The **Interpretation Paradox** refers to the problem that psychological differences between samples that vary along many different social, cultural and economic dimensions are easy to find, but it is then difficult to explain why these differences exist and what variables may cause them.

Guideline 3: Samples should be matched as closely as possible in order to rule out alternative explanations for observed differences in the outcomes being studied.

The Quest for Cross-Cultural Equivalence

As we have just seen, there are many challenges in making valid comparisons between groups. How confidently, then, can we use psychometric measures of values, traits, or abilities to test reliably (consistently) and validly (truly) whether two different populations are the same or different on the value, belief, trait or ability in question? Cross-cultural methodologists have developed guidelines for establishing four increasing levels of equivalence in measures of psychological processes and constructs (Van de Vijver & Leung, 1997; Fontaine, 2005; Matsumoto & Van de Vijver, 2011). The higher the level of equivalence, the more confidently we can claim to be measuring the same underlying construct across different cultural samples. Here, we use terminology adopted by Fontaine (2005). Van de Vijver and Leung (1997) put functional and structural equivalence together as construct equivalence.

Functional equivalence

The most general and broadest level of measurement equivalence is **functional equivalence**, that is whether the same underlying psychological construct can be said to exist across different cultural contexts. In operational terms, can the test behaviour (e.g., the behavioural

> **Functional equivalence** refers to the situation where the same theoretical variable accounts for the same measurement outcomes across cultural groups.

response of selecting a response category to a Likert-type item) be seen as an expression of the same theoretical variable? This issue is most easily described and discussed in relation to cognitive phenomena such as intelligence. As we have seen, intelligence is consensually defined more broadly or more narrowly in different cultures. The ability to solve abstract cognitive problems, typically emphasised in Western definitions of intelligence, is only one aspect of the much broader conceptualisation of intelligence that prevails among various African groups.

Functional equivalence is the most abstract and difficult level of equivalence to establish, as it requires an in-depth understanding of each cultural context and extensive qualitative and conceptual work. It is often assumed rather than tested, because it depends additionally on philosophical and theoretical considerations, and no statistical tests are available for making such judgments. Qualitative and ethnographic research is necessary if one is to make an informed judgment about the nature of a construct in each culture and thus to make claims about construct equivalence.

Structural equivalence

If functional equivalence is considered to be tenable, the second issue is whether the same items can be used in different cultural contexts as indicators of the underlying construct. This level of equivalence is called **structural equivalence**.

> **Structural Equivalence** refers to the situation where the same measurement instrument is a valid and sufficient indicator of a theoretical variable of interest to the researchers in two or more cultural samples.

To illustrate the use of comprehensive procedures for establishing both functional and structural equivalence, we describe here a cross-cultural study of emotion research. Breugelmans and Poortinga (2006) were interested in the hypothesis that all humans have the same physical and biological capacities to experience certain emotions, even though these capacities cannot be expressed through language in settings where the language does not have words for specific emotions. For example, members of the native American group of Raramuri in Mexico use the same word for 'shame' and 'guilt'. Does the absence of a specific word indicate that they cannot differentiate and respond appropriately to different social situations that would elicit either shame or guilt in another culture?

To assess this question, Breugelmans and Poortinga started by soliciting descriptions of typical situations that invoked either shame or guilt from Javanese villagers in Indonesia, chosen because they are comparable in many socio-economic characteristics to the Raramuri. They next found that both Dutch and Javanese students were able to differentiate these two types of scenarios. They then presented these scenarios to Raramuri villagers, asking them how they would feel in each situation. The results showed that they responded to the two kinds of situations in a very similar way to that of the Javanese. This demonstrates that the Raramuri were able to discriminate between culturally relevant scenarios of guilt and shame in very much the same way as other groups that do have separate words for shame and guilt. Hence, the non-availability of a word does not affect the differential emotional experience of shame versus guilt.

This example demonstrates that using culturally relevant scenarios can establish both a functional and structural equivalence of psychological processes, even if the observed behaviour (the lexical encoding of emotions) would indicate otherwise. Thus, the critical way to establish structural equivalence is to find indicators that tap the construct of interest in a culturally meaningful way. Indicators need to be relevant and representative of the construct in each cultural setting, but may vary between groups.

To develop meaningful indicators in each culture, extensive qualitative and ethnographic research is necessary, followed by sound psychometric analysis of the instrument. Unfortunately, many published cross-cultural studies have not followed these requirements and have instead used imposed-etic measures. Often, much work is spent in examining the simpler task of whether survey items load in psychometrically similar ways on the expected construct, but far less effort is dedicated to developing locally relevant measures. A major problem is that important aspects or indicators of the psychological construct are often missed when imposed-etic measures are used. This failure can be expected to lead to domain-underrepresentation.

Achieving structural equivalence suggests that the same items can validly be used to measure individual differences in the same underlying construct within both groups. However, this does not yet mean that one can validly compare correlational patterns or mean scores across groups. Before doing this, further levels of equivalence are required.

Metric equivalence

To compare correlational patterns across groups validly, **metric equivalence** is needed. Metric equivalence means that a difference of one scale point on a measure can be assumed to reflect the same difference in the underlying construct across groups. In the psychometric literature this is often called metric invariance. Because we cannot directly measure the underlying construct, metric invariance is inferred from the patterns of relationships among the items. If factor loadings for all items are found to be equal across groups, this supports the assumption that the items are related to the underlying construct in the same way. As the level of an individual on the **latent variable** (often defined as a latent factor) increases, so too does his or her endorsement of items in the questionnaire or test and, crucially, metric invariance suggests that this relationship between latent variable and observed indicator is the same in all cultural groups studied.

Cross cultural tests of metric invariance are often used to identify and remove problematic items from a scale. Panel (a) in Figure 4.3 shows an item that is performing acceptably for metric equivalence. In both groups, an increase in the latent variable is associated with the same increase in the observed variable. Compare this result with that in Panel (b), where the increases in group

Metric Equivalence refers to a situation where relative comparisons (e.g., mean patterns or correlations) are possible between two or more cultural groups. This result indicates that items have identical relationships with the latent underlying variable in all cultural groups.

A **Latent Variable** is a hypothetical variable that is not directly observable, but can be inferred from other variables that have been directly observed or measured. The inference of a latent variable is done through mathematical models, such as factor analysis.

Non-Uniform Item Bias is characterised by individuals not showing the same ordering on the measurement instruments as would be expected based on their ordering along the latent variable. Bias is present and the size of this bias for a respondent in a group depends on the position of that individual on the latent variable.

Uniform Item Bias is characterised by individuals in two cultural groups showing the same order on the observed measurement that corresponds to their ordering on the latent variable. However, there are some relative differences between the two groups that are not accounted for by the latent variable. The degree of bias is the same for all individuals.

1 are much larger than those in group 2. For example, the item 'working hard to achieve good grades in school' may be a valid indicator of achievement values in literate societies where achievement in school is a strong indicator of achievement, but it might not be as valid an indicator in a pastoral community where children may go to school but achievement is evaluated against non-school criteria. This differential relationship between the observed indicator and the latent variable is called **non-uniform bias**. The term 'non-uniform' emphasises that changes in the latent variable are not uniformly associated with changes in the observed item.

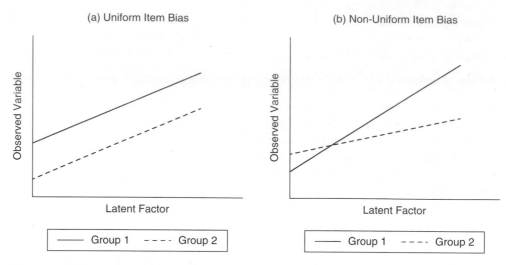

Figure 4.3   Examples of Item Bias

Psychometric tests for metric equivalence are available and discussed in detail elsewhere (Van de Vijver & Leung, 1997; Fischer & Fontaine, 2011). If we find metric equivalence, we can compare patterns of correlations across cultural groups. Differences within each group can be analysed, but absolute mean differences cannot yet be compared across groups. As is seen in Panel (a) in Figure 4.3, the means for group 1 are consistently higher independent of the latent variable. This difference is due to other factors independent of the latent variable of interest. This difference is called **uniform bias**, indicating that there is some difference that is not due to the latent variable (hence the term 'bias'), but this difference is constant (uniform) along the levels of the latent variable. However, the presence of bias means that we cannot make a comparison of scores and attribute them to the latent variable of interest. Only their correlations may be compared across groups.

Full Score or Scalar Equivalence refers to a situation where the scores can be directly compared between two or more cultural groups. It assumes that the measure taps the same base level or intercept in all cultural groups.

Scalar equivalence

The final level of equivalence is called **full score** or **scalar equivalence** (or scalar invariance in the psychometric literature) and allows us to compare group means directly. Full score equivalence requires that the scale is not affected by uniform bias: a score of 5 in one group indicates the same level on the underlying construct as a score of 5 in another group. As with metric equivalence, a full score equivalence cannot be tested directly, because we cannot directly measure the underlying construct. However, we can infer that particular items may suffer from a uniform bias if they show differential mean levels in relation to the other items across the groups being studied. In statistical terms, researchers can test whether the item intercepts, that is whether the points where the regression line of the latent variable on the observed indicator crosses the y-axis are identical or not. In other words, is the baseline of an instrument comparable?

This level of equivalence is the most difficult to establish, but is necessary if we want to make inferences about the mean levels of the latent psychological trait of interest. Unfortunately, until recently very few researchers have fully tested levels of equivalence and in particular full score or scalar equivalence. This means that many of the studies reported in this book are open to alternative explanations.

One of the most challenging of these explanations, as we mentioned in Chapter 2, is acquiescent responding. If people agree with an item more strongly than they actually believe, we have the pattern seen in Panel (a) in Figure 4.3. In this situation, the mean score reflects both the variable of interest *as well as* the group's average tendency towards acquiescent responding. To rule out such alternative explanations, researchers need to evaluate their data properly and use methods that can rule out this potential confound. This also applies to other aspects of response style such as extreme responding or moderate responding, where these are found to be culturally distinctive.

> **Guideline 4: Instruments need to be valid and reliable in all cultural groups in order to accurately detect cross-cultural similarities or differences. Researchers should try to ensure that instruments, measures, and manipulations are understood in comparable ways in each location.**

EXPERIMENTS

Internal Validity refers to the level of confidence that a researcher can place on the premise that changes in a dependent variable are caused by the experimental manipulation alone and that alternative causal explanations can be ruled out.

Up until now we have been dealing with methods that psychologists share with many other social science disciplines. The basis upon which psychology became distinguished from neighbouring social sciences was through its emphasis upon studying samples of individuals within controlled settings, rather than focusing upon larger groups, organisations or nations. Experimentalists test the specific effects of changes within controlled environments to which individuals have been randomly assigned so as to rule out alternative explanations. The issue of **internal validity** (establishing that changes in the dependent variable can only be attributed to the experimental manipulation) has been a primary concern for psychologists trying to establish our discipline by emulating the physical sciences in their rigor and objectivity.

Obviously, we cannot randomly assign individuals to cultural groups. However, culture is often treated as a quasi-experiment, as people are born and socialised into different cultural systems. Thus researchers often use the logic of experimental psychology to infer 'effects of culture' by comparing survey or test scores between samples from two different nations. Of course, individuals will also differ on a number of other dimensions that fall outside our definition of what is cultural (e.g., wealth and education) or are indirectly related to cultural variables (religion and political ideologies). This requires the experimenter to select tasks that can rule out alternative interpretations.

As we discussed in Chapter 1, one of the earliest applications of experimental methods to the charting of cross-cultural differences in psychological functioning was conducted by William Rivers (1901), investigating perceptual processes among Torres Straits Islanders. Today, experimental studies typically involve participants from two or a few cultural groups, most often comparing East Asian and US or other Western students. Participants are assigned to different experimental groups on the basis of their cultural background and will then perform one or more brief tasks designed to test explanations of the cultural contrasts that are found. These approaches have been used frequently by cultural psychologists residing in the USA and Canada. For instance, Peng and Nisbett (1999) compared Chinese (most of whom were studying in the United States) and US students in their preference for dialectical proverbs containing apparent contradictions. They presented dialectical and non-dialectical proverbs to students and asked them to rate how much they liked each proverb. They found that Chinese students preferred dialectical proverbs more than non-dialectical proverbs, compared to US students. They then asked their respondents to evaluate brief reports on pairs of scientific studies that appeared contradictory. The Chinese were more willing to conclude that both studies had merit, while the Americans were more disposed to judge the conclusions of one study correct and the other false. Experimental studies of this kind are frequently used to study contrasts in social cognition, and we review a broad range of such research in Chapter 6.

Studies of this type are quasi-experiments, because the independent variable that is hypothesised to represent cultural differences cannot be randomly assigned to respondents. They are simply categorised (e.g., as Asians versus Westerners), often without measuring the cultural dimensions or processes expected to explain the observed differences or paying attention to alternative explanations. Although these studies do appear frequently in mainstream social psychology journals today, they mark a return to what Bond (2009) called Aristotelian research (see Chapter 1). The theorising and methodological rigor is arguably richer than in equivalent studies conducted in the 1970s and 1980s, but unless some proposed psychological mediator is included and measured, we still cannot make any firm interpretations of cultural effects. The cultural background of the participants is the crucial variable that moderates the effect of an experimental manipulation, but it often remains 'packaged'. In other words, it is unclear what specific aspects of the differing cultural backgrounds of the samples are causing these effects.

It may well happen that an experimental manipulation is not as effective in one culture as in the other. Any claims about psychological processes involved therefore hinge on the success of the experimental manipulation, that is, on the researcher's ability to show that the manipulation was effective in both contexts. The better experiments are therefore the ones that include both an experimental manipulation check and measures of the psychological process variables that help to explain (i.e., unpackage) the cultural differences and rule out alternative cultural explanations.

In short, experimental studies select samples based on underlying cultural dimensions that are thought to influence the dependent variable of interest. Experiments in cross-cultural settings are quasi-experimental because participants cannot be randomly assigned to experimental conditions. They are always open to alternative explanations.

> Guideline 5: Experiments are more persuasive in their evidence if a) they include a manipulation check on the effectiveness of the crucial manipulation in all cultural samples, and b) the experimenter specifies the relevant psychological processes and relates them to the dependent variable of interest, to rule out alternative theoretical explanations for the observed cultural difference.

Priming Studies

A different group of experimental studies has focused on eliciting or 'priming' cultural processes rather than relying on country of origin as an independent variable. Priming is thought to temporarily activate procedural or tacit knowledge (cultural mindsets) and mental representations (including beliefs, values, goals or norms) in people's minds. The evoked mindset then serves as an interpretive frame for processing any subsequent information and switches on heuristics and processing strategies that are relevant and effective in the given context. Priming is therefore a short-term equivalent to the long-term 'chronic' activations that are produced by cultural products and cultural agents in one's socialisation environment.

In these studies, individuals typically engage in a series of tasks (Oyserman & Lee, 2007, 2008). In a first set of tasks, individuals are required to engage in a brief activity during which particular psychological concepts, knowledge or motivational goals are activated. They then participate in another task, in which the cues made salient in the previous activity are carried over and now influence the behaviour on the second task. The purpose of the first task is to prime particular responses which will then spill over into the next, apparently unrelated task, in which the actual dependent variable is embedded.

Given the widely reported differences between individualistic and collectivistic cultures, the various primes deployed typically focus on making either the individual or group mindset typical for another cultural sample salient in people's minds. Researchers randomly assign participants to one of two conditions, in which either individualism or collectivism is primed. Alternatively, one of the two primes is compared with a control condition of no priming. This between-subject design is intended to simulate salient cross-cultural differences. The idea is that priming targets the active ingredient of culture and can explain why previously reported differences in behaviour were found across national cultural groups. Researchers have sought to prime culture either by priming national symbols or languages, which we discuss in Chapter 6, or by priming the content of cultural dimensions such as individualism-collectivism or self-construals, which we discuss in Chapter 7. These studies can provide interesting information about processes that may help us to unpackage cultural differences but, as we discuss more fully in Chapters 6 and 7, their ecological validity and their explanatory reach have sometimes been greatly exaggerated.

Advocates of priming studies imply that the early focus of theorists on defining culture in terms of nation-level constructs can be dispensed with. For these researchers, culture is a mindset in our heads and is open to continuous and variable elicitation by everyday momentary events. In terms of our present discussion of research methods, the key issue raised by the work of these researchers is whether experimental primes are a striking instance of domain under-representation. Do the effects that they elicit fully represent the cultural differences that they seek to explain?

INDIVIDUAL-LEVEL AND NATION-LEVEL EXPLANATION

As we have stressed repeatedly, culture exists between individuals and would not exist if each human being was on some proverbial island, finding food by him- or herself, and only meeting a partner once a year to mate. Instead, humans live as a part of complex social systems, full of norms, taboos, and toys that allow us to fly to the moon, meet a romantic partner at the cinema, and find out the latest gossip on Facebook, Google+, Orkut or whatever other social network is currently in fashion. A continually intriguing question is whether the aggregated or averaged information gained from individual-level psychological measures from national samples can tell us anything about the norms that seem to influence us on a daily basis. Hofstede's (1980) lasting legacy was to take the bold step that led to the popularising of nation-level dimensions of culture. Thinking about nation-level dimensions raises two questions that need more detailed consideration here, namely whether instruments and constructs at the nation level still have the same structure as at the individual level (**isomorphism**) and whether the relationship between the psychological construct of interest and a third variable is the same at the nation level as it is at the individual level (**homology**). These two questions of isomorphism and homology are often confounded and difficult to answer.

Isomorphism is the extent to which a psychological construct, and the instrument that measures the construct, have the same meaning and dimensionality (i.e., 'internal' structure, for instance, factors) at the individual and the nation levels.

Homology is the extent to which a psychological instrument has the same relationship with an external variable ('external' structure) at the individual level and at the nation level (using aggregated individual scores).

In Chapter 2, we discussed the results of Schwartz's work, in which he emphasises the importance of the differences between the individual- and nation-level organisation of values. Despite striking differences in the positioning of some individual items, the overall value structures he obtained at the two different levels do look remarkably similar. Nevertheless it is important to maintain a theoretical distinction between these two levels as Schwartz (2010) maintains, and as we now explain. Cultural groups such as nations cannot be compared using individual-level scale means, and likewise, individuals within nations cannot be compared using nation-level value scales. Comparing the values endorsed in Germany, Kenya and Argentina, we need to use the means based on nation-level dimensions because we are dealing with representations of national groups rather than individuals. Using scores based on individual-level dimensions would confuse within-country and between-country variability. For instance, since the Schwartz values 'humble' and 'social power' refer to conflicting motivational orientations for individuals, we cannot compare individuals using a combination of uncorrelated items such as these two. These items refer to different and conflicting underlying latent dimensions (tradition values and power values). However, at the nation level, a statistical combination of values such as 'humble' and 'social power' into a single index does make sense because these values are positively related at the nation level and therefore do refer to the same underlying latent construct (hierarchy). Confused measures lead to confusion in results, because means can only be validly interpreted at the appropriate level. This point underlines a subtle, critical, yet largely unrecognised implication of the lack of isomorphism between individual and group levels of value organisation. We can compare individuals within nations using the individual-level dimensions described by Schwartz (1992) but we need to use the country-level dimensions (Schwartz, 1994) if we want to compare samples from different nations with each other.

The problem of homology is equally interesting and complex. For example, Pehrson, Vignoles, and Brown (2010) measured prejudice and identification with one's nation in samples from 31 nations. At the individual level, prejudice was weakly but positively associated with national identification. However, at the nation level these variables were strongly negatively correlated: in other words, nations with higher levels of national identification had lower levels of prejudice, the opposite pattern. For a more technical understanding of this knotty issue, see Box 4.4.

In practical terms, researchers have constructed nation scores by taking one of three options. Firstly, they have simply used the averaged scores of individuals on metrically-equivalent constructs within each nation as an indicator of its culture. We refer to scores of this type as a citizen mean. This option was taken by Leung and Bond (2004) in their social axioms study. Secondly, some researchers have aggregated items from all individuals within each sample to the nation level and then created nation-level versions of variables that had been validated at the individual level. This option was taken by the GLOBE researchers (House et al., 2004). Thirdly, some researchers have aggregated all items from all individuals within each nation and then examined the structure of items across nations. This last option was taken by both Hofstede (1980) and Schwartz (2004). Options 1 and 2 do not give us answers about the similarity of individual- and nation-level structures, because the individual-level structure was used at both levels. Only option 3 can allow us to compare the resulting structure with that found at the individual level.

Interpreting non-equivalent results

What are the implications of non-isomorphism for tests of invariance at the individual level? If the structure of a scale is not isomorphic across levels of analysis, this implies a failure to find full scale equivalence, because the group means across items differ in ways that cannot be accounted for by the individual-level structure of the items (see Figure 4.3). How, then, can we interpret the cultural dimensions?

A strict interpretation of the relationships between equivalence and isomorphism is that dimensions that have different structures at the individual and nation levels indicate artifacts of measurement bias at the individual level. A possible psychometric interpretation is therefore that these dimensions cannot be interpreted (and should not be used), because they reflect measurement bias in at least one or more samples.

A more lenient interpretation is that bias is of some relevance here because it shows that cultures operate differently. Therefore 'bias' can become a variable of interest. With recent advances in both theory and methodology, it is now possible to study this bias and identify the cultural dynamics leading to the differences in structure between samples. For instance, we can explore the tendency to respond acquiescently as a dimension of cultural variation (Smith, 2011a), and how the level of the human development index introduces bias into the structure of Schwartz's measure of universalism values (Davidov et al., 2012). Future research that explores when and how different structures emerge opens up a new field of research and can provide fascinating insights into how the context within which individuals are operating influences their psychological realities (see for example, Fontaine, Poortinga et al., 2008; Fischer, Ferreira et al., 2011; Fischer, Milfont & Gouveia, 2011).

A third viewpoint, which is advocated by more sociologically-minded researchers and by many cross-cultural researchers interested in national dimensions of culture, is that an exploration of nation-level dimensions is valid in its own right. This is because we are dealing with the properties of a social aggregate, which is captured in the average responses of individuals. Any bias found at the individual level is a kind of evidence of the 'existence' of cultural differences. Remember also that the nation-level correlation component is based on mean scores and is thus statistically independent from the individual-level correlation component, and can therefore be validly explored in its own right. What is crucial about this last position is that we are not dealing with analyses that are explicitly psychological any more. As Leung and Bond (2007) put it, 'eco-logic' is not the same as 'psycho-logic'. What is found at the nation level cannot be meaningfully linked directly to individuals. It is an aspect of the context within which people live (Schwartz, 2010). For instance, power distance refers to nations, and not necessarily to individuals' attitudes to power. This discussion has focused on isomorphism, but the same principles apply to questions of homology (that is, the similarity of the relationship between constructs at individual and nation levels).

Multi-level Modeling

Data that have been aggregated to the nation level, averaged within each nation and factor analysed yield dimensions at the nation level. We can then explore correlations with other indicators

Box 4.4   Portraying Non-Isomorphism

Let us step back for a second and consider the basics of what we are doing. Mathematically, the correlation in any sample can be broken down into two independent parts, a within-group (within-nation) and a between-group (between-nation) component. This is similar to any of the discussions of ANOVA that you will have seen in methods and statistics textbooks. These two components further entail information about the variability within and between groups and the correlation within and between groups.

Technically, it is possible that we will encounter different structures and correlations at the individual and nation level, leading to non-isomorphism and non-homology. Figure 4.4 shows this situation graphically. As you can see there, the regression in each group separately is positive. However, because the means between the groups are different, the correlation of the means (that is the nation-level correlation) will be different compared to the correlations within each group separately (Leung & Bond, 1989).

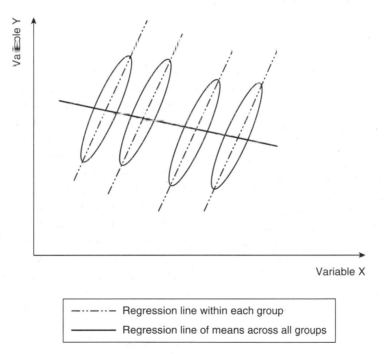

Figure 4.4   Effect of Within- and Between-Group Differences on Correlations

to establish their validity, as Hofstede (1980) did. Tables 2.2 and 2.3 showed some of the correlations that have been found between prominent nation-level dimensions.

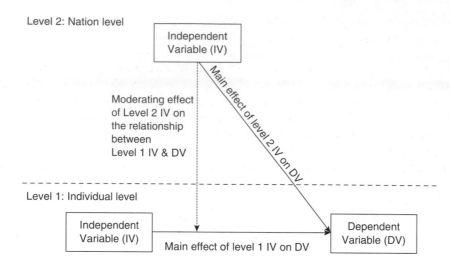

Figure 4.5   Example of a Hierarchical Linear Model with a Moderation Effect of the Level 2 Variable

More interestingly, advances in statistical methods now allow us to test whether these aggregated dimensions have an influence that goes back onto psychological processes at the individual level, while controlling for the corresponding variables at the individual level. We can therefore now truly examine the relative importance of individual versus aggregated cultural effects on psychological processes. For example, we can separate the effect of holding particular value priorities oneself from the effect of living in a context where certain values are normatively prioritised. In an increasing number of studies, researchers are examining the effects of nation-level variables in such multi-level models, but relatively few have so far also controlled for the equivalent individual-level processes. In Chapter 7, we shall discuss some recent studies that have used such multi-level approaches.

Moderators are either categorical (gender, race, class, nation, etc.) or continuously measured variables (e.g., personality or values) that affect the direction and/or strength of the relationship between a predictor and criterion. In a correlational framework, the moderator is the third variable that affects the zero-order correlation between two variables, whereas in an ANOVA framework, they are represented as interactions between two independent variables. Moderator effects therefore refer to interactions between the variables used to predict an outcome.

This method has much potential for moving our understanding forward, especially if we can separate the effects of individual-level processes from those at the aggregated national level. Figure 4.5 shows the logic of such a multi-level model schematically. One further feature of multi-level models is that they can also examine the strength of relationships, i.e., explore psychological processes, and whether these relationships differ across different cultural contexts. Variables that change the relationship between two other variables are called **moderators**. In later chapters, we will discuss a number of other studies that have identified such moderators in cross-cultural research. This is an exciting avenue for further research.

The Unpackaging of Culture

Returning to the level of the functioning individual, how can we study cultural processes if we have only a few samples and therefore cannot use multi-level modeling? What components of our

Unpackaging of culture is the process that explains why differences emerge between two or more cultural groups based on an explicit test of the psychological mediators of the observed cultural differences.

Mediators are variables that account for the relationship between an independent or predictor variable and the dependent or criterion variable. In psychological terms, they often explain how the external context takes on an internal psychological significance. Mediators more generally imply causal theoretical processes and explain how and why effects occur.

outcome are cultural and what can be explained by other processes? Here, an old idea becomes important, the idea of **unpackaging** culture. Whiting and Whiting (1975) orchestrated a large ethnographic study of child development among six communities: a New England Baptist community; a Philippine *barrio*; an Okinawan village; an Indian village in Mexico; a northern Indian caste group; and a rural tribal group in Kenya. Observing substantial differences in psychological processes, socialization and child-rearing patterns, they reasoned that there

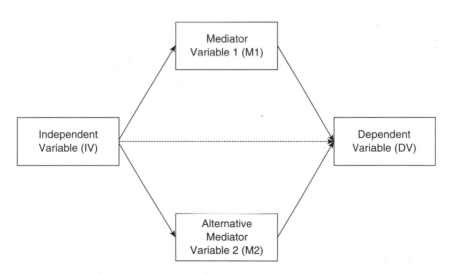

Figure 4.6 Example of a Mediator Relationship, with Two Potential Mediators

must be specific contextual variables that could explain the differences found, linking ecological constraints faced by these communities to psychological processes via adaptive socialisation practices. For instance, they compared the activities of children from the same families, some of whom were living in cities and others in villages. They also compared families in which young boys helped with baby-tending, with those in which girls did the helping. In ways such as these, the variability in observed behaviours could be broken down and associated with specific hypothesised mediators.

Hence, unpackaging studies are extensions of basic cross-cultural comparisons in which the active ingredient presumed to cause the observed differences in psychological processes is directly measured and explicitly tested for its efficacy in explaining the outcome. In the contemporary methodological literature, this process variable is called a **mediator**. Alternative names for unpackaging include 'linkage studies' (Matsumoto & Yoo, 2006), 'mediation studies' (Kirkman, Lowe & Gibson, 2006) or 'covariate studies/strategies' (Leung & van de Vijver, 2008).

Figure 4.6 shows a graphical representation of mediation. Most current mediation studies are conducted within a single nation, but we are especially interested here in those that have sampled several nations. Studies of this type provide a bridge between cross-cultural psychology and mainstream social/personality psychology, because they show that cross-cultural variations can be explained in terms drawn from both perspectives, without resorting to ill-defined constructs such as nationality (Brockner, 2003). For example, Tinsley (2001) found that differences in the conflict management strategies of German, Japanese and US managers were completely mediated by the values held by members of these cultural groups, and Felfe, Yan and Six (2008) reported that individuals' scores on a 'collectivism' scale mediated differences in organisational commitment across samples of Romanian, German and Chinese employees. Further studies testing mediation are discussed in Chapter 7.

In an ideal test of mediation, the researcher tests whether other relevant variables that are *not* related to the hypothesis also yield mediation effects. This provides greater certainty in establishing exactly what causes the results that are obtained. For instance, in a study discussed in Chapter 10, Y. Chen, Brockner, and Katz (1996) showed that a measure of individual-collective primacy mediated the intergroup effects that they had predicted and found. They then tested whether six other measures derived from the concept of individualism-collectivism also mediated these effects, and found that they did not. Studies of this kind help to clarify the loose and varied ways in which the psychological aspects of individualism and collectivism have been employed by different authors.

Another approach is illustrated by the work of Van de Vliert and Smith (2004), who tested predictions derived from Van de Vliert's theory of the effects of climate and wealth, which was discussed in Chapter 3. Across 76 nations, the climate and wealth predictions of variation in leader style were upheld. These authors then evaluated the distinctiveness of their findings by testing whether they were mediated by Hofstede's measures of uncertainty avoidance and power distance. No mediations were found, even though these Hofstede scores did each correlate significantly with leader style. This enabled Van de Vliert to sustain his claim that he had identified a distinctive predictor of cultural differences.

In summary, unpackaging has two inter-related features: identification of the theoretical factors or processes that may cause cultural differences in psychological outcomes of interest, and an explicit empirical test of the proposed processes leading to these outcomes (see Poortinga & Van de Vijver, 1987; Leung & Van de Vijver, 2008; Fischer, 2009, for more technical explanations).

META-ANALYSIS: A USEFUL TOOL FOR INTEGRATING RESEARCH

Thus far we have focused on methods that sampled individuals in different locations. In summarising the results of intensively researched fields with many independent studies, meta-analysis can be a fruitful tool with which to study cultural phenomena. A meta-analysis is a set of quantitative techniques that aggregates results across many (typically published) studies. In other words, it is an analysis of previous analyses. Meta-analysis can be conducted so long as you have an effect size, that is, a numerical measure of the expression of a psychological characteristic (a mean or frequency), or the strength of an association between two psychological constructs (typically a correlation), or the mean difference of a psychological characteristic between two or more groups.

The results reported from previous studies may need to be converted, so that they can be compared directly. For instance, they could be weighted by sample size, so as to ensure that a study with 1,000 participants receives more weight than a study with only ten participants in the conclusions. Each result could also be adjusted for criteria of quality, so as to give more weight to studies that were well designed compared to those that had many flaws. Once we have a combined mean effect, we can test whether the studies are homogeneous, that is whether they show the same effect. If there are differences between studies, we can search for moderator variables that can explain such variability. Meta-analysis is a sensitive tool for summarising and synthesising past research, testing novel hypotheses, and identifying gaps in the literature.

Throughout the book, we present various meta-analyses to summarise past research. Traditionally, cross-cultural meta-analysis has focused on cultural differences, requiring a comparison of at least two or more samples. With the increasing number of studies in single nations, we can also combine single-nation studies for cross-cultural meta-analyses. For example, we could examine whether the means of a variable vary systematically with nation-level indicators or we could examine whether two variables correlate differently in different ecological contexts. Meta-analysis in this context is essentially a multi-level analysis, allowing us to understand how psychological processes vary across samples and nations (e.g., Fischer & Mansell, 2009; Fischer & Boer, 2011; Boer & Fischer, 2013). Meta-analyses therefore provide another option for researchers who wish to unpackage the differences between nations.

CONCLUSION

Studying the Ik

If we were to understand the psychological processes that led Adupa's parents to starve their daughter, this chapter has provided many options. We could think of the value of children as a crucial variable that has some role to play in the process that Turnbull observed (see cross-cultural research into the value of children in Chapter 8). Alternatively, we could focus on the effect of resource availability on parenting behaviours. What other variables could you think of that might be applicable in this case?

We could undertake an ethnographic study and conduct interviews with mothers and fathers in a number of traditional and modern societies. We could conduct some simple experiments in which we give vignettes or scenarios to parents and ask how they might behave in a situation like that. We could use some form of economic game in which money or some other resource needs to be divided between themselves and their children (or between their children). We could develop tests that measure moral concerns or devise a questionnaire that captures the psychological value of children to their parents. We could adapt existing measures or develop new ones that fit each of the cultural contexts of our study. For example, does the number of children the parents already have make a difference? What about their gender, or their ages?

If we had only a few samples, we could use unpackaging at the individual level to see what psychological processes are implied. If we had studied more than ten samples from around the world, we could then use multi-level models to understand how features of the context affect such decisions. Obviously, we would need to consider carefully the samples that we should recruit and how we might control for any other variables that could influence our results. Alternatively, we might want to include such variables as additional independent variables, to further understand parental decisions in resource allocation to their children. For example, we could treat access to food as an independent variable in its own right. What other variables would we need to control or include in our design?

FURTHER READING

1 He, J., & Van de Vijver, F. (2012). Bias and equivalence in cross-cultural research. *Online Readings in Psychology and Culture.* Available at http://scholarworks.gvsu.edu/*orpc*

2 Matsumoto, D., & Van de Vijver, F. (2011). *Cross-cultural research methods in psychology.* Cambridge: Cambridge University Press.

3 Valsiner, J. (2003). Culture and its transfer: Ways of creating general knowledge through the study of cultural particulars. *Online Readings in Psychology and Culture.* Available at http://scholarworks.gvsu.edu/*orpc*

4 Van de Vijver, F. (2009). Types of comparative studies in cross-cultural psychology. *Online Readings in Psychology and Culture.* Available at http://scholarworks.gvsu.edu/*orpc*

5 Van Hemert, D.A. (2003). Cross-cultural meta-analyses. *Online Readings in Psychology and Culture.* Available at http://scholarworks.gvsu.edu/*orpc*

STUDY QUESTIONS

1 Should different research methods be used in studying different cultures or are there methods that can usefully be applied in all cultural contexts? Give examples.
2 Which research method holds the greatest promise for advancing our understanding of cross-cultural issues: fieldwork, psychometric tests and surveys, or experimentation? Explain why.
3 Select any one of the five guidelines for cross-cultural research and explain why it is important in the study of social psychology across cultures.
4 Explain the difference between mediation and moderation.

SECTION 2

Core Aspects of Social Psychology in Cross-Cultural Perspective

5

Personality and Social Context

'You will find, as a general rule, that the constitutions and the habits of a people follow the nature of the land where they live.'

(Hippocrates)

In the preceding chapters we have seen how values and beliefs vary across different nations and explored why these differences may arise. We shall next consider the role that the broader concept of personality can play in accounting for the evident differences in social behaviour around the world. In fact, it was the kaleidoscopic diversity of observable behaviours that led to our seeking explanations for cultural differences in the first place. In the early part of the chapter, we recount the stages that have been involved in developing globally valid measures of personality. In the later sections, we show how these measures can give us a fuller understanding of how individuals' personalities interact with the cultural contexts in which they are expressed. As we first discussed in Chapter 3, the processes by which cultures are created and maintained involve innumerable actions and reactions between causal agents. Within this framework, we shall see that personality can be considered both as a cause of culture and as a consequence of culture.

THE CULTURE AND PERSONALITY SCHOOL

Early anthropologists encountered especially dramatic differences in behavioural patterns during their residence in exotic places that were far removed from their cultures of origin. For instance, Malinowski (1927) in the Trobriand Islands, Bohannon (Bowen, 1964) in Nigeria, and Geertz (1973) in Bali, encountered an extraordinary range of behavioural differences in the societies that they studied and subsequently reported to an often-amazed readership. Some social scientists, many of them trained in psychoanalysis, turned to personality to explain these observed differences in behaviour, creating the 'culture and personality' school (e.g., Kardiner & Linton, 1945). Their position was that cultures train their members through early life experiences to assume a particular and distinctive personality profile that is common to most members of that culture. Thus, for instance, Muensterberger (1969) wrote,

> The Southern Chinese chooses ways of channelization and sublimation of drives which appear, on first sight, strange to us. To a greater extent than among Westerners, his pre-genital impulses and fantasy systems continue to find expression directly together with his reality adjustments. In avoidance of Oedipal conflicts it is culturally permitted to resolve inhibitions and tensions in daydreams, ideals, hallucinations, and pseudo activity. The dependence on each other is a culturally determined defense mechanism against instinctual demands. As a result of this psychic constellation the Chinese have created their art and philosophy and contribute so much to human civilization. (Muensterberger, 1969: 329)

This analysis was tightly grounded on close observation of daily life in a dramatically different non-Western cultural system, and constitutes a creative extension of Freudian constructs and dynamics into an alien reality. Three significant assumptions characterise this type of approach: the tendency to perceive considerable similarity in the personalities of a given culture's members; the presumption that this modal personality system exerts a pervasive influence on all aspects of social life, thus strengthening the impact of familial patterns of socialisation across other societal institutions; and the treating of distinctive behaviours as 'secondary' extensions of the 'primary' personality type that characterises that cultural group. As we shall explain through this chapter, each of these assumptions is open to question. In particular, we have noted already in Chapter 2 that there is much more variability in values between individuals than there is between nations (Fischer & Schwartz, 2011), so it does not make sense to represent nations as uniform personality prototypes.

MAPPING THE PERSONALITY OF INDIVIDUALS AND THEIR CULTURAL GROUPS

As McCrae (2000) has pointed out, the culture and personality school made little impact upon personality psychologists, in part because of the poor psychometric properties of the instruments that they used to measure personality, most of which were derived from psychoanalysis: the inter-judge reliabilities of the measures, used to tap constructs like ego strength and projected anger, were low. Furthermore, the Freudian theory underlying these measures has been superseded over time by social-learning and trait theories of personality. These theories encouraged the development of new personality measures, mostly in the form of written responses to written questions, which were amenable to factor analysis and yielded multi-faceted structures of constructs.

   These complex measures, like Cattell's 16 PF or Eysenck's EPN, could be used to compare individuals on a variety of broad dimensions. Their high test-retest reliabilities reassured psychologists that something consistent about individuals' character was being tapped. Their written nature and standardised response categories ensured that inter-judge reliabilities in their scoring were very high, hence addressing one of the major scientific concerns about psychoanalytically-derived measures. However, as personality tests of this type were developed in the decades following the Second World War there was little initial agreement even among personality researchers working in the USA and Europe as to how personality dimensions could best be identified. For instance, Cattell's measure yielded 16 dimensions, while Eysenck's yielded just three. So how many would be best?

The Lexically Derived Big Five

This problem was addressed by researchers who took an initial step back from the use of personality tests. They reasoned that we can best hope to summarise ways of describing people if we make 'lexical' studies, in other words by looking at all the words that exist in a given language to describe other people. Norman (1963) identified five robust dimensions of variation in the rated personality of acquaintances in fraternities at the University of Michigan. What made this work 'universal', to use Norman's word, was its diligent attempt to be comprehensive in the range of personality variation that was included in the assessment of people. This work was based upon thousands of personality descriptors originally culled from the English lexicon by Allport and Odbert (1936), subsequently reduced by Fiske (1949), and then summarised by Norman as five distinct or independent dimensions of personality variation that he labeled as Extraversion, Good-Naturedness, Conscientiousness or the will to achieve, Emotional Stability, and 'Culture'. Norman called these the 'Big Five' because of their robustness across the various samples from which they had been extracted.

Building on this approach, Goldberg (1990) formulated a 'lexical' hypothesis which states that, '... the most important individual differences in human transactions will come to be encoded as single terms in some or all of the world's languages' (p. 1216). This influential hypothesis has inspired considerable within-nation exploration of local languages, so as to identify indigenously-derived structures for personality. Around 15 single-nation studies examining local lexicons of personality terms, usually adjectives, have been analysed in terms of how they function in a given nation as descriptors of either oneself or others (e.g., Church, Katigbak & Reyes, 1996). As always with factor analysis and other multivariate techniques, there is some arbitrariness about the decision regarding how many factors to extract.

Integrating across some of this plethora of studies, De Raad, Perugini, Hrebickova, and Szarota (1998) concluded that '... using the American English solution as a target ... the congruences show replicability of the first four American English Big Five factors in the other languages' (p. 212). However, confirmation of a consistent fifth factor has not been found in several languages. More recently, De Raad, Barelds, Levert et al. (2010) have argued that by attempting to test for the generality of Big Five factors, alternative factor solutions may not have been adequately examined. Sampling a wider range of studies, they concluded that only three factors are always present. Nonetheless, they continue to argue that the Big Five model should be retained, since most factors are identified in most language traditions. The ones that are not found differ between studies. In their view, a lack of congruence across language systems occurs in part because only adjectives, rather than also nouns and verbs, are typically used, and ability terms, especially those related to intelligence, have not been consistently included in the various lexicons used for the ratings of personality. This oversight is significant, because as we shall see later in this chapter there are found to be cultural variations in whether persons are described more in terms of the abstract qualities that are captured by nouns and adjectives or more by specific actions that are better captured by verbs.

Thus it appears that variants of the Big Five do exist in all languages. The fifth factor is now referred to by researchers as 'Openness to Experience', rather than 'Culture', while Good-Naturedness is now referred to as Agreeableness, and Emotional Stability is now referred to by its opposite, Neuroticism. What is important for our present purposes is that these five have been extracted from the language-system-in-use in most contexts where it has been studied.

This universality in use suggests that there is a strong functional basis for the emergence and use of the Big Five factors in daily discourse to describe ourselves and others. Hogan (1982) has argued that these dimensions of personality description arise because they help people identify those persons who are capable of meeting the functional prerequisites of social integration and task coordination that all social systems must address because of our evolutionary heritage. As he argues:

> The problems of achieving status and maintaining peer popularity are biologically mandated … status … provides the opportunity for preferential breeding and reproductive success … popularity … has considerable survival value … The core of human nature consists of certain fixed, insistent, and largely unconscious biological motives … three of them give a distinctive style to human social behavior: (a) … needs for social approval, and at the same time they find criticism and disapprobation highly aversive … (b) … needs to succeed at the expense of others, modified … by the genetic relationships between them … (c) … needs for structure, predictability and order in their social environment … (1982: 56–57)

Hogan's perspective fits well with the eco-cultural perspectives explored in Chapter 3, but they do not lead us directly to an expectation that there would be five major personality factors. His conclusions do show an interesting and reassuring convergence with the listing of fundamental human needs that was used by Schwartz (1992) as the basis for his studies of the structure of values which we discussed in Chapter 2. A study of the structure of human goals by Grouzet and nine co-authors (2005) provides some further evidence of structural consistency across nations. Sampling 15 nations, they found that respondents' goals could be summarised in terms of a circular model defined by two dimensions: intrinsic versus extrinsic goals and self-transcendent versus physical goals. Just as we noted in the case of values, the structures of personality and of goals may be universal, but individual people will vary in the strength of their social needs and in their capacity to meet those needs in their particular social environment.

The Big Five in Personality Inventories

The lexical tradition and the questionnaire tradition in the study of personality have converged with the development in the United States of the Revised NEO Personality Inventory (NEO-PI-R) by Paul Costa and Robert McCrae (1992). In their manual for this widely used test of personality, these authors claim that their instrument,

> … is a concise measure of the five major dimensions, or domains, of personality and some of the more important traits or facets that define each domain. Together, the five domain scales and 30 facet scales of the NEO-PI-R allow a comprehensive assessment of adult personality … The NEO-PI-R embodies a conceptual model that distils decades of factor analytic research on the structure of personality. The scales themselves were developed and refined by a combination of rational and factor analytic methods and have been the subject of intensive research conducted for 15 years on both clinical and normal adult samples. (1992: 1)

Key Researcher Box 5.1   Robert McCrae

Figure 5.1   Robert McCrae

Robert R. McCrae (b. 1949) received his PhD in personality psychology from Boston University in 1976. After completing his training, he began working with Paul Costa at the National Institute of Health in Washington, DC. Working jointly with Costa, he developed the widely used *NEO-Personality Inventory*. The lengthy collaboration between Costa and McCrae has yielded well over 200 co-authored research articles and chapters, and several books. His publications have been cited overall more than 43,000 times. In recent years he has focused on the psychology of aging and on cross-cultural personality studies.

Details of the range of traits included within the NEO-PI-R are shown in Research Instrument Box 5.1, where each dimension is defined by a series of subsidiary facets. Given the extensive use of this instrument throughout the discipline, along with its demonstrated reliability and validity, it became an ideal starting point for addressing the earlier challenges to the culture and personality school that its methods were faulty and without empirical foundation.

Research Instrument Box 5.1   Dimensions and Facets in the Five Factor Model of Personality

Costa and McCrae's Five Factor Model provides a synthesis of broad overarching dimensions, each of which is defined by a series of more specific facets, that are in turn made up of items reflecting individual traits. We may expect evidence for cultural generality to be strongest at the level of dimensions, with greater cultural specificity attending the meaning of individual facets as well as individual items in particular. The facets making up each dimension give some indication of its meaning:

Agreeableness	Conscientiousness	Neuroticism	Extraversion	Openness to Experience
Trust	Competence	Anxiety	Warmth	Fantasy
Straightforwardness	Order	Angry hostility	Gregariousness	Aesthetics
Altruism	Dutifulness	Depression	Assertiveness	Feelings
Compliance	Achievement-striving	Self-consciousness	Activity	Actions
Modesty	Self discipline	Impulsiveness	Excitement-seeking	Ideas
Tendermindedness	Deliberation	Vulnerability	Positive emotions	Values

Starting with an early case study of Chinese culture (McCrae, Costa, & Yik, 1996) followed by Filipino and French surveys (McCrae, Costa, Pilar, Roland, & Parker, 1998), McCrae and his collaborators have gradually extended their investigation to cover perceptions of one's own and others' personality in 50 nations, with the respondents typically being college students and occasionally adults (McCrae, Terracciano, et al., 2005a, b). Individual-level factor analyses of NEO-PI-R data have demonstrated equivalence in the pattern of its facet groupings across all the nations examined. Furthermore, the balance between positively worded and negatively worded items in each facet has enabled these investigators to overcome the problem of acquiescent response style that might distort the meaningfulness of the resulting comparisons.

Following the techniques that we have discussed in earlier chapters, Allik and McCrae (2004) were also able to conduct a nation-level factor analysis using data from 36 nations. Their analysis revealed the important finding that the same five factors emerged at the nation-level as are consistently found at the individual-level. This similarity of structures at different levels (isomorphism) enabled them to calculate a modal personality profile for each nation, yielding a 'geography of personality traits'. This 'psychography' for social scientists could replace the scattered conclusions of the culture and personality school, if we can be sure that it rests on a defensible empirical basis.

A first step in verifying this map is provided by another very large-scale project, in which a shorter alternative measure of the Big Five was completed by students in 56 nations (Schmitt, Allik, McCrae & Benet-Martinez, 2007). A pan-cultural individual-level factor analysis yielded the same five-factor structure. Citizen scores were then computed for each factor by nation. This study sampled 27 nations that were also sampled by McCrae and his colleagues. Significant correlations averaging around 0.4 between the Big Five means for each dimension in the two studies were found.

Commenting on the national mean scores derived from their data on national personality, Allik and McCrae concluded that,

> ... cluster analysis showed that geographically proximate cultures often have similar profiles, and multidimensional scaling showed a clear contrast of European and American cultures with Asian and African cultures. The former were higher in extraversion and openness to experience and lower in agreeableness. (2004: 13)

These conclusions are drawn from statistical associations with the two-dimensional mapping of the personality profiles of typical cultural group members that are shown in Figure 5.2:
As the authors point out,

> ... the horizontal axis ... is positively associated with extraversion and openness to experience and negatively associated with agreeableness. People from European and American cultures thus appear to be outgoing, open to new experience, and antagonistic, whereas people from East Asian and African cultures are introverted, traditional, and compliant. Euro-American cultures are lower in power distance (i.e., they reject status hierarchies) and higher in individualism (i.e., they put self-interest before group interest) ... cultures (and their typical members) towards the top of the figure are high in neuroticism and low

in conscientiousness; (these cultures) are also high in uncertainty avoidance ... They are also low in interpersonal trust and subjective well-being. (2004: 21–22)

Schmitt et al. also examined the national means derived from their data, summarising them in terms of mean scores for ten regions of the world. The results for two of these regions were particularly striking: East Asians scored significantly lower than all other regions on extraversion, agreeableness, openness to change and conscientiousness, as well as significantly higher than all other regions on neuroticism. Africans scored significantly higher than persons from all other regions on agreeableness and conscientiousness and significantly lower on neuroticism. A third study drawing on nearly one million respondents to the Occupational Personality Questionnaire (Bartram, 2013) also showed East Asians scoring very low on conscientiousness and very high on neuroticism.

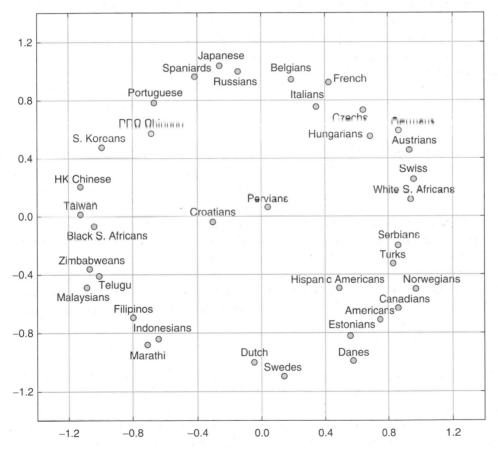

Figure 5.2   Multidimensional Scaling Plot of 36 Cultural Groups. North in the figure is associated with greater Neuroticism; East with greater Extraversion and Openness to Change; South with greater Conscientiousness; West with greater Agreeableness

Source: Allik & McCrae (2004).

These characterisations differ substantially from most people's expectations. One would find it difficult to locate many people who would concur with the view that the Japanese are among the least conscientious. Indeed, Terracciano et al. (2007) showed that when respondents in 49 nations were asked to rate what a typical person in their own nation would be like, these ratings did not correlate significantly with the nation-level means derived from the study by McCrae et al. (2005a) which used ratings of individuals' personality to derive their national averages. Therefore, these means do not accord with our everyday stereotypes of nations. Terracciano et al. concluded that the stereotypes are wrong and the national means are right.

In order to decide whether this interpretation is correct, we need to return to the issue of the **Reference Group Effect**, which was already touched upon in Chapter 2: are self-perceptions or the perceptions of others more likely to be accurate? Heine, Lehmann, Peng and Greenholz (2002) proposed that when individuals record their self-perceptions on Likert rating scales they have no uniform basis on which to make comparisons. If I am to say that I am conscientious, my judgment has to be in relation to my view of others, whom I believe to be either more conscientious or less conscientious. However, personality scales do not specify against whom the comparison is to be made, and depending on whom I choose this varying choice across respondents could introduce error into scores of this type.

> The **Reference Group Effect** occurs when respondents' descriptions of themselves or others on a series of Likert scales are influenced by which group they choose as a basis for comparison.

The reference group effect would be the case especially when comparisons are made across nations where different bases of comparison are prevalent. For instance, if the Japanese are prone to comparing themselves with others in more modest ways than those from other nations are, this could explain why their mean scores on ratings of the Big Five dimensions show a less socially desirable profile. Heine, Buchtel, and Norenzayan (2008) examined this possibility. They did so by correlating five nation-level behavioural indices that they considered to be representative of conscientiousness with mean Big Five scores from the studies by McCrae et al. (2005a) and Schmitt et al. (2007), as well as the national stereotypes provided by Terracciano et al. (2007). The stereotype ratings showed strong correlations with the behavioural indices, but the Big Five mean scores did not. Heine et al. therefore concluded that cross-national comparisons of personality do not give valid scores.

Both values researchers and personality theorists have argued against the conclusions of Heine et al. (2008). Fischer and Schwartz (2011) showed that cross-nation variability in values shows no consistent difference between values that refer to relations with others and those that do not. If reference group effects are salient, values that refer to others should vary more. Möttus, Allik, Realo, Pullman, et al. (2012) asked students in 21 nations to rate the level of different facets of conscientiousness that was present in a series of brief hypothetical scenarios. By comparing the means across nations they could see whether there was any evidence of a reference group effect. None was found, so they concluded that some other explanation was required for the low correlations between self-perceived conscientiousness and the indices used by Heine et al. (2008). Möttus, Allik, and Realo (2010) suggested that the poor correlations found by Heine et al. arose because their chosen indices were more likely to correlate with specific facets of conscientiousness rather than with the overall score for this Big Five factor. Reanalysing the nation-level means computed earlier for self-perceptions and the mean perceptions of others, they found some support for this proposition. Another possible source of error is cross-national variation in the use of extreme points on rating scales. The Big Five measures can discount variations in acquiescence but not in extremity. Möttus, Allik, Realo, Rossier et al. (2012) obtained estimates of extreme response style from students in 20 nations, and showed that when this factor was controlled, Big Five scores gave stronger correlations with independent criteria related to conscientiousness.

The recent study by Bartram (2013) is also relevant here. Bartram's measure of personality does not use Likert rating scales. Instead, his respondents are presented with a series of sets of four statements. Within each set, they are asked to select which statement best represents them and which least represents them. Thus, their judgments are intrapersonal rather than comparative across persons. Bartram's Big Five scores for nations do correlate with the results of the other Big Five surveys and show a similar pattern of relationships to Hofstede scores and objective indices, such as wealth and human development. In Bartram's data, the Japanese sample continue to be shown as very low on conscientiousness. We discuss more fully in Chapter 7 the meaning of the tendency of Japanese and other East Asian cultural groups to present themselves in modest ways across the conscientiousness, and probably other, domains of the Big Five. Debates will continue as to whether this socialised tendency may help to explain current findings.

The final implications of this debate remain unclear. As we shall see in Chapter 12, Heine et al's provocative analysis can also be interpreted in terms of alternative explanations of the content of national stereotypes (Fiske, Cuddy, Glick & Xu, 2002). There is continuing evidence for the validity of national mean scores for Big Five dimensions, and they remain useful for conducting individual-level studies because they have been shown to have a consistent structure across cultures. However, in characterising nations it may be preferable to use measures in which this ambiguity is not present. The measures of values and beliefs outlined in Chapter 2 are valuable because, as with Bartram's OPQ measure, their items are phrased in ways that do not require implicit comparisons of oneself with others (Fischer & Schwartz, 2011). Consistent with this, when McCrae, Terracciano, Realo & Allik (2008) correlated their stereotype ratings with the ratings on the perceived practices dimensions collected by the GLOBE researchers (House et al., 2004; see Chapter 2), they did find significant relationships with those GLOBE dimensions that relate to aspects of personality.

Is the Five-Factor Model of Personality Complete?

The Big Five dimensions of personality variation are found in almost all nations where the NEO-PI-R factor structure has been tested against the American norms (Allik & McCrae, 2004). These five distinct features of personality functioning are thus useful starting points for developing a pan-cultural model for social behaviour, involving both the characteristics of the actor and those of his or her interaction partner. Each of the five has a basis in our shared evolutionary history and provides information about a person's standing on an important aspect of interpersonal behaviour. But are they complete? Would additional dimensions emerge if measures are constructed that do not impose a perspective defined by a US starting point?

There are two reasons why the answer to the first of these questions is no, and to the second is yes. Firstly, personality dimensions do not in an objective sense exist. More or fewer of them can be differentiated depending on one's specific research purpose. For studies concerning global variation, we need dimensions that are fewer in number and phrased in more general terms. For studies focused on specific cultures, however, we need dimensions that pick up more adequately on whatever is locally salient. This is best done with items that refer to locally distinctive aspects of behaviour. Psychologists have developed increasingly sophisticated statistical techniques for judging how many factors best summarise a dataset, but opinions continue to differ between researchers. For instance, using lexical methods, Ashton et al. (2004) identified six replicable personality dimensions in data from seven, mostly European, nations. The factor additional to the Big Five was defined as honesty versus humility.

Secondly, it is possible that additional concerns are salient in different cultures from those that spawned the Big Five. By sampling those cultures, investigators may be able to identify indigenous items that define supplementary dimensions of personality (Cheung, Van de Vijver, & Leong, 2011). To prove the distinctiveness of these possibly unique dimensions, indigenous personality questionnaires must first be developed. The indigenous questionnaire then needs to be given along with the imported measure of the Big Five, and a joint factor analysis of the two instruments conducted in the indigenous culture. If a distinct dimension appears over and above the Big Five, then an emic local dimension has been isolated (see Yang & Bond, 1990, for the earliest example of this approach). Work can then proceed to establish its local utility, and whether that indigenous dimension can also be identified in other cultural populations. If so, this sixth dimension becomes a candidate for universal status as a 'Big Sixth' dimension of personality variation.

This is a demanding undertaking and understandably rare. It has been attempted by Church and his colleagues in the Philippines and by Cheung and her colleagues in China. Katigbak, Church, Guanzon-Lapena, Carlota, & del Pilar (2002) administered three indigenously developed Filipino personality inventories along with the Filipino translation of the NEO-PI-R to students in the Philippines. They concluded that,

> (a) most Philippine dimensions are well encompassed by the five factor model (FFM) and thus may not be very culture specific; (b) a few indigenous constructs are less well accounted for by the FFM; these constructs are not unknown in Western cultures, but they may be particularly salient or composed somewhat differently in the Philippines; (c) the structure of the ... FFM replicates well in the Philippines; and (d) Philippine inventories add modest incremental validity beyond the FFM in predicting selected culture-relevant criteria. (2002: 89)

Thus, there was only a modest yield from this extensive, meticulous programme of research aimed at discovering whether there are distinctive indigenous constructs of personality when placed in a head-to-head comparison with the standard Western measure of the Five Factor Model. On the basis of these findings, the Filipino inventories were not translated and tested in non-Filipino cultural groups.

Working within Chinese culture, however, Cheung et al. (2001) found clear evidence for the existence of an indigenous dimension of personality variation in three separate studies in which respondents completed both the NEO-PI-R and the Chinese Personality Assessment Inventory (CPAI) (Cheung, Leung, Fan, Song, Zhang, & Zhang (1996). They labeled their additional dimension as Interpersonal Relatedness:

> This factor, which was originally labeled as the Chinese Tradition factor, consists of the indigenous personality scales developed specifically for the CPAI, including *Ren Qing* (relationship orientation), Harmony, and face. In addition, this factor is loaded negatively by Flexibility. The characteristics associated with these personality scales reflect a strong orientation toward instrumental relationships; emphasis on occupying one's proper place and in engaging in appropriate action; avoidance of internal, external, and interpersonal conflict; and adherence to norms and traditions. (1996: 425)

Key Researcher Box 5.3   Fanny Cheung

Figure 5.3   Fanny Cheung

Fanny M. Cheung grew up in Hong Kong, and obtained her PhD from the University of Minnesota in 1975. Returning to Hong Kong, she joined the Chinese University of Hong Kong, where she is currently Psychology Department chair. She is also the current and founding director of the Gender Research Centre at the Hong Kong Institute of Asia-Pacific Studies. In the early 1990s she took the lead in developing the Chinese Personality Assessment Inventory. This was the first major initiative to develop a non-Western personality test. She has published more than 150 research articles and books and is currently editor of the *Asian Journal of Social Psychology*. She has been active in promoting rights and services for women and the disabled in Hong Kong, as well as spearheading the War on Rape campaign in the late 1970s and founding the first community women's centre in Hong Kong in the early 1980s. She mobilised women's groups to advocate the establishment of a women's commission and the extension to Hong Kong of the UN Convention on the Elimination of All Forms of Discrimination Against Women. From 1996 to 1999, she was the founding chairperson of the Equal Opportunities Commission of the Hong Kong government and established the research foundation of this organisation. Her work has led to increased opportunities for women and persons with disabilities and has been influential across Asia in the fields of both psychology and gender studies.

The next issue of importance for Cheung and her colleagues was to determine whether the Interpersonal Relatedness factor could also be isolated as an additional dimension of personality among non-Chinese, especially Western respondents. Cheung, Cheung, Leung, Ward, and Leong (2003) have provided such evidence by administering the NEO-FFI (a shorter measure of the Big Five) and an English-language translation of the CPAI both to Singaporeans and to

Caucasian-Americans. Their results replicated the earlier Chinese results: a sixth independent dimension of personality identified as Interpersonal Relatedness emerged from the joint factor analyses. As the authors suggest, '… the absence of Interpersonal Relatedness in a Western instrument may point to a 'blind spot' in Western personality theories, specifically the interdependent domains that receive relatively less attention in Western personality theories' (2003: 450).

There is a strongly hierarchical and collectivist theme to this dimension. Particularly noteworthy is the authors' highlighting of 'adherence to norms'. Such a dimension is crucially important for theories of social psychology. The social situation itself has been neglected by most social psychologists. Indeed, few of their theories have focused on social behaviour rather than cognitive processes. If we wish to explain behaviour, then a personality measure of responsiveness to interpersonal influence and normative situational force will be most helpful (Bond, 2013). Combined with some knowledge of what the appropriate norms might be, a psychologist would have a ready recipe for predicting the actor's behaviour. Cheung et al. signal this way forward by concluding, 'In future studies, we will validate the functional equivalence of Interpersonal Relatedness by examining its external behavioral correlates in different cultural contexts' (2003: 450).

WHAT CAN THESE UNDERSTANDINGS OF PERSONALITY HELP TO EXPLAIN?

As we have seen, the Big Five personality dimensions can provide an approximate psychography of the world, just as the studies of values and beliefs discussed earlier have shown. However, we must continue to bear in mind the distinction between individual variability and variability among nations. Just as Fischer and Schwartz (2011) showed in relation to values (see Chapter 2), Poortinga and Van Hemert (2001) found that there is much more variability in personality between individuals than there is between nations. Using data from the Eysenck Personality Questionnaire (a forerunner of some of the Big Five dimensions) from 38 nations, they obtained intra-class correlations of .14 for Psychoticism, .17 for Extraversion, .16 for Neuroticism, and .25 for the Lie scale. Thus, the variability of personality within nations compared to that across nations is of about the same magnitude as that of values.

These results are important, because cross-cultural psychologists tend to highlight cultural differences at the expense of individual variability. They sometimes forget that the mean scores used to represent differences themselves derive from the distributions of individual scores. Cross-cultural analyses are simply one way of pulling apart the full range of individual differences across the pan-cultural array of data. In personality and in values, intra-cultural variation is substantially greater than inter-cultural variation. There is a clear implication from this finding: we need to take account of individual-level variability when we make comparisons across nations, rather than simply comparing mean scores at the level of nations, as Hofstede did. We will examine individual-level studies in the next section, but first there are some types of study that do benefit directly from the availability of nation-level data.

National Differences

We have noted that there is a substantial source of error in personality scores for nations, but it remains worthwhile to consider where these personality differences originate. Distinctive perspectives are outlined in Research Debate Box 5.1. If personality is just an individual-level attribute, why are there any differences in personality between nations at all? If differences exist, there must be some type of selection pressure causing non-randomness.

Research Debate Box 5.1 Personality and Cultural Values

The availability of nation-level scores both for personality and for values makes it easy to test the correlations among them. All four Hofstede dimensions are significantly associated with scores on one or more of the Big Five personality dimensions as measured by Allik and McCrae:

Big Five Dimensions	Power Distance	Uncertainty Avoidance	Individualism (versus Collectivism)	Masculinity (versus Femininity)
Extraversion	−.57		.61	
Conscientiousness	.52			
Openness to Experience	−.39			.40
Neuroticism		.58		.57
Agreeableness		−.55		−.36

Note: The direction of these correlations refers to the variables that are not placed in brackets

In an unusual format, Hofstede and McCrae (2004) debated within a single publication how best to interpret the meaning of these correlations. McCrae sees personality as having a strong genetic component. Consequently, he expects that the predominance of a particular profile of genes in a given nation will encourage the development of cultural adaptations to whichever personality type prevails locally. He writes, for instance:

> ... [the] table suggests that higher Neuroticism and lower Agreeableness predict higher Uncertainty Avoidance. Consider a group of people who are temperamentally prone to these personality characteristics. They will, in general, be tense and irritable, and interpersonal interactions will be difficult. Each new decision will be a potential source of distressing conflict. Such people may find that they can co-exist only if they adopt a rigid set of rules and screen out new situations that would require new decisions—in other words, they would develop the values and institutions that typify high Uncertainly Avoidance countries'. (2004: 76)

McCrae also asserts that over centuries, those whose personalities do not fit well may also be more likely to emigrate or to reproduce less with local partners. Thus he sees cultures evolving to accommodate their genetic predisposition.

(Continued)

(Continued)

Hofstede concedes that there may be some genetic basis to personality, but points out that the variation of personality types and of differing ethnic origins within large nations indicates that other causes for cultural difference must be sought. We can expect that those who grow up within a given cultural context will be socialised to express their personality in culturally appropriate ways. For instance, he explains the high correlation between conscientiousness and Power Distance, by saying that persons in high Power Distance cultures need to be conscientious and to present themselves as conscientious, whereas those in low Power Distance cultures have a greater possibility to behave less conscientiously. Thus he sees cultures as socialising their members to express their genetic predispositions in acceptable ways.

This debate provides a new version of the long-running nature versus nurture debate in psychology. The two positions are not fully opposed to one another, and as was discussed in Chapter 3, it is possible to formulate a model of the co-evolution of genetic and social contributions of personality to culture (e.g., Church, 2010).

Gender Differences

Intriguing questions are also provoked when the *variability* of scores between nations is compared. Both in terms of self-perceptions (Allik & McCrae, 2004) and in terms of perception of another person (McCrae, Terracciano et al., 2005a), Big Five scores vary much less in data from African and Asian nations than they do in data from the rest of the world. This effect was found across all personality dimensions, but it was also found across genders. In other words, there is much more variability between male profiles and female profiles in Western nations than in African and Asian nations. The same findings for gender differences were also obtained in the other very large-scale survey that measured self-perceptions on the Big Five dimensions in 55 nations (Schmitt, Realo, Voracek, & Allik, 2008). The magnitude of the difference is correlated significantly with national wealth, Hofstede's individualism scores and the United Nations' Human Development Index.

These results contradict the expectations of most people in Western nations, who expect that the changes in women's roles in recent decades would have reduced rather than increased gender differences. Researchers have struggled to understand this effect since it was first detected (Williams & Best, 1990). Schmitt et al. favour an evolutionary explanation. They argue that modern economies are more similar to hunter-gatherer societies than are pre-industrial agricultural economies, and that this encourages men to express the more differentiated risk-taking approach to life with which they are hypothesised to be genetically endowed. In agricultural societies, this difference is said to be suppressed by the survival needs entailed in agricultural subsistence. McCrae et al. (2005b) suggest that gender differences are smaller in the less affluent societies because respondents think less in terms of traits and more in terms of roles when considering the behaviour of themselves and others. This account does not contradict the views of Schmitt et al. because it is likely that a system of integrated roles would have high survival value in pre-industrial societies. As we shall see, evidence exists that is relevant to this viewpoint.

Another possibility is that the effect is found because persons in individualistic nations compare themselves with those of the opposite gender, whereas in collectivist nations comparisons are made only within one's own gender. Although conducted using self-construal scores (see Chapter 7) rather than personality scales, experimental data in which respondents were asked either to rate themselves relative to their own gender or the other gender support this explanation (Guimond, Chatard, Branscombe, et al., 2006; Guimond, Branscombe, Brunot, et al., 2007).

Age Differences

Chan, McCrae, de Fruyt et al. (2012) asked students in 26 nations to rate the personality traits that would be typical of persons in their nation who were adolescent, adult or old. These scores were then compared with the average of self-reported and other reported personality profiles of individuals in these age groups. The stereotype ratings correlated well with averaged personality scores, with little variation across nations. Here we find an instance of a stereotype that has a 'grain of truth' (Allport, 1954), although the stereotype ratings exaggerate the differences between age groups.

Happiness and Subjective Well-Being

There has been considerable debate as to how best to describe variations in the overall happiness of the members of different nations. Some of the largest surveys have relied on mean responses to a single question, 'Taking everything together, how satisfied or dissatisfied are you currently with your life as a whole?' However, scores for responses to single items are subject to numerous sources of error and misinterpretation, even within a single culture. Some type of check similar to those made by Schwartz (1992) for values is required, to determine whether happiness has the same connotations in different cultures. Some researchers have added questions asking how often respondents experienced positive affective feelings and negative affective feelings in a given time period, while others have favoured including measures of living in a good environment, being able to cope with life, life expectancy, and being of worth in the world and enjoying life. Even discounting these elaborations, however, mean scores for the single item measure do correlate negatively with nation-level means for depression and for suicide (Veenhoven, 2010).

In an early study, Diener, Diener, and Diener (1995) showed that across 55 nations, national means for satisfaction with life were associated with high wealth, high scores on individualism rather than collectivism, and low reported levels of corruption. Subsequently, Steel and Ones (2002) found that national mean scores were strongly correlated with mean scores for extraversion and for low neuroticism, both as measured by Eysenck's Personality Questionnaire and with Big Five measures. However, when these authors included controls for differences in national wealth, the relationships with personality disappeared. Thus it appears that at the nation level, wealth is more important than personality in understanding life satisfaction, contrary to what is found at the individual level (Diener & Biswas-Diener, 2002). Furthermore, a meta-analysis of clinically validated scales related to well-being and life satisfaction showed nation-level individualism to be a stronger predictor of well-being than wealth (Fischer & Boer, 2011). The greater autonomy that is typically found in more individualistic nations helps people to express themselves with fewer constraints imposed on them by their in-groups. This fulfillment of one's aspirations is a crucial element of experienced happiness, as discussed in self-determination theory (Ryan & Deci, 2011). Furthermore, the eco-cultural theories outlined in Chapter 3 may be helpful here in clarifying how combinations of differing causal agents can elicit cultural profiles that favour greater or lesser life satisfaction depending on the availability of resources and the experienced challenges in one's environment (Fischer & Van de Vliert, 2011).

As we have noted in relation to other variables, it is important to understand the meaning of national-level scores for measures that were originally collected from individuals. Individual-level measures of variables related to satisfaction have shown the importance of distinguishing positive and negative affect as components of overall satisfaction. Using measures incorporating this more complex view of satisfaction, Lucas and Diener (2008) found evidence of isomorphism. Thus we can speak validly of national satisfaction, but we need to think clearly about what the concept means. The life satisfaction of individuals within any given nation varies greatly, and the national means in the many cross-national studies conducted by Diener and his colleagues also show great variation. We can best understand the relationship between the individual-level data and the nation-level data by considering both at once.

The classic study in this mould is Diener and Diener's (1995) examination of self-esteem and life satisfaction in 31 nations. They argued that a major part of the social agenda in individualist cultures is to enhance the perceived importance of the self as an actor in a world where one has been freed from binding association with collectivities. One's self-esteem will reflect one's success at achieving this goal, and one would be more satisfied with life in consequence. To test this idea, they simply correlated self-esteem with life satisfaction for individuals within each of their 31 national samples. The correlation was positive in every nation's data, but its strength varied. The size of each correlation was itself correlated with the nation's level of individualism – the more individualistic the nation, the stronger the correlation between self-esteem and satisfaction with life. The strong correlation between a nation's wealth and its individualism had already been established by Hofstede (1980) and subsequently confirmed, so one could thus argue that increasing wealth leads to increasing individualism in a nation's socialising institutions. This individualism makes self-esteem a more salient concern throughout socialisation and ties it more strongly to having a sense of satisfaction with one's life.

Note that self-esteem is itself also strongly associated with high extraversion, perhaps therefore accounting for the national-level correlations between this dimension of personality with both national-level individualism (Schmitt et al., 2007) and life satisfaction (Steel & Ones, 2002). National culture can thus be construed as a sensitising contextual agent, enhancing certain social processes and diminishing others. These processes differ between nations, leading to an effect on the average level of its citizens' satisfaction with life. In the remainder of this chapter we explore further the importance of context in relation to personality by looking at some other types of cross-cultural studies.

SITUATIONAL DETERMINANTS OF BEHAVIOUR

Personality is ordinarily discussed without much reference to the context in which it is expressed, perhaps because personality theory has been developed principally within the more individualistic nations of the world. Of course we know that the personality of an actor is one factor underpinning their interpersonal behaviour. However, when the actor's personality is considered without referring to context, we also know from Mischel's (1968) challenge that only a small proportion of the outcome variance is explained. This is not surprising. As Hogan put it, 'Personality is stable, but behavior varies; it varies largely because, in order to be consistent, people must change their actions when they deal with different people' (1982: 85). That is, the personality of one's interaction partner is also an important factor eliciting one's behaviour. The role behaviours required of one in different settings would be another important determinant. By pitching one's behaviour to the character of others (for instance their reputation, status or role) one's interpersonal behaviour can be more effective, even if apparently inconsistent across different target persons or situations. These issues have been debated in social psychology for some time, for example within the so-called personality vs. **situationism** controversy (see e.g., Bond, 2013).

> **Situationism** is a theory that persons' behaviours are determined more by situational contexts than by personality.

Self-monitoring (Snyder, 1987) is a construct that is relevant here in pointing to individual differences. Those persons who monitor themselves are more attuned to the evaluations and expectations of others than those who do not monitor themselves. High self-monitors are therefore more likely to be affected by variations in social context. So too, perhaps, will be those who are higher in Cheung et al.'s (2003) interpersonal relatedness. Beyond individual differences, there will also be cultural variations in situationism. People in collectivistic cultures tend to be more attuned to others, especially their in-groups, and will also tend to show greater variations in behaviour across different social situations.

As we described in earlier chapters, Gelfand et al. (2011) compared the level of reported situational constraint in 33 nations. Even though the *rank ordering* of situational constraint was found to be virtually identical in all nations, the *amount* of constraint varied greatly between nations. Thus we may expect that personality traits will have a larger effect on behaviour in some nations than others. This suggestion is empirically testable and indeed has been tested in a series of studies by Church and his associates, which are described in Key Research Study Box 5.1.

Further evidence relevant to cultural variations in the importance of situational context comes from the work of Owe, Vignoles et al. (2013). These authors devised a six-item measure of 'contextualism', which asks respondents to rate the extent to which they believe that one can best understand someone by knowing about the contexts from which they originate and which they currently inhabit (e.g., family, social group, social position). They define this measure as 'the belief component of collectivism', and across 19 nations it was most strongly endorsed in nations where their high school respondents more strongly endorsed Schwartz's conservation values, compared to openness to change values.

Perceiving and Interacting with Others

If behaviour is an outcome of both personality and the social context, then how do individuals make sense of those around them who comprise a major element of that context? McCrae,

Key Research Study Box 5.1
Cultural Variations in Traitedness

In a series of studies, Church and his colleagues have investigated whether there are cultural variations in the extent to which persons understand others in terms of traits or in terms of their context. Church, Ortiz, et al. (2003) developed a 74-item questionnaire measure known as the Personality Beliefs Inventory. Some items reflected a belief in the efficacy of traits as a basis for understanding others. For instance, one item was, 'People who are quite industrious when they are students will probably be quite industrious in their jobs as adults'. Other items reflected a belief in contextualism. For instance, one item was, 'It is hard to judge how timid a person is until you have interacted with him or her in many social situations'. Students in Mexico and the USA were asked to rate these items on scales ranging from 'strongly agree' to 'strongly disagree'. Factor analysis showed that beliefs in traitedness and beliefs in contextualism yielded separate factors. One set of beliefs is not simply the opposite of the other. No difference was found in endorsement of contextual beliefs, but traitedness scored higher among Americans than among Mexicans.

The results of two-nation comparisons are often ambiguous, because there are many reasons why two nations differ. Church, Katigbak et al. (2005) repeated their study, this time sampling two individualist nations, the United States and Australia, and two collectivist nations, Mexico and the Philippines. In this study, the Americans scored higher in trait beliefs and lower in contextual beliefs than both Mexicans and Filipinos. The results for Australians resembled those for the USA, but sample limitations prevented a comparison of mean scores.

Church, Katigbak et al. (2006) further extended the scope of this study, sampling more widely and including measures intended to test for the functions of cultural differences in traitedness. They predicted that those who scored high on contextualism beliefs would also score higher on self-monitoring, reasoning that if you believe in contextualism, you will want to make sure that your own behaviour conforms to the contextual requirements.

In this study, both Anglo-Australian and American students endorsed trait beliefs more than contextualism, whereas both Chinese Malays and Japanese showed the reverse pattern. The results for Mexicans, Filipinos, Chinese Australians and ethnic Malays were intermediate. US students reported less self-monitoring than respondents from five of the more collectivist samples. However, Mexican respondents also reported low self-monitoring. In addition, the measures predicted to mediate these differences did not succeed in doing so. Church et al. considered that this might be due to a failure to control acquiescent response style and other measurement problems. They therefore made a fourth study with improved measures (Church, Willmore, et al., 2012). Sampling Mexico, the Philippines, Japan and the USA, the contrasts in traitedness and self-monitoring were confirmed. These effects were partially mediated by measures of perceived collectivism, tightness-looseness and dialecticism. The last of these concepts is discussed in Chapter 6.

These results indicate that beliefs in both traits and contextual factors are endorsed in all cultures, but replicable cultural differences are found in the relative weight given to them. The results contribute toward our understanding of collectivism, and suggest limitations in the valid use of personality measures for assessment and selection purposes in more collectivistic cultures.

Terracciano et al. (2005a) examined the factor structure of other-rated personality traits, again using the NEO-PI-R questionnaire measure of personality. To do so, they asked college students in 42 nations to rate the personality of a man or woman whom they knew well. Within-nation factor analyses of the 30 facets constituting the NEO-PI-R replicated the organisation of the American self-report structure in most nations: in the remaining nations, the familiar five-factor structure was still clearly recognisable. Thus, the organisation of other-rated personality into the basic dimensions of extraversion, agreeableness, conscientiousness, neuroticism, and openness to experience paralleled the organisation of self-ratings using questionnaire items, just as the structure of trait terms used to describe others parallels the structure of trait terms used to describe the self. However the relevance of these trait perceptions is likely to vary, depending on the levels of traitedness or contextualism in a given context, and on the importance of each particular trait to the local context.

Consider first the local importance of traits. Williams, Satterwhite, and Saiz (1998) asked students in 20 nations to rate the importance of the Big Five dimensions. They concluded that across all these countries extraversion and agreeableness were the most important, emotional stability and openness to experience the least, with conscientiousness falling in between. There were, however, exceptions to this pattern with Singaporeans, for example, rating emotional stability as most important. The authors conclude that, '... sufficient variability was observed to warrant the further exploration of between-country differences in the qualities associated with psychological importance' (1998: 126–127). Presumably these variations in importance relate to the needs, values and beliefs of the citizens in the societies involved.

A more detailed illustration is provided by the work of Bond and Forgas (1984), who presented Australian and Hong Kong Chinese perceivers with descriptions of persons varying across four of the Big Five dimensions used in their culture to characterise others. In both cultural groups, perceivers indicated that they would be more likely to associate with a target described in terms indicating high extraversion and high agreeableness. People in both, and probably all, cultural systems prefer to interact with someone who is generally enthusiastic and broadly accommodating towards others. The respondents in both cultural contexts were also more inclined to trust someone higher on conscientiousness. However, culture-specific dynamics are also involved in this process. Hong Kong Chinese attached much greater weight to a target person's agreeableness in choosing whom they wished to spend time with and much more weight on conscientiousness in deciding whether to trust them than did the Australians. This difference in the weight placed on agreeableness and conscientiousness might well characterise any comparison between an individualistic and a collectivist nation.

Indeed, Kwan, Bond, and Singelis (1997) found that respondent extraversion and agreeableness predicted the achievement of relationship harmony in both US and Hong Kong samples, but that conscientiousness was a stronger predictor for the Hong Kong Chinese. Variations in aspects of conscientiousness – self-restraint, planfulness, achievement-striving and diligence – all seem relatively more crucial in guiding choices about whom to seek out and whom to avoid within a collectivist compared to an individualistic culture. Where in-group responsibilities are heavier, one chooses to associate with those who are more trustworthy.

Everyday Life Box 5.1　Personality in Advertisements

Advertisements seek to attract the attention of consumers in a variety of ways, one of which is by establishing a desirable brand image. Aaker (1997) reasoned that rather than impose Big Five personality dimensions, she should first identify the types of personality that existing advertisements evoked. In this way, she was able to identify five types of US brand images. These could be summarised as Sincerity, Excitement, Competence, Sophistication, and Ruggedness. For instance, ruggedness was defined by US raters in terms of outdoorness, masculinity, toughness, and Westernness. Examples would be advertisements for Levi jeans, Harley-Davidson motorcycles and Marlboro cigarettes.

Figure 5.4　Japanese Peacefulness; Spanish Passion
Images printed by arrangement with Shutterstock.

Aaker, Benet-Martinez, and Garolera (2001) then made similar types of study in Japan and in Spain. In Japan, they found four of the same types of brand image that they had found in the US, but there were no products emphasising ruggedness. Instead, there was a brand image that focused on peacefulness. The advertisements illustrating peacefulness were characterised by Japanese raters as shy, mild-mannered, peaceful, naïve, dependent, and childlike. In Spain, images characterised by sincerity, excitement and sophistication were again found, but the competence and ruggedness images were replaced by a brand image focused on passion. The advertisements illustrating passion were characterised by Spanish raters as fervent, passionate and intense, but also spiritual, mystical and bohemian.

The authors argue that there is a reciprocal relationship between culture and brand images. Exposure to particular brand images can be thought of as a series of attempts at priming by advertisers. Where the prime accords with one of the value types that Schwartz identified in different nations, the advertisement is more likely to be effective. Repeated use of brand images by advertisers may also influence the maintenance of or change in cultural values.

This contrasting emphasis is visible, not only when researchers focus their respondents' attention on particular qualities, but also in language use in everyday life. For instance, Zhang, Kohnstamm et al. (2002) compared free descriptions of children by their parents in Dutch and Mainland Chinese. The authors conclude that, 'Chinese parents of school-age children generated many more descriptors, mostly critical, in the domain of conscientiousness. The findings reflect the Chinese high achievement orientation and show that the classification system [for trait descriptions] … is sensitive to cultural differences' (2002: 165). Parental descriptions of their children are more numerous in the conscientiousness domain because academic achievement by children of school age is so crucial to the family at that point, relative to other life concerns. This emphasis on conscientiousness-related trait terms reflects the Chinese pre-occupation with inculcating self-discipline in school-age children and maintaining social order throughout the rest of their lives. The point here is that the salience of language terms for describing personality is responsive to cultural concerns, and that these concerns may be detected by comparing the relative frequencies of words-in-use across cultural systems. For further research underlining the linkage between language and the expression of personality, see Box 5.1.

Box 5.1   Do Bilinguals have Two Personalities?

In assessing the structure of personality across cultures, any inventory of personality must be translated from its language of origin into the language of the receiving culture. The accuracy of this translation procedure is usually ensured by having competent bilinguals translate and back-translate the questionnaire, and then resolve any discrepancies. The original and the translated versions of these questionnaires may then be given to a separate set of bilinguals to further check on the accuracy of the translation (e.g., McCrae, Yik, Trapnell, Bond, & Paulhus, 1998). Differences in the facet or dimension scores would then be used to adjust scores from the two language groups when comparisons are made.

However, an alternative way to conceptualise these differences is to use the shift in bilinguals' profile across their two languages as revealing their dual personalities – one learned for use in each language with its corresponding community of language users. The initial stimulus for exploring personality shift as a function of language was the linguistic relativity hypothesis of Whorf (1956), who argued that different languages provided different worldviews so that a language shift would entail a personality shift. More recently researchers have framed this process in terms of what they call the 'culture framing hypothesis' (Hong, Morris, Chiu, & Benet-Martinez, 2000).

The argument is that bilinguals are biculturals who have acquired two internalised cultures with personalities consistent with the two cultural systems. The language of the personality questionnaire cues the culturally appropriate personality, so that the bilingual's apparent personality shifts towards the modal personality found among native speakers of the bilingual's second-language. For example, Ramirez-Esparza, Gosling, Benet-Martinez and Pennebaker (2006) compared the responses of Spanish-English bilinguals to the Big Five Inventory. When responding in their second language of English, Spanish-English bilinguals 'were more extraverted, agreeable and conscientious in English than in Spanish and these differences were consistent [though not as strongly] with the personality displayed in each culture' (p. 19). Chen

(Continued)

(Continued)

and Bond (2010) showed that personality change in Chinese biculturals that is elicited by responding to questionnaires in English or Chinese is observable not just in survey responses but also in subsequent behaviour as perceived by a conversation partner.

Such shifts in responses towards the position of a cultural group when using one's second language as a first language have been observed in many studies. Occasionally, however, the opposite pattern of 'ethnic affirmation' occurs, i.e., the bilingual shifts away from the position of their second-language culture and gives responses even stronger than those produced by typical members of their first-language culture (Bond & Cheung, 1984). A given language shift can thus produce personality shifts in either direction. But how can bilinguals have such flexible personalities? Instead, it would seem more sensible to regard questionnaire responses of bilinguals in their second language as being unconscious self-presentations directed towards the audience that typically uses that language (Chen & Bond, 2010). The more familiar the bilingual is with that second culture, the greater the accommodative shift they may be expected to show. In cases of cultural conflict, however, they will affirm their ethnic identity by over-reacting, with the strength of that reaction dependent on the strength of the identification they wish to claim with their first-language culture.

These effects are a source of measurement error when researchers use English language questionnaires with respondents for whom English is a second language. As we described in Chapter 4, Harzing (2005) showed that when responding to a survey in English, participants from 26 nations gave answers that were closer to the answers given by English participants.

THE IF-THEN MODEL OF SOCIAL BEHAVIOUR

The studies that we have discussed in the preceding section indicate that the idea that personality variations drive social behaviour may not be as simple as we proposed at the outset of this chapter. Since Mischel's (1968) classic text, personality theorists have been struggling to develop models of behaviour that predict a higher percentage of the variance in observed behaviour than is provided by information about personality alone. In line with our previous discussion, the obvious solution is to incorporate measures of the situation into the predictive equation. The crucial element in the situation is often other persons, be they interaction partners or imagined reference groups. These others may be characterised in terms of their perceived personalities (Bond & Forgas, 1984), or the interpersonal norms they are expected to apply during an interaction (Pepitone, 1976), or the norms surrounding the behavioural expression itself (Gelfand et al., 2011). We shall discuss the effects of cultural norms in Chapter 8.

In terms of the issues we are exploring in this book, a key situational variation is the cultural context. To what extent would an individual who is high on extraversion behave in the same way in different parts of the world? We have seen that cultures vary in the extent to which they foster individual autonomy. Therefore extraverted behaviour needs to be expressed within the limits that a particular culture specifies as acceptable. Thinking in terms of roles can help us identify the ways in which cultural settings funnel the expression of personality: behaviour can be more completely explained by incorporating the type of role relationship characterising each interaction (for instance, father-son, same-gender friends and so forth: McAuley, Bond, & Kashima, 2002) or by the actor's beliefs about the world in which he or she must function (Leung & Bond, 2004). Each of these potential supplements to our prediction of social behaviour has been shown to vary across national groups, and so may help to explain social processes across cultures. Regardless of which situational factors are considered important, a predictive model will need to be more complex than the simplistic formula: personality predicts behaviour. Instead, it would need to be in the 'if-then' format, where the 'ifs' include some representation of situational context (Bond, 2013).

As an instance, we can consider what happens when a relatively introverted child goes to school in different nations. X.Y. Chen and his colleagues compared the school experiences of 2,000, 9–12 year old children in China, Brazil, Italy and Canada (Chen, He, De Oliveira et al., 2004; Chen, Zapulla, Lo Coco et al., 2004). They were particularly interested in the experience of 'shy-sensitive' children, compared to other children. The sampled nations were selected to illustrate the range from a strongly collectivist nation to a strongly individualist nation. Children reported their self-perceived competence and loneliness, while information on social behaviours was assessed by peer nominations and teacher ratings. Shyness-sensitivity was found to be positively associated with reported loneliness and negatively related with self-perceived social competence most strongly in Canada and less strongly in Brazil and Italy, but not at all in China. In China, the lonely children were the aggressive ones, not the shy ones. Overall levels of loneliness did not differ between nations after acquiescent response style had been discounted. Thus, we can say that *if* a child is shy and the cultural context is individualistic *then* he or she will be lonely. It is just as possible for a child to be lonely at school in a collectivist nation, but shyness and sensitivity are not the appropriate personality predictors, as they are within schools in more individualistic nations.

SUMMARY

Psychologists have attempted to explain the differences in typical behaviours of persons from different cultures by assessing the typical personalities of individuals from those cultures. Early attempts to do so were frustrated by the unreliable and unfamiliar instruments available for personality measurement. Psychometric progress in the last three decades has enabled psychologists to export translated versions of extensive personality questionnaires to many countries. Because the structure of these questionnaires has proven to be equivalent across cultures, personality psychologists can now compare the profiles of persons across cultural groups.

The results of this work have combined with those from lexical studies of various languages around the world to indicate that personality may be described across five basic dimensions – extraversion, agreeableness, conscientiousness, emotional stability, and openness to experience. These features of individual variation appear to derive from pan-cultural issues of interpersonal and societal functioning, so that the typical profile of individuals from a given nation represents that nation's solution to the challenge presented by its particular ecological-historical legacy. Nations can now be compared in terms of how they position their typical members' personality across the Big Five dimensions, but we cannot yet be sure how large are the measurement errors involved in comparing these means. Although persons in all nations do think of themselves and others in terms of personality traits, the extent to which they do so is stronger in individualist cultures than in collectivist cultures. Conversely, making one's behaviour fit the requirement of each particular social context is more important in collectivist cultures than in individualist cultures.

The indigenous study of Chinese personality indicates that the Big Five are an incomplete representation of personality variation. A sixth dimension named interpersonal relatedness has been found and replicated in other, non-Chinese cultural groups, and constitutes an important addition to the basic five. It may be especially relevant in more collectivist cultures. Differences in life satisfaction across nations are explained by differences in individualism and national wealth, rather than by personality.

FURTHER READING

1 Cheung, F.M., & Cheung, S.F. (2004). Measuring personality and values across cultures: Imported versus indigenous measures. *Online Readings in Psychology and Culture.* Available at http://scholarworks.gvsu.edu/*orpc*
2 Church, A.T. (2001). Personality measurement in cross-cultural perspective. *Journal of Personality, 69,* 979–1006.
3 Church, A.T., & Katigbak, M.S. (2002). Studying personality traits across cultures: Philippine examples. *Online Readings in Psychology and Culture.* Available at http://scholarworks.gvsu.edu/*orpc*
4 Heine, S.J., Buchtel, E. & Norenzayan, A. (2008). What do cross-national comparisons of personality traits tell us? The case of conscientiousness. *Psychological Science, 19,* 309–313.
5 Hofstede, G., & McCrae, R.R. (2004). Personality and culture revisited: Linking traits and dimensions of culture. *Cross-Cultural Research, 38,* 52–88.
6 McCrae, R.R. (2002). Cross-cultural research on the five-factor model of personality. *Online Readings in Psychology and Culture.* Available at http://scholarworks.gvsu.edu/*orpc*
7 Suh, E.M., & Oishi, S. (2002). Subjective wellbeing across cultures. *Online Readings in Psychology and Culture.* Available at http://scholarworks.gvsu.edu/*orpc*

STUDY QUESTIONS

1 What sorts of variation in personality are observed across the nations of the world?
2 What does the variation in personality observed across the nations of the world tell us about the national factors that affect this variation?
3 If most of the variation in personality occurs at the individual level, how scientifically useful is it to characterise the 'personality' of nations?
4 How would you explain the finding that gender differences are greater in European and North American nations than they are in the rest of the world?

6
Cognition, Motivation and Emotion

'But to persever In obstinate condolement … shows a will most incorrect to heaven,
A heart unfortified, a mind impatient'

(Shakespeare, *Hamlet*)

In several of the preceding chapters, we have examined studies in which researchers have attempted to measure differences between national cultures, whether these be measured in terms of values, beliefs or personality. Here we take a different perspective, considering in turn three domains of basic psychological processes. In each case we shall find evidence for the universality of these processes, but also for some ways in which this universality is tempered by the differing nature of local contexts. Rather than measure cultural dimensions, researchers working is this tradition have usually postulated ways in which particular cultural groups differ and then used these postulates to predict how participants in experimental settings will perform tasks that are designed to highlight the predicted differences.

The primary impetus for this type of work came from Markus and Kitayama (1991), who proposed that cultures differ in terms of independence and interdependence. These concepts closely parallel Hofstede's dimension of individualism versus collectivism, but Markus and Kitayama did not explicitly derive their hypothesis from his work. Their own reasoning is examined more fully in Chapter 7, but for the moment we may note that their particular focus was on contrasts in cognition, motivation and emotion between Japanese and Americans. Their focus on cognition has proved particularly fruitful.

INTERDEPENDENCE AND COGNITION

Markus and Kitayama (1991) proposed that in interdependent cultures (exemplified by Japan) a distinctive way of thinking prevails, characterised by a mode of comprehending the world which refers not just to oneself but also to all other aspects of one's ecological niche. Following this initiative, Nisbett and his colleagues were able to summarise a broad range of evidence indicating that East Asians tend to think **holistically**, while North Americans tend to think **analytically**

(Nisbett, Peng, Choi, and Norenzayan, 2000; Nisbett, 2003). Similar contrasts have also been proposed between North Americans and Africans (Nsamenang, 1992), and even between US ethnic groups, genders, and socioeconomic groups.

Key Researcher Box 6.1   Richard Nisbett

Figure 6.1   Richard Nisbett

Richard Nisbett (b. 1941) grew up in Texas and completed his PhD in social psychology at Columbia University in 1966. After teaching at Yale University for five years, he joined the faculty of the University of Michigan, where he has held a series of positions ever since, including the Directorship of the Research Center for Group Dynamics. From 1992 to the present he has been Theodore Newcomb Distinguished Professor, as well as a co-Director of the Culture and Cognition Programme. He has been a key pioneer in studying cultural variations in basic cognitive processes, particularly between Asian and Western cultures, and in understanding relationships between intelligence and culture, and cultural variations surrounding the concept of honour. His studies have been cited more than 43,000 times.

This proposition recalls much earlier cross-cultural research, such as Berry's (1976) eco-cultural framework, which proposed that survival in different types of environment calls for differing perceptual and cognitive skills. In particular, socialization into more relational or interdependent roles promotes more context dependency and holistic thinking. Early supportive evidence for this was obtained using Witkin's (1950) theory of perceptual differentiation and one of its key instrumentations, the Embedded Figures Test. Respondents to this test are asked to identify a series of shapes, each of which is hidden within a larger background. An example is shown in Figure 6.2. Respondents from groups whose survival requires individual enterprise, such as the Inuit in hunting seals and walrus, showed field independence, that is to say they were better able to pick out targeted figures from the confusing background. Respondents from groups whose survival required collective action, such as the Temne rice farmers of West Africa, showed greater field dependence and had trouble disembedding the targeted figures. The early studies showed substantial variations in field dependence among samples from many parts of the world (Witkin & Berry, 1975).

Holistic Cognition is a style of thinking and of perception in which a pattern of stimuli and their interrelationships are considered as a whole.

Analytic Cognition is a style of thinking and perception in which key components of a stimulus are identified and separated from their context.

The more recent studies enable us to explore more fully this contrast between field-dependent or holistic thinking and field-independent or analytic thinking. Ji, Peng, and Nisbett (2000) found East Asian students studying in the USA

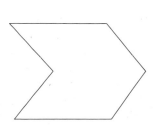

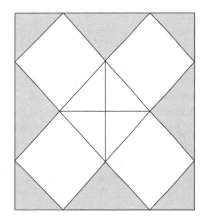

Figure 6.2   Embedded Figures Test
Source: Witkin et al. (1977).

to be more field-dependent than US students, while Kuhnen, Hannover, Roeder et al. (2001) found Malay and Russian students more field-dependent than German and US students. By the way, did you fail to find the hidden pattern in Figure 6.2? If you did, you may be field dependent: look again, and this time do not discount the shaded regions.

Masuda and Nisbett (2001) showed animated vignettes of underwater scenes and photographs of wildlife to Japanese and US students. The Japanese recalled the context in which they had been shown the animals better. They were also better at recognising whether they had been shown particular animals before, if they were shown again in the same context, but not if they were shown in new contexts. More recently, Masuda, Gonzalez, Kwan, and Nisbett (2008) studied differences between East Asian and US paintings portraying individuals in major museums in East Asia and the United States. The percentage of the canvas taken up by the individual being portrayed was greater in US portraits, whereas the context was more emphasised in the Asian portraits. Asked to take a photo of a fellow student, Caucasian US respondents selected a more close-up setting than did Asian American students. To check for similar effects in your own life, see Everyday Life Box 6.1.

An alternative procedure for detecting analytic versus holistic cognition is known as the Rod and Frame test. Kitayama, Duffy, Kawamura, and Larsen (2003) showed Japanese and US students a series of vertical lines ('rods'), each of which appeared within a square frame. In each trial, they were then shown a second square frame of different size. The task was to reproduce the line from the first square, either in the same absolute size as it had first been seen, or in proportion to the dimensions of the second square. In Figure 6.3, the upper part shows an example of the stimuli as presented to a participant. The lower part of Figure 6.3 shows what would be a correct response if the participant had been asked to match the absolute size (on the left of the figure) or the relative size (on the right of the figure). Americans were better at reproducing the absolute length and Japanese were better at producing a new version whose length was relative to the new square.

Evidently, Pacific Asians, who are from more collectivistic backgrounds, attend more to the context in processing visual stimuli. Further studies have focused on the context of other kinds of stimuli. Ishii, Reyes, and Kitayama (2003) tested whether Japanese and US students were more distracted in completing tasks by the verbal content of speech or by the tone of voice of the

Everyday Life Box 6.1   Facebook Self-Portrayals

How have you portrayed yourself on Facebook or other social media sites? Huang and Park (in press) tested the extent to which Facebook portrayals are consistent with some of the cultural differences discussed in the present chapter. Does the portrait of your face fill most of the picture that you have chosen to represent yourself? Alternatively did you include also some contextual background? A contextualised portrait would be more likely for someone from a cultural group in which holistic cognition was more strongly favoured. A decontextualised portrait would be more likely for someone from a cultural group that favours analytic cognition.

Huang and Park randomly selected 312 Facebook profiles of undergraduate students at six universities in East Asia (Hong Kong, Singapore, and Taiwan) and the United States (California and Texas). Their data showed that East Asian Facebook users are more likely to de-emphasise their faces compared to Americans. Specifically, East Asians included more context in their profile photographs, whereas Americans tended to prioritise their focal face at the expense of the background. East Asian Facebook users also had a lower intensity of facial expression than Americans on their photographs. If you included contextual information in your page, is its purpose to show where you are, or to show you with particular people? Would you expect these contrasts to be found also in other regions of the world?

speaker. Americans were more distracted by verbal content and Japanese were more distracted by the emotional tone in which the words were embedded. Ishii et al. consider tone to be more contextual than words. These results might be due to the differences between the English and Japanese languages, so Ishii et al. did a second study using bilingual Filipinos. The Filipinos were more distracted by verbal tone than by words, regardless of whether the speech was in English or in Tagalog. Thus, the effect appears to be cultural rather than linguistic.

Thinking in holistic ways also involves an awareness of complexity, whereby many causal factors impinge on and interact with one another. Thinking holistically is more systemic,

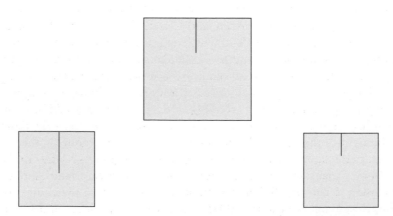

Figure 6.3   The Rod and Frame test used by Kitayama et al. (2003)

and gives less reason to expect the identification of direct causal links between what is happening now and what may come next. Ji, Nisbett, and Su (2001) showed Chinese and US students a series of shapes and asked them to predict whether each ensuing shape would be similar to or different from the last. The Americans predicted greater continuity, the Chinese more change. Choi and Nisbett (2000) presented descriptions of an individual's behaviour to Korean and US students. After being asked to predict what the individual would do next, they were then told what had actually occurred. When their predictions were proved false, the Koreans expressed less surprise, and were more likely to use hindsight to explain what had happened, perhaps because they were more accepting of uncertainty in the flow of events.

Because it is difficult to apply causal logic to complex systems, a focus on the interdependence of the elements in a social system or an abstract problem is likely to lead to a preference for intuitive problem solving. Norenzayan, Smith, Kim, and Nisbett (2002) compared preferences for formal reasoning versus intuitive reasoning among Chinese, Korean and US students. Problems were presented to them in a way that created a conflict between the two styles of reasoning. Faced with this conflict, the Chinese and Koreans used intuitive reasoning and the US students used more formal reasoning. However, when no conflict was created between reasoning styles, no cultural differences were found. In a similar way, Zhou et al. (2012) showed that when Chinese students received repeated feedback that they were failing on an experimental task, they shifted toward more analytic reasoning. When they did so they experienced a greater sense of personal control.

In understanding the nature of these differences in cognitive style, it is necessary to be clear that these are not differences in ability. As the Norenzayan et al. (2002) and the Zhou et al. (2012) studies indicates, holistic and analytic thinking are better thought of as culturally socialised habits. Most of us can reason in either way, but over time we may learn from the cultural context within which we are located to rely more on reasoning in one way than in the other. We can, however, revert to the other style if primed by a social situation to do so. As a further instance, Choi, Nisbett, and Smith (1997) showed that Americans made stronger inductive inferences when presented with sets of premises concerning animals, whereas Koreans made stronger inferences when presented with premises referring to persons. Choi et al. suggest that cognitive categories referring to persons are more accessible to Koreans because of their greater social interdependence.

Correspondence Bias

Further illustrations of the ability to switch between one cognitive style and another can be found in studies of correspondence bias. Numerous studies have been reported in which respondents are asked to explain an individual's behaviour, where either dispositional or situational explanations are possible. US respondents are typically found to attribute the cause to the individual rather than the contextual determinants. In other words, they see a correspondence between the individual's actions and their personality, attitude or intentions. This tendency has often been referred to as the Fundamental Attribution Error.

However, we follow those authors who refer to this phenomenon as correspondence bias because, as we shall see, cross-cultural studies have shown the phenomenon to be less fundamental than has often been thought. Interestingly, Ichheiser (1943), who first wrote about the bias, considered that it was shaped by 'ideologically conditioned patterns of interpreting personality which permeate [...] society'. Subsequently, North American theorists have mostly tried to understand the correspondence bias in terms of individual cognitive processes, but French social psychologists continue to study this process in terms of the social context in which it is presumed to be embedded, emphasising its social origins by referring to it as the internality *norm* (Beauvois & Dubois, 1988).

Shweder and Bourne (1982) asked Indian and US adults to describe their peers. They found that 72% of the qualities attributed by US respondents were context-free personality traits. Only 50% of the qualities attributed to Indians fell into this category. In a more detailed study, Miller (1984) found that Indian students gave many more situational explanations and fewer trait-based explanations than did US students for events in a series of scenarios that she provided. This tendency was found in adults as well as children, showing that the difference is not a matter of developmental maturity. Given the greater weight that Asians attach to the individual's context, it is not surprising that correspondence bias has been found to be much less evident in studies from this region (Choi, Nisbett, & Norenzayan, 1999).

However, Norenzayan, Choi, and Nisbett (2002) tested the proposition that whether or not correspondence bias is found will depend upon the type of information provided to respondents. When Koreans and Americans were provided only with information about individuals, both were equally willing to make predictions as to how the individual would behave in future. In contrast, when situational information was also provided, the Koreans drew upon it in making predictions much more than did the Americans. In a similar way, Miyamoto and Kitayama (2002) found that when respondents were told that the position taken in a student essay had been constrained by course requirements, Americans still showed a correspondence bias but Japanese did not. However, when respondents were told that although the individual had been constrained by course requirements the essay might nonetheless give some indication of real attitudes, both the Japanese and Americans showed equally strong correspondence bias. Thus cultural differences in the tendency for dispositional attributions can be induced or eliminated under experimental conditions.

Miyamoto and Kitayama (2002) also obtained evidence of respondents' 'on-line' reasoning styles while they were making their judgments. Codings were made of the extent to which respondents thought about the course requirements, the essay content, or both. The degree of thought about the course requirements was found to mediate whether correspondence bias occurred. Among the cross-cultural studies of cognition in relation to independence and interdependence that we have discussed so far, this is the only one that has attempted an explanation of the results obtained on a more precise basis than simply stating the nationality of respondents and then speculating on what might underlie the observed difference.

Broadening the Sampling Focus

The strong initial emphasis of social cognition researchers on contrasts between North America and East Asia has been both useful and problematic. It is useful because the contrasts between analytic and holistic cognition have been thoroughly explored. It is problematic because it leaves open the question of how fully this contrast compasses the variability of cognitive processes in other contexts. More recent studies have shown that contrasts between analytic and holistic cognition can be also be found both in other parts of the world as well as between distinctive samples located in the same parts of the world. For instance, Kitayama, Park, Sevincer, Karasawa, and Uskul (2009: see Chapter 7) found results from two European nations that were intermediate between those found in Japan and the USA. The contrast between analytic and holistic cognition is a matter of degree, not a simple dichotomy.

Nisbett and colleagues' basis for predicting that contrasts would be found in analytic and holistic cognition lies in a blending of eco-cultural theory with Markus and Kitayama's contrast between independence and interdependence. If this basis is correct, analytic cognition should prevail wherever there is or has been survival value in thinking and acting independently. Relevant to this, Kitayama, Ishii, Imada, Takemura, & Ramaswamy (2006) predicted greater use of analytic cognition in the northern Japanese island of Hokkaido than in the mainland Japanese island, since Hokkaido has a culture reflecting the pioneer spirit of the early settlers there. Supporting their prediction, Hokkaido participants showed a higher correspondence bias than participants from the mainland. Uskul, Kitayama and Nisbett (2008) administered the Line and Frame test to three samples in Eastern Turkey, namely farmers, herdsmen and fishermen. They reasoned that herding and fishing are more individualistic activities than farming, which requires more collective action. Consistent with eco-cultural theory, the farmers did best at judging the relative line lengths, while the herdsmen did better at judging absolute lengths.

Varnum, Grossmann, Kitayama, and Nisbett (2010) argue that these results from adjacent samples favour an explanation based on a distinction between independence and interdependence rather than on possible genetic or linguistic contrasts between much more broadly defined populations such as East Asians and North Americans. However, simple contrasts between samples can never provide a definitive test of explanations for the differences that have been found. As we discussed in Chapter 4, there are two principal ways in which we can test hypotheses about the causation of cultural effects. We can either unpackage effects by identifying the factors that mediate these effects, or we can use experimental primes to see if we can create changes in effects. In relation to the effects identified by the Nisbett group, we shall discuss some unpackaging studies in Chapter 7. Here we consider priming.

Priming Cognition

We noted above the finding of Norenzayan et al. (2002) that national differences in correspondence bias can be changed or eliminated by providing different types of information to respondents. This is a priming effect, but the prime that was used was not directly related to theories of cultural difference. The most basic cultural primes to have been used take images associated with a nation as primes. Take a look below at Key Research Study Box 6.1.

Aside from national icons, another frequently used prime with some linkage to nationality is language. Use of the English language as a prime has accomplished some very striking effects. For instance, Chen and Bond (2010) found that compared with a Chinese language prime an English language prime caused Hong Kong Chinese to change not just their response to a questionnaire but also their behaviour in ways that were noticeable to third parties who were unaware of the priming. Thus it appears that primes can lead respondents to produce responses that are more characteristic of cultures other than their own.

Oyserman and Lee (2007, 2008) reviewed the full range of primes used by researchers interested in culture. Priming experiments have been conducted with two different sets of participants, either with biculturals, who through heritage and socialisation experiences have been exposed

Key Research Study 6.1   Priming Culture

Hong, Morris, Chiu and Benet-Martínez (2000) sought to show that effects like correspondence bias could be reversed by using images representing different nationalities as primes. For experimental materials, they used the design first employed by Morris and Peng (1994) who compared American high school children of either European descent or Chinese descent. In this study, the students were shown videos depicting images of fish of various colours swimming around. A blue fish was further to the right on the screen than the others and moved in a slightly different direction. As Figure 6.4 shows, European Americans attributed the blue fish's moves to both internal and external forces, whereas the Chinese Americans saw external forces as much more important. Americans commented more frequently that the blue fish was influencing the others. The Chinese commented more frequently that the other fish were influencing the blue fish. This study showed how the European American children attributed individualistic motives to the blue fish, whereas the Chinese Americans saw the fish's movements as a response to the group context.

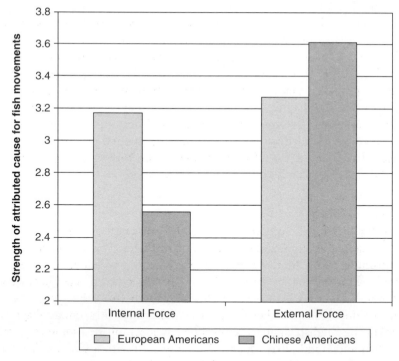

Figure 6.4   What causes the blue fish to move? (Morris & Peng, 1994)

In the studies by Hong et al. (2000), Hong Kong students were assigned randomly to one of three experimental conditions. They were then shown either American cultural icons, such as images of the Statue of Liberty, Mickey Mouse and so forth, or else the Great Wall, a

Chinese dragon and so forth. Those in the control condition were shown geometric figures. They were then asked which nation the pictures symbolised and what would be the characteristics of the persons in nations whose iconic images had been shown. This completed the priming phase of the study. Participants were next shown images of a fish swimming in front of other fish, and asked to indicate their confidence in reasons for the behaviour of the fish in front. As shown in Figure 6.5, those exposed to US primes made attributions that were more internal and those exposed to Chinese primes made attributions that were more external.

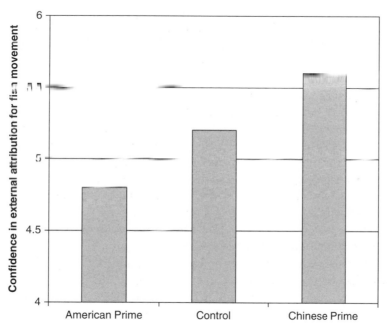

Figure 6.5   What Causes the Blue Fish to Move? (Hong et al., 2000)

In further studies, similar effects were obtained when attributions were made about the behaviours of humans rather than fish. In yet another study, Hong, Benet-Martínez, Chiu and Morris (2003) showed that the attribution effects were only obtained when the fish in front had a different colour. Thus, the success of priming depends on emphasising distinctive priming stimuli.

to more than one cultural context (typically Asians living in the USA), or with mono-cultural student samples in different contexts. The former design rests on the assumption that individuals who were brought up in one cultural context (e.g., Asian culture within the family or one's original heritage culture) but are then exposed to a different cultural context (e.g., US mainstream culture in school and work contexts) are able to draw upon two different cultural knowledge and value systems. Depending on which system is temporarily activated, they are predicted to show more stereotypically Asian or Western responses. The latter approach assumes that cultural knowledge that is typical of other (usually Western) cultures is internalised by participants in these samples to a sufficient extent that it can be used to activate a different cultural script or mental representation.

In their meta-analysis, Oyserman and Lee (2008) found 67 studies that had tested the effect of priming on measures related to the broadly defined concept of individualism-collectivism. Fifty-nine of these studies had been conducted within a single nation. Across all studies, they concluded that priming was successful in shifting attitude, value and belief measures that are often used in cross-cultural comparisons. The strongest effects were found for the prime where individuals were asked to imagine what they had in common with, or what made them different from, their family and friends (see Chapter 7). The least consistent findings were reported when language was used as a prime among bilingual samples. How priming is done (that is, how the independent variable is manipulated) therefore has some effect. The magnitude of priming effects also varied across different dependent measures. Medium effect sizes were obtained when the outcome variables were measured in terms of what Oyserman and Lee called relationality. This construct included measures of social obligation, perceived social support from others, social sensitivity and prosocial orientation. Effects were also strong on measures of cognition, such as measures of prevention–promotion focus and the inclusion or exclusion of others. Effects for values and self-concept, the instruments most typically used in cross-cultural psychology, were of smaller magnitude. The language in which the study was conducted had a significant effect, with the strongest priming effects being found when using English. This supports the findings of Harzing (2005) discussed previously. Importantly for our purposes, the effectiveness of priming also seemed to depend on who was sampled. Priming effects were less strong and less consistent in the few studies that were conducted with Asian participants who were residing in their nations of origin.

One of the more perplexing aspects of priming with mono-cultural participants is that some researchers have claimed that individuals can be manipulated to such an extent that they start behaving as if coming from a different culture (e.g., individualists behaving like collectivists and vice versa). Oyserman (2010) famously proclaimed that Chinese can be turned into Americans and Americans into Chinese by priming. This notion has resulted in the proposition that culture can be defined as a 'situated cognition' (Oyserman, 2011), in other words that culture can be thought of as a set of environmental cues that will trigger people to behave in culturally appropriate ways.

Some limitations of priming

What can we learn from the significant effects accomplished within this impressive body of research? One of the central assumptions is that relevant cultural knowledge is available to all participants. This is likely to be the case with bicultural individuals, and most priming studies have used biculturals, or else populations such as those in Hong Kong that have had extensive exposure to alternative cultural influences. Among mono-cultural samples, alternate forms of cultural knowledge are likely to be more superficial, stereotypic, and less elaborated. Hence, the impact of the prime will be weaker.

If priming is a strong determinant of behaviours in everyday life, it should make intercultural training highly effective and cross-cultural transition an easy process. We review the substantial literature on cross-cultural training and acculturation in Chapters 11 and 13 which shows that this is not the case. Settling into a new cultural environment is fraught with adjustment difficulties. If culture works as a set of situated cognitions and the information inherent in situational primes can switch individuals from one cultural mode into another, we should not find any of the problems that are associated with adapting to new cultural environments. It is more likely that cultural settings are complex and not easily decoded. Meanings need to be learned and abstracted from rich contextual settings. Fiske (2002) put this criticism clearly:

> Construct accessibility is a transient effect that cannot be equated with the enduring, objective social entity that is culture. Some individuals are flexibly capable of participating in multiple cultures, of course. But does a person's culture change in response to questions such as 'How are you different from other people?' Does reading that sentence change a Chinese communal farmer into a cowboy? Sort of, a little bit, for a moment? No. If it did, then IND and COL scales would alter culture instead of measuring it. Priming does not change institutions, practices, or systems of communication and coordination. Priming does not affect socially constituted entities, relations, and practices in relation to which a person lives. Rodeos, poker, cattle brands, Colt 45s, and gunfights. If one does not know Wyatt Earp and the OK Corral, they cannot be primed. Mere accessibility can hardly be an important factor mediating the effects of these constituents of culture on the psyche, unless one postulates that all humans have cognitive representations of all significant aspects of all cultures. (2002: 80–81)

A second difficulty is that, as we saw in Chapter 5, collectivist cultures are characterised by context and group dependency. Collectivists are more likely to adapt their responses to the situation and their interaction partner (Hui, 1988). Collectivists are therefore more likely to behave prosocially only with in-group members (often their immediate family and friends; see Fischer, Ferreira et al., 2009), whereas with out-group members they are more likely to behave like individualists (Leung & Bond, 1984). If priming is effective everywhere in the same way, independent of the origin of samples, it is unlikely to capture these distinctive aspects of culture. Instead, it may tap into the more general psychological processes related to social relationships, which may be influenced by the evolutionary processes that we discussed in Chapter 3.

We should also note that primes are not always interpreted by respondents in the way expected by experimenters. In several studies in Hong Kong, English language primes have been found to enhance students' distinctively Chinese responses rather than the more usual movement toward more Western responses (Yang & Bond, 1980; Bond & Cheung, 1984; Chen & Bond, 2007). Priming can generate reactance as well as accommodation. In the experiments by Zhou et al. (2012), while failure feedback initially primed Chinese participants to switch to analytic cognition, when the priming continued, they switched back to their more familiar holistic cognitive approach.

Oyserman and Lee's (2008) review also showed weaker effects of priming among Asians living in their home country than among those living in North America. These effects might be due to using weaker manipulations, as these particular studies have typically used different primes. Further research is needed using equivalent primes in Eastern and Western samples. This would not be possible using national icons or language as primes. If regional differences in priming effects do emerge when equivalent primes are used, this would indeed indicate cultural differences, but in a way that would require different explanations from those so far proposed. Priming is an exciting and growing area of research, but like other research methods it will be most valuable when we can unpackage the reasons for its effects. This will require primes that have been carefully selected on the basis of theory, rather than crudely undifferentiated primes such as national icons. (Studies using theoretically-based primes are addressed in Chapter 7.)

Research into cultural variations in cognitive processes has thus come a long way since the publication of Markus and Kitayama's (1991) seminal paper. We can now appreciate that there are indeed cultural variations in how people think, but we can also see that these variations are matters of habit and not biologically mandated differences. The differences can be shifted both experimentally and by experiences in everyday life.

MOTIVATION

Markus and Kitayama (1991) proposed that independent and interdependent cultures elicit a different spectrum of motives, just as they elicit different styles of cognition. The motives elicited are likely to be concordant with the differing patterns of prevailing values and personality that we reviewed earlier. Cross-cultural research into motivation has been of two types: some researchers have sought to test the universality of particular motives, while others have explored the way in which motives interact with cultural context. We shall explore the first of these perspectives here and examine the second in Chapter 7.

Achievement Motivation

Early research into the motivation to achieve assumed that achievement was something that brought credit to the individual. An individual's motivation was assessed by coding references to individual achievement and recognition produced by the person in describing a series of pictures. McClelland (1961) sought to apply this kind of thinking in accounting for the greater economic success of some nations over others. He reasoned that by encouraging individual achievement, a generation of entrepreneurs could be created who would find ways to foster economic development. In pursuit of this goal, he undertook some training programmes in India. However, this type of thinking can now be seen to rest on an imposed-etic conceptualisation. More interdependent persons are not likely to think of achievement solely in terms of individual gain and recognition. Indeed, McClelland did not succeed in getting his Indian managers to compete against fellow managers on an individual basis.

One strength of McClelland's work was that he pioneered the use of implicit rather than explicit measures of motives. Measuring motives in this way can overcome some of the measurement biases inherent in asking respondents directly about their motives, and some researchers have continued to develop this approach cross-culturally (Hofer, 2010).

Yu (1996) developed separate measures of individually- and socially-oriented achievement motivation and found them to be largely independent of one another among Chinese respondents. Those who score high on socially-oriented achievement motivation look to others in their group to define targets, to work toward those targets, and to evaluate how well those targets are achieved. Similar conceptualisations of socially-oriented achievement motivation have emerged from research in India (Agarwal & Misra, 1986) and from a comparative study of Turkish and Belgian adolescents (Phalet & Claeys, 1993).

Consistent with this analysis, Redding (1990) studied Chinese entrepreneurs. He found that the economic success of Chinese family firms was strongly dependent upon collaborative links between networks of interrelated family members. Church and Katigbak (1992) compared the work motivations of US and Filipino students. The Americans stressed getting good grades and personal achievement, while the Filipinos emphasised preparation for getting a good job and receiving approval from others. This differentiation among different types of achievement motivation parallels Bandura's (2002) acknowledgement that personal efficacy and group efficacy can have equally strong effects on human action.

There are further consequences of socially- rather than individually-oriented motivation. An independent person who fails may experience self-doubt in his or her abilities. Yu (1996) notes that failure among Chinese people is more often attributed to poor connections with others, fate, bad luck, or one's socially undesirable attributes. Accounts are thus expressed in terms of culturally salient causal agents.

Self-Determination

More recently, Ryan and Deci (2000) have developed an extensive research programme focused on the concept of autonomy, which they refer to as self-determination. Within their model, the experience of autonomy is considered to be a universal motive. Consistent with this, their studies indicate that the reported experience of autonomy is associated with enhanced performance and satisfaction in a wide variety of social contexts. Since autonomy values have been shown to be more strongly endorsed in Western or individualist cultures (Schwartz, 2004), one might expect that their theory would be supported only among samples from individualistic cultures. However, it has received empirical support in studies within Asia, Europe, and South America (Ryan & Deci, 2006). To understand why this is possible, we need to examine their conceptualisation and operationalisation of autonomy. Self-determination is defined in terms of one's choice as to how one behaves. A decision to conform with one's group could therefore be an act of self-determination, provided it is based upon one's on own motivation or will. Self-determination is assessed in terms of four progressive levels of internalisation: 'Did I take this action because of external rewards and punishments, because of approval by myself or others, because of a personal value, or because it fits in with my other values?' The last of these options is seen as fully internalised self-determination.

Chirkov, Ryan and Willness (2005) asked students in Brazil and Canada to rate the frequency of various cultural practices, and then to rate the reasons why they would engage in each of these behaviours. Those who scored higher on the more internalised reasons reported higher well-being, regardless of their cultural group. Chirkov, Ryan, Kim and Kaplan (2003) obtained similar results in Russia, South Korea, Turkey and the USA. The value of these studies is that they define some limits to the sometimes vague ways in which the concepts of individualism and independence are understood. Through the experience of autonomous or internalised choice one could achieve positive outcomes in all kinds of cultural context, just as the lack of autonomous choice could yield unfavourable outcomes in any context.

However, these researchers do acknowledge that some cultural practices are harder to internalise than others. They found that practices which they characterised as 'horizontal' were better internalised by their respondents than those characterised as 'vertical'. This result is reminiscent of the findings obtained when values researchers have examined cultural similarities rather than differences. Schwartz and Bardi (2001) found benevolence and self-direction values most popular universally and power values least popular universally. Thus, it may be more difficult to experience autonomy in more hierarchical cultures.

One way of conceptualising the experience of autonomy in different cultural contexts was proposed in an influential paper by Weisz, Rothbaum, and Blackburn (1984), who contrasted primary control and secondary control. By the use of primary control one seeks to influence events, whereas through secondary control one handles one's reactions to events over which one has no control. Weisz et al. proposed that both types of control processes occur in all cultures, but that primary control would be particularly frequent within individualistic cultures such as that of the USA, whereas secondary control would be more frequent within collectivistic cultures such as Japan's. No direct measures of primary and secondary control have been developed, but the differential distribution of secondary control across nations is illustrated by the variations in emotional display rules discussed in Chapter 8 (Matsumoto et al., 2008) and by the differences in the Asch conformity effect that we described in Chapter 1.

Hierarchy of Motives?

For many years, the hierarchical theory of motivation formulated by Maslow (1943) has been popular, even though it has not been extensively tested. Maslow proposed that, as the more basic motives for food and security are satisfied, additional needs for social inclusion and status become salient and that, as these needs in turn are satisfied, a need for self-actualisation emerges. Comparisons between nations provide a more adequate basis for testing this perspective, since a much greater range of personal circumstances can be included by sampling participants from different cultures.

Huang and Van de Vliert (2004) analysed responses from nearly 130,000 business employees from 39 nations, all of whom worked for the same multinational company. In individualistic nations, white-collar employees were more satisfied than blue-collar employees, especially if their job provided challenging opportunities to use their skills and abilities. However, in collectivist nations job satisfaction did not vary with type of job. Furthermore, where opportunities to use one's skills were low, blue-collar employees were the most satisfied. These effects were obtained after controlling statistically for differences in national wealth. This study provides strong evidence of differing work motivations between nations classified as individualistic and collectivistic, but it is not clear how well the results fit with Maslow's hierarchical theory. To accomplish this integration, it would be necessary to show that the incentive value of challenging opportunities among white-collar employees in individualistic nations rested on greater job security, and that the aversion to challenge of blue-collar employees in collectivist nations rested on lesser job security.

To address this problem, Huang and van de Vliert (2003) made a further study with another very large sample of employees drawn from 49 nations, in which they included a nation-level measure of job security as well as separate measures of intrinsic and extrinsic work motivations. They found that the strength of the positive link between intrinsic aspects of the job (for instance, chances to use one's skills) and job satisfaction was moderated by nation-level security and low power distance. In contrast, positive ratings of extrinsic job characteristics (for instance, pay) were associated with higher job satisfaction in all nations. The findings for security can in a general sense be said to support Maslow's theory, although the study lacked a measure of whether individuals actually felt secure or insecure. The findings that everyone likes more money may arise because money can be used to satisfy most of the motives in his theory. Alternative perspectives might become more apparent in studies that were not focused on work settings, or which included measures of socially-oriented achievement.

Kenrick, Griskevicius, Neuberg, and Schaller (2010) have suggested that Maslow's theory can be updated from the perspective of evolutionary psychology. They propose that through the individual's life-cycle the motives identified by Maslow are gradually added to one another, rather than replacing one another. They also specify additional motives relating to mate acquisition, mate retention, and parenting. A consequence of these modifications is that any of the proposed motives can be elicited by the different contexts within which we find ourselves. Thus, just as circumstances may elicit different aspects of basic cognitive processes, so may circumstances elicit different emphases upon a set of basic motives.

EMOTION

Markus and Kitayama (1991) proposed that while some types of emotion may be universal, there would also be differences in which emotions were most frequently experienced in those contexts in which independence is salient and those in which interdependence is salient. In independent contexts, socially-disengaging emotions that serve to sustain one's independence from others will be functional and will therefore be more frequently experienced: for instance, we should expect more frequent experience and expressions of pride, frustration and anger. In interdependent contexts, socially-engaging emotions such as friendly feelings, shame and guilt will be more functional. Kitayama, Markus, and Kurokawa (2000) found initial support for these propositions. Students were asked to keep diaries. Among US students, feeling good was associated with episodes in which respondents reported pride, whereas among Japanese students feeling good was associated with episodes in which friendliness was reported.

In evaluating Markus and Kitayama's (1991) propositions, two basic issues have to be addressed, each of which has been touched on in earlier sections of this chapter. Firstly, are there absolute differences in the emotions that are experienced by members of different cultures, or is it more the case that the emotions that humans can experience are universal, but occur more frequently in some contexts than others? Secondly, if we do find cultural differences in the frequency of reported emotions, do these differences arise because certain emotion-eliciting situations are more frequent in some cultural groups than others, or are they better interpreted in terms of differing cultural norms about the appropriateness of emotional expression? In the case of cognition, we concluded that differences in thinking in holistic or analytic ways were not absolute, but something more akin to culturally socialised habits of varying strength. The evidence relating to emotion points to a similar conclusion.

The Universality of Emotions

In addressing the question of the universality of emotions, it is necessary to consider the ambiguities involved in the concept of emotion (Matsumoto & Hwang, 2012). It is very likely that some basic emotional states have a biological basis which we share with other primate species, and that other emotional states are context-specific sets of feelings that arise through cultural socialisation. Early studies in this field focused on the more basic emotions.

An extensive series of studies has examined the ability of respondents to identify emotions portrayed in photographs of faces. Ekman (1972) found high percentages of correct recognition of faces portraying anger, joy, sadness, disgust, surprise, and fear among respondents in Brazil, Chile, Argentina, Japan and the USA. The stimuli used in the first studies were all American, so that the design had the weakness that it was imposed etic. However, Ekman, Friesen, O'Sullivan, et al. (1987) used faces taken from all nations and found a continuing high proportion of correct identifications. Furthermore, Ekman, Sorenson, and Friesen (1969) had earlier reported a study in which US faces were shown to respondents from West Irian in New Guinea, people who had minimal previous contact with modern societies. To balance their research design, they also showed New Guinean faces to US respondents. Even in this case, there was a high proportion of correctly identified emotions.

The implications of studies of this type have been much debated. The accuracy rates may be boosted by the fact that respondents are provided with the names of the emotions to be fitted to the faces, and by the fact that the faces portray emotions that are posed rather than natural. Verbal labels for emotions may not exactly correspond with the labels that are used in English. In everyday life, numerous cues are available that are not provided by static photographs of faces alone. In most languages, the number of words used to describe distinct emotions is very much larger than six.

In order to overcome the problems inherent in the use of photos of posed emotions, Matsumoto and Willingham (2006) coded photographs of the spontaneous expressions of Judo medal winners at the 2004 Olympic Games, taken at the moment of victory or defeat. No cultural differences were found between the winners' smiles or between the various expressions of the losers. Subsequent ratings of these photos for differing types of emotion by observers from UK, Japan and the United States showed strong consensus on which emotions were being displayed (Matsumoto, Olida, Schug, et al., 2009). As Figure 6.7 shows, similarly contrasting expressions of sighted winners and losers were also found among congenitally blind winning and losing judo competitors in the subsequent Paralympics (Matsumoto, Olida & Willingham, 2009). If congenitally blind persons show similar emotional expressions as sighted persons, there is no possibility that these expressions are due to socialisation.

Key Researcher Box 6.2   David Matsumoto

David Matsumoto (b. 1959) grew up in Hawaii, and obtained his degrees at the University of Michigan and the University of California, Berkeley, where he worked with Paul Ekman, receiving his PhD in 1986. Since 1989, he has been a Professor of Psychology at San Francisco State University, where he received a distinguished faculty award. He is also the founder and director of the Culture and Emotion research laboratory at San Francisco State, and holder of a seventh degree black belt in judo. He has published more than 16 books, some in Japanese, and many research articles concerning cultural aspects of emotional expression, non-verbal behaviours and acculturation. His professional involvement in the world of judo gave him the necessary access to obtain the photos of emotional expressions in Olympic winners and losers such as those that are shown in Figure 6.7. He recently completed a six-year term as editor of the *Journal of Cross-Cultural Psychology*.

Figure 6.6   David Matsumoto

Figure 6.7   Blind and Sighted Winners and Losers
Reprinted by permission of David Matsumoto and Bob Willingham.

Thus it appears that the sequence of studies initiated by Ekman does provide evidence for the cultural generality of a set of basic emotions. Broadening the support for this conclusion, Scherer, Banse, and Wallbott (2001) also showed high levels of correct identification of anger, fear, joy, and sadness by students from nine nations, when listening to actors' verbal expression of nonsensical phrases. Debate concerning the realism of emotional recognition studies has triggered several recent improvements in research methods. Some researchers have tried to determine effects of the intensity with which emotions are portrayed. In their 11-nation study, Ekman et al. (1987) already reported strong agreement as to which portrayed emotions were most intense. However these judgments were solely concerned with the actual intensity of emotional display.

Because of cultural differences in display rules, Matsumoto, Consolacion, Yamada et al. (2002) expected that Japanese people would make stronger inferences than Americans about the internal feelings of those who were portraying the emotions. They therefore asked respondents to rate separately how intense were the portrayals of each emotion and how intense was the subjective experience of the person portraying that emotion. Results for low intensity faces showed much stronger cultural differences, with the Japanese rating subjective experience as more intense. Matsumoto et al.'s study also included a measure of the interpersonal behaviours, values and attitudes associated with individualism-collectivism, which was found to mediate almost all of the differences that were found between Japanese and US responses. Participants with a more collectivist cultural orientation made stronger ratings of subjective experience. This is thus the first of the studies that we have discussed in this chapter that establishes a link with a mediator derived from cross-cultural theory.

The emphasis of the studies on the facial recognition of emotion has been on rates of recognition of specific emotions. If we change the focus toward an examination of who the perceiver of emotion is, some issues of practical importance become apparent. Look now at Research Debate Box 6.1.

Research Debate Box 6.1   Is There an In-Group Advantage in Person Perception?

An important attempt to extend our understanding of emotional recognition was made by focusing not simply upon the overall accuracy with which emotions were identified, but by taking greater account of interactions between who was the perceiver and whose face was being perceived. Elfenbein and Ambady (2002) conducted a meta-analysis of all previous studies of the facial recognition of emotions and reported that there was an 'in-group advantage', in other words, that accuracy was greatest when emotions were portrayed and perceived by persons from the same national or ethnic group.

In a further analysis, they then tested alternative explanations for this in-group advantage (Elfenbein & Ambady, 2003). Drawing on the four largest studies of visual and vocal emotion recognition, they showed that accurate recognition was significantly predicted by the overall *difference* between Hofstede scores for the nation of the perceiver and the nation of the person portraying the emotions. Larger differences in individualism, power distance and uncertainty avoidance each predicted decreased accuracy. We should note that this is a nation-level analysis and not an individual-level analysis, so it gives us no clues as to what it is about the similarity between persons from different nations that permits their more accurate decoding of emotions.

These conclusions were contested by Matsumoto (2002) who argued that an in-group advantage could only be validly detected if the faces in the photos that were being judged had the precisely correct muscle contractions that are associated with each of the major types of emotion. Most of the photos used in the studies in Elfenbein and Ambady's (2002) meta-analysis did not satisfy this criterion.

Marsh, Elfenbein and Ambady (2003) responded by using photographs of emotion portrayals by Japanese and Japanese-Americans that had earlier been equated for stimulus equivalence by Matsumoto. Japanese-Americans were used because they are visually similar to Japanese, but have been socialised within US culture. Respondents were then asked to guess whether the person in each photograph was Japanese or American. When the poser was showing a neutral expression, accuracy was at chance levels. However, when a specific emotion was being portrayed, accuracy became significant beyond chance. There must therefore be distinctive non-verbal accompaniments or 'accents' even within facial portrayals of basic emotions that US judges can detect, even though they cannot say what these cues are. In a further study, Elfenbein, Beaupre et al. (2007) found distinctive accents in the specific muscles that Canadians and Gabonese used to portray particular emotions. Moreover, when the photos with distinctive accents were compared with a control condition with posed photos that lacked the accents, greater in-group accuracy was found only where the accents were present.

Matsumoto, Olida and Willingham (2009) remain unconvinced of the presence of in-group advantage and attribute the effects that others have found to the use of posed photos. They found no in-group advantage among US and Japanese judges when using photos of Olympic winners and losers. Nevertheless, the results of Elfenbein and her colleagues may give us better guidance on the presence of in-group advantage because judges of posed photos will be looking at photos where the posers are thinking about how to present themselves to others, whereas Matsumoto's athletes provide better information on the most basic component of emotional processes.

The presence and extent of in-group advantage could have both positive and negative practical consequences. It could enhance perceptiveness skills within one's own culture, but it could also encourage one to think of cultural out-groups in stereotyped ways and to feel reduced empathy for their experiences.

The Component Theory of Emotion

The entire sequence of studies of emotional expression that we have reviewed so far extracts emotional expression from the context within which individuals normally occur. Considering that Markus and Kitayama (1991) stressed that context was of particular importance in interdependent cultures, it is not likely that this type of study can give a full picture of the relation between emotion and culture. Requirements as to how one should behave vary from one setting to another, and this may influence the extent to which one will express whatever emotions one is experiencing. Even within mainstream theories, the experience of emotion is no longer seen simply as something that is either present or absent. What is known as the component theory of emotion identifies a whole series of stages, comprising the appraisal and labeling of inner states and subsequent processing of choices as to how those states should be represented and expressed within a given social context (Scherer, 2009). Each of these stages is potentially subject to cultural variation (Mesquita & Leu, 2007).

An early illustration of these processes was provided by Friesen (1972). Friesen showed a short film depicting bodily mutilation to Japanese and US adults. They watched the film either on their own or in the presence of others. While watching the film, their facial expressions were videoed and later coded. It was found that when US participants watched the film their faces registered disgust, although not when they watched a neutral film. On the other hand, the Japanese showed disgust when watching the mutilation film alone, but not when being observed while they watched. Friesen concluded that Japanese display rules inhibit the direct expression of disgust.

However, the details of the Friesen study are often described incorrectly, and it appears that the US watchers also changed their expressions when watching mutilation scenes, though not in the same way as the Japanese (Fridlund & Duchaine, 1996). Matsumoto and Kupperbusch (2001) replicated Friesen's study, using only Caucasian-American women as participants, but also including a measure of individualist-collectivist cultural orientation. They found that participants higher on collectivism smiled more and expressed less negative emotion when watching the unpleasant film in the presence of an observer than when alone. The effects were in the same direction for respondents higher on individualism, but less marked. Thus, an effect originally described as cross-cultural can be reproduced within a US sample, when applying concepts and measures derived from cross-cultural studies. A multi-cultural perspective can enrich mainstream research and help contextualise its possibly indigenous results.

Cultural differences in the expression of emotion are discussed in Chapter 8. Here we focus on the prior question of whether there are cultural differences in the experience of different emotions. As we have seen, nations differ in prevailing values, beliefs and personality profiles. Each of these types of variation could be associated with differences in the experience of emotion (Scherer & Brosch, 2009). For instance, cultures may vary in the frequency of events that are likely to elicit fear, happiness, anger or other emotions. They may also differ in ways that would encourage a person to label emotional arousal in one way or another. What is excitement or challenge to one person may be fear or threat to another.

An extensive database that permits analyses of reported emotions in natural contexts has been provided by the International Study on Emotional Antecedents and Reactions (ISEAR), which included 37 nations (Wallbott & Scherer, 1986). Students were asked to keep a diary for one week, describing recent episodes when they had experienced joy, sadness, fear, anger, disgust, shame and guilt, as well as what happened before and after and who was present. Scherer (1997) later analysed these data in terms of the 'appraisal' stage within the componential model of emotion. In other words, he tested whether there was consistency in respondents' appraisals of the circumstances that led to each type of emotion.

The dimensions of appraisal were novelty, unpleasantness, obstruction of one's goal, external causation, one's ability to cope with the situation, immorality, and self-consistency. Scherer concluded that each emotion had a distinctive pattern of appraisal conditions that was equally applicable to the data derived from almost all nations. Of course, this does not mean that equal amounts of each emotion occurred everywhere, because the eliciting circumstances can occur more often at some locations than at others. The principal divergence from these culture-general conclusions was found among African nations, especially Malawi and Botswana. In the data from these nations, an appraisal of immorality, unfairness, and external causation had stronger effects on any of the emotions that were elicited, possibly because of the prevalence of beliefs in witchcraft (Scherer & Brosch, 2009).

A more systematic set of data has been collected through the use of the 'GRID' questionnaire. Respondents are asked to rate the extent to which 24 different emotion words are associated with each of 144 features that represent the overall sequence of an emotional experience (Fontaine, Scherer, Roesch, & Ellsworth, 2007). The rated features comprise aspects of appraisal, action tendencies, bodily reactions, expression (facial, vocal, gestural) and subjective feelings. Sampling students from Belgium, the UK and Switzerland, Fontaine et al. concluded that emotions can be summarised in terms of four dimensions: valence, power, arousal, and novelty. This approach has recently been extended to 34 samples from 27 nations covering a total of 24 different languages (Fontaine, Scherer, & Soriano, 2013). Substantial similarity in the four dimensional representation of emotions across cultures was again found, with some regional differences. For example, 'feeling submissive' had rather different concomitants in the UK than in Taiwan.

Oishi, Diener, Scollon, and Biswas-Biener (2004) found that among students from India and Japan as well as Hispanic American students there was greater cross-situational variability of reported negative emotions than among Caucasian American students. For positive emotions, only Japanese and Hispanic Americans showed more variability than the Caucasians. Thus, consistent with earlier sections of this chapter, context is a more important element in the appraisal of emotion in collectivist cultures, just as it is in relation to cognition.

SUMMARY

Evolution has endowed us with a range of ways in which we can think about and experience the contexts in which life positions us. These contexts may encourage use to think analytically or holistically, to prioritise different motives, and to experience different emotions to greater or lesser degrees. The contrasts in these basic processes around the world are contrasts in relative emphasis, not absolute differences. However, many of the studies that we have reviewed compare data from just two or three samples. This restricts the possibility of knowing why effects are obtained, because as we saw in Chapter 4, nations differ from one another in numerous ways. We need more direct tests of the processes that mediate these contrasts than has been provided by these studies, and some examples of such tests are explored in the next two chapters.

FURTHER READING

1 Altarriba, J., Basnight, D., & Canary, T. (2003), Emotion representation and perception across cultures. *Online Readings In Psychology and Culture.* Available at http://scholarworks.gvsu.edu/orpc
2 Hofer, J., & Chasiotis, A. (2011). Implicit motives across cultures. *Online Readings in Psychology and Culture.* Available at http://scholarworks.gvsu.edu/orpc
3 King, R.B., & McInerney, D. M. (2012). Including social goals in achievement motivation research: Examples from the Philippines. *Online Readings in Psychology and Culture.* Available at http://scholarworks.gvsu.edu/orpc
4 Nisbett, R.E., Peng, K.P., Choi, I., & Norenzayan, A. (2000). Culture and systems of thought: Holistic versus analytic cognition. *Psychological Review*, *108*, 291–310.

STUDY QUESTIONS

1 Describe the contrast between analytic and holistic thinking. Are these cognitive processes antagonistic or complementary? Are your own cognitive processes predominantly analytic or holistic? Is this similar to the processes of those you mostly spend time with?
2 How would you react if you were asked to look at cultural icons representing your nation? Or those of another nation? What impact would these exposures have upon your 'cultural mindset', momentarily or for a longer time?
3 What cultural differences do you think might be detected in cognition, motivation, or emotion, if other regions of the world were studied as intensively as North America and Pacific Asia have been?
4 What are the strengths and weaknesses of using photographs and diaries to study culture-general and culture-specific aspects of emotion?
5 In what ways are motivations culture-general or culture-specific?
6 Think about a recent situation when you experienced anger, joy or fear. Who was present in this situation and how did you display your reaction? Do you think the presence of others and who they were made a difference for your emotional display? To what extent is it useful to study the effects of others on emotional expressiveness?

7

Self and Identity Processes

'Ubuntu ungamuntu ngabanye abantu'

(People are people through other people)
Xhosa traditional saying

In Chapter 6, we reviewed the evidence for cultural differences in a variety of individual psychological processes, including many aspects of cognition, emotion, and motivation. We have seen that many studies are now available in which researchers have compared samples of individuals from two or more nations and reported the mean differences on some measure. But how can we explain the differences that are found? Frequently, cross-cultural researchers have focused their explanations for observed cultural differences on Hofstede's (1980) dimension of individualism-collectivism. But as we discussed in Chapter 4, we cannot simply assume the validity of such explanations without testing them: unpackaging studies are needed (Brockner, 2003; Bond & Van de Vijver, 2011).

Closely related to individualism-collectivism is Markus and Kitayama's (1991, 2003, 2010) distinction between independent and interdependent self-construals, and we shall devote much attention to their theoretical perspective within this chapter. Thus, our main focus in this chapter is on the contents and processes of personal identity. Although we touch briefly on group identities here, our main coverage of group identities, including the social identity perspective, is in Chapters 12 and 13. Markus and Kitayama's perspective has sometimes been associated with a relativist view of psychological functioning, whereby individual psychological processes are seen as bounded within particular cultural systems. However, in recent years, theorists have begun to propose that self and identity processes follow some universal underlying principles, which play out differently according to the peculiarities of different cultural contexts (e.g., Vignoles, Chryssochoou & Breakwell, 2000; Sedikides, Gaertner & Toguchi, 2003).

INDIVIDUALISM-COLLECTIVISM

We have seen that the literature of cross-cultural psychology includes a large number of studies comparing the responses of participants (usually university students) from pairs of nations, of which one nation is typically in North America or Western Europe and the other is most commonly in East Asia. The observed differences are then typically attributed to the researchers' portrayal of one nation as an 'individualist culture' and the other nation as a 'collectivist culture'. Sometimes these portrayals are based on Hofstede's (1980) ranking of nations for individualism-collectivism, but often they are assumptions based on geographical location alone, such as 'Western' versus 'Eastern' (or 'non-Western'). Some researchers have used individual-level measures of cultural orientation to unpackage the observed cultural differences, testing whether the participants they have sampled differed as expected on the cultural dimension of interest, as well as whether individual differences in cultural orientation accounted for the observed differences in outcomes of interest (e.g., Hui, Triandis & Yee, 1991; Matsumoto, Consolacion, Yamada et al., 2002).

Following the publication of Hofstede's (1980) research, Triandis, Leung, Villareal and Clack (1985) were among the first to develop individual-level measures related to individualism-collectivism. They used items developed in the USA by Hui (1988), describing aspects of one's relations with different groups (the 'INDCOL' scale). In order to reduce confusion between different levels of analysis, they named their individual-level measures as idiocentric (individualistic) and allocentric (collectivistic). Unfortunately, this helpful terminology has not been adopted by others, so that the terms 'individualism' and 'collectivism' are often used to refer both to individual-level concepts and nation-level concepts, confusing many as a result.

The INDCOL scale was subsequently modified to reflect not only the cultural contrast between individualism and collectivism, but also the contrast between high and low power distance (Singelis, Triandis, Bhawuk, & Gelfand, 1995). Separate scales were provided tapping individuals' preference for horizontal collectivism (collectivism + low power distance), vertical collectivism (collectivism + high power distance), horizontal individualism (individualism + low power distance) and vertical individualism (individualism + high power distance).

Since this pioneering work, a huge and bewildering variety of measures has been produced, purporting to measure individual differences in individualism-collectivism, as well as the closely related constructs of independent and interdependent self-construals, which we discuss shortly. Oyserman, Coon and Kemmelmeier (2002) undertook a series of meta-analyses of studies that had used any one of 27 such measures: they investigated whether scores differed between the USA and elsewhere, whether scores differed between different ethnic communities in the United States, and whether scores were found to predict variations in other dependent variables.

Key Researcher Box 7.1   Daphna Oyserman

Figure 7.1   Daphna Oyserman

Daphna Oyserman (b. 1960) completed her first degree in social work at the Hebrew University of Jerusalem, and then received her PhD in Psychology and Social Work from the University of Michigan in 1987. She subsequently held teaching and research positions at Wayne State University and at the Hebrew University of Jerusalem. Since 2004, she has been Edwin Thomas Professor of Social Work and Research Professor of Psychology at Michigan. Her research into culture and self-concept has emphasised situational influences on cognition and she has used priming studies extensively.

Oyserman and colleagues' (2002) comparisons of effect sizes for different nations yielded some startling conclusions. While representatives of some nations scored higher than the Americans on both individualism and collectivism, others scored lower on both. Egyptians scored lowest on both individualism and collectivism, and Peruvians scored highest on both. Convergence with Hofstede's nation scores was minimal. Oyserman and colleagues' paper was published in *Psychological Bulletin* with a series of accompanying commentaries, most of which suggested either that Hofstede's characterisation of nations was outdated or else that other, quite different approaches to cross-cultural study would now be more fruitful. However, if you have read closely the methodological precepts advanced in earlier chapters of this book, a study of Oyserman and colleagues' paper will reveal two weaknesses, both of which undermine the conclusions that they drew.

Firstly, Oyserman et al. (2002) did not consider the potential confounding influence of cultural differences in acquiescent response style. Since these differences are known to be substantial across national groups (Smith, 2004a; see also Chapter 2), it is advisable to use adjusted measures so as to account for this. Schimmack, Oishi and Diener (2005) utilised data from a 40-nation student survey to question this aspect of Oyserman and colleagues' conclusions. They showed that their nation scores, uncorrected for response style, correlated positively with those derived by Oyserman et al. Furthermore, their estimate of response style correlated strongly with Oyserman and colleagues' effect sizes for both individualism and collectivism. However, when Schimmack et al. adjusted their scores for response style, their individualism scores correlated substantially with nation scores from Hofstede (1980).

The second weakness in Oyserman and colleagues' (2002) meta-analysis is perhaps harder to grasp, but nevertheless important. The effect sizes that they calculated for nations were based on measuring individualism and collectivism as properties of individuals, which they then aggregated to the nation level. This contrasts with Hofstede's (1980) original portrayal of this dimension as capturing properties of national cultures, and not of individuals. As we discussed in Chapter 2, the ways in which variables relate to one another at different levels of analysis are not necessarily the same, and thus individual-level and nation-level analyses of the same data can often yield strikingly different conclusions.

To understand why this matters, we need to look more closely at how the contrast between individualist and collectivist cultures has been defined theoretically. Although Hofstede (1980) originally described individualism as a dimension of cultural values (see Chapter 2), subsequent research suggests a more complex and multifaceted definition. For example, Triandis (1993, 1995; see Key Researcher Box 1.2), one of the foremost researchers on individualism and collectivism, defined these two broad constructs as 'cultural syndromes':

> Cultural syndromes … reflect shared attitudes, beliefs, categorizations, norms, roles, and values organized around a central theme, that are found among individuals who speak a particular language, and live in a specific geographic region, during a specific historical period. (Triandis, Chan, Bhawuk, Iwao, & Sinha, 1995: 462)

Clearly, this broadens the definition of individualism-collectivism well beyond just a value dimension. In fact, it leads to a very specific theoretical prediction: that the attitudes, beliefs, categorisations, norms, roles, and values that make up these syndromes will tend to correlate with each other *at a cultural level of analysis*. However, this does not mean that the same attributes will necessarily go together at an individual level of analysis *within* each culture.

Owe, Vignoles et al. (2012) tested this reasoning by measuring three proposed facets of individualism-collectivism among high-school students in 19 nations: autonomy *vs.* embeddedness values (discussed in Chapter 2); decontextualised *vs.* contextualised beliefs about personhood (discussed in Chapter 6); and independent *vs.* interdependent self-construals (discussed later in this chapter). In nation-level analyses, these three variables were reliably correlated with each other, although not so strongly as to suggest that they were interchangeable ($r = .44$ to $.49$). However, correlations among the corresponding individual-level measures were very small ($r = -.01$ to $.21$), indicating that these variables did not form a coherent 'syndrome' at the individual level. Thus, especially at the individual level (and arguably also at the national level) it seems that the dimension of individualism-collectivism itself needs to be unpacked into its constituent parts. As Bond (2002) proposed in his commentary on Oyserman et al. (2002), in order for cross-cultural psychology to progress further, researchers must develop cross-culturally equivalent measures of individual variation in the many aspects of collectivism and individualism, and then link these measures to the outcomes whose variation across cultural groups we want to explain.

INDEPENDENT AND INTERDEPENDENT SELF-CONSTRUALS

In 1991, Hazel Markus, a British-born American social psychologist, and Shinobu Kitayama, a Japanese social psychologist working in the United States, published a theoretical article in *Psychological Review* that has come to define the way in which social psychologists have thought about cultural differences over the last 20 years. Drawing partly on their own different cultural origins, and reviewing a wide range of prior evidence and theories from anthropology as well as cross-cultural psychology, they introduced a theoretical distinction between **independent and interdependent self-construals**.

Key Researcher Box 7.2   Hazel Markus

Figure 7.2   Hazel Markus

Hazel R. Markus (b. 1949) was born in London, but grew up in California. In 1975, she received her PhD in social psychology from the University of Michigan, and later became one of the university's faculty members. During her time at Michigan she was a research scientist at the Institute for Social Research. In 1994, she was appointed Davis-Brack Professor of Behavioural Science at Stanford University, where she is co-director of the Stanford Research Centre for Comparative Studies in Race and Ethnicity. She has pioneered research into the self-concept and its consequences, both within and between cultures. With Shinobu Kitayama, she co-authored the influential 1991 paper on culture and the self. Overall, her publications have been cited more than 36,000 times.

Key Researcher Box 7.3   Shinobu Kitayama

Figure 7.3   Shinobu Kitayama

Shinobu Kitayama (b. 1957) grew up in Japan and received his Bachelor's and Master's degrees from the University of Kyoto. Interested in why psychology textbooks had no references to work by authors with Japanese names, he obtained funding that enabled him to complete his PhD in social psychology from the University of Michigan in 1987. While holding his first teaching appointment, which was at the University of Oregon, he collaborated with Hazel Markus in publishing their landmark paper on culture and the self-concept. More recently he taught at the Universities of Chicago and Kyoto and then returned to the University of Michigan in 2003, where he is now Professor of Psychology and the Director of the Culture and Cognition Programme. He has published many papers concerning cultural variations in cognition, emotion and motivation, and is co-editor of the *Handbook of Cultural Psychology*. He is currently studying cultural aspects of neuroscience.

Self-Construal Markus and Kitayama (1991) introduced this term to refer to what they later described as diverse 'modes of being' across cultures. The term was intended to encompass culture-level representations of 'self' as an abstract category and the social orientations linked to them (see Markus & Kitayama, 2003). Other researchers have mostly understood the term to refer to the self-concepts of individuals.

Independent Self-Construal The representation of the self as separate from the social context, bounded, unitary, and stable.

Interdependent Self-Construal The representation of the self as closely connected to others, embedded in, and varying across, contexts.

According to Markus and Kitayama (1991), an independent self-construal involves viewing the self as separate from the social context, bounded, unitary, and stable. Hence, a person with an independent self-construal will strive for self-expression, uniqueness and self-actualisation, acting autonomously based on his/her own thoughts and feelings, and pursuing his/her own goals. On the other hand, an interdependent self-construal involves viewing the self as closely connected to the social context and therefore flexible, fluid, and varying across contexts. Hence, a person with an interdependent self-construal will strive to fit in and maintain harmony with relevant others, basing their actions on expectations and social norms, rather than personal wishes and preferences.

Markus and Kitayama's (1991) central claim was that contemporary Western cultures are unusual in promoting an independent self-construal. In contrast, they suggested that an interdependent self-construal is more characteristic of human societies in most other parts of the world, as well as in previous historical periods: this self-construal was 'exemplified in Japanese culture as well as in other Asian cultures' (1991: 225). Notably, they did not explicitly link their constructs to individualism and collectivism. Nevertheless, their selection of North American and Japanese cultures as contrasting exemplars has resonated with a common tendency to think of the USA as the prototypical individualist nation and Japan as the prototypical collectivist nation. As we have seen in Chapter 2, data indicate that this characterisation is somewhat inaccurate. For example, Figure 2.5 suggests that US and Japanese cultures actually have quite similar value priorities: both nations emphasise autonomy over embeddedness, to a lesser extent than many European and English-speaking nations but more so than most other nations in Schwartz's survey.

Moreover, Markus and Kitayama (1991) predicted that these different ways of construing the self would have markedly different consequences for cognition, emotion, and motivation. Thus, they argued, understanding which form of self-construal is emphasised in different nations or geographical regions would provide the key to explaining cultural differences in cognition, emotion, and motivation, such as those we have reviewed in Chapter 6. As a result, Markus and Kitayama (1991) appeared to be claiming (although they did not spell this out explicitly) that cultural influences on cognition, emotion, and motivation would be mediated by independent and interdependent self-construals (see Figure 7.4).

Based on this reasoning, researchers began to create measures of self-construals for use in studies designed to unpackage cultural differences (e.g., Singelis, 1994; Gudykunst et al., 1996). We review some of this research shortly. Nevertheless, we should note at the outset that Markus and Kitayama expressed reservations in their original article about the possibility of measuring self-construals directly, and indeed they have never published their own measure of self-construals. In fact, both the empirical evidence reviewed in their original paper and most of their subsequent research in this area have been focused on documenting national (or

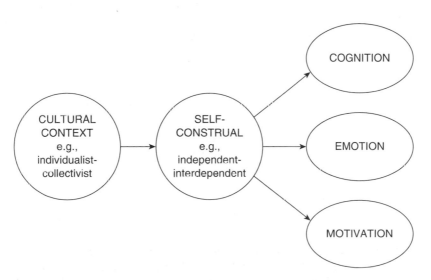

Figure 7.4   Self-construals as mediators of cultural differences (adapted from Matsumoto, 1999)

sometimes within-nation) differences in the *consequences* of self-construals that they have the-orised, rather than testing their implied mediation model (for a critique, see Matsumoto, 1999). We shall return to this key point shortly, but first we should examine some of the ways in which researchers other than Markus and Kitayama have attempted to measure cross-cultural differ-ences in people's self-views.

Measuring Independent and Interdependent Self-Construals

Direct attempts to measure cross-cultural differences in self-conceptions fall mostly into two groups: (1) content analyses of open-ended self-descriptions, and (2) Likert-type measures. In an attempt to produce measures that were emic rather than imposed-etic, several research-ers have asked participants to describe themselves using the open-ended 'Twenty Statements Test' (TST), first devised by Kuhn and McPartland (1954; see Research Instrument Box 7.1). In this task, participants provide up to 20 answers to the question 'Who am I?' as quickly as pos-sible and without thinking about the logic or importance of their responses (e.g., Bond & Cheung, 1983; Triandis et al., 1990; Bochner, 1994). Based on theorising about individualism-collectivism or about independent and interdependent self-construal, researchers have devised various coding schemes for content analysing responses to this task, with the broad prediction that members of individualist cultures would describe themselves more frequently in terms of individual characteristics such as traits and abilities, whereas members of collectivist cultures would provide a higher proportion of references to their social relationships, roles, and group memberships.

Research Instrument Box 7.1   Twenty Statements Test

There are twenty numbered blanks on the page below. Please write twenty answers to the simple question 'Who am I?' in the blanks. Just give twenty different answers to this question. Answer as if you were giving the answers to yourself, not to somebody else. Write the answers in the order that they occur to you. Don't worry about logic or 'importance'. Go along fairly fast, for time is limited.

1
2
3
[...]
19
20

Source: Kuhn & McPartland (1954)

Initial results were encouraging: in several studies, US respondents showed a greater frequency of trait-like self-descriptions, whereas East Asians referred somewhat more frequently to social roles and categories (e.g., Triandis et al., 1990; Trafimow, Triandis & Goto, 1991; Bochner, 1994), although trait-like responses were the most common responses among participants from both regions. However, as later studies began to include participants in a wider range of locations, it became clear that there was no simple correspondence between national levels of individualism-collectivism and the frequencies of different types of TST responses (Watkins et al., 1998; Del Prado, Church, Katigbak et al., 2007). So how can we explain this?

One possible explanation is methodological. Smith (2011b) argues that the TST is not nearly as emic as researchers had hoped. Far from providing a culture-free space in which participants can describe themselves freely, he suggests that the usual wording of the TST measure primes an individualised, decontextualised and introspective 'self' that may be much closer to Western than to other cultural conceptions of selfhood (see also Cousins, 1989; Kanagawa, Cross, & Markus, 2001). Moreover, the ambiguity of the question, as well as the request to write down the first thoughts that come to mind, may make this measure especially sensitive to minor contextual influences. This may be useful when researchers are interested in experimentally priming different kinds of self-content (e.g., Trafimow et al., 1991) as we discuss later in this chapter, but it could also inadvertently confound cross-cultural comparisons when participants in different parts of the world are tested by different researchers in settings that are not perfectly matched.

Although some of these problems can be reduced by a culturally sensitive rewording of the TST instructions (e.g., Becker, Vignoles et al., 2012), a further difficulty lies in the ambiguity of coding responses. Different coding schemes have been used in different TST studies. Researchers have also made differing predictions about exactly which kinds of response should be more prevalent in individualist or collectivist cultures (c.f. Trafimow et al., 1991; Bochner, 1994; Watkins et al., 1998; Parkes, Schneider & Bochner, 1999). Even within a single study, fitting participants' responses into predefined categories can be a difficult and rather subjective task, and it is relatively easy to be swayed by the linguistic properties of the responses rather than their substantive meaning (for example, one might code 'I love nature' as a personal characteristic but 'I am a nature-lover' as a category membership). Moreover, any such coding scheme may fail to capture what the responses mean to the participants themselves. For example, Brewer (2001) discusses her identity as a 'mother' as simultaneously carrying personal, relational, group, and collective meanings. Add to this that often either the participants or the coders will be working in a second language, or the responses will have been translated, and it is easy to see how biases can arise when trying to compare the frequencies of different types of responses!

A further question regarding the TST method is whether the *frequency* of different kinds of self-content is the most appropriate way to measure cultural differences in self-construal. Indeed, despite having pioneered the cross-cultural comparison of TST-based frequency scores, Triandis (1995) has noted that members of collectivist cultures tend to have relatively *few* in-groups, but that these are typically highly stable and thus influential. In contrast, members of individualist cultures often belong to a variety of different in-groups, in which their membership may be more transient and less personally involving. This suggests that it may not be the *number* of traits versus relationships and group memberships in one's self-concept that best differentiates members of individualist and collectivist cultures, It may be more productive to examine *which* relationships and groups people find most important and self-involving and, perhaps even more importantly, *how* people define the relationships and groups that they occupy and their implications for the self.

Based in part on these considerations, an increasingly popular approach has been to focus on structured measures of self-construal rather than the open-ended TST measures. Both Singelis (1994) and Gudykunst et al. (1996) created scales for independent and interdependent self-construal, designed specifically to measure the features described by Markus and Kitayama (1991). These measures have been used in many recent cross-cultural studies. The Singelis items include some that are descriptive of oneself and some that are closer to attitude statements. Gudykunst et al. attempted to create scales in which all items were self-descriptive, but some attitude items remain. The Gudykunst et al. scales are reproduced as Research Instrument Box 7.2.

Research Instrument Box 7.2   How do I See Myself?

Independent self-construal	*Interdependent self-construal*
I should be judged on my own merit	I consult with others before making important decisions
Being able to take care of myself is a primary concern for me	I consult with co-workers on work-related matters
My personal identity is very important to me	I will sacrifice my self-interest for the benefit of my group
I prefer to be self-reliant rather than to depend on others	I stick with my group even through difficulties
I am a unique person separate from others	I respect decisions made by my group
If there is a conflict between my values and the values of groups of which I am a member, I follow my values	I will stay in a group if they need me, even when I am not happy with the group
I try not to depend on others	I maintain harmony in the groups of which I am a member
I take responsibility for my own actions	I respect the majority's wishes in groups of which I am a member
It is important for me to act as an independent person	I remain in the groups of which I am a member if they need me, even though I am dissatisfied with them
I should decide my future on my own	I try to abide by customs and conventions at work
What happens to me is my own doing	I give special consideration to others' personal situations so I can be efficient at work
I enjoy being unique and different from others	It is better to consult with others and get their opinions before doing anything
I am comfortable being singled out for praise and rewards	It is important to consult close friends and get their ideas before making a decision
I don't support a group decision when it is wrong	My relationships with others are more important than my accomplishments

Source: W.B. Gudykunst & C.M. Lee, 'Assessing the validity of self-construal scales: A response to Levine et al.', *Human Communication Research* (2003). Reprinted by permission of John Wiley and Sons.

Both Singelis (1994) and Gudykunst et al. (1996) created separate subscales for independent and interdependent self-construal in their measures. In most studies, these two subscales appear uncorrelated at the individual level: in other words, individuals may score higher on independence and lower on interdependence, higher on interdependence and lower on independence, higher on both dimensions, or lower on both dimensions. However, in both measures, all of the items are phrased in a positive direction, making it hard to disentangle the substantive constructs from acquiescent response style. If an individual scores high (or low) on both independent and interdependent self-construals, is she *really* high (or low) on both dimensions, or is she simply high (or low) on acquiescent responding?

We should also note that many of the items in the Singelis (1994) and Gudykunst et al. (1996) scales overlap quite closely with measures of individualism and collectivism. This has led some researchers to suggest using the terms 'independence' and 'interdependence' as labels for individual differences in cultural orientation towards individualism and collectivism (e.g., Smith, 2011b). Not all theorists would agree with this labeling. Nonetheless, the similarity of items means that individualism-collectivism scales have sometimes been used to measure self-construals, and vice versa (Oyserman et al., 2002).

Unpackaging Cultural Differences with Self-Construal Measures

Despite these limitations and ambiguities, researchers have sometimes succeeded in using self-construal scales to unpackage cross-cultural differences in some of the outcomes theorised by Markus and Kitayama (1991). For example, Singelis, Bond, Sharkey, and Lai (1999) sought to explain cross-cultural differences in embarrassability. They compared self-reported levels of embarrassability among students from three cultural groups: Caucasian Americans on the US mainland, Asian Americans in Hawaii, and Hong Kong Chinese. On average, the Caucasian Americans reported significantly less embarrassment than members of the other two groups, and they averaged significantly higher on independent self-construal and lower on interdependent self-construal. At the individual level, those scoring higher on independent self-construal tended to report lower embarrassment, whereas those scoring higher on interdependent self-construal tended to report higher embarrassment. Finally, after accounting for the individual-level effects of independent and interdependent self-construals, cultural group membership predicted little more variance in embarrassability. Singelis and colleagues concluded that this pattern of results is consistent with viewing self-construals as mediating the influence of culture on embarrassability (for further details of this study, see Chapter 9).

These findings provided direct evidence for Markus and Kitayama's (1991) claim that differences in independent and interdependent self-construal could be used to explain cultural differences in emotion (see also Singelis & Sharkey, 1995). Studies have provided similar evidence for the theorised role of independent and interdependent self-construals in explaining ethnic and national differences in cognition and motivation.

Regarding differences in cognition, Singelis (1994) reported that individual differences in interdependent self-construal accounted for ethnic differences between Caucasian and Asian American students in the correspondence bias (see Chapter 6). Recent studies have extended the use of self-construal scores to explain ethnic differences in neuropsychological measures of cognition. Lewis, Goto and Kong (2008) showed that interdependent self-construal (measured using a 'collectivism' scale) accounted for differences between East Asian American and Caucasian American students in neural indicators of attention to context when processing visual stimuli. Na and Kitayama (2011) showed that independent versus interdependent self-construal (measured using the Singelis scale) partially mediated differences between Asian American and Caucasian American students in neural indicators of spontaneous trait inferences.

Regarding differences in motivation, Lam and Zane (2004) found that Caucasian Americans were more likely to use primary control strategies, whereas Asian Americans were more likely to use secondary control strategies (see Chapter 6), when coping with stressful events: they reported that ethnic differences in primary control were fully mediated by individual differences in independent self-construal, whereas differences in secondary control were fully mediated by individual differences in interdependent self-construal. Zhang and Mittal (2007) asked Chinese and American students to evaluate the attractiveness of two different vacation spots based on their ratings in a fictitious consumer survey. On average, American participants preferred an 'enriched option' (portrayed as excellent on some rated attributes and poor on others), whereas Chinese participants preferred an 'impoverished option' (portrayed as moderate across all rated attributes), and these differences were fully mediated by the relative proportion of interdependent to independent responses on a TST measure. In Chapter 9, we describe several further studies in which measures of independent and interdependent self-construals have been used to unpackage national differences in actual and desired closeness of relationships (Uskul, Hynie & Lalonde, 2004), and in communication styles (Kim et al., 1996; Sanchez-Burks et al., 2003).

Surprisingly, however, most published studies using measures of independent and interdependent self-construal have not reported mediation tests (for a review, see Cross, Hardin, & Gercek-Swing, 2011). Unfortunately, we cannot be sure in how many of these studies no mediation test was conducted and in how many studies the researchers may have chosen not to report a mediation test because the model was not supported. Nonetheless, considering that Markus and Kitayama's original (1991) paper has been cited in more than 9,000 published articles over the last 20 years, it is striking how few of these publications have reported successful mediation tests.

Why Doesn't the Mediation Model Work Better?

Because of the relative dearth of published mediation tests, reviews of the self-construal literature have usually treated the two steps of the mediation model in Figure 7.4 as separate questions: (1) 'Do independent and interdependent self-construals differ across national and ethnic samples in the expected direction?'; and (2) 'Are individual differences in independent and interdependent self-construal associated with cognitive, emotional and motivational outcomes in the expected manner?' Reviews have mostly answered the second question positively, but not the first one (Gudykunst & Lee, 2003; Levine, Bresnahan, Park et al., 2003; Cross et al., 2011).

Numerous studies (reviewed by Gudykunst & Lee, 2003; Cross et al., 2011) have shown that individuals' scores on measures of independent and interdependent self-construals show predicted correlations with a wide range of social and psychological variables, including context sensitivity in cognition (Newman, 1993), social anxiety (Okazaki, 1997), self-regulatory focus on promotion or prevention (Lee, Aaker, & Gardner, 2000), self-control (Seeley & Gardner, 2003), personal space (Holland, Roeder, van Baaren, et al., 2004), leadership styles (Hackman, Ellis, Johnson, & Staley, 1999), approaches to conflict resolution (Oetzel, Ting-Toomey, et al., 2001), and preferred communication styles (Gudykunst et al., 1996).

Studies using experimental primes of independence and interdependence (discussed later in this chapter) have often supported viewing these outcomes as causal outcomes of differences in self-construal. Moreover, a growing body of studies has begun to identify neurological correlates of individual differences in self-construals (e.g., Chiao et al., 2009; Goto et al., 2010; Ray et al., 2010; Na & Kitayama, 2011). In a recent review, Kitayama and Uskul (2011) noted that self-construal scales tend to correlate with neurological indicators of self-representation, person perception, attention and self-investment in choices *better* than they predict behavioural measures of the same outcomes.

In contrast, studies have provided much weaker evidence for the expected national differences in measures of independent and interdependent self-construal. Levine, Bresnahan, Park, et al. (2003) meta-analysed the results of eight studies comparing independent and interdependent self-construal scores of participants from 'Western' (the USA, Canada, Australia) and 'Asian' (Japan, Korea, Hong Kong, Taiwan, Mainland China) locations. Results weakly supported the prediction that Western participants would score higher than Asian participants in independent self-construal, but the differences were small (with national membership predicting on average just 4.2% of the variance in independent self-construal) and highly inconsistent across studies. Moreover, they found no support for the prediction that Asian participants would score higher than Western participants in interdependent self-construal: again the results varied greatly across studies, and some studies even showed significant effects in the wrong direction. Furthermore, many studies that were not included in this meta-analysis because they used different measures or focused on other parts of the world have also failed to show the expected pattern of differences (Matsumoto, 1999).

So how should we understand these unexpected findings? Of course, one possibility is that the theory is wrong, and self-construals in North America and East Asia do not differ in the ways that were thought (Matsumoto, 1999; see also Spiro, 1993; Holland & Kipnis, 1994; Lindholm, 1997). Nevertheless, a second possibility is that the studies reviewed above have not tested the theory adequately. In the following sections, we consider a number of reasons why this might be the case, as well as some ways that Markus and Kitayama have sought recently to clarify, and in some cases revise, the details of their perspective (e.g., Markus & Kitayama, 2003, 2010; Kitayama, Park, Sevincer, Karasawer, & Uskul, 2009).

Acquiescent response style

As we noted earlier, neither of the self-construal scales that have been most commonly used includes any reversed items, meaning that the scores will be confounded with acquiescent response style. This is a particular problem for comparing means across cultures, because people from different nations are known to show different levels of acquiescence (Smith, 2004a). Moreover, self-construal researchers have very rarely adjusted their measures for acquiescence.

Levine et al. (2003) did not consider acquiescent responding in their meta-analysis, so how might this have affected their results? Given that members of collectivist cultures often show more acquiescence (Smith, 2004a), we can speculate that acquiescent responding might have inflated the scores for both dimensions in the East Asian samples, compared to the 'Western' samples. This could make the measured differences in independent self-construal appear smaller than the true, underlying differences, because the scale content and the response style would be working at cross-purposes. On the other hand, this would not explain the failure to find the expected difference in interdependent self-construal. If anything, it suggests that the underlying differences may be even further from the expected pattern than Levine and colleagues' results already suggested.

Inadequate sampling

An important limitation of the research reviewed above is that the vast majority of studies focus either upon ethnic differences within the United States or upon contrasts between North America (in most cases, the USA) and Pacific Asia (in most cases, Japan). The reasons for this limited focus are not hard to find. They include the growing affluence of the 'Asian tiger' nations, migration in both directions of key researchers between Pacific Asia and North America, and journal editors' preference for papers reporting clear and significant contrasts between samples that are stereotypically regarded as different. We know that both Japan and the USA are relatively distinctive and unusual nations, in terms of how they score on many of the cultural dimensions explored in Chapter 2. In comparing them, we do not exhaust the range of global variations in values or in self-construal. Neither do we test fully the difference between individualism and collectivism. Indeed, despite being widely regarded by social psychologists as the prototypical collectivist nation, and having been the model for Markus and Kitayama's description of interdependent self-construals, Japan actually scored just above the median on Hofstede's (1980) original individualism dimension, which was based on data collected in the late 1960s, and there are good reasons to believe that the Japanese have become more individualistic in the intervening decades.

Moreover, most studies have been conducted with university students. University students are unrepresentative of most nations because of their youth and their relative affluence. We noted in Chapter 4 that they are more unrepresentative of some nations than others. Affluent young people may hold especially divergent cultural orientations from the mainstream in nations that are experiencing rapid economic or cultural change (Jensen, Arnett, & McKenzie, 2011). Markus and Kitayama (1991) explicitly stated that they expected self-construals to differ within as well as between nations (see also Snibbe & Markus, 2005). Thus, finding that Japanese university students are not more interdependent than American university students does not necessarily contradict their theory. To have derived such a prediction in the first place may simply be an example of the ecological fallacy of assuming that national differences necessarily apply to all individuals within those nations (Gudykunst & Lee, 2003). To test the prediction of national differences in self-construal, it would be better to use more representative, or more typical, samples of the nations in question, such as those provided by the World Values Survey.

Self-construal scores as ideological positions

The fact that East Asian university students often report construing themselves quite similarly to North American students might be understood in part as an attempt to signal their membership of a 'new generation' that does not share the traditional orientation of previous generations, rather than measuring their levels of independence or interdependence *per se*. There is evidence that scores on self-construal scales are linked to social identification. Jetten, Postmes and McAuliffe (2002) found that US students who identified more strongly with their nation scored *higher* on an individualism measure (reflecting independent self-construal), whereas Indonesian students who identified more strongly with their nation scored lower on the same measure. Thus, in the context of the individualist culture of the USA, those who described themselves as more independent were actually conforming with the cultural norms of their nation. Moreover, Salvatore and Prentice (2011) found in a study of US students that, when their mental resources were depleted by doing another task, those who scored higher on independent self-construal were *more* likely to change their attitudes to match a majority opinion, a finding that they termed the *ironic conformity effect*. We can make sense of these findings if we consider that, when people respond to self-construal scales not only are they reporting on their self-perceptions of independence and interdependence but they are also implicitly positioning themselves in relation to perceived cultural norms. In Chapters 2 and 5, we touched on a similar point when discussing the critique of data derived from rating scales by Heine et al. (2002).

One response to the complex meaning of explicit self-construal scales is to turn to implicit measures of self-representation. Zhu, Zhang, Fan et al. (2007) conducted a study using fMRI scanning to compare neural representations of the self, one's mother, and a well-known political figure, among Chinese and Western college students in China. In both samples, they found greater activation of the medial prefrontal cortex (MPFC) when participants were judging the applicability of trait adjectives to the self than when they were judging their applicability to the politician. However, significant differences emerged when participants were focusing on their mothers. Western participants showed significantly less MPFC activity when focusing on their mother than when focusing on themselves: in fact, the activation pattern for their mothers was quite similar, although not identical, to that for the politician. In contrast, the Chinese participants showed significantly more MPFC activity when focusing on their mothers than on the politician: in fact, they showed no less MPFC activity when focusing on their mothers than when focusing on themselves. These results suggest that neural representations of self and mother were much more closely linked (suggesting a more interdependent self-construal) for Chinese participants than for Westerners, although it is possible that the results could also have been influenced by the Westerners' greater physical distance from their mothers since they were studying abroad.

Finer Specification of Self-Construal Dimensions

A further possibility is that the constructs of 'independence' and 'interdependence' are too broad and diffuse to capture the important ways in which self-construals differ across particular cultural groups. Reported reliabilities of the Singelis (1994) scales are typically rather lower than the accepted level of 0.70. Scale structures vary between samples and between groups from different nations, and have been found to be more complex than the two-dimensional structure originally proposed (Hardin, Leong & Bhagwat, 2004; Fernández, Paez & González, 2005; Christopher, Norris, D'Souza & Tiernan, 2012). Thus, more work is required to determine the dimensions along which individual-level self-construals vary, and to instrument these dimensions accordingly.

Western theorists of identity have proposed that at different times people may think of themselves as an individual self, a relational self, or a collective self (Brewer & Gardner, 1996; Sedikides & Brewer, 2001). Based on this thinking, an increasing trend has been to divide the construct of interdependent self-construal into 'relational' and 'collective' facets, resulting in a three-dimensional model of individual (≈ independent), relational, and collective self-construals (e.g., Kashima & Hardie, 2000; Cross et al., 2011).

A *relational-interdependent* self-construal involves defining oneself in terms of interpersonal bonds or attachments to specific others, such as family members or a romantic partner. A *collective-interdependent* self-construal involves seeing oneself as part of a larger entity and does not necessarily entail personal bonds with members of that entity, similar to the concept of social identity in Western social psychology (see Chapter 12). Thus, it is argued that cross-cultural researchers may have confounded aspects of relational and collective self-construal within measures of interdependence. For instance, among the items in Research Instrument Box 7.2, 'I stick with my group even through difficulties' could refer to the group as a collective identity, whereas 'It is important to consult close friends and get their ideas before making a decision' seems more relational.

Several measures are now available that distinguish relational and collective forms of interdependent self-construal (e.g., Gabriel & Gardner, 1999; Cross, Bacon, & Morris, 2000; Kashima & Hardie, 2000; Harb & Smith, 2008). However, the conclusions that have been drawn so far using these dimensions have been rather contradictory. Some researchers have concluded that national groups differ on collective interdependence, whereas gender groups differ on relational interdependence (e.g., Kashima, Yamaguchi, Kim, Choi, Gelfand, & Yuki, 1995; Cross & Madson, 1997). In direct contrast, others have argued that observed differences in collectivism between Western and East Asian nations are best viewed as differences in relational collectivism (e.g., Kim, 1994; Brewer & Chen, 2007; Brewer & Yuki, 2007). Still others have concluded that women (in North America) are higher on relational interdependence, whereas men are higher on collective interdependence (Gabriel & Gardner, 1999).

One reason for these contradictory findings may be the ambiguity of distinguishing between a 'relationship' and a 'collective'. This distinction has been understood in varying ways by different researchers, and it may also be understood differently by different research participants, as we noted earlier when discussing the TST. For example, Gabriel and Gardner (1999) treated 'relationships' as *connections to other individuals* and 'collectives' as *any form of group*. In contrast, Harb and Smith (2008) operationalised relational and collective self-construals in terms of people's perceived connection to *different kinds of groups*: relational groups were face-to-face groups such as family and friends, whereas collective groups were broader social categories of membership such as universities, political or religious groupings.

These approaches involve categorising the social world into different kinds of *targets* to which people may feel connected, even if the categories are defined differently. But another possibility is that this category-based approach may be overly influenced by the analytical mode of thinking typical of Western cultures (see Chapter 6). An alternative approach is to focus on different ways of construing the same (or comparable) targets. Illustrating this approach, Yuki (2003) studied differences in the predictors of identification and loyalty to small groups and to the nation among Japanese and US students. Among Japanese students, identification and loyalty were predicted by their knowledge of relationships in the group. Among US students, identification and loyalty to the same groups were predicted also by perceived group homogeneity. Thus the US respondents drew on both collective and relational criteria to define these groups, whereas the Japanese used only relational criteria (see Chapter 12 for a further discussion of Yuki's work). Perhaps what may matter more is not *which* 'others' (individuals or groups) one relates to most strongly, but *how* one relates to these 'others'. This suggests that it may be productive to focus on different ways of being independent or interdependent (see Markus & Kitayama, 2003).

An important theoretical step in this direction was provided by Kağıtçıbaşı (2005). She argued that measures of independence and interdependence typically combine together two quite different dimensions: interpersonal distance (relatedness-separateness) and agency (autonomy-heteronomy). Independence is seen as entailing both autonomy and separateness and interdependence as entailing both heteronomy (dependency) and relatedness. Therefore, self-construal theorists often appear to view autonomy as being opposed with relatedness, whereas in fact these constructs are perfectly compatible with each other, as we have shown in our discussion of the work of Ryan and Deci (2000) and others on self-determination in Chapter 6. Kağıtçıbaşı suggests that an autonomous-related self may be the prevailing mode of self-construal among the more affluent groups within collectivistic cultures.

In the most extensive research into self-construal dimensions to date, Owe, Vignoles et al. (2012) factor analysed data from two studies, involving high-school students from 16 nations and non-student adults from 64 cultural groups in 36 nations. Their first study included items from several previous measures, but crucially they also created many reverse-scored items, making it possible for the first time to explore and test alternative dimensional structures while controlling for acquiescent responding. They identified seven individual-level dimensions of self-construal.

Unlike previous research, instead of clustering together into separate, higher-order factors of independence and interdependence, each of the dimensions contrasted a particular facet of 'independence' with a particular facet of 'interdependence'. In line with Kağıtçıbaşı's predictions, they found that self-perceptions of autonomy and relatedness formed separate dimensions, which they named respectively *self-direction versus reception to influence* and *boundedness versus connectedness*. Further dimensions contrasted *uniqueness versus similarity, consistency versus variability, self-expression versus harmony, self-reliance versus dependence*, and *self-centeredness versus other-centeredness*.

Interestingly, in their study with adults, participants from several world regions tended to show distinct profiles of self-construal. Participants from most European nations tended to score highly on uniqueness and self-expression, but also on other-centeredness; participants from Middle Eastern nations tended to score highly on connectedness and similarity, but also on self-reliance; participants from nations in Sub-Saharan Africa tended to score highly on dependence and variability, but also on boundedness and self-centeredness. US participants scored highly on self-expression, uniqueness, consistency, self-reliance, and self-direction, whereas participants from most Asian nations tended to score relatively highly on harmony, reception to influence, and other-centeredness. However, the Japanese participants showed a very different profile from that of the other Asian samples: they scored especially highly on dependence, variability, and connectedness, but also relatively highly on self-direction and uniqueness.

The Owe et al. (2012) model has yet to be used in unpackaging studies. Nevertheless, previous research by Y. Chen and colleagues has shown the value of adopting a finer-grained approach to measuring self-construals when seeking to explain cultural differences in outcomes. Y. Chen, Brockner, and Katz (1998) showed that cultural differences in patterns of in-group favouritism were explained by a measure of 'individual versus collective primacy' (similar to Owe et al.'s dimension of self-centeredness versus other-centeredness), but not by more general measures of independent and interdependent self-construal (for more details of this study, see Chapter 12). Morrison, Chen and Salgado (2004) showed that a measure of 'self-assertiveness' (similar to Owe et al.'s dimension of self-expression versus harmony) mediated national differences between US and Hong Kong Chinese samples in feedback-seeking at work, whereas measures of two other facets of independence, 'self-reliance' and 'preference for working independently', did not.

FROM SELF TO CONTEXT: CULTURAL MANDATES, VALUES AND TASKS

Kitayama, Park, Sevincer, Karasawa, and Uskul (2009; see also Markus & Kitayama, 2010; Kitayama & Uskul, 2011) have recently proposed a radically different explanation from those discussed above for the failure to find expected national differences on explicit self-construal measures. They reported a study showing that members of four nations (Japan, Germany, the UK and USA) differed as predicted in their performance on five experimental tasks designed to measure psychological tendencies towards independence and interdependence, but not on the Singelis self-construal scale. Key Research Study Box 7.1 describes their methods and findings in more detail.

Key Research Study Box 7.1   Implicit Interdependence

Kitayama et al. (2009) asked students in Germany, the UK, USA and Japan to complete five tasks that had been developed in earlier studies of cultural variations in cognitive style. In the first task, participants were presented with brief vignettes in which people had engaged in socially desirable and in socially undesirable behaviours. They were asked to rate the extent to which these people's behaviours were due to their dispositions or to the context, and whether these behaviours would have been different if the dispositions or context were different (from Norenzayan, Choi, & Nisbett, 2002, discussed in Chapter 6). This task measures correspondence bias. The second task was the Line and Frame test (as shown in Figure 6.3). In some trials, participants were asked to reproduce the absolute length of lines, and in other trials to reproduce the line in proportion to the size of the box in which it was to be placed. This task measures analytic versus holistic cognition.

In the third task, participants were given a list of everyday situations. Situations were either social (e.g., 'having a positive interaction with friends') or not social (e.g., 'being caught in a traffic jam'). They were asked to think of the last time they were in each of these kinds of situations, and then to record which of a list of emotions they had experienced. This task measures the frequency of 'socially engaging' and 'socially disengaging' emotions. Engaging emotions necessarily involve others, such as feeling friendly, ashamed or guilty. Disengaging emotions do not necessarily involve others, such as pride, frustration and anger. For the fourth task, participants rated their level of general happiness in each situation. This rating was correlated with their overall frequency of engaging and disengaging emotions to see which contributed more to overall happiness. Where happiness was more strongly correlated with engaging emotions, Kitayama et al. called it social happiness. Where happiness was more strongly correlated with disengaging emotions, they called it personal happiness.

In the fifth task, participants were asked to draw their social networks, using circles to represent themselves and their friends and lines to represent the relationships among them. This task yields a measure of 'symbolic self-inflation', which is operationalised as the extent that the 'self' circle was drawn larger than the average size of the other circles.

Consistent with earlier results, American participants showed more correspondence bias, more analytic cognitive style, more frequent disengaging emotions, happiness that was more personal than social, and more symbolic self-inflation, compared to Japanese participants. There were no significant differences between the results from Germany and those from the UK. The scores for the European students were intermediate between those from the USA and Japan, but they nonetheless differed significantly from the Japanese and US results in most comparisons. Thus the pattern of mean scores across the four national samples was quite similar for these separate tasks.

The researchers also computed correlations between the results for the five tasks within each country's sample. The correlations found were very low: in other words, the individuals within each country who scored highest on correspondence bias were not the same individuals who scored highest on analytic cognition or frequently experiencing personal rather than social emotions. This is to be expected given the differing nature of the five tasks, although it may be surprising to some researchers who would have expected these tasks to be alternative ways of assessing idiocentric or allocentric tendencies.

The researchers also included Singelis's (1994) self-construal scale in their study, which they scored as a single dimension by subtracting interdependence from independence. This measure showed a very different pattern of mean differences: German participants scored highest on independence, followed by the Japanese, and the US and UK participants showed the least independent (or most interdependent) responses.

In one sense, their study might be viewed as yet another failure to confirm the mediation model shown in Figure 7.4. However, Kitayama et al. argued that the divergent results for self-construal from the other tasks in their study had at least two important implications for how we should think about the nature of cross-cultural differences in independence and interdependence.

Their first implication, already foreshadowed by Markus and Kitayama (1991), is that cultural orientations towards independence and interdependence may not necessarily be measurable with explicit self-report scales. Kitayama et al. (2009) argue that these cultural influences will be manifested in people's implicit psychological tendencies, but not necessarily in their explicit ideas about how 'independent' or 'interdependent' they are. Why should this be the case? One possible reason, grounded in developmental psychology, is that implicit psychological tendencies will be socialised relatively early in the lifespan (see Chapter 8), whereas explicit and generalised self-perceptions of one's standing on abstract dimensions such as 'independence' and 'interdependence' are not likely to arise before adolescence. Moreover, as we discussed earlier, perhaps especially among young, middle-class students in a nation such as Japan that has undergone rapid economic and cultural change in recent decades, these explicit self-perceptions may be influenced by subcultural ideas that push towards identifying oneself as 'modern' or 'Westernised'.

This first implication might be viewed as rescuing the mediation model of Figure 7.4 at a theoretical level, although it implies that the model is not directly testable because of the impossibility of measuring independence and interdependence separately from their outcomes. Nonetheless, the arguments above suggest that explicit self-construal measures may be especially problematic among the student samples used by Kitayama et al. (2009), and perhaps even more so in the particular socio-historical context of contemporary Japan. Might an explicit self-construal measure have shown more convergent results if they had used adult, non-student samples from a wider range of national contexts?

Kitayama and colleagues' (2009) second, arguably more radical, implication stems from the finding that the five measures of implicit psychological tendencies showed a convergent pattern of mean differences across the four national groups, whereas the same five measures were almost entirely unrelated to each other at the individual level within each nation. Based on this pattern of findings, they propose that the broad constructs of independence and interdependence should be understood as 'cultural mandates', rather than as construals of the self. Cultural mandates are defined as 'the ideals or general goal states (such as independence and interdependence) positively sanctioned by a given cultural group' (2009: 238): in other words, independence or interdependence should be studied not as properties of individuals (as researchers have usually understood the term 'self-construal') but as properties of the cultural contexts in which the individuals are located.

Kitayama and colleagues' (2009) argument underlines the importance of a clear understanding of the distinction between levels of analysis that we have emphasised in earlier chapters. According to their perspective, a prevailing cultural context can provide incentives to think or behave independently or interdependently, but individuals within that context may select different ways of being independent or interdependent according to their own specific individual predispositions, which may be personality variables, values, beliefs, or self-construals (see also Bond, 2013). However, this argument also raises some significant questions. Theoretically, if independence-interdependence is now to be viewed as a culture-level dimension, it becomes important to know how this construct should be distinguished theoretically and empirically from the prior construct of individualism-collectivism. Indeed, the concept of an underlying cultural dimension, inferred from mean differences on various individual-level measures, seems very similar to Triandis's (1993) earlier conceptualisation of individualism and collectivism as 'cultural syndromes'.

Empirically, although the argument about levels of analysis helps to make sense of Kitayama and colleagues' (2009) findings, their culture-level sample size of just four national groups does not provide a firm empirical basis for inferring the presence of a culture-level dimension. Hence, it will be necessary to replicate their findings in the future with participants from a much larger number of cultural groups, sampled from a wider range of locations. Will their measures of implicit psychological tendencies towards independence and interdependence cluster together into a reliable dimension at the cultural level of analysis? If so, how will this dimension be related to indices of individualism-collectivism, or to culture-level variation on Owe and colleagues' (2012) dimensions of explicit self-construals?

Large-scale, multinational research will be one important way of testing ideas about pressures towards independence and interdependence as properties of the context, rather than as properties of individuals, but it is not the only way. Indeed, several other approaches are equally valuable, if we are to understand the processes by which individuals are influenced by, and reciprocally act on, their cultural contexts. These approaches have been used more commonly in cultural psychology than in cross-cultural psychology.

Analysing Cultural Products

One valuable way of examining the cultural contexts that people in different parts of the world inhabit is to analyse the contents of cultural products such as newspaper articles, advertisements, children's books, or song lyrics, as discussed in Chapters 2 and 4. Cultural products can be viewed as naturally occurring data produced by individual cultural members, but they are also notable features of the situations in which people in different parts of the world live their daily lives. For example, the average American adult is exposed to an estimated 3,000 advertisements every day (Kakutani, 1997, cited by Kim & Markus, 1999).

Kim and Markus (1999) analysed the content of 293 advertisements from US and Korean magazines, in order to examine the prevalence of messages related to conformity (an aspect of interdependence) and uniqueness (an aspect of independence). They found that conformity-related messages (e.g., 'Seven out of ten people are using this product') occurred in 95% of the Korean advertisements but in only 65% of the American advertisements; in contrast, uniqueness-related messages (e.g., 'The internet isn't for everybody. But then again, you are not everybody') occurred in 89% of the American advertisements but in only 49% of the Korean advertisements. Kim and Markus argued that the differing prevalence of these types of messages would provide a powerful route for transmitting and reinforcing the prevailing cultural values of uniqueness or conformity in these two nations.

Priming Independence and Interdependence

If cultures differ in the themes that they make salient for their members, then a logical next step for research is to try experimentally manipulating the salience of these themes. In Chapter 6, we reviewed studies that have used national icons or languages to prime different cultural frames among bicultural participants. However, a growing trend in the self-construal literature has been to test the effect of priming participants with messages or tasks designed to manipulate directly the salience of independent or interdependent self-construals.

In a first attempt at experimental manipulation, Trafimow, Triandis and Goto (1991) simply asked Caucasian and Chinese students in the United States to sit for two minutes and think either about everything they had in common with their family and friends, or about everything that made them different from their family and friends: participants then completed the Twenty Statements Test. The experimental manipulation had a substantial effect on how members of each group described themselves. When asked to think about their similarities, their TST scores showed greater interdependence. When asked to think about their differences, their TST scores showed greater independence.

Subsequently, researchers have developed several further priming methods. Among the most commonly used, Trafimow et al. (1991) developed a second task, in which participants read a story about an ancient Sumerian warrior who behaved in either an independent or an interdependent manner, and Brewer and Gardner (1996; Gardner, Gabriel, & Lee, 1999) developed a task in which participants are asked to read a story about a trip to the city and circle all the pronouns, which are either first person singular (I, me, mine) or first person plural (we, us, our). These methods typically show small, but reliable effects on TST responses (Oyserman & Lee, 2008), whereas their effects on self-construal scales have been inconsistent across studies (cf. Levine, Bresnahan, Park et al., 2003; Zhang, Feick, & Price, 2006; Zhang, & Mittal, 2007).

In the last decade or so, there has been a proliferation of research testing the effects of these priming techniques on a wide range of outcomes (reviewed by Cross et al., 2011; Oyserman & Lee, 2008). Participants primed with an interdependent (compared to an independent) self-construal have been shown to: pay more attention to context in both behavioural and neurological measures of basic cognition (Kühnen, Hannover & Schubert, 2001; Lin, Lin, & Han, 2008); to assimilate more and contrast themselves less to social comparison targets (Kühnen & Hannover, 2000) and to negative stereotypes (Bry, Follenfant, & Meyer, 2008); to take more account of another person's perspective when providing information (Haberstroh, Oyserman, et al., 2002); to report more social content when asked to recall their earliest childhood memories (Wang & Ross, 2005); to base judgments of their life-satisfaction to a greater extent on the perceived views of important others (Suh, Diener, & Updegraff, 2008); to focus more on prevention rather than promotion in self-regulation (Lee, Aaker, & Gardner, 2000); to sit closer to where they expect another person to sit (Holland et al., 2004); to exhibit greater non-conscious mimicry in social situations (Van Baaren, Maddux, Chartrand et al., 2003); and to present themselves in a more socially appropriate and less enhancing fashion (Lalwani & Shavitt, 2009).

Many of these findings directly mirror those that have been observed in correlational research using self-construal scales (Cross et al., 2011). Moreover, in their meta-analysis of priming studies, Oyserman and Lee (2008) commented that the average effect sizes for many findings are comparable to those observed in cross-cultural research comparing Western and East Asian participants. As we discussed in Chapter 6, it would be unwise to conclude from this paradigm for doing cross-cultural-like research that the many differences between individualist and collectivist cultural groups are reducible to variation in the environmental salience of cues that prime thoughts of independence and interdependence. Nonetheless, these findings provide suggestive evidence for the view that cultural differences in independent and interdependent thoughts, feelings, motivations, and behaviour are sustained at least in part by variable features of the social context, and not only by the internalised beliefs, values or self-construals of individual cultural members. Even so, to join up the dots of this argument with confidence, further evidence is needed.

Firstly, we need to establish exactly what the various experimental manipulations are actually priming. As noted by Oyserman and Lee (2008), it is currently unclear whether it is changes in self-construal that are the 'active ingredients' of these primes or changes in other dimensions such as values, beliefs or cognitive style. Moreover, as we have seen, independent and interdependent self-construals are multifaceted, and it seems likely that different priming techniques are emphasising different aspects of these constructs. Trafimow and colleagues' (1991) commonality-difference prime seems closely linked to the *uniqueness versus similarity* dimension identified by Owe et al. (2012). The Sumerian warrior story is harder to classify in terms of known self-construal dimensions: in terms of Schwartz's (1992) model of individual-level value priorities, the warrior appears to show *conservation values* in the interdependence condition, and *self-enhancement values* in the independence condition. The pronoun-circling task perhaps may be priming the *boundedness versus connectedness* dimension identified by Owe et al. (2012). However, one might also expect that the interpretation of 'I' and 'we' will depend on which forms of independence and interdependence are more prevalent in different cultural contexts. In future research, these techniques could be adapted, or new techniques devised, to prime different facets of independence and interdependence. Moreover, a majority of self-construal priming research to date has used Western samples, and those studies that have used non-Western samples do not always show comparable results (Oyserman & Lee, 2008). Hence, it will be essential to examine to what extent each technique is understood similarly or differently in other cultures.

Secondly, more could be done to establish the ecological validity of self-construal priming research. More extensive analyses of cultural products could establish the prevalence of messages similar to those of the priming manipulations within the everyday contexts experienced by members of different cultural groups. Kim and Markus's (1999) analysis of US and Korean advertisements provides a valuable first step, showing evidence of the differential prevalence of messages that seem related to the commonality-difference prime, albeit in only two nations. However, a further piece of the puzzle could be contributed by using naturally occurring messages from cultural products as priming stimuli. What if Kim and Markus had followed their content analysis by priming US and Korean participants with advertisements from their respective cultures that emphasised uniqueness or conformity?

Thirdly, research is needed to compare systematically the scope of the effects of different priming techniques across a range of different outcomes, since the effects observed so far are not uniform across outcomes and across priming techniques (Oyserman & Lee, 2008). In doing so, it would be valuable to compare the effect sizes obtained by priming with those that are observed in cross-cultural comparisons over a sufficiently wide range of cultural groups. The fact that priming methods often show comparable effect sizes to existing cross-cultural comparative studies may be a reflection of the narrow range of student participants typically sampled in cross-cultural research, rather than indicating that priming can truly produce effects of similar magnitude to the effects of global variation in individualism and collectivism.

MARKUS AND KITAYAMA: 20 YEARS ON

We began this chapter emphasising the value of unpacking culture by identifying dimensions of cultural orientation that mediate observed national differences in cognitive, affective, motivational or behavioural outcomes. Markus and Kitayama's (1991) theorising about independent and interdependent self-construals, especially as it has been interpreted by authors such as Singelis (1994) and Matsumoto (1999), has provided a major impetus for unpacking studies in cross-cultural psychology. However, support for the mediation model shown in Figure 7.4 has been surprisingly elusive. Based on the literature to date, it is hard to know to what extent the lack of support should be attributed to problems of sampling and measurement, or whether the theoretical model needs changing.

Notably, in a recent review paper, Kitayama and Uskul (2011) suggest that the key mediators of cultural differences in behaviour will be *culture-level value priorities and related practices*, rather than *individual-level self-construals*. Although they do not develop the point in much depth, they appear to believe that explicit self-beliefs about one's independence or interdependence will emerge mainly as a consequence of enacting cultural practices. They suggest that repeatedly enacting cultural practices will lead the underlying brain pathways to become stronger, giving rise in turn to the same practices being performed more automatically and spontaneously. As a further consequence, people will come to interpret these practices as reflecting their true nature, and thus they will form self-beliefs around them.

SELF AND IDENTITY PROCESSES IN CULTURAL CONTEXT

We will have much more to say about cultural practices in the next three chapters of this book. However, we shall now discuss studies that have taken a finer-grained look at cultural variation in self and identity processes, viewing these processes as outcomes in their own right, rather than as potential mediators in unpacking studies. In several studies, we shall see that observed differences in self and identity processes can be explained by the measures of *nation-level* value priorities that we introduced in Chapter 2.

In Western cultures, three constructs are often seen as especially important properties of identity: *distinctiveness* from others, *continuity* over time, and positive *self-esteem*. Both distinctiveness and continuity have been portrayed, by philosophers as well as psychologists, as defining features of identity (e.g., James, 1892; Erikson, 1968; Codol, 1981). However, in social psychology, they have also come to be seen as motivational principles, guiding the processes of identity construction, maintenance, and defence, together with the motive for positive self-esteem. Research conducted in Western cultures has shown numerous ways in which people strive to construct, maintain, and enhance identities that are characterised by feelings of distinctiveness, continuity and self-esteem, as well as satisfying other motives (reviewed by Vignoles, 2011).

A key question, then, is whether we should expect that similar motivational principles will underlie identity processes among people in different cultural contexts. There are several good reasons to think that they might not. In the following sections, we shall consider in turn each of these three particular identity motives.

Distinctiveness: Difference, Separateness and Social Position

Geertz (1975) famously described the Western concept of the person as 'a *bounded, unique*, more or less integrated motivational and cognitive universe, a dynamic center of awareness, emotion, judgment, and action organized into a *distinctive* whole and *set contrastively both against other such wholes and against a social and natural background*' (1975: 48, emphases added). A salient theme in this characterisation is distinctiveness, marked by separateness and difference from others. But Geertz emphasised that this concept of personhood was 'a rather peculiar idea within the context of the world's cultures' (1975: 48).

Hence, cross-cultural psychologists have suggested that the motive for distinctiveness may be culturally specific. Triandis (1995) proposed that the motive for distinctiveness would be stronger in individualistic cultures and weaker in collectivistic cultures, whereas a motive for belonging would be stronger in collectivist cultures and weaker in individualist cultures. His predictions were based on the underlying assumption that identity motives are derived from the internalisation of cultural values: people who live in cultures where distinctiveness is valued will come to internalise this value, and for this reason they will seek to construct distinctive identities (for a similar argument, see Snyder & Fromkin, 1980).

A few studies have found evidence of cross-cultural variation in explicit self-report measures of 'need for uniqueness' (NFU). Yamaguchi, Kuhlman and Sugimori (1995) reported somewhat lower mean NFU scores among Japanese and Korean undergraduates compared to Americans, although statistical significance was not tested. Burns and Brady (1992) found significantly lower mean NFU scores among Malaysian than US business students, however, this difference appeared only on the subscale of 'lack of concern for others', suggesting a cultural difference in concern for social acceptance, rather than in the desire for uniqueness *per se*. Tafarodi, Marshall and Katsura (2004) found no difference between Japanese and Canadian undergraduates in overall NFU scores, but Japanese participants scored lower on items reflecting 'desire to be different'. Apparently stronger support for Triandis's (1995) prediction comes from Owe and colleagues' (2012) study of self-construals described earlier: their dimension of uniqueness versus similarity was significantly predicted by indicators of nation-level individualism-collectivism.

However, as we have discussed earlier, explicit self-report measures are ambiguous. Do members of individualistic cultures report that they want to be unique because they have a stronger underlying motivation for distinctiveness, or because this is the normative thing to do in an individualistic culture? Are they 'standing out' explicitly, in order to 'fit in' at a more subtle, implicit level? Explicit self-reports may be valid and useful measures of how much people consciously want to be unique, but conscious wants do not necessarily correspond with underlying motives (Vignoles, 2009).

Vignoles, Chryssochoou, and Breakwell (2000) questioned the rationale underlying Triandis's (1995) prediction. They argued that some form of distinctiveness was logically necessary in order to establish a meaningful sense of identity: this should be the case in any cultural meaning system, suggesting that the motive for distinctiveness would be culturally universal. Nevertheless, different cultural systems may come to emphasise different forms of distinctiveness, and these emphases should be reflected in the identities of cultural members. Thus, they predicted that members of individualistic cultures would achieve a sense of distinctiveness mainly by seeing themselves as different and separate from others, consistent with the Western concept of the person (Geertz, 1975). In contrast, based on characterisations of personhood in East Asian cultures as emphasising the place of the individual within a network of social relationships (e.g., Hsu, 1985; Ho, 1995), they predicted that members of collectivist cultures would gain a sense of distinctiveness through their social positions within the relational networks of kinship ties, friendships, roles, and social hierarchies.

In a recent study, Becker, Vignoles et al. (2012) put these predictions to the test. Rather than comparing explicit self-reports of NFU, they used a more indirect measure of the motive for distinctiveness. Participants in previous Western studies had been shown to perceive the most distinctive aspects of their identities as especially central and self-defining, whereas they perceived less distinctive aspects as more marginal (e.g., Vignoles, Regalia, Manzi, et al., 2006). Across adolescent members of 21 cultural groups, Becker et al. tested whether this effect would be moderated by two facets of individualism-collectivism: value priorities of autonomy versus embeddedness (see Chapter 2) and decontextualised versus contextualised personhood beliefs (see Chapter 5).

Results showed that the distinctiveness motive was no weaker in collectivist than in individualist groups. Nevertheless, members of different cultural groups appeared to understand the concept of distinctiveness in different ways that largely matched the predictions of Vignoles et al. (2000). Participants typically saw as more distinctive those parts of their identities that made them more different from others, but this tendency was stronger in individualist than in collectivist cultures. Participants also typically saw as more distinctive those parts of their identities that gave them a particular social position in relation to others, and this tendency was stronger in collectivist than in individualist cultures. Separateness was a weaker source of distinctiveness overall; nevertheless, it was emphasised somewhat more in cultural groups that prioritised autonomy over embeddedness values.

Notably, Becker et al. (2012) used multi-level analysis to demonstrate that these differences in the construction of distinctiveness did not depend on individual-level personal beliefs or values: instead, they are better explained as effects of living in a cultural context where certain things are believed or valued. This provides a significant reminder that individualism and collectivism are properties of cultures and not of individuals. As we discussed earlier and take up more fully in Chapter 8, the effects of culture on individuals' psychological functioning can be mediated by participation in shared cultural practices and institutions, rather than by the cognitive internalisation of cultural beliefs, values, or self-construals (Kitayama & Uskul, 2011; Yamagishi, 2011).

Continuity: Stability Across and Within Contexts, and Narrative Coherence

The identity motive for continuity has also been portrayed as specific to Western cultures. One of the most important Western theorists of identity, Erikson, defined identity itself as 'a subjective sense of an invigorating sameness and continuity' (1968: 19). In contrast, according to Markus and Kitayama, central features of the interdependent self are flexibility and variability: 'An interdependent self cannot be properly characterized as a bounded whole, for it changes structure with the nature of the particular social context. Within each particular social situation, the self can be differently instantiated' (1991: 227).

What is the evidence for such an assertion? One way of assessing the changeability of the self-concept is to examine people's responses to feedback that is consistent or inconsistent with their prior self-views. Typically, Western participants show a tendency towards self-verification: that is, they tend to accept feedback that is consistent with, but resist feedback that contradicts, their pre-existing self-concepts (Shrauger, 1975). However, Spencer-Rodgers, Boucher, Peng, and Wang (2009) found that self-verification varied across cultures: in their study, Caucasian American students showed resistance to feedback that contradicted their prior self-views, whereas Asian American and Chinese students tended to change their self-views in the direction of the feedback they had received.

Another way of examining the fluidity of identity is to compare self-descriptions across different contexts. Cousins (1989) compared the TST responses of US and Japanese students. When he employed the normal format, he found that US students used more trait-like self-descriptions. However, when he adapted the TST format to specify context (e.g., 'When with my friends, I am ...', 'When at home, I am ...') the results were quite different. The Japanese now used more trait-like descriptions, whereas the US respondents more often qualified their responses in a way that suggested that although they acted in a certain way in this setting, this was not an indication of their overall self. In a similar way, Suh (2002) found that how Koreans characterised themselves across five different situations was much less consistent than US responses. Tafarodi, Lo, Yamaguchi, Lee, and Katsura (2004) asked respondents directly whether the beliefs that they held about themselves remained the same in different situations. Among the student participants they surveyed, a total of 65% of Canadians said yes, but only 46% of Japanese and 28% of Hong Kong Chinese did so. Thus, persons within East Asian collectivist cultures reported more short-term variation in their experienced identities as they moved between different social contexts.

However, variation between contexts is not the same as instability over time. English and Chen (2007) compared self-descriptions of Asian American and European American students across contexts and over time. As expected, the Asian Americans showed greater variability in how they described themselves in differing relationship contexts. Crucially, the self-descriptions by each group showed no difference in test-retest consistency 25 weeks later. Thus, Asian Americans show greater situational variability, not greater long-term instability. English and Chen interpreted this result in terms of an 'if-then' model for Asian Americans ('If I am in situation X, then I am like this'). Extending these findings, English and Chen (2011) examined consequences of consistency across contexts and over time among members of the same two groups. European Americans reported greater perceived authenticity and relationship quality, the more that their self-perceptions were consistent across relationship contexts, whereas Asian Americans did not show this trend. Nevertheless, both groups reported greater perceived authenticity and relationship quality, the more that their self-perceptions were consistent over time *within* relationship contexts. Thus, self-consistency was important for both cultural groups: what differed was the type of consistency that mattered.

In the preceding examples, we have focused on stability (versus change) as a source of subjective self-continuity. Yet change is an inevitable fact of life for all individuals and social groupings. In fact, self-continuity does not require the absence of change, rather that there is some conceptual thread connecting past, present, and future time-slices of our identity, despite the occurrence of change (Vignoles, 2011). Like distinctiveness, a sense of continuity can be constructed in various ways. Chandler, Lalonde, Sokol and Hallett (2003) explored the strategies used by adolescents to assert their continuity over time, when confronted with the fact that they have changed. They concluded that these strategies become increasingly sophisticated with age, but they also distinguished between two broad approaches to constructing continuity, termed *essentialist* and *narrativist*. The essentialist approach is based on the belief in some stable and enduring, essential 'core' of one's identity; thus, continuity is maintained by denying or trivialising change. In the narrativist approach, the sense of continuity is based on establishing a coherent storyline in order to connect together different parts of one's life; in this way, even major changes can be accommodated into a coherent story using narrative devices such as 'turning points', or through social procedures such as 'rites of passage'.

Chandler et al. (2003) also reported differences in ways of maintaining continuity between indigenous Canadian adolescents and Canadian adolescents of European descent. European Canadians were more likely to use essentialist approaches to justify their continuity over time, whereas indigenous Canadians were more likely to use narrativist approaches. Notably, the choice between essentialist and narrativist continuity was not predicted by measures of independent and interdependent self-construal. Further research is needed to examine the range of continuity maintenance strategies that may be used across a wider range of cultures, as well as the cultural beliefs and values that may moderate their use.

Self-Esteem: Enhancement, Criticism and Improvement

The identity motive that has received the greatest attention in cross-cultural research is the motive for self-esteem. Markus and Kitayama (1991) originally proposed that self-esteem would be based on different value dimensions in different cultures:

> For those with independent selves, feeling good about oneself typically requires fulfilling the tasks associated with being an independent self; that is, being unique, expressing one's inner attributes, and asserting oneself. [...] The motive to maintain a positive view of the self may assume a somewhat different form, however, for those with interdependent selves. [...] Positive feelings about the self should derive from fulfilling the tasks associated with being interdependent with relevant others: belonging, fitting in, occupying one's proper place, engaging in appropriate action, promoting others' goals, and maintaining harmony. (1991: 242)

A few years later, Heine, Lehman, Markus, and Kitayama (1999) published a theoretical paper, provocatively titled 'Is there a universal need for positive self-regard?', in which they appeared to argue for a more radical possibility: that the need for self-esteem might be wholly specific to North American and other Western cultures.

Heine and colleagues' (1999) argument was again grounded especially in a comparison of North American and Japanese cultures. Reviewing anthropological and indigenous psychological writings, they argued that Japanese culture does not foster positive self-views. Rather than being motivated to evaluate themselves positively, they stated that Japanese people are motivated to seek positive evaluation from others (see our discussion of 'face' in Chapter 9). They argued that this positive evaluation would be based on living up to several values that were important in Japanese culture. The Japanese value of *hansei* involves paying attention to one's weaknesses, rather than one's strengths: self-criticism is seen as important, because it provides a first step towards self-improvement. Three further values, *doryoku* (effort), *gambari* (persistence), and *gaman* (endurance), together indicate the emphasis that is placed on self-discipline in Japanese culture. Thus, according to Heine et al., instead of being motivated towards *self-enhancement* (seeking to view oneself as positively as possible in the present with minimal investment of effort) Japanese people are motivated primarily towards *self-improvement* (seeking to become a better self, in the eyes of others, in the future, through a long-term investment of effort and endurance).

Research has supported the view that the Japanese are more focused on self-improvement than Westerners are. Heine, Kitayama, and Lehman (2001) showed that Japanese student participants were more responsive than Canadian participants to failure feedback, adjusting their self-evaluations in the direction of the feedback. Moreover, Heine, Kitayama, Lehman, Takata et al. (2001) showed that Japanese participants were more likely to increase their efforts on a task following failure feedback, whereas North American participants were more likely to reduce their efforts. The latter results were explained in terms of cultural differences in implicit theories about the perceived role of effort versus abilities in achievement. In general, Japanese participants saw effort as more important than North Americans did, and the difference in persistence following failure was reduced when Japanese participants were led to believe that task performance depended mainly on fixed abilities, as well as when North Americans were led to believe that task performance depended mainly on effort.

Notably, these findings are consistent with Western research that has examined the impact of malleability beliefs on self-evaluation processes and task performance. For example, Western participants show a better memory for negative self-attributes that they view as modifiable (Green, Pinter, & Sedikides, 2005), they seek more additional information following negative feedback about traits that they view as modifiable (Dauenheimer, Stahlberg, Spreeman, & Sedikides, 2002), and they choose more challenging tasks and persist more after failures if they believe that relevant abilities are modifiable, rather than fixed (Dweck, 1999). This suggests that the Japanese focus on self-criticism and self-improvement may be understood as a particular instance of a more general principle about how people are affected by beliefs about the malleability or fixedness of human characteristics.

But does this mean that Japanese people also have no need for self-enhancement? Heine et al. (1999) noted that studies of Japanese participants have often failed to replicate the self-enhancement and self-protective biases previously found in North American samples; moreover, Japanese participants do not show the enormous preponderance of positive scores on measures of global self-esteem that is characteristic of North American samples. Nevertheless, there has been extensive recent debate as to whether Japanese persons are 'really' self-critical, whether it is merely that Japanese culture requires a more modest self-presentation, or whether the results obtained are an artifact of the research methods that are used. Some key issues are summarised in Research Debate Box 7.1.

Based on the studies reviewed in Research Debate Box 7.1, it is unsafe to conclude that members of Japanese or any other culture have no need to see themselves positively. In fact, a careful perusal of the Sedikides-Heine debate shows that there is more common ground in their perspectives than might at first appear. Both authors agree that people are universally motivated by self-esteem concerns, if self-esteem is defined in terms of living up to values that are important in one's cultural worldview (Pyszczynski, Greenberg, Solomon, et al., 2004). Both authors also agree that the specific ways in which people fulfil this motivation will look very different according to the cultural context. However, they disagree about the prevalence of certain ways of seeking self-esteem across cultures.

Perhaps surprisingly, researchers have only quite recently begun to identify different predictors of positive self-regard across cultures, as was originally proposed by Markus and Kitayama (1991). Although studies have shown that people self-enhance on culturally valued attributes, the researchers have not usually tested whether they derived feelings of self-worth from doing so, namely whether these attributes actually serve as bases for self-esteem. Several early studies failed to support a prediction that self-esteem would be correlated more closely with independent self-construals among North American participants and more closely with interdependent self-construals among East Asian participants (Heine et al., 1999; Singelis et al., 1999; Kwan et al., 1997). However, recent studies have begun to explore the predictors of global self-esteem across a wider range of cultures and using more sophisticated measures (e.g., Goodwin et al., 2012; Becker et al., 2013; Gebauer, Wagner Sedikides, & Neberich, in press).

Research Debate Box 7.1   Self-Enhancement in East Asian Cultures

Based on their theoretical portrayal of Japanese culture, Heine and colleagues (1999) argued that Japanese people would have no tendency for self-enhancement. However, several researchers have disputed this view. Notably, Sedikides, Gaertner, and Toguchi (2003) have proposed that members of all cultures are motivated to enhance their self-esteem, but that they do so tactically and in culturally desirable ways. This reasoning suggests at least two possible explanations for why Western self-enhancement findings would not be replicated in studies with Japanese samples.

A first possibility is that the measures of self-enhancement in these studies, typically designed by Western researchers, have failed to capture the dimensions of self-evaluation and mechanisms of self-enhancement that are most important in Japanese culture. Studies using the 'better-than-average' effect as a measure of self-enhancement appear to support this possibility. Brown and Kobayashi (2002) showed that Japanese students rated themselves as better than they rated 'most other students', and that Japanese non-student adults rated themselves as better than they rated 'a typical person of the same age and sex' on traits that they viewed as important, but not on less important traits.

Sedikides et al. (2003) took this a step further, by employing trait ratings that were pre-tested to be differentially important in individualist and collectivist cultures. American and Japanese students imagined working in a group with others of the same age, gender, ethnicity and educational level, and then rated how likely they were to perform each of a series of behaviours, as well as the extent to which they saw themselves as 'better' or 'worse' on a series of positive trait dimensions, compared to a typical group member. Since many of the behaviours were not socially desirable, we focus here on the trait ratings. Although they studied only participants studying at US universities, Sedikides et al. found that both American and Japanese participants rated themselves as better than average on all of the trait ratings. Crucially, when participants rated themselves on individualist traits (e.g., free, independent, unique), the Americans showed greater self-enhancement than the Japanese, which replicated previous findings; however, when participants rated themselves on collectivist traits (e.g., cooperative, loyal, respectful), the Japanese showed greater self-enhancement than the Americans.

Publication of these results triggered an animated exchange of papers between Heine and colleagues (Heine, 2005; Heine & Hamamura, 2007; Heine, Kitayama, & Hamamura, 2007a, 2007b) and Sedikides and colleagues (Sedikides, Gaertner, & Vevea, 2005; 2007a; 2007b), including four separate meta-analyses of the cross-cultural literature on self-enhancement that apparently supported opposite conclusions about which theory is supported. The different results of the four meta-analyses depend in part on the researchers having used different criteria to select which studies to include, and also on differing decisions about how to weight the conclusions of different studies within the meta-analysis. In other words, the findings in the literature are complex, and the conclusions one reaches will depend on which groups of studies one views as most relevant or trustworthy.

So what *can* we conclude here? First of all, both groups of authors now agree that members of East Asian cultures *do* tend to rate themselves as better-than-average, especially on dimensions that have been shown empirically to be personally or culturally valued (Heine & Hamamura, 2007; Sedikides et al., 2007a). However, Heine and colleagues have disputed whether the better-than-average effect provides a valid measure of self-enhancement. Ratings of this type have been shown to yield some spurious effects, since even a randomly chosen other person is found to be rated better than average. Hamamura, Heine and Takemoto (2007) have provided suggestive, but not conclusive, evidence that this confound may be artificially inflating measures of the better-than-average effect in Japanese samples.

Many alternative measures of self-enhancement provide evidence for the prevalence of self-criticism in Japanese samples. Discrepancies between ratings of the self and ideal self were shown to be larger for Japanese than for Canadians (Heine & Lehman, 1999). These discrepancies were greatest for attributes that were rated the most important. In a laboratory experiment, Canadians were reluctant to believe that they had performed worse than average, whereas Japanese were reluctant to believe that they had done better than average (Heine, Takata, & Lehman, 2000). Heine and Renshaw (2002) had school club members in the United States and Japan rate themselves and each other: Japanese respondents rated themselves lower than the ratings they received from their peers; Americans rated themselves higher.

Thus, with the exception of the better-than-average effect, Japanese participants do seem to view themselves in a self-critical rather than self-enhancing fashion. But is this modesty 'real' or is it a matter of self-presentation? According to Sedikides and colleagues' (2003) model, self-enhancement is always a tactical process: people enhance their self-esteem in whichever ways they can get away with in the social and cultural contexts that they inhabit. Thus, in cultural contexts such as Japan where modesty is an important value, their reasoning predicts not only that people will target their self-enhancement towards culturally valued attributes (e.g., rating themselves as 'more modest than average'), but also that they will self-enhance in more subtle and indirect ways, compared to North Americans, so as not to violate social norms of modest self-presentation.

Muramoto (2003) found evidence of an indirect form of self-enhancement in a study of Japanese students' attributions for past successes and failures. Contrasting with the self-serving attribution style typically found in North American samples, participants showed a self-effacing attribution style, making external attributions for their successes and internal attributions for their failures. However, Muramoto also asked her respondents to rate how their friends and family would evaluate the same successes and failures. Here, she found evidence of self-serving attributions. Respondents believed that friends and family would give them credit for successes and blame them less for failures; moreover, this tendency was especially pronounced to the extent that they believed that their friends and family knew them well. This suggests that participants implicitly gave credence to the self-serving pattern of attributions that they attributed to close others, but that a concern for modest self-presentation may have prevented them from reporting such attributions explicitly.

Kurman (2001; 2003; Kurman & Sriram, 2002) has sought to unpackage cultural differences in self-enhancement in several studies comparing groups of high-school students from different locations and ethnic groups in Israel and Singapore. She measured several types of self-enhancement and also asked her respondents to rate how important it was to be modest. Across all studies, differences in self-reported modesty partially or fully mediated differences

(Continued)

(Continued)

in self-enhancement. In contrast, differences in self-enhancement were not accounted for by measures of horizontal individualism and collectivism.

If people's explicit self-evaluations are affected by self-presentational norms that vary across cultural contexts, then it seems likely that traditional measures of self-esteem may fail to provide a true picture of how people in different cultures really feel about themselves. Heine et al. (1999) noted that around 50% of Japanese research participants showed neutral or negative scores on the Rosenberg self-esteem scale, in contrast with the strongly positive scores shown by the vast majority of Canadian participants. But what if one measures self-esteem using more implicit methods?

Yamaguchi et al. (2007) compared explicit self-esteem scores and two measures of implicit self-esteem among US, Japanese and Chinese students. Implicit self-esteem was measured by the extent to which participants were faster to associate positive words and slower to associate negative words with themselves, compared to their speed of associating these words with their best friends or an in-group. Replicating previous findings, the authors found considerably lower explicit self-esteem among their Japanese participants than among Americans, although interestingly their Chinese participants showed nearly as high explicit self-esteem as the Americans. However, the implicit self-esteem measures showed a very different pattern: on the first measure, the three groups did not differ significantly; on the second measure, the Japanese showed significantly higher self-esteem than the other two groups (for further evidence of high implicit self-esteem among Japanese participants, see Kitayama & Karasawa, 1997; Kitayama & Uchida, 2003).

Recently, Cai, Sedikides, et al. (2011) tested the prediction that modest self-presentation might ironically be a source of positive implicit self-esteem in Chinese culture. In two correlational studies, they showed that self-rated modesty was negatively associated with explicit self-esteem in both Chinese and US participants, but that it was *positively* associated with implicit self-esteem among Chinese participants only. In a third study, they manipulated participants' opportunities to describe themselves modestly or immodestly. After describing themselves modestly, Chinese participants (but not Americans) showed an increase in implicit self-esteem; in contrast, after describing themselves immodestly, Chinese participants (but not Americans) showed a decrease in implicit self-esteem. Thus, by expressing self-criticism, the Chinese participants were living up to the important cultural value of modesty, leading to higher rather than lower self-esteem on a more implicit level.

In the most extensive study to date, Becker, Vignoles et al. (2013) examined variation in the bases of self-esteem as a function of personal and cultural value priorities across 20 cultural samples of late adolescents. Participants were found to derive self-esteem especially from those aspects of their identities that were most consistent with the value priorities of their surrounding culture: controlling one's life was a stronger base for self-esteem in samples where openness to change values were emphasised, whereas doing one's duty was a stronger base for self-esteem in samples where conservation values were emphasised; achieving social status was a stronger base for self-esteem in samples where self-enhancement values were emphasised, whereas benefitting others was a stronger base for self-esteem in samples where self-transcendence values were emphasised. These effects were found while controlling statistically for the effects of individuals' personal value priorities. Thus, it seems that the bases for self-esteem were defined collectively, reflecting what was valued normatively within a cultural group, rather than being defined individually based on one's personal values.

SUMMARY: BEYOND RELATIVISM, BEYOND INTERNALISATION

By focusing on the role of distinctiveness, continuity, and self-esteem in self and identity processes across cultures, we can see that a common pattern emerges. Instead of viewing these three identity motives as culturally bounded, resulting from individuals' internalisation of relevant cultural values, beliefs, or self-construals, as depicted in Figure 7.4, they now appear to be universal requirements for a satisfactory sense of identity. But individuals must still negotiate how best to satisfy these motives within the particular cultural contexts that they inhabit.

Although individuals are influenced by their cultural contexts in numerous ways, we should remember that *individuals are not simply products of their cultural environments*. Their needs and motives transcend cultural boundaries, and different cultural environments may provide different ways of satisfying these needs and motives. In later chapters, we discuss how further aspects of self and identity processes play out across cultures and especially in multicultural contexts. Our focus here has been mainly on 'personal identity', but researchers have also begun to identify both universal and culturally variable features of social identity processes. Social identity processes become especially crucial in situations of cultural contact, because it is here that culture can become subjectively self-defining (that is, part of the content of identity) in addition to being a context for individual identity processes (see especially Chapters 12 and 13).

Equally, we should remember that *cultures are not reducible to individual cognitions*. Early attempts to unpackage cultural variation were based on the assumption that cultural differences in behaviour would be mediated by individuals' personal endorsement of the relevant self-construals, beliefs, or values, as exemplified by Figure 7.4. Yet, the assumption that individuals' thoughts, feelings, and behaviour are mainly driven by their self-construals, beliefs, and values may itself be the product of an individualist cultural worldview. Recent multi-level research has shown that key mediators of several cultural differences are to be found at the cultural level: individuals base their self-esteem and their distinctiveness on what is *culturally* valued and not necessarily on what they *personally* value. Seemingly, cultural values can be internalised at an implicit level, without necessarily requiring explicit endorsement. As a result, we must look beyond individual cognitions and study the role of social norms and institutions, interpersonal relations and group processes, in order to gain a fuller understanding of the mechanisms by which individual psychology is affected by cultural contexts. These mechanisms are the major focus of the next three chapters.

FURTHER READING

1 Cross, S.E., Hardin, E.E., & Gercek-Swing, B. (2011). The what, how, why, and where of self-construal. *Personality and Social Psychology Review*, *15*, 142–179.
2 Kitayama, S., & Uskul, A.K. (2011). Culture, mind, and the brain: Current evidence and future directions. *Annual Review of Psychology*, *62*, 419–449

3 Kurman, J. (2010). Good, better, best: Between culture and self-enhancement. *Social and Personality Psychology Compass, 4,* 379–392.

4 Markus, H.R., & Kitayama, S. (1991). Culture and the self: Implications for cognition, emotion, and motivation. *Psychological Review, 98,* 224–253.

5 Markus, H.R., & Kitayama, S. (2003). Culture, self, and the reality of the social. *Psychological Inquiry, 14,* 277–283.

6 Wang, Q. (2011). Autobiographical memory and culture. *Online Readings in Psychology and Culture,* Available at *http://scholarworks.gvsu.edu/orpc*

STUDY QUESTIONS

1 How do you construe yourself? Try describing yourself using the Twenty Statements Test in Research Instrument Box 7.1, and code each of your answers as 'independent' or 'interdependent'. Now try rating your agreement with the items in Research Instrument Box 7.2. How similar or different is the information you get from each measure?

2 Now look again at your answers to the Twenty Statements Test. Try giving each answer a score from 0 to 10 for (a) how important it is in defining who you are, (b) how much it distinguishes you in any sense from others, (c) how much it makes you feel close to, or accepted by others, and (d) how much it makes you see yourself positively. What patterns can you see in your responses to these different questions?

3 What types of self-construal are mostly favoured by people around you in the part of the world with which you are most familiar? What signs can you identify that people predominantly favour particular forms of independence or interdependence?

4 Compare and contrast Triandis's portrayal of *collectivism* with Markus and Kitayama's portrayal of *interdependence*. Are these just different words for the same concept, or are there important differences?

5 Close your eyes for a minute and think of some statements about yourself including the words 'we', 'us' and 'our'. About whom does this make you think, and what kind of relationship(s) do you have with them?

6 Identify aspects of your own culture that encourage modest or enhancing self-presentations.

8
Cultural Norms and Socialisation Processes

'By birth, the same; by culture, different'

(San Zi ing, *Three Character Classic*, thirteenth century)

In the preceding chapters, we have discussed a series of research programmes proposing different ways of conceptualising culture. Each of these approaches illuminates an aspect of the process whereby individuals interact with their cultural context. Their emphases may be on beliefs and values as a way of establishing meanings, on differing modal personalities characterising those cultures, on differing cognitive styles, on differing self-construals or differing identities, but in all cases there are one or more social contexts within which these aspects of the person are expressed in any given culture. This chapter brings social context into the foreground, but it does so in two rather separate ways. The first of these emphasises the transmission of cultural elements at particular points in the life cycle. The second treats culture transmission and culture creation as a continuous two-way process.

At birth, indeed before it, individuals are thrown into a lifelong process of learning and negotiation with those around them, resulting in the acquisition of a distinctive way of being. This process is not finite. It includes both the transmission of 'culture', and also the continuous re-creation of culture, as the outcome of myriad interactions among the many parties involved in any individual's life. At different points in the life cycle, individuals may be more active or more receptive, but there is always a two-way aspect to the process of social influence. Children influence parents, students influence teachers, employees influence managers, minorities influence majorities. The social structures that define and emphasise a particular cultural context may appear fixed and immutable, but they remain stable only so long as the protagonists involved behave in ways that sustain them. Individuals and groups quite often act to redefine these structures through taking political, economic, social and interpersonal action. Sometimes they succeed, sometimes they fail. Thus cultures can and do evolve, but they are likely to do so more slowly than occurs through the life cycle of individual persons. As Figure 8.1 emphasises, we are all contributors to culture and culture change.

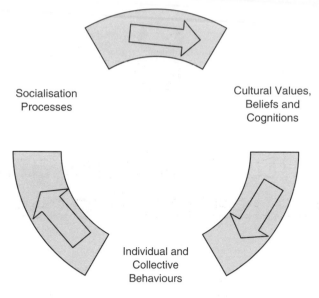

Figure 8.1   Processes Favouring Cultural Continuity

We explored in Chapter 3 some of the reasons why distinctive cultural patterns have arisen in different parts of the world. Here we look first at the experiences of individuals born into an existing cultural context, focusing in turn on particular points in the life cycle. In the second part of the chapter, attention is turned to the way that individuals experience their cultural context, usually referred to as subjective culture.

LIFE STAGES AND CULTURE

The way that we think about ourselves and the ways that we act are the result of lifelong adaptations shaped to a large extent by cultural influences. Furthermore, these adaptations are ever changing and themselves being adapted through feedback from continuing experience. This is the view introduced by lifespan perspectives in developmental psychology and it is widely shared today (Baltes & Smith, 2004). Continuous development is seen to span the whole spectrum from the prenatal period to old age and death. Nevertheless, through this lifelong process, infancy, childhood and adolescence are considered of special importance, as most growth, learning and change will occur in the early periods of human development (Super & Harkness, 1986). The lifespan developmental approach renders culture even more relevant, as the role of cultural factors shows variation at different phases of life, progressively increasing in their impact from infancy to adulthood (Bronfenbrenner, 1979).

The study of childhood in cultural context is seen not only in psychology, but has also traditionally been a central topic both for anthropologists (Whiting & Whiting, 1975; LeVine, 1989) and for sociologists (Elder, 1974). In psychology, ecological perspectives (Bronfenbrenner, 1979; Super & Harkness, 1986) situate child development and parenting in a socio-cultural context, the child being embedded within the proximal environment (family and immediate community) with these proximal environments being embedded within the distal environment (societal institutions, national economy, cultural norms and conventions). The place of the child in family and society, in combination with parental values and orientations, gives us important clues to understanding how socio-cultural variations come about in the development of the self, values and beliefs, mind, and behaviour, from a global perspective.

Infancy

There is much commonality across cultures in the construal of infancy and early childhood, based on biological needs for care, nutrition, protection and training. Accordingly, much infant care is based on biological/evolutionary functions, including universal 'intuitive parenting' which involves nursing and carrying infants in response to infant distress signals (e.g., crying) and smiling, and responding by talking a high pitched 'baby talk' (Keller, 2007). Keller, Lohaus, Volker, Cappenberg, & Chasiotis (1999) point to some basic components of parenting infants that have evolutionary bases and thus are present in all cultures. These are the primary care system (especially nursing), the body contact system (especially touching and carrying), the body motor-stimulation system (especially grasping), and the face-to-face interaction system (especially gazing).

Key Researcher Box 8.1   Heidi Keller

Figure 8.2   Heidi Keller

Heidi Keller (b. 1945) received her PhD at the University of Mainz, Germany, in 1975, and her Habilitation degree at the Technical University of Darmstadt, Germany. In 1984, she was appointed Professor at the University of Osnabrück, Germany, where she is currently Director of the Department of Culture, Learning and Development. Her main interest concerns the trajectories of development as the interface between biology and culture. Her research programme consists of cultural analyses of infants' early socialisation contexts and their developmental consequences in different family environments across cultures. She is also interested in culturally-informed family counselling. She has published two textbooks, as well as major German language handbooks of child development, and numerous papers and book chapters. From 2008-2010, she was president of the International Association for Cross-Cultural Psychology. She has also held the Nehru chair professorship at the MS University of Baroda, India, and has taught there and at the Universidad de Costa Rica, San Jose, and the University of California, Los Angeles.

However, in a series of studies, Keller and her colleagues have shown that there are variations in the prevalence of the last three systems across different cultural contexts (Keller, 2007; Keller, Borke, Lamm, et al., 2009). Utilising a form of eco-cultural theory, Keller and her colleagues show that within collectivistic agrarian traditional cultures in Africa, maternal body contact and body stimulation of the infant are more prevalent. In contrast, within middle-class individualistic families in urban European and Western societies, parents prioritise face-to-face interactions with their infants. Keller et al. further claim that childrearing characterised by close body contact is conducive to the development of relatedness with others, whereas face-to-face interaction along with child-directed language are considered to lead to the child's development of a sense of independent agency.

As a further test of this contrast, Keller et al. (2011) analysed the way that mothers who were German or Nso (an African tribal group) spoke to their infants. Talk was coded as either agentic or relational. Agentic talk included speaking about needs, wishes, or oneself as a person. Relational talk included speaking about the infant doing something with someone else, speaking about other persons, and speaking about moral correctness and social authority. German mothers spoke in more agentic ways and Nso mothers spoke in more relational ways. Even between less strongly contrasting cultural groups, differences in parenting are evident. Box 8.1 shows how paying close attention to mothers' behaviour can reveal subtle but significant cultural and historical differences.

Box 8.1   Childrearing Varies Even Between Western Nations and Across Time

There can be variations in childrearing even between educated urban populations within European societies that are otherwise similar in many respects. Comparing German and Greek urban middle-class mothers interacting with their three-month old babies, Keller, Papaligoura, Kuensemueller, Voelker et al. (2003) found that both groups used face-to-face contact and object play, and less body contact and body stimulation. These are interactional strategies that are considered to lead to the development of a sense of independent agency in the child. However, Greek mothers expressed more interactional warmth by smiling during face-to-face interaction than German mothers, who for their part were more responsive to babies' signals than were the Greek mothers. Thus, while both German and Greek mothers emphasised independence, Greek mothers also inculcated relatedness through warmth. According to the researchers, the Greek pattern is conducive to the development of 'autonomous-related' self-construal (Kağıtçıbaşı, 2007, discussed later).

Within a society significant changes can also occur over time. Keller and Lamm (2005) examined two comparable samples of German middle-class mothers over a 25-year period. They found a significant increase in face-to-face contact and object play, promoting independent agency and a significant decrease in body contact and warmth (expressed in smiling and tonal parameters of the voice), thereby downplaying relatedness.

Therefore, some developmental roots may be found even in very early mother-infant interactions that show variations across cultural contexts. An early consequence of mother-infant interactions is the formation of an emotional attachment between the two parties. Research into attachment has been much influenced by the early work of Ainsworth, conducted first in Uganda and later in the USA (Ainsworth & Bowlby, 1991). Ainsworth developed a procedure known as the 'Strange Situation' in which a mother leaves the room where her infant is located for a few minutes. While she is absent, a stranger enters the room. Subsequently, the mother returns. The reactions of the infant to these events enable a classification to be made of the type of emotional attachment to the mother that has been formed over the preceding months. Infants who quickly resume interacting with the mother are classified as securely attached. Those who ignore or avoid the mother are classified as anxious-avoidant, while those who behave in more inconsistent ways are classified as anxious-resistant.

The theory first advanced by Bowlby, and more fully disseminated by Ainsworth, sees secure attachment as the basis for the child's achievement of an individual identity and the confidence with which to explore his or her world. Many authors have concluded that the evidence supports the universal validity of this theory (Van Ijzendoorn & Sagi-Schwartz, 2008). However, the great majority of studies using the strange situation have been conducted within individualistic cultures. Results from more collectivistic cultures show equally large numbers of children achieving secure attachment, but differences in the frequencies of the insecure attachment types (Schmitt et al., 2004). In the United States, anxious avoidance is found more frequently than anxious resistance, but in Japan and several other more collectivistic nations, the anxious-resistant type has been found much more frequently than the anxious-avoidant (Rothbaum, Morelli, & Rusk, 2011). To understand why such differences might arise we need to consider parental values and beliefs about the right ways to bring up a child.

Parental Ethnotheories

The focus of developmental theories has long been predominantly eco-cultural. For instance, Bronfenbrenner (1979) emphasised the 'developmental niche', in other words, the way in which childrearing methods in specific circumstances tend to be tailored to providing the types of persons that environmental circumstances require and invite. In contrast to the broadly-defined values and beliefs examined in Chapter 2, parental **ethnotheories** specify parents' values and beliefs about the type of parent-child relations they desire and what would be good outcomes of the developmental process (Super & Harkness, 1997). Take a look at Key Research Study Box 8.1 overleaf.

The contrasting ethnotheories identified by Keller et al. are most strongly supported when observational studies are made of interactions between mothers and toddlers. For instance, Dennis, Cole, Zahn-Waxler, and Mizuta (2002) observed mother-child interactions among Japanese mothers temporarily residing in the United States, and US mothers with their respective preschoolers. US mothers had more conversations that emphasised individual experiences, more often acted as playmates, maintained more physical distance, and showed more positive emotions

An **Ethnotheory** is a set of values and beliefs distinctive to a particular cultural group. The term is usually employed in relation to childrearing.

Key Research Study Box 8.1   Predicting Socialisation Goals

Keller et al. (2006) studied parental ethnotheories in relation to socialisation goals in eight different cultural contexts that varied in their levels of collectivism. It was predicted that in more collectivistic contexts parents would endorse relational theories of parenting and relational socialisation goals, whereas in more individualistic contexts parents would endorse theories and socialisation goals that favoured the development of autonomy and self-direction.

Respondents were 204 mothers with three-month old infants, located in urban centres in Germany, Greece, the USA, China, Costa Rica, Mexico, India, and rural Cameroon. Parental collectivism was measured using a scale of Family Allocentrism developed by Lay et al. (1996). The other scales had been developed in earlier studies by Keller's research group. An example of an autonomous socialisation goal would be 'develop self-confidence', and a relational goal would be 'learn to care for the well-being of others'. An item illustrating autonomous parenting theory is 'react to positive infant signals', while a relational example is 'satisfy infant's physical needs'. Translation and back-translation procedures were used to provide locally appropriate measures. All the measures included reversed items, so that the scores obtained would not be distorted by cultural differences in acquiescent response style. All scales had adequate reliability in all locations.

The results obtained fell into three groups. Mothers in the United States, Germany and Greece were least collectivistic and most strongly endorsed autonomous parenting theories and their associated socialisation goals. The rural Nso mothers in Cameroon were most collectivistic and most strongly endorsed relational socialisation goals and parenting theories. In the remaining samples, the relational and autonomous items were both endorsed equally. In the sample as a whole, collectivism, relational parenting and relational socialisation goals were all strongly positively correlated, as predicted. In a further study by the same authors, mothers were asked to choose between a series of pictures showing aspects of child care. Analysis of the speech that they used showed a similar pattern distinguishing autonomy and relatedness (Kärtner et al., 2007).

Parents' accounts of their socialisation goals do not always accord with their parenting behaviours. Hofer, Schröder, and Keller (2012) used a projective test of motivation to gain a fuller understanding of parents' behaviour in Germany and Cameroon. Mothers were shown pictures of parenting and asked to make up stories that explained the pictures. The stories were then coded for the number of references to power and affiliation. German mothers scored higher on affiliation motives and Cameroonian mothers scored higher on power motives. It was found that the codings for power significantly predicted amount of parent-infant body contact in a free play situation. The implicit motives test was a better predictor than were parents' own accounts of their socialisation goals, indicating that we need a fuller understanding of how conscious and unconscious motives affect parenting.

Keller et al. interpret the results of their project in terms of Kağıtçıbaşı (2007) theory of family structure, discussed below. It emphasises that autonomy and relatedness are not polar opposites of one another, so that families in certain parts of the world may emphasise both autonomy and relatedness.

and more positive responses to the child's accomplishments. In contrast, Japanese mothers had more conversations that emphasised shared experiences, and maintained social role distinctions (between mother and child, not between playmates). The findings suggested an emphasis on autonomy in US dyads, and an emphasis on relatedness in Japanese dyads, but in a free play situation US mothers showed greater relational focus and Japanese mothers showed increased autonomous focus. Thus both autonomy and relatedness inductions are relevant in both cultures, although with different emphases in different interactional contexts.

Differing ethnotheories can also lead parents to use different approaches to praise and criticism, focusing either on the person or on the process. In an experimental study with 5-year old US children, Kamins and Dweck (1999) showed that praising a child's ability (e.g., 'You're really good at this') following the successful completion of a task resulted in more self-blame and reduced persistence following subsequent setbacks, compared to praising their effort (e.g., 'You must have tried really hard'). In another study, they found similar results for person-focused and praise-focused criticism. Based on our discussion of the focus on self-enhancement versus self-improvement in US versus Japanese culture (see Chapter 7), one might expect that person feedback would be more characteristic of US parenting, whereas process feedback would be more characteristic of Japanese parenting.

Jose and Bellamy (2012) set a series of tasks to 7- and 8-year old children in New Zealand, the USA, China and Japan. Some of the tasks were in fact impossible, and the dependent measure was how long the children persisted in attempting to complete them. Jose and Bellamy predicted that those who persisted would have parents who endorsed an incremental theory of intelligence ('how much you practise determines how successful you are') rather than an entity theory of intelligence ('you can't really change how intelligent you are'). As predicted, the Asian children were more persistent, and this effect was significantly predicted by parental endorsement of the items measuring an incremental theory of intelligence.

The role of parental ethnotheories in socialisation continues into young adulthood. Choi and Ross (2011) analysed the content of messages on greeting cards for university graduates in the United States and China. US cards were more likely to involve personal praise, whereas Chinese cards were more likely to involve process praise. Moreover, Chinese parents were more likely to select process-focused than person-focused cards for their children, whereas US parents were equally likely to select both kinds of cards.

Parenting Styles

While the focus of researchers into ethnotheories is a predominantly emic one derived from responses by each culture's parents, others have conducted work in the same area from a perspective that was at least initially imposed-etic, derived from measuring responses from children to behavioural styles tapped by established survey instruments. Working in the USA, Baumrind (1991) identified three styles of childrearing, which she called authoritarian, authoritative and permissive. These dimensions are defined in terms of the emphasis upon parental provision of warmth and the degree of their exercise of control: authoritarian parenting is defined by the presence of control without warmth; permissive parenting is defined by warmth without control; and authoritative parents are considered as intermediate, employing moderate degrees of both control and warmth. Thus, Baumrind treats parenting in terms of variations along a single dimension. Studies using this framework have sampled adolescents' or parents' descriptions of experienced warmth and control.

Outside of the USA, studies have uniformly supported the role of parental warmth in effective socialisation. Khaleque and Rohner (2012) conducted a meta-analysis with data from 22 nations, showing that perceptions of warmth as perceived by parents toward their children and as remembered by adult offspring about their parenting consistently predict positive adjustment indices of the offspring.

However, Baumrind's view of the role of control in child development as the opposite of warmth has been frequently challenged by non-US authors. One of the first studies challenging this view was conducted by Kağıtçıbaşı (1970), comparing the retrospective parenting experiences of Turkish and American late adolescents. While a difference in perceived parental control was found, with Turks reporting stronger control, no difference was obtained between the two national groups in perceived parental affection. Thus, Turkish adolescents reported having experienced both controlling *and* warm parenting. This was an empirical demonstration of the independence of the warmth and control dimensions of parenting.

Since then other researchers, in particular Rohner and his collaborators (Rohner & Pettengill, 1985; Trommsdorff, 1985), have come up with similar findings. They found that American and German adolescents associated parental control with parental rejection, but that Korean and Japanese adolescents associated perceived parental control with greater parental acceptance (warmth). Trommsdorff reported that Japanese adolescents even felt rejected by their parents when they experienced only modest amounts of parental control! Dwairy et al. (2006) sampled perceived parental roles across eight Arab samples. They identified three separate dimensions of Arab parenting, named as authoritarianism, authoritativeness and permissiveness, as have also been found in North America and elsewhere. However, in this sample authoritarian parenting was not associated with negative outcomes.

Thus it appears that parental control is understood in different ways in cultures that are more collectivist. A further distinction has been made by Lau and his colleagues between 'dominating control' and 'order-setting control' (Lau, Lew, Hau, Cheung, & Berndt, 1990). Working with Chinese adolescents and adults, they found dominating parental control to be associated negatively with perceived parental warmth, but 'order-keeping' and caring control to be positively associated with it. Chao (1994) suggested that what is termed authoritarian parenting in Baumrind's model may be an ethnocentric interpretation of Chinese parents' goal of 'training' in childrearing. Similarly, in a study with young adults in the United States, Hong Kong and Pakistan who were asked about the parenting they had experienced, Stewart, Bond, Kennard, Ho, & Zaman (2002) found this goal of training (*guan* in Chinese) to be common in the two Asian samples, and associated with parental warmth in all three cultural groups.

Studies of parenting do shed an important light on socialisation processes, but they implicitly reproduce the quasi-experimental perspective that is so much favoured by psychologists: parents as independent variable, children as dependent variable. We also need to test the implicit assumption of this type of study that parental style is a key factor in cultural transmission.

As part of the Value Of Children study (discussed below), Trommsdorff (2009) examined the attachment styles of mothers and their adolescent children in Germany and Indonesia. The attachment style of the mother was found to be significantly correlated with that of their off-spring in both samples. However, these correlations were not mediated by the mother's parenting style. This implies that other causal factors need to be considered in understanding the close relationship between attachment styles of parents and children. To take fuller account of the context for socialising children, we need to look at families as a whole, rather than simply abstracting what we may initially believe to be the key elements.

Family Structure

Research has shown that the familial roles of children and adolescents differ both between more and less affluent contexts and also between urban and rural contexts. We can take children's work as a case in point. Studies find that children in agrarian societies with subsistence agriculture start early to assume responsibilities for household chores, care of younger siblings, and care of animals (Munroe, Munroe, & Shimmin, 1984). The complexity and amount of work increases with age, and by middle childhood, most of children's waking hours are taken up by some sort of labour for their household. This is in contrast to children living in urban middle-class homes, and particularly in Western societies, which include a preponderance of play. For example, in their classic study of children in six cultures, Whiting and Whiting (1975) showed that among children aged between 3 and 10, 41% of Kenyan Nyansongo children's time was spent working, while only 2% of suburban American children's time was thus spent. Van de Vliert (2009) found that across 72 nations, child labour was most frequent in poor nations with harsh climates. Thus, child labour is not simply a concomitant of poverty, but is shaped by the combination of poverty and challenging climate, as Van de Vliert's eco-cultural theory predicts. In fact, nations that are very poor but have equable climates, such as Burundi and the Comoro islands, have *low* rates of child labour.

Child work contributes to the household economy, both in its own right, and also by freeing adults to put more time into economically productive work. Nsamenang (1992), an African psychologist, stresses that it is also a key way for children to learn their future social roles and responsibilities. Other work from Africa and similar socio-cultural contexts points to a similar understanding of how children are prepared for adulthood (Harkness, 1992). There are also variations in how children are taught and how they learn in everyday informal work contexts. Morelli, Rogoff, and Angelillo (2003) compared how 2-3 year old children spent their time in the Congo, Guatemala and the USA. In the Congo and Guatemala, children had frequent access to adults while the adults worked, and quite often observed them doing so. Even at this young age, their play with one another sometimes emulated adult work behaviours. US children had much less opportunity to observe adults actually working, and proportionally more of their playing time was spent playing with adults rather than with each other.

Studies thus point to different parental orientations toward child learning. Modifications over time are particularly notable, showing changes in socialisation practices within the same societies with their changing life styles (see Box 8.2).

Box 8.2   Changing Patterns of Childhood Socialisation in the Maya

Greenfield and her colleagues reported the effects of economic changes in a weaving community of the Zinacantec Maya, located in Chiapas, Mexico. This community shifted from a subsistence economy to a commercial cash economy over a period of two decades. This shift influenced the way the craft of weaving was taught and carried out. In 1969 and 1970, mothers taught their daughters weaving through careful guidance with detail-oriented representation and imitation. The repetitiveness in weaving patterns reflected a conservative, compliant orientation. In 1991 and 1993, the teaching and learning of weaving included a more independent apprenticeship, evidenced by more trial and error learning and less passive observation. The weaving patterns also reflected this change in orientation in that there was a shift from traditional patterns maintained over generations to novel designs involving individual creativity, as indicated below.

	1969–1970	*1991–1993*
Economy:	Subsistence economy	Commercial cash economy
Weaving apprenticeship:	Careful guidance, detail-oriented representation, imitation	More independent activity
Independent weaving:	47.98 (mean) 34.12 (SD)	59.16 (mean) 30.64 (SD)

Sources: Greenfield & Childs (1977); Greenfield, Maynard, & Childs (2003).

There is a current debate on the issue of when children's work stops being a positive social learning experience and starts to turn into child 'labour', or even child 'abuse'. In particular, from a [Western] 'human rights' perspective, international agencies and advocates for children's rights assail child labour practices that interfere with children's schooling. This is an example of the different cultural meanings that are assigned to the same behaviours in different settings, yielding differing judgments that can generate divisive debate. Cultural meanings associated with different life stages thus reflect life styles, social norms, values, beliefs about education, and the future roles for which children are being prepared.

Culturally differing roles of children reflect variations in the value placed on children in society. In the 1970s large, nationally representative samples comprising more than 20,000 married respondents in Indonesia, Korea, the Philippines, Singapore, Taiwan, Thailand, Turkey, the United States, and a women's sample from Germany were asked what they valued about having children (Kağıtçıbaşı, 1990). The value attributed by these parents to their children was found to vary significantly with the level of socio-economic development among the countries, as well as within countries. Parents in the less economically developed nations emphasised the economic/utilitarian benefits attached to children, especially sons. This value decreased in importance in the wealthier nations, where the psychological value attached to children, such as the love, joy, companionship, and pride that children provide, was emphasised more strongly instead.

Key Researcher Box 8.2

Çığdem Kağıtçıbaşı (b. 1940) grew up in Turkey, but completed her education in the United States, obtaining her PhD from the University of California, Berkeley, in 1967. She has held posts at academic institutions in Turkey from that time to the present, principally at Boğaziçi University, Istanbul, where she was appointed Professor in 1979, and at Koç University, Istanbul, where she is currently Director of the Centre for Gender and Women's Studies. In 1978, she began a programme of comprehensive pre-school education. By 1993, this initiative had evolved into a Mother-Child Education Programme. By 2010 more than 500,000 Turkish parents had participated in this programme, which has also been used by some centres in Belgium, Germany, France, and Switzerland. It is also being implemented in Bahrain, Jordan, Saudi Arabia, and Lebanon. She has published 13 books and 150 papers and chapters in English, as well as numerous books and papers in Turkish. She has been, and continues to be, a key figure in the development of psychology in Turkey, respected as a pioneer in representing the priorities of the majority (non-Western) world in cross-cultural research and in international psychology organisations.

Figure 8.3   Çığdem Kağıtçıbaşı

The Value Of Children study has been repeated more recently, sampling 10,000 parents in 15 nations (Trommsdorff & Nauck, 2005). The economic/utilitarian value of children is now less emphasised, especially within urban samples, whereas their psychological value is increasingly stressed. Kağıtçıbaşı (2007) has drawn on these studies to formulate a more comprehensive model of family relationships, which also takes account of contemporary social change. This model conceptualises the embeddedness of the family in its eco-cultural context and of the development of the child's self-construal within the family context. Cultural values, beliefs, conventions, urban-rural life styles and variations in affluence are all seen as key factors arising from this fundamental context for socialising children.

In socio-economic contexts where children's contribution to their family's material well-being is significant, an economic/utilitarian value is associated with one's children, a value derived from their material contributions. This is the case especially in societies with low levels of affluence, and particularly with rural agrarian people or low-income groups in urban or semi-urban areas, where having children work both in and out of the home is common and contributes to

In the **Family Model of Interdependence**, parents emphasise the induction of conformity and obedience, so that their children become dutiful. In the **Family Model of Independence,** parents seek to foster autonomy and initiative in their children.

the total family economy. When they have grown up, these children also provide old-age security benefits to their parents, who usually lack other resources such as the old-age pensions, insurance and retirement income that are provided in most economically advanced societies. Thus there is a dependence on children for a family-of-origin livelihood, both while they are young and when they grow up to be adults. This **family model of interdependence** (Kağıtçıbaşı, 1990, 2007) highlights what Arnett (1992) has categorised as 'narrow' socialisation, since it emphasises the induction of conformity and obedience, so that children become filial and dutiful.

This is also the cultural context where fertility is highest, because having more children means more material benefits and old-age security for declining parents. If one has five or six children, and each one contributes some form of benefit to their elderly parents, this accumulation of inputs gives greater security than depending on only one or two. Also, in the context of poverty, child mortality is high, underscoring the necessity of bearing many children to make sure that enough survive into adulthood to support their now-aged parents.

In the contrasting context of urban middle-class families living in more affluent contexts, children tend to be in school, rather than already at work. They become economic costs rather than assets for the family. Since children's economic value is negligible, their psychological value becomes salient for parents as a reason for having children, and often as the only reason. The psychological needs satisfied by children do not necessitate having many children, since their costs to the parents quickly come to outweigh their benefits. Parents can derive all the joy, love, and pride they need from only a few children and do not need more. This is the logic underlying the **family model of independence** (Kağıtçıbaşı, 1990, 2007), since there is little or no dependence on the material contributions of children. Arnett (1992) categorises the processes occurring within this model as 'broad' socialisation, since it seeks to foster autonomy and initiative.

The implications of the value attributed to children and the corresponding family dynamics are important for childrearing and for the resultant development of self-construal. In the family model of interdependence there tends to be obedience-oriented childrearing, which does not promote the development of independence and autonomy. This is because an autonomous child would be likely to develop into a separate, independent adult, who might look after his/ her own interests rather than those of the family. Therefore independence is not valued and may even be seen as a threat to family integrity and livelihood. Intergenerational interdependence, on the other hand, is manifested through the family life cycle, first in terms of the desired dependence of the child. This dependence is reversed later on, as the dependence of the elderly parents who in the course of the life cycle come to depend on their now-mature children for support.

The contrasting pattern within the family model of independence engenders self-reliance and independence in the growing child, as affluence and institutional welfare systems such as old age pensions render family interdependence less necessary. Going together with the objective conditions of life that support independence are cultural values that also foster independence and separation and normalise it as a requisite for 'healthy' human development. For example, in North America and Northern Europe it is expected that late adolescents/young adults will move out of their parents' home to live on their own, whereas in most of the rest of the world, they will remain in the parental home until they get married. Some will stay on even after marriage. Indeed, separating from one's family is not considered necessary for personal growth and maturity in non-Western cultures (Kağıtçıbaşı, 1982).

> In the **Family Model of Psychological Interdependence**, parents seek to foster both autonomy and relatedness in their children.

It is commonly assumed that as societies modernise and become more affluent with increasing levels of education, there is a simple shift from the family model of interdependence to that of independence. Recent research shows, however, that rather than a simple shift a more complex change is taking place, one that is associated with socio-economic development and especially with urbanisation, involving changes in life styles from traditional agrarian ones to urban ones. Among migrants to the cities, closely knit human/family relations appear to persist in the domain of emotional interdependencies, while material interdependencies weaken due to increased affluence and alternative old-age security resources. A third pattern, the **family model of** *psychological* **interdependence**, is proposed to characterise this change (Kağıtçıbaşı, 1990, 2007), an emerging development that produces socialised outcomes that are different from both the traditional (rural) family of total interdependence and the individualistic urban (Western middle-class) family of independence.

In this model, childrearing still involves control rather than permissiveness, because the goal is not the separated, individualistic independence of children. Together with control, however, there is also room for autonomy in childrearing, for two main reasons. Firstly, the autonomy of the growing child is no longer seen as a threat to family livelihood, given decreased material interdependencies – elderly parents have alternative sources of support in old age. Secondly, the autonomy of the growing child, rather than submissive obedience, becomes adaptive to urban life styles, for example, for independent decision-making in school and securing specialised jobs (see also Kohn, Naoi, et al., 1990). The effects of schooling appear to be particularly strong in promoting autonomy. Mayer, Tromsdorff, Kağıtçıbaşı, and Mishra (2012) found support for the distinctiveness of the three different models of family structure, sampling mothers and their adolescent children in Germany, Turkey and India. As expected, German respondents scored highest on independence, Turkish respondents scored highest on emotional interdependence, and Indian respondents scored highest on interdependence.

Similarly complex orientations towards children are also found in analyses of parental socialisation goals as assessed by the World Values Survey. Representative respondents from 55 nations were shown a list of 10 socialisation goals, and were then asked to choose up to five that they viewed as most important. Bond and Lun (2013) factor analysed these responses, finding two independent dimensions: 'self-directedness versus other-directedness' and 'civility versus practicality'. Self-directedness ('independence', 'imagination', 'feeling of responsibility' and 'determination and perseverance') versus other-directedness ('obedience' and 'religious faith') taps the independence thrust of the family independence model. Civility ('tolerance and respect of other people' and 'unselfishness') versus practicality ('thrift and saving money and things' and 'hard work') taps the interdependence thrust of the interdependence model, but distinguishes the range and way in which one relates. In nations socialising for civility, one inculcates norms for dealing openly and equally with all fellow citizens; in nations socialising for practicality, one inculcates norms for careful husbandry and careful instrumentality in dealing with one's fellow citizens. Nations in which both dimensions are endorsed would be those in which Kağıtçıbaşı's third family type would be most strongly endorsed.

In this way, each nation may be characterised by a profile indicating its emphasis on child socialisation across these two dimensions. This profile constitutes a context for development that will be reinforced and sustained by other institutions of socialisation and their agents across the lifespan. However, nation-level means from the World Values Survey do not test for the cultural change over time that is emphasised in Kağıtçıbaşı's model. Suggestive evidence for cultural change comes from studies comparing participants of different generations, or across urban versus rural locations. Mayer et al. (2012) found that adolescents in Germany, Turkey, and India emphasised independence more and interdependence less than their mothers did. Within-nation comparisons have shown lower interdependence and higher emotional interdependence among urban populations than in rural populations, both in Turkey (Mayer et al., 2012) and among the Canadian Inuit (McShane, Hastings, Smylie, & Prince, 2009).

Georgas, Berry, Van de Vijver, Kağıtçıbaşı, and Poortinga (2006) undertook a large-scale comparative study of families that also has potential relevance to Kağıtçıbaşı's family models. Students in 30 nations responded to a questionnaire in which they described numerous aspects of their family of origin. While the families of university students would not be wholly representative of the nations sampled as a whole, the sample nonetheless included nations that differed widely in terms of affluence. The results showed that emotional closeness with the nuclear family was rated equally highly throughout the sample. Closeness with the extended family was lower in some nations than others, but this outcome was not linked to affluence or religion. Children's roles were confirmed to be less instrumental in more affluent nations. The largest variations were found in endorsement of Schwartz's (2004) value domain of embeddedness, and in endorsement of hierarchical values about family relationships. These types of values were weaker in more affluent nations. There was also a striking similarity in the reported family roles, with mothers perceived as more expressive and nurturant, and fathers as more instrumental and controlling.

Family Structure and Self-Construal

The type of individual self-construal that is to be expected within Kağıtçıbaşı's model of interdependent families emphasises relatedness and mutual dependence. This is because in obedience-oriented childrearing there is no encouragement of autonomy. Instead, a 'heteronomous' self-construal would emerge, characteristic of a person who is dependent on others and lacks volitional agency (autonomy). In contrast, the self-construal fostered by independent families is predicted to be characteristic of a person who becomes autonomous and self-directing. Separation is often believed to be a requisite of autonomy. However, we discussed evidence in the previous two chapters that indicates they are better considered to be independent of one another, as portrayed in Figure 8.4. Thus, within Kağıtçıbaşı's third family type, the *psychologically* interdependent family, self-construal can be expected to be both autonomous and relational (Kağıtçıbaşı, 2005, 2007). The childrearing orientation that would contribute to the emergence of this type of self-construal involves autonomy, but there is also parental control, rather than permissiveness, as the goal is not separation of the growing child. Therefore a relational self that is also autonomous is the likely outcome.

The Georgas et al. (2006) study also included the Singelis (1994) self-construal scale, but the scales did not achieve adequate reliability in many samples. As we discussed in Chapter 7, this measure also does not control for acquiescent response style, so cross-national comparisons are not meaningful. More precise tests of Kağıtçıbaşı's model await more valid measurement. The study by Keller et al. discussed earlier does provide supportive evidence for the co-occurrence of ethnotheories favouring both autonomy and relatedness in non-Western urban samples. The multi-nation survey of self-construal and ways of achieving distinctiveness that was discussed in Chapter 7 (Becker, Vignoles, et al., 2012; Owe, Vignoles et al., 2012) has also yielded evidence that self-construals and related attributes do differ between rural, small town and urban locations in ways that are consistent with Kağıtçıbaşı's model (Easterbrook, Vignoles, et al., 2013).

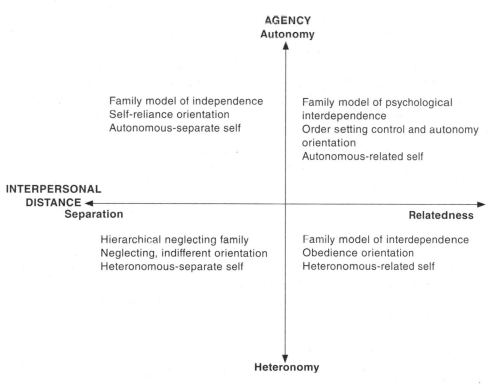

Figure 8.4   Agency, Interpersonal Distance and the Types of Self in Context

Adapted from Kağıtçıbaşı (2005).

Schooling

The proportion of children in the world who attend at least primary schooling has increased greatly over the past decade (United Nations, 2007). However, some 30% of children in sub-Saharan Africa still do not attend school. For them, the family continues preeminent as a source of socialisation into adult roles. For the remainder of the world's children, school begins to provide a series of alternative identities, both in terms of academic aspiration and in terms of peer-group affiliation. Crucially, in school, children learn to read and to write, and to think abstractly and critically in ways that do not arise directly from their family and immediate physical surroundings. Teachers may or may not be accepted as role models, but their very existence begins to enhance processes of identity choice.

In Chapter 6, we explored the consequences of differences between analytic and holistic cognition. Cultural contrasts in the nature of schooling can provide one factor sustaining this contrast. Schooling in East Asian cultures is said to give greater emphasis to rote learning than schooling in individualistic cultures (e.g., Purdie, Hattie, & Douglas, 1996). Even at early ages, contrasts are evident in approaches to learning. Li (2004) questioned Chinese and US 4-6 year olds on their understanding of learning. US children saw learning as a task, while Chinese children emphasised the relevance of effort in learning to the acquisition of moral virtue. Tweed and Lehman (2002) interpreted this contrast in terms of Socratic versus Confucian learning. In individualistic cultures, teachers encourage students to learn through analysis and criticism. The student establishes individual credibility by being good at questioning and debating. In contrast, in collectivist cultures, students give respect to the high status of teachers by putting effort into learning what is put in front of them. Only when they have mastered the material in its entirety would they feel it appropriate to ask questions about it. Pratt and Wong (1999) interviewed students and instructors in Hong Kong and concluded that Chinese learners see learning as a four-stage process: memorising, understanding, applying, and only finally questioning or modifying.

Peer pressures in schools also provide an increasingly important influence as the child ages. Attempts to define an appropriate basis for the comparison of peer pressures have proved problematic. For instance, the Anglo concept of bullying does not translate readily into many languages. Is this because the concept of bullying is indigenous to Anglo cultures? P.K. Smith et al. (2003) provided definitions of bullying for children in 14 nations. Using the terms judged most similar to the concept within each nation, they found widely varying reported frequencies of being bullied, and of being a bully, but it was not possible to deduce whether this varying frequency was attributable to variations in behaviour or variations in the meaning of the concept. To address this question, it might be easier to identify cultural variations in the types of behaviour that are found to elicit strong approval or disapproval. Some studies of this type are discussed later in this chapter.

Organisational Socialisation

Subsequent to schooling, individuals become affiliated with a variety of organisations, whether as university students, as business employees, or as participants in religious, military or sporting organisations. These organisations differ widely from one another, both within nations and between nations (e.g., Hofstede, Neuijen, Ohayv, & Sanders, 1990). However, they have in common with one another that there is typically a more substantive basis of choice than occurs during childhood as to whether to engage with them. Each is a source of distinctive socialisation processes, particularly those in which one commits to long-term membership.

All of them are likely to be affected by a series of processes identified in Schneider, Goldstein and Smith's (1995) ASA model (these initials stand for Attraction, Selection, and Attrition). As one approaches adulthood, certain organisations and occupations become attractive by virtue of their perceived compatibility with one's values, beliefs and aspirations. These organisations have their own priorities and selection procedures, so that the aspiring individual may or may not achieve membership of them. If membership is achieved, processes of induction and training, both formal and informal, will commence. If the organisation member responds positively to these socialisation processes and succeeds in contributing to the organisation's agendas, he or she will become an established contributor to that organisation's culture, identifying increasingly with its policies and practices. Among those for whom person-organisation fit is not accomplished, a process of attrition will occur: they will choose to leave, or will be discharged. Schneider et al. propose that in this way cultural groups will retain homogeneity in their membership character- istics over time. Thus a multitude of subcultures is created, not just within nations, but equally within organizations.

We can expect that these basic processes will be relatively similar around the world, but that they will differ in more specific ways that reflect cultural context. For instance, graduates hired by organisations in individualistic nations are typically appointed to a specific role that provides a distinctive form of technical or commercial expertise. In contrast, Japanese graduate recruits are typically required to work in many different organisational functions in turn, leading them to identify with the purposes of the organisation as a whole, rather than with a specific professional identity (Smith & Misumi, 1989).

Chow (2002) studied organisational socialisation in five East Asian nations. Respondents' predictions of career success were most strongly predicted by measures of organisational support and training. Earlier studies in Western nations have found measures of individual career tactics more strongly predictive. Ramesh and Gelfand (2010) compared labour turnover in call centres in the United States and India. Within the individualistic USA, employees' perception of a poor fit with their individual job was a significant predictor of turnover. In the more collectivistic India, employees' perceptions of poor fit, both with the organisation as a whole and with the local community, were significant predictors of turnover.

Therefore among those who experience socialisation in individualistic cultures, one's identity retains a stronger focus upon personal and professional attributes, with the consequent greater possibility of career mobility. Inkson and Khapova (2008) have distinguished bureaucratic careers and boundaryless careers: in a bureaucratic career, the individual stays with the same organisation and follows a career path provided by that organisation; in the increasingly frequent boundaryless career, individuals place their skills and experience on the market and make their own more opportunistic employment choices.

It is clear that some societies contain a much wider range of organisations than others, and that the boundaries through which individuals enter and leave organisations are more permeable in individualistic nations than in collectivistic nations. Nonetheless, organisations must be coun- ted alongside families as important contexts within which cultures are created and maintained.

SUBJECTIVE CULTURE

In Chapter 2 and again in Chapter 5, we examined debates between those who measure culture by aggregating individual self-perceptions of values, beliefs or personality characteristics and those who argue that we would do better to attend to individuals' perceptions of their context. In this section, we give fuller attention to this latter perspective. The basic reasoning in favour of attending to *perceptions* of context is that influence between ourselves and others mostly occurs on the basis of our subjective experience of what goes on around us (Bond, 2013).

The concept of **subjective culture** comprises all those elements of a small or large social grouping whose meanings are perceived to be shared. Thus it can refer to the values and beliefs that we have considered up to now, but equally it can encompass language, social roles and social norms. The first large-scale study to take this perspective was conducted by Osgood, May, and Miron (1975). These authors attempted to define the shared meaning of words within a given language by having people rate specific words or concepts on semantic differential rating scales (rating scales with opposing adjectives at each end of the scale). Factor analysis was used to summarise the ratings and three fundamental dimensions of meaning were identified: warm-cold, strong-weak, and active-passive. Osgood et al. obtained data from high-school students in 23 nations, and a factor structure resembling these three dimensions was found in all samples. This made it possible to identify which terms were consensually defined in a given culture and which were not. Consensus is indicated by a clear portrayal of a term in terms of the three dimensions of meaning. For instance, it was found that there was high consensus in defining the concept of 'duty' in nations that are now described as collectivistic, but not in nations that are more individualistic. In general, this study showed a contrast in the ways that word meanings were defined between the individualistic and collectivistic nations that were sampled. However, the individual-level factor analytic methods that were used mean that consensus is defined simply by the *average* of meanings in a particular sample. There is no measure of whether individuals actually share meanings.

> **Subjective Culture** is the individual's personal understanding of the terms that he or she uses to describe their context and life experience.

Triandis (1972) developed this approach further and was the first actually to use the term 'subjective culture'. For instance, he developed a 'role differential' measure, on which Greek and US respondents rated the types of behaviour that would be expected for example between fathers and sons, or between husbands and wives. The role differential measure is a direct precursor of those that were used by Gelfand et al. (2011) in their study of tight and loose cultures. As we noted in Chapter 3, these authors obtained direct ratings from their respondents as to how tightly bounded were the role requirements in their society, as well as ratings of how much latitude there was to behave in different ways in each of a range of social settings. These studies give a comparatively emic indication of the perceived norms that apply to specific roles and settings.

Measuring Norms

An alternative imposed-etic procedure is to specify a series of norms and ask respondents how strongly each norm is endorsed within their society. Argyle, Henderson, Bond, et al. (1986) compared the endorsement of 23 norms as applied to 23 different role relationships. They found a greater endorsement of norms restraining emotional expression in Hong Kong and Japan than in Italy and the UK. A more recent large-scale study also focused on norms concerning the expression of seven different specific emotions. Respondents were asked to rate whether, when they experienced a given emotion, they should express it toward each of 21 types of persons. Across 32 nations, Matsumoto, Hoo, Fontaine et al. (2008) found that citizen scores for norms restricting emotional expressiveness were more strongly endorsed in collectivist nations than in individualist nations. This was particularly true in relation to expressiveness within the in-group, and was most marked in relation to the expression of fear, happiness and surprise. Thus we find a clear convergence between a classification of cultures based on nation-level classifications of values and the actual measurement of subjective norms.

Having shown the importance of norms, it is particularly interesting to compare them more directly with the types of measures of cultural orientation that we have discussed in preceding chapters. Shteynberg, Gelfand, and Kim (2009) compared the predictive power of individualistic/collectivistic attitudes and individualistic/collectivistic norms in explaining Korean and American students' assignment of blame and amount of harm done in a series of hypothetical scenarios. Having controlled for national differences, perceived social norms accounted for differences in the amounts of blame and perceived harm that were assigned, whereas personal attitudes did not.

Fischer, Ferreira, Assmar, et al. (2009) took self-report survey items that had been used to measure different aspects of individualism-collectivism and rewrote them, replacing 'I' in each item with 'Most people', and asking respondents to think of most people in their family when completing the items. Data were collected from students in 11 nations. Four dimensions of perceived norms were identified, consistent with four different aspects of individualism-collectivism that had been specified by Triandis (1995). When the data were analysed at the nation level, four isomorphic dimensions were obtained. However, agreement between respondents in each nation as to the presence of the norms was only moderate.

Fischer et al. (2009) then examined the utility of their measures of subjective norms for predicting behaviour at the individual level. Students in New Zealand were asked to report the frequency with which they had engaged in 17 different behaviours over the preceding six months (e.g., 'lend something to a friend', 'obey my parents'). It was found that both subjective norms and personal cultural orientations of individualism-collectivism were significant predictors of actual reported behaviour. Overall, their predictive power was cumulative, suggesting that both norms and personal orientations were important. The results also varied between different behaviours: subjective norms were stronger predictors for social behaviours that had a normative element, whereas personal cultural orientation was more predictive for self-directed behaviours with no normative implications. Studying subjective norms can therefore help us to increase the amount of variance in behaviour that we can account for when combined with measures of the participants' own values, beliefs or self-construals.

The studies of norms that we have discussed so far are open to two kinds of interpretation. Firstly, it may be that nations do have rather strongly consensual norms, but that these norms are very situationally specific, just as behaviours tend to have very situation-specific meanings (Breugelmans, 2011). For instance, in Fischer et al.'s study, a typical item read 'When people have a need, they turn to others for help'. Even within the specified context of family, there may be very particular norms governing whether or not to ask for money, who to turn to for emotional support, what is a reasonable request to ask of particular types of person, and so forth. Thus, if we are predicting behaviour within a specific context, we then need to measure the norms perceived by the actors as applying in that context. These norms will be shaped by their broader national culture, but will be specific to the context whose interactions it reflects (Hofstede, Bond, & Luk, 1993).

The second possibility is that the objectively normative qualities of cultures are accessible to culture members only by way of their subjective perceptions, and that it is these subjective perceptions on which we must focus directly to gain the fullest understanding of culture. Studies taking this perspective are discussed next, but we first consider the work of Yamagishi (2011), whose model of culture is premised on the existence of situation-specific norms, although he does not directly seek to measure them and does not refer to them as norms. Yamagishi sees cultures as defined by a series of 'institutions', which comprise social niches that require the performance of specific behaviours. In using these terms, Yamagishi is not referring to institutions in the sense of schools, universities or hospitals. For him, an institution is an assemblage of self-sustaining beliefs, behaviours and incentives that enable an individual to interact effectively with those around them. He sees culture members as 'cultural game players' whose task it is to identify the particular behaviours that are required by a given setting. Their behavioural choices will not usually need to be consciously thought through, because there is long-established familiarity provided by an individual's reinforcement history with the many niches that make up a given culture.

Yamagishi and his colleagues have illustrated this perspective by following up on an earlier study by Kim and Markus (1999). These authors showed that, when given a choice of pens, Americans chose a distinctive one, whereas Japanese chose one that was similar to others. This result was interpreted as showing that Americans like to be different, whereas Japanese like to fit in. Yamagishi, Hashimoto, and Schug (2008) proposed that the Japanese would also have preferred a distinctive pen, but did not do so because to do so would contravene the implicit Japanese norm of *enryo*, that one should not offend others. They created an experimental procedure in which it was possible for the Japanese respondent to choose a distinctive pen without the risk of offending others, and found that under these circumstances, they did so as frequently as the Americans did. This effect was found not only in the more individualistic Northern Japanese island of Hokkaido, but equally in other parts of Japan (Hashimoto, Li, & Yamagishi, 2011). Thus they see the behaviour of the participants in their experiments as making choices that accord with 'commonsense' implicit norms. The impact of norms can be detected by devising informative experimental designs.

Intersubjective Culture

The second possible approach to the study of norms is to ask people to provide their subjective estimates of what is normative. Fischer (2006) asked students from ten nations to complete a modified version of the Schwartz Value Survey giving their perception of the values endorsed by most people in their country. When these scores were compared with means for self-reported values, the correlation was on average only 0.28. This correlation was much higher for embeddedness values and for affective autonomy values, and lowest for harmony values and intellectual autonomy values.

Fischer argued that autonomy and embeddedness were values that were socialised early in life and thus produced greater agreement between self-rated values and self-rated normative values (we discussed evidence supporting this view at the start of this chapter). Other values are socialised at later points in life and reflect more varied socialisation agencies. Consequently, there is less reason to expect them to be normative.

This interpretation received support from a further study in New Zealand. Students were asked to rate their own values and the values that they perceived to be normative in New Zealand. They were also asked to report on the frequency over the previous six months of six behaviours that were relevant to conformity values and universalism values. Here, Fischer showed that normative conformity values better predicted students' reports of their own conformity behaviours, whereas personal universalism values better predicted their reports of their own universalism behaviours. This finding suggests that self-reported values and self-rated normative values have different domains of predictive power; the same finding may apply to beliefs and other constructs used by social psychologists to predict behaviour.

Chiu et al. (2010) have popularised the term **intersubjective culture** to describe beliefs and values perceived to be normative. Wan, Chiu, Tam, et al. (2007) found that intersubjective values did in fact differ from values personally endorsed by samples of students in Hong Kong and the USA. The difference between one's values and the values that one perceives to be normative may be a key element in understanding an individual's behaviour. For instance, Wan et al. showed that students whose values were closer to their perceived campus normative values identified more strongly with their university and that this identification increased over time. Similar results were obtained in further studies focused on identifying with one's nation in China and in Singapore (Wan, Chiu, Peng, & Tam, 2007). Thus, norms are relevant to the achievement of the self-construals and identities discussed in Chapter 7. We explore more fully the links between groups and social identity in Chapter 12 and how this connection affects acculturation in Chapter 13.

Key Researcher Box 8.3   C.Y. Chiu

Figure 8.5   Chi-Yue Chiu

Chi-Yue Chiu (b. 1963) grew up in Hong Kong. He received his PhD in social-personality psychology at Columbia University in 1984, and taught at Hong Kong University before moving to the University of Illinois at Urbana-Champaign, and more recently to Nanyang Technological University, Singapore, where he is now full Professor of Management and Marketing. He is the author of four books and more than 200 journal articles and book chapters, some in English and others in Chinese. Some of his notable contributions to cross-cultural social psychology include pioneering work in developing the use of priming to study culture, and the development of the concept of intersubjective culture. With Ying Yi Hong, he is author of *Social Psychology of Culture* (2006).

Zou, Tam, Morris et al. (2009) replicated four published studies that had shown cultural differences in different aspects of social cognition, sampling students from Poland, Hong Kong and the United States (among them the attribution of fish movements and correspondence bias, which were discussed in Chapter 6). In the first three of these studies, they also included two measures of cultural orientation. The first of these obtained respondents' own cultural orientation. For the second, respondents predicted what they perceived would be the average ratings on the same scales by others in their cultural group. Zou et al. showed that in each of the four studies their measure of the perceived norm mediated the cultural effects that had been obtained, whereas respondents' own cultural orientation did not. In other words, respondents' subjective norms could explain the cultural differences that had been reported.

Why should this happen? The results obtained by Fischer (2006) indicated that norms will only be a stronger predictor of behaviour than individual values in circumstances where normative values are salient. In order to make the two sets of results consistent, we should need to determine that the specific circumstances of the studies by Zou et al. met this criterion. The alternative view, favoured for instance by Wan and Chiu (2009), is that cultural effects in all situations are better understood in terms of intersubjective norms than in terms of personal values. It is time to reexamine these alternative conceptions of how culture operates to affect individual social behaviour (Bond, 2013).

The position taken by intersubjective culture theorists is far removed from the approach taken by the theorists whose work was discussed in the early chapters of this book. They were concerned with identifying the dimensions of culture-level variation, whereas the subjective norm theorists often do not conduct comparative studies and analyse their data only at the individual level. Their position is consistent with major theories in social psychology such as social identity theory that make no specific reference to culture. In that sense, the intersubjectivists fulfil the aspiration championed by Bond (2002, 2013) that the goal of cross-cultural psychology should be to identify the sources of variation that would permit individual-level analyses of cultural differences.

As we have done in earlier chapters, Wan and Chiu (2009) note the difficulties in establishing the validity of cross-cultural measures of values and self-construals, due to the probable presence of reference group effects and other biases or confounds. However, many of these measurement problems are also likely to be present when respondents rate their subjective perceptions of others' values. The benefit of their approach lies not in improved measurement, but in the use of better constructs and more appropriate forms of data analysis. Rather than comparing mean scores from different nations, the relationship between variables within one or more samples can be unpacked using mediation analyses, as was done in Zou et al.'s study.

CONTINUITY AND CHANGE

This chapter commenced by examining the ways in which infants first encounter the normative aspects of the context into which they are born. It concludes by highlighting adults' experiences of the more varied contexts that make up life in contemporary society. In both sections, norms are treated as already existing before the interactions upon which researchers focus. However, in practice, the normative structures that one encounters rarely all point in the same direction, as illustrated in Everyday Life Box 8.1.

Everyday Life Box 8.1 Socialisation Experiences

I grew up in Eastern Germany, which is typically described as an individualistic, masculine non-traditional culture, in which analytical thinking and socialisation toward independence and autonomy are thought to be prevalent. Consequently, my parents raised me to be independent, encouraging me to take care of my own things, clean up my room, wash my own clothes and cook my own meals. Much to their dismay, I was actually quite lazy and did not act that independently. At the same time, to the outside world I was socialised to act rather collectivistically. I was told not to point at other people with my finger because this is rude, not to run around with dirty clothes when playing outside because this would embarrass my family, to greet strangers in a friendly fashion when walking to school or the small store because this was polite. All of this was to immature reflected well on my parents and good upbringing, and I was told that they were necessary in this small community of farmers. In school we were required to do a lot of rote learning. Problem solving was taught only occasionally, and instead of using analytic or empirical methods, we were encouraged to approach problems in a holistic fashion by identifying patterns, relationships and the overall gestalt, as well as using universal principles for the deduction of specific cases.

More confusing was that everyone was to take personal responsibility for their own actions (with transgressions being punished in various ways), while also stressing that the collective good was greater than the individual good and personal responsibility should be aligned with and contribute to the well-being of everyone in society. I will always remember an older friend telling me that nobody was unique and everybody was exchangeable and that the ultimate goal in life was serving the collective. In short, cultural socialisation was a confusing process, and messages and goals were not well aligned across contexts and situations. There was no coherent unified cultural press that socialised me into becoming a model German citizen.

Source: Fischer, 2011a.

The long-term distal causation of normative structures has been discussed in Chapter 3, but short-term proximal causation is of equal, and perhaps greater, importance. Norms do change and we examine evidence for major cultural change in Chapter 14, but the creation and maintenance of norms is an everyday event. Individuals who come together by chance or for some purpose may or may not achieve a shared understanding of purpose and procedures. If they do, values, beliefs or actions that contribute to that interactional success are more likely to be sustained. Elements that are distinctive, or are unrelated to success and continuation, are more likely to be lost. In this way, normative structures are subject to processes of selection over time, just as in biological evolution (Dutton & Heath, 2009). By participating in existing social structures, each of us contributes to their maintenance, and to the life and the death of those innovations in procedures and products that turn out to be passing fads and fashions.

SUMMARY

The role of parenting and the family is of key importance in the process of human development in context. Childrearing reflects cultural values and beliefs and thus ensures the making and the continuity of culture; however, it can also be an agent of change in the remaking of culture during socio-economic change, as seen in urbanisation and immigration. Variations in the value attributed to children, in family patterns and in the emergent self-concept of children make early contributions to the individual's understanding of prevailing norms. Adult experiences involve socialisation to the norms of additional subcultural contexts. The relative power of individual self-construals and of intersubjective norms in predicting behaviour in differing cultural contexts varies and appears to be a notable distinction that needs to be explored more extensively in these more proximal cultural contexts.

FURTHER READING

1 Chen, C., & Farruggia, S. (2002). Culture and adolescent development. *Online Readings in Psychology and Culture*. Available at http://scholarworks.gvsu.edu/*orpc*

2 Chiu, C.Y., Gelfand, M., Yamagishi, T., et al. (2010). Intersubjective culture: The role of intersubjective perceptions in cross-cultural research. *Perspectives on Psychological Science*, 5, 482–493.

3 Kağıtçıbaşı, Ç. (2002). A model of family change in cultural context. *Online Readings in Psychology and Culture*. Available at http://scholarworks.gvsu.edu/*orpc*

4 Kağıtçıbaşı, Ç. (2007). *Family and human development across cultures: A view from the other side.* Hillsdale, NJ: Erlbaum.

5 Keller, H. (2002). Culture and development: Developmental pathways to individualism and relatedness. *Online Readings in Psychology and Culture*. Available at http://scholarworks.gvsu. edu/*orpc*

6 Rohner, R.R., & Khaleque, A. (2002). Parental acceptance-rejection and lifespan development: A universalist perspective. *Online Readings in Psychology and Culture*. Available at http://scholarworks.gvsu.edu/*orpc*

7 Triandis, H.C. (2002). Subjective culture. *Online Readings in Psychology and Culture*. Available at http://scholarworks.gvsu.edu/*orpc*

8 Trommsdorff, G. (2002). An ecocultural and interpersonal approach to development over the lifespan. *Online Readings in Psychology and Culture*. Available at http://scholarworks.gvsu.edu/*orpc*

9 Vandermaas-Peeler, M. (2002). Cultural variations in parental support of children's play. *Online Readings in Psychology and Culture*. Available at http://scholarworks.gvsu.edu/*orpc*

STUDY QUESTIONS

1 How is a developmental perspective helpful in studying social behaviour across cultures?
2 Point to some possibly universal and some culturally bounded aspects of childhood.
3 What is the importance of the value of children in understanding family dynamics and changes in the context of socio-economic development?

4 What are the three different family models? Which one of these would you say is the most prevalent in the society/community where you live? Do you detect variations in these models across time?

5 What are some of the norms that obtain in your family of origin? Do you privately agree with them? When do you publicly conform to them and how do you make sense of your inconsistency?

6 Which values and beliefs would you say are normative among the groups with which you spend most time? Are these also the values and beliefs of your wider society? Are they your values and beliefs?

9

Interpersonal Behaviour

'When I use a word', Humpty Dumpty said, in a rather scornful tone,
'it means just what I choose it to mean – neither more nor less'.
'The question is', said Alice, 'whether you can make words mean so many different things'.

(Lewis Carroll, *Through the Looking Glass*)

In the preceding chapters, we have identified several ways to characterise individuals that take account of cultural differences. We have described cross-culturally valid measures of values, beliefs, self-construals, personality and aspects of emotional experience – what one might call 'the psychological software'. It is now time to move the focus away from the psychological interior and toward the ways in which individuals conduct their relations with one another. In doing so, we shall again emphasise studies in which researchers have used one or other of these earlier measures of cultural orientation, with the aim of unpackaging variations in interpersonal relationships in different cultural contexts.

Although cultural differences in some aspects of interpersonal behaviour appear to be mediated by measures of individual-level cultural orientation, other findings suggest that this may be a two-way relationship: communication and relationship processes can also be viewed as cultural practices or institutions, and participation in these practices may be a mechanism through which cultural differences in beliefs, values, and self-construals are sustained, rather than vice versa.

STYLES OF COMMUNICATION

Verbal Communication

We can expect that people's cultural orientation will be reflected in the ways that they communicate with one another, both verbally and non-verbally. Growing up within a given cultural context will provide socialisation as to what aspects of others' communications to attend to, as well as what it is worthwhile and appropriate for oneself to speak about, when to speak about it, and how to do so.

Language

A basic purpose of language is to draw attention to particular objects, actions, events or feelings (Semin, 2009). Furthermore, the way that we speak inevitably draws attention to ourselves, frequently announcing our identities for example in terms of ethnicity, nationality, social class, age, and gender (e.g., Labov, 2010). Perhaps the most basic way in which this complex set of considerations is accomplished is through the usages that have become integrated into different language systems.

For a long time the relationship between language and culture has been studied in terms of the different ways that languages classify items of experience. For example, the classification of kinship terms has been of great interest to anthropologists in reflecting the variations in the importance attributed to distinctions in kinship relations. In Turkish there are three words for aunt and three words for uncle, referring to whether the relationship is through the paternal or the maternal side or through marriage. In a similar way, some languages have more extensive provision for expressions of deference and hierarchy than do others. For instance, Japanese has three separate levels of formality and also requires men and women to speak in different ways. However, no available study has yet determined whether there is any systematic relation between these types of language features and nation scores on dimensions of culture, such as power distance.

Interestingly, Munroe, Munroe, and Winters (1996) have shown that words within languages spoken in hotter countries differ from those spoken in cooler parts of the world. Languages originating in hot countries contain many words with alternating vowels and consonants (Malawi, Malaysia, Panama), whereas speech in cold countries has many more consonants (e.g., in English – awkward, screech, stretch). Hot country languages are easier to decode because of their regularity, and Munroe et al. suggest that they evolved to permit easier communication over greater distances among persons interacting outdoors. Cold country languages were more likely to be spoken in sheltered or indoor settings that made speech discrimination easier. However, the locations in which the world's most widely spoken languages are spoken now bear little relation to the places in which they originated.

Language speakers also differ in the relative proportion of different parts of speech that they use. Semin, Gorts, Nandram, and Semin-Goossens (2002) predicted that in cultures where relationships and interdependence are salient, emotions serve as relationship markers and will be more often expressed concretely as verbs (for example, 'I like you', which implies a relationship). Conversely, they predicted that in cultures where emotions serve to identify the self, emotions will more often be represented abstractly as nouns and adjectives (for example, 'She is a friendly person', which does not imply a relationship). As predicted, they found verbs more frequent in Hindi and Turkish, but nouns and adjectives more frequent in Dutch. Since verbs are cognitively more accessible than nouns and adjectives, different languages may prime different ways of thinking. Kashima, Kashima et al. (2006) found a similar contrast when comparing Australian and Korean speech, as did Maass, Karasawa et al. (2006) when comparing Italians and Japanese.

Is it possible, then, that the parts of speech that we use will act as recurrent linguistic primes of the types of abstract and holistic social cognition that were discussed in Chapter 6? In that chapter, we noted limitations on the degree to which primes can elicit changed cognitions. Even so, because so much of everyday life is saturated by language, it seems plausible that language can sustain our habitual self-construals and self-presentations. For example, Kashima and Kashima (1998) found that use of the personal pronoun 'I' is more strongly required in languages spoken within individu-alist nations. Maybe this feature of language has been shaped by cultural values and beliefs, but it could also perhaps be instrumental in sustaining the same values and beliefs. In fact, there is a long history of controversy concerning linguistic effects on cognition, and more evidence is required of the ways in which such effects may occur, as illustrated in Box 9.1.

Box 9.1   Does Language Affect Cognition?

In 1956, Lenneberg and Roberts reported a link between language and cognition. They compared memory for colours of monolingual speakers of the Native American language Zuni and of Harvard undergraduates. Zuni has a single word for yellow and orange. Shown a series of colours, Zunis were unable to recall which were orange and which were yellow. Similar effects were later obtained by various researchers sampling cultural groups from hot countries that also lacked words for some colours. These studies are often cited as evidence for the Whorfian hypothesis, which states that language determines the way that we are able to think.

More recently it has been established that chronic high levels of ultraviolet radiation (UV-B) in tropical latitudes lead to a loss of sensitivity to blue and green. Lindsey and Brown (2002) showed that native English speakers viewing colours through lenses simulating these effects had a similar inability to name colours. This suggests that a lack of colour names in the languages of some cultural groups is a *consequence* of their inability to identify and remember certain colours, not a cause of it (Au, 2004). However, a loss of sensitivity cannot explain all the studies of language effects. Turkish has two words for blue, *mavi* (blue) and *lacivert* (dark blue). Turkish speakers have been found better able to discriminate differing shades of blue than English speakers. Moreover, it has also been shown that training improves the ability of English speakers to discriminate between shades of blue (Özgen, 2004). This finding suggests that the existence of an additional colour term in Turkish does over time encourage the development of greater colour sensitivity. Presumably, the availability of the term to language users means that they can reinforce one another for correct or incorrect colour identification, and thereby help develop discriminability of the colours in their cultural group.

Source: Au (2004).

Conversational constraints and goals

The studies of language discussed above suggested a link between language use and the cul-tural orientation of the speaker, but they did not make direct tests of this linkage. M.S. Kim (1994) developed a theory of what she called conversational constraints. These are ways in which one might wish to limit the effects of what one says. Kim proposed that speakers within collectivist cultures would constrain themselves in order not to hurt the hearer's feelings and not to impose themselves on others. Within individualist nations, on the other hand, she predicted a constraint favouring clarity of expression. Initial evidence showed support for the predictions among samples from Korea and the USA. In a further study, Kim, Hunter, Miyahara et al. (1996) included measures of self-construal and increased the range of specified

constraints. Respondents in Korea, Japan, Hawaii and mainland USA were asked how important each of five constraints would be in a series of imagined scenarios. Constraints favouring
the task outcome of the scenario were rated as being more important in the USA and this
difference was mediated by the respondent's level of independent self-construal. Constraints
favouring relationship harmony were rated more important in the Pacific Asian samples, and
this difference was mediated by the respondent's level of interdependent self-construal.

Service encounters of various sorts – such as getting a technician to repair a computer, obtaining
a room for a night at a hotel, or ordering coffee at a café – are occasions when the interdependency
of conversation becomes highlighted. Persons wishing to be served are dependent on the service
provider to deliver the desired service. They will want to obtain the service as quickly and fully
as possible without offending the service provider, thus maintaining the relationship for possible
future use. Chan, Bond, Spencer-Oatey, and Rojo-Laurilla (2004) examined how Filipinos and
Hong Kong Chinese seeking service would try to promote their relationship with service providers,
using scenarios involving five different types of service delivery. They found strong differences across
the five situations, with those seeking service more concerned to promote a relationship when the
service provider had discretionary authority in delivering that service. Filipinos were more concerned than the Chinese about relationship promotion in the scenario where they requested a
computer repair, where the difficulty of getting computers serviced in the Philippines put them
into a more dependent position than it did in Hong Kong. Endorsement of Schwartz's (1992)
dimension of self-transcendence values predicted the level of concern across all scenarios, regardless of nationality. Thus, those who valued interpersonal harmony more were generally more eager
to nurture and promote the relationship with the service provider by communicating in face-saving
and non-conflictual ways that were appropriate to their dependent status.

Directness

The contrast between communication styles that are preferred within individualist and collectivist cultures was discussed by Hall as long ago as 1966. Hall proposed a contrast between
low-context cultures and **high-context cultures**, by which he implied that in individualistic
cultures a communication is treated as a relatively
separate event, with little reference to the particular interpersonal context within which it occurs. In
contrast, in collectivist cultures he proposed that
communications are treated as integrally linked to
the context of the relationships within which they
occur, including the history of the parties involved,
their common ground of shared understandings,
and the setting of their interaction.

In **Low-Context Cultures,** communication is
typically through explicit direct messages. In
High-Context Cultures, communication is
typically through messages in which the meaning is implicit in the physical settings in which
they occur, or is internalised within the known
personal attributes of the senders, for example
their status and role. Very little of the message
is explicit.

This contrast has consequences for the ways
in which communication is likely to be expressed.
For instance, if one's relationships with others are
already well-established and there is high priority
given to maintaining the existing state of harmony, communication is likely to be less explicit and
more indirect, since the context carries meaning that does not need to be verbalised. There will be

no need to spell out those aspects of the relationship that are unchanging. On the other hand, in a low-context exchange of communication we can expect greater directness and less ambiguity.

Holtgraves (1997) developed a self-report measure of conversational indirectness. Separate scales assessed whether one spoke indirectly and whether one looked for indirect meanings in what others said. Koreans scored higher than Americans on both scales. Using Holtgraves' measure, Sanchez-Burks, Lee, Choi, et al. (2003) replicated these differences with Korean and Chinese business students, and showed that this effect was mediated by a measure of 'collectivist' cultural orientation. Similar mediation effects were also obtained among students in Hawaii (Hara & Kim, 2004). We should note, however, that indirectness is not only found in collectivist cultures (for a light-hearted account of British indirectness see Everyday Life Box 9.1).

Everyday Life Box 9.1   How to Understand the British

What the British say	What the British mean	What others understand
I hear what you say	I disagree and do not want to discuss it further	He accepts my point of view
With the greatest respect...	I think you are an idiot	He is listening to me
That's not bad	That's good	That's poor
That is a very brave proposal	You are insane	He thinks I have courage
Quite good	A bit disappointing	Quite good
I would suggest...	Do it or be prepared to justify yourself	Think about the idea, but do what you like
Oh, incidentally/by the way	The primary purpose of our discussion is...	That is not very important
I was a bit disappointed that	I am annoyed that	It doesn't really matter
Very interesting	That is clearly nonsense	They are impressed
I'll bear it in mind	I've forgotten it already	They will probably do it
I'm sure it's my fault	It's your fault	Why do they think it was their fault?
You must come for dinner	It's not an invitation, I'm just being polite	I will get an invitation soon
I almost agree	I don't agree at all	He's not far from agreement
I only have a few minor comments	Please re-write completely	He has found a few typos
Could we consider some other options	I don't like your idea	They have not yet decided

Source: Nannette Ripmeester (nd), *Looking for work in the United Kingdom*, ISBN 978-90-5896-059-7. Reproduced by permission.

Gudykunst, Matsumoto, Ting-Toomey, Nishida, Kim, and Heyman (1996) also drew on Hall's concepts to develop a broader range of measures of high- versus low-context communication styles, and to relate these measures to self-construal. Among students from the USA, Japan, Korea, Hawaii and Australia, independent self-construal was associated with using dramatic, feeling-oriented, precise and open communication, as well as a reduced ability to interpret 'indirect' messages. Interdependent self-construal predicted greater sensitivity, and more negative attitudes toward silence. As Gudykunst et al.'s results illustrate, the contrast between high and low context nations has broader applicability than Kim's model of constraints, because it focuses upon receiving communications as well as sending communications.

Yeung and Kashima (2012) reasoned that a preference for accurate and direct communication would cause Anglo Australians to transmit information that was relevant to stereotyping more accurately than Asian Australians would. Their hypothesis was supported. The Asian Australian messages were more distorted by stereotypic assumptions that had not been in the original messages. However, as was discussed in Chapter 6, differences in cognition between Anglos and Asians are better thought of as habits rather than as indelible differences. When Yeung and Kashima instructed their Asian Australian participants to transmit the information accurately, they became just as accurate as the Anglo Australians.

Each of these studies sampled just a few nations. Smith (2011a) reasoned that the way in which respondents agreed or disagreed with survey items would provide an indication of their habitual communication styles. Drawing on items within the World Values Survey (Inglehart, 1997) he constructed scores for citizens of 50 nations for agreement as well as disagreement. The strength of citizen agreement was significantly predicted by Hofstede's (2001) measures of collectivism, power distance and Schwartz's (2004) measure of embeddedness values; the nation-level strength of disagreement was most strongly predicted by cultural looseness rather than tightness on Gelfand et al.'s (2011) measures.

In-group speech and out-group speech

The results of the studies that we have discussed in the preceding paragraphs need to be evaluated cautiously because of an issue that we have discussed throughout this book: if collectivist cultures are high-context cultures, then the way that persons within those cultures choose to communicate with others will depend upon whom they are communicating with. Of course, communication style will also vary between contexts in low-context cultures. One speaks to one's romantic partner in a manner that is different from how one speaks to a teacher, a bank manager, or a stranger. However, the variation would be greater in high-context cultures (McAuley, Bond, & Kashima, 2002).

The in-group/out-group distinction is significant here. In general there is a greater difference between behaviours and communication within one's in-groups and with out-groups in collectivist societies than is the case in individualistic societies. We have seen already that interdependent self-construal is associated with seeing oneself or other persons differently in different contexts. Consequently, conclusions about differences in communication style that hold across all contexts are open to challenge. We may find that communication in high-context cultures is direct in some settings and indirect in others. The distinction between communication with known in-group members and out-group members is likely to be a particularly important one.

Gudykunst, Gao, Schmidt et al. (1992) compared in- and out-group communication among students in Hong Kong, Japan, Australia and the USA. When ratings for in-group and out-group persons were compared, several significant differences were found among the more collectivist samples from Japan and Hong Kong. Respondents reported more questioning of each other, more feelings of similarity, more shared networks, and more feeling that they could understand the others' feelings without their being explicit during in-group communication. By contrast, the US and Australian respondents did not show any significant differences between their in- and out-group communications. As suggested above, this difference between in-group and out-group communication outcomes may well be predicted by respondents' level of interdependent self-construal, and the different strengths of this self-construal by members of each cultural group may mediate the observed cultural differences.

Much remains to be learned about cultural differences in communication style. Self-report measures may have limited validity, particularly when they do not specify whom one is interacting with. There is also the problem that the instructions for any cross-cultural study of communication are themselves delivered to respondents, whether spoken or written, in a particular language and style and, as we saw in Chapter 6, this kind of variation in experimental procedure may act as an unintended prime (Oyserman & Lee, 2007).

Studies that sample actual dialogue may give us a richer understanding. Yeung (2003) compared business meetings in Australian and Hong Kong Chinese banks. In task-focused settings such as these, ways of disagreeing are required. Yeung found that members of both samples disagreed equally often, but did so in different ways. The Australians favoured the 'yes, but ...' format, while the Hong Kong Chinese asked more rhetorical questions. Each also had distinctive ways of not being seen as pushy. The Australians more often used phrases like 'somewhat', 'hopefully' and 'I think that ...'. The Chinese employed more questions, especially in the 'Can we ...?' form.

Nelson, al Batal, and el Bakary (2002) content analysed Egyptian and US spoken refusals to requests said to have been made by someone of a high, equal, or low status. Egyptian men were the most direct, but greater deference toward persons of higher status did not differ between the two nations. In a similar earlier study, Nelson, el Bakary and al Batal (1993) focused upon the giving of compliments. Here, too, they found the Egyptians at least as direct as the Americans. Egyptian compliments were more elaborated, often using metaphors.

The finding that Egyptians favour direct communication styles is noteworthy. It points again to the risks of generalising findings obtained in some collectivistic nations, mainly in East Asia, to all collectivistic nations. It may be that the indirect forms of communication commonly found in research with East Asian respondents are due more to the tact, modesty, or face-saving characteristic of Confucian-heritage cultures, rather than cultural collectivism *per se*. There may be other ways of communicating that function equally well to maintain the integrity of collectivist in-groups in other parts of the world.

Non-Verbal Communication

One could argue that an excessive focus on the verbal content of communication is itself culturally biased. Drawing on the contrast between high- and low-context cultures, Kitayama and Ishii (2002) compared the attention given to passages of emotional speech by Japanese and US listeners. Using a task where the emotional tone and words used were inconsistent with one another, they were able to show that Americans attended more to the content of the words that were used, but that the Japanese attended more to the vocal emotion that was expressed. Similarly, in previous chapters, we reviewed studies showing that collectivist cultures tend to have stronger display rules restricting the expression of intense emotions that might disturb relationship harmony (e.g., Matsumoto et al., 2008), but that members of these cultures are correspondingly more sensitive when judging the intensity of the underlying emotion from facial expressions (e.g., Matsumoto et al., 2002).

These results highlight that indirect communication is not necessarily any less effective than direct communication – it just works differently. However, they also highlight the importance of broadening our focus to include the various non-verbal aspects of the communication process, perhaps especially when studying participants in high-context cultural settings. These include facial expressions, gestures, speech volume, amount and speed, proximity and touching.

Research studies in these areas have only rarely drawn upon cross-cultural theory and mostly provide us with simple descriptive contrasts. The difficulty in this field of study may stem from some of the definitional issues that we discussed in Chapter 1. Non-verbal communication is most typically studied by the observation of behaviours. However, as we noted in that chapter, behaviours can have different meanings in different contexts, and consequently although some attempts have been made (Andersen, Hecht, Hoobler, & Smallwood, 2002), it is difficult to integrate these observations with conceptualisations of culture that stem from the meanings that are given to what goes on around us. For instance, someone who spends a high proportion of time looking at another person may be judged in one part of the world by that other person to be communicating friendliness, but in another to be showing insufficient deference or even hostility. H.Z. Li (2004) analysed video recordings of Canadian and Chinese students role-playing a doctor-patient interview. Canadian same-gender pairs showed more than twice as much mutual gaze as same-gender Chinese pairs. So how should we understand this dramatic difference? How should we best understand the variations in the meaning of silence that are explored in Everyday Life Box 9.2?

Proximity

The greatest amount of data on non-verbal communication concerns the preference for proximity or physical closeness when interacting with another person. Watson (1970) asked pairs of students from 31 nations attending the University of Colorado to sit at a comfortable distance and converse with one another. Arabs and South Asians sat closest, followed by Latin Americans and South Europeans. More distant were East Asians, and finally 'North Europeans' (who included North Americans and Australians). Although this study had some weaknesses, such as small sample size and variations in how well the partners said they liked each other, the range of nations sampled was unusually broad and entirely apt when studying this question.

Sussman and Rosenfeld (1982) found that previously unacquainted Venezuelan negotiators sat closer than did US negotiators, who in turn sat closer than the Japanese negotiators. The particular interest of the studies by Watson and by Sussman and Rosenfeld is that they array national samples in a different way from that implied by studies of individualism and collectivism. Despite being usually considered more collectivist than Americans, the Japanese

Everyday Life Box 9.2   Is Silence Golden?

Attitudes toward silence vary greatly around the world, as expressed in sayings in many societies. For example, a Turkish saying is 'if speech is silver, silence is gold', which reflects traditional values upholding reflection and caution before acting or speaking and frowning upon verbosity. It is often said that the Japanese make extensive use of silence, for instance to signal disagreement without the need for a direct contradiction. Hasegawa and Gudykunst (1998) compared US and Japanese attitudes toward silence. They proposed that silence can be thought of as an extreme example of high-context communication, which should therefore be more frequent in Japan than in the USA. Their study also included the key distinction between communicating with close friends and with strangers. Two dimensions were identified: using silence strategically and viewing silence negatively. As expected, the Japanese reported being silent more frequently. Their reactions to silence varied, depending on whether they were with friends or strangers. They were more uncomfortable being silent with strangers, whereas for the Americans it made no difference whether they were with friends or strangers. They reported more strategic use of silence than did the Japanese, which contradicts the stereotypic belief that it is the Japanese who use silence strategically. This stereotype may have arisen because American observers of the Japanese scene projected their own cultural logic about silence onto the Japanese. However, Hasegawa and Gudykunst proposed that their result was plausible, because low-context Americans will be more self-conscious during silences, whereas the Japanese will be less self-conscious and will therefore see the use of silence as natural rather than strategic.

Giles, Coupland, and Wiemann (1992) found a similar contrast between US and Chinese attitudes toward silence, but they found the Finnish to be even more comfortable than the Chinese with silence. Carbaugh (2006) made a detailed study of the Finns' distinctive propensity for silence, often interpreted by non-Finns as shyness. He identified an indigenous construct of *luonteva tapa alla*, which translates as 'natural way of being', implying that it is natural to feel no compulsion to speak. Within Finnish culture there is a preference not to speak unless one has something worthwhile to say, and a respect for others who stay silent even when in the company of others. At the same time Finns speak directly when they do speak up. As one of Carbaugh's interviewees put it:

> Communication in Finland can be described in one sentence - if you've got nothing to say: shut up. If you, on the other hand, have got something to say, say it straight, brutal but truthful, whatever it is. Don't try any slick small talk: Again the Finnish culture shows not only its elegance but also its efficiency. Wordless communication is in fact always the most truthful. (2006: 215)

Thus silence is valued in some individualistic cultures at least as much as it is in some collectivistic cultures.

negotiators preferred to keep their physical distance from one another. There may be several different explanations for proximity preferences in different parts of the world. One possibility, at least among Europeans, was indicated by Holland, Roeder, Van Baaren, Brandt, and Hannover

(2004), who found independent self-construal to predict greater actual spatial distance during seated conversations between German students. Similar distance effects were found by priming independence among Dutch students.

In the Sussman and Rosenfeld study, as in Nelson et al.'s (1993; 2002) Egyptian studies, gender effects were as large as the differences found between nations. We would similarly expect differences in proximity for different gender pairings across cultures, but at present we lack a clear understanding of how the meaning of proximity varies between nations that would help us explain the differences that are found.

Spatial positioning. Aside from simple distance, the positioning of people in relation to one another can convey different meanings in different locations. Marriott (1993) provided evidence concerning spatial positioning within Japanese business firms. Through observing meetings in Japan, she noted that seating position represented the relative seniority of each person present. In contrast, Australian managers took no account of status in determining where to sit. Thus, they failed to read contextual cues that would have enabled them to relate more effectively with the Japanese managers with whom they were meeting. From this, the Japanese would probably also be confused in their judgements of seniority among the Australians.

Touch

Together with his differentiation of high and low context cultures, Hall (1966) also proposed a parallel contrast between contact and non-contact cultures, referring to variations in the amount of touching. Proximity makes both touching and maintaining eye contact easier, and Watson (1970) also found that those who sat closer touched one another more frequently. Shuter (1976) also observed close proximity and frequent touching among Latin Americans. Remland, Jones, and Brinkman (1995) surreptitiously videoed people talking to one another while standing in public places in six European nations. Greeks and Italians showed more touching than did the French, Dutch, British and Irish. However, comparing overall touching rates is unlikely to be useful because different types of touch evidently have different meanings. Illustrating this difference in meaning, Dibiase and Gunnoe (2004) observed couples in nightclubs in Boston, Prague and Rome, distinguishing between hand touches and non-hand touches. Overall, men did more hand touching and women did more non-hand touching. Touch was more frequent in Italy and the Czech Republic than in the United States, with hand touching more frequent among the Czechs and non-hand touching among the Italians. However, hand touches were more frequent by Czech men than women but more by Italian women than men, suggesting that the meanings of different types of touch can be quite culture-specific.

Gestures

The frequency of using 20 different hand gestures across 40 locations in Western Europe has been documented (Morris, Collett, March, & O'Shaughnessy, 1979). Some were more widespread across nations than others. However, there are some relatively well-known variations in the meanings of many gestures, for instance 'V' signs and the 'A-OK' gesture, as well as head nodding and shaking. We lack a theory to explain the way in which such meanings have evolved. There is also substantially more gesturing in some nations than others. Graham and Argyle (1975) found that gesturing in Italy enhanced the effectiveness of communication more than in other locations. Low gesture rates are thought to be associated with greater formality and gesturing may therefore be less frequent in high power distance cultures. On the other hand, bowing may be largely restricted to hierarchical cultures, although it is not found in all such cultures, since relative status can also be signaled in many other ways, including variations in proximity, gazing and spatial positioning.

Crying

Crying sometimes occurs alone, but often occurs in interpersonal situations and has relational significance, for example augmenting a verbal communication. Becht and Vingerhoets (2002) obtained data on the frequency of adult crying across 37 nations. Crying was reported most frequently by Italian, Turkish and German men, and by Swedish, Brazilian and German women. It was least frequent among Malay men and Nigerian women. Van Hemert, Van de Vijver and Vingerhoets (2011) tested three alternative explanations for the nation-level frequencies that had been found. To test their theories, it was necessary to assume homology – in other words, that what causes individuals to cry can also explain which nations are more and least tearful (see Chapter 4). They found that crying was most frequent in nations with higher nation-level extraversion, with a loose rather than tight culture, and with weaker norms restricting emotional expression. However, the measures that they used to tap the last two of these variables were indirect estimates. Using Gelfand et al.'s (2011) measure of cultural tightness-looseness, they found that female crying was indeed more frequent in loose cultures, but there was no relationship for male crying. Neither did Matsumoto et al.'s (2008) measure of emotional display norms predict crying frequency, perhaps because the published scores did not differentiate between genders.

Becht and Vingerhoets (2002) also asked their respondents how they felt after they had cried. Most people felt better. Four factors were found to explain the extent to which people felt better: Hofstede's nation-level score for femininity, low feeling of shame, being from an affluent nation, and coming from a nation where crying was relatively frequent. Among these, the strongest predictor was Hofstede's femininity score. Crying works best in Finland and least well in Switzerland!

Facial expressions

In Chapter 6 we discussed evidence for the universal *recognition* of expressions of emotions. However, we may also make additional inferences from facial expressions. Matsumoto and Kudoh (1993) showed photographs of smiling and neutral faces to Japanese and Americans. Smiling faces conveyed sociability to all respondents, but the Americans also judged smiling faces as more intelligent. In a similar study, Albright, Malloy, Qi et al. (1997) compared Chinese and Americans. Both saw smiling faces as more sociable, but the Chinese also saw them as lacking in self-control and calmness. Thus, there was evidence for both universality and cultural distinctiveness in reactions to smiling and in the meanings attributed to it. Patterson, Iizuka, et al. (2007) compared Japanese and American responses to a confederate who smiled, nodded, or made a brief verbal greeting to strangers walking in a public place. Around 1% of the Japanese responded, whereas between 9% and 25% of Americans did so, depending on the type of greeting.

Emotional display

Non-verbal expressions are often associated with the experience of various emotions, with each emotion having its distinctive profile of observable behaviours. Wong, Bond and Rodriguez

Mosquera (2008) examined display profiles for the experience of seven emotions in relation to nation-level scores for Schwartz's (2004) values measures. Emotional reactions were measured by self-reported verbal and non-verbal responses across 25 of the national groups in the ISEAR database created by Walbott and Scherer (1986). Non-verbal expressions of emotion, for instance laughing or crying, were found to be more strongly related to values than verbal expressions, with fear, shame and guilt all expressed less in hierarchical cultures and joy expressed less in cultures high in embeddedness.

New ways of thinking about non-verbal behaviour

The studies reviewed in this section indicate considerable variability in the frequency and meaning of non-verbal aspects of communication. We do not yet have conceptual frameworks that enable us to unpackage most of this complexity in any systematic way. Indeed, it may be that the cultural specificity of non-verbal communication is closely related to the functions that it serves: correct usage of non-verbal communication conveys the communicator's authentic identity as a member of the in-group. This specificity is most obvious in the case of 'emblems' – culture-specific gestures communicating explicit meanings – and less obvious in the case of features of speech like volume and amount.

Throughout this section, we have followed the conventional assumption that non-verbal behaviours reflect the inner states of the communicator. However, there is an intriguing alternative possibility: our socialisation to employ particular types of non-verbal communication may affect our internal states. Cohen and Leung (2009) have reported studies in which persons asked to adopt certain postures 'for the purposes of the experiment' actually express different attitudes. For instance, those who were asked to stand tall and hold their heads high more strongly endorsed attitudes characteristic of honour cultures (discussed in Chapter 10). Thus, just as language may contribute to the priming of our cultural orientation, so may our habitual postures.

Learning a culture requires mastery of both verbal and non-verbal aspects of communication. In Chapter 11, we will discuss what can go wrong when out-group members fail to master both types of skills, since they are needed for effective interactions across group lines.

RELATIONSHIP SKILLS

An alternative approach to communication has been to develop and test theories that focus on successful and unsuccessful ways of relating to others. Specific theories of this type that focus upon processes such as leadership and negotiation are discussed in Chapter 10. Here we discuss a more general approach, which explores the related phenomena of face, politeness, and embarrassment. The parties to any communication process have a shared interest in achieving their relationship outcomes. As Goody put it:

> The basic constraints on effective interaction appear to be essentially the same across cultures and languages; everywhere a person must secure the co-operation of his interlocutor if he is to accomplish his goals. To secure cooperation, he must avoid antagonizing his hearer. (Goody, 1978: 6)

Politeness and Insults

An initial step toward achieving and sustaining cooperation is to be achieved by addressing the other party in a manner that will be judged appropriately polite to their role requirements. Holtgraves and Yang (1990, 1992) compared judgments of how polite were various ways of phrasing requests (e.g., 'Go, get the mail', 'Would you mind getting the mail?') by US and Korean students, in relation to status differences and closeness of the relationship. Americans showed a stronger preference for the more polite forms of address and were more likely to use them. Holtgraves and Yang explain this difference by noting that US respondents rated themselves as more distant from the person of whom they were making the request than the Koreans did. Greater distance required greater politeness. The effects of status and closeness were relatively similar in each sample. However, as we would expect, the Koreans took more account than the Americans of variations in the social context of their interaction when choosing which degree of politeness to use. Ambady, Koo, Lee, and Rosenthal (1996) coded videotapes of interactions, also sampling Korean and US respondents. By comparing codings of audio and video versions of the same interactions, they found variations in non-verbal 'circumspection' as well as in verbal behaviours, depending upon the degree of politeness that a particular context required. Consistent with Hall's (1966) theorising and studies reviewed earlier in this chapter, the Koreans' politeness strategies were again more affected by the relational aspects of the setting, whereas the Americans were more affected by the politeness of the actual words that had been addressed to them.

Dittrich, Johansen, and Kulinskaya (2011) compared the politeness of British and Norwegian adults. They predicted that because of the lower power distance and greater femininity of Nordic cultures compared to Anglo cultures, the Norwegians would use more egalitarian styles of address. Respondents were asked how they usually addressed a variety of other persons and how those same persons usually addressed them. Among family members and in unequal relations with others (e.g., a priest, one's doctor, a subordinate) no contrasts were found between Norwegians and British respondents. However, in equal relations with strangers (e.g., a waiter, a stranger, a taxi driver) Norwegians more often used a reciprocal address (John/John or Mr Johnson/Mr Johnson), whereas the British marked the presence of unequal status (Mr Johnson/John or John/Mr Johnson). British respondents reported greater distress if they had been addressed by another person in what they regarded as an impolite manner. Therefore, both context and cultural norms are involved in accomplishing effective communication. This study included no direct measure of respondents' cultural orientation, so we cannot make a more stringent test of the validity of the authors' hypotheses for the effects that they found.

Of course, not all communicators wish to be polite. What is found to be insulting is likely to vary in different cultural contexts. In particular we may expect that in individualist nations, insults will tend to be targeted at the individual who has given offence, whereas in collectivist nations insults could also focus on the group to which that individual belongs. Semin and Rubini (1990) found that insults addressed to a person as an individual (e.g., 'you're a stupid cretin') were frequently used in the more individualistic northern part of Italy, whereas relational insults (e.g., 'your sister is a cow') were more popular in the more collectivistic south of the country. Van Oudenhoven, De Raad et al. (2008) compared insulting terms used in ten European nations and the USA, finding some common terms used in most nations, but also some marked differences even between adjacent nations. For instance, Norwegians used more religious insults, Germans used more insults related to cleanliness, and the Dutch used more insults related to genitals. It is possible that broader sampling would show that favoured insults are related to cultural differences in conceptions of honour, with insults being selected in each culture that most threaten the recipient's sense of honour. Honour cultures are more fully discussed in Chapter 10.

Face

Politeness strategies and insult tactics may or may not succeed. If they fail, there will be some loss of face to the parties involved. In individualistic cultures, if my communication strategy fails, it is I who will risk losing face, unless I can engage in some form of defensive **facework** that alleviates the problem. Facework was first analysed in Western settings by Goffman (1959), who identified a range of actions, such as apologising, making excuses or shifting the blame, through which one might discount or redress a loss of face. In collectivistic settings the situation becomes more complex. Ting-Toomey (1988) formulated a theory of face negotiation that took account of collectivist issues. Her theory emphasised that if my identity is defined by my group rather than by myself as an individual, then *my* loss of face will also cause *you* to lose face. You and I therefore have a shared interest in avoiding loss of face. The preference for an emphasis on harmony in collectivist groups is focused around anticipating and forestalling any loss of face within one's dyad or group. The focus upon context and upon indirect styles of communication can therefore be seen as a form of preventive facework.

Languages spoken in collectivist cultures reflect concerns with face. For instance, Chinese has two characters, *lian* and *mianzi: lian* refers to personal or moral integrity, whereas *mianzi* refers to the social face that one displays in relation to others (Ho, 1976). *Mianzi* has parallels with *che-*

> **Facework** comprises a set of strategies for containing and neutralising threats to harmony within one's relations with others.

myon in Korean and *mentsu* in Japanese (Choi & Lee, 2002). In studies where Ting-Toomey and her colleagues have tested face negotiation theory cross-culturally, these concepts are referred to as self-face and other-face, and a third concept of mutual-face was also required. The need to invent new English phrases in order to adequately represent these concepts provides a timely reminder of the way in which any one language cannot necessarily capture key aspects of another culture. In this case the language of an individualistic cultural tradition, English, cannot encompass the complexities of collectivist relational concerns except by creating tailor-made words and phrases.

Hwang, Francesco, and Kessler (2003) compared students' reports of asking questions during class in Hong Kong, Singapore and the USA. Those who feared losing face asked less questions in all three nations, but only in the United States did those who hoped to gain face ask more questions. Kam and Bond (2008) compared the responses of students in Hong Kong and the USA to a face loss episode. Compared to the US respondents, the Hong Kong students felt *more* angry and that their relationship had been more damaged, but they were *less* likely to retaliate. In a further study, students reported on an event when someone had harmed them (Hui & Bond, 2009). Hong Kong students retaliated less, were more forgiving and more in favour of maintaining a good relationship with the offending party than were the US students. These studies suggest that a concern for face is present in all cultures, but elicits stronger effects in Chinese cultures.

However, it is not clear that the measures that were employed in any of these studies reflected the distinctive contrast between *mianzi* and *lian* that Chinese authors have described.

Oetzel et al. (2001) compared self-construals, face concerns and facework strategies employed during interpersonal conflicts in China, Germany, Japan, and the USA. As would be expected, they found that independent self-construal was associated with self-face concerns, whereas interdependent self-construal was associated with other- and mutual-face concerns in all cultural groups. However, self-construals did not account for the differences found between national samples. A further analysis by Oetzel and Ting-Toomey (2003) showed that a concern with self-face wholly mediated national differences in a form of facework referred to as 'dominating', whereby the threat to one's own face was averted by seeking to shift the blame to the other party. In contrast, other-face concern partially mediated national differences in types of facework referred to as 'avoiding' and 'integrating', whereby the threat to other-face was averted by downplaying the conflict or seeking joint solutions: persons with higher levels of other-concern were more likely to use these harmonising facework strategies.

Embarrassment

When facework fails, some degree of embarrassment is likely to occur. As we described more briefly in Chapter 7, Singelis, Bond, Sharkey, and Lai (1999) administered an embarrassability scale to students in Hong Kong, Hawaii, and mainland USA. In all samples, two factors were identified, self-embarrassability and empathetic embarrassability – defined as the shame that one feels for others who have violated social expectations. This distinction parallels Ting-Toomey's definitions of self- and other-face, providing a further illustration of the way in which concepts that derive originally from studies in collectivist cultures may nonetheless be applicable and useful in individualist cultures. As expected, the Caucasian-Americans scored lower on both of the embarrassment measures than did the Asian-Americans and the Hong Kong Chinese. Singelis et al. also obtained measures of independence and interdependence and showed that group differences in self-embarrassability and empathetic embarrassability were partially mediated by low independence and high interdependence, respectively.

Face concerns and embarrassability also need to be understood from a developmental perspective, since they are ingrained in the socialisation of children in any culture. Ridiculing and shaming are some of the socialisation strategies designed to develop a sense of embarrassment and face-concern toward others over time. Use of these strategies might well be linked to Bond and Lun's (2013) national dimensions of socialisation, discussed in Chapter 8: perhaps shaming would be used more readily in nations where civility (an orientation toward others) is a major socialisation goal, and blaming (to instill a feeling of guilt) would be more central in cultures where self-directedness is a stronger socialisation goal. Providing suggestive evidence for these ideas, Conroy, Hess, Azuma, and Kashiwagi (1980) compared the words that Japanese and US mothers said they would use to respond to a series of child misbehaviours. Japanese mothers stressed the feelings that misbehaviours would cause and the consequences for others, using phrases such as, 'it will be annoying to them if you misbehave'. US mothers much more often referred to infractions of rules and authority that the child was supposed to have internalised, using phrases such as 'you know better than that'. The former input emphasises interdependence and a concern for others, while the latter emphasises the child's independent responsibility for their actions.

RELATING TO OTHERS

We have emphasised at several points in this chapter that the process of relating to others is very much tied up with what kind of person the 'other' is. In the second half of this chapter we start with one of the most basic questions that are involved in relating to others: are strangers to be trusted? If they are, they may deserve our friendship or help. If not, defensive actions may be required. Subsequently, we consider issues arising from the establishment of increasingly intimate relations with others.

Trust and Altruism

The evolutionary theorists whose work was introduced in Chapter 3 proposed that the creation of cultures required the development of a capacity to trust one another. Paradoxically, Boyd and Richerson (1992) proposed that this state of affairs could only be achieved if persons had the capability of punishing one another. The shared norms necessary for social life will only arise if persons who deviate from these norms are punished. Henrich, McElheath, Barr, et al. (2006) reported gaming studies conducted in 14 traditional societies and one US student sample. Two types of gaming study were conducted at each location. In the first game, a respondent has to state which sums of money would be accepted if they were offered by another participant in the study. If this sum exceeds what is actually offered, neither party receives anything. Henrich et al. argue that a participant who accepts only the more generous offers is engaging in 'costly punishment', because the cost of punishing the other party's lack of generosity also punishes him- or herself.

In the second game, a participant is simply asked to decide what proportion of the money that the experimenter has provided will be shared with another participant. Henrich et al. describe this as a measure of 'altruism', although perhaps 'generosity' would be more accurate. Consistent with their expectation, the locations in which costly punishment was high were the same locations in which generosity was high. The identities of participants in these studies were not known to one another. If we suppose that participants' generosity can be interpreted as a sign of their trust that others would be similarly generous, then these results could provide a basis for predicting the incidence of trust in contemporary society: trust should be high where there are tightly enforced norms.

Muethel and Bond (in press) have compared 47 nations in terms of each nation's institutional strength for enforcing trust, scoring these nations for their observance of the rule of law. This construct was defined as 'perceptions of the extent to which agents have confidence in and abide by the rules of society, and in particular the quality of contract enforcement, property rights, the police, and the courts, as well as the likelihood of crime and violence' (http://info.worldbank. org/governance/wgi/pdf/rl.pdf). This study showed that, consistent with the argument of Boyd and Richerson (1992), the stronger the rule of law in a nation, the greater the trust of out-group persons shown by the citizens of that nation.

Generalised trust

Yamagishi and Yamagishi (1994) noted the importance of distinguishing between trust as a general approach to others, including strangers, and trust that derives from the assurance provided by some type of existing relationship. They proposed that generalised trust would be higher in individualistic nations than in collectivist nations. This should be so because in individualistic nations one's relative trust in strangers rests on an impersonal set of norms and laws, whereas in collectivist cultures, trust is relationally based and likely to be focused within the proximal in-group. An initial study by Igarashi, Kashima, Kashima, et al. (2008) compared attitudinal measures of generalised trust among students in Japan, Korea, Australia, Germany and the UK. No clear contrast was found between the samples from individualist and collectivist nations in this sample. However, an earlier study by Allik and Realo (2004) had shown that across 42 nations generalised trust was indeed higher in more individualistic nations.

Multi-level analyses can give a clearer understanding of these results. Gheorghiu, Vignoles, and Smith (2009) compared generalised trust in others across representative samples of adults in 31 European nations, using survey data taken from the European Values Survey. Yamagishi's theory was supported, with generalised trust lowest in the more collectivistic nations of Eastern Europe. Gheorghiu et al. were able to show that this effect was not reducible to differences in wealth or political history, and was attributable to nation-level differences in autonomy versus embeddedness values, not individual-level differences in the corresponding dimension of openness to change versus conservation values. Hamamura (2012) also compared the effects of individual-level and nation-level predictors. Using World Values Survey data from 57 nations, he found that high-income respondents had more generalised trust than low-income respondents, but only in wealthier societies, where trusting behaviours presumably led to more frequently positive outcomes. Therefore trust is again shown to be not an individual trait but a judgment about one's social context. These results appear consistent with the perspectives advanced by Henrich et al. and by Yamagishi, but future studies will need to take account of the fact that 'generalised' trust is not an all-or-nothing attribute. There are cultural variations in how wide is the circle of persons whom one is willing to trust (Delhey, Newton, & Welzel, 2011).

Helping

A generalised trust of others should predict a willingness to help others. Early studies provided some confirmation of travellers' subjective impressions that people were much more helpful to strangers in some parts of the world than in others. For instance, Feldman (1968) reported a higher percentage of helpful responses to a request for helping in Athens than he did in Paris or London. However, to understand such differences, we need a careful matching of locations and request procedures along with the inclusion of a broader sample of nations. For such a study, take a look at Key Research Study Box 9.1.

While Levine et al.'s study stands alone as an exemplar of the cultural aspects of actual prosocial behaviours toward strangers, there are of course many studies of *un*helpfulness to strangers (we consider studies of prejudice and intergroup relations in Chapter 12).

Once we move from considering relations with strangers to relations that have some more enduring component, additional issues become important. McAuley, Bond, and Kashima (2002) constructed a framework for all types of dyadic relationship, using data from Hong Kong and Australia. Their analysis contrasted four dimensions of relationship: complexity, equality, adversarialness, and what they called containment (separateness from other settings). In the succeeding sections we focus on just two types drawn from this broad range, both of which are typically complex and equal – namely friendship, and then intimate relationships.

Key Research Study 9.1   Prosocial Behaviour

Levine, Norenzayan, and Philbrick (2001) conducted an innovative cross-cultural study, in which they collected three separate measures of helping strangers who appeared to be in need of help, sampling persons from 23 nations. Data were collected in the largest city within each nation. In the first task, a trained accomplice accidentally dropped a pen while walking past a single pedestrian. In the second task, as a pedestrian approached, an accomplice who appeared to have hurt his leg dropped a pile of magazines and struggled to pick them up. In the third task, the accomplice, dressed as a blind person, waited at a pedestrian crossing as the light went green to see who might help.

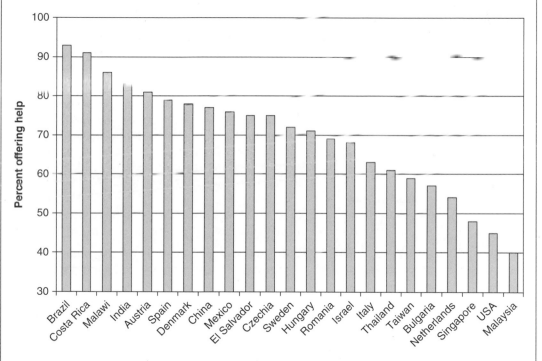

Figure 9.2   Prosocial Behavior across Nations (based on Levine et al., 2001)

The percentages of helpful responses in the three scenarios were moderately and positively correlated across the 31 nations, yielding an overall index of helpfulness. As shown in Figure 9.2, the helpfulness of passers by ranged from 45% to 93%. Levine et al. did not collect any other information that could help in choosing between possible explanations for these large variations in effect. Some caution is needed in interpreting these results, since the experimental accomplice was a different person, albeit a local, in each country sampled. Nonetheless, the

(Continued)

(Continued)

study focuses on an important social behaviour, and underlines the need for a richer theory in explaining cultural differences. Before considering explanations that can be derived from cross-cultural theory, we need to consider possible extraneous causes.

One possibility is that people in some locations are in more of a hurry than others. Cultural variations in orientation to time are widely believed to be important, but have rarely been studied. However, Levine and Norenzayan (1999) did attempt such a study, again using three separate measures. In each of 31 nations, the average speed of individuals walking on city pavements was recorded. Records were also made of the accuracy of clocks in public places, and the time taken by a clerk in a post office to sell a postage stamp. These three measures proved to be strongly correlated with one another, yielding an index of the national pace of life, which was higher in nations that were cooler, richer, and happier.

Drawing on these earlier results, Levine et al. showed only a weak and non-significant relationship between prosocial behaviour and the pace of life index. There was also no relationship with Hofstede's (1980) measure of individualism-collectivism. This leaves the way open to explore alternative explanations. In a subsequent analysis, Knafo, Schwartz and Levine (2009) found helpfulness was more frequent in nations low on Schwartz's (2004) measure of embeddedness and low in affluence. These two effects were independent of one another. The effect of low affluence was also explored by Van de Vliert, Huang, and Levine (2004). Van de Vliert's (2009) theory of the climato-economic origins of cultural differences was discussed in Chapter 3. Using measures from 33 nations included in the World Values Survey, Van de Vliert et al. (2004) showed that respondents who provided altruistic explanations for engaging in volunteer work were more frequently found in rich countries that were colder and in less rich countries that were hotter. These two contexts are among those that Van de Vliert's theory classified as more demanding, thus providing a further basis for understanding Levine et al.'s (2001) results.

Key Researcher Box 9.1

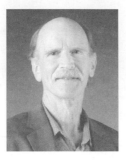

Robert V. Levine (b. 1945) obtained his PhD in social/personality and social psychology from New York University in 1974. Since that time he has been Professor at California State University, Fresno. He has published four books and more than 90 articles and book chapters. While most of his work has not been concerned with culture, he has conducted several important and distinctive cross-cultural studies, each of which relates to one of his major fields of interest: the pace of life and the practice of altruism. His cross-cultural work is distinguished by his use of behavioural measures rather than self-reports.

Figure 9.1   Robert Levine

Friendship

The current predominance of concepts derived from individualism and collectivism in cross-cultural research highlights the need to distinguish between in-groups and out-groups, especially if we are to understand the behaviours of members of collectivist cultures. But how shall the boundaries be drawn between in- and out-group membership, and do they differ between cultures? Brazilians distinguish acquaintances (*colegas*) from very close friends (*amigos*). In traditional Chinese culture, a distinction has been made between *jia-ren* (family members), *shou-ren* (relatives outside the family, neighbours, friends, classmates and colleagues), and *sheng-ren* (strangers) (Goodwin & Tang, 1996). In Japan, a *shin-yu* relationship (a lifelong confiding friendship) was reported to have characteristics more akin to the marriage relationship in Germany (Salamon, 1977).

A long time ago, Kurt Lewin, the pioneer of modern social psychology, commented on differences in the meaning of friendship in Germany and the USA (Lewin, 1936). He perceived German friendships to start more slowly but to be deeper and more permanent than their American variant. Subsequent findings referring to a lesser number of friends but greater closeness to one's best friend in collectivistic societies (e.g., Verkuyten & Masson, 1996, discussed below, Wheeler, Reis, & Bond, 1989) seem to point in the same direction, though Germany is much more individualistic today than in the 1930s. In individualistic societies, and especially in the United States, being sociable and having many friends is a good thing. Initiating contact with new people appears to come easily, as a part of being 'friendly', and self-disclosure is an established way of building new relationships. Thus the 'outer' layer of the self is more open or permeable, but then there is a rather less penetrable inner layer - the 'private' inner self. In collectivist contexts, on the other hand, the outer layer appears to be more impenetrable, but once the other person is accepted as a 'friend', self-disclosure will occur. Relationship formation may thus have a distinctive tempo and rhythm in different cultural contexts.

Schug, Yuki, and Maddux (2010) proposed that these differences can be explained by cultural differences in 'relational mobility'. Where relationships are more fluid, they need to be actively maintained, which is often accomplished through mutual self-disclosure. Where established relationships are unlikely to change, there is less need for disclosure. Schug et al. showed that a measure of perceived relational mobility mediated the differences that they found in self-disclosure among US and Japanese students. Self-disclosure to close friends is also less important in collectivist cultures, at least in East Asian ones. Taylor, Sherman, Kim et al. (2004) compared reported ways of handling stress among Korean, Asian American and European American students. The Asian respondents more frequently reported achieving support by just being with their friends, rather than by disclosing their difficulties explicitly. Such revelations were avoided because Asians associate explicit help-seeking with a loss of face and the disruption of relationship harmony.

In contrast to these categorical distinctions between relationship types, some researchers have recently used measures that assume relationships can be arrayed along a dimension of closeness. Fijneman, Willemsen, Poortinga. et al. (1996) asked students in Greece, Turkey, Hong Kong, the Netherlands, and the USA to rate how close they were to each of six types of family member, a close friend, a neighbour, an acquaintance, and a stranger. Closely similar rank orders of the ratings were found in all samples, with parents rated closest. Closeness ratings were found to correlate strongly with the degree to which respondents would be willing to support each person and how much they would expect support from them.

Fijneman et al. (1996) argued that these results negate individualism-collectivism theory, because no differences are found between samples, even though they span nations said to be both individualist and collectivist. This conclusion indicates the need for greater clarity as to what exactly we mean when we speak of individualism and collectivism. Different authors have used the terms in a variety of ways. Hofstede's (1980) original conceptualisation focused on the *reasons* we have for belonging to groups. In individualist cultures, group memberships are a consequence of choice, whereas in collectivist cultures memberships are to a greater extent predefined and central to one's identity. Closeness to one's groups may therefore have a different meaning in these contrasting contexts. Individualism-collectivism theory does not assert that families are unimportant to members of individualist nations, nor does it negate the fact that more emotional and material investments would be made in those closer to oneself than those distant from oneself. We must look in more detail at what this 'closeness' is.

Aron, Aron, and Smollan (1992) developed an 'Inclusion of Others in the Self' (IOS) scale in Canada. Respondents were asked to portray their closeness to various others by choosing between seven pairs of circles that varied between overlapping with one another to increasing degrees of separation. Uleman, Rhee, Bardoliwalla, Semin, and Toyama (2000) compared ratings on the IOS scales relating to family, relatives and friends by students from the USA, Japan, the Netherlands, and Turkey. The ratings were repeated using a series of different criteria for closeness, such as similarity, harmony and reputation. Across cultural groups, family and friends were rated closer than relatives. However, the basis of closeness varied between nations. Among Dutch and Caucasian-American respondents, closeness rested most on supportiveness and least on a similarity with others and their reputation. Among Turks and Asian-Americans, closeness was distinctively associated with reputation and harmony. For the Japanese, harmony alone was the strongest basis for closeness and similarity the weakest. So although the outcomes may be similar across cultural groups, the rationales for that outcome may vary and do so in ways that are consistent with the logic of individualism and collectivism.

Li (2002) compared the IOS responses of Chinese and Canadian students. The Chinese reported greater closeness to their families. Using a different measure, Claes (1998) found that Italian and Belgian adolescents reported a greater closeness to their families than Canadian adolescents did. Uskul, Hynie, and Lalonde (2004) compared IOS scores from Canadian and Turkish students for family members, romantic partners, friends and acquaintances. Ratings were completed once for actual closeness, and a second time for desired closeness. Turkish respondents scored higher on both actual and ideal closeness. Both samples placed a romantic partner ahead of family, then friends and then acquaintances. This study also included self-construal measures, and interdependence partially mediated the national differences in both actual and desired closeness.

The IOS studies help to clarify which relationships are most salient to respondents and the extent to which they may rest on different bases within different cultural contexts. However, more specific forms of measurement can help to pin down these differences. Verkuyten and Masson (1996) surveyed same-sex friendships among the various ethnic groups living in the Netherlands, while also measuring idiocentric and allocentric tendencies. Moroccans and Turks showed higher allocentrism than the Dutch and Southern Europeans. Allocentrism was found to be associated with greater closeness with one's best friend, but a lesser number of other friends. Allocentrism also predicted having more rules about how to represent one's best friend in dealing with third parties. These findings recall the description of a *shin-yu* friendship in Japan, as well as observations of the contrast between friendship in Hong Kong and the USA (Wheeler et al., 1989), and perhaps even Lewin's contrast between German and American friendship in the 1930s. Within collectivist societies, friendship appears to be more intense, more focused, and more exclusive.

We can see just how significant this type of friendship is by reflecting on a study of life satisfaction by Kwan, Bond, and Singelis (1997). These authors developed a measure of reported levels of harmony achieved in one's five most important relationships. As one would expect, some of the variance in life satisfaction was explained by respondents' self-esteem. However, additional variance in life satisfaction was predicted by relationship harmony, which in turn was higher among those with more interdependent self-construals. Furthermore, the amount of life satisfaction explained by relationship harmony relative to self-esteem was greater in Hong Kong than it was in the USA. Similarly, in a later study, relationship harmony was a stronger predictor of lower depression in Hong Kong than in the United States, even after controlling for self-efficacy (S.X. Chen et al., 2006).

Intimate Relations

The boundary between friendship and more complex forms of intimacy is not drawn in the same way everywhere. Seki, Matsumoto, and Imahori (2002) asked Japanese and US students to rate the intimacy level of their relations with their mother, father, lover, and same-sex best friend, and to also rate the frequency of various intimacy-related actions and feelings. Japanese intimacy was found to be more strongly associated with feelings such as appreciation, ease and 'bond', whereas American intimacy was more strongly associated with engaging in physical contact. However, differences existed that were dependent on relationship type. The Japanese preferred direct communication with their same-sex, presumably *shin-yu*, best friend and indirect communication with others, whereas the Americans preferred direct communication with lovers and indirect communication with parents and same-sex best friend.

While Seki et al. (2002) chose to apply the concept of intimacy to a wider range of relationships, the remainder of this section is focused upon relationships that have an explicitly sexual element. The major studies in this field have been conducted from the perspective of evolutionary theory. Researchers have therefore been particularly interested in identifying those universal aspects of male-female relationships that may contribute to the survival of the species. In discussing these studies, we give equal attention to the search for universals and the potential of cross-cultural theories for explaining aspects that are culturally variable.

Gender differences

Buss, Abbott, et al. (1989) surveyed gender differences in preferred qualities of a heterosexual partner among more than 9,500 students from 37 nations. Across the entire sample, men were found to prefer partners who were young, healthy and beautiful, whereas women preferred partners who were ambitious, industrious. and had high-earning potential. In a further analysis of the same data, Buss, Shackelford, and Leblanc (2000) found evidence among men that the greater the preferred difference between their own age and that of their (younger) partner, the larger their preferred number of children. As they had predicted, no such effect was found among women. Using samples from Korea, Japan, and the USA, Buss, Shackelford, Kirkpatrick et al. (1999) found that men were more threatened by the sexual aspect of infidelity, whereas women were more threatened by the emotional aspect of infidelity. In a 62-nation survey discussed more fully below, Schmitt, Alcalay et al. (2003) found men to report a greater desire for a variety of sexual partners than did women. Men were also found more frequently to report having seduced a partner from another relationship or to have allowed themselves to be seduced from their current relationship (Schmitt, Alcalay et al., 2004). The results of each of these studies are interpreted as evidence that men's behaviour is driven by a biological mandate to father as many children as possible, whereas women's behaviour is driven by their stronger priority to ensure the survival of their own genes by nurturing the children that they have already borne and sustain a relationship with a male who will provide for them.

Although each of these surveys has found the gender effects predicted, the very large samples employed have ensured that such effects will achieve statistical significance even if they explain only a modest amount of variance. In Buss's (1989) survey, gender differences accounted for just 2.4% of variance. In contrast, further analyses showed that national differences in the same dataset accounted for an average of 14% of variance (Buss, Abbott et al., 1990). The greatest variation was in preferences as to whether one's partner should be chaste or sexually experienced, where nationality accounted for 37% of variance. Buss et al. used multi-dimensional scaling to cluster the nations within which the desired mate characteristics were most similar. The principal contrast that they identified was between nations that they described as traditional and modern, but their data included no measures of cultural orientation for those nations they had sampled. Considering how much more variance was explained by national culture than by gender, it is rather ironic that this study is extensively cited as demonstrating the significance of evolutionary/biological determinants of partner preferences, rather than the greater power of cultural socialisation!

The Buss data have been re-examined in a more systematic way. Shackelford, Schmitt, and Buss (2005) factor analysed the 18 characteristics of a potential partner and identified four individual-level factors. These were labeled as: love versus status; dependable/stable versus good looks and health; education and intelligence versus the desire for home and children; and sociability versus a similar religion. Chan (2004) tested hypotheses about nation-level predictors of citizen scores on these factors. She found that, on average, persons from more affluent nations had a stronger preference for love, dependability, education, and sociability in their partner than did persons from less affluent nations. These correlations were strong to moderate, suggesting a powerful background role for economic development in shaping the basis by which the marriage bond is established. This result is reminiscent of Georgas and colleagues' (2006) finding of the powerful role of affluence in influencing family relations across cultures. Gender is important, but so, too, is culture – especially the priorities that result from economic development and the associated prevalence of individualistic rather than collectivist values. These effects can be understood by considering more recent studies that address cultural variations in the attractiveness of mates.

Physical attractiveness

A slender physique is currently rated as most attractive in Western nations, although it appears that this was not the case historically. Swami, Frederick and 59 co-authors (2010) asked men and women in 26 nations to make ratings of the attractiveness of a set of nine line drawings depicting women of differing size. Men were asked to rate the attractiveness to them of each body shape, whereas women were asked to rate how attractive they thought men would find each body shape. As shown in Figure 9.3, there were significant but modest variations in the body shapes that were rated as most attractive. Larger bodies were favoured in rural samples and the differences between rural and urban samples within those nations where both were sampled were larger than the differences between nations. Only about 10% of the variability was explained by exposure to western media that show predominantly skinny models. Swami et al. explained their results in terms of evolutionary theory. Where food is scarce, as in rural areas, a plump woman can signify an abundance of food. Where food is no longer scarce, a fleshy mate is no longer a priority. Women's preferred female body shape was more slender than men's preferred female body shape in all samples.

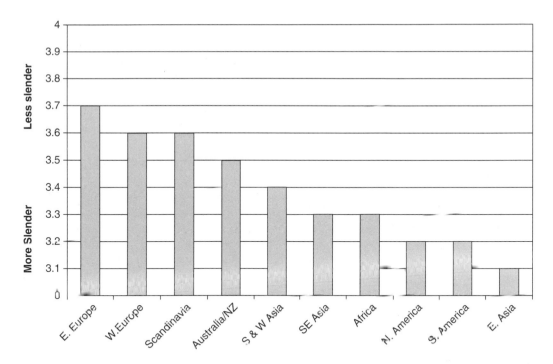

Figure 9.3   Most Attractive Body Shape across World Regions (based on Swami et al., 2010)

The hypothesis that women favour men who have 'masculine' facial features has received inconsistent support. De Bruine, Jones, Crawford et al. (2010) proposed that this is because women face conflicting priorities. On the one hand, more masculine men are likely to be less faithful, while on the other hand, the offspring of masculine men may be better able to survive in harsh circumstances. These authors conducted an online study in which women in 30 nations were asked to use a computer program to adjust the features of male faces until they were their most attractive. The faces could be adjusted toward more masculine or more feminine features. They predicted and found that more masculine features were favoured in nations where the health risks were more severe.

Attachment

In the 62-nation study by Schmitt and his colleagues discussed above (Schmitt et al., 2003, 2004), measures were also obtained of attachment style from the 18,000 respondents. The origins of the concept of attachment in childhood were discussed in Chapter 8. Attachment styles are expected to be relevant to the way that adults make relationships with one another. Respondents were asked a series of simple questions that were intended to tap their style of attachment to those with whom they had close relations, with scales reflecting the extent to which they had a positive view of the self and a positive view of others. These items are imposed-etic, being derived from earlier studies in the USA (Bartholomew & Horowitz, 1991). Combinations of responses to questions of this type yielded scores on four types of attachment: secure (positive view of both self and others), dismissive (positive view of self and negative view of others), preoccupied (negative view of self and positive view of others), and fearful (negative view of both self and others).

Having presented some evidence favouring the cross-cultural validity of their measures, Schmitt et al. (2004) reported that in most nations the secure type of attachment is endorsed more strongly than the other types of attachment. While this might be interpreted as evidence of a universal attachment style, Schmitt et al. noted that respondents from nine Asian nations, ranging from India to Japan, all reported a more positive view of others than of themselves. He concluded that gaining the romantic approval of highly-valued others will be a particular priority in this context. Schmitt (2005) next analysed the correlates of dismissive attachment, showing that persons from nations with a high mean dismissive attachment are high in short-term relationships and less-restricted sexuality. Finally, Schmitt (2008) predicted and found that the frequency of dismissive attachment styles would be higher in adverse environments, characterised by pathogen prevalence, poverty, a high pace of life, high mortality, and so forth.

In one further analysis of their data, Schmitt et al. (2003) compared the responses of men and women to their measure of attachment styles. Expectations based on earlier research that men would favour dismissive styles more than women were not fully upheld. Gender differences were small and differed by nation. Men were more dismissive than women only within the more affluent nations in the sample. All in all, the results of this large-scale survey found substantial evidence for evolutionary explanations of cultural variation in both partner choice and relationship type.

Again, however, culture enters the picture in terms of how types of attachment styles function. Adult attachment style can also be measured using two dimensions, reflecting avoidant and anxious ways of relating to both parents and partners: 'Persons who are highly avoidant have learned to avoid rejection by attachment figures by maintaining psychological and emotional distance and independence. Individuals who are highly anxious are convinced that their attachment figures are likely to abandon them either physically or emotionally' (Friedman, Rholes et al., 2010: 114). In a study comparing Americans, Mexicans, and Hong Kong Chinese, Friedman, et al. tested members of romantic partnerships that had lasted longer than three months. As predicted from attachment theory, they found that the avoidant attachment style 'was more strongly associated with relationship problems in more collectivist societies given the greater emphasis placed on closeness and harmony in relationships in collectivist cultures' (2010: 107). This outcome validated the authors' cultural fit hypothesis whereby an avoidant style of relating to others would clash with the collectivist interpersonal orientation in Mexico and Hong Kong.

In a related study, Mak, Bond et al. (2010) argued that anxious and avoidant attachment styles would be linked to depressive symptoms, but that the links would be mediated by perceived support from one's partner and satisfaction with that relationship. These hypotheses were supported in romantic relationships for both Americans and Hong Kong Chinese. However, the impact of an avoidant style of attachment was stronger for the Chinese partners. The greater impact of avoidant attachment in a collectivist cultural system again supports the position that one's attachment style will be more problematic when it is incompatible with the cultural logic of one's social context.

Marriage

Evolutionary psychologists have thus obtained substantial support for predictions about partner preference. However, marriages are not always based solely upon partner preference. In Chapter 8, we explored the manner in which different family structures have evolved within differing cultural environments. Family structure has a two-fold linkage with intimate relationships, in the sense that families are at the same time built around a relationship that is sexually intimate and to varying degrees relationally intimate between the parents. As described above, however, marriages are also designed to socialise offspring toward particular styles of attachment, which will in due course colour their later preferences for an adult partner.

Models of family thus predict varying bases of interpersonal attachment. Families built upon the model of interdependence are more likely to favour attachments for their offspring that are based upon the needs of the family as a whole. Marriages will often be arranged on behalf of offspring rather than by individual initiative. Even where they are not formally arranged, parents and other family members will be influential in partner choice. Families built upon the model of independence will encourage the autonomy and self-reliance of their offspring, and this autonomy will extend to partner choice. Romantic attachment will be the norm and will provide the basis for marriage. Everyday Life Box 9.3 provides an illustration of some rather striking contrasts in the qualities sought in partners within today's UK and India.

Everyday Life Box 9.3   Finding a Partner

What qualities are important in seeking a partner? In the UK, personality traits and interests are emphasised. In India, there is greater salience for caste, family status, qualifications, and sometimes compatible horoscopes. Note how, in the UK, individuals advertise themselves, whereas in India, it is often the family rather than the individual that seeks a partner. Note also that one of the UK advertisements is for a homosexual partner.

United Kingdom	India
Lots of energy and a lust for life. Eccentric, kind-hearted female, 35, 5'9", loves singing, dancing, reading and travel; would like to meet confident pragmatic, hard-working male, 33–38, who likes a joke and a hearty laugh.	**Smart,** very handsome Brahmin boy, 31, 180cm, BE,MBA, own established business, monthly income six figures, send biodata and photo (must).
Attractive 39yo black male, speaks five languages, would like to meet female, similar age, for long-term relationship. Likes walking by the sea, food, cooking and travel.	**Delhi**-based Punjabi Khatri family seeks professionally qualified girl from educated family for IT, MBA, 29 years, 5'7" working manager in leading company.
New here, looking around. I am a 32yo male seeking an honest, balanced, fun female 25–34 with good sense of humour.	**Hindu girl**, 23, 160cm, BTech working professional software engineer, only child, father senior bank executive, mother legal professional, seeks preferably BTech, MBA, below 28 from educated family. Caste no bar.
Tall, blonde, incredible hunk, 27, attractive handsome young male would like to meet older non-scene, distinguished gentleman, 65+, hopefully leading to friendship and relationship.	**Beautiful** working girl in Delhi sought for handsome Uttar Pradesh Khatri boy, born 3.2.1980/ 3.15am, 5'3", employed in a reputable company.

Sources: The Guardian (London), April 2010; *Sunday Times of India*, matrimonials, March 2010.

Consistent with these predictions, it is often stated that romantic love is characteristic of individualist nations, while 'companionate' love is more frequent within collectivist nations (Hatfield & Rapson, 1996). Levine, Sato, Hashimoto, and Verma (1995) provided a preliminary test of such a hypothesis. Students in 11 nations were asked, 'If a man (woman) had all the other qualities that you desired but you were not in love with them, would you marry them?' Substantial percentages of respondents from India, Pakistan and Thailand answered that they would. The percentage who agreed that they would across the 11 nations correlated +0.56 with Hofstede's collectivism scores for these nations.

However, such a simple equation of romantic love with individualism is not convincing. In Levine et al.'s study, a willingness to marry without love was almost as low in some samples said to be collectivist, such as Hong Kong and Brazil, as it was in the individualist nations that were sampled. The affluence of nations was a better predictor of an unwillingness to marry without love, correlating at +0.70 for this sample of nations. This result is consistent with Chan's (2004) finding that love was rated higher as a component of marriage in more affluent nations.

Arranged marriages are no longer so frequent as in times past, but cultural differences in the decision for a couple to marry remain. Zhang and Kline (2009) compared the marital intentions of Chinese and US students. For US respondents, the decision rested on the length of the existing relationship, a supportive and caring relationship, a belief that marriage would improve life, and the opinions of family and friends. For the Chinese, the opinions of family and friends were strong predictors, and the only factors that achieved significance. Thus norms as represented by the opinions of family and friends are shown to be important both in the USA and China, but more so in China.

In another study that highlights the role of social norms, Stavrova, Fetchenhauer, and Schlösser (2012) compared the happiness of married and cohabiting couples, drawing on representative samples in 30 nations. Male happiness did not differ by marital status, but married women were happier than cohabiting women. The magnitude of this difference varied between nations and was predicted by a *nation-level* index of liberal norms for gender roles, but not by the women's *own* gender role preferences. As would be expected, the women who were happier to be married were in the nations that did not have such liberal norms, again supporting the important role of a supportive social context for one's actions.

Weisfeld, Dillon, Novak et al. (2011) surveyed more than 3,000 married couples from Turkey, Russia, China, the UK and the United States, who had been together for an average of 12 years. Within each nation, the wives were more likely to say that their parents had played a role in choosing their husband, and also more likely to say that they had thought of divorcing their husband. In four nations, wives perceived their husband as more humorous, but in Russia the husbands perceived the wife as more humorous. Humour was a significant predictor of marital satisfaction, and especially for the wife's satisfaction (Weisfeld, Nowak, Lucas et al., 2011).

As evolutionary psychologists, these researchers were interested in their prediction that women would find humorous men more attractive because they would see humour as indicating the desirable quality of higher intelligence. Their interest was thus in gender differences, rather than in whether the absolute level of these sentiments differed between their five national samples, and no sample means were cited. The diverging results for Russia suggest an explanation based on socialisation rather than a universal evolutionary principle.

In an earlier analysis of the same data, Lucas et al. (2008) concluded that marital satisfaction had invariant components of romantic love and companionate love (which they termed partnership) in all samples, but that there would be cultural variations in how these qualities were achieved. For instance, in arranged marriages romantic love may develop over time.

To achieve an understanding of these variations, studies using an emic approach may be more useful. For instance, Rothbaum and Tsang (1998) have analysed the content of popular romantic songs in China and the USA. American songs focus more frequently on the present positive qualities of the loved one, while Chinese songs have more references to sadness, the future, and the context where love occurs. Romance may be universal, but the manner in which it is expressed may vary, dependent upon the broader context of interpersonal relations within different cultures. We need better measures before studies in this field can be linked adequately with cross-cultural theory.

We also need to bear in mind that romantic relations are not always harmonious. Archer (2006) compared rates of physical aggression between partners in 12 nations. He found that, within Western nations, physical aggression by women towards men was as frequent as physical aggression by men toward women, and especially among student samples. This effect was partly because women's aggression toward partners was greater than in non-Western nations, and partly because men's aggression toward their partners was less than in non-Western nations. However, physical aggression by men toward women predominated in India, Jordan, Japan, Nigeria, Korea, and especially in Papua New Guinea. A predominance of aggression by men was strongly and negatively correlated with an index of gender empowerment. These results are not consistent with the types of genetically-based evolutionary theory that have guided many researchers in this field, and suggest that a cultural evolution of gender roles occurs in response to changes in social power.

SUMMARY

The way in which we communicate with others is constrained by the language that we speak, the way in which we think about ourselves, and the degree to which this self-construal causes us to take account of our social context. Successful communication rests on shared assumptions about politeness, how to handle threats to face, and the transience or permanence of particular relationships. Communication is both a reflection of culture and an agent by which culture is continuously recreated. Cultures differ in respect of non-verbal behaviours, but we do not yet have clear explanations of the way in which these variations relate to values, beliefs, or self-construals.

There is a greater difference between communication with in-group and out-group members in collectivist cultures than there is in individualist cultures. Friendships are more focused, more intense, and more permanent within collectivist cultures, whereas in individualist cultures intimacy is more strongly associated with romantic love. Some aspects of gender relations are universal, but cultural variations in the preferred basis of gender relations outweigh these effects. The extent to which attachment processes vary between national groups shows promising connections to theorising about collectivism and individualism, but more culturally responsive measures are needed along with extensions of this work into less modernised social systems and their populations.

FURTHER READING

1 Chiu, C.Y. (2011). Language and culture. *Online Readings in Psychology and Culture.* Available at http://scholarworks.gvsu.edu/*orpc*

2 Goodwin, R. (1999). *Personal relationships across cultures.* London: Routledge.

3 Levine, R.V. (2004). Measuring helping behavior across cultures. *Online Readings in Psychology and Culture.* Available at http://scholarworks.gvsu.edu/*orpc*

4 Schmitt, D.P., et al. (110 co-authors) (2004). Patterns and universals of adult romantic attachment across 62 cultural regions: Are models of self and of other pancultural constructs? *Journal of Cross-Cultural Psychology, 35,* 367–402.

5 Singelis, T.M., Bond, M.H., Sharkey, W.F., & Lai, S.Y. (1999). Unpackaging culture's influence on self-esteem and embarrassability. *Journal of Cross-Cultural Psychology, 30,* 315–341.

STUDY QUESTIONS

1 How would you characterise your non-verbal behaviours, including how loud or softly you speak? In what way are your preferences in relation to proximity, touch, eye contact, and use of silence distinctive of your culture of origin?

2 Discuss the extent to which researchers have succeeded in making a convincing case that cultural differences in communication are different from gender differences in communication.

3 What are the factors that influence the level of trust of strangers in your culture? Consider the influence of collectivism, social norms, face concerns, politeness, and embarrassment.

4 How would you communicate with someone from a collectivist culture in a way that preserved the face of both parties?

5 In what circumstances is it permissible to tell lies in your culture, and how do those acceptable circumstances relate to your culture's logic?

6 How can the concept of attachment be applied validly to all cultures?

10

Group Processes

'No man is an island, entire of itself
Every man is a piece of the continent, a part of the main'

(John Donne, 1624)

When one of the authors of this book opened his email this morning, he had received a range of emails from students, colleagues and friends. Some students asked for advice about their assignments, while others requested extensions for their assignments. His boss asked him whether he would help with a faculty function later this week and, on a more positive note, a friend invited him to a party this weekend. Although seemingly unrelated, all these emails related to three fundamental psychological processes in groups that we discuss in this chapter.

As we recognised in Chapter 3, many of our current psychological processes evolved millions of years ago, when our ancestors were roaming the grasslands of East Africa. Humans were unable to survive alone because as individuals we were too weak a species to fight against stronger predators alone, or to find sufficient food on our own. Our bodies are also not well-adapted enough to cope on our own with the various climatic challenges of our planet. Our best survival strategy was to form small bands of blood-related individuals and cooperate in order to ensure survival.

The benefits of this sociality come with some associated challenges, however. Firstly, as we get involved in group life, we need to be careful not to be exploited by others in our group. This requires careful monitoring of social exchanges within the group to ensure that each member receives justice. Secondly, we want to benefit from being part of our group, so we need to influence others to give us help, to get some of those benefits that smarter, stronger and bolder members of our group can obtain, or to ensure that vulnerable members of the group are cared for. Thirdly, in dealing with the various members of our group, each member must make sure to maintain harmonious relations with all of them. If, for example, I respond to some of my e-mails but not to others, issues of in-group inclusion and exclusion may arise, inviting resentment or retaliation by those excluded. In this chapter, we discuss in turn how these three major aspects of group life (monitoring social exchanges, influencing others, and maintaining harmonious relationships with others) are handled in the context of different cultural systems, according to the broad dimensions of cultural variation that we have introduced in earlier chapters.

MONITORING SOCIAL EXCHANGES

One of the oldest theories in social psychology is social exchange theory. This theory assumes that humans are rational beings who will try to obtain rewards from social relations while keeping costs to a minimum and that we judge the relative ratio of costs versus rewards of our interaction through social comparisons with relevant others (Blau, 1964). More recently, Lind (2001) has argued that people are continuously faced with the fundamental dilemma of whether to trust a group and submit to its demands, or whether they should retain their distance so as to protect their self-interests and avoid potential exploitation by the group. In most social situations, these two goals are mutually exclusive and a balance needs to be negotiated. The best solution to this dilemma in Lind's view is to use principles of justice that specify boundaries for power abuse, provide criteria for decision-making, specify interactions that adequately limit the potential for exploitation, and allow individuals to engage in group activities without the fear that advantage will be taken of them. By this view, justice concerns are universal, and justice as a basic motive is independent of culture because it appears evolutionarily adaptive. In fact, rudimentary justice principles can be observed in higher primates such as chimpanzees, rhesus monkeys and gorillas (Brosnan, 2006; Price & Brosnan, 2012). Yet, as we shall see, how human cultures resolve justice issues varies between cultural groups, as do the criteria that are used to solve justice dilemmas.

Distributive Justice
Distributive Justice refers to the perceived fairness of the rewards that have been allocated.

Procedural Justice
Procedural Justice refers to the perceived fairness of the procedures used in deciding on the allocation of rewards.

Interactional Justice
Interactional Justice refers to the perceived fairness of the interpersonal interactions occurring during the process of reward allocation and distribution.

DIMENSIONS OF JUSTICE

Although social exchange theory discusses all aspects of social relations in terms of general costs and rewards, in practice most justice researchers have focused on allocations of money, usually in work settings. They have distinguished between the outcomes arising from resource allocations (**distributive justice**), the procedures used to allocate rewards (**procedural justice**), and the nature of interpersonal transactions involved in the allocation process (**interactional justice**). We consider these aspects in turn, but we need to ask first whether these distinctions as proposed and tested by Western researchers are also made by individuals in non-Western contexts. A large multinational study by Fischer, Ferreira et al. (2011) recently showed that employees from all continents do make these distinctions when responding to an imposed-etic questionnaire developed in the USA. At the same time, the correlations between perceptions of different types of justice were much stronger in nations higher in collectivism and power distance. It is possible that employees in these contexts are more likely to perceive that all forms of justice reflect the decision of a central authority: in other words, a single powerful individual or small group of individuals may make the decisions and see to it that they are implemented. It is not clear whether such perceptions are accurate and based on different decision-making and power structures or not. Independent of their origins, there is less variance in these perceptions and people distinguish less sharply between different dimensions of justice.

Let us consider how cultural processes influence some of these justice principles. When examining allocations of rewards in group settings, it is vital to take account of the relative roles and positions of those involved. Leung (1997) argued that it is important to distinguish studies in which participants are asked to allocate rewards between themselves and someone else from studies in which participants choose how to distribute rewards between two or more other people, but do not themselves benefit from the allocation. The first type (which we shall call 'reward sharing') is more similar to exchanges between friends or in small groups, whereas the second ('reward assignment') has been studied extensively in organisational contexts, as this is the typical situation for deciding on pay rises, promotions, or any other type of allocation relevant to human resource management. Most studies have focused on this latter type.

> **Reward Sharing**
> Reward Sharing refers to a person's allocation of rewards among peers, including oneself.
>
> **Reward Assignment**
> Reward Assignment refers to a person's allocation of rewards to other, typically more junior, persons.

Distributive Justice

Distributive justice has received the most attention from cross-cultural researchers. Many years ago, Deutsch (1975) proposed a distinction between three different bases for distributive justice, suggesting that each would be more prevalent in a particular type of interaction. In contexts where the first priority is economic profit, he predicted a preference for equity – in other words, an allocation of rewards that is proportional to the contributions made by each individual. In contexts where the development and maintenance of harmonious relations is the priority (as is common among friends), he predicted a preference for the egalitarian sharing of rewards. Finally, in settings where personal welfare is the priority (such as in families), he predicted a preference for an allocation of resources based on need.

Fischer and Smith (2003) conducted a meta-analysis of 25 cross-national comparisons of distributive justice effects, 21 of which involved comparing allocations by persons from the USA and by persons from another nation. Overall, respondents from 14 nations were involved in these studies. Fischer and Smith found a significantly stronger preference for equity over equality in samples from nations scoring higher on power distance and with greater income inequality. Individualism-collectivism was not a significant predictor, although several earlier researchers have used this concept to interpret their results. By drawing on a range of studies across time and cultural groups, this meta-analysis gives a more precise interpretation of the factors affecting the results of individual studies.

Fischer and Smith examined several factors of this type. Firstly, they found that there was a significant difference between the results of studies in which students had been asked to share or assign hypothetical rewards and those few studies that had actually sampled preferences for reward assignment by business employees. These latter studies concerned business-like decisions, so we are likely to obtain the most externally valid understanding by focusing on the two studies of business employees. Chinese managers were found to favour allocations based upon equity more strongly than US employees (C.C. Chen, 1995). Russian managers also favoured equity, but they nonetheless distributed rewards more equally than did US managers (Giacobbe-Miller, Miller, & Victorov, 1998).

Russia scores high on power distance, so allocations by Russians based on equality do not support the findings of the overall meta-analysis. However, Russia has also had a long history of state socialism, with an emphasis on collective rewards and equality. This suggests that there are further uncontrolled variables affecting the results that had been obtained by the time of this analysis. For example, only a few studies had measured the actual cultural orientation of participants, and some of the samples surveyed may have had values that did not accord with the Hofstede or Schwartz scores for their nation.

More recent studies have attempted to overcome some of these problems. He, Chen, and Zhang (2004) surveyed preferences for reward assignment among business employees in China. Using the measures of horizontal and vertical individualism-collectivism from Singelis et al. (1995), they found that those who endorsed vertical collectivism favoured differential reward allocation – in other words, allocation based upon job performance. In contrast, those who endorsed horizontal collectivism favoured more equal assignment. A direct link is thus established for the first time between different reward allocation preferences and cultural orientations.

Moving from preferences to allocations in real work organisations, Fischer, Smith, Richey et al. (2007) asked employees in the UK, USA, East and West Germany, New Zealand and Brazil to report what allocation principles were used in recent decisions in their organisation. They found that higher nation-level mastery values (Schwartz, 1994) were associated with greater use of assignments based on equity. Although the predictors found to be significant were different (power distance in the meta-analysis versus mastery values in organisations), both dimensions share a common emphasis on differentiating between individuals based on their status and abilities.

Focusing on the perceived fairness of various criteria, Fischer and Smith (2004) found that the scores of business employees in the UK and Germany on Schwartz's self-enhancement values predicted a favourable evaluation of reliance on equity and an unfavourable evaluation of reliance on seniority in both nations. Hence, values endorsing power differences and demonstrating mastery over others are consistently related to both preferences for, and the perceived fairness of, less equal distributions of rewards in both laboratory and field surveys.

Procedural Justice

Leventhal (1976) was the first to propose that decisions about allocations and other matters are perceived as fair when the procedures used to reach these decisions are perceived as unbiased and honest, when decision-makers are seen as benevolent and trustworthy, and when the recipients of decisions are treated with dignity and respect. As we discussed above, these concerns are probably universal, but may be shaped by cultural considerations. For example, Lind, Tyler, and Huo (1997) suggested that members of nations high in power distance are more accepting of interpersonal differentials and may therefore have lesser concerns about these aspects of procedure. Consistent with this reasoning, they found that in describing dyadic conflicts that they had experienced, US respondents reported having more concerns about their status in a group than did Japanese respondents.

Interactional Justice

A third concept, interactional or interpersonal justice, refers to the ways these decisions are transmitted to recipients in social interactions. This includes providing sufficient information about the procedures that are being used to reach these conclusions, and showing respect and dignity to individuals during these social exchanges.

It appears that a concern for interactional justice may also increase with changing economic and social conditions. In a study of Chinese managers working in joint venture hotels in China, Leung, Smith, Wang, and Sun (1996) found that perceptions of distributive justice and procedural justice, but not of interactional justice, predicted job satisfaction. However, three years later, distributive justice was no longer a significant predictor, whereas interactional justice had become predictive (Leung, Wang, & Smith, 2001). The authors explained these changes by showing that at the earlier time respondents compared their outcomes favourably with Chinese managers working in state-owned enterprises. Three years later, respondents believed that their increased level of expertise permitted them to make comparisons with the expatriate managers with whom they were working. In other words, the group with which they believed it was fair to compare themselves, their 'reference group' (Kelley, 1952), had changed.

Implementing Abstract Justice Criteria

It is important to note that all these studies have used Western instruments that portray relatively abstract criteria and ask respondents to indicate whether these abstract criteria and principles are used in their organisation. As Morris and Leung (2000) observed, we do not know how these justice principles may actually be implemented in group settings. For example, as we saw in Chapter 9, norms of politeness vary quite substantially between cultures, as do the norms allowing people to express their opinions during the decision-making process.

The aspects of behaviour that are seen as relevant when allocating rewards are also likely to differ across cultures. For example, in a study by Smith, Misumi, Tayeb, Peterson, and Bond (1989), employees had to indicate whether particular behaviours by their supervisor were seen as appropriate. They found that, if a supervisor discussed a worker's problems with co-workers in the worker's absence, this was considered supportive in Japan and Hong Kong, but not in the USA and UK. Hence, abstract dimensions of justice-related leadership styles can be implemented differently. This is a research area where a better understanding will require measures that tap more directly into what happens among relevant stakeholders in differing cultural contexts.

Justice Motives and Reactions to Injustice

We argued above that one of the principal issues that people have to consider when inter-acting with others in group settings is whether they can trust their group (for example, their organisation) and submit fully to the demands of the group, or whether they should remain more distant, retaining control and avoiding the risk of exploitation. These concerns will be influenced by how individuals around them habitually relate to their in-group – that is, by individualism-collectivism. Brockner et al. (2000) argued that procedural justice should be more important for individuals who assign greater importance to their relationships with others and those who more strongly believe that social interactions and relationships should affirm their basic moral values (Brockner, De Cremer, Van den Bos, & Chen, 2005). One option for affirming group moral values is to treat individuals fairly. Consequently, for individuals who are closely aligned with their in-groups, procedural justice effects should be stronger. In a series of single-nation studies in Japan and the Netherlands, Brockner et al. (2005) showed that the effects of procedural justice on cooperation, positive affect and the desire for future interaction were greater among students with more interdependent self-construals. Consistent with the pro-cedures recommended in Chapter 4 for eliminating alternative explanations for effects, Brockner et al. showed that the effects obtained using self-construal as a moderator were not obtained when self-esteem was used instead.

Self-construals were also used to unpackage cultural differences between Chinese and US students in the previous study by Brockner et al. (2000). They found that the buffering effect of procedural justice when distributive justice is low (e.g., the acceptance of undesirable outcomes in a negotiation exercise if the procedures that led to the negotiation outcome had been fair) was much stronger among students with more interdependent self-construals and that this unpack-aged the cultural difference in their reactions.

Reactions to procedural justice will also be relevant to power distance, but in a slightly differ-ent way. According to Lind (2001), justice provides information about whether one is included in a group or not. Tyler and Lind (1992) suggested that in-group justice perceptions can define one's identity in ways that are equivalent to the predictions made by social identity theory in intergroup contexts (see Chapter 12). However, as the study by Lind et al. (1997) showed, people socialised into more hierarchical social systems are well aware of their position within the sys-tem. Perceived justice is therefore less useful as a way of monitoring whether one is fully included or not, because in more hierarchical settings one's relative status as a group member would be clearer and more stable. In contrast, in more egalitarian settings, inclusion and status are less well-defined and more negotiable, so people may be more motivated to monitor their level of inclusion as a full-fledged group member via their perceived treatment by group authorities and other group members (that is, their perceptions of justice).

Most studies of the effects of justice on aspects of actual work outcomes so far have focused on power distance as a moderator, but some have examined variables such as indi-vidualism-collectivism and individual-level self-construal. A review of these studies by Fischer (2008) indicated that the results are inconsistent and it was not clear what accounted for the differing results. Fischer (2013b) therefore conducted a further meta-analysis, examining the relative strength of linkages between justice perceptions and different employee reactions (e.g., job satisfaction, commitment to the organisation, self-reported work behaviours). In order to examine the relative importance of cultural dimensions, he linked the findings to research into justice motives – that is, the reasons why people would pay attention to justice. The basic idea is that if justice concerns are related to human needs, then these effects can be expected to be stronger or weaker depending on the context, because different contexts allow for differential satisfaction and salience of needs (Kenrick, Griskevicius et al., 2010), as we discussed in Chapter 6.

At the beginning of this chapter, we identified three major issues relevant to group living. We may have concerns about justice for reasons of belonging (being included as a respected and valued group member) and for reasons of control (being sure that we are receiving the goods that we deserve and are not being exploited). Linking these motives to cultural and economic differences, individuals in different cultural and economic contexts may exhibit different justice-outcome relations depending on the relative salience of these two concerns, and therefore may react differently to violations of justice. This argument is consistent with studies of attitude-behaviour relations (e.g., Fazio & Powell, 1997; Cohen, Shariff, & Hill, 2008) demonstrating that attitude accessibility strengthens the attitude behaviour link. The salience or accessibility of needs and motives related to justice within a particular cultural context should therefore strengthen the link between justice perceptions and work outcomes. If individuals work in a context where motives such as belonging are a central concern, then the link between justice and work outcomes should be strengthened if a particular justice dimension is related to a need for affiliation or belonging.

The results of Fischer's (2013b) meta-analysis with 54,100 participants from 36 nations showed that macro-economic income inequality and nation-level values can systematically explain variability in the associations between justice and work outcomes. By assessing the pattern of associations with contextual variables, useful insights into the motives and concerns underlying justice effects can be found. For instance, the strongest finding was that national collectivism was associated with stronger reactions to perceived injustice. Individuals in more collectivistic settings are more concerned about maintaining positive and harmonious relationships, and therefore react more negatively if they are treated unfairly. As we have stressed repeatedly, individualism-collectivism is a central aspect of cultural variability. In collectivistic settings, individuals are socialised into valuing and maintaining close relationships with others and therefore are more satisfied if these values are upheld by the use of fair procedures and allocation of fair rewards in organisational contexts. This analysis therefore supports the previous reasoning by Brockner et al. (2005) and confirms the general importance of needing to belong.

People also showed stronger reactions to violations of procedural and interpersonal justice in contexts where income inequality was higher. This can be seen as support for control motives. In contexts with higher income inequality, people should be concerned about getting their fair deal because otherwise the possibility of falling down the social ladder is a real threat. Fairer procedures and treatment will ensure appropriate outcomes in the long run, increase predictability, and employees in more unequal economic contexts will reciprocate with greater job satisfaction, trust and commitment.

Perhaps you will have noticed that there are two different and somewhat opposing trends in these results. We had demonstrated that individuals in more power distant contexts are less concerned about justice overall, but that greater collectivism strengthens the effects of justice on work outcomes. The first line of results is concerned with whether paying attention to justice enables individuals to gauge their inclusion and status in valued in-groups, whereas the second line of results is concerned with how people react to an encountered injustice. The current findings suggest that these two processes involve different motives. If people are concerned about their standing in the group, they will pay more attention to indicators of whether they are valued members within the group hierarchy. However, collectivists will then express these perceptions in their attitudes and behaviours to a greater extent, because fair treatment upholds their cherished group moral values. Of course, it is necessary to test these conjectures more directly. It is also noteworthy that many individual-level studies have shown a positive moderating role of power distance, whereas at the nation level, collectivism is a stronger and more consistent moderator.

At the start of this chapter, we identified three principal issues affecting relations in groups. The studies that we have reviewed in this section show that the first of these, obtaining justice, is strongly influenced by cultural and contextual norms. However, once we have decided to engage in social interactions, we will also try to influence others to act in our favour and not to hurt or damage our interests. This involves processes of social influence, which we shall examine next.

TYPES OF SOCIAL INFLUENCE

Social influence is arguably one of the most important topics in social psychology. Some authors even argue that social psychology is nearly synonymous with social influence research (Hogg & Vaughan, 2011). All interpersonal behaviours involve some form of mutual influence, so that groups and societies can only exist and function because of effective, pervasive, and shared forms of social influence. In contrast to such general views, much research in the Western individualistic tradition has focused on more narrowly defined types of social influence. In Chapter 1 we touched on some of the classic studies of social influence, focusing on conformity and obedience (Asch, 1956; Milgram, 1961), and in Chapter 8 we explored the role of norms in the creation and maintenance of cultures.

Here, we consider influence that occurs in group settings from three different perspectives: informal influence, negotiation, and formal leadership. We start with informal influence, because it is the most widespread. The process of negotiation may occur on a formal or an informal basis, but is defined as a subcategory of influence processes where there is a substantive difference between the parties involved. Leadership can be considered as a subcategory of negotiation in which one party is formally endowed with greater power.

INFORMAL INFLUENCE PROCESSES

A wide variety of sources of influence is available to someone who wishes to influence others. However, which behaviour is effective will vary, depending on the relative power of the person whom one wishes to influence. As we shall see, it may also depend on the forms of influence that are distinctive within a particular context.

Ralston, Vollmer, Srinivasan et al. (2003) asked managers from six nations to evaluate the utility of six methods of influencing one's seniors (that is, upward influence strategies). After standardising the measures to eliminate differences between samples in acquiescent response style, it was found that US and Dutch managers favoured 'soft' tactics such as rational persuasion and a willingness to put in extra work. Mexican and Hong Kong managers were more willing to entertain 'hard' tactics such as withholding information or using information to manipulate others. German and Indian managers fell in between these two extremes.

A series of scenario studies conducted by Yukl and his colleagues also initially considered upward influence styles. Yukl, Fu, and McDonald (2003) found that US and Swiss managers favoured rational persuasion and inspirational appeals to persuade others and verbal objections to resist others. Chinese managers reported that informal approaches and avoidance of confrontation were more effective. Hong Kong managers were intermediate between these positions. Kennedy, Fu, and Yukl (2003) broadened their focus to include scenarios that referred to upward, lateral, and downward attempts. Managers from 12 nations were asked to identify which of 16 influence styles would be effective in each scenario. Rational persuasion, consultation and collaboration were rated effective in all samples. Gift-giving, socialising, the use of informal settings, and pressure were universally rated as relatively ineffective. After clustering the influence styles, it was found that national-level means for effectiveness of a cluster containing consultation and collaboration were significantly higher in low power distance, individualist nations.

Fu, Kennedy, Tata, Yukl et al. (2004) made a multi-level analysis predicting these responses as a function of Leung and Bond's (2004) individual-level measures of social axioms and nation-level scores derived from House et al.'s (2004) 61-nation GLOBE survey (both of which we described in Chapter 2). The 16 influence tactics yielded three broad factors that were named 'persuasive', 'assertive', and 'relationship-based'. At the individual level, persuasive tactics were rated more effective by those who endorsed Leung and Bond's measure of belief in reward for application. Assertive and relationship-based tactics were both rated more effective by those who endorsed social cynicism, fate control, and religiosity. At the nation-level, several significant moderations of these effects were found. For example, beliefs in the effectiveness of assertive and relationship-based tactics were more strongly linked with endorsement of fate control in nations that were low on uncertainty avoidance. Since low uncertainty avoidance refers to nations with a lesser degree of formalised rules and procedures, it appears that people in such nations who believe in fate see a greater value in having influence on those around them.

The strength of this series of studies is that respondents were asked for ratings of effective influence in specific settings, and toward specific types of person, rather than in general. Responses of this type are more likely to have cross-cultural validity, provided that the settings are representative. By measuring responses in a number of nations, the investigators were able to examine whether individual-level connections between beliefs and ways of influencing that were perceived to be effective were pan-cultural or were moderated by features of the national contexts in question.

Culture-Specific Influence Strategies

The research by Yukl's group used a culture-general approach, distinguishing broad types of influence strategies. However, within specific contexts, individuals may influence each other in ways that are culturally distinctive. This is a fascinating and growing research area, typically starting off with the type of emic research methods favoured by those who wish to develop local indigenous psychologies (Sinha 1997; Kim, Yang, & Hwang, 2006). This research is beginning to give rise to comparative studies of such influence strategies.

Guanxi

The most thoroughly researched indigenous influence strategy is *guanxi* ('connections'), a Chinese concept that describes the establishment, maintenance, and use of relationships within close social networks (X.P. Chen & Chen, 2012). It typically involves an implicit social contract between two individuals that leads to a long-term relationship characterised by mutual commitment, loyalty, and obligation. Links have traditionally been based upon being a relative, sharing ancestors, being neighbours, attending the same school, or having the same family name. Work relationships have become a more frequent basis in recent times. The linkage is based upon the connection of linked roles, not on personality. Persons engaged in *guanxi* relations are expected to remember and reciprocate favours given to one another over long periods of time. Typically, each party will seek to grant the other more favours than they receive, thereby enjoying a positive 'bank-balance' of favours to draw upon in future transactions.

Farh, Tsui, Xin, and Cheng (1998) surveyed 560 pairs of superiors and subordinates in Taiwan: 100 pairs concurred that they had a *guanxi* relationship with one another. Trust in the superior was found to be significantly higher among those who had *guanxi* relations based upon being a relative or upon being a former neighbour, but not for those with other types of *guanxi* relations. Farh et al. (1998) next surveyed a smaller sample of 32 managers in China who reported a total of 212 lateral business connections. Thirty-seven of these were identified as *guanxi* relations, based upon being former classmates, relatives, or those with a shared ancestry. Trust was again significantly higher within *guanxi* relations than in the remainder of the sample.

C.C. Chen, Chen, and Xin (2004) used a scenario study to investigate reactions to *guanxi* relations. Chinese business students were asked to rate how much trust in their supervisor they would have if he (or occasionally she) appointed someone to a job on the basis of a *guanxi* relationship. A large decrease in trust was found where the *guanxi* was based on being a relation or coming from the same town. A lesser and non-significant decrease was found where the *guanxi* was based on being a former schoolmate or close friend. Chen et al. suggest that this result occurred because respondents may have reasoned that the supervisor would know more about the actual abilities of the friend or schoolmate. Thus, there may be some forms of *guanxi* that are more compatible than others with the conduct of effective business relationships in China's contemporary economy.

Amae

Japanese persons quite frequently seek to influence one another in a distinctive manner referred to in Japanese as *amae*. In a first attempt to explain the phenomenon to a wider audience, Doi (1973) translated this term as 'indulgent dependence'. An *amae* episode typically occurs between two persons, and involves one relatively junior person making what would in most circumstances be considered an unreasonable demand on a more senior person. Furthermore, this demand is made with the presumption that the demand will in fact be accepted, as indeed it often is.

Yamaguchi (2004) has made a series of studies of *amae*. Initial surveys among the Japanese population indicated that a high percentage of respondents agreed that they do engage in *amae*-type relations, either in the family, at work, or among friends. Although *amae* relations most probably originate in childhood, *amae* episodes are also reported as frequent among adults. In an attempt to define what are the essential components of an *amae* relationship, Yamaguchi next asked participants to evaluate whether *amae* was present in each of a series of scenarios describing situations in which inappropriate demands or behaviours occurred: 87% reported that *amae* was present when the protagonists were described as presuming that their demands would be met, with lower percentages when no presumption was made. However, the scenarios did not yield direct evidence of how that presumption was actually communicated between the two parties.

Yamaguchi argues that *amae* provides an effective means for upward influence within Japan and possibly other collectivist cultures, because of the nature of attachment within collectivism. The presumption that the demand will be met affirms the strength of the attachment. To test his interpretation, adults were presented with descriptions of children's behaviour in the 'strange situation' that has been much used to study the attachment of infants to their caregivers (see Chapter 8). In this procedure, the caregiver temporarily leaves the child with a stranger, and the child's behaviour is noted during the separation and after the caregiver's return. Yamaguchi found that infants behaved in ways that characterise the 'secure-attachment' response were the ones that his respondents predicted would show most *amae* behaviour. In contrast, *amae*-type behaviour by a child within a Western nation might be expected to be more typical of insecurity (Rothbaum, Weisz, Pott et al., 2000).

Niiya and Ellsworth (2012) compared the responses of Japanese and American students to a request from a friend to stay in their apartment. The Japanese rated themselves as closer to a friend who asked to stay for a week than to a friend who asked to stay for three days. In contrast, the Americans were not affected by the duration of the request, but rated themselves closer to the requester if they felt in control of what was happening. Requests to stay for periods of longer than a week were increasingly less well received by both groups, but especially by the Americans. The authors interpreted these results as showing that the Japanese interpreted the situation in terms of *amae*, while the Americans focused more on considerations of power and control. Though initially assumed to be uniquely Japanese, *amae* may be relevant in other collectivistic societies as well. For example, there are terms in Turkish and Farsi with rather similar meanings.

Jeitinho

A different form of social influence strategy is typical of Brazilian culture. *Jeitinho Brasileiro* is widespread but highly controversial, because of its alleged links to corruption and the provision of favours. It can be best translated as the 'little way' of getting problems sorted out in a hierarchical and bureaucratic culture. Pilati, Milfont, Ferreira, Porto, and Fischer (2011) conducted qualitative studies with students and members of the public to understand how Brazilians constructed *jeitinho brasileiro*. These researchers found that it was seen as an innovative problem-solving strategy in which Brazilians used social status combined with cunning tricks to achieve personal goals, despite the fact that it broke formal rules. They originally identified seven major categories, which in a subsequent scenario study yielded factors labeled corruption, *malandragem* (social norm-breaking), and creativity (Ferreira, Fischer, Pilati, Porto, & Milfont, 2012: see also examples of each of these in Everyday Life Box 10.1).

Everyday Life Box 10.1   Social Influence Strategies in Brazil

Have a look at these examples of Brazilian *jeitinho* and consider how typical they may be in your own cultural context. Would you engage in these behaviours? If yes, under what circumstances would you behave like this?

Corruption Scenarios

- Every time José takes a taxi for company purposes, he has the right to request reimbursement for the amount paid. When he is without money, he requests a receipt for a greater amount than he has paid and submits this to the company. He keeps the extra money.
- A councillor, who is very well known in his city, was able to get building materials from companies around the region to rebuild a school. However, he diverted some of these materials to renovate the house of one of his sons.
- Pablo's car has a broken light. While driving at night on the highway, he is pulled over by the traffic police. To avoid receiving a fine, Pablo offers the policeman a bribe to continue his journey.

Creativity Scenarios

- It is the birthday of a very close friend of Joana and she has forgotten to buy him a present. She also has financial problems and believes that she will not find anything affordable at such short notice. As Joana is very clever, she uses free school material to create a beautiful card to give to her friend.
- Marília works as a general services clerk in a large company and cannot earn enough money to pay off all the debts on her house. To earn extra money, she talks to the boss and requests authorisation to sell sandwiches and snacks to other employees at her workplace.
- Tampinha earns a living as a delivery boy. To improve his earnings, he works enthusiastically as a waiter in a restaurant every night. With his pleasant ways, he is able to conquer the whole clientele.

Norm-Breaking Scenarios

- Parking at shopping centres is difficult during busy times. Knowing that it is very hard to find a place to park at these times, Camila speaks to her grandmother and invites her to go shopping, so that she can park in a space reserved for the elderly.
- Tickets to the last show on a tour by Edward's favourite artist have almost run out. When he arrives at the venue, he sees that there is a very long queue and it will be very difficult for him to get a ticket. At the front of the queue, however, he sees an old school colleague he hasn't seen for some time. As Edward is really keen to attend the show, he greets his friend and asks whether he can join him in the queue.
- Marina needs to go to the supermarket very quickly to buy just one litre of milk for her children's bottles. When she arrives at the supermarket, she sees that there are no parking spaces. She therefore puts the car along the pavement, switches on the emergency lights, and quickly goes into the market to buy the milk.

These authors found in their study of Brazilians residing in Rio de Janeiro that individual-level preferences were associated with both moral leniency and the social dominance orientation of individuals, especially for corruption and social norm-breaking. However, when *jeitinho* was conceptualised as an intersubjective norm perception (see Chapter 8) by asking what behaviours are typical for Brazilians, they found a higher endorsement of *jeitinho*, but the correlations with social dominance disappeared. This suggests that individuals engage in these behaviours to obtain some personal goal, but that at the normative cultural level, *jeitinho* is a positively valued cultural symbol.

Other social influence processes said to be culturally distinctive have been described (Smith, 2008), including *wasta* ('going in between') in Arab nations, 'pulling strings' in the UK, 'One-talk' (talking as one person) in Melanesian culture, and *'svyazi'* ('power') in Russia. So how do such processes differ and do they have a common psychological element? At the conceptual level, Ferreira et al. (2012) argue that *guanxi* and *jeitinho* were different processes. *Guanxi* is focused on a long-term and harmonious social relationship: partners are well-advised to avoid upsetting or upstaging the other partner. *Jeitinho* on the other hand is focused on achieving short-term goals that may even upset or strain relationships in the long run; it also involves a subversive strategy that negates traditional forms of power through deception, creativity, or social skills. The powerless in Brazilian folklore can trick the rich and powerful and achieve their short-term objectives through *jeitinho brasileiro* (namely, trickery and cunning).

A different approach was taken by Smith, Huang, Harb, and Torres (2012). They developed simple scenarios exemplifying *guanxi*, *wasta*, *jeitinho* and 'pulling strings', obtained from respondents in the nations in which these processes were said to be widespread. After disguising the cultural origins of these scenarios, the researchers distributed the complete set to students in Brazil, China, the Lebanon, and the UK. Although respondents did confirm that scenarios drawn from their own nation were adequately representative, little evidence was found for distinctiveness. *Guanxi* and *jeitinho*, for example, were both rated as more typical in the Lebanon than in China or Brazil, their countries of origin, respectively.

Similar results were obtained by Smith, Torres, Achoui et al. (2012), who sampled business managers in six nations and also included scenarios exemplifying Russian *svyazi*. Scenarios depicting *guanxi*, *wasta*, *svyazi* and 'pulling strings' were all rated as most frequent by Russians. This study did show evidence for the distinctiveness of *jeitinho*, but in general it appears that informal social influence processes are less distinctive than has been claimed and they probably vary between nations more in frequency than in kind. Smith, Huang et al. (2012) also found that individuals with more self-enhancing values rated all social influence strategies as more positive. This confirmed the Brazilian findings of Ferreira et al. (2012) across a more diverse set of nations and scenarios. These influence strategies may differ in their frequency and mechanisms, but they are used by individuals around the world for similar reasons, namely to achieve self-serving goals in a social interaction.

Evidence for these culture-specific influence strategies poses three groups of questions: Firstly, are they emic aspects of specific traditional cultures, or are parallel phenomena present in other cultures? If the answer is yes, how do they differ? Are they expressions of universal psychological processes within the context of a specific culture or do they express different psychological motives, and are therefore used for obtaining different goals? Secondly, how are such phenomena responding to the current rapid social change in many traditional societies? One argument is that these strategies have developed to overcome the barriers that are present in rigid and bureaucratic settings and contexts of scarcities and inequalities. Will these behaviours diminish over time with increasing development and access to resources? Thirdly, how might such culture-specific relationships best be handled by expatriate business persons, whose own value system may lead them to see some aspects of these influence strategies as nepotism or corruption?

CONFLICT AND NEGOTIATION

We turn now to look at ways of managing differences with others. Imagine you have had a dispute with your brother or sister. You probably reacted quite differently from when you were arguing with your lecturer about a grade. In considering studies of conflict then, it is necessary to specify the party with whom the conflict is occurring. Conflicts are unlikely to be handled in the same manner between these who are close and those who are strangers to one another, those who are of equal or unequal status, those who are adversaries or partners, those who are alone or in public (McAuley, Bond, & Kashima, 2002). It is also central to the concepts of collectivism and power distance that variations in the behaviours used to address different types of conflict will be larger in collectivist, high power distance contexts. The field of conflict research is also particularly interesting, because theorists working in various parts of the world have formulated separate models of conflict and negotiation, which produce predictions that are sometimes mutually contradictory. Take a look at Research Debate Box 10.1 below.

Research Debate Box 10.1 demonstrates that there is some evidence in favour of both the dual-concern model and the Leung model, but neither has been extensively tested. Contrasts between Asian and Western approaches to conflict management are evidently oversimplified. We therefore need to look at a broader range of studies. Van Oudenhoven, Mechelse, and De Dreu (1998) asked managers from five European nations to describe episodes of conflict with their superiors and colleagues. Dutch, British and Danish managers reported more problem-solving behaviours than did Belgian and Spanish managers. Dutch managers reported giving more consideration to the other party's viewpoint. There are thus behavioural differences in conflict management, even within the more culturally homogeneous area of Europe.

Morris, Williams, Leung et al. (1998) moved the field forward by making a direct test of whether negotiation style is predicted by the individual negotiator's cultural orientation. Their samples comprised business students in India, Hong Kong, the Philippines, and the USA. Using Schwartz's value measures, they confirmed that achievement values partially mediated national differences in competitive bargaining, while conservation values wholly mediated national differences in avoidance behaviours. Since conservation values represent protection of the status quo rather than a concern for others, this study does not directly test cross-cultural validity of the dual-concern model. However, it does indicate that across several nations, avoidance is predicted by variables other than those specified in the dual-concern model. The Morris et al. study did not include a distinction between in- and out-group negotiations, so there is some uncertainty as to whether the effects that were found are equally applicable to both types of setting.

Research Debate Box 10.1   Avoidance and Conflict Resolution

Researchers in North America have mostly conceptualised conflict in terms of a series of 'dual-concern' models. Negotiation styles are seen as a product of how strong the concern is for one's own outcomes and how strong the concern is for the other party's outcomes (e.g., Pruitt & Carnevale, 1993). If the concern for oneself outweighs a concern for others, a tough competitive stance is predicted, whereas if the concern for others is high, a more accommodating or yielding approach is thought likely. Where a concern for both oneself and others is high, a more integrative or 'problem-solving' approach is predicted. Finally, a low concern for both oneself and others is expected to lead to avoidance of the conflict situation. Problem solving is predicted to be most effective.

A contrasting East Asian model was proposed by Leung (1997). Leung identified two principal concerns relating to conflict, which he labeled 'animosity reduction' and 'disintegration avoidance'. He hypothesised that the strength of these two motives would vary, dependent upon whether the conflict is with an in-group or an out-group party. Within the in-group, a primary concern would be to avoid the disintegration of the relationship, since the group is central to one's own identity. Consequently, all kinds of tactical avoidance and face-saving behaviours would be engaged with. With the out-group, a concern for others is lower, but the risk of animosity is much higher. Leung therefore predicted greater use of compromising and collaborative behaviours in this kind of interaction.

The point of contention between these two models lies in their conceptualisation of avoidance. Western models see avoidance as occurring when the parties are indifferent to one another. In the East Asian model, avoidance is maximal where concerns for the self and for others are highest. No studies have been reported that have directly tested these predictions against one another. However, existing studies have tested the range of nations within which each model can account for the effects obtained.

Cross-cultural tests of the dual-concern model are provided by a series of studies in which business persons participated in an hour-long simulation of a buyer-seller negotiation. The simulation permits an objective evaluation of negotiators' success in achieving an optimal outcome. Data from 16 nations showed that a problem-solving approach was employed more frequently by negotiators from collectivist nations, such as Japan, Korea and Taiwan, whereas European and North American negotiators were more competitive (Graham, Mintu, & Rodgers, 1994).

However, these studies also yielded effects indicating that prevalence of negotiation style is a poor guide to eventual outcome (Graham & Mintu Wimsat, 1997). Although US negotiators were less inclined to use a problem-solving approach, best outcomes were achieved when they did so, provided the other party reciprocated. In Spain, on the other hand, a problem-solving approach resulted in a less positive outcome. In Japan, buyers invariably obtained a better bargain than sellers did regardless of the approach, because sellers in Japan owe deference to buyers.

(Continued)

(Continued)

The Leung model differs from the dual-concern model in that it specifies the *reasons* why negotiators would behave in particular ways in a given context. Consequently, tests of the model require not just choices between negotiation style but also measures of preference for animosity reduction or disintegration avoidance. His theory is more socially responsive.

Leung (1987) obtained ratings of the extent to which Hong Kong and US students favoured various procedures for conflict resolution, such as negotiation, mediation, and adjudication. He found that the preferred procedures were those rated as most likely to reduce animosity across both samples. Gire and Carment (1993) conducted a similar study with Canadian and Nigerian students. In this case, both groups favoured negotiation. However, while Canadians rated negotiation as most likely to reduce animosity, Nigerians also perceived that the issuing of threats would do so. This distinctive result from Nigeria is one of the few in this book drawn from African respondents, and it would be valuable to understand more fully how the Nigerian respondents conceptualised the negotiation process and why threats play this distinctive role in their culture.

Bond, Leung, and Schwartz (1992) used a similar research design, sampling Hong Kong and Israeli students. The Israelis were more likely to make threats than the students in Hong Kong. In this case, the Israeli preference for threats was explained in part by their lower concern about the animosity reduction it would generate. Additionally, however, Israelis preferred arbitration. This preference arose because of the stronger Israeli belief that arbitration would result in a greater animosity reduction. Therefore, both the value placed on animosity reduction and the belief that using a given negotiation tactic will lead to greater animosity reduction are involved in predicting the choice of negotiation tactics. Cross-cultural differences arise because each of these factors (values and beliefs) varies between national groups.

These studies do not provide a full test of the Leung model, but they illustrate once more the various ways in which specific behaviours may vary between cultures, but may be linked by common explanatory concepts, in this case their perceived utility in reducing animosity and the value of animosity reduction itself. No studies have yet been reported in which measures of disintegration avoidance were included.

Pearson and Stephan (1998) compared student ratings of how they would negotiate with strangers and with friends in Brazil and the USA. As predicted, the Brazilians scored higher on measures of collectivist cultural orientation than the Americans, and preferred non-competitive ways of handling conflict. Furthermore, they differentiated more sharply than US respondents between the in-group and out-group scenarios. In a further study comparing Mexicans and Americans, Gabrielidis, Stephan, Ybarra, Pearson, and Villareal (1997) obtained similar results, but they also reported correlations between self-construal measures and their measures of negotiation style. Contrary to predictions from the dual-concern model, they found significant positive correlations in both nations between a measure of interdependent self-construal and preference for avoidance.

Reward sharing studies, where the allocator divides money between him- or herself and another person, are in essence also studies of negotiation. Relatively few studies of this type have directly compared in- and out-group allocations. In a scenario study, Leung and Bond (1984) found that among Hong Kong students rewards were shared equally among friends, but that sharing based on equity was favoured when rewards were allocated to strangers. US students did not differentiate allocations in this way. In a similar study, also comparing Hong Kong and the United States, Hui, Triandis, and Yee (1991) showed that differentiation in reward sharing between in-group and out-group was partially mediated by an individual-level measure of collectivist cultural orientation.

Some more recent studies have attempted to describe cultural understandings of conflicts in a way that captures the complexity of most conflict situations in additional detail. Gelfand, Nishii, Holcombe et al. (2001) analysed descriptions of conflict episodes provided by US and Japanese students. Respondents from both nations assessed the conflicts in terms of compromising versus winning. However, Americans also construed the negotiations in terms of threats to their preferred individual identity, whereas the Japanese saw negotiations in terms of meeting their relational obligations to others. Ohbuchi, Fukushima, and Tedeschi (1999) obtained ratings of the conflict experiences of Japanese and American students. The Americans saw assertion as a way of achieving justice, while the Japanese saw avoidance as a way of preserving harmony.

The results from the studies with students that have just been cited differ somewhat from those that have used managers. Tinsley (2001) observed pairs of German, Japanese, and US managers negotiating in an intra-cultural simulation. She predicted that the Americans would prefer to seek ways of integrating both their own and their opponents' preferences (in other words, to satisfy both negotiators rather than simply optimising one's own preference). The Japanese were predicted to emphasise power, and the Germans to emphasise adherence to the rules. Her predictions were upheld and she found that her results were completely mediated by individual-level measures of individualism, hierarchy and directness, respectively. The predicted linkage between German directness and their focus on rules was based upon her expectation that the Germans would challenge deviations from the rules.

In a similar study of pairs of Hong Kong and US business students negotiating intra-culturally, Tinsley and Brett (2001) again found that the Americans more often achieved outcomes that integrated the preferences of both parties. They also more frequently achieved agreements that involved tradeoffs between the different elements in a negotiation, rather than negotiating each issue separately. More frequent Hong Kong outcomes were referring decisions to the supervisor or leaving the situation unresolved. Hong Kong respondents endorsed collectivism and a respect for authority more, but neither of these measures predicted the outcomes, leaving it unclear which cultural process led to the observed difference. Van de Vliert, Ohbuchi, Van Rossum, Hayashi, and Van der Vegt (2004) obtained ratings from Japanese business employees of how well they had handled disputes with their superiors. A combination of having first 'contended with' (i.e., disputed) and then accommodated to the superior's wishes predicted effectiveness. Van de Vliert et al. contrasted this finding with earlier results showing that for Dutch employees a combination of contending and then integrating their own and their superior's wishes was most effective. They speculated that the Japanese-Dutch differences arose because of the greater Japanese need to preserve face.

The separate stages of effective negotiation identified in the study by van de Vliert et al. suggest the value of looking at negotiations as a process that occurs over time. Take a look now at the series of studies described in Key Research Study Box 10.1, which explore this important aspect more fully.

Key Research Study Box 10.1   The Importance of Timing in Negotiation

Adair and Brett (2005) constructed a complex, one-hour long simulation of a commercial negotiation. This enabled analyses of actual negotiation behaviours over time rather than simple summaries of negotiation style. The collectivist negotiations comprised dyads drawn from Russia, Japan, Hong Kong and Thailand, and the individualist negotiations comprised dyads from Germany, Israel, Sweden and the USA. In all of these instances, each dyad comprised two persons from the same nation. The negotiations were audiotaped, transcribed, and coded into a series of predetermined categories. In order to examine the sequential development of the negotiations, the transcripts were divided into quarters.

In studies that use a complex content analysis of this kind, the numbers of dyads from each individual nation is necessarily low, so Adair and Brett analysed the results for all individualist dyads in contrast to the results for all collectivist dyads. Negotiators from the individualistic nations showed more direct exchange of information through questions (e.g., 'We could offer 40% upfront') and answers (e.g., 'We couldn't possibly accept that offer'). Only during the last quarter did they make actual offers focused on a possible agreement. Negotiators from collectivistic nations used indirect information exchange more frequently. In other words, they made a mixture of offers and more generally phrased persuasive arguments (e.g., 'Everyone knows our company makes the finest products and we plan to continue introducing new ones') during the early stages, and inferred what must be the more important priorities of the other party from the relatively indirect responses (e.g., 'This deal is very important for me. I'm up for promotion and the budget is really tight') that they obtained to their offers.

Information exchange during the first section of the negotiation was associated with greater joint gains by the two protagonists, whether the exchange was direct or indirect. Developing our knowledge of this cultural contrast further, Adair, Weingart, and Brett (2007) showed that early direct offers by American negotiators resulted in a lower joint gain, as did early direct information exchange by Japanese negotiators. Therefore, the strategy that worked best within each nation did not work well in the other nation. On this basis, we can anticipate the problems that would be experienced in intercultural negotiations, where the two ways of gaining information would not be compatible with one another. Studies that examine this process cross-nationally are considered in Chapter 11.

In addition to the effects of time, we may expect that other aspects of interpersonal relations such as face concern and interpersonal trust will also be operative in conflict settings. For instance, Brew and Cairns (2004) compared Anglo-Australian and Chinese students' responses to conflict scenarios that involved threats to one's own face and to others' face.

The type of face threat accounted for more variance than did the nationality of the respondents. Both groups favoured direct communication in relation to threats to one's own face. The Chinese responded more strongly to threats to others' face, however, primarily by using more cautious styles of communication. Gunia, Brett, et al. (2011) compared the negotiation strategies of US and Indian business managers, using a 75-minute simulation similar to those described in Key Research Study Box 10.1. On the basis of Yamagishi's (2011) analysis of institutional trust, and Gelfand et al.'s (2011) mapping of tight versus loose cultures, they predicted that the Indians would be less trusting than the Americans and that their suspicion would lead them to use less of the technique shown in earlier studies to lead to an optimal joint outcome – that is, asking more early questions and giving more early answers. Their hypotheses were supported.

In this section we have seen that approaches to negotiation do differ in terms that can be predicted on the basis of collectivism, power distance, and related concepts. A strength of studies in this area is that researchers have started to identify the timing and nature of specific behaviours that will result in beneficial outcomes in different cultural contexts. A weakness in that insufficient attention has been given to whether one is negotiating with an in-group or an out-group member. Cross-national negotiations will have characteristics that are more similar to out-group negotiations. For some of the additional factors that become challenging in such settings, see Everyday Life Box 10.2.

Everyday Life Box 10.2   Cross-National Negotiation

The world summit on climate change held in Copenhagen in 2009 provided numerous instances of cultural differences in negotiation style and their consequences (Vidal & Watts, 2009). President Obama delayed his arrival at the summit until his advisers judged that there was a possibility of agreement with the Chinese. When he arrived he joined the group of predominantly Western leaders who were attempting to rescue the stalled negotiations. However, the Chinese and Indian governments sent only middle-ranking protocol officers to these meetings, thereby preventing the flexibility that might have been possible within a meeting of heads of state. Obama reacted by leaving these meetings and twice having one-to-one negotiations with Chinese premier Wen Jia Bao, thus illustrating his preference for direct communication. He returned from the second of these meetings announcing agreement on certain points. The Chinese responded by introducing new demands into the group discussions through their protocol officers, thus regaining control of the negotiation. Obama responded by once more seeking out the Chinese, and this time found them engaged in an alternative negotiation with a small group of key non-Western nations. Obama joined these negotiations uninvited, and a new agreement was announced. The new rather modest deal was in turn much criticised by nations that had not been party to any of these discussions, but was eventually accepted. Chinese indirectness had proved most effective in achieving the goals they desired, but there would have been no agreement at all without the more direct initiatives of several Western leaders.

FORMAL LEADERSHIP

The effectiveness of different styles of leadership has been very extensively studied, both within North America and globally. Many cross-cultural studies have followed the mainstream perspective of seeking effective qualities of leaders as individuals without reference to context, finding a variety of effects (Aycan, 2008). Here we focus first on a major study that retains the perspective of mainstream studies, but which developed new measures intended to be cross-culturally valid.

The GLOBE Project

The GLOBE project, directed by Robert House, involved nearly 200 collaborators from 62 nations (House et al., 2004). The GLOBE (Global Leadership and Organisational Behavior Effectiveness) researchers surveyed more than 17,000 managers, drawn from the telecommunication, financial services, and food supply industries during the 1990s. Respondents were asked to select from a list those traits that they perceived characterised an effective leader. With further ratings, they also described, in terms of nine dimensions, their nation and their organisation, both as they understood it (in other words, as a measure of current practices) and also as they would like it to be (in other words, as a measure of values). Many of these dimensions were intended to tap concepts similar to those that arose from the work of Hofstede (1980).

Key Researcher Box 10.1   Robert House

Figure 10.1   Robert House

Robert J. House (1932–2011) was born in Toledo, Ohio, and completed his doctorate in management at Ohio State University in 1960. After holding positions at Ohio State University, the University of Michigan, City University of New York and the University of Toronto, he was appointed professor of organisation studies at the Wharton School of Business, University of Pennsylvania, in 1988. Throughout his career, he was concerned with the study of leadership, developing first a model of role conflict, then a path-goal theory, and later an emphasis on the charismatic qualities of effective leaders. In the early 1990s, he brought together and directed the cross-national team of researchers whose research into leadership in more than 60 nations became known as the GLOBE project. He was the author of more than 130 research papers, many book chapters, and six books.

Den Hartog, House, Hanges, Dorfman, and Ruiz-Qintanilla (1999) reported the initial GLOBE results for effective leader traits. Substantial worldwide consensus was found, favouring charismatic-type leaders who were seen as trustworthy, dynamic, encouraging and intelligent, but rejecting those held to be non-cooperative, egocentric and irritable. These and other traits were first summarised in terms of 21 clusters, and these clusters in turn were summarised in terms of six styles of leadership.

Table 10.1   National- and Organisational-Level Predictors of Desired Leader Styles

Leader style	Clusters where this style is seen as more effective	Values that predict endorsement of this style
Charismatic	Anglo Germanic Nordic Southern Asia Latin Europe Latin America	High Performance Orientation (O) High In-Group Collectivism (N, O) High Gender Egalitarianism (N)
Team-oriented	No difference between clusters	High Uncertainty Avoidance (N, O) High In-Group Collectivism (O)
Participative	Germanic Anglo Nordic	Low Uncertainty Avoidance (N, O) High Performance Orientation (O) High Gender Egalitarianism (N, O)
Humane	Southern Asia Anglo Sub-Saharan Africa Confucian Asia	High Humane Orientation (O) High Uncertainty Avoidance (N, O)
Autonomous	No difference between clusters	High Performance Orientation (O) Low Institutional Collectivism (N, O)
Self-Protective	Middle East Confucian Asia Southern Asia Eastern Europe Latin America	High Power Distance (N, O) High Uncertainty Avoidance (N, O)

N = Nation-level; O = Organization-level.

Source: adapted from House et al. (2004).

In order to present their complex findings most clearly, the GLOBE researchers also formed ten clusters of nations in their sample whose respondents were judged to be relatively similar to one another with respect to values. The leader styles identified as charismatic and team-oriented were most positively endorsed in all clusters, while the self-protective and autonomous were least favoured. However, there were variations in endorsement across clusters for four of the six styles. The most crucial findings of this study concerned the extent to which the differences in the styles of leadership perceived to be effective in each cluster of nations could be explained in terms of the value dimensions that were strongly endorsed in those clusters. Significant links between preferred leader style and values were found at both the organisation level and the nation level.

Table 10.1 summarises the organisation- and nation-level results for each of the leadership styles. Although all of the effects shown in the box are statistically significant, the majority of effects were not strong. At these levels of aggregation, styles are necessarily somewhat heterogeneous. We should expect to find stronger effects at the level of single nations, industries and organisations. Indeed, Paris, Dorfman, Howell, and Hanges (2009) showed that within the GLOBE data there were consistent gender effects of preferred leader types. Women more strongly preferred participative, team-oriented and charismatic leaders than did men.

An indication of the type of results that we may expect from more specifically-targeted samples is provided by Spreitzer, Perttula, & Xin (2005). These authors tested the impact of traditional values on the effectiveness of 'transformational' leadership in two organisations in Taiwan and the United States. Transformational leadership (Bass, 1997) is similar in conception to the charismatic style identified by the GLOBE researchers, and some evidence does support the claim that it is effective in many contexts (Bass, 1997). Spreitzer et al. showed that a measure of traditional Chinese values moderated the impact of transformational leadership on performance negatively (in other words, transformational leaders were less effective with more traditional employees).

Overall, leadership researchers concur with one another that there are elements of effective leadership that are universal and other elements that are more specific to certain cultures. There is less agreement as to whether it is the universal or the specific elements that are relatively more important, and this question awaits testing. The GLOBE project was originally conceptualised in terms of the models of charismatic or value-based leadership that have been espoused by many recent US leadership researchers, and it was expected that some universal effects would be obtained. The use of an initially unstructured listing of the traits that provided the basis for the clusters has permitted the additional emergence of some quite marked culture-specific results.

However, a listing of traits is itself an imposed-etic approach, because as we saw in Chapter 5, traitedness varies between cultures. Leadership in high power distance, collectivist contexts may have more to do with role obligations than with personal traits or styles. Leaders may actually have to work harder to achieve influence in low power distance nations, because those around them are less responsive to normative obligations and more responsive to the influence styles that leaders employ. This was confirmed in a recent meta-analysis of studies on leader-member exchange relations (Rockstuhl, Dulebohn, Ang, & Shore, 2012). The relationship between the leader and subordinate was more strongly related to positive work attitudes and behaviours in Western business samples compared to Asian samples. Studies that detect aspects of leadership specific to high power distance nations would need to start with the distinctive qualities of role relationships, which we discuss below in terms of 'paternalism'.

Contextualising Leadership

A further series of studies has emphasised that leadership involves the management of one's relations with a whole set of the key parties with whom leaders interact, not just one's subordinates. Smith, Peterson, and Schwartz (2002) surveyed the extent to which around 7,000 managers in 43 nations reported that they relied on each of eight different sources of guidance in handling each of eight frequently occurring work events, for example, the appointment of a new subordinate. In most nations, the most frequent sources of guidance were found to be one's own experience and training, one's superior, and formal rules and procedures.

Nonetheless, the relative extent of reliance on each source varied across nations. An index of reliance on 'vertical' sources was constructed, weighting positively a reliance on one's superior and on formal rules and procedures, and weighting negatively a reliance on oneself and one's subordinates. Nation-level means for this index correlated strongly with Hofstede's scores for collectivism and power distance, and Schwartz's scores for hierarchy. Thus, the ways in which leaders handle work events do vary between nations in ways that we can explain in terms of national dimension scores.

The more vital practical question is whether these variations enhance leaders' effectiveness in these cultural settings. A multi-level analysis (Smith, Peterson, Thomason et al., 2011) showed that the rated effectiveness of relying on different sources in introducing changes to work procedures was significantly moderated by scores for different nations from the Hofstede and GLOBE projects. Reliance on unwritten rules and co-workers was perceived as more effective in collectivistic nations. In contrast, relying on personal experience and subordinates was more strongly associated with effectiveness in nations that are individualistic, masculine, and low on power distance. Reliance on formal rules was linked with effectiveness in nations high on uncertainty avoidance, whereas reliance on superiors was rated more effective in nations high on power distance. Effective ways of handling critical situations in everyday working life therefore relate in interpretable ways to known types of cultural variation.

Paternalism

The perspectives of both the GLOBE researchers and Smith et al. still exemplify Western perspectives insofar as they treat leaders as individuals who are somehow separate from the groups that they lead. Controversial leaders from Mao Zedong to Fidel Castro exemplify leadership processes that are embedded in distinctive ways within their specific cultural contexts. Recent voices from the non-Western world, with alternative models of leadership, are emerging.

In particular, the concept of paternalism has provoked considerable interest. In Western societies with their strong Protestant history, paternalism has had a negative connotation. The famous German sociologist Weber (1947) described paternalistic leadership as a form of traditional authoritarian domination and predicted its demise with increasing bureaucratisation and economic development. Yet in non-Western contexts, paternalism is defined as a hierarchical relationship in which the superior provides guidance, nurturance, protection and care, and in return the subordinate is loyal and deferent (Aycan, Kanungo, Mendoca et al., 2000). Aycan and her colleagues conducted a ten-nation study of paternalism and found it to be highest in India, Pakistan, Turkey and China, and lowest in Israel and Germany. Multiple regression indicated that in seven nations, endorsement of paternalism was associated with a heightened sense of obligation toward others, and in five nations it was linked with an expectation of employee participation. Thus the consequences of paternalism will differ depending on one's culture, suggesting that the role played by paternalism in some nations is replaced by other ways of handling hierarchical relationships in those cultural systems where paternalism has negative connotations.

There is continuing debate as to the dimensions that may underlie paternalism. Farh and Cheng (2000) distinguished two components: authoritarianism – the element of paternalistic leadership that has so many negative connotations in the Western world – and benevolence – the parent-like caring element of paternalistic leadership that makes it so attractive and effective in non-Western societies. The importance of this caring aspect was confirmed in a study of leaders' empathic emotions on effectiveness in 38 nations (Sadri, Weber, & Gentry, 2011). Subordinates rated the empathy shown by their leaders. For each of these leaders, the respective superior of the leader provided a rating of the leader's performance. The ratings of both the predictor (empathy) and the dependent variable (performance) were therefore obtained from different sources, a procedure which enhances the validity of the results. More empathic leaders were seen as better performers overall. It is notable that this relationship was stronger in samples from nations that had higher power distance values (as measured by the GLOBE researchers). Thus the caring and empathic aspect of leadership is more important for leadership effectiveness in more hierarchical, non-Western, nations.

Research Instrument Box 10.1   Paternalistic Leadership

The Paternalism Questionnaire of Cheng et al. (2004) contains 28 items. Below are three sample items from each of his three scales.

Authoritarian leadership

My supervisor has the last say in meetings.
My supervisor asks me to obey his/her instructions completely.
My supervisor scolds us when we cannot accomplish our tasks.

Benevolent leadership

My supervisor is like a family member when he/she gets along with us.
My supervisor takes good care of my family members as well.
My supervisor devotes all of his/her energy to taking care of me.

Moral leadership

My supervisor does not take advantage of me for personal gain.
My supervisor employs people according to their virtues and does not envy others' virtues or abilities.
My supervisor does not take credit for my achievements/contributions for himself/herself.

Cheng, Chou, Wu et al. (2004) proposed that morality was a third component of paternalistic leadership in Chinese business organisations. They predicted that a high score on each dimension of paternalism would augment the impact of the other dimensions. Morality in their view included integrity and fulfilling one's obligations, not taking advantage of others and being a selfless leader. Research Instrument Box 10.1 shows examples of some of the items in their measures. In a study of employees in Taiwan, Cheng et al. found significant positive effects of all three dimensions on subordinates' responses on indices of identification, compliance, and expressed gratitude.

The most culturally distinctive aspect of these results is the positive relation between authoritarian leadership and the dependent measures. However, this particular effect has not always been replicated in subsequent studies with Chinese samples (Wu & Xu, 2012). Niu, Wang, and Cheng (2009) found that high scores on benevolent and moral leadership induced high deference to the supervisor, even in the absence of authoritarian leadership. In summary, the negative notions of paternalistic leadership that are emphasised in Western societies can be counterbalanced by strong social and moralistic components in Asian and other non-Western societies. It would be valuable next to examine whether the emphasis on benevolence and morality by Chinese leaders would have similar effects in low power distance cultures. The results obtained by Sadri et al. (2011) suggest that if any effects were to be found they would be weaker.

HONOUR CULTURES

Thus far in the chapter, we have focused on processes that are probably universal but are shaped by the cultural and social norms of each group. We now focus on some processes that are more often seen as culture specific, but which have received a significant amount of media and research attention in recent years. These processes nevertheless involve the same issues that have been a central focus of this chapter: reputation, status, and control of in-group members.

We are concerned here with groups whose distinctive culture is built upon having pride in one's group, with the consequence of particularly strong in-group conformity as well as resistance to insults from outsiders. These are known as honour cultures (Nisbett & Cohen, 1996). If some offence to the dignity or reputation of a member of one's group is given, it will be the responsibility of appropriate members of one's group to exact a suitable penalty from the person or group that has given offence. Honour cultures are said to exist in parts of Mediterranean Europe and the Middle East, Latin America, South Asia, and the southern United States.

In cultures of this type, the concept of honour has a distinctive meaning. In order to contrast the understanding of honour in an individualist and a collectivist culture, Mosquera, Manstead, and Fischer (2000, 2002) obtained free descriptions of situations having relevance to honour, its loss, or its enhancement, from schoolchildren and adults in the Netherlands and Spain. In the Netherlands, honour was understood to be associated with personal achievements and autonomy. In contrast, in Spain, honour was linked with one's family and an interdependence with others. Honour was considered a more important concept in Spain and was more strongly associated with the emotions of pride, shame, and anger.

The Spanish concept of *pundonor* and related concepts such as the Greek *philotimo* refer to a personal dignity or honour, which is maintained by fulfilling one's obligations to the members of one's in-group. These obligations include loyalty and showing generous hospitality to those who are favoured, but also a firm defence of the group's honour in the face of a threat or insult. As we noted in Chapter 9, an interesting reflection of this different understanding is found in comparisons of insults. In Northern Italy, swearwords mostly target the individual, but in Southern Italy they also target the person's family members, stressing the entanglement of the individual's honour with that of the immediate family (Semin & Rubini, 1990). Similarly, in the northern United States one might cause someone to lose honour by insulting or criticising them directly, whereas in Turkey it would be more effective to make false accusations or physical or sexual attacks that would affect someone's reputation (Uskul et al., 2012). Using descriptions of typical US and Turkish honour loss episodes, these authors also found that Turkish types of honour loss would be felt more strongly by themselves and by a person's family in Turkey than they would in the USA, whereas US types of honour loss would be felt equally in both cultures. Everyday Life Box 10.3 underlines the extremes to which people will go to defend honour in some sections of the Pakistani population.

Everyday Life Box 10.3　The Honour of One's Family

A Pakistani couple accused of killing their 15-year old daughter by pouring acid on her carried out the attack because she sullied the family's honour by looking at a boy, the couple said in an interview broadcast by the BBC in November 2012. The girl's death underlines the problem of honour killings in Pakistan, where women are often killed for marrying or having relationships that are not approved by their families or because they are perceived to have somehow dishonoured their family.

The girl's parents, Mohammad Zafar and his wife Zaheen, recounted the incident from jail. Television footage of the couple showed them standing behind bars in adjoining jail cells. The father said that an older daughter had already disgraced the family and they did not want to be dishonoured again. He said the girl had turned to look twice at a boy who drove by on a motorcycle, and he told her it was wrong.

'She said, "I didn't do it on purpose, I won't look again". By then I had already thrown the acid. It was her destiny to die this way,' the girl's mother said.

According to the Human Rights Commission of Pakistan, 943 women were killed in the name of honour in 2011, 100 more than in 2010. Only 20 of these women were reported to have been given medical care before they died, the report said. The real toll is believed to be higher, because many honour killings go unreported. 'Women are callously killed in the name of honour when they go against family wishes in any way, or even on the basis of suspicion that they did so. Women are sometimes killed in the name of honor over property disputes and inheritance rights,' the BBC report said.

Sources: http://www.iol.co.za/news/world/girl-s-death-highlights-honour-killings-1.1418052#.UJ0TXsXeS7I; http://www.bbc.co.uk/news/world-asia-20202686

Traditional honour cultures are said to have developed in pastoral ecologies (Peristiany, 1965). The dispersed nature of pastoral herds makes the theft of cows, sheep, or camels relatively easy and traditional law enforcement difficult. Informal means of sanctioning those who offended against one's group therefore arose. Central values in such cultures were male valor and especially the protection of female virtue. Breaches of the honour code would elicit vengeance, including honour killings where the offence given was great, for instance in a case of sexual infidelity, or a flight from a marriage that had been arranged by one's family or elders.

While honour killings are less frequent than in former times, they continue to occur, both within traditional communities and within ethnic migrant communities where these values retain currency within industrialised societies. Such events have received significant media attention, but it is important to note that such killings often provoke strong reactions and disapproval from within those same communities that are said to have an honour culture. It is often impoverished and marginalised community members who engage in extreme actions such as honour killings as a last resort, in hope of regaining some perceived cultural standing within a changing world.

It is also important to note that not all traditional and collectivistic cultures are honour cultures. The elements of honour cultures have not been identified in East Asian cultures, for example. Indeed, A. K. Y. Leung and Cohen (2011) have proposed a distinction between dignity cultures, honour cultures and face cultures, defining face cultures as those in which there is no direct response to insults. Even in the USA, elements of honour cultures can be identified, particularly in the southern United States (Nisbett & Cohen, 1996). Vandello and Cohen (2003) asked students in Brazil and the USA to rate the damage to a man's reputation that would be caused by his female partner's infidelity. They also rated the extent to which that reputation could be restored through the use of violence and the extent to which the woman should accept her partner's violent response. Responses to these questions were significantly more in accord with the norms of an honour culture among respondents from Brazil and the southern USA than were those from respondents in the north of the United States.

Similar results were obtained when Vandello and Cohen (2003) staged an experiment in which a naïve subject witnessed a man's apparent violence toward a woman. Both the man and the woman were actually experimental accomplices. Respondents from the southern USA expressed more tolerance of the violence than did those from the northern United States and formed a less favourable impression of the victim when she condemned the violence rather than blaming herself for its occurrence. In a further study, Vandello, Cohen, Grandon, and Franiuk (2009) refined their analysis by showing that respondents condoned a husband's reported violence toward his wife more in Chile (an honour culture) than in Canada (a non-honour culture), but only when the violence was related to an honour issue. In this study, the honour issue concerned the wife having flirted with another man, and the non-honour issue concerned her spending too much money.

Cohen and Nisbett (1997) mailed job application letters to companies from someone who had supposedly participated in an honour-related killing. Responses from companies in the south and west of the USA were more tolerant than were those from the north and east. They also sent information relating to an honour killing to newspapers. The stories created by newspapers in the south and west were more sympathetic. Cohen and Nisbett were able to show that these results were not simply attributable to a more favourable response to violence in general – the differences found were distinctive to honour-related episodes. Traditions can even influence the law. Until quite recently, saving one's own or one's family's honour was considered an ameliorating circumstance for homicide in the Turkish penal code.

WORKING IN TEAMS

Honour cultures are typically built upon a base of longstanding family relationships. In contrast work teams are often but not always composed of persons who are not members of the same family. Collaborative working does not necessarily exclude some of the elements of conflict and negotiation that were previously discussed, but Smith, Peterson, Leung, and Dugan (1998) found that across 23 nations conflict in business organisations was reported more frequently between departments than within departments. To the extent that they are relatively permanent, teams have a shared interest in the development of a collaborative team culture. Within certain types of organisation, such as small family businesses, the team and the organisation are likely to be synonymous and relatively permanent. While businesses based upon families are found in all parts of the world, they have been particularly characteristic of ethnic Chinese in South East Asia and Indians in many locations. Redding (1990) has delineated the way in which collaborative family linkages have contributed to the particular economic success of Chinese entrepreneurs.

Within larger organisations, the creation of collaborative linkages within teams becomes the primary responsibility of appointed managers. However, the emergent culture of a work team is not simply a product of leadership: it is also a product of prevailing cultural values and organisational procedures. In Chapter 1, we discussed Earley's (1993) pioneering studies on social loafing, but the explanation of the mediation effects he obtained had to be deferred until we had introduced the necessary concepts. He found that team members with a more collectivist cultural orientation actually worked harder when they were collaborating with others, whereas those with a more individualist cultural orientation worked less hard in teams than individually. This finding was supported by a meta-analysis of social loafing studies. Karau and Williams (1993) found that social loafing was considerably reduced in East Asian samples compared to US samples, implying that members of presumed collectivist cultures were more invested in their group and worked harder when together than when alone.

A key issue for teams is how to optimise performance without jeopardising cohesion, and we should be cautious about assuming that teams with collectivistic members always accomplish this best. Man and Lam (2003) surveyed 471 work teams located in Hong Kong and the USA, all of whom were working for the same multinational bank. Teams that faced more complex tasks and were more autonomous from the overall organisation were more cohesive and performed better. As they had predicted, Man and Lam found that these effects were moderated *positively* by a measure of individualist attitudes that had been aggregated to the team level. They argued that autonomy and task complexity required a greater differentiation of individual roles and that individualists were better able to make the individually distinctive contributions that were required in this type of setting than were collectivists.

Kirkman and Shapiro (2001) tested for cross-cultural influences on the effectiveness of 81 self-managed work teams in Belgium, Finland, the Philippines and the USA. They reasoned that the collaborative work procedures used by self-managed work teams would be congenial to those with collectivist values, but that the lack of formal leadership would be threatening to those who favoured high power distance. Since power distance and collectivism are strongly allied at the nation level, this may appear to be a challenging pair of hypotheses. However, as we continue to emphasise, variables may relate to one another in different ways at different levels of analysis. Kirkman and Shapiro used individual-level measures of collectivism and power distance, aggregated to the team level. At this level, the two cultural predictors were not significantly related to one another, and both hypotheses received significant support, using independent ratings of team effectiveness provided by more senior management.

Teams are also likely to vary in the extent to which they draw upon the contributions of different team members. Earley (1999) tested the effect of status on contributing to a team decision task among managers attending training programmes in the UK, France, Thailand and the United States. Senior members, defined by age, had a greater impact within teams that scored higher on an aggregated measure of individual-level power distance. Regardless of nation, teams with more hierarchically oriented members deferred more to their team leaders.

Feedback processes

Whatever the specific dynamics occurring within them, individuals and their teams will require feedback on their individual or collective performance in order to be effective. If the feedback is not to jeopardise cohesion, it will need to be given in a form that is compatible with the prevailing culture. Earley, Gibson, and Chen (1999) used a managerial simulation to study differences in the response to feedback of managers from China, the USA, and the Czech Republic. Feedback indicating that task performance had been either above average or below average was provided, either individually or to groups. Individual positive feedback yielded the strongest effect on personal efficacy among those who scored high on a measure of individualistic values, regardless of their nationality. However, those endorsing collectivist values showed enhanced efficacy following either individual- or group-based positive feedback.

In a similar study, Van de Vliert, Shi, Sanders, Wang, & Huang (2004) compared the reactions of Dutch and Chinese students to various types of feedback. Interdependent self-construal predicted a significantly more favourable response to feedback that was concerned with the work of the whole team, particularly when it was delivered to the team as a whole, but much greater variance was explained simply by whether the feedback was positive or negative. Those who received positive feedback, in this case praise and encouragement, reported more positive affect and less destructive intentions.

As is the case with many of the findings reported in this book, caution is required when assuming that the results obtained in a few intensively researched locations would necessarily prove applicable in other locations. Gausden (2003) studied feedback processes among Albanian staff employed by the BBC's World Service. She noted that feedback was often expressed in forceful and negative ways, and that her respondents believed that solely positive feedback had no value.

Morrison, Chen, and Salgado (2004) compared the extent to which students from Hong Kong and the USA had actually sought feedback from their superiors while in a former job. As predicted, the US employees sought more feedback than the Hong Kong employees and this difference in feedback-seeking was positively and wholly mediated by individual-level measures of low power distance and a high preference for working independently. Thus, the expectation that

Americans would favour the direct types of communication that were entailed in explicit feedback was successfully unpackaged as attributable to their individual cultural value orientations.

Morrison et al. did not investigate how the Hong Kong employees had obtained the necessary guidance in their jobs, but we may expect it was accomplished through peers and more indirect forms of communication, such as comparisons against established standards. An illustration of this type of contrast is provided by Tinsley and Weldon (2003), who asked Chinese and American managers how they would react to a colleague who had taken credit for work that had actually been done by the respondent. The Americans stated that they would give feedback to the colleague by confronting them directly, while the Chinese said they would speak to others, in an attempt to shame the delinquent or to teach them a moral lesson.

Multicultural teams

It is now an everyday occurrence that work teams comprise members from different nations, often from many different nations. Such teams may meet face-to-face, but frequently they will work together as virtual teams, through various forms of electronic mail. Both the differing cultural expectations of what is required for effective teamwork and the lack of face-to-face contact can pose problems for such teams (Earley & Gibson, 2002).

Studies of multicultural student work teams have the advantage that they more readily permit the collection of longitudinal data. Several researchers have hypothesised that a homogeneous team faces lesser problems and in the short run will prove more effective. However, they proposed also that a heterogeneous team has greater potential, if it is able to create a team culture that draws upon the diverse skills and perspectives that are available. Watson, Kumar, and Michaelsen (1993) found culturally heterogeneous student teams in the USA had surpassed homogeneous teams in problem identification and the generation of alternative solutions after 17 weeks during which course tutors provided consultation on team dynamics and development.

This result proved replicable by Watson, Johnson, and Zgourides (2002), also in the USA, but not by Thomas (1999) over ten weeks in New Zealand. These contrasting results could be due to the different tasks involved, or to the lesser time period, or to differences in the amount or quality of interventions by tutors. A further possibility is that we need clearer theorising about the ways in which cultural diversity achieves its effects. Van der Zee, Atsam, and Brodbeck (2004) explored the interaction of personality variables and team diversity among 43 culturally diverse student teams in the UK over ten weeks. A multi-level analysis showed that more diverse team membership and individuals' flexibility interacted to predict higher final grades for individual team members. Team diversity and individuals' emotional stability also interacted to predict the ratings of members' well-being.

An alternative way forward is provided by the work of Earley and Mosakowski (2000), who proposed that a simple contrast between homogeneity and heterogeneity was too limited. If the requirement is for a multicultural team to develop an effective team culture of its own, this may be easier to achieve if members come from many different nations, rather than just from two. Both these types of team would be considered heterogeneous, but a team derived from just two nations risks a polarisation that is much less likely in a team drawn from multiple nations. Earley and Mosakowski confirmed their predictions using four-person business school teams in the UK, with team members drawn from many nations. Their result suggests that intra-team divisiveness around culturally defined blocs of members can undercut the accommodation and flexibility needed to make multi-cultural teams effective.

Further evidence of the problem of polarisation in groups with just a few cultural groups present comes from another study with students in the UK. Brodbeck, Guillaume, and Lee (2011) studied the effects of group diversity on learning performance in culturally diverse student teams and whether these effects depended on individual, group, or cultural differences. They found that individual- and group-level variables had an effect and interacted with each other in the prediction of learning outcomes. At the individual level, non-Anglo students in diverse teams performed worse, but at the group level more diverse teams had higher learning outcomes. Integrating the two levels, the highest learning outcome was shown by non-Anglo students who worked in diverse groups but were less different from others than most members of their group. This study demonstrates that results from previous studies showing different impact of cultural diversity may be due to a mixing of the impact of variables at different levels. It is vital to consider the differential impact of diversity variables for individuals, groups, and the origins of group members.

Another variable that is necessary for understanding group processes is the stage that a group has reached in its life cycle. Cheng, Chua, Morris, and Lee (2012) investigated longitudinal changes in the effect of Hofstede's cultural value orientations on the performance of 67 student teams. The measures of performance were based on independent assessments of two tasks performed by the teams at different points in time. Team scores were created by aggregating the nation-level Hofstede scores for each team member. Low uncertainty avoidance was associated with better team performance at the beginning, especially if there was some variability of uncertainty avoidance within teams. Once the teams were well established (four months later), relationship orientation (defined as Hofstede's masculinity-femininity) became important. As with uncertainty avoidance, a higher relationship orientation was associated with more effective teams, but this effect was strongest in teams with a moderate degree of variance in relationship orientation.

These findings suggest that cultural orientations have different impacts on team effectiveness over time, but require replication because the team tasks varied at the two points in time: uncertainty avoidance may have been more relevant to the first task and relationship orientation to the second. A more secure conclusion, confirming earlier studies, is that moderate variability in cultural diversity can be beneficial. If there is no variability, 'group-think' may lower performance, but if the variability is very high, the team may need to focus more on maintaining cohesion within itself, which then distracts from performance. Moderately diverse teams may be most effective because they are able to create their own distinctive culture, in which individuals can reap the benefits of diversity, while not being challenged by too many factions and frictions (Adair, Tinsley, & Taylor, 2006).

None of the studies of multi-cultural student teams that we have discussed had formally appointed leaders. Within less temporary types of teams such an unstructured situation is less likely, and it would be important to take account also of the manner in which leaders address the multi-cultural issues faced by their teams. Fewer studies are available on teams in the workplace. Elron (1997) surveyed 22 top management teams in multinational corporations. Members of the more culturally diverse teams felt less satisfied with their performance, but their teams were nonetheless shown to be more effective than the more homogeneous teams, presumably because they had better represented the conflicting priorities that the overall organisation needed to reconcile if it was to do well.

The studies reviewed in this section indicate that diversity in the national cultures of team members affects team functioning. However, nationality is most probably a distal cause of these effects. Individual values, gender, ethnicity, sexual orientation, language skill and intelligence could all matter. In future studies, we need to unpackage what it is about nationality that makes the most difference for teams.

SUMMARY

Fairness and justice concerns differ between cultural contexts. In egalitarian nations and for individuals with more self-transcending values, justice communicates whether individuals are included and esteemed in their group. Perceived injustice is associated with poorer outcomes in work settings, but these effects are stronger in nations characterised by collectivism, high power distance, and greater inequality. However, we need to know more about the specific behaviours that are seen as fair in a given setting. Formal leaders who are perceived as charismatic, team-oriented and participative are perceived as effective globally, but the strength of these effects varies in relation to collectivism and power distance. Effective negotiation differs in terms of cultural context and is dependent on timing. To gain a full understanding of social influence, we need to draw on the existing imposed-etic multiple nation studies of formal leaders and supplement them with more qualitative accounts of indigenous processes. Teams are most effective when they are neither too homogeneous nor too heterogeneous in terms of cultural orientation.

FURTHER READING

1 Aycan, Z. (2002). Leadership and teamwork in developing countries: Challenges and opportunities. *Online Readings in Psychology and Culture.* Available at http://scholarworks.gvsu.edu/orpc
2 Earley, P.C., & Gibson, C.B. (2002). *Multinational work teams: A new perspective.* Mahwah, NJ: Erlbaum.
3 House, R.J., Hanges, P.J., Javidan, M., Dorfman, P.W., Gupta, V., & GLOBE associates (2004). *Leadership, culture and organizations: The GLOBE study of 62 nations.* Thousand Oaks, CA: Sage.
4 Leung, K. (1997). Negotiation and reward allocation across cultures. In P.C. Earley & M. Erez (Eds), *New perspectives on international industrial organizational psychology* (pp. 640–675). San Francisco, CA: New Lexington.
5 Pearson, V.M.S., & Stephan, W.G. (1998). Preferences for styles of negotiation: A comparison of Brazil and the US. *International Journal of Intercultural Relations, 22,* 67–83.

STUDY QUESTIONS

1 On what basis would you say that rewards should be allocated to a work team in your country? Distribute 100 points to show what priority you would give to allocations based on performance, equality, need, and seniority.
2 What considerations should be taken into account when preparing to negotiate a business deal with a party from another culture?

3 Is it more useful to focus on culture-general or culture-specific aspects of social influence processes? How does each focus assist our understanding?

4 Which of the styles of leadership identified by the GLOBE project researchers would prove most effective in two different types of organisation with which you are familiar?

5 There have been recent reports of honour killings among migrant communities in Western Europe. Find out more about the background of these families and discuss whether traditional cultural norms can explain these killings. If not, what other variables could explain these crimes?

6 What criteria does a manager of a multi-cultural work team need to consider in order to obtain the best team performance? How could a manager increase effectiveness in existing teams?

SECTION 3

The World in Flux

11

Intercultural Contact

And what should they know of England who only England know?

(Rudyard Kipling, *The English Flag*)

Most of the studies that we have reviewed in the preceding chapters have been concerned with describing and attempting to explain the differences in various psychological phenomena that occur in different parts of the world. In the remaining chapters of this book, we give more direct attention to the processes that occur during the increasingly frequent occasions when persons who have been socialised in different cultural contexts interact with one another. Intercultural interactions can be studied at each of the levels of analysis that we have distinguished. At the most basic level, we can consider what happens when one individual meets another individual, and this will provide the focus for the present chapter.

However, when two individuals interact, the outcome will be determined not just by the attributes of those two individuals, but also by the nature of relations between the larger group-ings with which they are affiliated – in other words, their intercultural context. Cross-cultural aspects of intergroup relations are examined in Chapter 12. These issues become especially significant in relation to the current large-scale population movements within and between the nations of the world. Migration and acculturation are discussed in Chapter 13. Finally, the myriads of intercultural interactions that have been occurring over recent decades have the potential to influence the global changes that are currently underway, and these are explored in Chapter 14.

A fictitious example of a particularly unsuccessful intercultural interaction is given in Everyday Life Box 11.1. As you read though this case study, note the numerous bases for misunderstanding. Perhaps the most striking is the way in which Mrs Robertson, a language teacher, nonetheless fails to express herself with English words that are simple, unambiguous and well-known, choosing instead many complex, idiomatic phrases, including some that would be understood only in her native Scotland. However, there are many other ways in which com-munication is hindered by the socialisation of Mr Chan and Mrs Robertson into their respect-ive cultural backgrounds: Mrs Robertson's background is one characterised by individualism and low power distance, whereas Mr. Chan has grown up in the cultural context of collectivism and high power distance. Based on what you have read in earlier chapters, how many of these cultural differences can you identify for yourself? You will find our own analysis of the case in Table 11.1 below.

Everyday Life Box 11.1   Learning a Language and Learning a Culture

Chan Chi Lok, a Chinese freshman at a Hong Kong university, has taken a course in Business English from Mrs Jean Robertson, a divorced British teacher recently arrived from Scotland. Mr Chan has failed his final exam and Mrs Robertson has made an appointment to meet him at 12 o'clock to discuss his poor performance. She has a 12.30 p.m. lunch date with the department chair, George Davis.

Chan arrives with a friend at 12.20, knocks on Mrs Robertson's door, and they both enter without waiting for a response. Mrs Robertson looks up in surprise. Chan and his friend approach her chair and stand right beside her.

Chan smiles and asks, 'Have you had your lunch yet, teacher?'

Mrs Robertson replies sternly, 'Chan, sit y'rsel doon over there,' pointing to a chair positioned about two metres from her desk. 'I doubt you are 20 minutes late', she complains, 'and we had best speak alone.' She points at Chan's friend. 'Ye can wait outwith the door.'

'Huh?' Chan asks, his mouth remaining open.

Mrs Robertson repeats herself slowly and Chan's friend leaves.

'We all feel you very good ... teacher.' Mrs Robertson's mouth drops. 'We all like to invite you to class party tomorrow. You contribute your precious time, yes?'

Mrs Robertson stares at Chan in astonishment. 'I cannae do that; I book well ahead', she retorts, with furrowed eyebrows.

'Don't you like books, teacher?' asks Chan smiling and gazing attentively.

'Chan, ye must realise that we have serious matters to discuss. Ye have yet to explain your lateness.' Chan looks at his teacher blankly and waits. 'Chan, why were ye late?'

Chan laughs and then pauses. 'Well, ah, the train was delayed', he lies, looking down, 'and the school bus was crowded, so I walk all the way to your office', he explains, telling the truth.

'Did anyone ever tell ye that ye are a wee bit slippery, Mr Chan?'

'Huh?'

'Mr. Chan, it's impolite to say "huh". Ye should say, "I beg your pardon".'

'Sorry, teacher', mutters Chan, eyes downcast.

'Never bother', she continues, 'your exam mark was none too good. What way have ye done so poorly?' Chan sneezes twice.

'D'ye have a cold?' asks Mrs Robertson.

'No, teacher – you stink', replies Chan, referring to her perfume.

Mrs Robertson's eyes widen.

Chan responds to her apparent distress by switching back to her earlier question and explains, 'It's very difficult. But I tried very hard and reread the b-b-b-book f-f-four times before the exam,' Chan stammers. 'All we found your test very difficult and …', Chan continues, referring to his classmates, ' and …'

'It's nae good hiding behind the others. Ye must stand on your own two feet', interrupts Mrs Robertson, 'and effort is nae enough for a pass '

'But my English has improved so much from you. Your teachings are so good. I have to pass out from this course for being promoted'.

'I'm not caring about any of that, Mr Chan. What is at issue is your ability at English. And it was nae helped by your frequent absence from class.'

'My mother was in the hospital during this term times. 'I had to …', (Chan pauses lengthily while he searches for the word) '… visited her every day'.

'Your first responsibility is your studies, Mr Chan. Ye could well have visited your mother fine in the evenings.'

'But who watches after my younger sister?' Chan retorts.

'Ye dinna get it, do ye?' Mrs Robertson sighs.

'Yes', answers Chan, puzzling his teacher still more.

'Mr Chan, I'm away now, as I have a previous appointment.'

'Couldn't you just give me a compassionate pass, teacher? I really need to pass out of your course.'

'What?! A *compassionate* pass? I've never heard of the like! Anyway, I've got to run. Phone me for an appointment if ye want to have a wee word about retaking the exam.'

Mrs Robertson then goes to the door and holds it open as Mr Chan walks out to find his friend, eyes downcast.

'Don't be late next time, Chan. If ye canna get here on time, you'll never get anywhere.'

Source: Modified from Smith and Bond (1998).

Table 11.1   A Failure to Meet – Mrs Robertson and Mr Chan

Mrs Robertson	Mr Chan
Values disciplined timekeeping	Sees harmonious interpersonal relations as more important than timeliness
Is monochronous – she wants to discuss only one issue at a time	Is polychronous – he sees passing the exam, getting a job and caring for family as interrelated
Values her personal space	Feels comfortable approaching closer
Keeps her door closed and expects others to enter only when she invites them in	Does not understand the need for this type of deference
Sees Chan's exam failure as a failure of him as an individual	Sees no reason to exclude his friend from the meeting and prefers having his friend's support when dealing with his remote and difficult teacher
Feels insulted by Chan's apparent lack of acceptance of her control of the interaction and asserts her status by using only Chan's family name	Defers to Mrs Robertson by using the honorific 'teacher'
Judges Chan as trying to ingratiate himself	Seeks to give Mrs Robertson status by reporting the class's favourable evaluation of her teaching, and referring to her time as 'precious'
Believes that exams measure performance and ability	Believes that evidence of effort is of equal importance to evidence of ability
Considers her professional role to be one of upholding an absolute standard of quality, in this case the quality of written English	Considers it appropriate to ask his teacher to use her discretion, by referring to family problems, giving her praise, and referring to his career needs
Is critical of the telling of lies	Uses lying and indirectness as ways of trying to restore harmony
Seeks to take control of the interaction by determining the only topic to be discussed, but fails to achieve what she wants in the time remaining	Finds all of his preferred ways of handling the situation ineffective
Asks a negative question, which in English requires a negative response to indicate agreement	Indicates agreement to a negative tag question by saying 'yes', as is the way in Cantonese
Takes offence at unintended language errors	Refers to Mrs Robertson as 'stinking' because of her perfume, which is rarely used in Cantonese culture

LANGUAGE ISSUES

Many of the key issues contributing to the failures of communication in Everyday Life Box 11.1 have been explored in earlier chapters and here we shall mostly only explore further difficulties relating to language use. If we consider first the situation where two strangers meet, many of the issues that arise are equally applicable to meetings between strangers from within the same culture and meetings between those from different cultures. In both cases, a process of first impression formation will occur, as a way of coping with the inherent uncertainty of the situation. These first impressions will be strongly influenced by the physical appearance of each party, by whatever is knowable about their group memberships, and by the circumstances under which they meet. However, in cross-national encounters an additional issue very frequently arises: what language shall be spoken? The two parties may share a single language, more than one language, or of course, no spoken languages at all. We shall consider these situations in turn.

The Single Language Option

Where only one language is shared, there is little choice in how to converse. Once interaction commences, a process of communication accommodation is inevitable – in other words, a pressure arises on both parties to align their speech patterns (vocabulary, accent, style of speaking) with one another (Giles, Coupland, & Coupland, 1991), and discover a minimum ground of knowledge, beliefs and assumptions that is sufficient to enable them to communicate effectively (Clark & Brennan, 1991). Most typically, the chosen language will be the first language of one speaker but a second language of the second speaker. This entails a series of consequences for both parties.

First language speakers

First language speakers are provided with an affirmation of their identity through speaking their natural language, but are under pressure, that is not always appreciated, to communicate in ways that differ from their normal speech with other native speakers of that first language. Their vested interest in being understood argues in favour of simplified speech, the avoidance of idioms, and slower speaking with more pauses. Gass and Varonis (1985) identify these effects as 'foreigner talk'. Some studies confirm that first language speakers do accommodate in these ways more when speaking to second language speakers than with other first language speakers (Pierson & Bond, 1982).

However, this helpful accommodation does not always occur as there may be factors in the situation that will encourage first language speakers to resist accommodation – for instance, if they see themselves as representing groups that are in conflict with one another, or if they need to assert their superior status. Smith, Torres, Hecker et al. (2011) analysed 1,497 problem events reported by business employees who were interacting with someone from a different nation. Language difficulties were the most frequent reported problem, and markedly so for non-English speakers from collectivist nations. While 'under-accommodating' to one's partner may be particularly frequent, first language speakers may also 'over-accommodate'. In other words, they may use 'foreigner talk' needlessly or excessively in a way that is similar to persons who use 'babytalk' when addressing persons who are very old (Williams, Garrett, & Tennant, 2004). Under- and over-accommodation are likely to occur when first language speakers view second language speakers as representative of groups that are less competent and less likeable than their own group. As we discuss in Chapter 12, the dimensions of competence and likeability are found to summarise well the stereotypes that members of different groups hold about one another (Cuddy et al., 2009). Within the model of Cuddy et al. both under- and over-accommodation can be seen as forms of passive harm.

Studies of simulated and naturalistic conversations between Chinese students in Australia and native Australians showed that first language speakers who did accommodate were better liked (Jones, Barker, Gallois, & Callan, 1994). This series of studies also illustrated the rich variety of ways in which accommodation could be achieved by first language speakers (Gallois, Giles, Jones, Cargile, & Ota, 1995). In speaking with Chinese students, female Australian students responded more slowly and paused more often, whereas male Australian students asked more questions to check on their interlocutor's comprehension, and Australian faculty members steered the conversation toward topics with which their interlocutors would be more familiar. Which strategy is used by whom under which social circumstances is a key future topic for research.

Second language speakers

The interpersonal situation of second language speakers is somewhat different. To speak or write in a language other than our own may cause us to think in different ways. Depending upon the context of the interaction, one might think of oneself as less identified with one's language community, or as even more identified with it. As we noted earlier, Harzing (2005) showed that respondents described their values differently when responding to a survey in English than when responding in their local language. When responding in English, their reported values became more similar to those reported by native English speakers – an outcome known as cross-linguistic accommodation (see, for example, Chen & Bond, 2010).

However fluent second language speakers may be in their second language, it is rare that their speech cannot be discriminated from that of a first language speaker, either by vocabulary, accent, or distinctive language usage. For instance, Al Issa (2003) asked US and Jordanian students to refuse requests while speaking in English. Even though they were speaking in English, the Jordanians used an Arab style of speaking, indicated by more frequent references to the defining of one's relationship with the other, a greater emphasis upon the reciprocation of favours, more requests for understanding, and more emphasis on removing negative feelings. We noted in Chapter 9 the findings by Nelson et al. (1993, 2002) that Egyptians spoke directly. Al Issa's findings suggest that Arabs speak directly about relational issues.

In a further study of accommodation, this time between Chinese students and Australians, the Chinese who accommodated were judged more positively by the Australians. This was particularly true for accommodation involving the markers of one's group membership, such as language use, accent and voice register, rather than for the markers of one's individual attributes, such as gaze and gestures (Hornsey & Gallois, 1998).

Because of the various distinguishing features of their speech, second language speakers are likely to be rated lower in competence by first language speakers, even where their competence for a given task is equally high (Hui & Cheng, 1987; Cargile & Bradac, 2001). Many unfortunate consequences can stem from misperceptions of this type and conscious strategies are required on the part of first language speakers to eliminate or at least minimise them. The problem is compounded by the fact that while English is not the most widely spoken first language in the world, it is the most widely used language for international communication. The current profile of cross-national contacts means that the first language speaker is rather often a speaker of English. Consequently, the first language speaker is often also from a nation that is economically or politically more powerful, thereby introducing considerations of relative power into the conversational dynamic. Considerations of relative power may be handled differently by persons from cultures varying in their degree of hierarchy or power distance.

The Language Choice Option

Where the parties share more than one language, a separate set of issues becomes relevant. The choice of language in which to converse is likely to be guided by the **ethnolinguistic vitality** of the languages in question. The concept of ethnolinguistic vitality refers to the relative numbers of speakers of a language in a given community, its prestige, and its use within relevant local institutions. Ethnolinguistic vitality can be assessed in terms of objective indicators of inter group power, but in many circumstances the subjective perceptions of speakers of a particular language as to its vitality are more important in predicting their actions (Yagmur, 2011).

The **Ethnolinguistic Vitality** of a language is defined by its status within a community, how many people speak it within a multi-lingual community, how much support a community provides to speakers of that language, and how much control they have over its use in various social settings.

In Canada, perceived vitality positively predicts the preference for speaking a language and predicts the willingness to learn a second language negatively (Harwood, Giles, & Bourhis, 1994). Noels, Clément, and Gaudet (2004) asked French Canadian students to imagine themselves speaking with someone from a particular ethnolinguistic group. Evidence for accommodation (change toward the other party) was found: in speaking with an English language person, their English identity was raised and their French identity lowered. Noels et al. (2004) also had respondents rate their confidence in speaking English, the vitality of the English and French languages, and how much they identified with the English and French communities in Canada. Where English language confidence was low, identification with the French community was consistently high. However, among those with increased confidence, vitality was associated with enhanced French identity at home and enhanced English identity in public settings. Indeed the primacy of the mother tongue in the private realm is probably a universal pattern. Thus, the ethnolinguistic vitality of one's first language can be a protective factor against the predominance of English and other languages widely spoken outside one's home.

A further option where conversation partners share two languages is code-switching. This term refers to the use of single words or longer utterances from the shared second language, when conversing in the first. Scheu (2002) studied a group of bilingual students in a school in Spain. Conversations occurred in both German and Spanish, but code-switching within sentences was most often used for emphasis, for instance when swearing. More generally, code-switching can serve to define one's identity in relation to those with whom one is conversing. Lawson and Sachdev (2000) sampled code-switching between French and Arabic by Tunisians, using both diaries and field observation of street conversations. They concluded that code-switching defines more informal discourse between in-group members and was much less frequent when

Tunisians spoke with their teachers and non-Arabs. However, code-switching is frequent among Lebanese students, even when conversing with non-Arabs.

Code-switching can also have a valuable function in immigrant families. Ng and He (2004) studied Chinese families in New Zealand. Grandparents tended to switch the conversation from English to Chinese and children tended to switch from Chinese to English. The middle parental generation more frequently switched within an utterance, rather than between utterances. Their code-switching often served to aid grandparents' understanding of English and children's understanding of Chinese, so the middle generation were serving as linguistic mediators.

No Common Language

Circumstances also arise when it is necessary that persons communicate with one another when they do not have a shared language. In these situations, a third party interpreter is essential for effective communication, but the use of a third party introduces a host of further difficulties. How should interpreters represent each party to the other? Should they provide literal translations of what is said, or should they also use their own knowledge of either culture to interpret and communicate what they believe to be the intentions behind what either party says?

Everyday Life Box 11.2   The Hazards of Translation

Business companies have to struggle with the difficulty of reproducing the meaning of their advertising slogans into other languages. They do not always succeed:

- In marketing their pens in Latin America, the Parker Pen company initially chose to use the word *bola* to refer to their ballpoint pen. This conveys the intended meaning at some locations, but in one nation *bola* refers to a revolution, in another it is an obscenity, and in a third it describes a lie.
- A mistranslation meant that a US shirt manufacturer advertised its shirts in Mexico with the slogan, 'Until I used this shirt, I felt good', rather than the US version, 'When I used this shirt I felt good'.
- Advertisements for face cream were markedly unsuccessful in some Arab countries. The ad featured photographs of a woman's face before and after using the cream. The text was correctly translated, but the 'before' picture remained on the left-hand side of the ad, with the 'after' picture on the right. Since Arabic is read from right to left, the photos indicated that the cream made one's face worse, not better.
- Advertisement in a French clothing store: 'We sell dresses for street walking'.
- Advertisement for a Japanese garden: 'The Japanese garden is the mental home of the Japanese'.

Source: Ricks (1993).

It is often the case that an interpreter is of the same nationality as one of the parties, thereby leaving the other party faced with not one but two protagonists, who can converse with one another in a private manner, dramatically changing the power balance in the conversation and often provoking suspicions by the excluded party. This can be particularly problematic in relation to health issues, where the interpreter is often another family member, and often a younger one, and this is likely to impose barriers on which issues can be spoken about openly. A different issue is salient in military and political settings, where trust between the parties is often tenuous. Often in these settings, each party will have an interpreter from his or her own cultural group. Translators can then be decisive factors influencing the outcome of negotiations. The USA dropped the atomic bombs on Hiroshima and Nagasaki in Japan in 1945 after the Japanese had responded to a US ultimatum for unconditional surrender using the ambiguous word *mokusatsu*. This can mean 'silent contempt', 'ignore', or 'we need more time' (www.wikipedia.org/wiki/mokusatsu). In this instance, it was translated as 'ignore'. However, the Japanese emperor had already agreed to surrender. Conflicts within his government needed to be resolved before they were ready to respond.

In the field of diplomacy, achieving agreement may often rest upon the degree to which one or more crucial words can be translated in a manner that has equally acceptable connotations in two or more languages. In less public settings, the difficulties will be less exclusively focused on what is said and include also those aspects of the communication process that cannot be verbally translated. In medicine or psychotherapy, for instance, a therapist or other practitioner working with a patient from a different cultural background may be unable to rely on an accurate interpretation of non-verbal cues that would ordinarily be important sources of information. So, for example, Li-Ripac (1980) found that Caucasian-American therapists compared to Chinese-American therapists 'over-diagnosed' depression in Chinese-American clients, and much of this 'misdiagnosis' probably arose from a culture-derived 'misreading' of non-verbal cues – for instance, the lack of gaze during conversation (H.Z. Li, 2004).

Levels of eye-contact may also be impeded or misunderstood by the propensity of both therapist and client to address the interpreter (Hillier, Huq, Loshak, Marks, & Rahman, 1994). Where interpreters are addressed directly, they are at risk of feeling directly responsible for trying to overcome the problems that are under discussion. For instance, interpreters in medical settings addressing life-threatening issues in Australia reported often feeling threatened by the emotional intensity of the setting. This led them to want to amend and improve on the cultural sensitivity of the health professional's central role in achieving a rapport with the patient (Butow et al., 2012).

TOWARDS INTERCULTURAL EFFECTIVENESS

In discussing the dilemmas faced by interpreters, we are touching on issues that have a more general importance. How can one 'read' (i.e., accurately interpret) the words and actions of someone from a cultural background other than one's own? Conversely, how will the other party read one's own words and actions? Language fluency is a necessary but not sufficient condition for effective interactions. One needs to know also how one's words will be interpreted within the context of the other party's cultural assumptions. In Table 11.1, when Chan asks Mrs Robertson whether

Everyday Life Box 11.3   Cultural Issues in Counselling

During the late nineties, the Milosevic regime in the former Yugoslavia orchestrated the attempted 'ethnic cleansing' of Albanians from the province of Kosovo. More than half a million refugees were forced to flee, as their homes were burnt to the ground, some family members were killed, and many family members lost touch with one another. Within Western nations, it is expected that counselling would contribute toward more positive outcomes to post-traumatic circumstances of this kind. However, within a very traditional and strongly collectivist cultural community, individual counselling is unlikely to be the best form of intervention, particularly if it is provided by foreigners working through interpreters. Cavill (2000) describes how the training of local group leaders from the refugee camps enabled them to conduct single-gender, single-clan group meetings that addressed the shared experience of trauma in culturally appropriate and hence more effective ways.

Similarly, Dwairy (2006) identifies distinctive challenges in conducting counselling among Palestinian Arabs. Arab identity is closely interwoven with one's family. Consequently, an intervention is far more likely to be effective if it is conducted with the participation and approval of family members. Furthermore, therapeutic interventions must differ from Western styles of family therapy, giving respect to the hierarchical nature of Arab family relationships and the way in which true feelings are often hidden behind a positive, diplomatic face (*mosayara*). Less direct forms of therapeutic intervention can include the use of drawings, metaphors, and allegorical stories.

Cultural Intelligence is defined as the possession of the relevant knowledge, motivation, behavioural flexibility, and awareness of cultural differences that enables us to interact effectively with persons from other cultures.

she has had lunch, his English is correct, but he has misjudged the appropriateness of making that specific enquiry at that time. When a Dutch visitor uses his fluent Portuguese to ask his Brazilian host when he should *really* arrive for dinner, he has met his need to avoid uncertainty, but has violated Brazilian hospitality norms. When a Chinese professor states to a visiting Irish teacher that his wife (who is present) did not attend university because she is stupid, he is adhering to Chinese norms of modesty, but failing to give consideration to European norms about public criticisms of one's family when those family members are present (Wei & Yue, 1996). They are all committing errors in socio-pragmatics. To overcome such errors, we need a set of skills that have in recent years become known as **cultural intelligence**.

Cultural Intelligence

Numerous authors have sought to identify the skills required to interact effectively with persons from other cultures (Thomas & Fitzsimmons, 2008). Earley and Ang (2003) have summarised these skills in terms of what they call cultural intelligence, which is defined in terms of cognitive, motivational, behavioural, and metacognitive skills. The last of these concepts refers to the ability to monitor a cross-cultural interaction to see how well one's cultural knowledge is helping to achieve a positive outcome. There is a widely available self-report inventory that can be used to assess these skills. Example items include 'I enjoy interacting with people from other cultures', 'I know the legal and economic systems of other cultures', 'I am conscious of the cultural knowledge I use when interacting with people from different cultural backgrounds', and 'I vary the rate of my speaking when a cross-cultural situation requires it'. The value of this type of measure rests on the degree to which the respondent has gained insight into his or her behaviour. The instrument requires validation before we can be sure that it captures cross-cultural skills rather than acquiescent responding to the types of socially desirable survey items that are included in it. An important early validity study is described in Key Research Study Box 11.1.

Key Research Study Box 11.1   Does CQ Predict Cross-Cultural Effectiveness?

Ang et al. (2007) conducted studies testing the validity of their measure of cultural intelligence (CQ), collecting data in Singapore and the USA. In preliminary studies with student respondents, they found that the scores on all their four facets of CQ correlated moderately but significantly with McCrae and Costa's Big Five personality dimension of Openness to Experience.

Next they examined the relationship between CQ and measures of performance in cross-cultural settings. Most of the measures they employed were completed by the same persons who had rated themselves on CQ. Although these analyses showed promising results, we focus here only on those that used independent measures of performance, as these provide firmer evidence for validity. Students in Singapore and the United States were asked to select culturally-appropriate actions in a series of scenarios for each of which there was a correct solution. After controlling for personality differences like openness to experience, general mental ability and emotional intelligence, respondents on cognitive CQ and on metacognitive CQ scored significantly higher.

In a second study, CQ scores were obtained from executives from many nations attending a training programme in Singapore. Cognitive and metacognitive CQ predicted independent ratings of the executives' individual analyses of a case study involving a cross-cultural problem. The executives also worked on a task in pairs. Behavioural and metacognitive CQ was a significant predictor of task performance as rated by one's partner, even after controlling for levels of cognitive ability and social desirability. Finally, CQ scores were obtained from 103 professionals from many nations who were working for a consultancy firm in Singapore. Metacognitive and behavioural CQ predicted independent ratings of their task performance by the professionals' supervisors.

These and similar subsequent results (Ang & Van Dyne, 2008) have provided some evidence in favour of the validity of the CQ measures. However, personality and ability were measured and controlled only in the first and second study, respectively. Consequently, we cannot know whether the task performance that was rated highly by the supervisors in the final study was due to specific instances of cross-cultural effectiveness or to a more general reaction to particular personality types or skills that would have been equally highly valued in someone from one's own culture.

The studies of CQ suggest that behavioural and metacognitive skills may be particularly important in cross-cultural effectiveness. This is plausible because behaviour change and an awareness of the need for behaviour change are often more difficult to accomplish than a simple awareness of cultural difference. Molinsky (2007) describes the making of changes in one's cross-cultural behaviour as a form of code-switching. If one is accustomed to communicating indirectly, an awareness of the need to be more direct with a person from a culture that communicates more directly is challenging. There can be some degree of identity threat in perceiving oneself as behaving in the more 'unnatural' direct manner that the context requires – might one have 'crossed over', 'gone native', or otherwise sacrificed one's cultural integrity?

Understanding the need for behaviour change

We have some evidence for the extent to which persons understand that behaviours can have different meanings in different contexts. Pittam, Gallois, Iwawaki, and Kroonenberg (1995) asked Australian and Japanese students to rate the extent to which a series of non-verbal behaviours would be associated with each of eight different emotions, as expressed by both Australians and Japanese. Some culture-general effects were found. For instance, smiling was said by both the Japanese and Australians to be associated with love, respect, elation and relief, but not with anger, fear or grief, regardless of the nationality of the person observed. Other effects were ethnocentric. For instance, the Japanese associated a fast speech rate with anger and fear and a slow speech rate with love, respect and relief, regardless of which nationality they observed. In contrast, the Australians did not link speech rate with any particular emotions. Finally, a few instances of awareness of cross-cultural differences were also detected: the Japanese perceived walking about as characteristic of anger and fear among the Australians, but not so among their fellow Japanese. The Australians associated soft speech with love among the Japanese, but not so among fellow Australians. Awareness of difference may have been low because the students sampled had little experience with persons from one another's nationality and such differences may well be more evident for persons with greater inter-cultural experience.

Albert and Ha (2004) asked Anglo and Latino 10-15 year old students within the USA and their teachers to give their interpretation of 12 school-based scenarios that highlighted instances of various types of touching by Latino students and of silence and the avoidance of touching by an Anglo teacher. Even though these respondents had much more day-to-day inter-cultural contact, the results indicated that the scenarios were mostly interpreted in ways that took no account of cultural differences in interpretation. The Anglos tended to interpret behaviours in terms of personal qualities, whereas the Latinos made more reference to the context. For instance, Anglo teacher silence was perceived as meanness by the Anglos, but as an attempt to punish a naughty boy by the Latinos. The teacher's request that students remain at their desks rather than crowd around her was more often seen as a need for personal space by Anglos and as the exercise of authority by Latinos.

Changing behaviour

If one understands that behaviours have different meanings in different cultural settings, it is likely that at least some of the time it will be necessary to modify one's own behaviours, so as not to be misunderstood by persons from the other culture. The extent to which respondents are found to have an understanding of this need no doubt rests on the inter-cultural experience and maturity of those who are sampled. Rao and Hashimoto (1996) surveyed 202 Japanese managers working in Canada. They assessed inter-cultural adaptation by comparing how the Japanese managers acted when seeking to influence the Canadian managers or other Japanese managers who were also in Canada. It was found that when working with the Canadians, the Japanese reported speaking more assertively, appealing more to reason, making more threats, and appealing more to higher authorities. With their fellow Japanese they communicated more indirectly, as would be the case back in Japan. Thomas and Ravlin (1995) played US managers a videotape of a Japanese manager who had either adapted his behaviour toward US styles of communication or not done so. The culturally accommodating Japanese manager was judged as more trustworthy and more effective.

In a similar way, Adair, Okumura, and Brett (2001) found that when Japanese negotiators were negotiating with other Japanese, they relied on indirect information exchange and direct influence attempts (as discussed in Chapter 10), but when they were negotiating with Americans they moved toward the US style of direct information exchange and fewer attempts at direct influence.

It is noteworthy that all three of these studies illustrate Japanese managers adapting their behaviour. We discussed in Chapter 6 the way that persons from collectivist nations are more inclined to adapt their behaviour to its context in their own cultures. Another example is provided by H.Z. Li's (2004) study of eye-contact (discussed in Chapter 9). Canadians made eye contact with one another much more frequently than did Chinese. However, in mixed Canadian-Chinese pairings, the Chinese increased their level of eye-contact to the Canadian level. This accommodation of others can be seen as an instance of 'self-monitoring' – a personality dimension along which there are both individual and cultural differences (see Chapter 5).

Further studies are required to determine how well and how frequently persons from individualist nations will adapt their behaviours when interacting in a different cultural context. One early study indicated that US managers in Hong Kong did not do so (Black & Porter, 1991). More recently, Smith, Torres et al. (2011) obtained brief descriptions of problematic cross-cultural work episodes from employees in many nations. Respondents were also asked to rate the extent that they had changed their behaviour in attempting to handle the episode. No significant relation was found between the collectivism of the respondent's nation and amount of reported behaviour change, but respondents from collectivist nations did report significantly more positive outcomes in these inter-cultural encounters, and one wonders why this was so. Perhaps their more collective socialisation led them to accommodate without being aware of doing so. Alternatively, they might be preserving face by making a more positive rating.

Stereotypes and Essentialism

In deciding how to act toward a previously unknown person from another culture, we are faced with a choice of strategies. On the one hand, it is possible to approach that person from a 'culture-blind' perspective – in other words, to assume that there is much in common between

> **Essentialism** is the belief that all members of a group share the same psychological characteristics.

the ways in which people around the world communicate with one another. From this perspective, it makes sense to act normally until such time as one becomes aware that some miscommunication is occurring. This would be analogous to a researcher who uses an imposed-etic research strategy modifying instruments only when it becomes clear that they are not functioning as expected. On the other hand, one could approach the previously unknown person in a way that was guided by the assumption that because they come from a particular nation they will have certain core characteristics that define members of that nation. Assumptions that all members of a group will be the same have been described as **essentialism** (Prentice & Miller, 2007) – a concept that underlies the process of stereotyping. Stereotypes specify the specific qualities that are attributed to a given group, by those who endorse essentialism.

Stereotypes can contain a 'kernel of truth' (Allport, 1954), and so long as they are treated as a *provisional* basis for one's interactions with others, they can assist inter-cultural effectiveness. Relatively accurate stereotypes may be derived from many sources, including direct experience, talking to other travelers, exposure to information in the media, or attending training programmes. Taking a course in cross-cultural social psychology can increase cultural essentialism beliefs, but reduce to more realistic levels one's self-rated cultural intelligence (Fischer, 2011b). One could also construct a set of expectations based upon the nation-level characterisations that have been provided by the empirical investigations outlined in this book. Relevant expectations might include knowing how individualistic, how hierarchical, and how expressive are typical interpersonal interactions within the stranger's nation. In drawing upon these characterisations we should be engaging in some initial stereotyping, and we might find that our stereotypic expectations did not fit the individual in question too well. On average, though, we should expect fewer misunderstandings to arise than would occur with the culture-blind approach, provided one's expectations are seen as a basis for initiative rather than as an explanation for insoluble difficulties.

> Members of **Monochronous** cultures prefer to do things one at a time sequentially, in contrast to members of **Polychronous** cultures, who are comfortable with doing several things at the same time.

Stereotypic beliefs are often defined in ways that suggest they involve prejudiced and negative perceptions of others. While such beliefs can certainly be the basis for all kinds of intolerance, they can also sometimes facilitate inter-cultural interactions. For instance, Lee and Duenas (1995) made a study of meetings between Mexican and US business people. Each party had a stereotype of the other's orientation toward time. The Mexicans described the Americans as 'machines', referring to their preference for conducting business in a linear, ordered, '**monochronous**' fashion. For their part, the Americans referred to the Mexicans as 'banana people', referring to their more relaxed way of working on several issues concurrently without any strict time regulation. These stereotypic characterisations, however apparently disparaging, provided the basis on which both parties were able to negotiate how they could work effectively together, by accommodating on important aspects of interpersonal style.

Cross-Cultural Skills

The process whereby awareness of difference is converted into the effective handling of cross-national interactions is not yet well understood. Those researching cultural intelligence have treated skill as a trait-like generic quality. For instance, Liu, Friedman, Barry et al. (2012) used intra-cultural Chinese and US negotiations as a baseline against which to assess effective cross-national negotiation. They found that a measure of concern for face derived from the Chinese Personality Assessment Inventory (Cheung et al., 1996; see also Chapter 5) enhanced the outcome of inter-cultural negotiations, whereas a measure of need for closure (Neuberg, Judice, & West, 1997) was detrimental to their outcome.

However, it is not clear how much an individual's learning of skills in relating to others across a given cultural boundary can generalise across other cultural boundaries. If I develop some expertise in relating to persons from Latin America, am I likely also to be more skilled in relating to South Asians or East Europeans? We saw in Chapter 5 that social context has powerful effects on the ways in which personal attributes are expressed. Some skills may have cultural-general effectiveness while others may be valuable only in specific contexts. In the study by Smith, Torres et al. (2011) some reported coping behaviours that were significantly associated with a positive outcome in the sample as a whole. Focusing on task-related aspects of the problem and adjusting one's language showed this pattern. In contrast, actions designed to promote harmony were significantly associated with a positive outcome only where the other party involved in the episode was from a more collectivist culture.

Van der Zee and Van Oudenhoven (2002) created a measure described as the Multicultural Personality Questionnaire (MPQ), which comprises scales of self-reported skills that are somewhat more specific than those tapped by measures of cultural intelligence: Cultural Empathy, Open-mindedness, Emotional Stability, Social Initiative, and Flexibility. Self and peer ratings showed that Dutch students with prior international experience obtained higher MPQ scores than those who had not left the Netherlands. MPQ scores also predicted personal, professional and social adjustment among expatriates in Taiwan (Van Oudenhoven, Mol, & Van der Zee, 2003).

However, since the MPQ taps qualities that are also likely to have value in relating to members of one's own nation, if it is to be judged as a valid measure of distinctively *cross-cultural* skills, it must be shown to predict the outcomes of cross-cultural experience better than a conventional measure of personality does. Van Oudenhoven and Van der Zee (2002) reported that the MPQ was a better predictor of the adjustment of foreign students at a Dutch business school than was a measure of self-efficacy. In a similar way, Matsumoto, LeRoux, Bernhard, and Gray (2004) developed a scale of potential for inter-cultural adjustment. Scores on this scale measured before Japanese students' departure to the United States successfully predicted their subsequent self-rated adjustment, degree of culture shock, and life satisfaction in their host culture, even after variance explained by a Big Five personality measure had been discounted.

Thus we have some preliminary indications that it may be possible to measure specific cross-cultural skills, but the conclusions so far achieved mostly rest on self-reported skills and self-reported adjustment. Independent criteria of behavioural effectiveness are required before firm conclusions can be drawn. Early studies that did use such criteria (e.g., Hawes & Kealey, 1981) have been neglected. In one study that points the way forward, Imai and Gelfand (2010) focused on 20-minute cross-cultural negotiations between US and East Asian student negotiators, using a design similar to that employed by Adair et al. (2001) discussed earlier. This study included also measures of cultural intelligence (CQ), cognitive ability, emotional intelligence, and the Big Five personality variables of extraversion and openness. The negotiations were tape recorded and subsequently coded. Greater amounts of offering and asking for 'integrative information' (initiatives toward a joint solution) were found for high CQ scorers, but not for those who scored higher on the other measures of ability and personality. High CQ scores predicted positive outcomes, but the outcome was best predicted by the CQ score of the *lower* scoring negotiator within each pair. Presumably this person was a limiting factor in achieving still better outcomes. In this context, the effects achieved were best explained by the scores for motivational CQ.

Cross-Cultural Training

Most of those who visit another culture experience no form of preparatory training for their encounter. However, one way of enhancing the prospects for successful cross-cultural interactions is to provide such training, particularly for those who will be spending extended periods of time abroad. The methods that are used can be divided into three types (Brislin, 1989). Firstly, low-involvement activities such as lectures can provide trainees with basic information. Secondly, somewhat more involving activities can include simulations and the study of critical incidents to sensitise trainees to the nature of differences between national groups and their own nations of origin. Finally, sessions can be created that will give trainees direct practice in behaving in ways that would be more effective in a given cultural context. Provision of information by itself is unlikely to have a marked effect on successful outcomes, because information rarely matches up with the specific circumstances that one encounters and may frequently be forgotten. However, it may usefully be combined with the more involving types of training.

Programmes focused upon understanding attempt to sensitise trainees to the existence of cultural differences and the consequent need to attend to the way one's behaviour is interpreted by locals. This can be achieved through the use of simulations, such as 'BaFa BaFa' (Shirts, 1995). Trainees are randomly assigned to one of two simulated cultures, in each of which trainees are required to behave in accordance with a set of rules provided by the trainers. Meetings between members of the two cultures typically give rise to a series of misunderstandings that are later used to illustrate the way in which we all tend to interpret the behaviours of others using the preconceptions of our own mother cultures. There is little evidence, however, as to whether the effects of this and similar simulations have a lasting impact on one's intercultural effectiveness (Ward, 2013).

Skill-oriented programmes come much closer to the requirements for effective training intervention. This chapter has emphasised the crucial importance of language in cross-cultural interactions, and there can be little doubt that the most effective form of cross-cultural training is to learn the local language. However, language learning takes a long time, and attempts have been made to provide briefer opportunities to develop relevant skills. These can be based upon meetings with members of a local culture prior to one's own departure, where such a possibility is available. Alternatively, trainees are presented with descriptions of one or more critical incidents that have occurred when others have visited the same destination. Through group discussion they can learn to interpret what went wrong and how the incidents could have been handled more effectively.

Collections of critical incidents have also been used to develop what are known as culture-assimilators. These comprise a series of brief descriptions of critical incidents each of which is accompanied by four or more different interpretations, one of which is correct, as judged by experienced professionals, and the remainder incorrect. An example is given in Box 11.1. By working though an assimilator composed of varied descriptions of this type, trainees can increase their understanding of how to behave, particularly where the assimilator is focused on a particular target culture and based on accurate knowledge about that culture.

Box 11.1   The Culture Assimilator

OH SO PROPER!

The English class that Martha Anderson is helping to teach is going very well. The Vietnamese, Cambodian and Central American students seem to enjoy being with one another and are adjusting to each other well. The men and women frequently help one another. Having had very little exposure to other cultures, Martha is amazed at their ease of interaction and often asks the instructor about the various behaviours she observes in the classroom. They are all very polite to each other even when they do not seem to be able to understand each other. They are also especially polite when they are talking to her or to the other instructors, always addressing them with very formal, polite titles.

Martha would like to develop relationships with some of the students and make them feel more at home. In one particular instance she is talking with Vien Thuy Ng in private. She asks him to call her by her first name, saying, 'My name is Martha, please call me Martha!' Vien responds by acknowledging that he does indeed know her name, but 'Would it not be good to call you by your proper title?' She persists by saying that is too formal and that they can just be good friends and go by first names. Vien just smiles and nods, but he does not return to the English class the following week.

What could explain this situation? (Choose an answer from the four listed below before turning to Box 11.2 on page 298.)

1 Vien Thuy Ng thought that Martha was too aggressive and forward to him, as women do not talk to men.
2 Martha should not have singled out an individual person. Vien did not like being singled out.
3 The English class is too complicated for Vien and he does not really know what is going on.
4 Martha violated a rather intricate system of hierarchy that exists in South Asian countries.

Source: Brislin, Cushner, Cherrie & Yong (1986).

Behaviourally-focused forms of training use behaviour modification to increase specific skills such as making contact with a new person or expressing disagreement with someone. In the EXCELL (Excellence in Cultural Experiential Learning and Leadership) design (Buckingham, Barker, Logan, & Millman, 1999), models first display the required behaviours and trainees then repeatedly practise them, each time receiving feedback on their performance. This design has been used to prepare student sojourners before their departure (Mak & Buckingham, 2007).

Evaluations of the effectiveness of cross-cultural training have yielded modest but positive results. In a meta-analysis, Deshpande and Viswesvaran (1992) concluded that cross-cultural training for managers was effective. However, the indices of success in many of the studies were completed immediately after training, rather than when the trainee went on assignment or after its completion. Gannon and Poon (1997) compared information-giving plus watching a video, watching several videos, and participation in BaFa BaFa. No differences were found in students' increased cultural awareness, but their participation in BaFa BaFa was enjoyed more. Earley (1987) compared different versions of a three-day programme preparing 80 US managers for an assignment in Korea. As part of the programme, trainees either received documentary information on Korea followed by a group discussion, or else they spent an afternoon visiting an Asian-American community, or did both with a subsequent group discussion. Performance ratings by the trainees' managers in Korea showed that both forms of training were more effective than no training at all. However, those who received both forms of training did best of all. Hawes and Kealey (1981) found that pre-departure training of Canadians working on overseas development projects did have significant effects on their subsequently observed project behaviour. Bhawuk (1998) compared four types of training for US students prior to their departure for Japan. He found that a culture-assimilator that was explicitly designed in terms of contrasts between the USA and Japan in individualism-collectivism had superior effects to culture-general assimilators and to a reading-only control group.

The difficulty in reaching conclusions about the effectiveness of cross-cultural training is that the outcome is assessed in a multitude of different ways in different studies, each of which may be appropriate for a different type of inter-cultural contact. Thus the best that we can say is that there is some evidence that training can be beneficial, if the training design is well adapted to trainees' needs. We would however need some clarification of which forms of training show improvement on which criteria of inter-cultural success. In particular, it is important to determine when it is best to opt for generalised training intended to increase cultural intelligence, and when it is preferable to train skills specific to the cultural context to which the trainee is adapting (Brislin, Macnab, & Nayani, 2008).

Psychological and Socio-Cultural Adaptation

Terms such as 'adjustment', 'adaptation', 'acculturation' and 'effectiveness' have been much used in the analysis of the outcomes of inter-cultural contact. We shall see in the remainder of this chapter and in the next that care is needed in thinking through how these terms can be most usefully employed, just as has been the case in studying issues of stress, strain and adjustment in psychology more generally. Ward (2013) distinguishes three categories of response to spending time with members of another cultural group. Firstly, there will be affective reactions, ranging for instance from pleasure through confusion to anxiety or depression. Ward defines these types of reaction as '**psychological adaptation**'. Secondly, there will be a process of culture learning, which will include learning (or

> **Psychological Adaptation** refers to achieving successful mental balance in a novel cultural context.

failing to learn) both how the other cultural group functions, and how to operate within that culture oneself. Ward defines these processes as '**socio-cultural adaptation**'. Finally, if cross-cultural contact is prolonged, issues will arise as to the extent to which one thinks

> **Socio-Cultural Adaptation** refers to learning and using the behavioural skills that are required to be effective in a novel cultural context.

of oneself as part of the local community or as separate from it. Ward discusses these more cognitive processes in terms of 'acculturation'. In this chapter, we are concerned only with the first two of these adaptations, since at this point our focus is upon individuals who stay for relatively brief periods of time. We cover acculturation processes in Chapter 13.

Key Researcher Box 11.1   Colleen Ward

Figure 11.1   Colleen Ward

Colleen Ward (b. 1952) grew up in the United States, but obtained her PhD from the University of Durham in the UK in 1977. Since that time, she has held research and/or teaching positions at the University of the West Indies, Trinidad; the Science University of Malaysia; the National University of Singapore; the University of Canterbury; and most recently Victoria University of Wellington where she was formerly Head of Psychology and is currently Director of the Centre for Applied Cross-Cultural Research. She is author of more than 120 journal articles and book chapters. After making early studies of spirit possession in the Caribbean and altered states of consciousness cross-culturally, she has focused more recently on research into acculturation and inter-cultural relations.

TYPES OF CONTACT

Those who spend time within a cultural group other than their own, but nonetheless expect to return home before long, are usually referred to as sojourners, to distinguish them from migrants. As long ago as 1954, Allport proposed that contact between members of different cultural groups would have positive effects, provided certain conditions were met. These conditions were that contacts should be between persons of equal status, that the parties had shared goals, and that contacts had institutional support from

> The **Contact Hypothesis** specifies the conditions under which contact between members of different ethnic or cultural groups will have positive effects on inter-group relations and interactions.

Box 11.2   Explanations for Answers to the Culture Assimilator

1   In many Southeast Asian countries, the roles of women may be restricted in some ways, such as approaching men. However, this class is in the United States and there are some students from other countries as well as the instructors interacting together. The fact that the class is mixed and that the students seem to get along fairly well suggest that this is really not the reason for Vien's disappearance from class.

2   It is true that individuals from Asian societies do not like to be singled out. However, in this instance, this minor correction was not a singling out. Martha was talking with Vien alone, so there would be no great embarrassment involved, since others were not present.

3   This conclusion can hardly be drawn, as the scenario states that all seemed to be going well in the class.

4   This is the best answer. South East Asians have a very intricate system of status hierarchy. Martha violated it by trying to downplay her role or perceived status. Her attempt may not have been the total cause for Vien's not wanting to return, however. Probably if she had just suggested it and left it open for Vien to choose he may have felt more comfortable. Her persistence in the matter forced him into a situation where he had to relinquish a value that affected his whole worldview or lifestyle.

Source: Brislin, Cushner, Cherrie, & Yong (1986).

---

the contexts in which the parties were involved. This '**contact hypothesis**' has been extensively researched, and we consider the most relevant studies in Chapter 12. Preliminary to that discussion, we first consider in turn some issues distinctive to the three most frequent types of sojourners.

Tourists

Tourism is currently the largest single source of cross-national contact in the world. In 2010, 940 million cross-national tourist visits occurred (World Tourism Organisation, 2011). Tourist visits are frequently of quite short duration and are often undertaken with groups of co-nationals. For these reasons, direct contact between tourists and those who live in the locations that they visit is quite often restricted to structured visitations and routines. Furthermore, contact is frequently buffered by representatives of the hospitality industry, whose task it is to guide, interpret for, and entertain tourists.

The impact of tourism on tourists themselves will vary widely depending upon their motivations for undertaking the tourism involved. Those engaging in beach holidays, skiing vacations or sex tourism are least likely to be interested in the local populations of the areas that they visit. Heritage tourism, visits to locations in which films were shot, backpacker holidays and ecotourism all have a greater potential to increase awareness and appreciation of cultural differences (Ward, 2013). Despite this diversity, there are some elements common to all forms of tourism, namely one's absence from one's normal location, and the consequent increased likelihood of encountering unfamiliar bacteria, foods, accommodation, and companions. Consequently, tourists do experience some degree of 'culture shock' to varying degrees (Berno & Ward, 2005).

More importantly, the sheer scale of contemporary tourism ensures that it has a substantial impact on host populations, particularly where the ratio of tourists to local population is high. The most immediate effect is a restructuring of the economy, so that an ever higher proportion of the population is engaged in servicing the needs of tourists, with the consequent loss of previous, less profitable occupations and skills. These changes in turn cause a series of stresses and uncertainties that challenge pre-existing cultural values. Berno (1999) compared the impact of tourism on different destinations within the Cook Islands in the Pacific. Within the less visited islands, tourists were treated as guests. In Rarotonga, where tourist visits outnumbered locals by 3.6 to 1, traditional language and practices were lost and there was evidence of the local population adopting the behaviours demonstrated by tourists. Local and even national economies benefit from tourism, while some sectors of the host population also benefit economically and welcome these changes. Host population attitudes have been surveyed in a wide variety of locations (Reisinger & Turner, 2002; Jurowski & Gursoy, 2004), with a balance that differs by location as well as by distance from major tourist destinations between those who applaud the economic benefits and those who regret the environmental and cultural effects.

Urry (1990) has identified what he termed the 'tourist gaze', in other words the desire among tourists to emphasise the fact that they have traveled to somewhere different by looking at and photographing sites and spectacles that are exotic and different. In many cases, the very presence of so many tourists has resulted in the extinction of culturally distinctive ceremonies, events and crafts, so that a pressure then arises to recreate these for the benefit of tourists. Although the revival of traditional skills has a positive aspect, the need to adapt ceremonies in directions that tourists will enjoy watching and to modify cultural artifacts in ways that enhance sales can often distort the very cultural processes being marketed. As Moscardo and Pearce (1999) note, 'ethnic tourism is in danger of consuming the commodity on which it is based'.

The cultural impact of tourism is therefore felt much more by host nations than by the tourists themselves. In some cases, the pressure of tourism has led to the development of cultural training for members of the host nation. For instance, Bochner and Coulon (1997) developed culture assimilator training to help Australian hospitality workers respond more effectively to Japanese tourists. Members of the host culture with culture-specific skills then become valued resources as employees in businesses catering for tourists from relevant cultural groups.

Student Sojourners

There are currently estimated to be more than a million student sojourners, sometimes known as international students, at any one time. Since student sojourners tend to be away from their home country much longer than tourists, research has focused more upon the types of relations that they develop during their stay, and how these relationships contribute to their adjustment. It is useful to distinguish between relations with one's co-nationals, relations with host nationals, and relations with student sojourners from nations other than one's own.

Rather consistent patterns of findings are reported, but we should note that these studies have all been done in relatively similar cultural settings, such as the USA, Australia, Israel, the UK, and other European nations (Ward, 2013). Results may differ when the student destination is non-Western. Sojourners in the existing studies are most likely to report that their best friend during their visit is a co-national. Relations with host nationals are primarily instrumental, that is to say focused on fulfilling academic requirements and gaining help with language. Relations with non-compatriot sojourners, in other words fellow sojourners who are from nations other than one's own, mostly provide social support. Measures of psychological adjustment are predicted by student sojourners' better relations with host nationals and with co-nationals.

The difficulty in interpreting these types of results is that we have no way of determining causal relationships between the variables. Does forming relationships cause satisfaction, or are those who are more satisfied better able to form supportive relationships? Or is there a third component, a personality variable (like optimism, openness to change or cultural intelligence), that drives both outcomes? Studies that have obtained pre-departure measures from student sojourners can help to clarify this confusion. They confirm that personality is indeed a significant predictor of later adjustment. Ying and Liese (1991) found that a pre-departure level of depression predicted the adjustment of Taiwanese students in the USA negatively. Ward, Leong, and Low (2004) found that among Australian and Singaporean sojourners, low neuroticism and high extraversion were associated with both psychological and socio-cultural adaptation. Bardi and Guerra (2011) showed that the coping styles employed by student sojourners from many nations in the UK could be predicted by nation-level indices of the Schwartz values for the nations from which they came, even when personality measures were controlled.

As discussed earlier, there is a current debate as to whether measures of cultural intelligence tap qualities that are not equally well measured by more established personality measures. Ward, Fischer, Lam, and Hall (2009) found that the psychological and sociocultural adjustment of student sojourners in New Zealand was predicted just as strongly by a measure of generalised emotional intelligence as it was by Earley and Ang's (2003) measure of cultural intelligence. In a further study Ward, Wilson, and Fischer (2011) found that, although motivational cultural intelligence was a significant predictor of adjustment, the region from which sojourners had come was a stronger predictor.

Thus it is not likely that personality and other individual attributes by themselves are sufficient to predict adjustment. We must take account also of the type of culture to which the sojourner is moving. Oguri and Gudykunst (2002) predicted that the match between sojourners' self-construals and those favoured in the local culture would predict adjustment in the United States. Independent self-construal was found to predict psychological adjustment. Socio-cultural adjustment was predicted by use of more direct communication and greater acceptance of silences. This style was judged to accord with local US norms. Ward, Leong, and Low (2004) tested the 'cultural fit' hypothesis in a different way, comparing the Big Five personality of sojourners with average Big Five norms within the nations where they were sojourning. They found no indication that Australians with a personality more similar to that of Singaporeans or Singaporeans with a personality more similar to that of Australians achieved better psychological adjustment. The contrast between the results of these two studies may be caused by differences in the circumstances of sojourners in the locations studied, or by the different types of 'fit' that were tested.

Indeed, circumstances vary greatly, making for much diversity in sojourning experience. Among the variables that appear significant are the age of the sojourners, the duration of the sojourn, the degree of similarity between the home and the host culture, the opportunities for meaningful interpersonal relations with host nationals, and the level of perceived acceptance-rejection by the host nationals. For example, if the sojourner sees that his/her country does not enjoy a positive image in the eyes of host country nationals, he/she may experience a 'loss of status'. In an early study, Kağıtçıbaşı (1978) examined some of these factors among two groups of Turkish high school students spending a school year in the United States, living with host families. She used both pre-departure and post-return measures of attitudes, self-concepts and world views. Especially because they lived in accepting families, these sojourners showed positive growth and adjustment, involving a greater belief in internal control, higher self-confidence, less authoritarianism, and more world-mindedness compared with matched control groups who spent the same period in Turkey. The sojourners also showed a positive readjustment to the home country even one to two years after their return.

This study appears to have tapped a particularly optimal sojourner experience. There is some evidence that student sojourners also quite frequently have some difficulties on returning to their country of origin, experiencing 're-entry' problems. Ward, Berno, and Main (2002) showed that among Singaporean students returning from Australia, psychological adjustment in Australia predicted psychological adjustment back in Singapore. However, socio-cultural adjustment in Australia did not predict socio-cultural adjustment back in Singapore. This makes good sense, since psychological adjustment is strongly influenced by the personal attributes that one travels with, whereas socio-cultural adjustment has more to do with the quite different situational challenges that one would face in Australia and in Singapore.

Organisational Sojourners

Business travel has changed somewhat over the past two decades. In former times, the focus was largely upon expatriate managers, who undertook assignments of anything up to five years, working typically within a subsidiary of a multinational organisation. Expatriation does continue on a substantial scale, with more than around 100,000 business expatriates currently on placement around the world (Mercer Consulting Group, 2008). However, the advent of email, video-conferencing and improved travel facilities means that many business trips have become very much shorter. As we noted in Chapter 10, much business may be conducted by multinational teams, who communicate either by email or video-conference, and only rarely meet face-to-face. We focus here on those employees of business and other types of organisation, for example aid agencies and the diplomatic service, who continue to fit the more traditional expatriate role.

Some of the issues facing organisational sojourners parallel those faced by students. However, there are also additional, distinctive challenges. Being, on average, older, organisational sojourners are more frequently accompanied by spouses and children. The adjustments achieved are necessarily tempered by the adjustment of all those who travel, not just the individual directly employed by the organisation. Early reports that substantial percentages of business expatriates returned prematurely from their placements have proved to be untrue (Harzing, 1995). Nevertheless, it remains the case that a premature return is often associated with spousal dissatisfaction (Thomas, 2008). Although a spouse may provide support to an expatriate, there is also the risk that the spouse may not be able to find additional meaningful roles within the local community. Indeed, the spouse may discover quite a different and unwelcome set of role prescriptions for spouses in the new culture! Among Japanese managers working in the United States, work-family relations were found to affect adjustment in both directions: work pressures affected spouse adjustment, and poor spouse adjustment predicted the intention to return early to Japan (Takeuchi, Yun, & Tesluk, 2002). A second hazard faced by organisational sojourners is that they are at the same time required to perform satisfactorily as judged both locally and in their country of origin. Since the criteria for success at home and in the new location will often vary from one another, this new set of employment challenges can be problematic. For instance, locals may expect behaviours that are respectful of local cultural norms, while head offices will often apply global performance criteria. Consequently, it can often be the case that the sojourners judged as most successful in their assignment also experience the most adjustment problems (Thomas & Lazarova, 2006). Consistent with our earlier discussion, foreign language fluency is one of the most consistent predictors of success in handling adjustment problems (Thomas & Fitzsimmons, 2008). This may not simply be a matter of making oneself better understood: language fluency can contribute to the development of mutual respect.

The distinction between psychological adjustment and socio-cultural adjustment has also proved fruitful in studies of organisational sojourners. In a study of aid workers in Nepal, identifying with the sojourner's co-nationals predicted psychological adjustment, whereas identifying with local Nepalese predicted socio-cultural adjustment (Ward & Rana-Deuba, 1999). Poor psychological adjustment was best predicted by personality as measured by external locus of control, low identification with the Nepalese, and high reported loneliness (Ward & Rana-Deuba, 2000). However, as in the case of student sojourners, while high socio-cultural adjustment no doubt contributes to effectiveness during the placement, it is likely to be of no help to returning expatriates. Sussman (2002) found that among US teachers returning from Japan, those who had identified more strongly with the Japanese were those who experienced greatest distress on returning to the United States.

The studies of different types of sojourners that we have reviewed indicate that all those who cross cultural boundaries are faced with varying degrees of role conflict. Some will find ways of handling this tension better than others, but the problem is inescapable. This occurs not just because of sojourners' individual attributes, but also because of the particular groups with whom they identify. We shall explore these processes more fully in the next chapter.

SUMMARY

Although first language speakers of English frequently fail to appreciate it, language use is by far the most important influence on the outcome of cross-cultural interactions. Language fluency determines power relations and also influences the degree to which persons like one another. Language can be used to define one's identity in relation to others. The absence of a shared language severely constrains the success of a cross-cultural interaction. However, use of a shared language does not ensure that one understands the other party's goals or perspectives. Cross-cultural skill requires an awareness that others' assumptions may differ from one's own and the ability to adapt behaviours in ways that enhance mutual understanding.

It is not yet clear whether cross-cultural skill is primarily general or more situation-specific. Nor is it certain whether cross-cultural skill is a component skill of any socially intelligent person or a separate competency. Cross-cultural contacts are increasing through tourism, which has become a major component of cultural change. In evaluating the experiences of sojourners who stay longer and interact more widely with locals than tourists, the distinction between psychological adjustment and socio-cultural adjustment has considerable promise. In organisational settings, cross-cultural contact assumes added importance in terms of the organisational goals served by the interactions and takes on a longer-term basis and a dynamic less chosen by the predilections of the individual sojourner. These considerations provide a distinctive context for within-organisation interactions, and influence their outcomes.

FURTHER READING

1 Bochner, S. (2004). Culture shock due to contact with unfamiliar cultures. *Online Readings in Psychology and Culture*. Available at http://scholarworks.gvsu.edu/orpc
2 Brislin, R. (2004). Encouraging depth rather than surface processing about cultural differences through critical incidents and role plays. *Online Readings in Psychology and Culture*. Available at http://scholarworks.gvsu.edu/orpc
3 Reisinger, Y., & Turner, L.W. (2002). *Cross-cultural behavior in tourism: Concepts and analysis*. Oxford, UK: Elsevier.
4 Spencer-Oatey, H., & Franklin, P. (2009). *Intercultural interaction: A multidisciplinary approach to intercultural communication*. New York: Palgrave Macmillan.
5 Sussman, N.M. (2002). Sojourners to another country: The psychological roller-coaster of cultural transitions. *Online Readings in Psychology and Culture*. Available at http://scholarworks.gvsu.edu/orpc
6 Thomas, D.C., & Peterson, M.F. (2013). *Cross-cultural management: Essential concepts* (3rd edn). Thousand Oaks, CA: Sage.
7 Wang, J. (2011). Communication and cultural competence: The acquisition of cultural knowledge and behavior. *Online Readings in Psychology and Culture*. Available at http://scholarworks.gvsu.edu/orpc
8 Ward, C. (2004). The A, B, Cs of acculturation. In D. Matsumoto (Ed.), *Handbook of culture and psychology* (pp. 411–445). New York: Oxford University Press.

STUDY QUESTIONS

1 If you are bilingual, how different does it feel to express yourself in one language rather than in the other? What are some of the things that you can say and do better in each of your two languages? Why is this?
2 If you are monolingual, how do you modify your behaviour when talking to those who are conversing with you in their second language, and what impact will these forms of

accommodation have upon your relationship with the second-language user? If you are bilingual, what changes do you make when working in your first language? And in your second?

3 Is cross-cultural skill broadly applicable, or is it more important to know how to be effective in a particular cultural context? What is the reason for this?

4 If you are a sojourner, what factors will help or hinder your adaptation?

5 What are the different types of cross-cultural interaction, and how do they differ in their social psychological dynamics?

12

Intergroup Relations

'There are truths on this side of the Pyrenees that are falsehoods on the other side'

(Blaise Pascal, 1679, *Pensées*)

In this chapter, we look first at some basic aspects of why individuals differentiate between in-groups and out-groups, and then discuss whether there are cultural uniformities in the ways that different types of in-groups and out-groups are characterised. Finally, we explore research into the ways in which relations between different cultural groups can be improved.

SOCIAL IDENTITY PROCESSES

In Chapter 7, we discussed the ways that individuals in differing cultural contexts come to construe themselves, focusing especially on the distinction between independence and interdependence. While this distinction has value to cross-cultural psychologists, it should not be taken to mean that only those who construe themselves as interdependent are concerned about their relations with others. Social psychologists have long maintained that processes of group identification are central to everyone's definition of who one is. Indeed, the 'social identity approach', based on social identity theory (Tajfel & Turner, 1979; Tajfel, 1981) and its close relative, self-categorisation theory (Turner, Hogg et al., 1987), has become a major focus for contemporary social psychological research in Western nations (for a recent review, see Spears, 2011).

According to this perspective, each of us is able to define ourselves in terms of both social and personal identities. Social identities involve perceiving oneself as a member of a particular social grouping or category. People have available a range of social identities, based upon age, gender, family, ethnicity, nationality, occupation, friendship groups, religious affiliation, and so forth. Equally, one can define one's personal identity on the basis of perceived differences between ourselves and other individuals, which may be in terms of personal characteristics or in terms of the distinctive combination of group memberships that each individual simultaneously occupies.

According to social identity theory (Tajfel & Turner, 1979), people will generally strive to see their social identities, like their personal identities, as positively distinguished from the identities of other groups or categories. This need for **positive group distinctiveness** can lead one to a more negative view of groups other than one's own. However, social identity theory is often misrepresented as being exclusively or mainly concerned with in-group favouritism and prejudice: in fact, Tajfel and Turner emphasised that people may adopt several different strategies in order to strive for, or maintain, a positively distinct social identity (see Spears, 2011). We touch on some of these strategies in the current chapter, but we discuss them in greater depth in Chapter 13.

An important question left unanswered by social identity theory is how we come to see ourselves in terms of group memberships in the first place. Self-categorisation theory (Turner et al., 1987) proposes that the self-concept is highly fluid. In an average day we may perceive ourselves in terms of many different identities, and these identities may take on different meanings depending on our individual and social circumstances at the time. Across situations, the salience and meaning of a given aspect of identity are predicted to depend on a combination of 'bottom-up' considerations of **comparative fit** (akin to categorical perception: the extent to which perceived between-group differences are greater than perceived within-group differences), 'top-down' considerations of **normative fit** (the extent to which observed differences between the groups are consistent with prior expectations about the groups concerned), and **perceiver readiness** (pre-existing characteristics of the individual, including motives, goals, and prior identification with the group) (Oakes, Turner, & Haslam, 1991; Spears, 2011).

Positive Group Distinctiveness Seeing my group as better than other groups in terms of one or more attributes chosen by myself.

Comparative Fit Are the differences among members of this group smaller than the differences between members of this group and members of another group?

Normative Fit How well does this particular group fit with my understanding of what groups of this type are like?

Perceiver Readiness How do my goals, motives, and previous links with this group predispose me to feel about it now?

If the social identity approach is to provide us with a useful basis for considering relations between ethnic groups and between nations, we need first to consider what evidence there is that its main ideas are applicable to cultural contexts that differ from the primarily European settings in which it was originally formulated and tested. On the surface, one might intuitively predict that social identity theory would be *more* applicable in collectivist cultural contexts than in individualist cultures. The results of self-construal priming studies (see Chapter 7) seem consistent with viewing collectivist cultures as contexts where relational and/or collective identities are frequently salient. Similarly, within the framework of self-categorisation theory, individual differences in self-construal might be interpreted as an aspect of perceiver readiness: thus people who score higher on relational-interdependent or collective-interdependent self-construal would be chronically more likely to see themselves in relational or collectivist terms when the situation affords it.

However, there are several reasons why we should be cautious about these intuitively appealing ideas. In Chapter 7, we questioned the popular view that interdependent self-construal means simply that relationships and group memberships are more important, suggesting that it may be more profitable instead to examine the different *ways* of being independent or interdependent within different cultural systems. From this perspective, portraying groups as 'social categories', formed by comparing the similarities and differences among individuals, may seem like a distinctively 'Western' way of thinking about groups, grounded in an analytic cognitive style (see Chapter 6). A conceptualisation of the group that is grounded in holistic thinking would likely focus to a greater extent on the relationships among the group members; therefore the defining characteristic of a group, rather than the similarities of group members, would be their *interdependence* (Lewin, 1939).

Critics of the social identity approach have argued that even in Western cultures many groups do not function as social categories. Researchers have consequently stressed the importance of distinguishing between *social categories* (also known as common identity groups) and *social groups* (also known as interpersonal network groups or common bond groups: e.g., Rabbie & Horwitz, 1988; Prentice, Miller, & Lightdale, 1994; Easterbrook & Vignoles, 2012). As we noted in Chapter 7, Yuki and colleagues have conducted a series of studies comparing social identity processes among US and Japanese student participants: crucially, their findings converge to show that social identity processes among Japanese participants are mainly focused on intra-group relationships, and less focused on comparing similarities and differences with out-groups (Yuki, 2003, 2011; Yuki, Maddux, & Brewer, 2005; Takemura, Yuki, & Ohtsubo, 2010). Understanding groups as 'social categories' may be more appropriate in some cultural settings than others.

A second concern about the applicability of self-categorisation theory to non-Western settings is the theory's emphasis on the extreme fluidity of the definitions of group identities. On the surface, this might seem to resonate with arguments that the self-concept is more fluid and context-dependent in East Asian nations (although much less is known about self-concept fluidity in other non-Western locations). However, as we discussed in Chapter 7, the fluidity that is characteristic of East Asian self-concepts involves a temporary fluctuation across a range of context-specific identities that are themselves relatively stable and clearly defined over time. The fluidity proposed by self-categorisation theory is of a much more radical kind, suggesting that the entire basis and meaning of group memberships is constructed and re-constructed from moment to moment, depending on temporary features of the comparative context (see Spears, 2011). This seems much more likely to occur in contexts of high relational mobility and the loosely-defined social structures that are typical of contemporary Western nations, rather than in the relatively stable and tightly-defined social structures that are more typical of traditionally collectivist nations (see Yuki, 2011).

Thinking of oneself as a group member also has behavioural consequences. Many studies undertaken in individualistic nations have shown that groups behave in more competitive ways than individuals do. Wildschut et al. (2003) have summarised the behavior of US students making decisions individually or as a group in a series of different experimental games: groups are consistently more competitive. Takemura and Yuki (2007) replicated one of the studies by Wildschut et al. with Japanese participants. They found that Japanese groups were also more competitive than individuals, but the effect was less strong than in the USA.

If the meanings of social identities in East Asian nations are more stable than in the West, then we might expect to find less of a chronic need to defend against possible losses of positive distinctiveness. Consistent with this view, and against the intuitive view that in-group favouritism will be necessarily stronger in collectivist rather than individualist cultures, Yamagishi, Mifune, Liu, and Pauling (2008) also found less in-group bias among Japanese students in minimal groups than among New Zealanders. A minimal group is a group to which an experimental participant is told that he or she has been assigned, but which never actually meets. Thus minimal groups may be especially useful for studying the processes of group formation, rather than what happens in established groups. Heine and Lehman (1997) also found differences in group-serving biases in two studies comparing Japanese and Canadian students: in these studies, Canadians showed a more positive bias than Japanese when evaluating either their family members or their universities.

However, a different pattern of results is found in situations when positive group distinctiveness is undermined. Y.R. Chen, Brockner, and Katz (1996) compared the behaviour of randomly composed groups of US and Chinese students. Group members were led to believe that their group had performed either poorly or well, or that each had individually done either poorly or well, relative to others. In the poor group performance condition, the US respondents reacted by rating their in-group lower than was found in other conditions of the experiment. The Chinese respondents reacted by rating the out-group lower than was found in other experimental conditions. In other words, the US respondents sustained their personal identity by dissociating themselves from their in-group, whereas the Chinese acted to sustain their in-group affiliation by derogating the out-group. These effects were found to be mediated by a measure of *individual-collective primacy* (similar to the self-construal facet of self-centeredness versus other-centeredness, discussed in Chapter 7). Among those told they had done poorly, respondents higher in collective primacy favoured their in-group more and their out-group less than those who were higher in individual primacy. In a second similar study, participants were also given feedback about the performance of the out-group. When the out-group did well and the in-group did not, participants who were higher in collective primacy were again found to sustain in-group favouritism to a greater extent (Y.R. Chen, Brockner, & Chen, 2002).

Focusing on real rather than artificial groups, Derlega, Cukur, Kuang, and Forsyth (2002) asked US and a heterogeneous set of non-US students to rate how they might handle various scenarios involving interpersonal, intergroup, and international conflicts. Interdependent self-construal predicted a greater acceptance of the other's viewpoint during interpersonal conflicts, but a greater use of threats during conflicts with out-groups. Those with high interdependence also reported a greater negative affect in relation to the out-group conflicts. Derlega et al. suggest that this pattern could arise because those who are high on interdependence identify more strongly with their in-groups and defend their in-group accordingly.

Taken together, these studies support the prediction of social identity theory that intergroup discrimination will be strongest in situations where the boundaries and meanings of group membership are relatively fluid, uncertain, or under threat, whereas it will be weaker where group boundaries and meanings are more clearly and securely defined, as well as showing that self-construal measures can help us to understand the effects that are found. Hogg (2007) has argued that one of the main functions of group identities is to protect group members against uncertainty. Supporting this view, a recent meta-analysis of minimal group studies by Fischer and Derham (2013) showed that in-group bias was highest in those nations that scored higher on Hofstede's (1980) dimension of uncertainty avoidance, whereas indicators of individualism-collectivism showed a more complex pattern of effects.

The lack of a clear relationship between individualism-collectivism and in-group favouritism may be easier to understand if we consider that 'collectivism' encompasses an extremely diverse range of cultural values, beliefs, and practices. As we discussed in Chapter 10, the 'collectivist' label has been applied not only to East Asian cultures where modesty is a key social value that seems to affect how people portray their social identities as well as their individual selves, but also to honour cultures in different parts of the world, where people are sometimes prepared to kill their own offspring in order to protect the positive reputation of their family or another in-group (A.K.Y. Leung & Cohen, 2011).

Many of the effects described above have been obtained using experimentally-contrived small groups. However, for the remainder of this chapter we will focus on groupings that have a long-term relevance to one's identity, such as religion, ethnicity and nationality. Self-categorisation theorists propose that one is increasingly likely to adopt a given social identity the more similar one is to a prototypical member of a given group. Thus judgments about one's own group identity will draw on images of what is typical of members of different groups. Our concern here is primarily with widely shared images of larger groupings based upon political groups, ethnicity, 'race', and nationality.

We place 'race' in quotation marks because there is no biological evidence for the existence of separate human races (Segall, 1999). Proportions of genetic markers, such as blood groupings and HLA antigens in different human populations, reveal gradual transitions rather than the sharp differences that would be required to identify different races. The continued mingling of populations subsequent to our common origin in Africa has ensured that all persons derive from a common genotypic stock. Each one of us is to some extent African *and* Asian *and* European. Among the many thousands of human genes, social conventions have been created so that a few (such as those concerning skin colour and facial characteristics) shall be used to define 'racial' groups. However, such groupings have been constructed socially and not biologically. The concept of ethnicity provides a better way to describe these different social groupings, because it comes closer to reflecting their culturally-constructed basis, even if 'race' is the more readily apparent one. Both ethnicity and nationality are therefore social constructs, reflecting the differing social contexts within which persons are socialised. The point at issue in this chapter is to gain an understanding of the factors that lead us to treat these entities as real, identifying with some and rejecting others.

Why do humans have a need to distinguish between in-groups and out-groups? Based on anthropological data, Gil-White (2001) proposed that all humans make distinctions between in-groups and out-groups, because it has been vital for our survival as a species to distinguish between people belonging to our kin group and others who may threaten to kill us or take our resources. Others have suggested that the extent to which people will pay attention to 'race' or other markers of group identity will depend on the context and whether other persons are potential coalition partners (Cosmides, Tooby, & Kurzban, 2003). These theories suggest that we cannot escape our cognitive proclivity to notice differences between in-groups and out-groups, but the relative differentiations that we make will depend on the local social, cultural, and political context.

VIEWS OF THE 'OTHER'

At the most basic level lies the question of how we define humanity. What is the humanness with which we identify and what is the quality of non-humanness? Bain et al. (2012) asked students in Australia, China, and Italy to list the characteristics that came to mind when they thought about humanness. When their responses were content-analysed, a distinction was found between emphasising core elements of human nature (such as abilities, emotions and personality) and emphasising contrasts with other animal species. The Chinese more frequently made contrasts with animals, whereas the Italians and Australians gave a greater emphasis to human nature.

This study formed part of a sequence of earlier single-nation investigations into what is perceived to be essential about human nature and the extent to which we attribute types of humanness to groups other than our own (Haslam, Loughnan, Kashima, & Bain, 2008). Bain, Park, Kwok, and Haslam (2009) asked ethnic Chinese and Australian students to rate personality traits, as well as values drawn from the Schwartz values survey, in terms of whether they were distinctive to humans, and whether they were part of human nature. Subsequently, their participants rated how typical these various traits and values were of Chinese and Australians. By combining these two sets of ratings, Bain et al. were able to show that the Australians rated the Chinese high on qualities that they saw as less typical of human nature. In contrast, the Chinese rated the Australians higher on qualities that they felt could also be found in animals. Apparently, each group 'de-humanized' the other group to some extent. Wider sampling will be required to determine how great are the in-group versus out-group distinctions in humanness and whether these national contrasts relate to other dimensions of cultural variation. It is also clear that the types of genocide and warfare that we discuss later in this chapter involve each party perceiving the other as less than human.

The concept of essentialism may also prove central to our understanding of prejudice against out-groups (Haslam, Bastian, Bain, & Kashima, 2006) and can provide a basis for justifying the immutability of caste and gender relations (Mahalingam, 2007). We return to it after discussing studies that have focused on various specific types of out-group. In a pioneering study of this type that sampled widely across cultural groups, Brewer and Campbell (1976) questioned the members of 50 tribal groups in East Africa as to what was good and bad about neighbouring groups, whether they would be willing to be related to them by marriage and so forth. The results were clear: groups that were viewed more favourably were those perceived as more similar and were physically closer. Attraction and rejection were reciprocal: we like groups that like ours.

POLITICAL GROUPS

Political parties have greater salience in some nations than others, depending on the degree of trust that both majority and minority individuals hold in the processes whereby political parties do or do not contribute to national governance (McLaren, 2012). The policies espoused by political parties are necessarily focused on issues that are locally relevant. However, it is possible that there is an underlying structure to the types of beliefs and attitudes that are debated within and between political parties. Ashton, Danso et al. (2005) surveyed students' political attitudes in the USA, Canada, Wales, Hong Kong, and Ghana. Two dimensions were identified, somewhat consistent with our everyday understanding of left- and right-wing political attitudes. The first dimension contrasts a preference for regulation based on morality with a preference for individual freedom. The second dimension contrasts a preference for compassion with a preference for competition. These two dimensions were found within the data for the first four nations surveyed, but not in Ghana. In Ghana the items defining the two dimensions were intermingled and a second dimension was comprised of items indicating that respondents would dislike their government whatever its policies.

Within their Canadian data, Ashton et al. found that a positive endorsement of moral regulation was correlated with Schwartz's measure of conservation values, whereas a positive endorsement of competition was correlated with Schwartz's measure of self-enhancement and the social dominance measure of Sidanius and Pratto (2001) which is discussed next. In this way political parties can be seen as drawing together persons whose values and beliefs favour particular ways of handling the conflicts between different groups in society. These values and beliefs are frequently associated with differing understandings of morality as well as religious belief, which serve to entrench the positions espoused (Graham & Haidt, 2010).

Social Dominance Orientation

Sidanius and Pratto (2001) have formulated Social Dominance Theory to explain the emergence and persistence of hierarchies in all human societies. Their argument is that all human groups will establish hierarchies based on age, gender, and culture-specific characteristics (e.g., education, and caste). These hierarchies are internalised by individuals in the form of social dominance orientation (SDO) and socially supported through legitimising ideological myths. Individuals endorsing SDO in a socially stable system will typically justify these hierarchies, with dominant group members showing higher levels of intergroup prejudice (sexism, ethnic prejudice, hegemonic beliefs, etc.) and low status group members showing out-group favouritism. Interestingly, nations scoring high on SDO are those in which Schwartz's egalitarianism values are rated as low (Fischer, Hanke, & Sibley, 2012).

SDO theory was initially formulated within the United States, and support for its validity was found there in relation to both gender and ethnicity. SDO predictions have been subsequently tested in Canada, Israel and Taiwan (Levin & Sidanius, 1999; Pratto, Liu, Levin, & Sidanius, 2000). In each nation, the researchers developed locally relevant measures of sexism, ethnic prejudice, conservatism, and support for hegemony. The SDO measure was positively correlated with these measures and with an identification with high status in-groups in almost all instances. Exceptions were that SDO did not predict ethnic prejudice in relation to marriage partners in Taiwan, whereas in Israel it did predict ethnic prejudice in relation to marriage partnerships with Jews, but not with Arabs. Thus there is evidence for the general validity of predictions derived from SDO theory, but full testing requires paying greater attention to the stability and meaning of local hierarchy systems. Take a look at the discussion of this issue in Box 12.1 on page 312.

More recently, SDO measures have been used to compare responses by students in Lebanon and the USA to the 2001 attack on the World Trade Centre in New York and the subsequent conflicts in Iraq and Afghanistan. Consistent with earlier results, US students high in SDO favoured anti-Arab violence more strongly. However, within the Lebanese sample it was those who scored low on SDO who most strongly supported anti-American violence (Henry, Sidanius, Levin, & Pratto, 2007). Identifying with an Arab identity correlated with a low score on SDO and positively with the belief that the September 11 attack was justified (Levin, Henry, Pratto, & Sidanius, 2003). The authors argue that the results support SDO theory, because they show that those who are dominant will favour violence to maintain their dominance, while those who are not dominant will favour violence to eliminate the dominance of the other party.

Box 12.1   Some Nations are More Equal than Others

We have discussed numerous studies in which cultural differences are associated with levels of national wealth. However, wealth is also distributed between the groups in a society more equally in some nations than in others. Gini (1921) devised an index to represent this. Scores fall between 1, where one individual in a nation has all the money, and 0, where the money is held equally by all. In all nations there is substantial inequality and the mean Gini index globally is 0.80. National wealth and national inequality are independent of one another. The table below shows examples of nations scoring at each extreme:

	Rich Nations	Less Rich Nations
Most Equal Nations	Japan	Yemen
	Norway	India
	Ireland	China
	Australia	Sri Lanka
Least Equal Nations	The United States	Zimbabwe
	Switzerland	Namibia
	Denmark	Gabon

The analysis by Fischer, Hanke, and Sibley (2012) showed that across 27 nations social dominance orientation was correlated with wealth. However, the relationship with the GINI index was more complex. In rich nations SDO was endorsed more where inequality was high, but in less rich nations SDO was endorsed more where inequality was low. Therefore in rich societies (where egalitarian values tend to prevail) high SDO may be a way of legitimating inequality. In contrast, in less rich societies (where hierarchical values tend to predominate) low SDO may be a way of opposing inequality.

Staerkle, Sidanius, Green, and Molina (2010) used the International Social Survey Programme to test the consistency of group dominance within each of 33 nations. In the sample as a whole, members of ethnic, linguistic and religious majority groups identified more strongly with their nation and also endorsed nationalistic ideologies more than minority groups did. These effects were also stronger in nations that were ethnically diverse. National identification and nationalism were both higher in more economically unequal nations, but the difference between scores on these variables for the majority and the minority was actually greater within nations characterised by greater economic equality. We can speculate that this surprising result might arise (a) because levels of welfare provided to minority groups in these nations gave rise to expectations of inclusion that remain unfulfilled, or (b) because majority groups would feel a greater threat to their positive group distinctiveness in contexts where minority groups had greater economic power.

NATIONAL STEREOTYPES

If the types of social inequality between groups in society or between nations that are favoured by those who endorse SDO or similar sets of attitudes and beliefs are to emerge and be sustained, two requirements must be met. Firstly, derogatory or dismissive stereotypes should exist. Secondly, those who endorse these stereotypes should also subscribe to essentialism. As we have discussed, the concept of essentialism refers to the belief that all members of a given social category are the same. Conversely, to create more equal societies, ways must be found of challenging derogatory stereotypes, or at least of reducing their impact on behaviour.

In earlier chapters, we examined evidence indicating that national groups differ from one another in terms of prevailing values, beliefs, and the personality of their citizens. These findings provide us with what might be considered as relatively accurate, empirically derived stereotypes. So how do these compare with the lay stereotypes prevailing within the general populations of different nations? As we noted in Chapter 5, some lay stereotypes may contain more than a grain of truth. In discussing the studies reported below, it is necessary to bear in mind that other stereotypes that researchers have detected are not necessarily accurate. More often than not they are derived from indirect sources such as the mass media rather than from direct experience. We are not endorsing them, just studying what they are, how they form, how they may affect the behaviours of those who do endorse them, and whether they can be changed.

Hetero-Stereotypes

Early research found relative consensus across a number of major industrialised societies (Peabody, 1985, Stephan, Stephan, Abalakina et al., 1996) in **hetero-stereotype** ratings, that is, ratings of nations other than one's own. There was agreement for instance that Americans are self-confident, competitive and materialistic, the English are self-controlled, Germans are hard-working, and the Japanese are also hard-working.

It is not plausible that those who responded to these surveys had visited all the nations that were rated or had met many persons from them. So the question arises here as to how these representations of nations are created. We can say that they derive from the media, but that does not answer the question of what sources were drawn upon by those who construct the images portrayed by the media. Linssen and Hagendoorn (1994) tested a series of alternative hypotheses as explanations of West European hetero-stereotypes provided by students. By factor analysing sets of trait ratings, they identified four dimensions characterising the ways in which persons from other nations were perceived, naming them as efficiency, dominance, empathy, and emotionality. These dimensions were then correlated with objective national attributes. Understandably, perceived efficiency was predicted by national wealth, and dominance by a nation's political power. Less straightforwardly, empathy was predicted by a nation's smaller size, and emotionality by a nation's more southerly European latitude.

The equation of emotionality with southerly latitude, which is often also found within single nations, is most probably related to temperature, and should therefore be reversed in the southern hemisphere. In Chapter 3, we discussed some

> **Hetero-Stereotypes** are stereotypes held by group members about groups other than one's own group.

> **Auto-Stereotypes** are stereotypes held by group
> members about one's own group.

possible linkages between climate and the types
of culture that emerge in warmer climates. These
may provide a logical basis for the belief that persons from warmer nations differ on average from
those from cooler climates. Sampling students
from 26 nations, Pennebaker, Rimé, and Blankenship (1996) tested the belief that persons from
the southern part of one's own country are seen as more emotional than those from further north.
The predicted effect was found across 21 northern hemisphere nations, but there was no effect in
either direction among the five southern hemisphere nations. The effect was stronger in nations
further from the equator and stronger in Europe than it was in North America. Pennebaker et al.
also asked their respondents to rate themselves using the same scales, and found that there was
a significant but weak tendency for those from more southerly locations to see themselves as
more emotional than those from further north. Thus, there is a modest overlap between these
auto-stereotypes and the hetero-stereotypes.

It is interesting that national stereotypes are often expressed in terms of personality traits.
However, as we discussed in Chapter 5, Heine et al. (2008) found that stereotypes of national
conscientiousness were unrelated to the nation-level means for conscientiousness reported by
McCrae, Terracciano et al. (2005b). McCrae, Terracciano, Realo, and Allik (2007) propose that
this is because national stereotypes are based on widely shared information, such as how wealthy
a nation is and how warm the climate, rather than on the much less easily judged attributes of
median personality. Although the national stereotypes thus far considered exhibit a broad range
of different content, it is now possible to summarise them in more systematic, theory-driven
ways. Take a look here at the stereotype content model described in Key Research Study 12.1.

Key Research Study Box 12.1 Universal Stereotype Content?

In a series of studies, Fiske, Cuddy, and their colleagues have proposed that when encountering
persons from previously unknown groups, one would ask oneself two basic questions: 'Does this
person intend to harm me?' and 'Is this person capable of harming me?' These types of questions
refer to two evaluation dimensions that have been found to be important in many studies of person perception, namely warmth and competence. Fiske, Cuddy, Glick, and Xu (2002) used cluster
analysis to show that a Stereotype Content Model (SCM) based on these dimensions could be
used to summarise perceptions of different occupational and ethnic groups within the USA.

More recently, Cuddy et al. (2009) tested the cross-cultural validity of the same framework by comparing national stereotypes held by student respondents in seven European
nations, asking them to rate how they thought persons in the European Union perceived
their own and all of the other European Union nations. Warmth, competence, status, and
competition were each measured using four-item scales. Combinations of high and low perceptions of warmth and competence defined three possible forms of prejudice, which they
named as paternalism, contempt and envy, as well as positive stereotyping which they name
as admiration. The results from the European study are portrayed in Table 12.1. The results

also confirmed Cuddy et al.'s hypotheses that competence ratings would be predicted by a measure of the perceived status of each nation and warmth ratings would be related to a perceived lack of competition with one's own nation. These conclusions concur with those of Linssen and Hagendoorn (1994) in relation to competence, and provide an alternative explanation of the results for warmth.

Table 12.1   Positioning of Shared European Hetero-Stereotypes on Two Dimensions

	Low Competence	*High Competence*
High Warmth	('Paternalistic prejudice') • Spain • Italy • Portugal • Greece • Ireland Belgium • • Sweden • France Denmark • • The Netherlands Finland • • Luxembourg • Austria	('Admiration')
		• The UK • Germany
Low Warmth	('Contemptuous prejudice')	('Envious prejudice')

Source: Based on Cuddy et al. (2009).

Cuddy et al. (2009) next extended their studies to include South Korea, Japan, and Hong Kong. At each of these sites, students were asked to make ratings of differing demographic and occupational groups within their nation, as had been done earlier in the USA. Again, the results could be fitted with the two-dimensional SCM framework based on warmth and competence. Warmth was also again predicted by a perceived lack of competition with one's own group and competence was again associated with perceived status.

Finally, Cuddy et al. examined their data in relation to in-group preference, by comparing the stereotype for students with all other stereotypes. In the Asian samples the in-group ratings were no more positive than the out-group mean ratings, which contrasted with the earlier results from Europe and the United States. This result could be explained by low Asian self-enhancement or modesty, as we discussed in Chapter 7. However, further results from Europe that are discussed shortly suggested alternative explanations.

Although there is broad agreement on national hetero-stereotypes and how they may be best summarised, there are also specific factors that will influence the ways in which members of particular nations will characterise each other. Van Oudenhoven, Askervis-Leherpeux,

Hannover et al. (2001) used social identity theory to predict that students' images of one another's nation will reflect the degree to which other nations threaten one's national identity. They proposed that the identity of small nations will be threatened by the existence of larger ones, especially when they speak similar languages, whereas the identity of large nations will not be threatened by the existence of small ones. They took advantage of the fact that Belgium is a smaller nation than its neighbours Germany and France. Furthermore, among Belgians, the first language of the Flemish community is Dutch while the first language of the Walloon community is French. As expected, the Flemish image of Germans comprised more arrogance and less sympathy than did the German image of the Flemish. The contrast between Walloon perceptions of the French and French perceptions of the Walloons was even stronger, a finding that supported the predicted results because both these groups speak French. Thus, in terms of Cuddy et al.'s stereotype content model, size is associated positively with competence and negatively with warmth.

There is substantial evidence of consensus regarding those national stereotypes that have been most studied, and on some of the factors that influence their formation. However, Box 12.2 serves to remind us that we should not assume that stereotypes are always fixed and immutable.

Auto-Stereotypes

There is value in knowing the prevailing hetero-stereotypes for particular nations. Such information may help for instance in understanding individuals' migration decisions or the dynamics of international diplomacy. However, for most individuals the principal relevance of national hetero-stereotypes is that they provide a contrast with one's national auto-stereotype. At least at those times when one is thinking of oneself in terms of one's nationality, social identity theory asserts that we will seek to define our nation and co-nationals more positively than other nations and their co-nationals. Consistent with this reasoning, Smith, Giannini, Helkama et al. (2005) found that identifying with one's nation varied substantially between their student samples from nine European nations, with the lowest scores being from German respondents. However, in all samples individuals' identification with their nation correlated with a more positive auto-stereotype. As the study by Cuddy et al. discussed in Box 12.1 lacked a measure of identification, we do not know whether the Asian respondents were most strongly identified with being students, or with alternate identities.

There are some negative aspects of most nations' identity that cannot be readily denied. Social identity theory predicts that one strategy for dealing with such circumstances is to seek out alternative bases of comparison between one's group and other groups. Poppe and Linssen (1999) reported an instance of this type. Sampling schoolchildren from six nations in Central and Eastern Europe, they found that persons from Italy, Germany, and the UK were perceived as higher on a series of positive qualities that the researchers summarised as greater competence. However, the school children's auto-stereotypes emphasised a second set of traits that were summarised as representing the superior moral qualities of their nation. These effects were strongest where the rater saw his or her own nation as small and powerless. Poppe (2001) was able to confirm some of the causal relationships between these variables by collecting further data one year later. Where the economic circumstances of the raters' nation had declined, the schoolchildren perceived persons from the more successful nations as even less moral. It therefore seems that stereotypes do change as contextual factors evolve, but they do so in ways that continue to sustain a positive in-group identity and are consistent with Cuddy et al.'s stereotype content model.

Box 12.2   How Changeable Are Stereotypes?

Although national hetero-stereotypes may be predictable on the basis of enduring historical, political, and geographical features, they are also open to influence by media coverage of major political events. Haslam, Turner, Oakes et al. (1992) measured Australian students' stereotypes of Americans at the outbreak of the first Gulf crisis, when Iraq invaded Kuwait. They repeated their measurements six months later, after the military conflict had commenced. The repeat measure showed significant decreases in Australians' ratings of Americans as industrious, straightforward and scientifically-minded, and significant increases in perceptions that they were arrogant, argumentative and tradition-loving.

However, the principal purpose of Haslam et al.'s study was to demonstrate that stereotypes can be changed much more readily by a simple adjustment to the experimental design. Self-categorisation theory predicts that our expressed attitudes will vary depending upon the way we categorise ourselves at a specific point in time. Haslam et al. showed that they could elicit similar and equally large changes in Australian stereotypes of the Americans simply by mentioning the names of other nations, such as Iraq, in the course of their experimental instructions. Of course we do not know how long these changes would persist, but the finding that stereotype positivity could change so readily suggests the possibility of constructive interventions in this field

This study qualifies earlier work that pointed to the stability of stereotypes over time. For example, a series of studies conducted over a period of 50 years with students in the United States pointed to the stability of stereotypes regarding ethnic and national groups despite world events that could have changed some of them (Katz & Braly, 1933; Gilbert, 1951; Karlins, Coffman, & Walters, 1969; Singleton & Kerber, 1980). The work of self-categorisation theorists suggests that through life we acquire many differing stereotypic representations of other groups. Which ones are elicited will depend on the social context at a given time. While some persons may hold chronic prejudices, others will focus on the positive attributes of another group at some times and negative attributes at other times, depending on the presence or absence of a threat, differing audiences, and so forth. By using experimental methods, Haslam et al. enlarge our understanding of stereotyping processes. While their study provides some basis for hope that the negative national stereotypes that frequently accompany international conflicts are amenable to change, it is unfortunately equally true that such stereotypes can be fostered and strengthened by contrary media coverage based on traditional stereotypes.

Constructing Nationhood

A positive sense of one's national identity can also be fostered by focusing on key events within one's nation's history. Liu, Lawrence, Ward, and Abraham (2003) asked students within Malaysia and Singapore to identify the ten key events in their nation's history. The events listed by ethnic Chinese, Indian and Malay respondents within these two nations were rather similar, focusing mainly on the achievements of independence and national statehood. Liu et al. argue that this 'hegemonic' view of shared history enhances identification with one's nation rather than with one's ethnic identity within that nation. However, in Taiwan, although there is a shared view of history, that history is evaluated in contrasting ways, depending on the point in history at which the respondent's family moved to Taiwan, leading to alternative identifications with either a Chinese or Taiwanese identity and representation of Taiwanese history (Huang, Liu, & Chang, 2004).

These representations of a nation's history are not simply constructed by individuals. Governments and special interest groups within a nation will strive to interpret history in ways that favour their goals for that nation's political future (Liu & Hilton, 2005). In a series of studies, Liu and his collaborators mapped the events and historical persons that were regarded as most salient in a broad sample of nations (Liu, Goldstein-Hawes et al., 2005; 2009). Major events such as the Second World War are seen as continuingly salient in many nations, but are interpreted in diverse ways. Paez, Liu et al. (2008) examined World Values Survey data on reported willingness to fight for one's nation in relation to the views of world history in 22 nations that had been collected by Liu and his colleagues. Willingness to fight was highest in nations that were higher in power distance and in which respondents saw the Second World War as a significant event, were on the winning side and evaluated it positively. In a further study, Liu, Paez, Hanke et al. (2012) used multidimensional scaling to summarise nation-level evaluations of 40 world historical events across 30 nations. Nations were found to differ in the ratings that they gave to calamities (e.g., wars and terrorism), progress (e.g., the digital revolution, space travel, the industrial revolution) and resistance to oppression (e.g. the abolition of slavery, decolonisation). Willingness to fight for one's nation was highest in nations that rated progress most positively and calamities least negatively (e.g., Malaysia, China, Tunisia, Fiji).

Some types of historical circumstance can foster contested views of history. For instance, Liu, Wilson, McClure, and Higgins (1999) found that *Pakeha* (New Zealanders of British descent) and Maori New Zealand students gave very different listings of key events in their nation's history and their significance. These authors suggest that Maori empowerment and the acknowledgement of the legitimacy of Maori claims of past injustices have generated a contested rather than a hegemonic view of New Zealand history. The denial by *Pakeha* New Zealanders of the contemporary relevance of historical injustices to the Maori can provide them with a basis for opposing reparations to Maoris. Sibley and Liu (2012) distinguish between reparations that involve the transfer of specific resources and reparations that are symbolic. In a longitudinal study, they showed that *Pakehas* who negated the relevance of historical injustices were more likely to oppose resource specific reparations one year later, but would not oppose symbolic reparations, such as public apologies. Sibley and Liu interpreted these results as showing that symbolic reparations enhanced a positive *Pakeha* sense of nationhood, whereas the transfer of resources was seen as an economic threat. A similar dynamic may emerge in other nations with a post-colonial history once the original inhabitants become economically and psychologically empowered.

Nations can also be mapped in terms of their peacefulness. The Global Peace Index based on 25 different indicators is published annually by the Economist Intelligence Unit (www.visionofhu manity.org). Fischer and Hanke (2009) examined correlations between the Global Peace Index and the nation-level endorsement of Schwartz's (2004) measures of values. Figure 12.1 shows that high egalitarianism of teachers and students is most negatively associated with violence, whereas both embeddedness and hierarchy values are highly correlated with greater violence at the nation level.

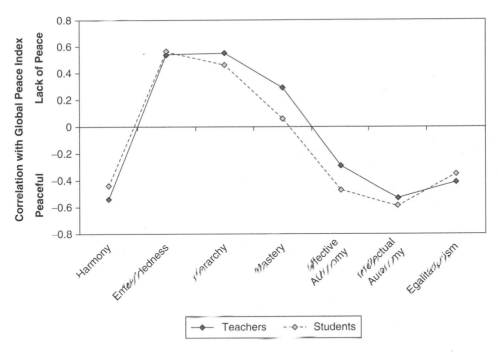

Figure 12.1   Values and the Global Peace Index
Source: Fischer & Hanke (2009).

Many inhabitants of European nations currently see no conflict between identifying with their nation and identifying with the supranational identity of being a European, perhaps as a way of overcoming their extensive historical legacy of wars with one another. In smaller European nations such as Portugal and the Netherlands, those who identify more strongly with their nation also identify more strongly with being European (Gonzalez & Brown, 2006). In contrast, identifying with being British is negatively correlated with identifying with being European (Cinnirella, 1997; Smith et al., 2005). At a still more global level, the questions comprising the World Values Survey include one that asks each respondent whether they consider themselves to be a citizen of the world. The proportion who respond that they strongly agree varies greatly between nations, shown in Figure 12.2. This variation is no doubt attributable to a blending of the contemporary political discourse within each nation, their political history, inward and outward migration, and many others factors. Some time ago, Gergen (1973) argued that social psychology should be seen as a type of social history, recording how we currently relate to one another, without assuming that what researchers find now will necessarily remain the same in the future. Studies of national and supranational identities reveal a further role for history in psychology: the way that we represent our past national history can constrain our contemporary identity choices and how we may now wish to relate to other nations. This is a strong reminder that cross-cultural psychologists need to take political and historical factors into account when examining group processes within and across nations.

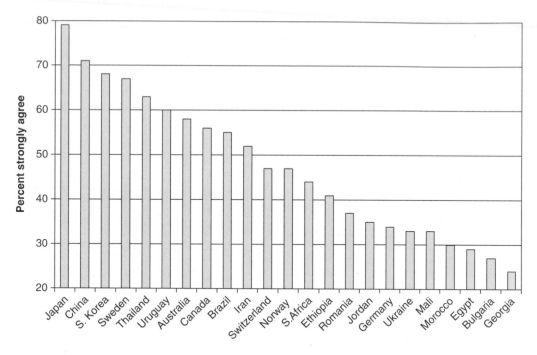

Figure 12.2   Do you See Yourself as a Citizen of the World? (based on World Values
             Survey data)

ETHNIC STEREOTYPING

Research into ethnic stereotypes differs substantially from that into national stereotypes. The focus has been largely upon hetero-stereotypes and even within that field has strongly emphasised negative attitudes, which are more typically described as prejudices, following the pioneering work of Gordon Allport (1954), or contemptuous prejudice as defined by Cuddy et al. (2009). Furthermore, ethnic communities within different nations are rarely the same, so that stereotypes have typically been studied within a single nation, which gives little detailed information as to the extent to which such stereotypes transcend national boundaries.

Key Researcher Box 12.1   Gordon Allport

Gordon Allport (1897–1967) was born in Indiana, but obtained a scholarship to Harvard University, where he completed his PhD in 1922. He remained at Harvard for almost all of his career. He was an early advocate of personality psychology, rejecting both psychoanalysis and behaviourism and contributing to the early development of trait-based theories of personality. His pioneering 1954 monograph initiated contemporary research approaches to intergroup relations by treating prejudice and stereotyping as exaggerated instances of normal cognitive functioning. He was an early advocate of the view that essentialism was a core aspect of prejudice.

While the early US research into the authoritarian personality by Adorno et al. (1950) has been subject to much later criticism, it has encouraged subsequent researchers to pay attention to the fact that those who endorse prejudiced stereotypes of one ethnic community are often also prejudiced against other minority communities. Some current measures preserve the view that prejudice is unidimensional, although now allowing that it may be more strongly held against some groups than others (Pettigrew & Meertens, 1995). However, Duckitt (2001) has more recently proposed a 'dual-process' model of prejudice which identifies two different motivations that may underlie prejudice. Right-wing authoritarians (Altemeyer, 1988) are seen as prejudiced because they are reacting to a perceived threat from out-groups. Those who are high on social dominance orientation (Sidanius & Pratto, 2001) are seen as prejudiced because they are competitive with out-groups. Prejudice will take different forms depending on the relative balance of these motivations.

Stereotypes and Behaviours

Generalised measures of prejudice do have their usefulness, but they also risk diverting attention from the way in which we will maintain images of ethnic groups other than our own. Going beyond personal factors, there are also *situational* factors that play a role, particularly with regard to prejudiced *behaviours*. For example, an early study of ethnic prejudice showed that the majority of Caucasian-Americans in a southern US town interacted with African-Americans in the work situation where interaction was required and expected, but did not interact with them in the town outside of work, where segregation was the norm (Minard, 1952). Indeed, the distinction that Pettigrew draws between subtle and blatant prejudice (Pettigrew, 1998) combines a personality and a situational perspective on prejudice. In societies such as the Netherlands where it is not 'politically correct' among the more educated middle classes to express blatant prejudice, situational pressures cause prejudice toward ethnic minorities to be expressed in more subtle and indirect ways.

By using measures of generalised prejudice, we also direct our attention toward particularly prejudiced persons and away from the specific content of the stereotypes attributed to particular groups. In thinking about the ways in which particular ethnic groups may actually be perceived, it is useful to draw again on Cuddy and Fiske's SCM model of types of prejudice. Table 12.2 shows the different ways in which ethnic groups within the USA were rated (Fiske, Cuddy, Glick, & Xu, 2002). Berry and Kalin's (1995) analysis of a Canadian national survey also indicated that the population as a whole had a shared evaluation of their relative preference for different ethnic groups, with European ethnicities being most favoured. In their sample, the difference between more tolerant and more intolerant individuals was that the intolerant made much sharper distinctions between those ethnic groups they favoured and those they rejected.

Asbrock, Nieuwodt, Sibley, and Duckitt (2011) compared the role of stereotypes and of personal factors in legitimating behaviours toward different ethnic and demographically defined groups. Students in Germany and New Zealand were asked to rate how acceptable it was to behave in various facilitative and harmful ways towards each group. The groups had previously been described in terms of Fiske et al.'s (2002) SCM dimensions of warmth and competence. In both nations, respondents felt it was more acceptable to engage in both passive and active harm towards groups rated low on warmth. They also felt it was more acceptable to be less actively

Table 12.2 Positioning of US Ethnic Stereotypes along Two Dimensions

	Low Competence	High Competence
High Warmth	('Paternalistic prejudice')	('Admiration')
	Migrant Workers • Hispanics •	Black Professionals • Asians • • Jews
	• Poor Whites • Poor Blacks • Arabs	
Low Warmth	('Contemptuous prejudice') ('Envious prejudice')	

Source: Fiske, Cuddy, Glick, & Xu (2002).

facilitative and less passively facilitative toward these groups. Asbrock et al. also compared the strength of effects attributable to the two aspects of the dual process model of prejudice: right-wing authoritarianism and social dominance orientation. In this instance, most of these effects were stronger among those who scored high on social dominance orientation (which supports Social Dominance Theory discussed above).

Determinants of Ethnic Prejudice

In this section, we explore the factors that enhance ethnic prejudice. In a later section we look at the factors that can reduce prejudice. Ethnic prejudice varies between populations and over time. Stereotyped perceptions are likely to contribute to prejudice, but other factors such as personality and the social context are also likely to be involved, both as causes of stereotyping and as direct contributors to prejudice. Hence it is important to try to elucidate how all these processes interact in creating and sustaining prejudice. Figure 12.3 shows the different factors that can contribute to prejudice. Researchers have yet to clarify the reasons for variations in the strength and directionality of the arrows in the diagram.

Media portrayals of ethnic groups can certainly contribute to this process, through repetitive portrayals of association between ethnicity and social problems. Similar processes occur in face-to-face relations. Verkuyten (2001) conducted focus groups in which Dutch adults were asked to discuss their multicultural neighbourhood. Four reasons for arriving at critical judgments of ethnic minorities were identified: describing their behaviour as abnormal, identifying their behaviour as violating moral standards, presenting extreme examples of their behaviours as typical, and asserting that certain behaviours deviated from basic commonsense. Other researchers have sought to explain prejudice by examining some of the more specific beliefs

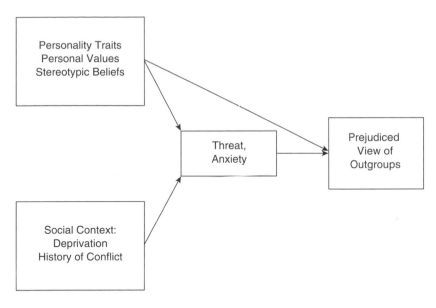

Figure 12.3   Determinants of Prejudice

that are associated with prejudice. Several lines of investigation have been developed, which we examine in turn.

Integrated threat theory

Stephan and Stephan (1996) hypothesised that prejudice toward ethnic groups may be associated with any or all of four different perceived threats, namely, realistic threats, symbolic threats, intergroup anxiety, or negative stereotypes. Realistic threats could include perceived competition for jobs, threats to one's health, or environmental pollution. Symbolic threats would be perceived threats to the values, beliefs, and norms of one's cultural group. Intergroup anxiety would be a threat related, for instance, to past conflicts or minimal prior contact. Negative stereotypes could lead to expectations of difficult or unpleasant contact.

Stephan, Ybarra, Martinez et al. (1998) asked students in Spain to rate their level of negative emotions toward Moroccan immigrants, while students in Israel rated their negative emotions toward Ethiopian and Russian immigrants. They also rated each of the four types of threat that they experienced. For perceptions of Moroccans and Ethiopians, the strongest predictors of the respondents' negative emotions were intergroup anxiety and negative stereotyping. For perceptions of the Russians, the significant predictors were intergroup anxiety and symbolic threat. In a similar study, Stephan, Diaz-Loving, and Duran (2000) found that the attitudes of US students toward Mexicans were best predicted by intergroup anxiety, while Mexican student attitudes toward the US were predicted by both intergroup anxiety and negative stereotypes. Intergroup anxiety is thus the most consistent predictor of negative emotion, but all of these studies sampled students and each of them treated the four bases of threat as independent predictors. It is more likely that these factors are interrelated with one another or shaped by the specific local context (remember the differential support for a symbolic versus resource-specific redressing of past injustices among the *Pakeha* discussed above).

Curseu, Stoop, and Schalk (2007) asked Dutch workers to rate their perceptions of immigrant workers and used structural equation modeling to examine the relations between the four types of threat. The best explanation of their results was achieved by postulating negative stereotypes as a mediator of the other three types of threat. In other words, those who experienced symbolic and realistic threats were more likely to develop negative stereotypes, which would lead in turn to prejudiced perceptions and behaviour. In a study also conducted in the Netherlands, Gonzalez, Verkuyten, Weesie, and Poppe (2008) sampled school children's prejudice against Muslims. In this case, the most satisfactory model gave the predictors of prejudice as symbolic threat and stereotyping. Thus the predictors of prejudice vary between populations in ways that are plausible. For instance, a realistic threat was perceived to be important by workers, but not by schoolchildren.

Esses, Dovidio, Jackson, and Armstrong (2001) have conducted studies in North America that focus upon the first of Stephan and Stephan's four threats. The 'zero-sum' belief that more jobs for immigrants necessarily means that there are fewer jobs for non-immigrants has been repeatedly found to predict levels of rated reluctance to admit immigrants. Furthermore, when messages endorsing or denying the truth of zero-sum beliefs are given to respondents, their rated reluctance to admit immigrants is caused to rise or to fall in accordance with the effect of these messages on zero-sum belief. Thus, like stereotypes, the expression of prejudiced attitudes can be experimentally manipulated by challenging its bases.

System justification theory

Jost and Banaji (1994) proposed that the propensity to stereotype high status groups in society as agentic, and low status groups as communal can provide a basis for prejudiced persons to justify existing social inequalities. Their use of the terms agentic and communal are equivalent to Cuddy et al.'s dimensions of competence and warmth. Jost, Rivetz, Rubini et al. (2005) reported several tests of predictions from this theory. Students in Italy were asked to make ratings of Northerners and Southerners, to estimate the magnitude of economic differences between the north and south of Italy and to complete a scale measuring system justification. This contained items such as: 'Laws of nature are responsible for differences in wealth in society'. It was found that endorsement of system justification and high estimates of economic differences predicted more agentic-communal stereotyping.

Jost et al. next conducted a similar study in the UK, where Northerners rather than Southerners are the less wealthy region. The hypotheses were again supported, which made it possible to exclude a simple geographic explanation of their Italian results. These authors then made a final study in Israel, focusing this time on stereotypes of the higher status Ashkenasim and lower status Sephardim groups. In this study they also included an experimental manipulation of the level of threat said to be currently experienced in Israel. The predictions were again supported, with the effects being stronger when the threat was said to be high than when it was low. Thus system-justification theory predicts and finds effects that are somewhat similar to those predicted by social dominance theory.

Cross-national predictors

The types of threat that enhance prejudice may also vary in relation to distinctive aspects of national culture. Jackson, Brown, Brown, and Marks (2001) drew on data from the Eurobarometer, an annual public opinion survey focused upon representative samples from each nation within the European Union. Jackson et al. compared various predictors of whether respondents had asserted that immigrants should be returned to their country of origin. In 14 of the 15 nations sampled, the perceived threat of 'encroachment' was a significant predictor. Encroachment is defined in terms that place it within Stephan and Stephan's category of symbolic threats – a threat to our values and normal ways of life. In contrast, self-rated racism proved to be a significant predictor in only 11 nations, while a belief that some limits should be placed on the acceptance of immigrants, and a belief that immigrants do not make valued contributions, were predictive in nine nations. The differing cultural contexts of nations in Europe and varying rates of immigration are reflected in the fact that these predictors accounted for markedly different amounts of variance in each nation, ranging from 11% in Ireland to 45% in France. This study also illustrates the way in which specific beliefs can account for more variance in effects than a simple overall measure of prejudice.

Cohrs and Stelzl (2010) extended this line of analysis by examining the circumstances in which right-wing authoritarianism and a social dominance orientation would most strongly predict out-group attitudes to immigrants. Across 17 nations, right-wing authoritarianism was the strongest predictor in nations where immigrants were perceived as increasing the crime rate and failing to benefit the economy (e.g., Germany and Italy). Social dominance orientation was a stronger predictor where the unemployment rate for immigrants was relatively high (e.g., Belgium and Sweden).

Sampling more broadly, Pehrson, Vignoles, and Brown (2009) analysed survey data from 31 nations on national identification and negative perceptions of immigrants. They reasoned that the implications of national identification for rejecting or welcoming immigrants would depend on how national identity was conceptualised in different nations. In nations where nationality is thought of in essentialist terms such as a specific language or ancestry, those who identify with their nation are likely to reject immigrants. In nations where nationality is thought of simply in terms of citizenship, those who identify with their nation are much more likely to be welcoming of immigrants. The hypothesis was supported, with national identification and prejudice being unrelated in nations such as Canada, Israel and New Zealand, but significantly positive in, for example, Switzerland, Germany and Denmark. Thus multiculturalism may be more readily accomplished in some nations than others. Take a look at Research Debate Box 12.1, and Research Instrument Box 12.1.

Research Debate Box 12.1   What is Multiculturalism?

Political rhetoric in Europe in recent years has reflected a growing rejection of multicultural-ism, which is said to have been tried and to have failed. Following an influential statement by Chancellor Merkel in Germany, we can take as an instance this essentialist account in a 2011 speech by UK premier David Cameron:

> Under the doctrine of state multiculturalism, we have encouraged different cultures to live separate lives apart from each other and apart from the mainstream. We've failed to provide a vision of society to which they feel they want to belong. We've even tolerated these segregated communities behaving in ways that run completely counter to our values. So, when a white person holds objectionable views, racist views for instance, we rightly condemn them. But when equally unacceptable views come from someone who isn't white, we've been too cautious frankly – frankly even fearful – to stand up to them. The failure for instance of some to confront the horrors of forced marriage, the practice where some young girls are bullied and sometimes taken abroad to marry someone whom they don't want to is a case in point. The hands-off tolerance has only served to reinforce the sense that not enough is shared. And this all leaves some young Muslims feeling rootless. And the search for something to belong to and something to believe in can lead to this extremist ideology. Now, for sure they don't turn into terrorists overnight, but what we see – and what we see in many European countries – is a process of radicalization.

Cameron thus appears to equate multiculturalism with ethnic separation and hypothesises various detrimental consequences. How does this compare with the definitions employed by social psychologists? Berry, Kalin, and Taylor (1977) formulated a 'multiculturalism hypothesis', which states that confidence in one's identity will lead to sharing, respect for others, and the reduction of discriminatory attitudes. Moghaddam (2008) identified three separate subsequent formulations of the multiculturalism hypothesis:

- in-group confidence and security leads to the acceptance of other groups
- a strong in-group affiliation does not lead to out-group rejection
- an endorsement of multiculturalism has different implications for majority and minority groups

The social psychological approach to multiculturalism focuses on the preconditions for its cre-ation, while the political approach has been to highlight phenomena that may be more frequent in its absence. Research relevant to the multiculturalism hypothesis is discussed later in this chapter and in Chapter 13.

Research Instrument Box 12.1   The Multicultural Ideology Scale

The Multicultural Ideology Scale was first formulated by Berry and Kalin (1995) for use in Canada. The items below are adapted from a version used in the Netherlands by Arends-Toth and Van de Vijver (2003).

1   We should recognise that our society consists of groups with different cultural backgrounds.
2   Ethnic minorities should be helped to preserve their ethnic heritage in this country.
3   It is best for this country if all people forget their cultural backgrounds as soon as possible.
4   A society that has a variety of cultural groups is more able to tackle new problems as they occur.
5   The unity of this country is weakened by people of different cultural backgrounds sticking to their old ways.
6   If people of different cultural origins want to keep their culture, they should keep it to themselves
7   We should do more to learn about the customs and heritage of different cultural groups in this country.
8   Immigrant parents must encourage their children to retain the culture and traditions of their homeland.
9   People who come to live here should change their behaviour to be more like us.

Each item has a seven-point response scale, with answers ranging from strongly agree to strongly disagree. To avoid the effects of acquiescent responding, scores for items 3, 5, 6 and 9 are reversed.

VARIATIONS IN IN-GROUP BIAS

The preceding sections have examined domains of social behaviour in which intergroup relations are both important and problematic. Next we consider work that cuts across these domains, discussing whether there are variables that directly affect the magnitude of in-group bias in a more general way.

Essentialism

The results of Pehrson, Vignoles, and Brown (2009), and the multicultural hypotheses outlined in Research Debate Box 12.1, are relevant to an interesting question which is important both for social psychological theory and for practical issues related to overcoming prejudice. Social identity theory has often led researchers to expect in-group bias where group members identify with their group (but see Spears, 2011), yet formulations of the multiculturalism hypothesis suggest that in-group affiliation and secure attachment to one's identity will be associated with a lower amount of in-group bias and not more. The results of Pehrson et al. suggest a way in which this apparent contradiction can be resolved. Their findings indicated in-group bias to be greatest in circumstances when identification with the national in-group was high *and* it was defined in terms of essentialist categories.

In a second study, conducted just in the UK, Pehrson, Brown, and Zagefka (2009) again found that identification with one's nation and in-group bias were significantly related only among high school students who defined nationality in essentialist terms. In this study, in-group bias was assessed in terms of the rejection of asylum seekers. Longitudinal data showed that an essentialist definition of one's nationality at time 1 predicted enhanced in-group bias six weeks later. Meeus, Duriez, Vanbeselaere, and Boen (2010) obtained a similar increase in the effects of essentialism over time on the relation of in-group identification and ethnic prejudice among Flemish high-school students. Therefore we have evidence that the endorsement of essentialism is a key explanatory variable that complements and adds to the capacity of social identity theory to explain problematic aspects of intergroup relations.

Religion and Intergroup Relations

In the contemporary world a substantial number of violent conflicts are found between groups for whom religious affiliation is a major source of identity. Often, one protagonist in these conflicts is an individualistic group or nation in which Judaeo-Christianity is espoused, while the other is a relatively collectivistic group or nation in which Islam is espoused, although other conflicts between groups defined on the basis of religion are also important. Analysing these conflicts requires a more detailed treatment than can be provided here. Atran, Axelrod, and Davis (2007) note that a core element in such conflicts is an example of what they define as sacred values. Sacred values are seen as non-negotiable and cannot be traded for material or economic incentives (Tetlock, 2003). Atran et al. propose that an effective resolution of conflicts will often require mutual recognition of each party's sacred values before negotiators can address substantive issues. Ginges, Atran, Medin, and Shikaki (2007) tested these ideas by asking samples of Israeli settlers, Palestinian refugees and Palestinian students to rate their reactions to a series of hypothetical resolutions of the current Israeli-Palestinian conflict. They found that violent opposition to a compromise over sacred values *increased* when material inducements were offered, but *decreased* when a symbolic compromise of one's own party's sacred values was included. In this particular instance, the values involved were not sacred in the sense of religious, but had to do with land rights, which are entangled with religious affiliations in the region.

In a more direct test of the association of religion and intergroup conflict, Ginges, Hansen, and Norenzayan (2009) tested alternative explanations of the relation between religion and support by Palestinians and Israelis for suicide attacks. They predicted that support for such attacks could not be associated with religious belief itself, but with an involvement in communal religious activity. Consistent with this expectation, the frequency of religious attendance predicted the endorsement of attacks, but the frequency of prayer did not.

These results have implications for Huntington's (1996) portrayal of the fundamental clash of civilisations, with religion as a central component in that clash. As we saw in earlier chapters, there is indeed a contrast in the nation-level distribution of values around the world. However, this distribution does not map very closely onto the distribution of religious affiliations. Furthermore, an individual-level study sampling from 11 nations showed no significant differences in the correlation between self-rated religiosity and the Schwartz values espoused by adherents to the monotheistic religions of the world, Christianity, Islam and Judaism (Huismans, 1994). Those who rated themselves as more religious endorsed tradition, conformity

Figure 12.4   Cruel Culture by permission of Malcolm Evans

and benevolence most strongly, irrespective of which religious tradition they belonged to. Boer and Fischer (2013) supported these claims in a cross-cultural meta-analysis of the relationship between values and attitudes.

It may also be the case that those who become most actively involved in intergroup conflicts differ from the general population. Khan and Smith (2003) compared the individual-level Schwartz values espoused by members of two groups in Pakistan. Both groups had a Muslim membership, but one group was actively engaged in politically-motivated terrorism. Members of the terrorist group scored significantly higher on hedonism, stimulation and power values, while the other group scored higher on benevolence, universalism and conformity values. Terrorist group members also scored high on independent self-construal.

Montiel and Shah (2004) investigated the ways in which our perspective on such conflicts is coloured by relevant group loyalties. They chose to sample students from the Philippines, which has a Christian majority and a Muslim minority, and from Malaysia, which has a Muslim majority and a Christian minority. Christian and Muslim respondents from both countries were asked to respond to one or other version of a scenario in which a suicide bomber, described either as a terrorist or a freedom-fighter, bombs a building and kills many people. As they predicted, Montiel and Shah found no effect of nationality or of religious affiliation on ratings of the qualities of the bomber. However, members of minority groups in both nations responded significantly more positively to the freedom-fighter label and more negatively to the terrorist label than did members of the majority groups. Thus, it is the experience of being a minority group member rather than religious affiliation that proved to be a key causal factor in this setting. The implication of these studies is that it is an oversimplification to analyse contemporary conflicts in terms of clashes based upon religion: they are better thought of as intergroup conflicts, driven by some of the factors discussed earlier in this chapter such as social dominance, inequality, and realistic threat.

National Tendencies Towards In-Group Favouritism

Aside from the variations in relations between the various different types of groups that we have discussed, there is also some evidence that nations differ in terms of the extent to which priority is given to in-groups in general. In-group favouritism has long been discussed by sociological theorists (e.g., Parsons & Shils, 1951) in terms of a contrast between particularism and universalism. Those endorsing particularistic values would say that it is good to give preference to one's close associates, while those endorsing universalistic values would say that everyone should have equal rights. This contrast in values finds expression in contemporary debates about nepotism, corruption, and equality of opportunity. Across 178 nations, Van de Vliert (2011) drew from existing data sources to construct three indices of nation-level in-group favouritism: a preference for jobs being given to persons of one's own nationality; the perceived frequency of jobs being given to relatives; and the endorsement of preferential treatment for family members. Van de Vliert found support for his eco-cultural theory (discussed in Chapter 3) as an explanation for variations in in-group favouritism. More extensive testing will be required to establish the relative explanatory value of his theory in comparison with other relevant dimensional measures.

THE CONTACT HYPOTHESIS

This chapter has documented extensively the ways in which intergroup relations can be problematic. Researchers have frequently and rightly been concerned to study practical ways in which this situation can be remedied. In light of everyday experience, it is evident that simply having contact with persons from other groups does not guarantee improved relations with them. There is a long history of investigations into the types of interpersonal and intergroup contact that do foster positive outcomes for both parties. The contact hypothesis was first advanced by Allport (1954), who proposed that good outcomes would occur where contact between groups was on the basis of equal status, where contact was approved or encouraged by higher authorities, where that contact was cooperative rather than competitive, and where it lasted long enough for the parties to get better acquainted.

By 2006, Pettigrew and Tropp were able to report a meta-analysis of more than 700 tests of the contact hypothesis, some of which concerned intercultural contact. They concluded that the hypothesis was supported, but that it was important to determine how contact was perceived by those involved. For instance, the parties may not agree as to whether a series of contacts is based on equal status. Key situations involving contact with immigrants, such as schooling and work, can provide the circumstances for prolonged cooperative contacts that are approved by authority. Achieving a perceived equality of status can be more problematic, however, even where such equality is mandated by government or by institutional policies. Despite these matters of detail it is clear that the contact hypothesis is no longer just a hypothesis: it is a theory with substantial empirical support (Hewstone & Swart, 2011). It remains to be seen whether it is supported equally strongly in all cultural contexts.

More recent studies have been concerned with trying to understand more precisely when contact is beneficial and what might be the intervening variables that lie behind successful outcomes. Possible mediators of the effectiveness of contact could be any one of the elements of Stephan and Stephan's (1996) integrated threat theory discussed earlier. That is to say, the positive effects of contact would be more likely where the perceived real and symbolic threats are lower, and there is less anxiety and less firmly-held stereotypes: for instance, Ward and Berno (2011) found that positive attitudes toward tourists in Fiji and New Zealand were predicted by each of these factors. In the case of more consistently problematic forms of contact, the effects of anxiety have most frequently been examined. If contact with an out-group actually raises anxiety, it is unlikely to reduce prejudice (Brown & Hewstone, 2005). Take a look at Key Research Study 12.2.

Key Research Study 12.2   Does Contact Reduce Prejudice or Does Prejudice Eliminate Contact?

Binder, Zagefka, Brown, Funke et al. (2009) made one of the relatively few longitudinal studies of the relations between intergroup contact and prejudice. Longitudinal studies are crucial in determining the direction of causal relationships between the variables that have been studied. In Binder et al.'s work, 1,100 majority and 500 minority schoolchildren in the UK, Germany and Belgium completed a survey twice. Minority respondents came from a wide variety of ethnic groups, which also differed across national samples. Those whose data were analysed were those who reported having at least one out-group friend. Measures collected included quantity and quality of out-group friendship, whether their out-group friend was typical of that out-group, negative emotions toward out-groups, desire for social distance from out-groups, and anxiety about being with out-group members.

The contact hypothesis was evaluated first. By controlling statistically for prejudice at Time 1, the causes of increases or decreases in prejudice at Time 2 can be tested. It was found that more and higher quality contact with one's friend at Time 1 gave rise to reduced prejudice at Time 2. The alternative hypothesis that prejudice reduces contact can also be tested. Controlling for contact at Time 1, it was found that prejudice reduced the amount of contact at Time 2. Thus, there was evidence both that contact decreased prejudice, and that prejudiced persons avoided contact with those against whom they were prejudiced. These effects were found to be stronger among the schoolchildren from the majority culture, and among those who perceived their friend to be a typical member of the out-group. The authors also found that reductions in prejudice were attributable to reduced anxiety about intergroup contact.

As we discussed at the beginning of this chapter, each of us has available a range of alternate identities that can be elicited by different circumstances. Groups in conflict with one another may be able to unite in the pursuit of a superordinate shared goal, as illustrated by Sherif's (1961) classic experimental studies of boys attending summer camps in the USA. Successful collaborations can foster a shared identity and reduced prejudice, and several models have been proposed as to how shared identities are best created and whether their effects will persist (Gonzalez & Brown, 2006). At issue is the question of whether an identity that is unified and shared is preferable to an identity that is unified but acknowledges separate components: for instance, if I identify strongly as European, does that threaten my national identity? Gonzalez and Brown found that it did so only among student respondents from smaller European nations. Guerra, Rebelo et al. (2010) arranged nine and ten year-old Portuguese children in groups that included majority European Portuguese and minority Portuguese-African members. The groups worked on a task for a prize, either with team members labeled with their ethnic identity, or with teams recategorised into one of two types of superordinate Portuguese label. The recategorised groups achieved more positive attitudes toward out-group members. Majority group members responded more favourably to the label 'Portuguese team with Portuguese and African origin members', while minority members favoured the label 'Portuguese team'. Hence in this study, as in those by Gonzalez and Brown and by Binder et al., majority and minority members responded to superordinate goals in different ways reflecting their majority or minority status.

Asbrock, Christ, Duckitt, and Sibley (2012) have proposed and tested a 'dual-process' model of the individual differences that will also affect the outcomes of intergroup contact. They reasoned that prejudice as represented by right-wing authoritarianism will be responsive to intergroup contact, because prejudice is based on perceived threat, and contact can reduce threat. In contrast, they argued that social dominance orientation is based on a competitive search for dominance in intergroup relations, and there is no reason to expect that contact would reduce this motive. Drawing on cross-sectional and longitudinal surveys representative of the adult German population, they showed that the interaction between right-wing authoritarianism and contact with an out-group member at Time 1 yielded *reduced* prejudice at Time 2. In contrast, the interaction between social dominance orientation and contact at Time 1 yielded *increased* prejudice at Time 2. This study used very brief two or three item measures of the variables involved, but it illustrates the continually increasing way in which the original contact hypothesis must be modified and extended to accommodate what we now know about the circumstances in which intergroup relations can be enhanced.

Intergroup Reconciliation

In the case of severe and long-lasting intergroup conflicts, such as those for instance in South Africa, Northern Ireland, Bosnia and elsewhere, the priority is initially not so much on creating contact as on creating the conditions in which tolerance and beneficial contact would become possible. One possibility is through 'extended' contact: in other words, even if there is little intergroup contact, my attitude toward the out-group may improve if a friend of mine has contact with out-group persons. Increased out-group trust of this kind has been established across the long-standing divide between Protestants and Catholics in Northern Ireland, especially when my friend is a close friend (Tausch, Hewstone, et al., 2011). In South Africa, Swart, Hewstone, Christ, and Voci (2011) found that increased affective empathy and decreased intergroup anxiety among Coloured schoolchildren mediated more positive attitudes toward White majority students. Both of these studies also used longitudinal designs, thus ensuring the directionality of the causal effects that were detected.

A second possibility is to make interventions with each group separately. Brown and Cehajic (2008) found significant relationships between expressing shame and guilt about one's in-group's misdeeds toward an out-group and willingness to endorse items recommending reparation toward the out-group. The respondents were Serbian students in Bosnia, where massacres of Bosnian Muslims had occurred during the 1992–1995 war. The effects of expressing collective guilt were mediated by empathy with the out-group, while the effects of expressing collective shame were mediated by both empathy and self-pity. Exploring this dynamic more fully, Cehajic-Clancy et al. (2011) found that these effects occurred if their student respondents were first asked to affirm their individual identity, but were not found if respondents instead first affirmed their group identity. Therefore, taking on personal responsibility is an essential component of a willingness to endorse reparation. This second study was conducted both with Bosnian Serbs and also with Israeli Jews, thus demonstrating that the results obtained were not distinctive of a particular conflict.

Everyday Life Box 12.1   When Life Chooses Your Research Topic for You

When I was twelve I was forced to flee my home. I managed to escape on the last plane leaving Sarajevo with my mother and younger brother. I wouldn't see my father, who bravely stayed and survived under Europe's longest modern-era siege, for almost three years. I wouldn't see my city, almost reduced to ruins, for over five years. I was not allowed to return to my home, divvied up by the Dayton Peace Accords, until I was twenty.

For many, the long and brutal war that ravaged Bosnia and Herzegovina literally destroyed their lives. For over 100,000 people – it ended theirs. The war and its consequences have, in so many ways, shaped the person I am and inspired the research that I do. I never tire in the quest to know how ordinary people deal with a past marked by such gross human rights violations and how we, as members of a post-conflict society, can restore broken ties and trust.

I research these issues not only because of their general and practical importance. I am examining these processes because I feel that it is also my obligation to personally contribute to the process of reconciliation in my country. Coming from and living in a country which to this day continues to deal with the reality of mass killings, deportations, mass graves, rape, and even genocide on a daily basis, I feel a strong sense of responsibility to be part of the process of how to deal with the past and create a brighter future.

In some ways I did not choose my work, it chose me. And I am glad it did. Having personally experienced deportation, refugee life, separation from family, and the seemingly eternal anxiety of not-knowing-what-will-happen-next, the work I do, the questions I address both with my research and teaching, were a natural response to my personal and communal experiences.

The large majority of people from Bosnia and Herzegovina did not choose war. It was forced upon us through an ideology of false hatred and fear. But this is the hand we were dealt. That left me with two options to deal with what happened. I could remain a disempowered victim with the hope that things would miraculously change, or I could let this experience strengthen my determination to shape my identity, work, and life in a more positive way. I chose the latter. I chose to appreciate and be grateful for my, and indeed our, unfortunate experience, which has added more meaning and purpose to everything I do.

Sabina Cehajic-Clancy

These results are impressive, but we cannot yet say whether the requirements for the accomplishment of forgiveness are culturally invariant. Ho and Fung (2011) note that differences in the fundamental attribution error between individualistic and collectivistic imply that the acknowledgement of personal responsibility may be a stronger requirement in individualistic cultures. Instances of what may occur in more collectivistic groups are illustrated by the truth and reconciliation tribunals subsequent to major collective violence that have now been employed in more than 30 nations. Rimé, Kanyangara, Yzerbyt, and Paez (2011) evaluated the effectiveness of this process in Rwanda in 2006, subsequent to the genocide that occurred there in 1994. Perpetrators, victims, and control groups from both sides who had not been involved were sampled before and after the tribunals were held. The process increased negative emotions among both the involved parties. Among perpetrators, shame increased whereas anger and disgust decreased. Among victims, shame decreased and anger and disgust both increased. After the tribunals, both the involved parties were found to have reduced their in-group identification and their stereotype of the other party had become more positive. Rimé et al. observed that the re-elicitation of negative emotions was a key element in the ultimate success of this process. It may also have been aided by the prior existence in Rwandan culture of the *Gacaca* reconciliation procedure. Staub, Pearlman, Gubin, and Hagengimena (2005) tested their hypothesis that traditional procedures such as *Gacaca* could be made more effective by prior training of facilitators in theory related to genocide and trauma as well as practical work on empathic responding. Their hypotheses were supported, with the groups conducted by trained facilitators showing better evidence of lasting benefit.

In this chapter, we have focused on relations between groups in a relatively general manner, without noting the origins of the minority groups to whom we have referred. Many of these groups are in fact composed of immigrants, and we shall explore the dynamics attending their circumstances more fully in the next chapter.

SUMMARY

Our identities are partly rooted in the groups with which we are affiliated, and in the way that we compare these groups with other relevant groups. We maintain stereotypic conceptions of other groups in society and of nations, which have some value in guiding relations with their members, but can amount to prejudice where they are resistant to contrary evidence. An in-group preference in general may be more directly linked to threat and uncertainty avoidance than to collectivism. In practical terms, it is more important to focus on the factors that determine levels of prejudice against minorities. Prejudice derives from perceiving a threat from other groups, anxiety about out-group members, and a desire to maintain existing forms of social dominance. Contact can reduce prejudice, especially in circumstances that reduce threat and anxiety, but prejudice can often restrict contact.

FURTHER READING

1 Khan, S., Bender, T., & Stagnaro, M. (2012). Stereotyping from the perspective of perceivers and targets. *Online Readings in Psychology and Culture*. Available at http://scholarworks.gvsu. edu/*orpc*

2 Levy, S., West, T., Rosenthal, L. (2012). The contributing role of prevalent belief systems to intergroup attitudes and behaviors. *Online Readings in Psychology and Culture*. Available at http://scholarworks.gvsu.edu/*orpc*

3 Liu, J.H. (2002). A cultural perspective on intergroup relations and social identity. *Online Readings in Psychology and Culture*. Available at http://scholarworks.gvsu.edu/*orpc*

4 Nisbett, R., & Cohen, D. (1996). *Culture of honor: The psychology of violence in the south.* Boulder, CO: Westview.

5 Segall, M.H. (2002). Why is there still racism when there is no such thing as 'race'? *Online Readings in Psychology and Culture*. Available at http://scholarworks.gvsu.edu/*orpc*

6 Yuki, M. (2011). Intragroup relationships and intergroup comparisons as two sources of group-based collectivism. In R.M. Kramer, G.J. Leonardelli, and R.W. Livingston (Eds), *Social cognition, social identity, and intergroup relations: A Festschrift in honor of Marilynn Brewer* (pp. 247–266). New York: Taylor & Francis.

STUDY QUESTIONS

1 How do you account for the stereotypes that you hold about persons from your own nation and the ways in which you believe that persons from your nation are seen by those from other nations?

2 Discuss the extent to which ethnic prejudices toward one or more minority groups in your nation or political unit are underpinned by Stephan's four types of threat: realistic threats, symbolic threats, intergroup anxiety, and negative stereotypes. What are the likely origins of these four threats in your nation or political unit?

3 Construct a full listing of the circumstances under which the contact hypothesis has been shown to be valid.

13

Acculturation

...in your 50 groups, with your 50 languages and histories and your 50 blood hatreds and rivalries. But you won't be long like that, brothers, for these are the forces of God you've come to.... Germans and Frenchmen, Irishmen and Englishmen, Jews and Russians – into the crucible with you all! God is making the American.

(Israel Zangwill, *The Melting Pot*, 1909, p. 33)

MIGRATION

People move from one cultural context to another for a wide variety of reasons. These range from the coercive impetus of fleeing from war or persecution to the freely taken choice to move to another location for a new job or to live closer to one's relatives. The largest element in contemporary migration is movement from rural to urban locations. Ruback, Pandey, et al. (2004) surveyed migrants who were slum dwellers in New Delhi, Dhaka, and Islamabad. The most frequent reason for moving to the city was to search for work, but many respondents also attributed their move to fate. This attribution to fate was related to a perceived lack of personal control and was not associated with religion or the degree of poverty.

Migrants from rural to urban contexts can experience many of the difficulties that are faced by those who migrate from one nation to another. However, most studies of migration have been focused upon international migration. Migration has occurred throughout human history but rarely on the scale that is currently evident. As Figure 13.1 shows, the total current number of international migrants in the contemporary world exceeds the population of all but the four most populous single nations in the world.

Persons from a great range of cultural backgrounds are to be found in the larger cities of the twenty-first century. In addition to nations such as Canada, Israel, Australia, New Zealand and the USA that are openly seeking certain kinds of immigrants, many other nations are experiencing population movements. We find Japanese people in Brazil, Bangladeshis in Japan, Vietnamese in Finland, Senegalese in Italy, Turks in Germany, Croatians in Sweden, Surinamese in the Netherlands, Filipinos in Hong Kong, and North African Arabs in France. We find Kazakh Poles who speak no Polish, and Russian Germans who speak no German, re-migrating

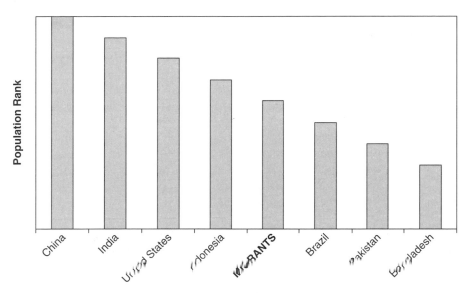

Figure 13.1   World Migrant Numbers Compared to Individual Nations

to Germany and Poland respectively. The nations most frequently discussed in relation to migration are those that have received the most migrants, but there are other smaller nations whose populations include much larger proportions of migrants. The United States has just 13% of migrants, Canada has 19% and Australia has 20%, but Switzerland has 23% and Israel has 37%. Kuwait has more than 60% of migrants, while Qatar and the United Arab Emirates have more than 70% (United Nations, 2006). The contemporary world is a kaleidoscopic mix of epic proportions!

> **Acculturation**
> Acculturation is the process of change that occurs when groups or individuals from differing cultural backgrounds interact with one another for extensive periods of time.

In order to gain the best understanding of the processes that attend these cultural transfusions, we need conceptual models that can capture the core processes involved. In the early part of the twentieth century, the concept of a 'melting pot' was popularised by Zangwill (1909), who envisaged an inexorable blending of European nationalities into the creation of the modern American. We now know that there is nothing inexorable about this process and that blending is only one of the possible outcomes. Concepts that we have explored in earlier chapters, such as self-construal, social identity and intergroup relations, can provide a firmer basis for understanding. Current research is mostly formulated in terms of the process of **acculturation**.

DEFINING ACCULTURATION

Given the magnitude and practical importance of immigration, it is no surprise that the study of acculturation has become a major area of investigation in recent years. Indeed, much of the

impetus for the study of cross-cultural psychology derives from the scale and political significance of such population movements. We focus first on how best to define acculturation.

Conceptual Issues

Although there was some earlier interest in the topic, a widely accepted definition of acculturation
is the one first formulated by three anthropologists – Redfield, Linton and Herskovits – in 1936:

> Acculturation comprehends those phenomena which result when groups of individuals hav-
> ing different cultures come into continuous first-hand contact, with subsequent changes in
> the original culture patterns of either or both groups … Under this definition acculturation
> is to be distinguished from culture change, of which it is but one aspect, and assimilation,
> which is at times a phase of acculturation. (1936: 149–152)

A notable aspect of this definition is that it is focused upon cultures, not upon individuals, and
that it envisages acculturation as a process in which either one or both parties experiences cultural change. Thus, we need to keep in mind our discussions of the issue of levels of analysis in
earlier chapters. Extensive migration into a particular nation may or may not cause changes in
the culture patterns of that nation. For instance, in recent decades, migration has had a major
influence on the range of cuisine that is offered by restaurants in many nations. This change can
in turn affect also what people choose to eat at home. However, the major focus of acculturation
researchers has been upon the immigrants rather than members of the host nation. Culture-level
processes tell us little about the experiences of these individual migrants, or those of the host-
nation persons with whom they have varying degrees of contact.

In order to focus on these personal experiences, we need to conceptualise the process of
psychological or individual-level acculturation. We already discussed Ward's (2013) distinction
between psychological adaptation and socio-cultural adaptation in Chapter 11, and these concepts give a valuable indication that worthwhile measures of acculturation require our paying
attention both to the individual's experience and to that individual's contact with other cultural
groups.

Acculturation is a long-lasting process. Researchers have sometimes attempted to address
the challenge that this timeframe poses by surveying samples that include earlier and later generations of immigrants into a country. Unfortunately, this gives only a partial solution to the
problem, because those who migrate to a given country at various points in history may often
do so for different reasons and may also experience different types of response from majority
groups when they arrive. They are therefore not directly comparable with one another. In the
absence of long-term follow-up studies, we can at best gain snapshots of the various processes
that may occur.

Consider some of the myriad possibilities: a single adult arrives and after some delay finds
employment; a couple arrives and one partner finds work while the other remains at home; a
family arrives, one parent finds work and the children begin attending school; a three-generation
family arrives and locates within a community that already includes relatives and co-nationals; a
couple arrives, one of whom is already a national of the nation in which they arrive. Each of these
scenarios will elicit a distinctive profile of acculturative processes.

The simplest conceptualisation of acculturation used by researchers has been to equate it
with assimilation into, usually, American culture. Scales have been devised that comprise, for

instance, items measuring the extent to which members of a specific immigrant group speak English, eat typical American foods, watch English language television stations, and so forth. An example of this type is the widely used Suinn-Lew Asian Self-Identity Acculturation Scale (Suinn, Ahuna, & Khoo, 1992).

Scales of this type have been increasingly criticised on the ground that they fail to separate adequately those who are actively engaged in both their group of origin and their new cultural group from those who are not much involved in either group. For instance, in answer to the question 'With whom do you now associate in your community?', the answer on a five-point scale 'About equally Anglo groups and Asian groups' scores three, and confounds some respondents who are isolated from both communities with others who are actively engaged in both. In answer to the same question, 'Almost exclusively, Anglos, Blacks, Hispanics and other non-Asian groups' scores five, and would identify those who are actively avoiding their own ethnic group. Because of these anomalies, scores on this scale would be unlikely to predict the degree of socio-cultural adaptation.

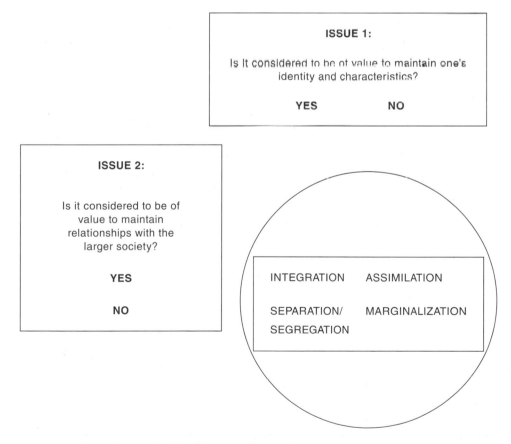

Figure 13.2   Berry's Model of Types of Acculturation

Source: Berry (1997).

The Bi-Dimensional Model of Acculturation

Berry (1997, 2006) has popularised an alternative model of acculturation that is depicted in Figure 13.2, and which has been used frequently by researchers from many nations. He distinguishes four orientations toward acculturation on the basis of the degree to which an immigrant seeks to maintain the characteristics of his or her culture of origin and the degree to which he or she seeks to engage with the majority culture.

Key Researcher Box 13.1   John Berry

Figure 13.3   John Berry

John W. Berry (b. 1939) grew up in Canada but completed his PhD at the University of Edinburgh in the UK. His dissertation was focused on the cultural adaptations of the Inuit and Cree nations to differing environments in Northern Canada. This led to his early formulation of eco-cultural theory (Berry, 1976). After teaching at the University of Sydney for three years, he held a series of appointments at Queens University, Kingston, Canada. He is currently Emeritus Professor of Psychology at Queens University. He was a founding member of the International Association for Cross-Cultural Psychology and principal editor of the second edition of the *Handbook of Cross-Cultural Psychology* (1997). He also co-authored *Cross-Cultural Psychology*, the first textbook covering the field as a whole (Berry et al., 1993). Overall, he has authored or edited almost 30 books and over 180 journal articles and book chapters. During the past three decades he has developed his model of acculturation processes, supervised the dissertations of many researchers now active in this field, and assisted the Canadian government in the development of their policies relating to immigration.

As Figure 13.2 shows, Berry conceptualised acculturation in terms of *values*. In the past two decades, his overall 2X2 model has been preserved but differing researchers have focused instead on acculturation in terms of different *attitudes* toward one's own and others cultural practices, and in terms of differences in *identification* with one's own and others cultural groups (S.J. Schwartz, Unger, Zamboanga, & Szapocznik, 2010; Brown & Zagefka, 2011).

   Berry identifies a multitude of factors that may lead particular immigrants to adopt one or other of these four orientations toward acculturation. It is likely that all immigrants face considerable difficulties when first arriving at their chosen destination. The most obvious ones are those associated with language skills, the loss of former support networks, the need for accommodation, and the need for employment. Numerous studies have now been reported which test the proposition that immigrants whose responses fall into the '**integration**' category will fare best on a variety of measures of adjustment, while those who favour assimilation will also do better than those who favour separation or marginalisation (Sam & Berry, 2006; Nguyen & Benet-Martínez, 2013).

> **Integration**
> Integration is the term used in Berry's model of acculturation to describe a preference for both the maintenance of one's own culture and inclusion in the majority culture. It is synonymous with biculturalism.

Although it is widely believed that these hypotheses are supported, the associations found between favoured acculturation style and measures of adaptation have varied from one study to another and are not always in the predicted direction (Rudmin, 2006). Integration may indeed often be the optimal acculturation style, but if it is, we need a clearer understanding of why the measures that have been used have failed to yield clearer results. We discuss several reasons in the sections that follow.

The use of the verb 'favour' in the preceding paragraph reflects the way in which Berry describes his model. As Figure 13.2 shows, the acculturation strategies are defined by what the immigrant *values*. However, immigrants are rarely able to make an entirely free choice as to the position that they can take up at their chosen destination. The positions open to them will be constrained by the attitudes of the majority population, the policies of their host nation, and the resources that are consequently made available to them. As the studies reviewed in Chapter 12 have underlined, majority populations are by no means always welcoming to those immigrants whom they perceive as out-groups, and may be willing to accept them only if they accept a substantial status loss and take up more menial roles than those they held in their country of origin. They are often also more inclined to accept those minorities whom they consider to be not very different from themselves.

Including majority attitudes

To understand these issues more clearly, some recent researchers have followed Berry's early lead (Berry & Annis, 1974) by surveying the preferences of majority nation respondents as well as those of immigrant groups. Van Oudenhoven, Prins, and Buunk (1998) found that Moroccan and Turkish immigrants in the Netherlands both favoured integration, while majority Dutch respondents favoured assimilation most strongly, but were also favourable to integration. Zagefka and Brown (2002) found that Turks in Germany favoured integration, and that Germans preferred that the Turks integrate. However, the German respondents believed that the Turks preferred separation. In fact, some other studies have found that separation is indeed favoured by Turks in Germany (Piontkowski, Florack, Hoelker, & Obdrzalek, 2000) as well as by lower status Turks in Canada (Ataca & Berry, 2002). German and Israeli majority respondents have been found to favour the integration of ethnic Germans and Jews re-migrating from Russia, respectively, whereas Finns favoured the assimilation of ethnic Finnish returnees (Jasinskaya-Lahti, Liebkind, Horenczyk, & Schmitz, 2003).

An alternative measure of majority preferences has been developed by Bourhis, Moise, Perreault, and Senecal (1997). This measure parallels Berry's four categories, but adds a fifth, individualism. Those who endorse the individualism option would be those who assert that immigrants should be evaluated on the basis of their personal qualities, rather than on the basis of their affiliation with ethnic categories. Using this measure, it has been found that majority preferences also vary, depending upon whether a particular minority is positively valued by the majority. Montreuil and Bourhis (2001) found that French Canadian students endorsed integration and individualism more strongly for European French immigrants, but assimilation, segregation or exclusion more strongly for Haitians. Similarly, Israeli students favoured integration and individualism for Russian and Ethiopian immigrants, but assimilation, segregation or exclusion for Israeli Arabs (Bourhis & Dayan, 2004).

Majority attitudes toward ethnic minorities rest on the degree of perceived difference of the 'other' (Montreuil & Bourhis, 2001), which together with perceived social status of the immigrant group, serves as the basis of an 'ethnic hierarchy' (Schalk-Soekar, Van de Vijver, & Hoogsteder, 2004). In general, the more different an immigrant group is perceived to be, the greater is the rejection of that group. A paradox inherent in integration rather than assimilation is that the maintenance of original cultural features tends to reinforce the immigrant's perceived 'difference' from the majority culture. This is particularly true where religious difference is the case. For example, Islamic schools, dress codes and other religious activities of Muslim immigrants are supported by multicultural policies in many European states, but Muslim immigrants are rejected more when they assume a more overt Muslim identity, often as a consequence of these activities (Kağıtçıbaşı, 1997).

The reciprocal perspective

These variations in minority and majority attitudes indicate that the process of acculturation is best thought of as a specific instance of intergroup relations, rather than as something unique and distinctive (Brown & Zagefka, 2011). This change of conceptualisation has important consequences. For instance, rather than positing that integration is the optimal acculturation strategy, it can be predicted that outcomes will be most favourable when both the minority and majority favour the same acculturation option. Outcomes will be still more positive where each group *perceives* that the other group favours the same option that they themselves favour (Piontkowski, Rohman, & Florack, 2002). This reconceptualisation may help us to understand why integration is not always more strongly associated with positive outcomes.

Zagefka, Brown and their colleagues have made a series of studies in this field, using separate measures of preferred minority group culture maintenance and preferred minority group adoption of majority group practices. These concepts are equivalent to the two components of integration as defined by Berry (1997), but are here treated as separate dimensions. Zagefka and Brown (2002) surveyed majority and minority children in German schools. In both samples, those who favoured integration also perceived current intergroup relations more positively. However, these are correlational results and, as Zagefka and Brown point out, it is just as likely that positive intergroup relations cause a preference for integration, as it is that preference for integration causes better intergroup relations.

As we discussed in relation to the contact hypothesis in Chapter 12, longitudinal studies can address this problem. Zagefka, Binder, and Brown (2010) surveyed large samples of majority and minority adults in Belgium, Germany and the UK, repeating their measurements after six months. A desire by majority members for minority culture maintenance led to less negative emotions toward the minority over time. A desire for the adoption of majority group practices led to more negative emotion among the majority, but reduced negative emotion among the minority. Thus it is possible to identify the causal direction of changes over time, but these changes turn out to be complex and do not simply favour integration (see also Binder et al., 2009, featured in Chapter 12). Since the reactions of both minority and majority group members are likely to be most directly influenced by their perceptions of what the other party favours, it may clarify the results if this aspect is measured directly.

Zagefka et al. (2010) did also ask their respondents for their perceptions of the other party's acculturation preferences. They then computed an index of the fit between own and other party's preference. Fit on preference for the adoption of majority group practices was found to be a significant predictor of more positive intergroup emotion over time, while fit on preference for the maintenance of minority group culture over time had no effect. Further progress in this field will require clarification of why some types of fit are predictive while others are not, and what are the best ways to measure fit.

Measurement Issues

While Berry's typology of strategies does capture key aspects of the immigration experience, a second aspect of current debate on its validity concerns how these orientations may best be validly measured. The four acculturation strategies have typically been assessed by asking respondents to what extent they agree with a series of statements, each of which includes *both* of the elements that define that strategy. For instance, one of the statements used by Montreuil and Bourhis (2001) was, 'Immigrants should maintain their own heritage culture while also adopting the Quebecois culture'. This was one of three statements that the authors used to measure preference for integration. Items like this contain two separate elements, a conflation which poses difficulties for respondents, since they may agree with one half more than with the other half. Overlap between the questions defining each strategy also means that the measures are not independent of one another (Rudmin, 2009).

Items representing marginalisation are even more problematic, because they ask respondents whether or not they agree with two negative statements that take the form, 'Immigrants should not do X and they should not do Y'. In some languages, like Mandarin, one indicates agreement with a negatively worded question by saying 'Yes', but in others including English, one would indicate agreement by saying 'No'. For instance, an English speaker would answer 'Should Muslim immigrants not have Islamic schools?' with 'No', if they agreed that they should not. The scope for confusion is evident. Sampling Turkish Dutch school children as well as adults, Arends-Toth and Van de Vijver (2007) compared the predictive ability of measures of this type with simplified measures that asked one question at a time. The simplified items proved more psychometrically satisfactory.

Berry and Sabatier (2011) have further advanced the utilisation of simpler measures by comparing the predictive validity in France and in Canada of three measures of minority respondents' preference for involvement in one's own culture and three measures of preference for involvement in the majority culture. The first pair of measures concerned culture maintenance and *adoption* of the majority culture, the second pair concerned contact with the minority and *contact* with the majority, and the last pair concerned minority identity and majority *identity*. These differing ways of operationalising acculturation attitudes yielded very different percentages of persons classified as holding an integration attitude. In a similar way, Ward and Kus (in press) found that among minority respondents in New Zealand integration was much more strongly favoured when defined in terms of contact than when defined in terms of adoption of the majority culture.

If acculturation orientations can now be more validly measured, this still leaves us with a second measurement problem, which has to do with defining exactly what psychological component is distinctive to the acculturation process. Most typically, measures of reported behaviours or reported stress have been employed. However, many other aspects of life are associated with changing levels of these types of indices. Consequently, if we wish to determine what is specifically associated with acculturation, we have three options. Firstly, we could make studies that include control groups of non-migrants. Secondly, we could include statistical controls derived from reports by members of groups in society who are not migrants but who are members of equivalent ethnic or socio-economic groups. These types of controls have not often been included in studies. The third option is to focus attention on acculturating groups over time, so as to determine what causes increases or decreases in the dependent measures that are employed, as has been done on the studies of the contact hypothesis discussed in Chapter 12.

Non-migrant controls

Georgas et al. (1996) administered a measure of endorsement of family values to urban and rural Greeks, Greeks who had migrated to Germany, the Netherlands and Canada, and to English Canadians. Family values were most endorsed by the Greeks, especially those still in Greece, and least endorsed by the European Canadians. Younger respondents in all samples endorsed family values less strongly. Greeks who had migrated to Canada showed a stronger retention of family values than those who had migrated to Germany or the Netherlands. This confirmed the prediction by Georgas et al. that, because Canadian government policy favours integration, values of the heritage culture would be more strongly retained there.

Ataca and Berry (2004) surveyed Turkish married couples in Turkey and in Canada, as well as Canadian married couples. The Turkish couples in Canada favoured separation (from Canadian culture, not from each other!). They scored lower on measures of both psychological and sociocultural adaptation than did the Canadian couples, and unsurprisingly were also lower on sociocultural adaptation than the couples back in Turkey. The integration strategy was shown to be a significant predictor of high socio-cultural adaptation, while marginalisation predicted poor psychological adaptation. This study is of particular value because it focuses upon couples, and family relations are frequently important in providing a secure base within which familiar languages and practices can be sustained during the acculturation process, as we shall see in a later section.

Perceived discrimination

Not all migrants find the process stressful. The experience of discrimination is associated with stress, whether among migrants or among non-migrants. For instance, in a large Swedish study that included both migrants and non-migrants, Wamala, Bostrom, and Nyquist (2007) found that the experience of humiliation and low socio-economic status were the strongest predictors of stress indicators for both groups. In a study of ethnic minority youth in 13 nations, perceived discrimination was a much stronger predictor of poor mental health, low self-esteem and low life satisfaction than were acculturation styles (Vedder, Van de Vijver, & Liebkind, 2006). Thus acculturation stress may be attributable to those migrants who enter low status roles where they experience discrimination. Migration is a distal cause and discrimination is a proximal cause of stress.

ACCULTURATION PROCESSES

The preceding emphasis on contrasts in majority and minority attitudes towards migrants make it clear that it is preferable to think of acculturation in terms of intergroup relations. Doing so is consistent with the perspective that we have argued for in preceding chapters: we cannot adequately analyse cultural processes if we ignore the context within which they occur. In the sections that follow, we simplify the situation by focusing in turn on the perspectives of majority groups and minority groups, but we first acknowledge that the situation is often more complex than that implied by such a simple split. In many nations there are numerous differing minority groups, and in locations such as South Africa, Israel, some of the states in the Persian gulf, and the south-western United States, minorities are actually a numerical majority. In some of these locations, particular groups are not faced with a simple choice as to whether to sustain links with their culture of origin or to seek links with the majority: in Israel, for instance, religious affiliations and ethnic affiliations are interwoven in a way that poses dilemmas to groups with multiple minority status. Horenczyk and Munayer (2007) clarified this situation by obtaining measures not only of group members' preferred strategies, but also of their perceptions of what other groups wanted them to do. They studied Christian Arabs, who preferred separation from Muslim Arabs, but whom they perceived as wanting them to integrate or assimilate. Conversely, Christian Arabs favoured integration with the Jewish population, but perceived Jews as preferring separation from them. In a social nexus, one's options are not only a matter of one's own preferences, they are also constrained by what members of the various other groups prefer.

A second caution is also in order. Many of the migrants in the contemporary world move from a collectivistic culture to a richer, more individualistic one. We have only fragmentary information about the processes involved in migration in the reverse direction, or between nations that are relatively similar in their levels of individualism or collectivism. The processes involved in these types of context may have similar components, but there are likely to be substantial differences as well, given the varying range of motives for these different types of migration.

In the preceding chapter, we examined intergroup relations in terms that were derived from social identity theory (Tajfel & Turner, 1979) as well as integrated threat theory (Stephan & Stephan, 1996). We now use these frameworks to analyse the processes that occur in nations receiving substantial numbers of migrants (for a more extensive discussion, see S. J. Schwartz, Vignoles, Brown, & Zagefka, in press).

THE MAJORITY PERSPECTIVE

As we discussed in Chapter 12, social identity theory predicts that people will experience identity threat (and thus engage in identity maintenance strategies) to the extent that the *positive distinctiveness* of their social identities is undermined by a given situation (Tajfel & Turner, 1979).

This suggests that members of a nation's majority group will feel threatened if the image of their nation is insufficiently positive and distinctive in relation to relevant comparison groups. In terms of the identity motives that we considered in Chapter 7, people would be expected to engage in identity maintenance strategies in situations where their nation is compared with a higher-status outgroup (undermining self-esteem) or with a group that is highly similar to their own (undermining distinctiveness). Hence, members of higher-status cultural groups would be expected to avoid such comparisons by preserving the lower status of minority groups in their society and by maintaining clear boundaries between their own and different groups. This implies that powerful majority groups will typically favour a separationist acculturation strategy for minority groups, thus maintaining their group's distinctiveness (by making boundaries impermeable) and positive evaluation (by reasserting their higher status). Salient historical examples of this intergroup dynamic include segregation in the United States, and apartheid in South Africa. This could also account for the prevalence of rhetorical demands for the deportation of migrant groups in numerous contemporary societies.

In direct contrast with social identity theory, integrated threat theory proposes that people will feel especially threatened by groups that are different from, rather than similar to, their own group (e.g., Stephan, Ybarra, & Bachman, 1999). Indeed, in most contemporary multicultural societies, the behaviour of cultural majorities does not match the pattern predicted by social identity theory. Seemingly against the interests of preserving positive group distinctiveness, cultural majorities are typically more comfortable with the presence of relatively *high*-status minority groups, especially those that are *similar* to themselves in their practices and values. In contrast, cultural majorities show greater hostility toward those minorities that they perceive as *dis*similar to themselves, and often favour these groups adopting an assimilationist acculturation strategy, making them more similar to the mainstream culture. Examples of these perceptions on the part of receiving-society members are evident in a number of countries, for

Figure 13.4 I'll help you back

Source: San Diego Union Tribune newspaper (1994). Reproduced by permission of U-T SanDiego.

instance in Canada (Berry & Kalin, 1995). Similarly, in many European nations, migration by other Europeans is not viewed as a threat, but migration by individuals from outside the European Union, and especially Muslims, is viewed negatively by many Europeans (Licata, Sanchez-Mazas, & Green, 2011).

These findings are difficult to reconcile with the original version of social identity theory. If members of cultural majorities are primarily concerned with maintaining the positive distinctiveness of their ethnic/cultural groups, we should expect more frequent segregationist social policies, in which cultural minorities would be encouraged to maintain their different (and supposedly 'inferior') cultural practices, beliefs and values in order to highlight the distinctiveness and superiority of the cultural majority. So why does this not happen?

A possible explanation is that, from the perspective of cultural majority members, immigrant minorities are not simply members of a cultural *out*-group: they are also members of the national *in*-group. Therefore, what is at stake here is not just the competitive *inter*group relations between *ethno-cultural* groups, but also the *intra*group processes of negotiating the meaning and boundaries of membership in a common *national* group. Viewed from a purely inter-ethnic perspective, immigrant minorities might simply be seen as out-group members, different and perhaps inferior, but certainly not threatening. However, viewed within the context of national identity, cultural minorities have the status of in-group members, whose presence has the potential to transform the meaning of national membership.

Research into intra-group dynamics (e.g., Marques, Abrams, & Serodio, 2001) has shown very clearly that in-group members who deviate from group norms are evaluated much more harshly than are out-group members who display the same characteristics or behaviours (the so-called 'black-sheep effect'). The black-sheep effect is understood to occur because the opinions or practices of the deviant individual threaten to undermine the group identity in question. Thus, once immigrant minorities are evaluated in terms of their status as national in-group members rather than as cultural out-group members, it is much easier to understand why minorities who are more different would be perceived by majorities as more threatening, and why majority members might seek to protect their national identity by pressuring minority members to conform with national group norms (an assimilationist policy).

Beyond the focus on self-esteem and distinctiveness implicit in social identity theory, another identity motive, the need for continuity, seems highly relevant to these processes. Over and above motives for self-esteem and for distinctiveness, people are typically motivated to maintain a sense of connection between past, present, and future in their personal and group identities (Sani, 2008; Vignoles, 2011: see also Chapter 7). This concern shifts the motivational emphasis away from social comparison of one's group with other competing groups towards a focus on temporal comparison between past, present, and possible future identities of one's own group. To what extent does the inclusion of cultural minorities *change* (or threaten to change) the perceived meaning of national group membership? To what extent can such perceived changes be reconciled with the historical roots of the national identity in question, or is that identity perceived as changed beyond recognition? This suggests that cultural majorities will feel most threatened to the extent that they believe that the existence of their in-group *per se* is endangered, for example following large waves of migration or in situations where there is a perceived danger of a 'hostile takeover', potentially resulting in the in-group as they know it ceasing to exist (González et al., 2008; Wohl, Branscombe, & Reysen, 2010). Potent current examples include anxiety about the Spanish language as a threat to the place of English as the official language of the United States (Barker et al., 2001), and about Muslim religious practices in Europe (Licata et al., 2011).

In this section, we have examined the attitudes of majority groups toward minorities as though these attitudes are equally endorsed by all majority group members and in all nations. In practice, nations differ both because of the migrants they receive and because of differing government policies toward immigration. Furthermore, some members of majority groups are more hostile to immigrants than others. In Chapter 12, we have already explored the predictors of individual-level variations in prejudice toward out-groups. The nation-level perspective helps us to understand the challenges posed by contemporary multicultural societies. Studies focused at the individual level provide the optimal basis for understanding how best psychologists can address specific problems.

THE MINORITY PERSPECTIVE

The low status position of many migrant groups in their host cultures is also a likely source of identity threat, potentially frustrating several identity motives. *Self-esteem* is threatened among migrants by the low status they typically occupy. This may be especially problematic for migrants from collectivist cultural backgrounds, given the high value and emphasis placed on hierarchy and social status in traditionally collectivist cultures (e.g., Hofstede, 1980). Feelings of *efficacy* are also likely to be undermined by occupying a low status position, which can lead to feelings of helplessness or incompetence, and perhaps especially among migrant men, who often find it harder to find employment than migrant women, thereby failing to fulfil their expected gender role as family breadwinner. Lower-status groups are often unwanted and derogated in the receiving society (Kosic & Phalet, 2006), and this experience of social rejection is likely to frustrate their identity motive for *belonging*.

However, an additional pressure is placed on many acculturating minority groups by assimilationist policies in their receiving nations, which typically ask them to shed or change important aspects of their ethnocultural identities in order to gain acceptance by the majority group. Such policies have become increasingly prevalent in Western Europe (and to a lesser extent in North America) in recent years, fuelled in part by terrorist attacks by radical Islamists. Assimilationist pressures from the majority, even when these are well-intentioned, aim by definition to reduce the *distinctiveness* of the minority group's identity (Berry, 1997). These policies and pressures require significant and often unwanted cultural change by the minority, potentially undermining feelings of collective *continuity* (Chandler et al., 2003). As a result of these changes, members of minority groups may often end up uncertain of what it means to be a member of their group in the larger national context where they reside, and this uncertainty may undermine the sense of *meaning* that minority group members might otherwise derive from their cultural-group identity.

Thus, Licata et al. (2011) characterise the situation of cultural minorities as a 'struggle for recognition'. In addition to a need for recognition in terms of material resources and social status, Licata et al. argue that minority group members need to have their cultural identities acknowledged and supported by the cultural majority if their successful integration into mainstream society is to be possible. Paradoxically, assimilationist policies and pressures often have the *opposite* effect to that which was intended (minority groups may resist identifying with the majority cultural group). This response has been labeled as **reactive ethnicity** (Rumbaut, 2008; see also Yang & Bond, 1980), and we shall return to this intergroup dynamic in the forthcoming sections.

Coping with Cultural Identity Threat

Social identity theory (Tajfel & Turner, 1989) specifies three types of strategies that people can use to establish or restore a satisfactory social identity when such an identity is lacking: individual mobility, social competition, and social creativity. Although social identity theory focuses on positive group distinctiveness, these strategies may also help with re-establishing satisfaction of the motives for efficacy, belonging, continuity, and meaning (Vignoles, 2011). Viewing the acculturation styles of migrants as strategies for coping with identity threats can help to explain which styles they adopt, as well as the emergence of more complex and diverse strategies than the four possibilities initially identified by Berry (1997).

Individual mobility

This is a strategy where a person attempts to become, or be accepted as, a member of the higher-status group, and is analogous to assimilation within Berry's (1997) typology. To the extent that their physical features and foreign accents will allow, migrants may try to 'pass as' majority group members. However, 'passing' is not available to visible- and auditory-minority individuals. Indeed, even those who were born into the society of settlement and speak the native language without an accent may be treated as foreigners, a phenomenon that Wu (2001) refers to as *perpetual foreigner syndrome* (see also Huynh, Devos, & Smalarz, 2011). Wu describes experiences of being asked where he was from and what life in China was like, even though he was born and raised in the United States and had never been to China. Perpetual foreigner syndrome is a subtle, and often unintended, form of discrimination, but it reminds the person that she or he is not considered to belong to the receiving society. Hence, individual mobility is rarely an option for individuals who can be classified either visually or by their accents into a migrant or minority group.

In some cases, migrants may also be mistaken for native minorities to whom they are physically similar: for example, Haitian and West Indian immigrants to the United States are often treated as though they were African American (Waters, 1994). As a result, these migrants are likely to be exposed to African American culture more than to the majority culture. More generally, migrants will often settle in inner-city areas, where they are likely to have more contact with other migrants, as well as members of ethnic minorities, than with majority group members.

This can lead to **segmented assimilation** (Portes & Zhou, 1993), whereby members of migrant groups (especially in the second generation) will often adopt the cultural characteristics of the native ethnic groups to whom they are most similar, or with whom they have the most

Reactive Ethnicity
Reactive Ethnicity is an assertion of one's minority ethnicity in reaction to assimilationist pressures or policies.

Segmented Assimilation
Segmented Assimilation occurs when a migrant is assimilated into an existing ethnic minority group rather than into the majority group.

contact, rather than engaging in acculturation processes and strategies in relation to the majority culture, as has been more commonly assumed in the acculturation literature. For example, US Hispanic adolescents will often use 'African American vernacular English' rather than standard American, and assimilate toward African American rather than White American practices and values (Stepick, Dutton Stepick, et al., 2001).

Segmented assimilation is an example of how acculturation can provide many more options than just the four possibilities shown in Figure 13.2. However, assimilating toward a given native ethnic group may have complex implications for power and social status within the receiving society: for example, although African American music and other forms of entertainment have achieved worldwide popularity, the use of African American vernacular English is associated with educational disadvantages and social exclusion (Labov, 2010). Notwithstanding these potential disadvantages, assimilation into an ethnic culture that is more established and more prevalent than one's culture of origin may provide more opportunity to use additional strategies for identity maintenance, which we discuss next.

Social competition

When individual mobility is not a viable option, social identity theory predicts that members of disadvantaged groups will use group-based strategies to establish positive distinctiveness, either by engaging directly in *social competition* with the majority group or by using *social creativity* to reframe the social comparison in more positive ways. In terms of Berry's (1997) model, both strategies involve maintaining the identification with one's culture of origin: hence, they will typically be linked to the acculturation styles of integration or separation. However, from a social identity perspective, it is likely that migrants whose identities are under threat, and are unable to engage in individual mobility, will actually increase the identification with their cultural groups. This is the reactive ethnicity phenomenon that Rumbaut (2008) has discussed, where migrants show a heightened attachment to their cultural groups as a consequence of an actual or perceived rejection by the dominant group.

In a similar vein, Branscombe, Schmitt, and Harvey (1999) found that perceptions of discrimination led to heightened ethnic identification among African Americans, and that this ethnic identification in turn gave rise to greater well-being, thereby buffering the otherwise negative implications of perceiving oneself to be a victim of discrimination. Similar effects were found among Muslim women in New Zealand (Jasperse, Ward, & Jose, 2012). Women among the sample who wore *hijab* dress perceived greater discrimination, but had higher life satisfaction and fewer symptoms of stress.

Given that migrant groups are typically in a disadvantaged position in material as well as symbolic terms, direct competition with the majority group is often very difficult, especially if 'success' is measured in terms of re-establishing a positive distinctiveness. Nevertheless, the increasing academic achievement of Asian Americans is one example of a minority group competing successfully to achieve positive distinctiveness, even in terms of the values of the majority, and this positive distinctiveness seems to be increasingly emphasised in Asian Americans' discourse about the meaning of their own cultural identity (i.e., the 'model minority' stereotype; Chua, 2011).

Social creativity

As an alternative to direct competition, members of minority groups may re-establish their cultural identities through various forms of *social creativity*, essentially reinterpreting the situation so that their group is no longer perceived in negative terms. One approach is to change the frame of reference for social comparison: if one belongs to a low status group, one might compare one's group with other low-status minorities, rather than comparing with the majority group, or one might isolate one's group in order to avoid intergroup comparison entirely and focus only on intragroup comparisons. Another option is to change the basis of comparison. For instance, as we discussed in Chapter 12, Poppe and Linssen (1999) found that children in nations in Central and Eastern Europe saw members of Western nations as more competent but themselves as more moral.

One salient way of avoiding comparisons with the majority group is to adopt a separationist acculturation strategy, or even to live in ethnic enclaves where the migrant group has a greater amount of social and political power. For example, in cities such as Bradford (UK), Marseille (France), and Miami (USA), migrants and their immediate descendants comprise considerable proportions of the population, and these cities are home to large ethnic enclaves dominated by migrant cultures. Adult migrants settling in these enclaves can live their daily lives without learning the language or adopting other cultural practices of the larger country to which they have migrated (S.J. Schwartz, Pantin, et al., 2006; Caldwell, 2008). Ethnic enclaves in these and other cities are often large enough that minority groups can challenge policies and decisions enacted by the larger nation in which the enclave is located, especially when they are granted the right to vote.

Migrants can also engage in group-based identity management strategies from the position of their new ethnic group, following a strategy of segmented assimilation. Especially for members of the smallest groups, identifying with a larger 'pan-ethnic' group (e.g., Hispanics in the United States, Muslims in Europe, Chinese in Australia) can provide greater opportunities for collective action or 'voice' than would otherwise be possible from the position of one's group of origin. For example, French Muslims in Islamic enclaves around Paris have protested, sometimes violently and occasionally effectively, against various laws and policies that have been enacted by the local and national governments (Caldwell, 2008).

It is important to recognise that intragroup dynamics within migrant communities play a key role here, not just intergroup relations with the majority. Group leaders may sometimes act as 'entrepreneurs of identity', advocating a version of social reality that makes particular social categories salient, or that emphasises particular intergroup contrasts and thus defines the in-group in a way that suits their personal goals or interests (Reicher & Hopkins, 1996; Reicher, Haslam, & Hopkins, 2005). Just as leaders within the majority community may attempt to sway public opinion by portraying migrants as a threat to the larger society, leaders within the migrant community may also seek to gain favourable social positions by denigrating or vilifying the majority ethnic group.

The distinction between the individual (i.e., mobility) and collective (i.e., social competition and creativity) strategies of identity management discussed above may seem reminiscent of the early, unidimensional view of acculturation as a straightforward choice between assimilation and separation. It may seem to point toward a relatively bleak view as to possible outcomes of the acculturation process. However, more radical forms of social creativity are also possible, involving the creation of new and hybridised forms of social identity, as suggested by the acculturation style of integration. In the next section, we discuss some of the complexities of adopting a bicultural identity.

BICULTURALISM

As we have noted earlier in this chapter, integration (which we now refer to by the more precise term biculturalism) has been treated implicitly or explicitly by most researchers as the most adaptive acculturation style, despite continuing evidence that a more complex view is required. On the surface biculturalism may seem the obviously preferable strategy, offering the 'best of both worlds' to the acculturating migrant. However, a bicultural migrant may often become caught between two worlds. Although social identity theory itself has little to say about these issues, subsequent research within the social identity tradition may be helpful in understanding some of the barriers to adopting a bicultural or integrated acculturation style, as well as some of the pitfalls for those who do adopt such an approach.

Earlier in this chapter, we noted the possibility of predicting an acculturation outcome on the basis of examining the fit between majority and minority acculturation preferences (Piontkowski et al., 2002; Brown & Zagefka, 2011). Biculturalism may be especially difficult to achieve in situations where there is a majority preference for migrants to assimilate. When assimilationist expectations are present, the distinctiveness and continuity of the migrant group's cultural identity are threatened (Sam & Berry, 2010). Hence, not only will the majority group be sensitive to behaviour by an individual migrant that might suggest that he or she is 'not one of us', but the minority group will also be especially sensitised towards behaviour that deviates from *their* cultural norms, and they may potentially reject or punish individuals who exhibit signs of biculturalism in order to protect the distinctiveness and continuity of their group membership. Thus, as Berry memorably put it, the 'Melting Pot … becomes more like a Pressure Cooker' (1997: 10).

Migrants may react to such stressful receiving contexts by withdrawing from the larger society altogether and interacting mostly with other members of their ethnic group, or with members of other minority groups, in ethnic enclaves, as we discussed earlier. Nonetheless, there is another sense in which almost every migrant has to be bicultural, at least to some extent. In most cases, majority group members expect migrants to adopt at least some of the aspects of the receiving culture (Piontkowski et al., 2002; Rohmann, Florack, & Piontkowski, 2006). Moreover, most migrants typically do elect to preserve their cultural heritage in their homes, at least to some extent, and to transmit this heritage to their children (e.g., Umaña-Taylor, Bhanot, & Shin, 2006).

Therefore, most migrants and their children must straddle at least two cultures: their heritage culture in the home (and perhaps in their ethnic community), and the receiving culture outside the home (Arends-Tóth & Van de Vijver, 2007). Of course, the extent to which migrants must interact with the receiving culture depends on the extent to which they reside in ethnic enclaves that insulate them from the larger society, and some adults who settle in ethnic enclaves and who do not attend formal schooling in the society of settlement may have little or no involvement with the receiving culture (S.J. Schwartz, Pantin, et al., 2006). Nevertheless, in most cases, migrants must reconcile, or at least balance, their 'heritage' and 'receiving' cultures.

The outcome of this balancing act depends on the context in which it occurs. Baysu, Phalet, and Brown (2011) asked young Turkish adults in Belgium to rate how much discrimination they had experienced in school. Respondents were classified into one or other of Berry's (1997) acculturation styles on the basis of how strongly they identified with being Belgian and how strongly they identified with being Turkish. It was found that among those who had experienced low discrimination, respondents with an integrated acculturation style had the greatest subsequent academic success. However, among those who had experienced high discrimination, assimilationists and separatists had done better.

> **Bicultural Identity Integration**
> Bicultural Identity Integration is the merging rather than the separation of alternative ethnic identities of bicultural persons.

As we saw in Chapter 7, adjusting one's identity to fit with the setting in which one is currently located is particularly characteristic of persons from collectivist cultures. This may be less easily accomplished within more individualistic cultures, where behavioural consistency is more highly esteemed. Thus, perhaps especially if they are living in individualist societies, biculturals may cope most effectively with the demands of living in a multicultural society by finding ways of integrating rather than separating their alternative identities. Take a look at Key Research Study 13.1, which investigates **bicultural identity integration (BII)**.

Key Researcher Box 13.2   Veronica Benet-Martinez

Figure 13.5   Veronica Benet-Martinez

Veronica Benet-Martinez (b. 1966) grew up in the Catalan region of Spain. She completed her Bachelor's degree in psychology at the Universitat Autonoma de Barcelona in 1989, and her PhD in social/personality psychology at the University of California at Davis in 1995. She then held positions at the University of California, Berkeley, the University of Michigan, and the University of California, Riverside. In 2010, she was appointed research professor in the Department of Social and Political Sciences at Pompeu Fabra University in Barcelona, Spain. She has conducted studies in the fields of culture and personality constructs, cultural transmission through social symbols, and dynamic models of identity. She has also pioneered the concept of bicultural identity integration.

BII has been shown to have predictive validity in additional cultural settings, and improved measures have been developed, as shown in Research Instrument Box 13.1 (Huynh, Nguyen, & Benet-Martinez, 2011). S.X. Chen, Benet-Martinez, and Bond (2008) sampled mainland Chinese migrants and Filipino sojourners in Hong Kong, as well as student sojourners there. Indices of successful adjustment for migrants (but not for sojourners) were predicted by BII, as well as by bilingual competence, after controlling for personality differences.

Key Research Study Box 13.1   Bicultural Identity Integration

Given the increasing frequency of biculturalism in many nations, Benet-Martinez and her colleagues (Benet-Martinez, Leu, Lee, & Morris, 2002) were interested in alternative ways of handling bicultural identities. How does someone think and feel if they perceive their identities as incompatible with one another? Do compatible identities facilitate cultural integration? Can experimental methods illuminate these issues? The authors tested two main hypotheses about how Chinese Americans, who are low versus high on identity integration, respond when faced with an attribution task. Firstly, because their identities are not in conflict, those who are high on identity integration were expected to respond to a US prime by making the more internal attributions that are typical of Americans, and to a Chinese prime by making the more external attributions that are typical of Chinese. Secondly, and in contrast, because of the identity conflict that they experience, respondents low in identity integration were expected to respond defensively, making external attributions in response to the US primes and internal attributions in response to the Chinese primes.

The sample was split between those who were low or high on bicultural identity integration (BII). The primes were either American (e.g., Mickey Mouse, a cowboy, the Statue of Liberty), Chinese (e.g., the Summer Palace in Beijing, a rice farmer, the Great Wall), or control items unrelated to culture. Participants first received one of these primes and then viewed a series of videos showing a fish moving ahead of a group of other fish that was used by Morris and Peng (1994), discussed in Chapter 6. They were asked to rate the extent to which 'the one fish is being influenced by the group (e.g., being chased, teased or pressured by others' and to rate the extent to which 'the one fish is influenced by some internal trait (such as independence, personal objective or leadership)'. Next, each participant was asked to make a single rating of the extent to which they perceived themselves as a Chinese person who lives in America, rather than as a Chinese American. This provided a measure distinguishing between low and high bicultural identity integration. Finally, participants also completed the measure of Berry's (1997) four acculturation modes.

The predictions were supported. The left-hand side of Figure 13.6 indicates the results for respondents with low bicultural identity integration (BII). They show the reverse pattern of attributions from those that were found by Hong et al. (2000). With the Chinese prime they made more internal attributions and with the American prime they made more external attributions. In contrast the results for the respondents with high BII shown on the right of the figure replicate the results of Hong et al., as shown earlier in Figure 6.5. Despite the differing effects for high and low identity integration, both groups scored equally high on Berry's measure of integration.

This study indicates that the concept of bicultural identity integration can advance our understanding of the processes of acculturation. Berry's favoured concept of the integration mode of acculturation is broadly defined and can encompass quite different types of bicultural person. Someone with low bicultural integration is in some ways like a person who can speak two languages fluently. Whichever language or identity they choose to express at a particular time, they place themselves on the outside of the other identity.

The study by Benet Martinez et al. supports the view that low BII persons feel the need to compensate for that outsiderness. So, a low BII Chinese American responds to a Chinese prime by emphasising his or her Americanness, and to an American prime by emphasising his or her Chineseness. A high BII person does not feel the need to show this reactance or ethnic affirmation, and such accommodation facilitates their relations with others. For instance, in later studies by the same group, Mok, Morris, Benet-Martinez, and Karakitapoglu-Aygun (2007) showed that high BII Chinese Americans tended to have networks of friends of varying ethnicity, many of whom also knew each other. Those with low BII had separate networks of friends who did not know each other.

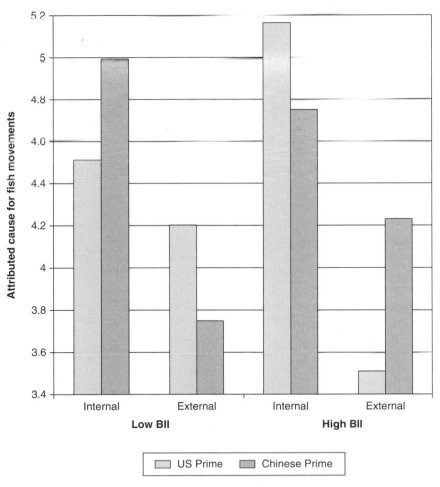

Figure 13.6   Attributions made by Biculturals High and Low in Identity Integration (based on Benet-Martinez et al., 2002)

Research Instrument Box 13.1   Bicultural Identity Integration

The Bicultural Identity Integration Scale Version 2 now comprises 19 items measuring two different components. Example items for each component are shown below:

Blendedness versus Compartmentalisation

1 I feel _____ and American at the same time.
2 I do not blend my _____ and American cultures. (reverse scored)

Harmony versus Conflict

3 I find it easy to harmonise _____ and American cultures.
4 I feel that my _____ and American cultures are incompatible. (reverse scored)

In a further study, S.X. Chen, Benet-Martinez, Wu et al. (2013) compared migrant and non-migrant samples in Hong Kong. In both types of sample, BII was a significant predictor of measures of psychological adjustment. Respondents also completed a measure of dialectical self-construal (Spencer-Rodgers, Boucher, Mori et al., 2009): this refers to the tendency among members of collectivistic cultures to be more tolerant of contradictions in how they see themselves (see Chapter 7). Although dialectical self-construal is more strongly endorsed in collectivist cultures, it has been shown to be linked with poor adjustment in both Anglo and Chinese US samples (English & S. Chen, 2007). S.X. Chen et al. found that among their non-migrant Hong Kong sample dialectical self-construal wholly mediated the effect of BII on adjustment: in other words, in non-migrant samples, BII does not detect significant issues additional to those tapped by other measures associated with poor adjustment. In contrast, among samples of migrants from mainland China and of Filipino sojourners, the authors found a different result. Here, both BII and dialectical self-construal explained separate amounts of variance in poor adjustment: in other words, BII did capture some of the distinctive difficulties faced by the migrants and sojourners who were sampled.

Adjustment to biculturalism can occur over long time periods. One of the most critical points in the acculturation process is the boundary between immigrant parents and their children. While separation may be preferred at least in the home domain, schooling prepares students for social and economic participation in the wider society and provides an incentive toward more comprehensive assimilation or integration. Phalet and Schonpflug (2001) showed that immigrant parents were more successful in transmitting their beliefs about the importance of education to their children in Germany than in the Netherlands. Across samples of Turkish migrants in Germany and the Netherlands and Moroccan migrants in the Netherlands, the extent to which parents endorsed collectivist values was relatively successfully transmitted to their children, whereas the extent to which they endorsed individualist values was not. Knafo and Schwartz (2001) compared the similarity between the values of adolescents and their parents within demographically matched samples of immigrant and non-immigrant families in Israel. Values differed more between adolescents and their parents in the immigrant families, but there was no difference between the samples in the accuracy with which the adolescents perceived what their parents' values were. Thus, the divergence in values cannot be attributed to parents' failure to communicate their values. Alternative socialisation processes must be implicated.

The key role of second generation youth in the acculturation process led a group of researchers to initiate the International Comparative Survey of Ethno-Cultural Youth, sampling several immigrant groups within each of 13 nations (Berry, Phinney, Sam, & Vedder, 2006). Analysing data from this project, Phinney and Vedder (2006) showed that the discrepancy between the views of adolescents and their parents on family obligations was significantly greater in immigrant families than in majority culture families. Furthermore, among the minority families, these differences were greatest where the adolescents endorsed assimilation and least where they endorsed separation. Conversely, the differences were greatest where the parents endorsed separation. Larger differences also predicted poor psychological and sociocultural adaptation.

A further stage in the process of cultural retention or loss is illustrated by a study comparing the mate preferences of South Asians born in Canada with Euro-Canadians. The South Asians had a significantly stronger preference for attributes traditionally favoured in India, namely good social class, family reputation, dowry, parental approval, and association with persons from the same caste (Lalonde, Hynie, Pannu, & Tatla, 2004). A preference for these attributes was mediated by the respondent's level of interdependent self-construal, being stronger the more interdependent the respondent. Within the South Asian sample a preference for these traditional qualities was also predicted by a measure of family connectedness.

In a study that also emphasised the role of the family, Rosenthal and Feldman (1992) contrasted first, second, and third generation Chinese migrants to Australia and the USA, including in addition a control group in Hong Kong. Maintenance of Chinese cultural practices within the family declined in the first generation of migrants, but fell no further in later generations, whereas ethnic identification did not fall at all. This set of findings is consistent with an integration strategy, with the maintenance of Chinese culture in private settings and the adoption of local practices in public settings, although this study included no actual measure of acculturation strategies.

Detailed analyses of conversations within multigenerational Chinese families in New Zealand give further clues as to some of the ways in which an intergenerational balance can be achieved. Ng, He, and Loong (2004) identified instances of what they called 'brokering': in other words, communications that encourage members of the family to speak in a language that the other party can understand. Typically, a child might describe in English an achievement one day at school. The parent would then encourage the child to explain the achievement to a grandparent in Chinese, so that it could be shared with all. In an earlier study, Ng, Loong, He et al. (2004) showed that in families with a shorter history in New Zealand, there was a greater proportion of remarks addressed to the family as a whole, whereas in families with a longer history in New Zealand the proportion of remarks addressed to individuals was greater. Thus, the overall process of acculturation is marked and sometimes fostered by subtle differences in communication patterns.

Other factors may also be associated with progress toward sociocultural adaptation, although it is difficult to know whether they are best thought of as contributing to its cause or as one of its consequences. Kurman and Ronen-Eilon (2004) tested the extent to which a knowledge of majority Israeli beliefs, as measured by Leung and Bond's (2004) Social Axioms Survey, predicted the socio-cultural adaptation of Ethiopian and Russian immigrants in Israel. Interestingly, positive adaptation was more strongly predicted by the difference between immigrants' beliefs and beliefs that immigrants *attributed* to the majority than by the actual differences between their beliefs.

Who Does the Acculturating?

In evaluating what acculturation researchers have achieved, it is useful to think back to Redfield et al.'s (1936) definition of acculturation. This specified that acculturation involved changes in either or both of the cultural groups in contact. Acculturation research to date has focused almost entirely on the changes made by immigrants. So in what way have majority populations changed in response to increased ethnic heterogeneity? We have reviewed some evidence in this chapter that majority members sometimes feel that their national identities are under threat from the presence of immigrants. In the next chapter, we discuss evidence relating to overall changes in national populations, but we currently have little evidence for the influence of multiculturalism on these types of change.

SUMMARY

The study of acculturation has until recently been hindered by a lack of clarity in conceptualisation and the use of measures with weak validity. There is modest empirical support for the prediction that integration and biculturalism have more positive outcomes for migrants than assimilation or separation. The experiences of migrants are best understood in terms of theories of intergroup relations, the multiple factors influencing majority and minority group attitudes toward one another, and the resulting identities that are consequently available to migrants of various ethnicities. The concept of bicultural identity integration provides a basis for understanding successful migrant acculturation. Acculturation poses continuing intergenerational dilemmas, which can be more or less acute, depending on factors such as the distance between migrant and host ethnicities, the presence of ethnic enclaves, and variations in governmental policies toward migrants.

FURTHER READING

1 Berry, J.W. (1997). Immigration, acculturation and adaptation. *Applied Psychology: An International Review, 46*, 5–34.
2 Brown, R.J., & Zagefka, H. (2011). The dynamics of acculturation: An intergroup perspective. In J. Olson & M. Zanna (Eds), *Advances in experimental social psychology* (Vol. 44, pp. 129–184). Burlington, MA: Academic Press.
3 Celenk, O., & Van de Vijver, F. (2011). Assessment of acculturation: Issues and overview of measures. *Online Readings in Psychology and Culture.* Available at http://scholarworks.gvsu.edu/orpc
4 Sam, D., & Berry. J. (Eds) (2006). *The Cambridge handbook of acculturation psychology.* Cambridge, UK: Cambridge University Press.

STUDY QUESTIONS

1 Discuss the identity approach to the analysis of acculturation and assess the evidence in support of this approach.
2 Is it better to measure acculturation in terms of preferences, identities or behaviours? Why?
3 How would you characterise your attitude toward the acculturation of ethnic minorities in the majority culture within which you are located? Why? How is your viewpoint influenced by your own situation as a majority or minority member?
4 What are key aspects of the public discourse about immigration in your nation? How could the research studies cited in this chapter be used to create a better informed public?
5 What are the features of an ideal national immigration policy in light of the current available evidence?

14

Globalisation and Cultural Change

'Change is the only constant.'

(Heraclitus, 5th century BCE)

In preceding chapters, we have explored the processes whereby differing environments and restricted contacts have led to the creation of many cultures in different parts of the world, characterised by differing emphases on a wide variety of social phenomena. In Chapters 12 and 13, we reviewed evidence suggesting that increasing contacts may be pushing us towards developing integrated, multicultural nations rather than hegemonic, mono-cultural nations. However, there is no current consensus that this process is occurring and some hold the contrary belief that current globalisation is generating different cultural adaptations in different regions of the world (Berger & Huntington, 2002). In this chapter, we consider the current evidence for and against claims that people in different parts of the world are currently undergoing a global process of cultural homogenisation.

INDUSTRIALISATION AND MODERNITY

Researchers in the 1960s devoted considerable attention to the study of what they termed **modernity**. Their focus rested upon the imperatives created by the industrialisation and consequent urbanisation of society. For instance, Kerr, Dunlop, Harbison, and Myers asserted that '… the logic of industrialism will eventually lead us all to a common society, where ideology will cease to matter' (1960: 12). In a systematic test of such ideas, Inkeles and Smith (1974) surveyed the presence of 'modern' attributes among adults in six nations experiencing economic development, namely Argentina, Chile, India, Israel, Nigeria and Pakistan. Box 14.1 summarises the attributes found in this and other studies conducted in developing nations during the 1960s and 1970s that the researchers concluded were more often present among 'modern' persons than among less 'modern' persons.

Box 14.1   Twenty Correlates of Modernity

A sense of personal efficacy
Cognitive and behavioural flexibility
Low integration with relatives
Future orientation
Egalitarian attitudes
Field independence
Openness to innovation and change
Empathetic capacity
Belief in gender equality
Need for information
Achievement motivation
Propensity to take risks
Individualistic orientation
Non-local orientation
Independence or self-reliance
Secularised beliefs
Active participation
Preference for urban life
Tolerance of and respect for others
Educational and occupational aspirations

Source: Yang (1988).

In the terms that we have been using in this book, the modern person appears to have a good deal in common with a person with independent rather than interdependent self-construal. However, reviewing this research, K.S. Yang (1988) pointed out that few of the studies sampled more than one nation, and the results actually varied substantially from one study to another. The historical circumstances of a nation are likely to restrain the degree that modernity will occur, and colour the ways in which it is expressed. Previously, Yang (1986) had described the personality changes occurring in Chinese individuals as they emerged from their distinctive cultural heritage. He contrasted the traditional, 'social-oriented' character with the modern, 'individual-oriented' character. He noted changes from a submissive disposition to an enjoyment orientation, from an inhibited disposition to an autonomous disposition, and from an effeminate disposition to an expressive disposition. None of these Chinese changes appears in his 1988 overall summary of the modern person, however, since they were not reflected in the studies from other nations that he reviewed.

As we shall see, modernity is not so much a convergence on a single point, more a process of parallel evolution with convergence on some characteristics and continuing distinctiveness on others. The modern person is more of an abstraction than a template for individualism. Furthermore, as we saw in Chapter 13, those who migrate from rural settings to urban settings, within their nation or internationally, do not simply change all their prior beliefs, values, and behaviours. Yang

(1988) concluded that convergent aspects of modernisation are best summarised in terms of what he called **specific-functional adaptations**. In other words, in order to survive in an urban industrial setting rather than a rural agrarian setting, certain adaptations are essential for effective adaptation, whereas others are not. To hold down a job in a factory or office requires many of the listed attributes of modernity. In contrast, living with one's family within an industrialised society does not require the same degree of change, so that we may expect family life to show fewer changes than aspects of life that are related to employment.

GLOBALISATION

Recent academic and popular discourse describes cultural change in terms of **globalisation** rather than modernity. D. Yang, Chiu, Chen et al. (2011) found that samples of students in China, Hong Kong, Taiwan and the USA each perceived globalisation as similar to but distinct from modernity, westernisation and Americanisation. Globalisation was understood in terms of information technology, a global consumer culture, international travel, and so forth. It was perceived as enhancing persons' competence, but not their warmth. Marsella (2011) summarised globalisation as a process and a product that were reciprocally determined: 'The primary drivers of globalization are all events, forces and changes that are transnational, transcultural and transborder, especially capital flow, ownership, trade, telecommunications, transportation, political and military alliances and international agencies' (2011: 460–461).

Within globalisation, industrialisation is thus not the only contemporary force for cultural change. Other socio-economic factors, including migration, urbanisation, developments in communication technology and climate change, all entail important modifications in life styles that will have a bearing on individual and collective change. Moreover, theories of globalisation, more strongly than theories of modernity, do not necessarily imply cultural convergence: possible outcomes include cultural convergence but also resistance against convergence, as well as the creation of new and hybridised forms of culture.

Geographical Mobility

Groups of humans have frequently travelled long distances since prehistoric times. Nonetheless, as we have noted in Chapters 11 to 13, the contemporary world offers unprecedented opportunities for direct contact between individuals from very different cultural backgrounds, for reasons ranging from mass tourism, overseas study or work, and economic migration, to escaping from

Modernity is an aspect of capitalist societies characterised by industrialisation, a market economy, and bureaucratic institutions. Associated changes such as urbanisation, social mobility, and occupational differentiation are thought to lead to changes in values, aspirations, and the increased psychological autonomy of individuals.

Specific-Functional Adaptation is a form of cultural change that arises because it is distinctively useful to persons within a changed environment. For instance, factory shift workers who are required to clock in are likely to become more skilled in aspects of time management.

Globalisation refers to an increasing integration and interdependence of world views, ideas and cultures, driven by changes in mass transportation and communication (including the internet). Although authors often link technological changes in the last 200 years with the emergence of globalisation, many societies over the last 3,000 years have shown characteristics of globalisation.

conflict or political persecution. We described in those chapters how these experiences of inter-cultural contact can result not only in the diffusion of alternative cultural ideas and practices, suggesting a trend towards convergence, but also in social identity processes that can lead people to defend the distinctiveness and continuity of what they come to see as defining features of their cultural identities.

Globalised Media

As well as these trends in face-to-face intercultural contact, communications media have become much more heavily internationalised in recent decades, and may be expected to have as great an impact within the home as at work. Already in 2004, 85% of all film audiences throughout the world watched films made in the USA, and the percentage has almost certainly increased since then (United Nations Development Programme, 2004). India's Bollywood currently makes more films than are made in Hollywood and these also reach a huge audience. In 2004, the number of television sets in the world was already equal to 24% of the world's population (United Nations Development Programme, 2004). Household sizes vary between nations, thereby affecting the numbers who have access to a set. The global audience for television was estimated in 2011 at 4.2 billion (61% of the world's population: www.brightsideofnews.com). This diffusion of technology thus gives exposure of popular channels to very large numbers of people. Furthermore, satellite communication technology has enabled the creation of a small number of channels with a global reach, such as CNN, the BBC, and Al-Jazeera. Television networks also buy one another's footage and programmes, as well as creating programmes that copy popular formats developed by other networks.

Cumulatively, this centralisation of the sources of media output provides a strong impetus towards the adoption of 'modern' values, and the rejection of values that are locally distinctive or 'old-fashioned'. However, in some circumstances, it may also trigger a reaction in favour of preserving local distinctiveness, as has occurred in some parts of Latin America. The style and content of this standardised media coverage is mostly Western, and the penetration of its coverage increases with a nation's wealth. So, much of the value and other psychological change arising from exposure to such mass media will not only reinforce the changes arising directly from economic modernisation, it will also impinge on areas of behaviour that are less directly related to the acquisition of wealth.

For instance, Boski, Van de Vijver, Hurme, and Miluska (1999) showed video clips to students in Poland, the USA, Finland, and the Netherlands. The clips showed various Polish persons greeting one another, and included shots of men (both young and old) greeting women by kissing their hand. This has been a customary procedure in Poland for the past several hundred years and the clips were actually recorded in 1994. Respondents were asked to estimate when the video clips were shot and rate how typical they were. Poles estimated that the clips were contemporary and saw them as more typical of scenes that they were familiar with than did respondents from the other nations. Non-Polish respondents rated the clips as having been filmed between seven and nine years ago: in other words, they saw them as not typical of contemporary behaviour. Ten years later, hand kissing in Poland had become restricted to rather formal occasions, just as men in the UK and other Western nations have long since given up greeting women by raising their hat (if they wear one at all), Christmas has become a holiday in non-Christian

Japan, Christmas trees have become New Year trees in Turkey, and the Brazilian martial art of *capoeira* is popular with Polish students (and those in many other nations).

None of these diffusions of cultural practices and many other similar changes can be attributed to industrialisation, but they can plausibly be linked to the globalisation of the media. These changes can be thought of as instances of the ways that specific behaviours take on new meanings over time, such that what is 'modern' or popular at one time is not so at a later time. Hence they may not indicate an underlying value change, but a continuing wish to appear to be modern or in fashion. The more standardised media content comes to define how one acts in modern ways.

Climate Change

Climate change provides incentives for adverse cultural changes in ways that are already apparent. Global warming threatens especially the food security of nations located in environments that are already threatened, such as Ethiopia and Kenya in East Africa and Mali and Niger in the Sahel region of West Africa. It also leads to changes in agricultural practices by the major food suppliers of the world, for instance from growing wheat to growing biofuel. This response in turn accentuates world food shortages, threatening economic security and leading to the increased attractiveness of migration from impoverished states toward nations that are more affluent. These nations are in turn challenged by increasing resistance to high rates of legal and illegal immigration. Future threats include conflict over scarce water resources, unpredictable flash flooding, and the long-term inundation of low-lying cities. World Values Survey data from 47 nations indicate widespread concern about these issues, especially in the more affluent nations that are less immediately vulnerable to its effects (Kvaloy, Finseraas, & Listhaug, 2012). Initial research into the relationship between climate variations and increased social conflict in Africa does indicate some causal effects, but also suggests that other factors currently have stronger effects (Gleditsch, 2012).

In Chapter 12, we discussed the role of threat in exacerbating intergroup relations. Fritsche, Cohrs, Kessler, and Bauer (2012) asked students in Germany and the UK to review either a list of the predicted consequences of global warming within their nation or a list of climate-related facts that did not refer to climate change. After some delay, they completed measures of authoritarianism and out-group derogation. Respondents who had earlier been reminded of the threats posed by climate change were significantly more rejecting of out-groups and more in favour of law and order. Current and future threats may thus negate or contradict cultural changes in terms of individual freedoms that have been under way during recent decades.

Contending with these threats requires international agreements on policies that will mitigate the effects of warming. However, agreements on equitable solutions are bedeviled by the intergroup dynamics discussed in Chapter 12. Perceived equity is subject to in-group bias. Kriss, Loewenstein, Wang, and Weber (2011) asked students in China and the USA to rate what would be equitable reductions in GDP for each nation to contribute toward reduced greenhouse gas emissions. Each group favoured a lesser percentage reduction for their own nation. However, when students from the same nations were asked to rate equitable contributions to the same problem from 'Country A' and 'Country B', there was no difference in what was perceived as fair. Willingness to sign up to restrictive international agreements is also likely to be affected by cultural differences in generalised trust. As we saw in Chapter 9, general-ised trust is higher in individualistic nations. Current contributions of psychologists toward the effective management of climate-induced change have mostly not addressed cross-cultural aspects of the problem (Stern, 2011).

EVALUATING NATION-LEVEL CHANGE

An important task for this chapter is, therefore, to clarify the extent to which global changes are occurring and to seek evidence as to which are the key factors that drive this process. The attempts to identify modernity and globalisation that we have reviewed thus far in this chapter have provided some initial guidelines, but if we are to understand the processes of cultural change, we require data that have been collected over a suitable period of time. It is also necessary to dis-tinguish between individual-level change and nation-level change. Nation-level change can occur over time even when individuals are not showing changes. This will typically occur as generations succeed one another, if younger generations are socialised to different sets of values from those of the generations that preceded them. In practice, individual-level change often also occurs and where such changes are widespread they may accelerate the process of nation-level change.

A preliminary indication of nation-level change was already provided by Hofstede (1980). The first survey providing data that contributed to his classic study was conducted between 1967 and 1969, while the second took place between 1971 and 1973. Comparing nation-level means for data collected during these two time periods, Hofstede found that significant increases in the items defining individualism occurred in 18 of the 19 nations for which he had data from both surveys. During this four-year period, the national wealth of every one of these 18 nations had increased. The nineteenth nation was Pakistan. During this period Pakistani national wealth had decreased, and Hofstede noted that individualism scores also decreased.

To understand change more adequately, we need data collected over longer time periods. Taras, Steel, and Kirkman (2012) made a meta-analysis of nation-level mean scores that had been obtained over the past 30 years in 451 different studies by numerous researchers who had used measures that related to Hofstede's four dimensions. The new cultural dimension scores obtained in this way correlated strongly with Hofstede's original scores, ranging between 0.74 and 0.86, which indicated that although many different measures had been used, the essence of the concepts defined by Hofstede had been successfully approximated.

Taras et al. next subdivided their data on the basis of each separate decade during which the studies had been conducted. They then found that the strength of the correlations between their new scores and Hofstede's original scores decreased as the time interval increased. For the most recent decade, the correlations had reduced to between 0.46 and 0.73. Furthermore, as time has passed, the Hofstede scores have correlated less strongly with external variables, whereas some of the newer measures have tended to be more predictive. Thus there is substantial evidence for cultural change, but Taras et al did not comprehensively test what processes may lead to these value changes.

THE INGLEHART PROJECT

Collaborative work by social scientists over the past few decades has now made it possible to form a much more comprehensive picture of cultural change. This development has occurred because the opinions on a wide variety of topics of representative samples of adults in an increasing range of nations have been surveyed on a periodic basis. The first development in this direction was the initiation of the 'Eurobarometer' survey in 1970. The nations included in these surveys have increased as the European Union has been expanded to include additional nations, and the surveys continue to the present time. The World Values Survey (WVS), a similar project focused upon a broader range of nations, was initiated in 22 nations in 1981 and repeated in 43 nations in 1990–1993, with 1,000 respondents from each nation. Wave 5, the most recent survey involving representative samples from 67 nations, has been completed, and Wave 6 results will be accessible in 2013. Much of the raw data from these surveys is available on a series of websites as a freely available resource to researchers (http://wvs.isr.umich.edu; www.worldvaluessurvey.org; http://www.europa.eu.int/comm/public_opinion). The country means for the earlier waves of the WVS are also available in book form (Inglehart, Basanez, & Moreno, 1998). Several of the multiple-nation studies discussed in previous chapters have derived their data from this source, but have focused solely on the data collected at a single point in time.

Key Researcher Box 14.1   Ronald Inglehart

Ronald F. Inglehart (b. 1934) obtained his PhD in political science from the University of Chicago in 1967. He has held a series of posts in political science at the University of Michigan throughout his career, with visiting positions at the Universities of Mannheim and Geneva. He has been a key figure in the creation and subsequent development of the World Values Survey, whose original purpose was to map the involvement of the populations of different nations in the political processes of their nation. The subsequent progressive inclusion of additional questions and nations has greatly enhanced the survey's usefulness to cross-cultural psychology more generally. He has been the author of eight books documenting aspects of social and political change, and of more than 200 publications. His work has been cited more than 41,000 times.

Figure 14.1   Ronald Inglehart

The first comprehensive analysis of cultural change derived from these data was reported by Inglehart (1997), an American political scientist whose original attraction to the field was focused on attempts to understand changing voting patterns. Over two decades of research, his project has achieved a much broader relevance. Inglehart's hypothesis is that global value change currently comprises not one but two types of change. Firstly, he identifies the types of change delineated by earlier investigations of modernity. Secondly, he identifies the emergence of a set of 'post-modern' values, especially among the richer nations in his sample. Post-modern values are expected to arise in circumstances where economic security and political stability

> **Post-Materialist Values** are values that emphasise quality of life, protection of the environment, and life style issues. These values emerge in the process of post-modernisation, as societies move from industrialised modern societies to a reliance on service industries that demand greater skill, autonomy, and creativity.
>
> **Pancultural Factor Analysis** derives a factor structure from a total data set without considering the origins of those data. Such an analysis mixes variability due to individuals and variability due to their country or culture of origin, which can result in misleading conclusions (see Figure 4.4). We do not recommend pancultural factor analysis.

have become sufficiently established that people start to take them for granted. The concept of post-modernity has been much debated by social scientists, but has received little attention from psychologists.

There is little current agreement as to the defining characteristics of post-modernity. For present purposes it is sufficient to focus on a set of values that Inglehart identifies as **post-materialist**, characterised by a shift away from concerns about material well-being to concerns about life style and quality of life, which comprise a core element within the broader conceptions of post-modernity that have been debated. To test his formulation, Inglehart first selected items within the databank of the WVS that were relevant to these concepts, and then conducted both a **pancultural factor analysis** of the individual-level data and a nation-level factor analysis of country means for these items. The first procedure does not yield valid individual-level scores, because the technique of pancultural factor analysis does not control for differences between nations (Leung & Bond, 1989). However, the second procedure does yield valid nation-level mean scores, comparable to those obtained by Hofstede (1980) and other investigators. In the present instance, the findings of the Inglehart group that we are interested in focus on these nation-level scores.

The first factor was named as Rational-Legal Authority versus Traditional Authority. The rational-legal pole of this factor corresponds to modernity and is defined by high loadings on achievement motivation, thrift, determination, an interest in politics, and an acceptance of abortion. The traditional pole is defined by high loadings on respect for authority, national pride, obedience, and the importance of God in one's life. The second factor was named as Well-being versus Survival. In later analyses to be described shortly, the well-being pole was renamed as Self-Expression (capturing the core idea of post-materialistic values), and the specific items defining it were also changed. In terms of the more recent definition, agreement with the positions summarised below defines the post-materialistic Self-Expression pole, whereas disagreement defines the Survival pole (Welzel, 2010):

- Independence and imagination are preferable to faith and obedience.
- In times of job scarcity, men do not have greater rights to a job than women.
- It is acceptable for a woman to bear a child as a single parent.
- Men do not make better political leaders than women.
- University education is not more important for men than for women.
- Homosexuality, abortion and divorce are justifiable.

The databank that Inglehart has analysed is even larger than those collected by Hofstede and Schwartz, exceeding 165,000 responses. It also includes a much broader range of items and is derived from nationally representative samples. The nations surveyed have not been the same within each wave of data collection, but across all the five waves so far completed, data have been obtained on at least one occasion from more than 80 nations. Both of Inglehart's dimensions correlate positively with Hofstede's individualism-collectivism dimension and with national wealth (per capita GDP), as his model would lead us to expect. The correlations with GDP are rather higher than those with individualism: +0.60 with rational-legal authority and +0.78 with self-expression values. Diener and Oishi (2003) have already established a linkage between subjective well-being and national GDP. Consistent with this, nations with high scores for post-materialism have populations that express greater happiness. Similarly high correlations are obtained between subjective well-being and Schwartz's (2004) nation-level scores for Autonomy. Joint factor analysis of well-being, individualism and autonomy scores at the nation level yields a first factor accounting for as much as 78% of the overall variance (Inglehart & Oyserman, 2004). At the individual level, self-expression values correlate most strongly with Schwartz's measures of universalism and benevolence (Welzel, 2010).

Value Change over Time

Having identified suitable dimensions to test his model of change, Inglehart (1997) then compared the scores obtained in the 1990 survey with those obtained in the 1981 survey. This was only possible for the 21 nations that were common to both surveys. For each nation, the percentage of respondents who endorsed materialist values was subtracted from the percentage who endorsed post-materialist values. Table 14.1 shows that in 18 of the 21 nations there was an increase in the proportion of those endorsing post-materialist values. The exceptions were South Africa, Iceland, and South Korea. Although materialists in 11 of the nations still outnumbered post-materialists, the trend was clear. The magnitude of change did vary but was not noticeably greater in the less affluent nations than in the more affluent ones. The large change in the reverse direction in South Africa is likely to be attributable to the violence and instability that prevailed there during the relevant nine-year period.

An alternative way of judging the importance of a change is to assess the breadth of attitudes and behaviours that are affected. Inglehart (1997) returned to the World Values Survey databank and searched for additional opinion items or reports of particular behaviours that were positively correlated with endorsement of post-materialist values. Forty such items were identified, many of them related to forms of political participation, which had been included in the survey because of the original interests of those who constructed it. In order to obtain the broadest possible summary of change toward post-materialism, Inglehart then determined the proportion of changes on these 40 items that had occurred toward or away from post-materialism within each of the 21 nations. Figure 14.2 shows that within 18 of the 21 nations a very high proportion of the changes on this enlarged range of indicators were indeed in the predicted direction. However, in Argentina, Hungary and South Africa, there were reversed trends. Inglehart points out that each of these nations experienced political upheaval during the 1980s, whereas the remaining nations, whose data are summarised in Figure 14.2, did not.

More recently, these conclusions have been tested with a larger sample of nations and over longer periods of time. Inglehart and Baker (2000) drew upon data collected in the third World

Table 14.1   Percentage Endorsement of Post-Materialist Values

Nation	1981	1990	Net Shift
Finland	21	23	+2
The Netherlands	−2	26	+28
Canada	−6	14	+20
Iceland	−10	−14	−4
Sweden	−10	9	+19
West Germany	−11	14	+25
The UK	−13	0	+13
France	−14	4	+18
Belgium	−16	2	+18
South Africa	−16	−33	−17
Mexico	−19	−14	+5
Ireland	−20	−4	+16
Argentina	−20	−6	+14
Norway	−21	−19	+2
The USA	−24	6	+30
Japan	−32	−19	+13
South Korea	−34	−34	0
Italy	−39	7	+46
Spain	−41	−6	+35
Northern Ireland	−45	−7	+38
Hungary	−50	−41	+9

Percentages are for those members of national groups endorsing post-materialist values minus those endorsing materialist values.

Source: Inglehart, Ronald, Modernization and post-modernization. © 1997, Princeton University Press. Reproduced by permission of Princeton University Press.

Values Survey, which was conducted in 65 nations between 1995 and 1998. Within this enlarged sample, they identified a further 24 items whose nation-level scores correlated with the traditional versus secular-rational dimension, and 31 items that correlated significantly with the survival versus self-expression dimension. Clearly, these dimensions are not dependent upon the idiosyncrasies of the wording of one or two constituent items. The directional trends identified in the earlier data were confirmed. Within the enlarged sample, Inglehart and Baker were able to show that a change from traditional authority toward endorsement of secular-rational authority was correlated with a lower percentage of agricultural workers and a higher percentage of industrial workers. On the other hand, endorsement of the cluster of self-expression values correlated +0.72 with the percentage of the labour force employed in organisations providing services.

They also once again found that responses within a minority of nations had moved in the reverse direction. Movement away from secular-rational authority was found in South Africa,

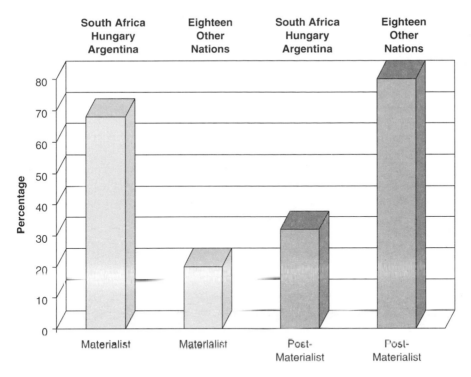

Figure 14.2   Percent of Items Showing Value Shifts Toward and Away from Post-
Materialist Values, 1981–1990.

Source: Inglehart, Ronald, *Modernization and post-modernization.* © 1997, Princeton University Press.
Reproduced by permission of Princeton University Press.

Brazil, Argentina, and Bulgaria. Movement away from self-expression was found in Russia, Belarus, Estonia, Lithuania, and Latvia. These were all nations that had experienced economic adversity during the relevant period and the effects found within them underline that the current overall trends are not irrevocable and can be reversed.

Inglehart and Baker (2000) also caution against the view that what is occurring is a simple convergence of values. They note that while values in many nations are changing in a parallel direction, the positioning of nations within the two-dimensional space defined by their dimensions retains the regional groupings that were found in former times. These groupings are defined by an historical affiliation with differing religious beliefs. Thus, we continue to observe clustering of nations that are historically Protestant, Catholic, Orthodox, Confucian, and Islamic. These continuities concur with the conclusions of Georgas, Van de Vijver, and Berry (2004) that religion can account for cultural variance additional to that explained by differences in wealth. Wealth is clearly implicated in cultural change while religion has more to do with stability. Inglehart and Baker also find evidence that, after accounting for other predictors, having experienced a period of communist rule shows a significant effect on the values that are currently espoused (for similar results using Schwartz values, see Schwartz, Bardi, & Bianchi, 2000; Gheorghiu et al., 2009). Look below at the most recent development of this type of study in Key Research Study Box 14.2.

Key Research Study Box 14.2
The Postmodernisation Hypothesis

Inglehart's (1997) postmodernisation hypothesis was further developed by Welzel and Inglehart (2010) into a universal theory of human development. Inglehart's original idea was that increasing income leads to major improvements in well-being and health, which level off when the further income does not contribute to further improvements. At this point, citizens start to focus more on their life style and begin to give priority to values emphasising environmental protection and personal growth. In this way, economic development is postulated to result in changes in people's values, moving from traditional to modern and ultimately postmodern values. In turn, these value shifts are associated with greater well-being and more effective societal institutions (e.g., higher democracy and lower corruption).

Welzel and Inglehart's (2010) elaboration of this theory goes into more detail as to the precise mechanisms that are predicted to drive these changes. The material and economic conditions of the environment in which a population is situated are said to provide a mix of opportunities and threats, which will lead people to value whatever is most helpful in handling their situation. In contexts where threats predominate, values shift towards obedience to authority and protection, whereas in contexts where perceived opportunities are greater, individuals shift toward values that emphasise emancipation from authority and individual self-expression. These changes in values are then predicted to cause changes in the cognitive strategies that individuals employ to realise these valued opportunities. In emancipated contexts, people will explore and accumulate more novel knowledge, which in turn will lead to higher well-being.

The major difference between this theory and Inglehart's earlier ideas of cultural evolution is that Welzel and Inglehart's model specifies the important context variables that influence psychological and social processes and explicitly acknowledges the dynamic nature of these processes. The model was tested concurrently at the nation level and at the individual level, with data from 83 nations. Nation-level opportunities were defined by an index of 'cognitive mobilisation', which summarised the provision of tertiary education, research activity and the use of communication technologies. Cognitive mobilisation was found to be a significant predictor of self-expressive values, which in turn was a significant predictor of reported levels of individual personal control, and this in turn was a significant predictor of life satisfaction. In this case, self-expressive values were measured by a composite of 13 value statements from within the World Values Survey, but personal control and life satisfaction were measured by just one item each. Caution is required in interpreting results obtained with single-item variables, since it is difficult to establish their reliability and validity.

The universal applicability of Welzel and Inglehart's conclusions has been questioned by Bomhoff and Gu (2012). These authors presented evidence showing that in East Asia the components of self-expressive values, such as generalised trust, the tolerance of minorities and a preference for quality of life over hard work, do not correlate strongly with one another. This recent debate is reminiscent of much earlier discussions as to whether there is a single form of modernity. Modern societies such as those of Japan, Korea and Taiwan remain distinct from modern Western nations.

As Welzel and Inglehart (2010) acknowledge, studies correlating measures that are all collected at a single point in time can do no more than suggest causal relationships between them.

Inglehart, Foa, Peterson, and Welzel (2008) began to address this problem in a previous study, by examining changes in reported subjective well-being in 52 nations for whom there were data available for more than one point in time. They found that subjective well-being had increased over time in 45 of these nations, and that the magnitude of this increase could be predicted from a measure of gross national product taken five years before the survey. We could be more sure of the causal role of wealth in this effect if we knew whether GNP had also increased over time. Increasing subjective well-being was most strongly predicted by concurrent increases in perceived personal freedom. Thus, wealth is confirmed as a probable causal factor in cultural change, but these data do not test the more specific aspects of Welzel and Inglehart's (2010) model. Take a look now at Research Debate Box 14.1.

Research Debate Box 14.1   Wealth and Culture

How should we best understand the relationship between wealth and culture? As we have seen, Hofstede (1980) considered wealth to be something separate from culture and partialled its effects out when computing correlations between his dimensions and other variables. Georgas et al. (2004), Van de Vliert (2009), and Welzel and Inglehart (2010) all see it as a major factor in the creation and maintenance of specific cultural adaptations. Smith (2004b) argues that the way in which we all agree to treat wealth as real when it is in fact a symbolic entity with no substantive basis indicates that money and wealth are themselves an integral part of the system of meanings that makes up a culture. We need to think more about whether wealth is best thought of as a cause of culture or as a correlate of culture.

Fischer and Boer (2011) sought to clarify the relation between wealth and culture by comparing their impact on indicators of well-being. Although well-being is often measured in terms of positive indicators such as subjective well-being and satisfaction with life, Fischer and Boer argued that negative indicators of well-being have been better measured and validated in previous research. They therefore used nation-level aggregated measures of poor general health, anxiety, and burnout as their dependent measures. In three separate meta-analyses spanning 63 nations, they found that a measure of individualism derived from the data of Hofstede (1980) and Schwartz (2004) was a stronger predictor of well-being than was a measure of nation-level wealth. They concluded that the impact of nation-level wealth on well-being occurs only because wealth enhances a nation's individualism. These results support the model of cultural change advanced by Welzel and Inglehart (2010), but do not test it directly because the available data do not permit the measurement of change over time.

O'Connor and Fischer (2012) compared the relative ability of measures of values, size of government and wealth to predict changes over time in nation-level differences in corruption. They were able to do this by using measures of the self-expression values that have been derived from responses to the World Values Survey. Across 59 nations, the only predictor that was associated with decreasing levels of corruption was nation-level wealth. It is plausible that corruption will decrease when wealth is relatively accessible in more legitimate ways, and that values will have a less direct impact on this process. Thus, the relative impact of wealth and values appears to depend on which type of cultural change we attempt to predict. Greater use of studies that include longitudinal data will further enrich our understanding of how wealth and values interact.

OTHER WAYS OF EXAMINING CULTURAL CHANGE

The data derived from the World Values Survey provide by far the most extensive information currently available on value change. However, no single survey can provide comprehensive coverage, and one weakness of this database is that the change measures that have been analysed concern a mixture of values, attitudes and beliefs, rather than looking at these components separately. A second weakness is that, to be able to include a sufficient number of nations in the analysis, change can only be surveyed over relatively short time-periods: ten years in the case of the analysis by Welzel and Inglehart (2010).

Li and Bond (2010) sought to clarify the ambiguity created by the fact that the dimensions defined by Inglehart and his colleagues confound together values, attitudes and beliefs. Analysing only those ten of the WVS items that had been used initially by Inglehart that refer to values, they found that his two dimensions could be reduced to one, which they named as secularism versus traditionalism. Using data from 69 nations represented in the first four WVS waves, they found increasing secularism over time in the sample as a whole, but no reduction in the variability of secularism across nations. The increased secularism was restricted to those nations that were already somewhat secular and that had increasing scores on the Human Development Index (which is a composite measure of wealth, life-expectancy, and educational enrolment: see the United Nations Development Programme, 2004).

Leung, Lam, Bond, et al. (2012) evaluated the stability of beliefs over eight years, using the Social Axioms survey discussed in Chapter 2. The rank order of eight nations on belief dimensions showed relatively high stability, especially for religiosity. The authors suggest that the changes attributable to changing wealth would have lesser impact on religiosity, since this aspect of a person's worldview is sustained by established institutional structures.

Allen, Ng, Ikeda, Jawan, et al. (2007) attempted to survey cultural change in eight nations over 20 years. They were able to draw on a survey of values reported by Ng, Hossain, Ball, Bond et al. (1982). In this early study, students in nine East Asian and Pacific island nations completed a 40-item version of the Rokeach Value Survey, the instrument that later provided a basis for Schwartz's well-known value survey. Two value dimensions were identified within the 1982 data, which were characterised as representing Submissive versus 'Dionysian' values and Inner Strength versus Materialistic values. The first of these dimensions is the one that is of particular interest. Examples of submissive values were obedience, politeness, and an emphasis on national security. Examples of Dionysian values were the endorsement of an exciting life and mature love.

In testing for culture change, Allen et al. (2007) replicated the same survey, aiming to sample students who were studying the same subjects at the same universities that had previously been sampled in each nation. This proved possible in some nations, while in others the most similar available option was selected. Data were received from eight of the nine nations originally sampled. Analysis of the new data set indicated that the first of the two value dimensions could be used to partially summarise the data, whereas the second dimension could not because it had a different structure. Change scores were therefore computed on the first dimension. The results showed that students from those nations that had endorsed Dionysian values in 1982, namely Australia, New Zealand and Japan, did so even more strongly in 2002. Students in Hong Kong and Taiwan were positioned midway between Dionysian and submissive values in 1982, but by 2002 they had moved toward a greater endorsement of Dionysian values. In contrast, values among students in the three remaining nations, Bangladesh, Malaysia and Papua New Guinea, which were already submissive, had become more so by 2002. Therefore, in sampling nations that ranged from very wealthy to much less wealthy, Allen et al. identified a trend toward a polarisation of values rather than a unidirectional change. We can only speculate as to the closeness of the linkage between Dionysian values and Inglehart's concept of self-expression, but there is at least some overlap. In both studies, we find value change moving in opposite directions when we compare the richest and the poorest nations within each sample – divergence, not convergence.

Like Inglehart, Allen et al. were interested in testing alternative explanations for the changes that they detected. Given the strong association between nations' wealth and the cultural values that prevail within them, a key question is whether we can establish any kind of causal relationship between the two. The most effective way to do this is through cross-lagged panel analysis, which draws on measures of both the variables in which one is interested, both from an earlier date and from a later date. By exploring the different correlations between these measures one can infer which causal linkages are the more plausible. Allen et al. used this method, finding that their values measure in 1982 did not predict per capita GDP in 2002, whereas per capita GDP in 1982 did predict value change in 2002. Thus, the conclusions drawn from the studies discussed earlier (e.g., Inglehart & Baker, 2000) are supported.

The simple statement that wealth has a significant effect on cultural change leaves open the question of how that change may occur. Allen et al. suggest that a nation's wealth affects at least some of the values that individuals form during childhood. To test this prediction, they computed correlations between national per capita GDP in every alternate year from 1959 to 2000 and each sample's endorsement of Dionysian values. As predicted, Dionysian values in the 1982 sample correlated most strongly with GDP in the late 1960s and the early 1970s, in other words in the first ten years of respondents' lives. In a similar way, Dionysian values in the 2002 sample correlated most strongly with GDP from the late 1980s onward, again during the first ten years of these respondents' lives. This type of data analysis leaves open various possible causal mechanisms, but also encourages us to examine family dynamics and early schooling practices. For instance, one could hypothesise that wealth affects the type of family dynamics that develop, or that wealth affects the presence or absence of schooling, or that wealth affects exposure to the more globalised media.

Political Change and Cultural Change

A further way in which we can seek an understanding of cultural change is to examine the consequences of some of the major political changes that have occurred in recent decades. From the perspective of psychology, these events can be thought of as large scale and poorly controlled field experiments. We consider three here: the reunification of Germany, the return of Hong Kong to China, and the Chinese government's one-child policy.

German reunification

Oettingen, Little, Lindenberger, and Baltes (1994) compared the self-efficacy perceptions and school performance of schoolchildren in East and West Berlin, shortly after the reunification of East and West Germany in 1989. The children in the formerly communist eastern sector of the city had much lower perceptions of their own ability to influence their levels of achievement than did the children in West Berlin. However, among East Berlin children there was a much stronger correlation between perceived efficacy and actual school grades. Oettingen et al. suggest that these differences are caused by different teaching methods. In East Berlin, children would receive public performance feedback in class, with this feedback being based on the teacher's evaluation. In West Berlin, the factors affecting efficacy and school grades were more diverse, and feedback was not given publicly, so that the correlation between the two was weaker. In a further study, Little, Oettingen, Stetsenko, and Baltes (1995) reported similar data collected from schoolchildren in Moscow and Los Angeles. As expected, the correlation between grades and self-efficacy from the Moscow children resembled that from East Berlin, whereas the correlation from Los Angeles was even lower than that from West Berlin.

In the years following the reunification of Germany, this group of researchers has continued to sample schoolchildren within Berlin, where teaching is now conducted throughout the city in the manner previously restricted to the Western sectors. They have found that East Berlin children continue to experience lower personal efficacy, but that the correlations between efficacy and school grades have declined to the levels found in West Berlin (Little, Lopez, Oettingen, & Baltes, 2001). In a similar way, repeated surveys of German factory workers by Frese, Kring, Soose, and Zempel (1996) showed a gradual increase in initiative-taking among East German workers, rising to the level found among West German workers. These studies thus demonstrate the capacity of liberal political change to create cultural change. However, not all such changes are positive. Fischer, Maes, and Schmitt (2007) surveyed the effects of contact between East and West Germans in 1996, 1998, and 2000. Contact at earlier time-points led to enhanced self-esteem at later time points among both East and West Germans. However, contact in business settings led at later times to decreased job satisfaction among East Germans, presumably because of unfavourable comparisons of their work outcomes.

Hong Kong's transition

The change in the status of Hong Kong in 1997 from British colony to a Special Autonomous Region within China also provided researchers with an opportunity to conduct informative research. Since the change in Hong Kong's political status guaranteed its continuing autonomy, the change was less radical than that which occurred in East Germany. As the time for change of status approached, the issue facing Hong Kong Chinese was either to sustain their identity as a Hong Kong Chinese or see themselves more inclusively as Chinese. Choices as to how to identify oneself with changing political contexts are likely to be crucial to an understanding of cultural change, because identifications will influence whom one seeks to associate with and consequently what types of influence one will be exposed to. Those who changed toward the more inclusive identification, as Chinese, were those who favoured Confucian values over modern values and who saw human nature as fixed rather than malleable (Chiu & Hong, 1999; Hong et al., 1999; Lam et al., 1999). Hence political change opens up possibilities for value change.

China's one-child policy

A third instance of politically-driven cultural change is provided by the one-child policy of the Chinese government. Reviewing relevant studies, Chang, Schwartz, Dodge, and

McBride-Chang (2003) concluded that parents in one-child families are less authoritarian and more concerned that their children do well in school, and that 'only-children' are more self-centred, aggressive, and extroverted than is found in Chinese multiple-child families. Chang (2004) interviewed the parents of 328 Chinese single-child families, asking them what types of social behaviours were desirable in their child. Only 24% endorsed traditional Chinese 'good child' behaviours, such as self-constraint, obedience, and listening to others. In contrast, 87% of parents endorsed 'pro-social leadership' behaviours, such as making friends, getting along with others, and being a leader. Most strikingly, there were hardly any gender differences in the behaviours that parents preferred to see in their child, or in the behaviours that they would regard as problematic. Asked whether their parenting was guided by the Confucian values of collectivism and self-restraint, not one parent agreed that they were. Some of these emphases no doubt reflect the trends toward modernity that we have discussed in this chapter. However, the apparent reduction in gender differences is more likely to be a consequence of the single-child policy.

The studies of political change that we have reviewed indicate some significant cultural effects. However, there are other studies that indicate no such effects. Silbereisen and Wiesner (2002) reviewed a broad range of studies of German reunification and their conclusion mirrored Yang's (1988) concept of specific-functional adaptation: that is to say, political changes only create cultural change where specific institutional changes directly require those changes. An example is the studies of Berlin schoolchildren's response to a centrally imposed change in teaching styles, including the abandonment of public performance feedback. In the changed environment, children's performance became dependent on a more diverse set of feedback sources, some of them probably contradictory of others, requiring a broader range of coping skills.

In other domains of life, political change does not have such immediate effects. For instance, the timing of adolescents' first romantic attachment showed no effect of the political change. Furthermore, Silbereisen and Wiesner provided instances of the ways in which established culture patterns may persist, even when the original reason for their existence is gone. The traditional *jugendweihe* youth initiation ceremony, much promoted under the disliked state communist regime, remained a popular event, perhaps because it provided an opportunity for sociability and celebration despite adverse economic circumstances. In evaluating the studies of the effects of German reunification, we must bear in mind that it is possible that changes may have occurred which preceded the start of the research studies. Clandestine watching of West German television in East Germany was widespread before reunification and may have contributed to some types of adolescent value change. Field experiments have their limitations as a source of unambiguous causal connections.

Families and Cultural Change

We have discussed the role of family in maintaining cultural continuity in Chapter 8. In considering the current global change, we need to discuss whether the family is less influential than it was in former times. In many of the nations of Europe and in North America, a large and growing proportion of children are born to unmarried mothers, and many children grow up living with a single parent. Furthermore, in many of the nations where the family model of interdependence has prevailed for generations, schooling has become much more widespread. Both of these social changes open up alternative sources of socialisation influences on the child. In his analysis, Inglehart (1997) predicted that one element in the emergence of postmodern values would be a decline in emphasis on the family. However, this prediction was contradicted by the data. In 16 of the 19 nations surveyed, the percentage agreeing that 'a child needs a home with both a father and a mother to grow up happy' increased between 1981 and 1990. Other survey items also detected increased support for the value of the family. Inglehart interprets this result in terms of a widespread public belief that the children of single parents are at greater risk of a variety of social pathologies. This knowledge itself is derived from the increased dissemination of psychological knowledge that is associated with widely adopted educational curricula in modern economies.

Rather than seeing family breakdown simply as a cause of cultural change, it is preferable to see families as subject to processes of cultural evolution that parallel those occurring in other segments of society. In Chapter 8, we presented evidence for the emergence of the family model of psychological interdependence. This model asserts that a decreased level of material interdependency among family members does not necessarily imply emotional distance (Kağıtçıbaşı, 2007). A study of family relations in 16 nations confirmed these expectations. Georgas, Mylonas, Bafiti, Poortinga, et al. (2001) found no differences between frequency of communication among family members in more and in less affluent nations. Among more geographically dispersed families in the more affluent nations, communication was more often by telephone or e-mail, whereas in the less affluent nations it was more often face-to-face. These results held true not just for the nuclear family but also for the extended family. A more recent study with samples from 30 nations (Georgas, Berry, Van de Vijver, & Poortinga, 2006) also confirmed the distinction between material and emotional family interdependencies and showed that material family interdependence is stronger in collectivistic societies, whereas emotional interdependence is important everywhere. The human functions served by families appear to be resilient across recent times.

Technology and Cultural Change

Most of the preceding discussion of change is based on analysis of nation-level data. We have seen that increasing wealth is associated with changes in values and increased individualism, but we have not yet examined all of the ways in which such changes may take place. In the contemporary world, communication occurs increasingly through a range of electronic media that would have been inconceivable to preceding generations. One consequence of increasing wealth is that there is an enhanced possibility of purchasing and using television sets, personal computers, mobile phones and so forth. Using these media provides access to a hugely increased range of information and modes of communication, and offers choice as to how to use these increased opportunities. In earlier chapters, we reviewed studies that showed how independent self-construal can be primed experimentally. Does the use of electronic communication itself constitute a quasi-experimental prime?

Rossette, Brett, Barsness, and Lytle (2012) studied the effect of negotiating electronically rather than face-to-face, using a type of buyer-seller negotiation similar to those that were discussed in Chapter 10. In negotiations between US and Hong Kong students, it was found that the Hong Kong sellers made opening offers that were significantly more demanding when negotiating electronically. Opening offers by the American sellers did not differ between experimental conditions. In order to establish more clearly the causes of this effect, Rossette et al. conducted a second study which included only negotiators from Hong Kong. Opening offers were again found to be more demanding in the electronic condition. Thus, the more assertive demands were not attributable to the intercultural basis of the first study. They argued that electronic communication eliminated the use of the rich variety of non-verbal cues that were available during face-to-face communication. In their absence, members of a cultural group for whom such cues would be relatively important are found to act in ways that appear more self-serving.

Assertive behaviour is not synonymous with individualism. It is one among many behaviours that might signal individualism in a specific context. An innovative study was conducted by Hansen, Postmes, Van der Vinne, and Van Thiel (2012). These authors studied a scheme in which laptop computers were given to 93 Ethiopian school children aged 12 to 16. Ethiopia is a nation in which less than 1% of the population owns a laptop. The laptops were given to children in some classes in a school, but not to those in other classes in the same school. All students were taught by the same teachers. One year later, the researchers compared those children whose laptop was still functioning with a control group who had received no laptop, as well as those students whose laptop had broken down. They found that after this year the children with functioning laptops had increased their score on a single-item measure of independent self-construal and endorsed more of what Schwartz et al. (2012) now define as personally-focused values (based on a composite of achievement, self-direction, and power values). This change was mediated by a change in self-construal, showing that the children had changed their values because of changes in how they saw themselves as individuals. Hansen et al. also found that the children's more traditional cultural beliefs and norms, as represented by scores for socially-focused values (based on a composite of tradition, conformity, benevolence, and universalism) and interdependent self-construal, were unchanged.

Hansen et al. proposed three alternative ways in which these changes may have occurred. Firstly, successfully mastering how to use a personal computer could enhance self-efficacy. Secondly, although the students had no access to the internet, by using and sharing their laptop they could have experienced success taking initiatives in their social relationships. For instance, some of them taught their parents to use their computer, which was a big change from a conventionally submissive role. Finally, possession of a prestigious object may also have enhanced their reputation within their existing social network, building their reputation as effective social actors. It is possible that all three of these factors may have contributed to the effects that were found. Further studies will be required to determine whether similar effects would occur in other cultural contexts, but the results provide intriguing indications of the ways in which media usage can contribute to cultural change. For another instance of technology as a trigger for change, look at Everyday Life Box 14.1.

Everyday Life Box 14.1   Adapting to the Introduction of Guns

Warfare among the highland tribes of Papua New Guinea was until quite recently conducted with bows and arrows. Among the half-million population of the Enga tribe wars were frequent but the average number of deaths per war was 3.7. Courts for the resolution of disputes had been established by the Australian colonial administration in the 1970s, but were rarely used. In 1990, guns were acquired by the Enga. The number of wars per year rose from less than five to more than 20, and average deaths per war rose to 17.8. Military tactics were radically changed and ambushes by 'Rambos' became frequent. As the social disorganisation caused by these innovations rose, support for warfare waned and it became easier for tribal leaders to encourage the use of courts for the resolution of disputes. Wars continue but they have become shorter and are frequently referred to the courts. Death rates have consequently declined, from 81 per 100,000 to 19 per 100,000 by 2011. Thus a technological innovation has enhanced the development and utilisation of a civil structure, as may have happened in other cultures in earlier times (Wiessner & Pupu, 2012).

Ethnic Diversity and Cultural Change

We must also take account of the important issue of migration and its implications for ethnic diversity. In Chapter 13, we noted that the acculturation process does not entail changes only within migrants, but also within the majority population. In surveying such cultural change, we must take account of two factors relating to migration. Firstly, when Inglehart analysed the data from representative national samples of different nations, the samples surveyed in 1990 would have been more ethnically diverse than those surveyed in 1981. Migrants from collectivist nations are not especially likely to have contributed to the growth of postmodern values in the more wealthy nations to which they have mostly migrated. More likely, their presence in these samples may have masked a stronger effect among majority groups within those nations. Across 24 European nations, Schiefer (2013) confirmed that migrants' attitudes were less typical of means for their nation as a whole.

More significantly, the increasing presence and visibility of ethnic minorities within previously homogeneous populations poses challenges to the majority population. Just as was the case for the Hong Kong Chinese in 1997, members of majority populations find themselves faced with an increasing choice of identities. Should they adopt a more inclusive multi-ethnic identity or a more exclusive, ethnically-restrictive identity? As we saw in the preceding chapter, adherence to exclusive majority identities creates problems for minorities. It also postpones rather than resolves the contemporary problem of how best to address cultural difference. If improvements are to occur, majorities will need not only to reject exclusive identities, but also to reconstrue what it means to say that one is, for instance, French, German, American, or Australian. Does a majority person's construal of nationalities such as these include implicit assumptions about skin colour, language fluency, or knowledge of historically-rooted conceptions of politeness?

Governments of some nations with particularly long experience of diversity have found ways to encourage the adoption of inclusive multiple identities. For instance, in Belgium, more than 90% of the population identify themselves as either Flemish or Walloon *and* Belgian, while 75% of those living in Spain see themselves as having both a regional identity *and* a Spanish identity (United Nations Development Report, 2004). Arnett (2002) suggests that globalisation will encourage all of us to think of ourselves in terms of a broader range of identities. Focusing specifically upon the young, he notes an increasing tendency to think of oneself as a citizen of the world, as well as a citizen of a specific nation. In this way, holding a bicultural identity could become the norm rather than the exception. Consistent with this, Gelfand, Lyons, and Lun (2011) found that among respondents to the World Values Survey in several nations, those who endorsed both a local and a global identity were more accepting of out-groups than those who endorsed either a local identity or or a global identity. However, it would be premature to assume that this pattern of dual identities will become widespread in the foreseeable future.

CONVERGENCE RECONSIDERED

Finally, it is worth reflecting on whether globalisation may ever eliminate the cultural differences that we have been examining in this book. For several reasons, we can see no reason to predict the imminent global demise of cultural differences.

Global Inequality

Firstly, we should remember that the cultural changes that we have identified appear to be driven substantially by increasing wealth. Yet in the contemporary globalised world, inequality remains high and, according to some indices, it is increasing (Milanovic, 2007). Moreover, the world's population currently faces the enormous challenges posed by uncontrolled climate change, by environmental degradation, and by failures in disease control. If adequate responses to these challenges are not forthcoming in future years, a reverse in economic fortunes could well be followed by the collapse of postmodern values and the evolution of values that are more reflective of adversity.

We have noted already the ways in which values in those parts of the world that have experienced particular turbulence or economic failure moved in a contrary direction. History is not reversible, but nor is the future that we face a simple extrapolation of the present. Van de Vliert (in press) has used his climato-economic model to predict the particular regions of the world that are most likely to be adversely affected by climate change over the next 100 years. Those most at risk will be hot nations in Africa, unless they can generate the wealth to meet new challenges, and some rich nations whose climate will become more demanding. Sadly, it seems very probable that poverty, disease and natural disasters will continue to preoccupy large segments of the world's population, rendering those among them who do not migrate relatively immune to the factors currently inducing cultural change.

Cultural Identity Processes

Secondly, if theories of social identity are to be believed (see Chapter 12), increases in intercultural contact and communication will make culture increasingly salient as a basis for identity. In Chapter 13 we described the phenomenon of 'reactive ethnicity', whereby pressures toward cultural assimilation within nations often lead cultural minorities to an increased identification with, and defence of, their cultural identities. We suggest that the same is likely to be true on a global level. One important consequence of globalisation has been the apparently paradoxical resurgence of individuals' ethnic consciousness and seeking of distinctiveness (Berger & Huntington, 2002). Paralleling the growth in demands for freedom and human rights are insistent voices claiming the right to protect and honour one's cultural heritage and traditions. There is a growing awareness that 'cultural identities have been suppressed, sometimes brutally, as state policy—through religious persecutions and ethnic cleansings, but also through everyday exclusion and economic, social and political discrimination' (United Nations Development Program, 2004: 1).

Even where there is greater freedom, many people are unwilling to embrace the prospect of 'one homogeneous worldwide culture in which all children grow up wanting to be like the latest pop music star, eat Big Macs, vacation at Disney World, and wear blue jeans, baseball caps, and Nikes' (Arnett, 2002: 779). Arnett argues that people can resist pressures towards global homogenisation by participating in what he calls 'self-selected cultures'. This can help to explain the growth of religious fundamentalism in Christian and Muslim communities, the genesis of anti-globalisation protest movements, the development of new musical subcultures, and the revival of traditional cultural practices such as tattooing rituals in Samoa (see also Jensen, Arnett, & McKenzie, 2011).

Notably, what these movements have in common is not resistance to cultural change *per se*, but resistance to convergence. Cultural distinctiveness can be achieved through innovative and 'hybrid' cultural forms, such as Bhangra music and Chicken Tikka Masala, both of which are understood to have originated in the British South Asian community in the late twentieth century. As we noted in Chapter 11, such cultural creativity may also occur in the context of tourist destinations, where local people may revive, and sometimes embellish, local traditions in order to provide an experience of cultural 'authenticity' for their visitors (AlSayyad, 2001). Commentators have similarly understood the rise of Christian fundamentalism in the late twentieth-century USA as a distinctively postmodern cultural innovation, combining elements of the contemporary culture with claims to an historical continuity with a reinvented past (e.g., Miller, 1999).

SUMMARY

Early studies equated modernity with the development of industrialised, individualistic cultures. More recent studies confirm wealth as a significant causal factor of cultural change, but identify different types of change in more affluent and less affluent contexts. The communications revolution and its globalisation may be as potent a cause of change as industrialisation. Post-materialist values have become more salient, especially within affluent nations over the past decade. The types of value change that have occurred are best thought of as specific-functional adaptations to the requirements of contemporary societies. Consequently, not all values are changing. The impetus for change is provided by globalised media, political change and migration, while the role of the family in maintaining cultural continuity is less clear. On the other hand, not all peoples share the conditions that are thought to lead to cultural change: moreover, the increased intercultural contact in globalisation can result in increased awareness and defence of cultural identities, which may lead people to resist the pressures toward cultural convergence.

FURTHER READING

1 Arnett, J.J. (2002). The psychology of globalization. *American Psychologist, 57,* 774–783.
2 Gelfand, M., Lyons, S., & Lun, J. (2011). Towards a psychological science of globalization. *Journal of Social Issues, 67,* 841–853.
3 Inglehart, R. (1997). *Modernization and post-modernization: Cultural, economic and political change in 43 societies.* Princeton, NJ: Princeton University Press.
4 Schultz, P.W. (2002). Environmental attitudes and behaviors across cultures. *Online Readings in Psychology and Culture.* Available at http://scholarworks.gvsu.edu/*orpc*
5 United Nations Development Program (2004). *Human development report: Cultural liberty in today's diverse world.* New York: Oxford University Press.

STUDY QUESTIONS

1 Discuss the concept of specific-functional adaptation. What adaptations have you made to your behaviour since becoming a student at university and why?
2 What do you understand to be post-materialist values and what evidence do you see for their growth in your country?
3 What are the consequences of distributing personal computers to children in non-industrialised societies, and is the practice beneficial?
4 How can migration become a stimulus to cultural change?

15

The Unfinished Agenda

'There is a tide in the affairs of men,
Which, taken at the flood, leads on to fortune.
Omitted, all the voyage of their life
Is bound in shallows and in miseries.'

(Shakespeare, Julius Caesar)

Having read the preceding chapters, you will have become acquainted with a broad range of studies that have advanced our understanding of how culture informs social psychological processes. We should like to conclude this book by discussing some of the issues that you may have confronted in making sense of the complex material we have placed before you.

The way in which most of us try to make sense of a new body of information is to relate it to conceptual frameworks with which we are already familiar. Sometimes these frameworks can help, but if they do not match well enough with the new material they can be a hindrance. Since we do not have the opportunity to hear your questions, we propose instead to share some comments on particular issues relating to the field that we have encountered frequently in discussions both with students and with colleagues. We cannot claim to have any irrefutable grasp of these issues, but we do claim to have relevant experience in thinking them through over long periods of time. We comment in turn on six frequently raised reactions and challenges to our field.

WHY FOCUS SO MUCH ON NATIONS? IT SUSTAINS STEREOTYPING, AND EVERYONE KNOWS THAT NATIONS INCLUDE DIVERSE POPULATIONS

We have focused on individualism-collectivism and related nation-level dimensions and examined how these dimensions are associated with psychological reactions of a nation's population in a variety of ways. Focusing on nations is a convenient starting point, as considerable political, social and economic data are available about groups of people organised by nation. We have also highlighted the importance of the norms for behaviour that char-acterise national populations. National institutions, and especially the laws enforced within nation states, play a significant role in regulating human behaviour. Although borders are relatively arbitrary demarcation lines which often separate people of similar historical and cul-tural descent, the laws that are applied to these separated groups of people can differ dramatically depending on where they reside. Similarly, education systems pass on the norms, beliefs, and values that are deemed desirable within the boundaries of a given nation. Education systems and their associated curricula are shaped by the political, social, economic, religious and historical conditions of the nation state, and play a significant role in the socialisation of a nation's human capital.

Even the prevailing economic system provides a framework that shapes individual actions and attitudes. Compare the role of incentives in a free-market economy that relies on entre-preneurship and individual initiative with the rigid planning that characterised state-socialist economies and de-emphasised, sometimes even criminalized, the entrepreneurial and eco-nomic activities of individuals (Landes, 1998). Nations and their institutions therefore can be expected to influence many aspects of human behaviour strongly. Thus, nations provide a relatively coherent institutional framework within which we can start to unravel the differ-ences between people.

However, this convenient starting point entails a significant risk and challenge. Emphasising national differences along specific cultural dimensions and identifying associated individual-level psychological variables poses the risk that we essentialise differences. In other words, we may start to see differences as static, fixed, objective, and uniformly applying to all individuals within a nation (or to those having associated individual-level characteristics). Allport (1954) argued that essentialist thinking contributes to prejudice and stereotyping, and research has confirmed this view (Prentice & Miller, 2007). Cross-cultural training embedded in university courses may increase essentialist interpretations of culture (Fischer, 2011b). Such essentialist thinking can be driven by positive intentions. Social workers might ask questions such as, 'My client has beaten his wife and/or children, but says it is normal in his culture. What can we do?', or a lawyer could represent the situation in a similar way: 'I understand that my client has beaten his wife and/or children, but I understand that it's in his culture, therefore …' (Wikan, 1999). These are extreme examples, but cross-cultural work on psychological differences lends itself easily to such thinking, with potentially far-reaching consequences for groups and the individuals within them.

Stereotypic thinking affects individuals. Chao, Chen, Roisman, and Hong (2007) demon-strated that Chinese Americans who essentialise ethnic differences are slower to switch between Chinese and American cultural frames and show greater stress responses when talking about their cultural experiences in the USA. In emphasising the differences between nations, between ethnic groups, and between individuals with specific cultural orientations (including values, beliefs, and thinking styles), we risk contributing to greater auto- and hetero-stereotyping, preju-dice, and ultimately greater conflict and misunderstandings between groups, as well as increasing individuals' stress when they encounter people from different groups.

It is important for social scientists to remember that national differences typically account for a relatively small proportion of the total variance in most measures of values, beliefs, self-construals, and other dimensions of 'cultural orientation'. Commonly less than 10% of the variance in these measures is between nations, leaving 90% of the variance to be found within nations. Our cognitive systems as humans may be fine-tuned to detect such small differences, because they are connected to the different languages, dress, foods, and physiognomic features often found across groups. Cross-cultural psychology as a discipline was born in response to this source of salient variability in humans, but as a consequence our field has often tended to amplify and over-generalise the differences and neglect the similarities among people from different parts of the world.

We need more balance in reporting our findings, both within our profession and to the media. Matsumoto (2001) has challenged researchers to include measures of effect sizes when reporting cross-cultural work. We need to educate students and other researchers more about the relative size of differences that we are talking about. Concurrently, we should also monitor how our research is understood by the public and tailor our communications accordingly (Abelson, 1995).

We also need to understand better how differences *within* nations can contribute to our understanding of psychological processes. Operationalising culture only at the national level may mean that we miss many interesting and important phenomena. Van Herk and Poortinga (2012) found significant variability in value priorities across regions within nations in Europe. Similarly, the culture of other kinds of social groupings needs more of our attention. Cohen (2009) challenged psychologists to study cultural differences due to socio-economic status and religion. In Chapter 8, we considered the role of families and schools as sources of cultural variability. Work organisations also generate cultures. Dickson, Resick, and Hanges (2006) showed that after controlling for national differences in the GLOBE study data, preferred leader styles could be predicted by organisation type. Broadening our attention to consider a wider variety of social groupings would greatly help to overcome the challenge that we essentialise differences between nations.

Breidenbach and Nyiri (2008) have encouraged practitioners dealing with intercultural issues to avoid negative implications based on incorrect cultural assumptions by asking a series of questions: for instance, 'Do cultural categorisations overemphasise differences, but neglect variability in values, norms and practices within these groups?', 'Who speaks on behalf of what interest group, what could be their interests, and what perspectives are potentially ignored or neglected?', and 'How much are cultural norms and practices shared and binding, and do members of this community have the possibility and right to behave differently?'

NOW THAT WE HAVE VALID INDIVIDUAL-LEVEL MEASURES OF BELIEFS AND VALUES, WHY DO WE NEED HIGHER-LEVEL MEASURES?

Psychologists have traditionally focused on analysing the cognitions and behaviour of individuals, as this level of analysis lends itself to favoured empirical methods and resonates with the individualistic cultural assumptions that have shaped empirical psychology more generally. However, we have encountered throughout this book compelling reasons why the understanding of culture cannot be successfully accomplished just by looking at individual behaviour. At the individual level, values explain relatively little variance in attitudes, beliefs, and behaviour.

Correlations seldom exceed .30, explaining less than 10% of the variability in other variables (Taras, Kirkman, & Steel, 2010; Fischer & Boer, 2012). As Lewin, Heider, and Heider (1936) famously proposed many years ago, behaviour is a joint product of person and situation, so in understanding cultures we must address the social contexts in which individuals are embedded. In Chapter 5, we noted that national cultures vary in terms of the perceived importance of traits (Church, Katigbak et al., 2006), but context remains important even in those cultures in which perceived traitedness is strong.

Within mainstream psychology, attempts have been made to understand individuals' behaviour changes based on the theory of planned behaviour (Ajzen & Fishbein, 1980). Researchers in this field have found it necessary to include a measure of the individual's subjective norms in order to achieve predictive success. First attempts to develop measures approximating subjective culture cross-culturally have been reported by the GLOBE researchers (House et al., 2004), who asked respondents to rate how typical behaviours were in their nation, and by Fischer (2006), who asked respondents to predict the values that were typical in their nation. However, as we emphasised in the preceding section, looking at differences between nations is only a first approximation to identifying the contexts that are important to individuals. Each nation is likely to comprise a myriad of loosely correlated subjective cultures that are somewhat different from those of other nations.

In several chapters, but especially in Chapter 7, we have emphasised the importance of unpackaging cultural differences using mediation studies. Most attempted mediation tests have used self-construal measures, and we have seen that these are not always successful. One possible explanation is that these measures have been insufficiently precise. If I construe myself as interdependent, it remains unclear with whom I am interdependent and what kind of interdependence is involved, so the predictive validity of 'interdependence' in broad terms may vary. Notably, although independent and interdependent self-construals are typically thought of as properties of individuals, they can also be understood as ways of thinking about one's relation to aspects of one's social context. Hence, these constructs also provide a bridge toward taking greater account of social context.

Multi-level analyses sampling respondents from many nations provide a novel way of unpackaging cultural differences, making it possible to disentangle the effects of individuals' personal values, beliefs or self-construals from the effects of the prevailing 'climate' of values, beliefs or self-construals within each group of respondents. Studies of this kind have shown some striking results. Although we noted earlier that national profiles of values and beliefs are far from consensual (contradicting early expectations that these constructs would be 'shared': Triandis, 1993), the small part of the variance that *is* shared appears to be especially important for predicting differences in trust and in ways of achieving distinctiveness or self-esteem (e.g., Gheorghiu, Vignoles, & Smith, 2009; Becker, Vignoles et al., 2012, 2013). Once these effects of cultural climate are accounted for, individual-level differences typically account for little or no further variation. Therefore we do not actually improve our ability to explain differences between nations by adding in individual-level measures.

We need studies that address more directly the mechanisms by which cultural context relates to individuals. We have explored three research designs in which this can be done. Firstly, by using experiments we can induce persons to think of themselves for a while in terms of differing types of subjective culture, and assess the consequences. The effectiveness of such primings will depend on the ability and knowledge of individuals about the various cultural constructs being activated.

Secondly, in Chapter 8 we examined current attempts to address social context in ways that move away from contrasts between nations. Yamagishi (2011) attempts to do this by creating experiments that test whether respondents react to particular experimental contexts in ways that imply their immersion in his understanding of the practices and institutions of Japanese culture. Chiu and his colleagues ask respondents to rate the subjective culture of more immediate membership groups to which they belong, and then measure the beliefs, attitudes and behaviours associated with identifying with these subjective cultures (Chiu et al., 2010; see also Wan, Chiu, Peng and Tam, 2007; Wan, Chiu, Tam et al., 2007; Wan & Chiu, 2009). Yamagishi's and Chiu's approaches differ from one another in their view of whether subjective culture is directly accessible or more implicit, but they both hold promise for future developments in specifying cultures.

Finally, our theories of culture can benefit from areas of investigation that are traditionally thought of as 'applied' topics, rather than sources of theory. Intergroup contacts, whether between groups in society or between migrants and host cultures, are situations where individuals encounter a choice of cultural contexts and are required to negotiate some kind of linkage with them. Choices about cultural identity signify one's association with one or another type of social grouping, through the implicit or explicit matching of self and social context (Benet-Martinez et al., 2002). Matching processes of this kind can also be unpacked through mediation studies. For instance, in Chapter 13 we noted Kurman and Ronan-Eilon's (2004) finding that successful acculturation among Israeli immigrants was mediated by their perceptions of typical beliefs held by the majority Israeli population, but not by the actual typical profile of majority Israeli beliefs. Thus, we believe that the way forward is found not by focusing exclusively on individuals or on nations, but by examining the subjectively experienced spaces produced by the myriad interactions between individuals and groups that make up larger entities such as nations, as well as organisations, schools, families and so forth.

ARE RESEARCHERS STILL FOCUSING TOO NARROWLY ON INDIVIDUALISM-COLLECTIVISM?

There are good reasons why a focus on the cultural dimension of individualism-collectivism and its two important correlates, power distance and wealth, has been fruitful. As we have seen, changes in wealth appear to be major determinants of contemporary changes in values, beliefs and behaviours. However, the multiple ways in which individualism-collectivism has been understood by different investigators can be considered both as too broad and also as too narrow. It is now clear that a cross-cultural psychology with such an imprecise focus cannot hope to explain the world's continuing diversity. We consider these two perspectives in turn.

Too Broad

As we have described in earlier chapters, the overall syndrome of individualism-collectivism entails numerous components. At the nation level, we noted in Chapters 5 and 7 the recent identification of separate dimensions of individualism-collectivism related to beliefs and self-construals (Owe, Vignoles, et al., 2012, 2013). At the individual level, researchers have tried to identify key components in the expression of individualism-collectivism for individual culture members. These individual attributes may entail the various values, beliefs, personality traits, and views of self that are particularly prevalent in a given cultural context. However, if we are to explain rather than merely describe cultural differences we need to identify which of these elements are most central to the contrasts that are found between cultural groups. This requires the unpackaging of cultural differences using mediation designs. As we explored in Chapter 7, the researchers who have examined mediation using self-construal measures derived from individualism-collectivism have operationalised their measures in different ways. To test the proposed causal role of particular measures of cultural orientation, however defined, in the creation and maintenance of cultures, it will be essential to test alternative mediators against one another, so that we can better specify the processes involved.

Too Narrow

Researchers have identified a considerable number of further ways in which national cultures differ from one another, beyond individualism-collectivism. Some of these differences have been conceptualised as dimensions, whereas others such as religious affiliation are categorical in nature. Among the dimensions identified by Hofstede (1980), uncertainty avoidance has been neglected, perhaps because different measures of the concept yield conflicting scores (House et al., 2004). Masculinity-femininity has been neglected because the naming of the dimension is often construed as sexist. Only Hofstede himself has championed it (Hofstede & Associates, 1998). A more recent analysis has identified a distinctive nation-level dimension of variability derived from World Values Survey data, named as Monumentalism-Flexumility (Minkov, 2011, 2012).

In terms of the variability associated with religion, we noted in Chapter 12 that, at the individual level, religious persons from all monotheistic religions have similar value profiles (Huismans,1994). However, at the nation level, Georgas et al. (2004) found the preponderant religious affiliation to be a correlate of cultural variation that is independent of the cluster of attributes associated with individualism-collectivism and wealth. Consequently, we cannot explain Georgas et al.'s results solely in terms of economic differences. The fact that nations in which one or other of these religious affiliations predominates have a shared distinctiveness must derive from something other than the value endorsements that we have shown in Chapter 14 to be substantially dependent on economic forces (Fischer & Boer, 2011; Inglehart & Baker, 2000).

A likely candidate is the intricately interwoven patterns of individual religious observance and institutional supports for that observance that exist within a given nation. These supports include the use of particular types of curriculum and distinctive styles of schooling associated with different religious traditions (Hofstede, 1986), provision of public holidays based upon religious observances, along with the belief and value emphases provided by the media and by mosques, temples, ashrams, and churches that enable particular kinds of observance.

Some researchers exploring alternative dimensions of national culture have followed a strategy that parallels one of the paths taken by those studying individualism-collectivism. For instance, individual-level measures have been created for power distance (Earley, 1993; Shavitt, Torelli, & Riemer, 2011), uncertainty avoidance (Sorrentino, Otsubo, Yasanaga, Nezlek et al., 2005), tightness-looseness (Gelfand et al., 2011) and, of course, multiple dimensions of values (Schwartz, 1992) and beliefs (Leung & Bond, 2004). Each of these can be, and in most cases has been, tested as a potential mediator of particular cultural effects. In future studies, it will be increasingly important to test these mediators against one another competitively.

Paying increased attention to dimensions such as these may aid the further development of the field. However, in our search for additional dimensions relevant to culture, we must avoid the assumption that all dimensions have equal relevance to what occurs in all parts of the world. Hofstede (2001) suggested that the reason why Uncertainty Avoidance emerged in his analysis, but not in the later study by the Chinese Culture Connection (1987) of predominantly Asian nations, is because Uncertainty Avoidance is more relevant to a strong concern with truth in Western nations. Conversely, he suggested that the dimension of Confucian Work Dynamism identified in the latter study (later renamed by him as Long Term Orientation) has more relevance to Pacific Asian nations, where he claims there is greater concern with virtue. His suggestion may or not prove correct, but it underlines the importance of also seeking out those aspects of culture thought to have more local emic relevance, as we discuss next.

HAVE WE PAID ENOUGH ATTENTION TO INDIGENOUS, EMIC APPROACHES?

In this book, we have emphasised studies that analyse comparative data from a set of nations, mostly using concepts derived from the overarching conceptual frameworks that have emerged over the past several decades. During this same time period, other researchers have sought to identify distinctive ways of understanding the psychological processes that occur within their own specific national groups. We have noted examples of such emic analyses, particularly from Japan (Yamaguchi, 2004), the Philippines (Enriquez, 1993; Pe-Pua, 2006), Brazil (Ferreira et al., 2012), the southern United States (Cohen & Nisbett, 1997), and China (Cheung et al., 1996; Chen & Chen, 2012). More extensive summaries of the achievements of indigenous psychologists are also available (Sinha, 1997; Kim, Yang, & Hwang, 2006).

From our perspective, indigenous studies pose two especially important questions. Firstly, are the processes that have been identified in specific locations actually unique to those locations, or can similar processes be identified in other cultures, even though they may be less salient there? If emic processes are actually more general than was first thought, then we may hope that they can contribute to the development of the cross-cultural field as a whole. Secondly, can indigenous psychologies draw our attention to further areas of study that would repay broader attention? We shall address these questions in turn.

There are at least seven instances in which concepts first identified indigenously have proved to have some degree of validity when operational measures of these concepts are incorporated into studies undertaken in wider cultural contexts. Yamaguchi's (2004) measure of the *amae* relationship style has shown significant relationships to hypothesised constructs in the United States, as has Cheung et al.'s (1996) Chinese personality dimension of interpersonal relatedness and Kwan et al.'s (1997) measure of relationship harmony. Diaz-Guerrero's (1993) measures of Mexican 'historic socio-cultural premises' were endorsed in Turkey (Ayçiçegi, 1993). Leung's (1987) measure of animosity reduction as a predictor of conflict resolution style was formulated in Hong Kong, but showed significant effects in Israel (Bond et al., 1992), and in Nigeria and Canada (Gire & Carment, 1993). Cohen and Nisbett's (1997) US concept of honour culture was found to be applicable in Brazil (Vandello & Cohen, 2003). *Guanxi*-like influence is found in several non-Chinese nations (Smith, Huang et al., 2012; Smith, Torres et al. 2012).

It is also possible that indigenous concepts within cultures can be linked to general psychological processes that have relatively universal applicability, thereby making the emic concept within cultures understandable from a broader, pan-cultural perspective (Ferreira et al., 2012). We should note also that if the theories and measures employed in mainstream social psychology are thought of as comprising an indigenous psychology of the USA, many of these concepts and measures have found extensive and valid application elsewhere. If US social psychology can be exported successfully, why should other social psychologies also not be exported? Recognising the emic nature of mainstream North American psychology underlines the mutual benefit of linking emic to etic approaches everywhere.

Numerous other indigenous studies draw attention to novel constructs that are likely to merit further exploration. Some researchers have identified values thought to be distinctive to particular nations or regions. Hamid (2004) developed a measure of *budi* values in Malaysia. *Budi* values concern generosity, respect, sincerity and rightcousness. Hamid found that, among his Malay student respondents, *budi* values accounted for variance additional to that explained by the Schwartz value survey. Boski (2006) identified *sarmatism* as a key Polish value. *Sarmatism* entails a mix of impulsive self-assertion and social hedonism, deriving from values espoused in times past by the Polish nobility, and is less clearly linked with other more widely used value measures. Noorderhaven and Tidjani (2001) investigated whether there were distinctive values among students in six nations in sub-Saharan Africa, compared to those in eight other nations. Nation-level analysis indicated that among the Africans the strongest emphases were on the importance of religion, respect for rules, the value of sharing with others, and a pessimistic view of human nature. Some of these values may relate to the concept of *Ubuntu* which is said to encapsulate key values prevalent in sub-Saharan cultural groups (Broodryk, 2006). These culture-specific values may also capture relevant aspects of abstract values better than the directly translated concepts in widely used instruments, such as the Schwartz Value Survey or the World Values Survey.

While there may prove to be some distinctive values that can account for variance not captured by existing comprehensive value surveys, it is more likely that indigenous psychologies will deepen our understanding by identifying distinctive norms and roles than by identifying distinctive values or beliefs. This is because, particularly in the less studied regions of the world, behaviour is likely to be governed less by prevailing values and beliefs and more by traditional role and norm requirements. Even in Western nations the role of norms has been inadequately explored.

Dols (1993) identified the frequent presence of what he termed 'perverse norms' in Spanish society. These are norms that are widely endorsed but not consistently enforced.

Traffic speed limits are a notable example in many cultures. The existence of such norms enables persons in positions of authority to maximise their discretionary power over others, by choosing when norms shall be enforced and when deviance shall be tolerated. Perverse norms are likely to be characteristic of cultures that are high on power distance but low on situational constraint, though no cross-cultural studies assessing their characteristics have yet been reported.

In lower power distance nations, a different type of norm, first identified by Feather (1994) in Australia as the 'tall poppy syndrome' is more likely to prevail. This describes the negative reactions that individuals may receive if they are excessively assertive or successful. In Scandinavian nations this phenomenon is often referred to as the *Jante* law (Fivelsdal & Schramm-Nielsen, 1993) and in Hong Kong as 'red eye disease' (Bond, 1993). More attention to the distinctiveness of roles and norms across cultures is required. It reflects our discipline's individualistic and subjective bias (Sampson, 1981) that so little attention has been paid to these external, shared determinants of social behaviour.

Two further points are significant in relation to this issue. A contrast is often made between quantitative cross-cultural comparisons and qualitative indigenous studies. We noted in Chapter 4 that hardly any cross-cultural studies have established a full-score equivalence of their measures across cultures. In that sense, we could argue that most studies in this book have an emic element. Moreover, especially when dealing with the complexities of cultures, it is not beneficial to limit particular areas of research to particular methods. As the studies discussed in this section illustrate, both kinds of method can be used in the same study, even if that study is predominantly qualitative or predominantly quantitative. In addressing a research issue, it will often be preferable to use a sequence of methods as the project unfolds.

HOW CAN CROSS-CULTURAL PSYCHOLOGISTS CREATE A BETTER FUTURE?

There are five principal ways in which cross-cultural psychology is already able to make substantive practical contributions toward creating a better society. In each of these areas, we have the capability to do more, if the necessary resources are made available and if key persons become aware of what we can contribute.

Providing Information on the Nature of Cultural Differences and Their Importance

A basic goal of any scientific investigation is to provide accurate information. Cross-cultural psychology has two tasks in this area. Firstly, studies can and do challenge the validity of derogatory or ill-informed ethnic and national stereotypes, by publicising empirically-based information on the values, beliefs, and life experiences of different groups. Secondly, studies can and do challenge those who adopt a culture-blind perspective, asserting that cultural differences either do not exist or can be ignored with impunity. This book can be seen as a challenge to those who assert that a valid psychology can be created by conducting studies within a single cultural group or nation. More specific challenges to psychologists are to move away from imposed-etic uses of psychometric instruments and develop locally valid instruments (Harkness, 2003; Hambleton & Zenisky, 2011).

Information and concepts derived from cross-cultural psychology are available to all, for use in ways that may serve their specific needs. Opinion surveys such as the annual Eurobarometer inform political debate within the European Union. Research into culturally varying definitions of human rights in 35 nations (Doise, Spini, & Clemence, 1999; Doise 2001) provides a basis for formulating ethical codes and for evaluating UN programmes. Advertisers have taken much note of the concepts of individualism and collectivism, designing advertisements to appeal to the prevailing values within their target populations (Aaker & Williams, 1998; De Mooij, 1998; Aaker & Schmitt, 2001; Wyer & Hong, 2010).

Training Persons in the Skills of Cross-Cultural Interaction

As we have seen, an increasing number of people are engaged in activities where cross-cultural effectiveness is required. Preparatory training programmes have been provided and evaluated for expatriate business persons, student sojourners, aid and development workers, tourist hospitality providers, police officers, military personnel, immigrants and many others (Brislin, 1990; Ward, 2013). Providing information on cultural differences is necessary, but rarely sufficient to facilitate effective cross-cultural interactions. As we explored in Chapter 11, while briefings and cultural assimilators can provide information, different forms of experiential training can enhance their effectiveness (Earley, 1987). Key elements in the success or failure of training programmes appear to be their duration and the degree to which they focus closely on the circumstances in which the trainees will be involved. A token investment of time and resources is unlikely to have more than a short-term effect and may induce an ungrounded sense of confidence.

Contributing to Programmes of Conflict Resolution

We have described several programmes in which psychologists with an understanding of the dynamics of intergroup relations have designed and carried through interventions relevant to the aftermath of warfare and genocide (Staub et al., 2005; Cehajic-Clancy et al., 2011; Rimé et al., 2011), as well as those that derive their rationale from applications of the contact hypothesis in a variety of less intensely contested settings. It is more typical that such interventions would involve multidisciplinary teams, but they have undoubted potential for the amelioration of society.

Working Multiculturally

There have been many applications of cross-cultural psychology in the fields of health and education in different parts of the world and also within multicultural nations such as the USA (Harkness & Keefer, 2000). A general lesson from these types of interventions is that not much is accomplished unless a culturally sensitive approach is used. In this context there is a growing need for culturally informed psychologists to take part in efforts to promote health, education, poverty reduction, gender parity and the like in the majority, non-Western world. Together with health workers, pediatricians, education specialists and others, psychologists can and should work in the projects of international agencies such as UNICEF and the World Health Organisation to contribute to human well-being globally.

It has long been lamented that cultural psychologists and anthropologists have benefited more from children in developing nations than those children have benefited from social scientists (Jahoda, 1986). It is high time to repay this debt by serving them better with our accumulated knowledge and expertise. An instance of a particularly effective intervention is the Turkish Early Enrichment Programme pioneered by Kağıtçıbaşı (2007), which has involved more than 100,000 disadvantaged mothers and their young children in Turkey. Its effects have been documented over 20 years (Kağıtçıbaşı, Sunar, Bekman et al. (2009), and the programme has been adopted in six further nations. There is now considerable expertise available in how to apply a culturally sensitive psychology usefully (Poortinga, 2009). As proposed by UNESCO, programmes should contribute to *endogenous* (that is, from within) development at human and societal levels (Tripathi, 1988; Huynh, 1979). This type of approach must encompass *both* culturally relevant *and* globally shared knowledge.

Achieving this type of collaborative linkage is never easy. A key element in the situation is that one party to the collaboration is typically of higher social status and paid much more than the other party. This differential can set in motion a downward spiral (Carr, 2003). The less well-recognised parties feel unjustly treated and therefore hold back their contribution, or even undermine the project. This leads the well-recognised party to evaluate the less well-recognised parties negatively and sometimes to compensate by increasing his or her own contribution. This dynamic in turn leads to further reduced ownership of the project and contribution from the less well-recognised parties. Unless this cycle is halted, both groups will become disillusioned and the project will fail, because the involvement of the less-well recognised parties is crucial to its long-term success. Carr's analysis was focused on technical aid workers in Africa, but is equally applicable to all types of multinational enterprise.

Equally important issues arise within the fields of psychotherapy and counseling. The effective diagnosis and treatment of distress requires an awareness of the cultural context in which it arises. If therapists and counsellors do not share the same cultural background as their clients, they require additional trained expertise in identifying culturally appropriate styles of understanding and response, so as to intervene more effectively (Pedersen et al., 1996; Dwairy, 2006).

Advising Key Negotiators and Decision-Makers

We have discussed in previous chapters the recent and massive increase in travel and migration. Researchers into the processes of acculturation are able to provide crucial information on the consequences of different government policies concerning immigration and community relations. While many governments have recently been implementing more restrictive policies concerning the admission of migrants, the policies in force concerning minority groups already present vary more widely between nations. Those nations such as Canada, Australia and New Zealand that have established official policies of multiculturalism have done so with knowledge of the relevant work of acculturation researchers.

Diplomacy and business negotiations provide a second field in which advice from specialists is crucial. Published accounts of negotiations tend to emphasise occasions when spectacular misunderstandings have occurred, due either to mistranslations, the misreading of non-verbal cues, or an incompatibility between negotiation styles (Glenn, Wittmeyer, & Stevenson, 1997). Given the vital consequences of such negotiations, these shortcomings make for dramatic reading. Factors contributing to successful negotiations are less newsworthy, but there is little doubt that culturally-informed negotiators more often succeed. These factors require greater attention.

In some cases, advice can be more methodological than substantive. A multinational business company running the same training programme for its employees throughout the world asked one of the authors of this book to help them work out why the programme was always less successful in Europe than in North America and Asia. The explanation turned out to be that European trainees, consistent with their cultural socialisation in assertiveness, showed a lower acquiescent response style in their ratings of the training programme. The evaluation form was redesigned, so that the training could be more accurately and hence validly assessed.

HOW CAN CROSS-CULTURAL PSYCHOLOGY BEST MOVE FORWARD?

Here, we illustrate the fact that the research process requires continuing dialogue and debate by offering separate views from each of the authors of this book.

Ron Fischer

I think there are two separate opportunities for progress. First, we need to get involved in more applied projects in which we test our theoretical insights in the field. If our current understanding of culture is valid and realistic, we should be able to make changes in people's lives that enhance their well-being and psychological functioning. At the same time, starting to address issues that people in different cultural environments grapple with will help us to focus on those things that are of greatest importance to individuals around the world. Following recent high-profile cases of scientific fraud and the relative lack of contribution by psychologists to public debates about domestic and global concerns, psychology faces the challenge of being regarded as an untrustworthy and irrelevant academic discipline. Applying our knowledge with scientific rigor in the field and addressing those challenges that people face will help to redress this perception and sharpen our theories, methods and understanding of psychology as a discipline with real-world applications.

The second avenue is to use more interactionist models that integrate psychological perspectives with biological, ecological and historical perspectives. Recent work in biology suggests that there are more basic biological differences between different populations around the world, whether in the distribution of specific genes or the gut microbes that are implicated in personality or disease. Such biological differences may directly shape psychological traits in different contexts. More likely though, such biological differences will interact with the environment in which people are situated. We need to understand how basic biological predispositions are played out in specific ecological, social, and historical contexts.

We reviewed some general frameworks related to this perspective in Chapter 3. The climato-economic model of Van de Vliert (2009; in press) shows the interdependency between climate and wealth in a wide range of psychological functions. The existence of genetic vulnerabilities to the experience of stress and anxiety between different ethnicities raises questions about how cultural and environmental variables interact in reducing this risk (see Chiao & Blizinsky, 2010; Fischer, 2013a). Historical changes in climates and ecological conditions have produced radical evolutionary changes in different populations (Diamond, 1997, 2005). Including non-psychological variables in our thinking and research designs can help us address long-standing questions in cross-cultural psychology. For example, testing the combined and interactive effects of climate and wealth has helped to shed some light on the relative importance of wealth versus individualism in predicting well-being across societies (Fischer & Van de Vliert, 2011). Giving greater attention to the non-psychological variables that these researchers have highlighted and their interactions with one another can move our understanding of cultural phenomena forward.

In addition to the direct and interactive effects of these variables on psychological variables, we need a better understanding of how psychological processes operate in different environments. Boer and Fischer (2013) found that although values are related to attitudes and behaviours in currently studied samples, the strength of these relationships is moderated to a large extent by their social and biological context. For example, in contexts with greater disease stress, people are less likely to express their values (particularly those relating to openness to change versus conservation) in terms of specific attitudes and behaviours, compared to contexts where people are less threatened by diseases. This suggests that psychological processes are responsive to environmental variables, but we do not understand well the mechanisms of how such external variables would influence the translation of values into attitudes. Earlier in this chapter, we discussed how little variance is explained in current cross-cultural research. By focusing on how relatively small differences in otherwise similar processes are played out in different ways in environments with differing constellations of ecological, social, economic, and historical conditions, we can move away from static interpretations of culture and embrace more fully how continuity and change in people's environments shape psychological functions.

Viv Vignoles

First of all, I endorse the main points made by Ron Fischer in the preceding paragraphs. In particular, I strongly agree with him that cross-cultural psychology can only advance if it engages with the real issues that matter to diverse groups of people in all parts of the world (not just in North America and East Asia). However, my main comments here are focused on theoretical and methodological issues.

I believe that an important challenge for cross-cultural psychologists seeking to unpackage cross-cultural differences will be to look beyond individual-level constructs and measures. In some respects, the focus on individual-level mediation tests in recent years has been a significant step forward, but it rests on an implicit model of cultures as reducible to collections of persons who happen to have similar beliefs, values, or self-construals. Multi-level research is increasingly showing this implicit model to be erroneous: for example, people appear to base their self-esteem on dimensions that are valued within their surrounding cultural contexts, but these effects are not mediated by individuals' own, personal value priorities (Becker, Vignoles, et al., 2013). If important effects of the cultural climate on psychological functioning are not reducible to the effects of people's individual cultural orientations, how then can they be explained? I believe that the answers will lie in exploring cultural practices and institutions involving communication and social relationships among cultural members, rather than focusing on processes within the heads of individual cultural members. Cultures are social contexts, and we forget this reality at our peril (Bond, 2013).

This focus implies that we need a rapprochement between the various subfields of psychology and other disciplines that are interested in culture. Cross-cultural psychologists have much to learn from the focus of cultural psychologists and social anthropologists on the social processes of cultural formation, reproduction, and change. These researchers, in turn, have much to learn from cross-cultural psychologists about the knowledge to be gained from systematic comparative research, including large-scale multinational surveys. All of us will fail dismally if we do not pay attention to the ideas of researchers from the cultures we are interested in studying, not only through collaborating in research but also by engaging seriously with indigenous psychological writings. These cultural products form the best defence available against basing our thinking on half-baked ideas and stereotypes.

Finally, we must recognise that contemporary trends of globalisation increasingly turn 'cultures' into 'cultural identities'. An important outcome of increased intercultural contact through travel, migration, or mediated communication is that cultural beliefs, values, and practices that once may have been taken for granted can now be recognised as distinctive to one's group, and thus they take on a new significance in defining who one is, as a member of a given cultural group. This substantially complicates the study of culture, because it gives the dimensions of culture an added motivational significance. In a globalised context, we can expect that some members of cultural groups will vigorously defend their beliefs, values, and practices against change or dilution, because they see this as the only way to maintain their cultural identities, to protect their sense of who they are. Other members of the same culture will disagree, so that 'our culture' becomes a political football. Developing a full account of the complexities of cultural identities and how they are influenced by global and local change is an important task for cultural and cross-cultural psychologists.

Michael Bond

Ron Fischer and Viv Vignoles have set apt but demanding agendas for doing state-of-the-art cross-cultural social psychology in this twenty-first century. I endorse their suggestions of ways forward 100%, as they reflect many of my own conclusions, hard won in the trenches of scientific practice during the previous century.

However, 'it is easy to say, but hard to do', as the Chinese adage puts the matter. Meeting even some of the components of the agendas they set for us will require achieving levels of academic competence and receiving institutional support as yet unheralded. Post-graduate training programmes will need to provide and encourage the acquisition of statistical sophistication, cultural literacy, research savvy and intellectual passion that is rare. These programmes must be carefully structured and inter-disciplinary; supervision by faculty must be reliable, informed and visionary; a collaborative, encouraging departmental or faculty culture must sustain the students and younger faculty undertaking cross-cultural research, since they face new challenges in the contemporary academic context. Cross-cultural data collection takes more time and requires greater collaborative skill than other social psychological research. It can also be done by exploiting the data sets collected by others and available for this purpose. What are the realistic expectations and assessment procedures for psychologists involved in doing this kind of research work at any stage of their career? Academic programmes should be developed accordingly.

Distinctive personal values, beliefs, and temperamental orientations will also be essential and will need to inform our research enterprise (Bond, 1997). Openness to experience, cognitive complexity, interpersonal understanding, attentiveness to procedural and distributive justice, sensitivity to cultural nuances, reliability, optimism and tenacity are key qualities. This is an exacting list, but these virtues are manifested in the lives of the key researchers profiled throughout our book; they stand as living examples to us of what is possible if we grasp the nettle of cross-cultural research mindfully.

Peter Smith

We envisaged the closing section of this chapter as illustrating the continuing debate as to how best to do cross-cultural psychology. Now we find that we agree with one another rather more than we had thought, partly through our collaborative working on this edition of the book. The team contributing to this edition differs from its predecessors in spanning two separate generations of cross-culturalists. This innovation is welcome and timely, but it also highlights the fact that cross-cultural psychology has arrived at a crossroads, as we have explored in preceding chapters. The framework that has guided the field for the past 30 years has been challenged.

Cultures can only to a limited extent be defined by shared values or shared meanings. The linkages between individuals and their contexts are certainly there, but they are less explicit than we had thought. To discern them, we need to conceptualise and use more sophisticated measures and analytical programmes. I have in mind two types of improvements or growth points. Firstly, our measures must address the individual's awareness of his or her social context, rather than simply tapping self-perceptions. If we forget context (be it at the nation level or any other more immediate level) we are losing sight of the essence of culture. We have noted a variety of new developments in this direction involving measures of perceived culture, norms, forms of interdependence, traitedness and differing identities as well as the use of multi-level modeling.

My second concern is more mundane and it has relevance to new ways of measuring culture, just as it has had to the older ones. We mostly use questionnaires to glean our data, and we have never reached agreement on the question of how to distinguish valid measures of cultural orientation from the distinctive response styles used by those whom we survey. For some researchers, the tendency of respondents to agree with all items in a survey is a measurement error that must be partialled out. For others, acquiescent responding is a part of what we are trying to measure. For them, taking it out makes our measures less valid and it must be left in. It is essential that the new generation of measures involves a more clearly reasoned basis for this aspect of measurement.

In Chapter 1, we cited Bond's (2009) portrayal of stages in the development of cross-cultural psychology, mapping a progression from a descriptive (Aristotelian) stage through a mapping (Linnaean) stage to an explanatory (Newtonian) stage. The Linnaean stage is exemplified by the early work of Hofstede (1980) and Schwartz (1994). The Newtonian stage is exemplified by the unpackaging studies that we have described. Bond's model actually includes a fourth 'Einsteinian' stage, one that was too complex for us to present in our opening chapter. In this stage, we move beyond the unpackaging of two-nation comparisons to address data that have been collected from a substantial range of sampled nations. Multiple samples greatly increase the possibility of discounting explanations that are distinctive to the peculiarities of one or two particular cultures. A full range of mediators and moderators can be explored, and researchers can begin to test complex predictions of the interplay between variables across multiple levels of analysis. Recent studies indicate that we have now arrived at the point where research of this type is being accomplished.

Back in the Aristotelian stage in 1984, Michael convened a small workshop with the goal of exploring the challenge that cross-cultural psychology could present to mainstream social psychology. He did his best to assemble the brightest and best among those who were working in the field at the time. He also invited three mainstream social psychologists to advise us on what we would need to do if we were to successfully challenge the mainstream. The outcome of the workshop (Bond, 1988b) made it plain that, in relation to the mainstream (if indeed there was one at the time), we were not a challenge. We were a small island visible only after the mainstream had travelled far out to sea.

Thirty years later, it can be argued that we are one of many elements within that mainstream. Sophisticated cross-cultural studies appear with some regularity in all the leading social psychology journals, and there is a substantial intermingling of the concepts that are used by those who say they are studying culture and by those who do not. We can hope for a further globalisation of the mainstream, both in terms of the locations of those who contribute to its corpus of research and in terms of researchers paying greater attention to context. In exchange, the mainstream has taught us and can continue to do so that in order to understand culture and its impact on individual processes we need also to study the differences between collectivities that are smaller in scale than nations.

As the process of acculturation of cross-cultural psychology within the mainstream proceeds, the much broader issue of globalisation will continue to unfold. As we discussed in Chapter 14, it is unclear whether cultural diversity will become more or less salient in the future. If the protection of cultural identities becomes more rather than less salient, we can expect that the interest in cross-cultural studies will escalate. More relevant for present purposes, we would also expect that the emphasis on ethnicity will occur in those domains of social life where ethnic group practices do not break the laws of the state or threaten the sovereignty of the nation. These domains are currently being negotiated in those many nations where culture and ethnicity are part of the contemporary public discourse. We expect that more and more nations will become involved in these issues. Forces of diversification rather than convergence will then become a salient theme in future cross-cultural studies.

> Where harmony is fecund, sameness is barren. Things accommodating each other on equal terms is called blending in harmony, and in so doing they are able to flourish and grow, and other things are drawn to them. But when same is added to same, once it is used up, there is no more. [...] There is no music in a single note, no decoration in a single item, no relish in a single taste. (*Discourses of the States*, China, 4th Century B.C.E.)

Glossary

Acculturation is the process of change that occurs when groups or individuals of differing cultural backgrounds interact with one another for extensive periods of time.

Acquiescent Response Style is the tendency to agree with rather than disagree with many or all of the statements that are provided by a researcher.

Analytic Cognition is a style of thinking and perception in which key components of a stimulus are identified and separated from their context.

Auto-Stereotypes are stereotypes held by group members about one's own group.

Back-Translation is the translation of a survey into a second language, followed by its translation back into the original language by a different bilingual person, who has not seen the original version.

Bicultural Identity Integration is the merging rather than separation of alternative ethnic identities of bicultural persons.

Citizen Mean is a score representing an attribute of the average member of a nation, computed using data that have been analysed at the individual level and then aggregated to the nation level.

Comparative Fit asks the question are the differences among members of this group smaller than the differences between members of this group and members of another group?

The **Contact Hypothesis** specifies the conditions under which contact between members of different ethnic or cultural groups will have positive effects on inter-group relations and interactions.

Cross-Cultural Psychology is an approach to the study of culture that focuses on comparisons between different groups and testing theories as to why they do or do not differ from one another.

Cultural Intelligence is defined as the possession of the relevant knowledge, motivation, behavioural flexibility and awareness of cultural differences that enables one to interact effectively with persons from other cultures.

Cultural Orientation is a general term used in this book to refer to any one of the various measures that are currently used to characterise culturally relevant individual-level attributes, such as self-construal, values or beliefs.

Cultural Psychology is an approach to the study of culture that emphasises the interrelatedness of persons and their specific contexts. This requires culturally appropriate research methods and makes no assumption that the results will be cumulative or will lead to the identification of causal relationships.

Culture is a concept applicable to all levels in the analysis of social systems – nations, ethnicities, organisations, teams, families, dyadic relationships. The culture of a social system comprises similar ways of responding to context, similar ways of processing information, and shared interpretations of the meanings of events occurring within the system. In this book we avoid labelling nations as cultures, even though very many of the studies that we discuss do base their sampling on nations. Nations do have many of the characteristics of cultures, but many nations are too diverse to fully satisfy their definition as having a unified culture. They are better thought of as political systems in which many types of other systems are embedded.

Cultures, High Context In high-context cultures, communication is typically through messages in which the meaning is implicit in the physical settings in which they occur or is internalised within the known personal attributes of the senders, for example their status and role. Very little of the message is explicit.

Cultures, Low Context In low-context cultures, communication is typically through explicit direct messages.

Decentering involves replacing culturally specific expressions in the initial version of an instrument with alternative wordings that are more translatable, but still preserve the underlying meaning.

Distal causes are longer-term and further-removed causes which may exercise their effect through one or more proximal causes.

Distributive Justice refers to the perceived fairness of the rewards that have been allocated.

Domain Under-Representation is present in a measure if an aspect of the domain that is important to the function of a theoretical variable is missing from that measuring instrument in at least one of the sampled groups.

Ecological Fallacy is the false belief that the relationship between two variables must be the same at different levels of analysis. Usually used to refer to the invalid extrapolation from nation-level relationships to individual-level relationships.

Emic and Etic Studies. Emic studies are those that draw material from the immediate context being studied and make no assumption about the cultural generality of what is discovered, while etic studies are those that make a provisional assumption that the phenomena being studied are universal and attempt to establish their validity everywhere.

Epigenetics refers to a wide range of processes that involve changes in gene expression and modifications in the genome that are not caused by genetic mechanisms. This involves the regulation of gene expression by environmental factors that does not change the underlying DNA sequence.

Epistemology is a branch of philosophy that discusses the nature, limits and scope of knowledge. It addresses questions such as 'What is knowledge?', 'What is a truth?' or 'How do we acquire knowledge?'

Essentialism is the belief that all members of a group share the same psychological characteristics.

Ethnicity/Ethnic Group Ethnicity is a problematic concept widely used in some parts of the world to identify sub-cultural groups on the basis of criteria such as ancestry, skin colour and other attributes. A person's self-identified ethnic identity does not always coincide with his or her ethnicity as identified by others.

The **Ethnolinguistic Vitality** of a language is defined by its status within a community, how many people speak it within a multi-lingual community, how much support a community provides to speakers of that language, and how much control they have over its use in various social settings.

An **Ethnotheory** is a set of values and beliefs distinctive to a particular cultural group. The term is usually employed in relation to childrearing.

Facework comprises a set of strategies for containing and neutralising threats to harmony within one's relations with others.

Factor Analysis is a statistical technique which indicates the extent to which different survey items have received similar responses and can therefore be grouped together as 'factors'.

In the **Family Model of Independence**, parents seek to foster autonomy and initiative in their children.

In the **Family Model of Interdependence**, parents emphasise the induction of conformity and obedience, so that their children become dutiful.

In the **Family Model of Psychological Interdependence**, parents seek to foster both autonomy and relatedness in their children.

Focus Groups are a form of qualitative research in which a group of individuals is asked to discuss their opinions, beliefs, attitudes or perceptions judgments about a particular object, construct, or topic of interest with each other and the researcher.

Full Score or Scalar Equivalence refers to a situation where the scores can be directly compared between two or more cultural groups. It assumes that the measure taps the same base level or intercept in all cultural groups.

Functional Equivalence refers to the situation where the same theoretical variable accounts for the same measurement outcomes across cultural groups.

Genetic Drift refers to changes in the frequency of genes or alleles in a particular population that are due to random fluctuations.

Your **Genotype** is the set of genes with which you are born. It is the complete hereditary information of an organism.

Globalisation refers to an increasing integration and interdependence of world views, ideas and cultures, driven by changes in mass transportation and communication (including the internet). Although authors often link technological changes in the last 200 years with the emergence of globalisation, many societies over the last 3,000 years have shown characteristics of globalisation.

Hetero-Stereotypes are stereotypes held by group members about groups other than one's own group.

Holistic Cognition is a style of thinking and of perception in which a pattern of stimuli and their interrelationships are considered as a whole.

Homology is the extent to which a psychological instrument has the same relationship with an external variable ('external' structure) at the individual level and at the nation level (using aggregated individual scores).

Independent Self-Construal is the representation of the self as separate from the social context, bounded, unitary, and stable.

Indigenous Psychology is an approach whose goal is to achieve understanding of a particular national or cultural group, using concepts that are developed locally rather than drawing on those provided from mainstream psychology.

Individualism-Collectivism refers to Hofstede's description of a nation-level dimension, derived from earlier writing by Kluckhohn and Strodbeck (1961), and defined by many authors in varying ways. The central element concerns the continuity of and commitment to group affiliations in collectivist cultures, compared with the negotiability of group affiliations and their rule-based operation in individualist cultures.

Individual-Level Studies involve studies in which the data from each individual respondent are treated as a separate case.

Integration is the term used in Berry's model of acculturation to describe a preference for both the maintenance of one's own culture and inclusion in the majority culture. It is synonymous with biculturalism.

Interactional Justice refers to the perceived fairness of the interpersonal interactions occurring during the process of reward allocation and distribution.

Interdependent Self-Construal is the representation of the self as closely connected to others, embedded in, and varying across, contexts.

Internal Validity refers to the level of confidence that a researcher can place on the premise that changes in a dependent variable are caused by the experimental manipulation alone and that alternative causal explanations can be ruled out.

The **Interpretation Paradox** refers to the problem that psychological differences between samples that vary along many different social, cultural and economic dimensions are easy to find, but it is then difficult to explain why these differences exist and what variables may cause them.

Intersubjective Culture refers to shared perceptions of the psychological characteristics that are widespread within and characteristic of a culture.

Interviews are used in qualitative research to capture the meaning and significance of particular themes, events, or experiences in the life of individuals by asking each respondent a series of relevant questions.

Intra-Class Correlation is an estimate of how much variability there is in subsamples within a dataset, compared to the variability in the dataset as a whole.

Isomorphism is the extent to which a psychological construct, and the instrument that measures the construct, have the same meaning and dimensionality (i.e., 'internal' structure, for instance, factors) at the individual and the nation levels.

A **Latent Variable** is a hypothetical variable that is not directly observable, but can be inferred from other variables that have been directly observed or measured. The inference of a latent variable is done through mathematical models, such as factor analysis.

A **Likert Scale** is a rating scale used in questionnaires that is named after an American psychologist, Rensis Likert. Respondents are asked to specify their level of agreement or disagreement with a specific statement on a symmetric agree-disagree rating scale (typically a 5- or 7-point graded scale). The response is taken as indicating the intensity of their reaction towards the stated topic.

Mediators are variables that account for the relationship between an independent or predictor variable and the dependent or criterion variable. In psychological terms, they often explain how the external context takes on an internal psychological significance. Mediators more generally imply causal theoretical processes and explain how and why effects occur.

Meta-Analysis is a statistical technique for summarising the results of a large group of related studies. Even though studies may have used different measurement scales, each can be analysed to yield an 'effect size', which is an estimate of the extent of change reported on whatever measure was used, minus the change found on any control or comparison group.

Metric Equivalence refers to a situation where relative comparisons (e.g., mean patterns or correlations) are comparable between two or more cultural groups. This result indicates that items have identical relationships with the latent underlying variable in all cultural groups.

Moderators are either categorical (gender, race, class, nation, etc.) or continuously measured variables (e.g., personality or values) that affect the direction and/or strength of the relationship between a predictor and criterion variable. In a correlational framework, the moderator is the third variable that affects the zero-order correlation between two variables, whereas in an ANOVA framework, they are represented as interactions between two independent variables. Moderator effects therefore refer to interactions between the variables used to predict an outcome.

Modernity is an aspect of capitalist societies characterised by industrialisation, a market economy and bureaucratic institutions. Associated changes such as urbanisation, social mobility and occupational differentiation are thought to lead to changes in values, aspirations and the increased psychological autonomy of individuals.

Members of **Monochronous** cultures prefer to do things one at a time sequentially, in contrast to members of **Polychronous** cultures, who are comfortable with doing several things at the same time.

Nation-Level Studies refer to studies in which all the data from each nation on each available variable are first averaged and then analysed, thereby treating each nation as a single case.

Non-Uniform Item Bias is characterised by individuals not showing the same ordering on the measurement instruments as would be expected based on their ordering along the latent variable. Bias is present and the size of this bias for a respondent in a group depends on the position of that individual on the latent variable.

Normative Fit asks the question how well does this particular group fit with my understanding of what groups of this type are like?

Objectivity refers to the absence of bias in the measurement process. The measurement process should yield equivalent results independent of the researcher or the instrument used.

Ontology is the philosophical discussion of being or reality. It is concerned with questions about what entities exist, how we know that an entity exists and what is its meaning, and how any entities may be grouped or related to each other.

Pancultural Factor Analysis derives a factor structure from a total data set without considering the origins of those data. Such an analysis mixes variability due to individuals and variability due to their country or culture of origin, which can result in misleading conclusions (see Figure 4.4). We do not recommend pancultural factor analysis.

Perceiver Readiness asks the question how do my goals, motives, and previous links with this group predispose me to feel about it now?

Phenotype refers to the form in which genes are expressed once environmental influences have taken effect.

A **Polymorphism** is a situation where two or more phenotypes exist in the same population, that is, there is more than one form (morph). In biological studies of personality, it often refers to variations in the DNA sequence. Single nucleotides (A, T, C or G) are changed in the alleles and this leads to differences between paired chromosomes in an individual.

Population Genetics is the study of the frequency and interaction of alleles and genes in a population.

Positive Group Distinctiveness means seeing my group as better than other groups in terms of one or more attributes chosen by myself.

Positivism is a philosophy of science that is based on empirical observation and the verification of data that can be derived from sensory experiences. It is assumed that general laws about the physical and social world can be formulated and that the researcher proceeds in an objective manner to draw conclusions from the collected data.

Post-Materialist Values are values that emphasise quality of life, protection of the environment and life style issues. These values emerge in the process of post-modernisation, as societies move from industrialised modern societies to a reliance on service industries that demand greater skill, autonomy, and creativity.

Postmodernism is a broad philosophical movement that rejects scientific or objective efforts to describe (in our context: psychological) processes. Reality is not independent of human understanding, but is socially constructed by humans. There is no absolute truth, and the way people perceive the world is subjective and shaped by language and power relations.

Post-positivism shares with positivism the meta-theoretical assumption that reality exists, but does not assume that reality can ever be known perfectly. Instead, it is recognised that the process of scientific research, like everyday understanding, is biased by the theoretical background, knowledge and values of the observer or researcher. Karl Popper, an influential proponent of this approach, argued that theories can only be falsified (that is, rejected based on empirical data), and never verified. One important implication is that theories need to be amenable to falsification for them to be assessed scientifically.

Procedural Justice refers to the perceived fairness of the procedures used in deciding on the allocation of rewards.

Proximal causes are the immediate causes of behaviour.

Psychological Adaptation refers to achieving successful mental balance in a novel cultural context.

Reactive Ethnicity is an assertion of one's minority ethnicity in reaction to assimilationist pressures or policies.

The **Reference Group Effect** occurs when respondents' descriptions of themselves or others on a series of Likert scales are influenced by which group they choose as a basis for comparison.

Reliability refers to the consistency of a measure, both in terms of its component parts and in terms of its repeated use over time. A measure has high reliability if it produces consistent results under consistent conditions.

Reward Assignment refers to a person's allocation of rewards to other, typically more junior, persons.

Reward Sharing refers to a person's allocation of rewards among peers, including oneself.

Segmented Assimilation occurs when a migrant is assimilated into an existing ethnic minority group rather than into the majority group.

Self-Construal was a term introduced by Markus and Kitayama (1991) to refer to what they later described as diverse 'modes of being' across cultures. The term was intended to encompass culture-level representations of the 'self' as an abstract category and the social orientations linked to them (Markus & Kitayama, 2003). Other researchers have mostly understood the term to refer to the self-concepts of individuals.

Situationism is a theory that persons' behaviours are determined more by situational contexts than by personality.

Smallest Space Analysis is a statistical technique analogous to factor analysis. It does not make the same statistical assumptions that are made in factor analysis, since the technique rests on ordinal measurement rather than interval scale measurement.

A **Social Axiom** is a widely shared belief as to what is true rather than false. It is distinct from values, which concern what is desirable versus what is undesirable.

Socio-Cultural Adaptation refers to learning and using the behavioural skills that are required to be effective in a novel cultural context.

Specific-Functional Adaptation is a form of cultural change that arises because it is distinctively useful to persons within a changed environment. For instance, factory shift workers who are required to clock in are likely to become more skilled in aspects of time management.

Structural Equivalence refers to the situation where the same measurement instrument is a valid and sufficient indicator of a theoretical variable of interest to the researchers in two or more cultural samples.

Subjective Culture is the individual's personal understanding of the terms that he or she uses to describe their context and life experience.

Translation-Back Translation is the classic translation procedure. An instrument is first translated from the source language into the target language and then independently translated back into the source language. The original and the back-translated versions are then compared and changes are made so as to improve accuracy.

Uniform Item Bias is characterised by individuals in two cultural groups showing the same order on the observed measurement that corresponds to their ordering on the latent variable. However, there are some relative differences between the two groups that are not accounted for by the latent variable. The degree of bias is the same for all individuals.

Unpackaging of culture is the process that explains why differences emerge between two or more cultural groups based on an explicit test of the psychological mediators of the observed cultural differences.

Validity in the statistical sense refers to whether a measure is fit for its intended purpose. Several subtypes can be distinguished. Predictive validity is concerned with whether the measure can predict some other construct of interest (sometimes called utility). Construct validity is the extent to which a measure accurately reflects the variability and relative position of test takers on the underlying construct that the measure is designed to measure.

References

Aaker, J.L. (1997). Dimensions of brand personality. *Journal of Marketing Research, 34*, 342–352.

Aaker, J.L., Benet-Martinez, V.L., & Garolera, J. (2001). Consumption symbols as carriers of culture: A study of Japanese and Spanish brand personality constructs. *Journal of Personality and Social Psychology, 81*, 492–508.

Aaker, J., & Schmitt, B. (2001). Culture-dependent assimilation and differentiation of the self: Preferences for consumption symbols in the United States and China. *Journal of Cross-Cultural Psychology, 32*, 561–576.

Aaker, J., & Williams, P. (1998). Empathy versus pride: The influence of emotional appeals across cultures. *Journal of Consumer Research, 25*, 241–261.

Abelson, R.P. (1995). *Statistics as principled argument*. Mahwah, NJ: Erlbaum.

Abubakar, A. (2008). *Infant-toddler development in a multiple risk environment*. Ridderkerk, Netherlands: Ridderprint.

Adair, W.L., & Brett, J. (2005). The negotiation dance. Time, culture and behavioral sequences in negotiation. *Organizational Science, 16*, 33–51.

Adair, W.L., Okumura, T., & Brett, J.M. (2001). Negotiation behavior when cultures collide: The United States and Japan. *Journal of Applied Psychology, 86*, 371–385.

Adair, W.L., Tinsley, C., & Taylor, M. (2006). Managing the intercultural interface: Third cultures, antecedents and consequences. In Y. Chen (Ed.), *Research on managing groups and teams, 9*, 205–232.

Adair, W.L., Weingart, L., & Brett, J. (2007). The timing and significance of offers in US and Japanese negotiations. *Journal of Applied Psychology, 92*, 1056–1068.

Adorno, T.W., Frenkel-Brunswik, E., Levinson, D.J., & Sanford, R.N. (1950). *The authoritarian personality*. New York: Harper.

Agarwal, R., & Misra, G. (1986). A factor analytic study of achievement goals and means: An Indian view. *International Journal of Psychology, 21*, 717–731.

Ainsworth, M., & Bowlby, J. (1991). An ethological approach to personality development. *American Psychologist, 46*, 333–341.

Ajzen, I., & Fishbein, M. (1980). *Understanding attitudes and predicting social behavior*. Englewood Cliffs, NJ: Prentice-Hall.

Albert, R.D., & Ha, I.A. (2004). Latino/Anglo-American differences in attributions to situations involving touching and silence. *International Journal of Intercultural Relations, 28*, 253–280.

Albright, L., Malloy, T.E., Qi, D., Kenny, D.A., et al. (1997). Cross-cultural consensus in personality judgments. *Journal of Personality and Social Psychology, 73*, 270–280.

Al Issa, A. (2003). Sociocultural transfer in L2 speech behaviors: Evidence and motivating factors. *International Journal of Intercultural Relations, 27*, 581–602.

Allen, M.W., Ng, S.H., Ikeda, K., Jawan, J.A., Sufi, A., Wilson, M., & Yang, K.S. (2007). Two decades of cultural value change and economic development in eight East Asian and Pacific island nations. *Journal of Cross-Cultural Psychology, 38*, 247–269.

Allik, J., & McCrae, R.R. (2004). Toward a geography of personality traits: Patterns of profiles across 36 cultures. *Journal of Cross-Cultural Psychology, 34*, 13–28.

Allik, J., & Realo, A. (2004). Individualism-collectivism and social capital. *Journal of Cross-Cultural Psychology, 35*, 29–49.

Allport, G.W. (1954). *The nature of prejudice*. Reading, MA: Addison-Wesley.

Allport, G.W., & Odbert, H. (1936). Trait names: A psycho-lexical study. *Psychological Monographs, 47*(1), (whole no. 21).

AlSayyad, N. (Ed.) (2001). *Consuming tradition, manufacturing heritage: Global norms and urban forms in the age of tourism*. London: Routledge.

Altemeyer, B. (1987). *Enemies of freedom: Understanding right-wing authoritarianism*. San Francisco, CA: Jossey-Bass.

Ambady, N., Koo, J., Lee, F., & Rosenthal, R. (1996). More than words: Linguistic and non-linguistic politeness in two cultures. *Journal of Personality and Social Psychology, 70*, 996–1011.

Amir, Y., & Sharon, I. (1987). Are social psychological laws cross-culturally valid? *Journal of Cross-Cultural Psychology, 18*, 383–470.

Andersen, P.A., Hecht, M., Hoobler, G.D., & Smallwood, M. (2002). Nonverbal communication across cultures. In W.B. Gudykunst & B. Mody (Eds), *Handbook of international and intercultural communication* (pp. 88–106). Thousand Oaks, CA: Sage.

Ang, S., & Van Dyne, L. (Eds) (2008). *Handbook of cultural intelligence: Theory, measurement and applications*. New York: Sharpe.

Ang, S., Van Dyne, L., et al. (2007). Cultural intelligence: Its measurement and effects on cultural judgment and decision-making, cultural adaptation and task performance. *Management and Organization Review, 3*, 335–369.

Apicella, C.L., Marlowe, F.W., Fowler, J.H., & Christakis, N.A. (2012). Social networks and cooperation in hunter-gatherers. *Nature, 481*, 497–501.

Archer, J. (2006). Cross-cultural differences in physical aggression between partners: A social-role analysis. *Personality and Social Psychology Review, 10*, 133–153.

Archer, J. (2009). Does sexual selection explain human sex differences in aggression? *Behavioral and Brain Sciences, 32*, 249–266.

Arends-Toth, J., & Van de Vijver, F. (2003). Multiculturalism and acculturation: Views of Dutch and Turkish-Dutch. *European Journal of Social Psychology, 33*, 249–266.

Arends-Toth, J., & Van de Vijver, F. (2007). Acculturation attitudes: A comparison of measurement methods. *Journal of Applied Social Psychology, 37*, 1462–1488.

Argyle, M., Henderson, M., Bond, M.H., et al. (1986). Cross-cultural variations in relationship rules. *International Journal of Psychology, 21*, 287–315.

Arnett, J.J. (1992). Reckless behavior in adolescence: A developmental perspective. *Developmental Review, 12*, 339–373.

Arnett, J.J. (2002). The psychology of globalization. *American Psychologist, 57*, 774–783.

Arnett, J.J. (2008). The neglected 95%: Why American psychology needs to become less American. *American Psychologist, 63*, 602–614.

Aron, A., Aron, E.N., & Smollan, D. (1992). Inclusion of Other in the Self scale and the structure of interpersonal closeness. *Journal of Personality and Social Psychology, 63*, 596–612.

Asbrock, R., Nieuwoudt, C., Duckitt, J., & Sibley, C. (2011). Societal stereotypes and the legitimation of intergroup behavior in Germany and New Zealand. *Analyses of Social Issues and Public Policy, 11*, 154–179.

Asbrock, R., Christ, O., Duckitt, J., & Sibley, C. (2012). Differential effects of intergroup contact for authoritarians and social dominators: A dual-process model perspective. *Personality and Social Psychology Bulletin, 38*, 477–490.

Asch, S. (1956). Studies of independence and conformity: A minority of one against a unanimous majority. *Psychological Monographs, 70*(9), whole no. 416.

Ashley-Koch, A., Yang, Q., & Olney, R.S. (2000). Sickle haemoglobin (HbS) allele and sickle cell disease: A HuGE review. *American Journal of Epidemiology, 151*, 839–845.

Ashton, M.C., Danso, H., Maio, G., Esses, V., Bond, M., & Keung, D. (2005). Two dimensions of political attitudes and their individual difference correlates: A cross-cultural study. In R. Sorrentino, D. Cohen, J. Olson & M. Zanna (Eds), *Culture and social behavior: The Ontario symposium* (Vol. 10, pp. 1–29). Mahwah, NJ: Erlbaum.

Ashton, M.C., Lee, K., Perugini, M., et al. (2004). A six-factor structure of personality-descriptive adjectives: Solutions from psycholexical studies in seven nations. *Journal of Personality and Social Psychology, 86*, 356–366.

Ataca, B., & Berry, J.W. (2002). Psychological, sociocultural, and marital adaptation of Turkish immigrant couples in Canada. *International Journal of Psychology, 37*, 13–26.

Ataca, B., & Berry, J.W. (2004). Comparative study of acculturation and adaptation among Turkish immigrants in Canada. Unpublished manuscript, Bogaziçi University, Istanbul.

Atkinson, Q., & Whitehouse, H. (2011). The cultural morphospace of ritual form: Examining modes of religiosity cross-culturally. *Evolution and Human Behavior, 30*, 50–62.

Atran, S., Axelrod, R., & Davis, R. (2007). Sacred barriers to conflict resolution. *Science, 317*(5841), 1039–1040.

Atran, S., & Henrich, J. (2010). The evolution of religion: How cognitive by-products, adaptive learning heuristics, ritual displays, and group competition generate deep commitments to prosocial religions. *Biological Theory, 5*(1), 18–30.

Atran, S., Medin, D. & Ross, N. (2005). The cultural mind: Environmental decision-making and cultural modelling within and across populations. *Psychological Review, 112*, 744–776.

Atran, S., & Norenzayan, A. (2004). Religion's evolutionary landscape: Counterintuition, commitment, compassion, communion. *Behavioral and Brain Sciences, 27*, 713–770.

Au, T.K. (2004). Making sense of differences: Language, culture and social reality. In S.H. Ng, C.N. Candlin, & C.Y. Chiu (Eds), *Language matters: Communication, culture and identity* (pp. 139–153). Hong Kong: City University of Hong Kong Press.

Aycan, Z. (2008). Cross-cultural approaches to leadership. In P.B. Smith, M.F. Peterson, & D.C. Thomas (Eds), *Handbook of cross-cultural management research* (pp. 219–238). Thousand Oaks, CA: Sage.

Aycan, Z., Kanungo, R.N., Mendonca, M., You, K., Deller, G., Stahl, G., & Kurshid, A. (2000). Impact of culture on human resource management practices: A ten country comparison. *Applied Psychology: An International Review, 49*, 192–221.

Ayçiçegi, A. (1993) *The effects of the mother training program.* Unpublished Master's thesis, Bogaziçi University, Istanbul, Turkey.

Bain, P., Park, J., Kwok, C., & Haslam, N. (2009). Attributing human uniqueness and human nature to cultural groups: Distinct forms of subtle dehumanisation. *Group Processes and International Relations, 12*, 789–805.

Bain, P., Vaes, J., Kashima, Y., Haslam, N., & Guan, Y. (2012). Folk conceptions of humanness: Beliefs about distinctive and core human characteristics in Australia, China and Italy. *Journal of Cross-Cultural Psychology, 43*, 53–58.

Baltes, P., & Smith, J. (2004). Lifespan psychology: From developmental contextualism to developmental biocultural co-constructivism. *Research in Human Development, 1*, 123–144.

Bandura, A. (2002). Social cognitive theory in cultural context. *Applied Psychology: An International Review, 51*, 269–290.

Bardi, A., Calogero, R., & Mullen, B. (2009). A new archival approach to the study of values and value-behavior relations: Validation of the value lexicon. *Journal of Applied Psychology, 93*, 483–497.

Bardi, A., & Guerra, V. (2011). Cultural values predict coping using culture as an individual difference variable in multicultural samples. *Journal of Cross-Cultural Psychology, 42*, 908–927.

Barker, V., Giles, H., Noels, K., Duck, J., Hecht, M., & Clément, R. (2001). The English-only movement: A communication analysis of changing perceptions of language vitality. *Journal of Communication, 51*, 3–37.

Bartholomew, K., & Horowitz, L.M. (1991). Attachment styles in young adults: A test of a four category model. *Journal of Personality and Social Psychology, 62*, 226–244.

Bartram, D. (2013). Scalar equivalence of OPQ32: Big Five profiles of 31 countries. *Journal of Cross-Cultural Psychology, 44*, 61-83 .

Bass, B.M. (1997). Does the transactional-transformational leadership paradigm transcend organizational and national boundaries? *American Psychologist, 52*, 130–139.

Baumeister, R. (2005). *The cultural animal: Human nature, meaning and social life.* New York: Oxford University Press.

Baumrind, D. (1991). The influence of parenting style on adolescent competence and substance use. *Journal of Early Adolescence, 11*, 56–95.

Baysu, G., Phalet, K., & Brown, R. (2011). Dual identity as a two-edged sword: Identity threat and minority school performance. *Social Psychology Quarterly, 74*, 121–143.

Beauvois, J.L., Courbet, D., & Oberlé, D. (2012). The prescriptive power of the television host: A transposition of Milgram's obedience paradigm in the context of a TV gameshow. *European Review of Applied Psychology*, *62*, 111–190.

Beauvois, J.L., & Dubois, N. (1988). The norm of internality in the explanation of psychological events. *European Journal of Social Psychology*, *18*, 299–316.

Becht, M., & Vingerhoets, A. (2002). Crying and mood change: A cross-cultural study. *Cognition and Emotion*, *16*, 87–101.

Becker, M., Vignoles, V.L., et al. (2012). Culture and the distinctiveness motive: Constructing identity in individualistic and collectivistic contexts. *Journal of Personality and Social Psychology*, *102*, 833–855.

Becker, M., Vignoles, V.L., et al. (2013). *Cultural bases of self-esteem: Seeing oneself positively in different cultural contexts*. Manuscript submitted for publication.

Benedict, R. (1932). Configuration of culture in North America. *American Anthropologist*, *34*, 1–27.

Benedict, R. (1946). *The chrysanthemum and the sword*. Boston, MA: Houghton Mifflin.

Benet-Martinez, V., Leu, J.X., Lee, F., & Morris, M.W. (2002). Negotiating biculturalism: Cultural frame switching in biculturals with oppositional versus compatible cultural identities. *Journal of Cross-Cultural Psychology*, *33*, 492–516.

Berger, P.L., & Huntington, S.P. (Eds) (2002). *Many globalizations: Cultural diversity in the contemporary world*. New York: Oxford University Press.

Bering, J. (2010). *The God instinct: The psychology of souls, destiny and the meaning of life*. London: Brealey.

Berno, T. (1999). When a guest is a guest: Cook islanders view tourism. *Annals of Tourism Research*, *26*, 656–675.

Berno, T., & Ward, C. (2005). Innocence abroad: A pocket guide to psychological research on tourism. *American Psychologist*, *60*, 593–600.

Berry, J.W. (1967). Independence and conformity in subsistence-level societies. *Journal of Personality and Social Psychology*, *7*, 415–418.

Berry, J.W. (1969). On cross-cultural comparability. *International Journal of Psychology*, *4*, 119–128.

Berry, J.W. (1976). *Human ecology and cognitive style: Comparative studies in cultural and psychological adaptation*. New York: Sage.

Berry, J.W. (1997). Immigration, acculturation and adaptation. *Applied Psychology: An International Review*, *46*, 5–34.

Berry, J.W. (2006). Contexts of acculturation. In D.L. Sam & J.W. Berry (Eds), *Cambridge handbook of acculturation psychology* (pp. 27–42). Cambridge, UK: Cambridge University Press.

Berry, J.W. (2011). The eco-cultural framework: A stocktaking. In F. van de Vijver, A. Chasiotis & S. Breugelmans (Eds), *Fundamental questions in cross-cultural psychology* (pp. 95–114). Cambridge, UK: Cambridge University Press.

Berry, J.W., & Annis, R.C. (1974). Acculturative stress: The role of ecology, culture and differentiation. *Journal of Cross-Cultural Psychology*, *5*, 382–406.

Berry, J.W., & Kalin, R. (1995). Multicultural and ethnic attitudes in Canada: An overview of the 1991 national survey. *Canadian Journal of Behavioral Science*, *27*, 301–320.

Berry, J.W., Kalin, R., & Taylor, D. (1977). *Multiculturalism and ethnic attitudes in Canada*. Ottawa: Ministry of Supply and Services.

Berry, J.W., Phinney, J., Sam, D., & Vedder, P. (Eds) (2006). *Immigrant youth in cultural transition: Acculturation, identity and adaptation across national contexts*. Mahwah, NJ: Erlbaum.

Berry, J.W., Poortinga, Y., Breugelmans, S., Chasiotis, A., & Sam, D. (2011). *Cross-cultural psychology: Research and applications*. Cambridge: Cambridge University Press.

Berry, J.W., Poortinga, Y., Segall, M., & Dasen, P. (1993). *Cross-cultural psychology: Research and applications*. Cambridge, UK: Cambridge University Press.

Berry, J.W., & Sabatier, C. (2011). Variations in the assessment of acculturation attitudes. *International Journal of Intercultural Relations*, *35*, 658–669.

Bhawuk, D. (1998). The role of culture theory in cross-cultural training: A multi-method study of culture-specific, culture-general and culture theory-based assimilators. *Journal of Cross-Cultural Psychology*, *29*, 630–655.

Binder, J., Zagefka, H., Brown, R., Funke, F., et al. (2009). Does contact reduce prejudice or does prejudice reduce contact? A longitudinal test of the contact hypothesis among majority and minority groups in three European countries. *Journal of Personality and Social Psychology*, *96*, 843–856.

Black, J.S., & Porter, L.W. (1991). Managerial behaviors and job performance: A successful manager in Los Angeles may not succeed in Hong Kong. *Journal of International Business Studies*, *22*, 99–113.

Blass, T. (1999). The Milgram paradigm after 35 years: Some things we now know about obedience to authority. *Journal of Applied Social Psychology*, *29*, 955–978.

Blau, P.M. (1964). *Exchange and power in social life*. New York: Wiley.

Bochner, S. (1994). Cross-cultural differences in the self-concept: A test of Hofstede's individualism-collectivism distinction. *Journal of Cross-Cultural Psychology*, *25*, 275–283.

Bochner, S., & Coulon, L. (1997). A culture assimilator to train Australian hospitality industry workers serving Japanese tourists. *Journal of Tourism Studies*, *8*, 8–17.

Boer, D., & Fischer, R. (2012). Towards a holistic model of functions of music listening across cultures: A culturally decentered qualitative approach. *Psychology of Music*, *40*, 179–200.

Boer, D. & Fischer, R. (2013). When do personal values guide our attitudes and sociality? Explaining cultural variability in attitude-value linkages. Unpublished manuscript, Jacobs University, Bremen, Germany.

Bohannon, L. (1964). *Return to laughter*. New York: Doubleday.

Bomhoff, E., & Gu, M.M. (2012). East Asia remains different: A comment on the index of 'self-expression' values by Inglehart and Welzel. *Journal of Cross-Cultural Psychology*, *43*, 373–383.

Bond, M.H. (1988a). Finding universal dimensions of individual variation in multi-cultural studies of values. *Journal of Personality and Social Psychology*, *55*, 1009–1015.

Bond, M.H. (Ed.) (1988b). *The cross-cultural challenge to social psychology*. Newbury Park, CA: Sage.

Bond, M.H. (1993). Emotions and their expression in Chinese culture. *Journal of Nonverbal Behaviour*, *17*, 245–262.

Bond, M.H. (1996). Chinese values. In M.H. Bond (Ed.), *The handbook of Chinese psychology* (pp. 208–226). Hong Kong: Oxford University Press.

Bond, M.H. (1997). Preface: The psychology of working at the interface of cultures. In M.H. Bond (Ed.), *Working at the interface of cultures: 18 lives in social science* (pp. xi–xix). London: Routledge.

Bond, M.H. (2002). Reclaiming the individual from Hofstede's ecological analysis: A 20-year odyssey. *Psychological Bulletin*, *128*, 73–77.

Bond, M.H. (2004). Culture and aggression: From context to coercion. *Personality and Social Psychology Review*, *8*, 62–78.

Bond, M.H. (2008). Culture and collective violence: How good people, usually men, do bad things. In B. Drozdek & J.P. Wilson (Eds), *Voices of trauma: Treating psychological trauma across cultures* (pp. 27–57). Springer: New York.

Bond, M.H. (2009). Circumnavigating the psychological globe: From yin and yang to starry, starry night. In S. Bekman & A. Aksu-Koc (Eds), *Perspectives on human development, family and culture* (pp. 33–49). Cambridge, UK: Cambridge University Press.

Bond, M.H. (2013). A general model for explaining situational influence on individual social behavior: Refining Lewin's formula. *Asian Journal of Social Psychology*, *16*, 1-15.

Bond, M.H., & Cheung, M.K. (1984). Experimenter language choice and ethnic affirmation by Chinese trilinguals in Hong Kong. *International Journal of Intercultural Relations*, *8*, 347–356.

Bond, M.H., & Cheung, T.S. (1983). The spontaneous self-concept of college students in Hong Kong, Japan and the United States. *Journal of Cross-Cultural Psychology*, *14*, 153–171.

Bond, M.H., & Chi, V.M.Y. (1997). Values and moral behavior in Mainland China. *Psychologia*, *40*, 251–264.

Bond, M.H., & Forgas, J.P. (1984). Linking person perception to behavioral intention across cultures: The role of cultural collectivism. *Journal of Cross-Cultural Psychology*, *15*, 337–352.

Bond, M.H., Leung, K., & Schwartz, S.H. (1992). Explaining choices in procedural and distributive justice across cultures. *International Journal of Psychology*, *27*, 211–225.

Bond, M.H., Leung, K., et al. (2004). Culture-level dimensions of social axioms and their correlates across 41 cultures. *Journal of Cross-Cultural Psychology, 35*, 548–570.

Bond, M.H., & Lun, V. (2013). Citizen-making: The role of national goals for socializing children. Unpublished manuscript, Hong Kong Polytechnic University.

Bond, M.H., & Van de Vijver, F. (2011). Making scientific sense of cultural differences in psychological outcomes. In D. Matsumoto & F. van de Vijver (Eds), *Cross-cultural research methods in psychology* (pp. 75–100). Cambridge, UK: Cambridge University Press.

Bond, R., & Smith, P.B. (1996). Culture and conformity: A meta-analysis of studies using Asch's (1952b, 1956) line judgment task. *Psychological Bulletin, 119*, 111–137.

Boski, P. (2006). Humanism-materialism: Centuries-long Polish cultural origins and 20 years of research in cultural psychology. In U. Kim, K.S. Yang & K.K. Hwang (Eds), *Indigenous and cultural psychology: Understanding people in context* (pp. 373–402). New York: Springer.

Boski, P., Van de Vijver, F.J.R., Hurme, H., & Miluska, M. (1999). Perception and evaluation of Polish cultural femininity in Poland, the United States, Finland and the Netherlands. *Cross-Cultural Research, 33*, 131–161.

Bourhis, R.Y., & Dayan, J. (2004). Acculturation orientations towards Israeli Arabs and Jewish immigrants. *International Journal of Psychology, 39*, 118–131.

Bourhis, R.Y., Moise, L.C., Perreault, S., & Senecal, S. (1997). Towards an interactive acculturation model: A social psychological approach. *International Journal of Psychology, 32*, 369–386.

Boyd, R., & Richerson, P. (1985). *Culture and the evolutionary process.* Chicago: University of Chicago Press.

Boyd, R., & Richerson, P. (1992). Punishment allows the evolution of cooperation (or anything else) in sizable groups. *Ethology and Sociobiology, 13*, 171–195.

Boyd, R., & Richerson, P. (2005). *The origin and evolution of cultures.* New York: Oxford University Press.

Bowen, E.S. (1964). *Return to laughter.* Garden City, NY: Doubleday.

Boyer, P. (1994). *The naturalness of religious ideas: A cognitive theory of religion.* Berkeley: University of California Press.

Branscombe, N., Schmitt, M., & Harvey, R. (1999). Perceiving pervasive discrimination among African Americans: Implications for group identification and wellbeing. *Journal of Personality and Social Psychology, 77*, 135–149.

Breidenbach, J., & Nyiri, P. (2008). *Maxikulti. Der Kampf der Kulturen ist das Problem – zeigt die Wirtschaft uns die Loesung?* [Maxicultural. The war of cultures is the problem – Can business show us answers?] Frankfurt/Main: Campus.

Breugelmans, S.. (2011). The relationship between individual and culture. In F. van de Vijver, A. Chasiotis & S. Breugelmans (Eds), *Fundamental questions in cross-cultural psychology* (pp. 135–162). Cambridge, UK: Cambridge University Press.

Breugelmans, S., & Poortinga, Y. (2006). Emotion without a word: Shame and guilt among the Rarámuri Indians and rural Javanese. *Journal of Personality and Social Psychology, 91*, 1111–1122.

Brew, F.P., & Cairns, D.R. (2004). Styles of managing interpersonal workplace conflict in relation to status and face concern: A study with Anglos and Chinese. *International Journal of Conflict Management, 15*, 19–94.

Brewer, M.B. (2001). The many faces of social identity: Implications for political psychology. *Political Psychology, 22,* 115–125.

Brewer, M.B., & Campbell, D.T. (1966). *Ethnocentrism and intergroup attitudes: East African evidence.* New York: Sage.

Brewer, M.B., & Chen, Y.R. (2007). Where (who) are the collectives in collectivism? Toward conceptual clarification of individualism and collectivism. *Psychological Review, 114*, 133–151.

Brewer, M.B., & Gardner, W. (1996). Who is this 'we'? Levels of collective identity and self-representations. *Journal of Personality and Social Psychology, 71*, 83–93.

Brewer, M.B., & Yuki, M. (2007). Culture and social identity. In S. Kitayama & D. Cohen (Eds), *Handbook of cultural psychology* (pp. 307–322). New York: Guilford.

Brislin, R.W. (1989). Intercultural communication training. In M.K. Asante & W.B. Gudykunst (Eds), *Handbook of international and intercultural communication* (pp. 441–457). Newbury Park, CA: Sage.

Brislin, R.W. (Ed.) (1990). *Applied cross-cultural psychology*. Newbury Park, CA: Sage.

Brislin, R.W., Cushner, K., Cherrie, K., & Yong, M. (1986). *Intercultural interactions: A practical guide*. Beverly Hills, CA: Sage.

Brislin, R.W., Lonner, W.J., & Thorndike, R.M. (1973). *Cross-cultural research methods*. New York: Wiley.

Brislin, R.W., Macnab, B., & Nayani, F. (2008). Cross-cultural training. In P.B. Smith, M.F. Peterson & D.C. Thomas (Eds), *Handbook of cross-cultural management research* (pp. 397–410). Thousand Oaks, CA: Sage.

Brockner, J. (2003). Unpacking country effects: On the need to operationalize the psychological determinants of cross-national differences. In R.M. Kramer & B.M. Staw (Eds), *Research in organizational behavior* (Vol. 25, pp. 333–367). Greenwich, CT: JAI Press.

Brockner, J., Chen, Y.R., Mannix, E.A., Leung, K., & Skarlicki, D.P. (2000). Culture and procedural fairness: When the effects of what you do depend on how you do it. *Administrative Science Quarterly, 45*, 138–159.

Brockner, J., De Cremer, D., Van Bos, K., & Chen, Y.R. (2005). The influence of interdependent self-construal on procedural fairness effects. *Organizational Behavior and Human Decision Processes, 96*, 155–167.

Brodbeck, F., Guillaume, Y., & Lee, N. (2011). Ethnic diversity as a multi-level construct: The combined effects of dissimilarity, group diversity and societal status on learning performance in work groups. *Journal of Cross-Cultural Psychology, 42*, 1198–1218.

Bronfenbrenner, U. (1979). *The ecology of human development: Experiments by nature and design*. Cambridge, MA: Harvard University Press.

Broodryk, J. (2006). *Ubuntu: Life-coping skills from Africa*. Randburg, South Africa: Knowres.

Brosnan, S. (2006). Non-human species reactions to inequity and their implications for fairness. *Journal of Social Justice, 19*, 153–185.

Brown, D.E. (1991). *Human universals*. New York: McGraw-Hill.

Brown, G., Dickins, T., Sear, R., & Laland, K. (2011). Evolutionary accounts of human behavioral diversity: Introduction. *Philosophical Transactions of the Royal Society B: Biological Sciences, 366* (1563), 312–324.

Brown, J.D., & Kobayashi, C. (2002). Self-enhancement in Japan and America. *Asian Journal of Social Psychology, 5*, 145–167.

Brown, R.J., & Cehajic, S. (2008). Dealing with the past and facing the future: Mediators of the effects of collective guilt and shame in Bosnia and Herzegovina. *European Journal of Social Psychology, 38*, 669–684.

Brown R.J., & Hewstone, M. (2005). An integrative theory of intergroup contact. In M. Zanna (Ed.), *Advances in Experimental Social Psychology* (Vol. 37, pp. 255–343). San Diego, CA: Academic.

Brown, R.J., & Zagefka, H. (2011). The dynamics of acculturation: An intergroup perspective. In J. Olson & M. Zanna (Eds), *Advances in Experimental Social Psychology* (Vol. 44, pp. 129–184). Burlington: Academic Press.

Bry, C., Follenfant, A., & Meyer, T. (2008). Blonde like me: When self-construals moderate stereotype priming effects on intellectual performance. *Journal of Experimental Social Psychology, 44*, 751–757.

Buckingham, K., Barker, M., Logan, G., & Millman, L. (1999). Benefits of cultural diversity for international and local students: Contributions from an experiential social learning program (the EXCELL program). In D. Davis & A. Olsen (Eds), *International education: The professional edge* (pp. 63–76). Sydney: IDP Education.

Bulbulia, J., & Sosis, R. (2011). Signalling theory and the evolutionary study of religions. *Religion, 41*, 363–388.

Burns, D., & Brady, J. (1992). A cross-cultural comparison of the need for uniqueness in Malaysia and the United States. *Journal of Social Psychology, 132*, 487–495.

Buss, D.M. (1989). Sex differences in human mate preferences: Evolutionary hypotheses tested in 37 cultures. *Behavioral and Brain Sciences, 12*, 1–49.

Buss, D.M., Abbott, M., et al. (1990). International preferences in selecting mates: A study of 37 cultures. *Journal of Cross-Cultural Psychology, 21*, 5–47.

Buss, D.M., Shackelford, T.K., Kirkpatrick, L.A., Choe, J.C., et al. (1999). Jealousy and the nature of beliefs about infidelity: Tests of competing hypotheses about sex differences in the United States, Korea and Japan. *Personal Relationships, 6*, 125–150.

Buss, D.M., Shackelford, T.K., & Leblanc, G.J. (2000). Number of children desired and preferred spousal age difference: Context-specific mate preference patterns across 37 cultures. *Evolution and Human Behavior, 21*, 323–331.

Butow, P., et al. (2012). A bridge between cultures: Interpreters' perspectives of consultations with migrant onco-
logy patients. *Supportive Care in Cancer, 20*, 235–244.

Cai, H., Sedikides, C., Gaertner, L., Wang, C., et al. (2011). Tactical self-enhancement in China: Is modesty at
the service of self-enhancement in East Asian culture? *Social Psychological and Personality Science, 2*, 59–64.

Caldwell, C. (2008). *Reflections on the revolution in Europe: Immigration, Islam, and the West.* New York: Doubleday.

Campbell, D.T. (1960). Blind variation and selective retention in creative thought as in other knowledge processes. *Psychological Review, 67*, 380–400.

Carbaugh, A. (2006). Coding personhood through cultural terms and practices: Silence and quietude as a Finnish
'natural way of being'. *Journal of Language and Social Psychology, 25*, 203–220.

Cargile, A., & Bradac, J. (2001). Attitudes toward language. In W.B. Gudykunst (Ed.), *Communication yearbook,
25* (pp. 347–382). Mahwah, NJ: Erlbaum.

Carr, S.C. (2003). Poverty and justice. In S.C. Carr & T.S. Sloan (Eds), *Poverty and psychology: Emergent critical
practice* (pp. 45–68). New York: Kluwer Academic/ Plenum.

Cavill, S. (2000). Psychology in practice: Welfare of refugees. *The Psychologist, 13*, 552–554.

Cehajic-Clancy, S., Efron, D., Halperin, E., et al. (2011). Affirmation, acknowledgement of in-group responsibility, group-based guilt and support for reparative measures. *Journal of Personality and Social Psychology, 101*,
256–270.

Chan, H.L. (2004). *The relationship between societal factors and universal mate preferences: A cross-cultural study.*
Unpublished Bachelor's thesis, Chinese University of Hong Kong.

Chan, S.K.C., Bond, M.H., Spencer-Oatey, H., & Rojo-Laurilla, M.A. (2004). Culture and relationship promotion in service encounters: Protecting the ties that bind. *Journal of Asia-Pacific Communication, 14*, 245–260.

Chan, W., McCrae, R., De Fruyt, et al. (2012). Stereotypes of age differences in personality traits: Accurate and
universal? *Journal of Personality and Social Psychology*, 103, 1050-1066.

Chandler, M.J., Lalonde, C.E., Sokol, B., & Hallett, D. (2003). Personal persistence, identity development, and
suicide: A study of Native and Non-Native North American adolescents. *Monographs of the Society for Research
in Child Development, 68*(2).

Chang, L. (2004). Socialization and social adjustment of single children in China. *International Journal of
Psychology*, 39, 390.

Chang, L., Schwartz, D., Dodge, K., & McBride-Chang, C. (2003). Harsh parenting in relation to child emotion
regulation and aggression. *Journal of Family Psychology, 17*, 598–606.

Chao, M.M., Chen, J., Roisman, G.I., & Hong, Y.Y. (2007). Essentializing race: Implications for bicultural
individuals' cognition and physiological reactivity. *Psychological Science, 18*, 341–348.

Chao, R.K. (1994). Beyond parental control and authoritarian parenting style: Understanding Chinese parenting
through the cultural notion of training. *Child Development, 65*, 1111–1120.

Chen, C.C. (1995). New trends in reward allocation preferences: A Sino-US comparison. *Academy of Management
Journal, 38*, 408–428.

Chen, C.C., Chen, Y.R., & Xin, K.R. (2004). *Guanxi* practices and trust in management: A procedural justice
perspective. *Organization Science, 15*, 200–209.

Chen, S.X., Benet-Martínez, V., & Bond, M.H. (2008). Bicultural identity, bilingualism, and psychological
adjustment in multicultural societies: Immigration-based and globalization-based acculturation. *Journal of
Personality, 76*, 803–838.

Chen, S.X., Benet-Martinez, V., Wu, W.C.H., Lam, B.C.P., & Bond, M.H. (2013). The role of dialectical self
and bicultural identity integration in psychological adjustment. *Journal of Personality. 81*, 61–75.

Chen, S.X., & Bond, M.H. (2007). Explaining language priming effects: Further evidence for ethnic affirmation
among Chinese-English bilinguals. *Journal of Language and Social Psychology, 26*, 398–406.

Chen, S.X., & Bond, M.H. (2010). Two languages, two personalities? Examining language effects on the expression of personality in a bilingual context. *Personality and Social Psychology Bulletin, 36*, 1514–1528.

Chen, S.X., Chan, W., Bond, M.H., et al. (2006). The effects of self-efficacy and relationship harmony on
depression across cultures: Applying level-oriented and structure-oriented analyses. *Journal of Cross-Cultural
Psychology, 37*, 643–658.

Chen, X.P., & Chen, C.C. (2012). Chinese *guanxi*: The good, the bad, and the controversial. In X. Huang & M.H. Bond (Eds), *Handbook of Chinese organizational behavior: Integrating theory, research and practice* (pp. 415–435). Cheltenham, UK: Elgar.

Chen, X.Y., He, Y.F., De Oliviera, A.M., et al. (2004). Loneliness and social adaptation in Brazilian, Canadian, Chinese and Italian children: A multinational comparative study. *Journal of Child Psychology and Psychiatry*, *45*, 1373–1384.

Chen, X.Y., Zapulla, C., Lo Coco, A., et al. (2004). Self-perceptions of competence in Brazilian, Canadian, Chinese and Italian children: Relations with social and school adjustment. *International Journal of Behavioral Development*, *28*, 129–138.

Chen, Y.R., Brockner, J., & Chen, X.P. (2002). Individual-collective primacy and in-group favoritism: enhancement and protection effects. *Journal of Experimental Social Psychology*, *38*, 482–491.

Chen, Y.R., Brockner, J., & Katz, T. (1996). Towards an explanation of cultural differences in in-group favoritism: the role of individual versus collective primacy. *Journal of Personality and Social Psychology*, *71*, 613–625.

Cheng, B.S., Chou, L.F., Wu, T.Y., Huang, M.P., & Farh, J.L. (2004). Paternalistic leadership and subordinate responses: Establishing a leadership model in Chinese organizations. *Asian Journal of Social Psychology*, *7*, 89–117.

Cheng, C., Chua, R., Morris, M., & Lee, L. (2012). Finding the right mix: How the composition of self-managing multicultural teams' cultural orientation influences performance over time. *Journal of Organizational Behavior*, *33*, 389–411.

Chentsova Dutton, Y., & Heath, C. (2008). Cultural variants: Why are some cultural variants more successful than others? In M. Schaller, A. Norenzayan, S. Heine, T. Yamagishi & K. Kameda (Eds), *Evolution, culture and the human mind* (pp. 49–70). New York: Psychology Press.

Cheung, F.M., Cheung, S.F., Leung, K., Ward, C., & Leong, F. (2003). The English version of the Chinese Personality Assessment Inventory. *Journal of Cross-Cultural Psychology*, *34*, 433–452.

Cheung, F.M., Leung, K., Fan, R., Song, W.Z., Zhang, J.X., & Zhang, J.P. (1996). Development of the Chinese Personality Assessment Inventory (CPAI). *Journal of Cross-Cultural Psychology*, *27*, 181–199.

Cheung, F.M., Leung, K., Zhang, J.X., et al. (2001). Indigenous Chinese personality constructs: Is the five factor model complete? *Journal of Cross-Cultural Psychology*, *32*, 407–433.

Cheung, F.M., Van de Vijver, F., & Leong, F. (2011). Toward a new approach to the study of personality in culture. *American Psychologist*, *66*, 593–603.

Chiao, J.Y., & Blizinsky, K. (2010). Culture-gene co-evolution of individualism-collectivism and the serotonin transporter gene. *Proceedings of the Royal Society B: Biological Sciences*, *277* (1681), 529–537.

Chiao, J.Y., Harada, T., Komeda, H., Li, Z., Mano, Y., Saito, D., Parrish, T. B., Sadato, N., & Iidaka, T. (2009). Neural basis of individualistic and collectivistic views of self. *Human Brain Mapping*, *30*, 2813–2820.

Chinese Culture Connection (1987). Chinese values and the search for culture-free dimensions of culture. *Journal of Cross-Cultural Psychology*, *18*, 143–164.

Chirkov, V., Ryan, R., Kim, Y., & Kaplan, U. (2003). Differentiating autonomy from individualism and independence: A self-determination theory perspective on internalization of cultural dimensions and well being. *Journal of Personality and Social Psychology*, *84*, 97–110.

Chirkov, V., Ryan, R., & Willness, C. (2005). Cultural context and psychological needs in Canada and Brazil: Testing a self-determination approach to the internalization of cultural practices, identity and well-being. *Journal of Cross-Cultural Psychology*, *36*, 423–443.

Chiu, C.Y., Gelfand, M., Yamagishi, T., et al. (2010). Intersubjective culture: The role of intersubjective perceptions in cross-cultural research. *Perspectives on Psychological Science*, *5*, 482–493.

Chiu, C.Y., & Hong, Y.Y. (1999). Social identification in a political transition: The role of implicit beliefs. *International Journal of Intercultural Relations*, *23*, 297–318.

Choi, I., & Nisbett, R.E. (2000). Cultural psychology of surprise: Holistic theories and recognition of contradiction. *Journal of Personality and Social Psychology*, *79*, 890–905.

Choi, I., Nisbett, R.E., & Norenzayan, A. (1999). Causal attribution across cultures: Variation and universality. *Psychological Bulletin*, *125*, 47–63.

Choi, I., Nisbett, R.E., & Smith, E.E. (1997). Culture, category salience and inductive reasoning. *Cognition, 65*, 15–32.

Choi, K., & Ross, M. (2011). Cultural differences in process and person focus: Congratulations on your hard work versus celebrating your exceptional brain. *Journal of Experimental Social Psychology, 47*, 343–349.

Choi, S.C., & Lee, S.J. (2002). Two-component model of chemyon-oriented behaviors in Korea: Constructive and defensive chemyon. *Journal of Cross-Cultural Psychology, 33*, 332–345.

Chow, I. (2002). Organizational socialization and career success of Asian managers. *International Journal of Human Resource Management, 13*, 720–737.

Christopher, M.S., Norris, P., D'Souza, J.B., & Tiernan, K.A. (2012). A test of the multidimensionality of the self-construal scale in Thailand and the United States. *Journal of Cross-Cultural Psychology*. 43, 758–773.

Chua, A. (2011). *Battle hymn of the tiger mother*. New York: Penguin.

Church, A.T. (2010). Current perspectives on the study of personality across cultures. *Perspectives on Psychological Science, 5*, 441–449.

Church, A.T., & Katigbak, M.S. (1992). The cultural context of academic motives: A comparison of Filipino and American college students. *Journal of Cross-Cultural Psychology, 23*, 40–58.

Church, A.T., Katigbak, M.S., Del Prado, A.M., et al. (2006). Implicit theories and self-perceptions of traitedness across cultures: Toward integration of cultural and trait psychology perspectives. *Journal of Cross-Cultural Psychology, 37*, 694–715.

Church, A.T., Katigbak, M.S., Ortiz, F.A., et al. (2005). Investigating implicit trait theories across cultures. *Journal of Cross-Cultural Psychology, 36*, 476–496.

Church, A.T., Katigbak, M.S., & Reyes, J-A.S. (1996). Toward a taxonomy of trait adjectives in Filipino: Comparing personality lexicons across cultures. *European Journal of Personality, 10*, 3–24.

Church, A.T., Ortiz, F.A., Katigbak. M.S., et al. (2003). Measuring individual and cultural differences in implicit trait theories. *Journal of Personality and Social Psychology, 85*, 332–347.

Church, A.T., Willmore, S.L., et al. (2012). Cultural differences in implicit theories and self-perceptions of traitedness: Replication and extension with alternative measurement formats and cultural dimensions. *Journal of Cross-Cultural Psychology, 43*, 1268–1296.

Cinnirella, M. (1997). Towards a European identity? Interactions between the national and European social identities manifested by university students in Britain and Italy. *British Journal of Social Psychology, 36*, 19–31.

Claes, M. (1998). Adolescents' closeness with parents, siblings and friends in three countries: Canada, Belgium and Italy. *Journal of Youth and Adolescence, 27*, 165–184.

Clark, H., & Brennan, S. (1991). Grounding in communication. In L.B. Resnick, J.M. Levine, & S.D. Teasley (Eds), *Perspectives on socially shared cognition* (pp. 127–149). Washington: APA Books.

Codol, J.P. (1981). Une approche cognitive du sentiment d'identité [A cognitive approach to the sense of identity]. *Social Science Information, 20*, 111–136.

Cohen, A.B. (2009). Many forms of culture. *American Psychologist, 64*, 194–204.

Cohen, A.B., Shariff, A., & Hill, P. (2008). The accessibility of religious beliefs. *Journal of Research in Personality, 42*, 1408–1417.

Cohen, D., & Leung, A. (2009). The hard embodiment of culture. *European Journal of Social Psychology, 39*, 1278–1289.

Cohen, D., & Nisbett, R.E. (1997). Field experiments examining the culture of honor: The role of institutions in perpetuating norms about violence. *Personality and Social Psychology Bulletin, 23*, 1188–1199.

Cohrs, J.C., & Stelzl, M. (2010). How ideological attitudes predict host society members' attitudes toward immigrants: Exploring cross-national differences. *Journal of Social Issues, 66*, 673–694.

Cole, M. (1996). *Cultural psychology: A once and future discipline*. Cambridge, MA: Harvard University Press.

Conroy, M., Hess, R.D., Azuma, H., & Kashiwagi, K. (1980). Maternal strategies for regulating children's behavior: Japanese and American families. *Journal of Cross-Cultural Psychology, 11*, 153–172.

Cosmides, L., & Tooby, J. (1992). Cognitive adaptations for social exchange. In J. Barlow, L. Cosmides & J. Tooby (Eds), *The adapted mind: Evolutionary psychology and the generation of culture* (pp. 163–229). New York: Oxford University Press.

Cosmides, L., Tooby, J., & Kurzban, R. (2003). Perceptions of race. *Trends in Cognitive Sciences*, *7*, 173–179.

Costa, P.T., Jr., & McCrae, R.R. (1992). *Revised NEO Personality Inventory (NEO-PI – R) and NEO Five Factor Inventory (NEO – FFI)*. Odessa, FL: Psychological Assessment Resources.

Cousins, S. (1989). Culture and selfhood in Japan and the US. *Journal of Personality and Social Psychology*, *56*, 124–131.

Cross, S.E., Bacon, P.L., & Morris, M.L. (2000). The relational-interdependent self-construal and relationships. *Journal of Personality and Social Psychology*, *78*, 791–808.

Cross, S.E., Hardin, E.E., & Gercek-Swing, B. (2011). The what, how, why, and where of self-construal. *Personality and Social Psychology Review*, *15*, 142–179.

Cross, S.E., & Madson, L. (1997). Models of the self: Self-construal and gender. *Psychological Bulletin*, *122*, 5–37.

Cuddy, A., Fiske, S., Kwan, V., et al. (2009). Stereotype content model across cultures: Towards universal similarities and some differences. *British Journal of Social Psychology*, *48*, 1–33.

Currie, T.E., Greenhill, S.J., Gray, R.D., Hasegawa, T., & Mace, M. (2010). The rise and fall of political complexity in island S.E. Asia and the Pacific. *Nature*, *476*, 801–804.

Curscu, P., Stoop, R., & Schalk, R. (2007). Prejudice toward immigrant workers among Dutch employees: Integrated threat theory. *European Journal of Social Psychology*, *37*, 125–140.

Darwin, C. (1859). *The origin of species*. New York: Random House.

Dauenhauer, D.G., Guhlberg, D., Spreemann, S., & Sedikides, C. (2002). Self-enhancement, self-verification, or self-assessment? The intricate role of trait modifiability in the self-evaluation process. *Revue Internationale de Psychologie Sociale, 15*(3–4), 89–112.

Davidov, E., Dülmer, H., Schlüter, E., Schmidt, P., & Meuleman, B. (2012). Using multilevel structural equation modeling to explain cross-cultural measurement non-invariance. *Journal of Cross-Cultural Psychology*, *43*, 558–575.

De Bruine, L., Jones, B., Crawford, J., et al. (2010). The health of a nation predicts their mate preferences: Cross-cultural variations in women's preference for masculinised faces. *Proceedings of the Royal Society B*, *277*, 2405–2410.

Delhey, J., Newton, K., & Welzel, C. (2011). How general is trust in 'most people'? Solving the radius of trust problem. *American Sociological Review*, *76*, 786–807.

Del Prado, A.M., Church, A.T., Katigbak, M.S., et al. (2007). Culture, method and the content of self-concepts: Testing trait, individual-self-primacy, and cultural psychology perspectives. *Journal of Research in Personality*, *41*, 1119–1160.

De Mooij, M. (1998). *Global marketing and advertising: Understanding cultural paradoxes*. Thousand Oaks, CA: Sage.

Den Hartog, D.N., House, R.J., Hanges, P.J., Dorfman, P.W., & Ruiz-Qintanilla, S.A. (1999). Emics and etics of culturally-endorsed implicit leadership theories: Are attributes of charismatic-transformational leadership universally endorsed? *Leadership Quarterly*, *10*, 219–256.

Dennis, T.A., Cole, P.M., Zahn-Waxler, C., & Mizuta, I. (2002). Self in context: Autonomy and relatedness in Japanese and U.S. mother-preschooler dyads. *Child Development*, *73*, 1803–1817.

De Raad, B., Barelds, D., Levert, E., et al. (2010). Only three factors of personality description are fully replicable across languages: A comparison of 14 trait taxonomies. *Journal of Personality and Social Psychology*, *98*, 160–173.

De-Raad, B., Perugini, M., Hrebickova, M., & Szarota, P. (1998). Lingua franca of personality: Taxonomies and structures based on the psycholexical approach. *Journal of Cross-Cultural Psychology*, *29*, 212–232.

Derlega, V.J., Cukur, C.S., Kuang, J.C.Y., & Forsyth, D.R. (2002). Interdependent construal of self and the endorsement of conflict resolution strategies in interpersonal, intergroup and international disputes. *Journal of Cross-Cultural Psychology*, *33*, 610–625.

Deshpande, S.P., & Viswesvaran, C. (1992). Is cross-cultural training of expatriate mangers effective? A meta-analysis. *International Journal of Intercultural Relations*, *16*, 295–310.

Deutsch, M. (1975). Equity, equality, and need: What determines which value will be used as the basis of distributive justice? *Journal of Social Issues*, *31*, 137–150.

Diamond, J. (1997). *Guns, germs and steel: A short history of everybody for the last 13,000 years*. New York: Viking.

Diamond, J. (2005). *Collapse: How societies choose to fail or succeed*. New York: Viking.

Diaz-Guerrero, R. (1993). Mexican ethnopsychology. In U. Kim & J.W. Berry (Eds), *Indigenous psychologies: Research and experience in cultural context* (pp. 44–55). Thousand Oaks, CA: Sage.

Dibiase, R., & Gunnoe, J. (2004). Gender and culture differences in touching behavior. *Journal of Social Psychology, 144*, 49–62.

Dickson, M., Resick, C., & Hanges, P. (2006). Systematic variation in organizationally-shared cognitive proto-types of effective leadership based on organizational form. *Leadership Quarterly, 17*, 487–505.

Diener, E., & Biswas-Diener, R. (2002). Will money increase subjective well-being? *Social Indicators Research, 57*, 119–169.

Diener, E., & Diener, M. (1995). Cross-cultural correlates of life satisfaction and self-esteem. *Journal of Personality and Social Psychology, 68*, 653–663.

Diener, E., Diener, M., & Diener, C. (1995). Factors predicting the subjective well-being of nations. *Journal of Personality and Social Psychology, 69*, 851–864.

Diener, E., & Oishi, S. (2003). Money and happiness: Income and subjective well-being across nations. In E. Diener & E. Suh (Eds), *Culture and subjective well-being* (pp. 185–218). Cambridge, MA: MIT Press.

Dittrich, W., Johansen, T., & Kulinskaya, E. (2011). Norms and situational rules of address in English and Norwegian speakers. *Journal of Pragmatics, 43*, 3807–3821.

Doi, T. (1973). *The anatomy of dependence.* Tokyo: Kodansha.

Doise, W. (2001). *Droits de l'homme et force des idées.* Paris: Presses Universitaires de France.

Doise, W., Spini, D., & Clemence, A. (1999). Human rights studies as social representations in a cross-national context. *European Journal of Social Psychology, 29*, 1–29.

Dols, J.M.F. (1993). Perverse norm: Theoretical hypotheses. *Psicothema, 5*, 91–101, Supplement S.

Duckitt, J. (2001). A dual-process cognitive-motivational theory of ideology and prejudice. In M. Zanna (Ed.), *Advances in Experimental Social Psychology* (Vol. 33, pp. 41–113). San Diego, CA: Academic.

Dutton, Y.C., & Heath, C. (2009). Cultural evolution: Why are some cultural variants more successful than others? In M. Schaller, A. Norenzayan, S. Heine, T. Yamagishi & T. Kameda (Eds), *Evolution, culture and the human mind* (pp. 49–70). New York: Psychology Press.

Dwairy, M. (2006). *Counseling and psychotherapy with Arabs and Muslims: A culturally sensitive approach.* New York: Teachers College Press.

Dwairy, M., Achoui, M., Abouserie, R., et al. (2007). Parenting styles in Arab societies: A first cross-regional research study. *Journal of Cross-Cultural Psychology, 37*, 230–247.

Dweck, C. S. (1999). *Self-theories: Their role in motivation, personality and development.* Philadelphia: Psychology Press.

Earley, P.C. (1987). Intercultural training for managers: A comparison of documentary and interpersonal methods. *Academy of Management Journal, 30*, 685–698.

Earley, P.C. (1993). East meets West meets Mideast: Further explorations of collectivistic versus individualistic work groups. *Academy of Management Journal, 36*, 319–348.

Earley, P.C. (1999). Playing follow the leader: Status-determining traits in relation to collective efficacy across cultures. *Organizational Behavior and Human Decision Processes, 80*, 192–212.

Earley, P.C., & Ang, S. (2003). *Cultural intelligence: Individual interactions across cultures.* Palo Alto, CA: Stanford University Press.

Earley, P.C., & Gibson, C.B. (2002). *Multinational work teams: A new perspective.* Mahwah, NJ: Erlbaum.

Earley, P.C., Gibson, C.B., & Chen, C.C. (1999). 'How did I do, versus how did we do?': Cultural contrasts in performance feedback use and self-efficacy. *Journal of Cross-Cultural Psychology, 30*, 594–619.

Earley, P.C., & Mosakowski, E. (2000). Creating hybrid team cultures: An empirical test of international team functioning. *Academy of Management Journal, 43*, 26–49.

Easterbrook, M., & Vignoles, V.L. (2012). Different groups, different motives: Identity motives underlying changes in identification with novel groups. *Personality and Social Psychology Bulletin, 38*, 1066–1080.

Easterbrook, M., Vignoles, V.L., et al. (2013). Urbanisation, culture, and the distinctiveness motive: Constructing distinctive identities in different contexts. Unpublished manuscript, University of Sussex.

Ekman, P. (1972). Universals and cultural differences in facial expressions of emotion. In J. Cole (Ed.), *Nebraska Symposium on Motivation* (Vol.19, pp. 207–282). Lincoln, NE: University of Nebraska Press.

Ekman, P., Friesen, W.V., O'Sullivan, M., et al. (1987). Universals and cultural differences in the judgment of facial expressions of emotion. *Journal of Personality and Social Psychology, 53*, 712–717.

Ekman, P., Sorenson, E.R., & Friesen, W.V. (1969). Pan-cultural elements in facial displays of emotion. *Science, 164*, 86–88.

Elder, G.H. (1974). *Children of the great depression: Social change and life experience.* Chicago: University of Chicago Press.

Elfenbein, H.A., & Ambady, N. (2002). On the universality and cultural specificity of emotion recognition: A meta-analysis. *Psychological Bulletin, 128*, 203–225.

Elfenbein, H.A., & Ambady, N. (2003). Cultural similarity's consequences: A distance perspective on cross-cultural differences in emotion recognition. *Journal of Cross-Cultural Psychology, 34*, 92–110.

Elfenbein, H.A., Beaupre, M., Levesque, M., & Hess, U. (2007). Toward a dialect theory: Cultural differences in the expression and recognition of posed facial expressions. *Emotion, 7*, 131–146.

Elron, E. (1997). Top management teams within multinational corporations: Effects of cultural heterogeneity. *Leadership Quarterly, 8*, 393–412.

English, T., & Chen, S. (2007). Culture and self-concept stability: Consistency across and within contexts among Asian Americans and European Americans. *Journal of Personality and Social Psychology, 93*, 478–490.

English, T., & Chen, S. (2011). Self-concept consistency and culture: The differential impact of two forms of consistency. *Personality and Social Psychology Bulletin, 37*, 838–849.

Enriquez, V. (1993). Developing a Filipino psychology. In U. Kim & J.W. Berry (Eds), *Indigenous psychologies: Research and experience in cultural context* (pp. 152–169). Thousand Oaks, CA: Sage.

Eppig, C., Fincher, C., & Thornhill, R. (2010). Parasite prevalence and the worldwide distribution of cognitive ability. *Proceedings of the Royal Society B: Biological Sciences, 277*(1701), 3801–3808.

Erikson, E.H. (1968). *Identity: Youth and crisis.* London: Faber & Faber.

Esses, V.M., Dovidio, J.F., Jackson, L.M., & Armstrong, T.L. (2001). The immigration dilemma: The role of perceived group competition, ethnic prejudice and national identity. *Journal of Social Issues, 57*, 389–412.

Farh, J.L., & Cheng, B.S. (2000). A cultural analysis of paternalistic leadership in Chinese organizations. In J.T. Li, A.S. Tsui & E. Weldon (Eds), *Management and organizations in the Chinese context* (pp. 84–127). London: Macmillan.

Farh, J.L., Earley, P.C., & Lin, S.C. (1997). Impetus for action: A cultural analysis of justice and organizational behavior in Chinese society. *Administrative Science Quarterly, 42*, 421–444.

Farh, J.L., Tsui, A.S., Xin, K., & Cheng, B.S. (1998). The influence of relational demography and *guanxi*: The Chinese case. *Organization Science, 9*, 471–498.

Farr, R.M. (1996). *The roots of modern social psychology.* Oxford, UK: Blackwell.

Faulkner, S.L., Baldwin, J.R., Lindsley, S.L., & Hecht, M.L. (2006). Layers of meaning: An analysis of definitions of culture. In J.R. Baldwin, S.L. Faulkner, M.L. Hecht, & S.L. Lindsley (Eds), *Redefining culture: Perspectives across the disciplines* (pp. 27–51). Mahwah, NJ: Erlbaum.

Fazio, R., & Powell, M. (1997). On the value of knowing one's likes and dislikes: Attitude accessibility, stress and health in college. *Psychological Science, 8*, 430–436.

Feather, N.T. (1994). Attitudes toward high achievers and reactions to their fall: Theory and research concerning tall poppies. In M.P. Zanna (Ed.), *Advances in Experimental Social Psychology* (Vol. 26, pp. 1–73). Orlando, FL: Academic Press.

Feldman, R.E. (1978). Response to compatriot and foreigner who seek assistance. *Journal of Personality and Social Psychology, 10*, 202–214.

Felfe, J., Yan, W., & Six, B. (2008). The impact of individual collectivism on commitment and its influence on organizational citizenship behavior and turnover in three countries. *International Journal of Cross-Cultural Management, 8*, 211–237.

Fernández, I., Paez, D., & González, J.L. (2005). Independent and interdependent self-construals and socio-cultural factors in 29 nations. *Revue Internationale de Psychologie Sociale*, *18*, 35–63.

Ferreira, M.C., Fischer, R., Pilati, R., Porto, J.B., & Milfont, T. (2012). Unravelling the mystery of Brazilian jeitinho: A cultural exploration of social norms. *Personality and Social Psychology Bulletin*, *38*, 331–344.

Fijneman, Y., Willemsen, M., Poortinga, Y.H., et al. (1996). Individualism-collectivism: An empirical study of a conceptual issue. *Journal of Cross-Cultural Psychology*, *27*, 381–402.

Fincher, C.L., & Thornhill, R. (2008). Assortative sociality, limited dispersal, infectious disease and the genesis of the global pattern of religion diversity. *Proceedings of the Royal Society B: Biological Sciences*, *275* (1651), 2587–2594.

Fincher, C.L., & Thornhill, R. (2012). Parasite stress promotes in-group assortative sociality: The case of strong family ties and heightened religiosity. *Behavioral and Brain Sciences*, *35*, 61–79.

Fincher, C.L., Thornhill, R., Murray, D., & Schaller, M. (2008). Pathogen prevalence predicts human cross-cultural variability in individualism/collectivism. *Proceedings of the Royal Society B: Biological Sciences*, *275*(1640), 1279–1285.

Fischer, R. (2006). Congruence and function of personal and cultural values: Do my values reflect my culture's values? *Personality and Social Psychology Bulletin*, *32*, 1419–1431.

Fischer, R. (2008). Organizational justice and reward allocation. In P.B. Smith, M.F. Peterson, & D.C. Thomas (Eds), *Handbook of cross-cultural management research* (pp. 135–150). Thousand Oaks, CA: Sage.

Fischer, R. (2009). Where is culture in cross-cultural research? An outline of a multilevel research process for measuring culture as a shared meaning system. *International Journal of Cross-Cultural Management*, *9*, 25–48.

Fischer, R. (2011a). About chickens and eggs: Four methods for investigating culture-behavior links. In F. van de Vijver, A. Chasiotis & S. Breugelmans (Eds), *Fundamental questions in cross-cultural psychology* (pp. 190–213). Cambridge, UK: Cambridge University Press.

Fischer, R. (2011b). Cross-cultural training effects on cultural essentialism and cultural intelligence. *International Journal of Intercultural Relations*, *35*, 767–775.

Fischer, R. (2012). Value isomorphism in the European social survey: Exploration of meaning shifts across levels. *Journal of Cross-Cultural Psychology*, *43*, 883–898.

Fischer, R. (2013a). Gene-environment interactions influence the endorsement of social hierarchy values and beliefs across cultures. *Journal of Cross-Cultural Psychology*, in press.

Fischer, R. (2013b). Belonging, status or self-protection? Examining justice motives in a three-level cultural meta-analysis of organizational justice effects. *Cross-Cultural Research*, in press.

Fischer, R., & Boer, D. (2011). What is more important for national well-being: Money or autonomy? A meta-analysis of well-being, burnout and anxiety across 63 societies. *Journal of Personality and Social Psychology*, *101*, 164–184.

Fischer, R., & Derham, C. (2013). Is in-group bias culture-dependent? A meta-analysis across 18 societies. Unpublished manuscript, Victoria University of Wellington, New Zealand.

Fischer, R., Ferreira, M.C., Assmar, E., et al. (2009). Individualism-collectivism as descriptive norms: Development of a subjective norm approach to culture measurement. *Journal of Cross-Cultural Psychology*, *40*, 187–213.

Fischer, R., Ferreira, M.C., Jiang, D.Y., et al. (2011). Are perceptions of organizational justice universal? An exploration of measurement invariance across thirteen cultures. *Social Justice Research*, *24*, 297–313.

Fischer, R., & Fontaine, J. (2011). Methods for investigating structural equivalence. In D. Matsumoto & F. van de Vijver (Eds), *Cross-cultural research methods in psychology* (pp. 179–205). Cambridge, UK: Cambridge University Press.

Fischer, R., & Hanke, K. (2009). Are societal values linked to global peace and conflict? *Peace and Conflict: Journal of Peace Psychology*, *15*, 227–248.

Fischer, R., Hanke, K., & Sibley, C. (2012). Cultural and institutional determinants of social dominance orientation: A cross-cultural meta-analysis of 27 societies. *Political Psychology*, *33*, 437–467.

Fischer, R., Maes, J., & Schmitt, M. (2007). Tearing down the 'wall in the head': Culture contact between Germans. *International Journal of Intercultural Relations*, *31*, 163–179.

Fischer, R., & Mansell, A. (2009). Commitment across cultures: A meta-analytical approach. *Journal of International Business Studies, 40,* 1339–1358.

Fischer, R., Milfont, T., & Gouveia, V. (2011). Does social context affect value structures? Testing the within-country stability of value structures with a functional theory of values. *Journal of Cross-Cultural Psychology, 43,* 252–270.

Fischer, R., & Schwartz, S.H. (2011). Whence differences in value priorities? Individual, cultural or artefactual sources. *Journal of Cross-Cultural Psychology, 42,* 1127–1144.

Fischer, R., & Smith, P.B. (2003). Reward allocation and culture: A meta-analysis. *Journal of Cross-Cultural Psychology, 34,* 251–268.

Fischer, R., & Smith, P.B. (2004). Values and organizational justice: Performance and seniority-based allocation criteria in the United Kingdom and Germany. *Journal of Cross-Cultural Psychology, 35,* 669–688.

Fischer, R., Smith, P.B., Richey, B., Ferreira, M.C., et al. (2007). How do organizations allocate rewards? The predictive validity of national values, economic and organizational factors across six nations. *Journal of Cross-Cultural Psychology, 38,* 3–18.

Fischer, R., & Van de Vliert, E. (2011). Does climate undermine subjective well-being? *Personality and Social Psychology Bulletin, 37,* 1031–1041.

Fischer, R., Vauclair, M., Fontaine, J., & Schwartz, S.H. (2010). Are individual and country-level value structures different? Testing Hofstede's legacy with the Schwartz value survey. *Journal of Cross-Cultural Psychology, 41,* 135–151.

Fiske, A.P. (2002). Using individualism-collectivism to compare cultures: A critique of the validity and measurement of the constructs. A comment on Oyserman et al. (2002). *Psychological Bulletin, 128,* 78–88.

Fiske, D.W. (1949). Consistency of the factorial structures of personality ratings from different sources. *Journal of Abnormal and Social Psychology, 44,* 329–344.

Fiske, S.T., Cuddy, A.J.C., Glick, P., & Xu, J. (2002). A model of (often mixed) stereotype content: Competence and warmth respectively follow from perceived status and competition. *Journal of Personality and Social Psychology, 82,* 878–902.

Fivelsdal, E., & Schramm-Nielsen, J. (1993). Egalitarianism at work: Management in Denmark. In D.J. Hickson (Ed.), *Management in Western Europe: Society, culture and organisation in 12 nations* (pp. 27–45). Berlin: de Gruyter.

Fontaine, J. (2005). Equivalence. In K. Kempf-Leonard (Ed.), *Encyclopedia of social measurement* (Vol. 1, pp. 803–813). New York: Academic.

Fontaine, J. (2008). Traditional and multi-level approaches to cross-cultural research: An integration of methodological frameworks. In F. van de Vijver, D. Hemert & Y. Poortinga (Eds), *Multilevel analysis of individuals and cultures* (pp. 65–92). New York: Erlbaum.

Fontaine, J., Poortinga, Y., Delbeke, L., et al. (2008). Structural equivalence of the values domain across cultures: Distinguishing sampling fluctuations from meaningful variation. *Journal of Cross-Cultural Psychology, 39,* 345–365.

Fontaine, J., Scherer, K., Roesch, E., & Ellsworth, P. (2007). The world of emotions is not two-dimensional. *Psychological Science, 18,* 1050–1057.

Fontaine, J., Scherer, K., & Soriano, C. (Eds) (2013). *Components of emotional meaning: A sourcebook.* Oxford: Oxford University Press.

Forde, D. (1934). *Habitat, economy and society.* New York: Dutton.

Frese, M., Kring, W., Soose, A., & Zempel, J. (1996). Personal initiative at work: Differences between East and West Germany. *Academy of Management Journal, 39,* 37–63.

Fridlund, A.J., & Duchaine, B. (1996). 'Facial expressions of emotion' and the delusion of the hermetic self. In R. Harré & W.G. Parrott (Eds), *The emotions: Social, cultural and biological dimensions.* London: Sage.

Friedlaender, J.S., Friedlaender, F.R., Reed, F.A., Kidd, K.K., Kidd, J.R., et al. (2008). The genetic structure of Pacific Islanders. *Public Library of Science, Genetic, 4*(1): e19.

Friedman, M., Rholes, W.S., Simpson, J.A., Bond, M.H., Diaz-Loving, R., & Chan, C. (2010). Attachment avoidance and the cultural fit hypothesis: A cross-cultural investigation. *Personal Relationships, 17,* 107–126.

Friesen, W.V. (1972). *Cultural differences in facial expressions in a social situation: An experimental test of the concept of display rules.* Unpublished doctoral dissertation, University of California, San Francisco.

Fritsche, I., Cohrs, J.C., Kessler, T., & Bauer, J. (2012). Global warming is breeding social conflict: The subtle impact of climate change threat on authoritarian tendencies. *Journal of Environmental Psychology, 32,* 1–10.

Fu, P.P., Kennedy, J.C., Tata, J., Yukl, G.A., et al. (2004). The impact of societal cultural values and individual social beliefs on the perceived effectiveness of managerial influence strategies: A meso approach. *Journal of International Business Studies, 35,* 284–305.

Gabriel, S., & Gardner, W. (1999). Are there 'his' and 'hers' kinds of interdependence? The implications of gender differences in collective versus relational interdependence for affect behavior and cognition. *Journal of Personality and Social Psychology, 77,* 642–655.

Gabrielidis, C., Stephan, W.G., Ybarra, O., Pearson, V.M.S., & Villareal, L. (1997). Cultural variables and preferred styles of conflict resolution: Mexico and the United States. *Journal of Cross-Cultural Psychology, 28,* 661–677.

Gallois, C., Giles, H., Jones, E., Cargile, A.C., & Ota, H. (1995). Accommodating intercultural encounters: Elaborations and extensions. In R.L. Wiseman (Ed.), *Intercultural communication theory* (pp. 115–147). Thousand Oaks, CA: Sage.

Gannon, M.J., & Poon, J.M.L. (1997). The effect of alternative instructional approaches on cross-cultural training outcomes. *International Journal of Intercultural Relations, 21,* 429–446.

Gardner, W., Gabriel, S., & Lee, A.Y. (1999). 'I' value freedom, but 'we' value relationships: Self-construal priming mirrors cultural differences in judgment. *Psychological Science, 10,* 321–326.

Gass, S.M., & Varonis, E.M. (1985). Variation in native speaker speech modification to non-native speakers. *Studies in Second Language Acquisition, 7,* 37–58.

Gausden, J. (2003). *The giving and receiving of feedback in central Eastern European cultures.* MSc dissertation, University of Salford, UK.

Gebauer, J.E., Wagner, J., Sedikides, C., & Neberich, W. (in press). Agency-communion and self-esteem relations are moderated by culture, religiosity, age, and sex: Evidence for the "self-centrality breeds self-enhancement" principle. *Journal of Personality.*

Geertz, C. (1973). *The interpretation of cultures.* New York: Basic Books.

Geertz, C. (1975). On the nature of anthropological understanding. *American Scientist, 63,* 47–53.

Geertz, C. (2000). *Available light: Anthropological reflections on philosophical topics.* Princeton, NJ: Princeton University Press.

Gelfand, M., Lyons, S., & Lun, J. (2011). Towards a psychological science of globalization. *Journal of Social Issues, 67,* 841–853.

Gelfand, M., Nishii, L.H., Holcombe, K.M., Dyer, N., Ohbuchi, K.I., & Fukuno, M. (2001). Cultural influences on cognitive representations of conflict: Interpretations of conflict episodes in the United States and Japan. *Journal of Applied Psychology, 86,* 1059–1074.

Gelfand, M., Raver, J.L., et al. (2011). Differences between tight and loose cultures: A 33 nation study. *Science, 332,* 1100–1104.

Georgas, J., Berry, J.W., Shaw, A., Christakopoulou, S., & Mylonas, K. (1996). Acculturation of Greek family values. *Journal of Cross-Cultural Psychology, 27,* 329–338.

Georgas, J., Berry, J.W., Van de Vijver, F., Kağıtçıbaşı, C., & Poortinga, Y.H. (2006). *Families across cultures: A 30-nation psychological study.* Cambridge, UK: Cambridge University Press.

Georgas, J., Mylonas, K., Bafiti, T., Poortinga, Y.H., et al. (2001). Functional relationships in the nuclear and extended family: A 16-culture study. *International Journal of Psychology, 36,* 289–300.

Georgas, J., Van de Vijver, F., & Berry, J.W. (2004). The ecocultural framework, ecosocial indices and psychological variables in cross-cultural research. *Journal of Cross-Cultural Psychology, 35,* 74–96.

Gheorghiu, M., Vignoles, V., & Smith, P.B. (2009). Beyond the United States and Japan: Testing Yamagishi's emancipation theory of trust across 31 nations. *Social Psychology Quarterly, 72,* 365–383.

Giacobbe-Miller, J.K., Miller, D.J., & Victorov, V.I. (1998). A comparison of Russian and US pay allocation decisions, distributive justice judgments and productivity under different payment conditions. *Personnel Psychology, 51,* 137–163.

Gilbert, G.M. (1951). Stereotype persistence and change among college students. *Journal of Abnormal and Social Psychology, 46,* 245–254.

Giles, H., Coupland, N., & Coupland, J. (1991). Accommodation theory: Communication, context and consequence. In H. Giles, N. Coupland, & J. Coupland (Eds), *Contexts of accommodation: Developments in applied sociolinguistics* (pp. 1–68). Cambridge, UK: Cambridge University Press.

Giles, H., Coupland, N., & Wiemann, J. M. (1992). 'Talk is cheap, but my word is my bond': Beliefs about talk. In K. Bolton & H. Kwok (Eds.) *Sociolinguistics today: Eastern and western perspectives.* London: Routledge.

Gil-White, F. (2001). Are ethnic groups biological 'species' to the human brain? Essentialism in our cognition of some social categories. *Current Anthropology, 42,* 515–554.

Ginges, J., Atran, S., Medin, D., & Shikaki, K. (2007). Sacred bounds on rational resolution of violent political conflict. *Proceedings of the National Academy of Sciences, 104*(18), 7357–7360.

Ginges, J., Hansen, I., & Norenzayan, A. (2009). Religion and support for suicide attacks. *Psychological Science, 20,* 224–230.

Gini, L. (1921). Measurement of inequality in incomes. *Economic Journal, 31,* 124–126.

Gire, J.T., & Carment, D.W. (1993). Dealing with disputes: The influence of individualism-collectivism. *Journal of Social Psychology, 133,* 81–95.

Gleditsch, N.P. (2012). Whither the weather? Climate change and social conflict. *Journal of Peace Research, 49,* 3–7.

Glenn, E.E., Wittmeyer, D., & Stevenson, K.A. (1997). Cultural styles of persuasion. *International Journal of Intercultural Relations, 1,* 52–66.

Goffman, E. (1959). *The presentation of self in everyday life.* New York: Doubleday.

Goldberg, L.R. (1990). An alternative "Description of personality": The Big-Five factor structure. *Journal of Personality and Social Psychology, 59,* 1216–1229.

Golder, S., & Macy, M. (2011). Diurnal and seasonal mood vary with work, sleep and day length across diverse cultures. *Science, 333,* 1878–1881.

González, K., Verkuyten, M., Weesie, J., & Poppe, E. (2008). Prejudice towards Muslims in the Netherlands: Testing integrated threat theory. *British Journal of Social Psychology, 47,* 667–685.

Gonzalez, R., & Brown, R.J. (2006). Intergroup contact and levels of categorization: Effects on intergroup emotions. In R.J. Brown & D. Capozza (Eds), *Social identities: Motivational, emotional and cultural influences* (pp. 259–277). Hove, UK: Psychology Press.

Goodwin, R., Marshall, T., Fulop, M., Adonu, J., Spiewak, S., Neto, F., & Hernandez Plaza, S. (2012). Mate value and self-esteem: Evidence from eight cultural groups, *PLoS One, 7*(4), e36106.

Goodwin, R., & Tang, C.S.K. (1996). Chinese personal relationships. In M.H. Bond (Ed.), *Handbook of Chinese psychology* (pp. 294–308). Hong Kong: Oxford University Press.

Goody, E.N. (1978). Introduction. In E.N. Goody (Ed.), *Questions and politeness.* Cambridge, UK: Cambridge University Press.

Goswami, U., Porpodas, C., & Wheelwright, S. (1997). Children's orthographic representations in English and Greek. *European Journal of Psychology of Education, 3,* 273–292.

Goto, S., Ando, Y., Huang, C., Yee, A., & Lewis, R.S. (2010). Cultural differences in the visual processing of meaning: Detecting incongruities between background and foreground objects using the N400. *Social Cognitive and Affective Neuroscience, 5,* 242–253.

Graham, J., & Haidt, J. (2010). Beyond beliefs: Religions bind individuals into moral communities. *Personality and Social Psychology Review, 14,* 140–150.

Graham, J.A., & Argyle, M. (1975). A cross-cultural study of the communication of extra-verbal meaning by gesture. *International Journal of Psychology, 10,* 56–67.

Graham, J.L., Mintu, A.T., & Rodgers, W. (1994). Explorations of negotiation behaviors in ten foreign cultures, using a model developed in the United States. *Management Science, 40,* 72–95.

Graham, J.L., & Mintu Wimsat, A.T. (1997). Culture's influence on business negotiations in four countries. *Group Decision and Negotiation, 6,* 483–502.

Green, J., Pinter, B., & Sedikides, C. (2005). Mnemic neglect and self-threat: Trait modifiability moderates self-protection. *European Journal of Social Psychology, 35,* 225–235.

Greenfield, P. (2000). Three approaches to the psychology of culture: Where do they come from? Where can they go? *Asian Journal of Social Psychology, 3*, 223–240.

Greenfield, P., & Childs, C.P. (1977). Weaving, color terms, and pattern representation: Cultural influences and cognitive development among the Zinacantecos of Southern Mexico. *International Journal of Psychology, 11*, 23–48.

Greenfield, P., Maynard, A.E., & Childs, C.P. (2003). Historical change, cultural learning, and cognitive representation in Zinacantec Maya Children. *Cognitive Development, 18*, 455–487.

Gregory, R.J. (1996). *Psychological testing: History, principles, and applications.* Needham Heights, MA: Allyn & Bacon.

Grouzet, F., Kasser, T., et al. (2005). The structure of goal contents across 15 cultures. *Journal of Personality and Social Psychology, 89*, 800–816.

Gudykunst, W.B., Gao, G., Schmidt, K.L., Nishida, T., et al. (1992). The influence of individualism-collectivism, self-monitoring and predicted-outcome value on communication in in-group and out-group relationships. *Journal of Cross-Cultural Psychology, 23*, 196–213.

Gudykunst, W B., & Lee, C.M. (2003). Assessing the validity of self-construal scales: A response to Levine et al. *Human Communication Research, 29*, 253–274.

Gudykunst, W.B., Matsumoto, Y., Ting-Toomey, S., Nishida, T., Kim, K., & Heyman, S. (1996). The influence of cultural individualism-collectivism, self-construals and individual values on communication styles across cultures. *Human Communication Research, 22,* 510–543.

Guerra, R., Rebelo, M.., et al. (2010). How should intergroup contact be structured in order to reduce bias among majority and minority group children? *Group Processes and Interpersonal Relations, 13*, 445–460.

Guimond, S., Branscombe, N., Brunot, S., et al. (2007). Culture, gender and the self: Variations and impact of social comparison processes. *Journal of Personality and Social Psychology, 92*, 1118–1134.

Guimond, S., Chatard, A., Branscombe, N., et al. (2006). Social comparisons across cultures II: Change and stability in self-views – experimental evidence. In S. Guimond (Ed.), *Social comparison and social psychology: Understanding cognition, intergroup relations and culture* (pp. 318–344). Cambridge, UK: Cambridge University Press.

Gunia, B., Brett, J., Nandkeolyar, A., & Kamdar, D. (2011). Paying a price: Culture, trust and negotiation consequences. *Journal of Applied Psychology, 96*, 774–789.

Haberstroh, S., Oyserman, D., Schwarz, N., Kuhnen, U., & Ji, L.J. (2002). Is the interdependent self more sensitive to question context than the independent self? Self construal and the observation of conversational norms. *Journal of Experimental Social Psychology, 38*, 323–329.

Hackman, M.Z., Ellis, K., Johnson, C.E., & Staley, C. (1999). Self-construal orientation: Validation of an instrument and a study of the relationship to leadership communication style. *Communication Quarterly, 47*, 183–195.

Hall, E.T. (1966). *The hidden dimension.* New York: Doubleday.

Hamamura, T. (2012). Social class predicts generalized trust but only in wealthy societies. *Journal of Cross-Cultural Psychology, 43*, 498–509.

Hamamura, T., Heine, S., & Takemoto, T. (2007). Why the better-than-average effect is a worse-than-average measure of self-enhancement: An investigation of conflicting findings from studies of east Asian self-evaluations. *Motivation and Emotion, 31*, 247–259.

Hambleton, R., & Zenisky, A. (2011). Translating and adapting tests for cross-cultural assessments. In D. Matsumoto & F. van de Vijver (Eds), *Cross-cultural research methods in psychology* (pp. 46–73). Cambridge, UK: Cambridge University Press.

Hamid, A.H. (2004). *Cultural values as a predictor of personality, work values and causal attributions in Malaysia.* Unpublished doctoral dissertation, University of Sussex, UK.

Hansen, N., Postmes, T., Van der Vinne, N., & Van Thiel, W. (2012). Information and communication technology and cultural change: How ICT usage changes self-construal and values. *Social Psychology, 43*, 222–231.

Hara, K., & Kim, M.S. (2004). The effect of self-construals on conversational indirectness. *International Journal of Intercultural Relations, 28*, 1–18.

Harb, C., & Smith, P.B. (2008). Self-construals across cultures: Beyond independence-interdependence. *Journal of Cross-Cultural Psychology, 39*, 178–197.

Hardin, E.E. (2006). Convergent evidence for the multidimensionality of self-construal. *Journal of Cross-Cultural Psychology, 37*, 516–521.

Hardin, E.E., Leong, F.T.L., & Bhagwat, A.A. (2004). Factor structure of the self-construal scale revisited: Implications for the multidimensionality of self-construal. *Journal of Cross-Cultural Psychology, 35*, 327–345.

Harkness, J. (2003). Questionnaire translation. In J. Harkness, F.J.R. van de Vijver & P. Mohler (Eds), *Cross-cultural survey methods* (pp. 35–56). New York: Wiley.

Harkness, S. (1992). Parental ethnotheories in action. In I.E. Sigel, A.V. MacGillicuddy-DeLisi, & J.J. Goodnow (Eds), *Parental belief systems* (pp. 373–391). Hillsdale, NJ: Erlbaum.

Harkness, S., & Keefer, C. (2000). Contributions of cross-cultural psychology in research and interventions in health and education. *Journal of Cross-Cultural Psychology, 31*, 92–109.

Harkness, S., & Super, C. (1977). Why African children are so hard to test. *Annals of the New York Academy of Sciences, 285*, 326–331.

Harper, J.E.T., & Cormeraie, S. (1992). 'C'est trop Anglais, Monsieur'. CRICCOM Papers, 2. Horsham, UK: Roffey Park Management Institute.

Harwood, J., Giles, H., & Bourhis, R. (1994). The genesis of vitality theory: Historical patterns and discoursal dimensions. *International Journal of the Sociology of Language, 108*, 167–206.

Harzing, A.W. (1995). The persistent myth of high expatriate failure rates. *International Journal of Human Resource Management, 6*, 457–474.

Harzing, A.W. (2005). Does the use of English-language questionnaires in cross-cultural research obscure national differences? *International Journal of Cross-Cultural Management, 5*, 213–224.

Hasegawa, T., & Gudykunst, W.B. (1998). Silence in Japan and the United States. *Journal of Cross Cultural Psychology, 29*, 668–684.

Hashimoto, H., Li, Y., & Yamagishi, T. (2011). Beliefs and preferences in cultural agents and cultural game players. *Asian Journal of Social Psychology, 14*, 140–147.

Haslam, N., Bastian, B., Bain, P., & Kashima, Y. (2006). Psychological essentialism, implicit theories and intergroup relations. *Group Processes and Interpersonal Relations, 9*, 63–76.

Haslam, N., Loughnan, S., Kashima, Y., & Bain, P. (2008). Attributing and denying humanness to others. *European Review of Social Psychology, 19*, 55–85.

Haslam, S.A., Turner, J.C., Oakes, P.J., et al. (1992). Context-dependent variation in social stereotyping: 1. The effects of intergroup relations as mediated by social change and frame of reference. *European Journal of Social Psychology, 22*, 3–20.

Hatfield, E., & Rapson, R.L. (1996). *Love and sex: Cross-cultural perspectives.* Needham Heights, MA: Allyn & Bacon.

Hawes, K., & Kealey, D. (1981). An empirical study of Canadian technical assistance. *International Journal of Intercultural Relations, 5*, 239–258.

He, W., Chen, C.C., & Zhang, L.H. (2004). Reward allocation preferences of Chinese employees in the new millennium: The effects of ownership reform, collectivism and goal priority. *Organization Science, 15*, 221–231.

Heine, S.J. (2005). Where is the evidence for pan-cultural self-enhancement? Reply to Sedikides, Gaertner and Toguchi (2003). *Journal of Personality and Social Psychology, 89*, 531–538.

Heine, S.J. (2007). *Cultural psychology.* New York: Norton.

Heine, S.J., Buchtel, E., & Norenzayan, A. (2008). What do cross-national comparisons of personality traits tell us? The case of conscientiousness. *Psychological Science, 19*, 309–313.

Heine, S.J., & Hamamura, T. (2007). In search of East Asian self-enhancement. *Personality and Social Psychology Review, 11*, 4–27.

Heine, S.J., Kitayama, S., & Hamamura, T. (2007a). Inclusion of additional studies yields different conclusions: Comment on Sedikides, Gaertner, & Vevea (2005), Journal of Personality and Social Psychology. *Asian Journal of Social Psychology, 10*, 49–58.

Heine, S.J., Kitayama, S., & Hamamura, T. (2007b). Which studies test whether self-enhancement is pancul-tural? Reply to Sedikides, Gaertner, & Vevea, 2007. *Asian Journal of Social Psychology*, *10*, 198–200.

Heine, S.J., Kitayama, S., & Lehman, D.R. (2001). Cultural differences in self-evaluation: Japanese readily accept negative self-relevant information. *Journal of Cross-Cultural Psychology*, *32*, 434–443.

Heine, S.J., Kitayama, S., Lehman, D.R., Takata, T., et al. (2001). Divergent consequences of success and failure in Japan and North America: An investigation of self-improving motivations and malleable selves. *Journal of Personality and Social Psychology, 81,* 599–615.

Heine, S.J., & Lehman, D.R. (1997). The cultural construction of self-enhancement: An examination of group-serving biases. *Journal of Personality and Social Psychology*, *72*, 1268–1283.

Heine, S.J., & Lehman, D.R. (1999). Culture, self-discrepancies and self-satisfaction. *Personality and Social Psychology Bulletin*, *25*, 915–925.

Heine, S.J., Lehman, D.R., Markus, H.R. & Kitayama, S. (1999). Is there a universal need for self-regard? *Psychological Review*, *106*, 766–794.

Heine, S.J., Lehman, D.R., Peng, K.P., & Greenholz, J. (2002). What's wrong with cross-cultural comparisons of subjective Likert scales? The reference group effect. *Journal of Personality and Social Psychology, 82,* 903–918.

Heine, S.J., & Renshaw, K. (2002). Interjudge agreement, self-enhancement and liking: Cross-cultural diver-gences. *Personality and Social Psychology Bulletin*, *28*, 578–587.

Heine, S.J., Takata, T., & Lehman, D.R. (2000). Beyond self-presentation: Evidence for self-criticism among Japanese. *Personality and Social Psychology Bulletin*, *26*, 71–78.

Henrich, J., Heine, S.J., & Norenzayan, A. (2010). The weirdest people in the world. *Behavioral and Brain Sciences*, *33*, 61–83.

Henrich, J., & Henrich, N. (2010). The evolution of cultural adaptations: Fijian food taboos protect against dangerous marine toxins. *Proceedings of the Royal Society: Biological Sciences, 277,* 3715–3724.

Henrich, J., McElheath, R., Barr, A., et al. (2006). Costly punishment across human societies. *Science, 312,* 1767–1770.

Henry, P., Sidanius, J., Levin, S., & Pratto, F. (2007). Social dominance orientation, authoritarianism and support for intergroup violence between the Middle East and America. *Political Psychology*, *26*, 569–583.

Herrnstein, R., & Murray, C. (1994). *The bell curve: Intelligence and class structure in American life*. New York: Free Press.

Herskovits, M. (1948). *Man and his works: The science of cultural anthropology*. New York: Knopf.

Hewstone, M., & Swart, H. (2011). Fifty-odd years of intergroup contact: From hypothesis to integrated theory. *British Journal of Social Psychology*, *50*, 374–386.

Higgins, E.T. (1987). Self-discrepancy: A theory relating self and affect. *Psychological Review*, *94*, 319–340.

Hillier, S., Huq, A., Loshak, R., Marks, F., & Rahman, S. (1994). An evaluation of child psychiatric services for Bangladeshi parents. *Journal of Mental Health*, *3*, 332–337.

Ho, D.Y.F. (1976). On the concept of face. *American Journal of Sociology*, *81*, 867–884.

Ho, D.Y.F. (1995). Selfhood and identity in Confucianism, Taoism, Buddhism, and Hinduism: Contrasts with the West. *Journal for the Theory of Social Behaviour*, *25*(2), 115–134.

Ho, M.Y., & Fung, H.H. (2011). A dynamic process model of forgiveness. *Review of General Psychology, 15,* 77–84.

Hodges, B., & Geyer, A. (2006). A non-conformist account of the Asch experiments: Values, pragmatics and social dilemmas. *Personality and Social Psychology Review*, *10*, 2–19.

Hofer, J. (2010). Research on implicit motives across cultures. In O. Schultheiss & J. Brunstein (Eds), *Implicit motives* (pp. 433–467). New York: Oxford University Press.

Hofer, J., Schröder, L. & Keller, H. (2012). Motivational basis of body contact: A multi-cultural study of mothers with their three-month old infants. *Journal of Cross-Cultural Psychology, 43,* 858–876.

Hoffman, E. (1990). Lost in translation: *Life in a new language*. New York: Penguin.

Hofstede, G. (1980). *Culture's consequences: International differences in work-related values*. Beverly Hills, CA: Sage.

Hofstede, G. (1986). Cultural differences in teaching and learning. *International Journal of Intercultural Relations, 10,* 301–320.

Hofstede, G. (2001). *Culture's consequences: Comparing values, behaviours, institutions and organizations across nations.* Thousand Oaks, CA: Sage.

Hofstede, G. (2006). What did GLOBE really measure? Researchers' minds versus respondents' minds. *Journal of International Business Studies, 37,* 882–896.

Hofstede, G., & Associates (1998). *Masculinity and femininity: The taboo dimension of national cultures.* Thousand Oaks, CA: Sage.

Hofstede, G., Bond, M.H., & Luk, C.L. (1993). Individual perceptions of organizational cultures: A methodological treatise on levels of analysis. *Organization Studies, 14,* 483–583.

Hofstede, G., & McCrae, R.R. (2004). Personality and culture revisited: Linking traits and dimensions of culture. *Cross-Cultural Research, 38,* 52–88.

Hofstede, G., Neuijen, B., Ohayv, D.D., & Sanders, G. (1990). Measuring organizational cultures: A qualitative and quantitative study across 20 cases. *Administrative Science Quarterly, 35,* 286–315.

Hogan, R. (1982). A socioanalytic theory of personality. In M. Page (Ed.), *Nebraska symposium on motivation* (Vol. 30, pp. 56–89). Lincoln, NB: University of Nebraska Press.

Hogg, M. (2007). Uncertainty-identity theory. In M. Zanna (Ed.), *Advances in experimental social psychology* (Vol. 39, pp. 69–126). Orlando, FL: Academic.

Hogg, M., & Vaughan, G. (2011). *Social psychology.* London: Pearson.

Holland, D., & Kipnis, A. (1994). Metaphors for embarrassment and stories of exposure: The not-so-egocentric self in American culture. *Ethos, 22,* 316–342.

Holland, R.W., Roeder, U.R., Van Baaren, R.B., Brandt, A.C., & Hannover, B. (2004). Don't stand so close to me: The effects of self-construal on interpersonal closeness. *Psychological Science, 15,* 237–242.

Holtgraves, T. (1997). Styles of language use: Individual and cultural variability in conversational indirectness. *Journal of Personality and Social Psychology, 73,* 624–637.

Holtgraves, T., & Yang, J. (1990). Politeness as universal: Cross-cultural perceptions of request strategies and inferences based on their use. *Journal of Personality and Social Psychology, 59,* 719–729.

Holtgraves, T., & Yang, J. (1992). Interpersonal underpinnings of request strategies: General principles and differences due to culture and gender. *Journal of Personality and Social Psychology, 62,* 246–256.

Hong, Y.Y., Benet-Martinez, V., Chiu, C.Y., & Morris, M. (2003). Boundaries of cultural influence: Construct activation as a mechanism for cultural differences in social perception. *Journal of Cross-Cultural Psychology, 34,* 453–464.

Hong, Y.Y., Chiu, C.Y., Yeung, G., & Tong, Y.Y. (1999). Social comparison during political transition: Interaction of entity versus incremental beliefs and social identities. *International Journal of Intercultural Relations, 23,* 257–279.

Hong, Y.Y., Morris, M.W., Chiu, C.Y., & Benet Martinez, V. (2000). Multicultural minds: A dynamic constructivist approach to culture and cognition. *American Psychologist, 55,* 709–720.

Horenczyk, G., & Munayer, S. (2007). Acculturation orientations toward two majority groups: The case of Palestinian Arab Christian adolescents in Israel. *Journal of Cross-Cultural Psychology, 38,* 76–86.

Hornsey, M., & Gallois, C. (1998). The impact of interpersonal and intergroup communication accommodation on perceptions of Chinese students in Australia. *Journal of Language and Social Psychology, 17,* 323–347.

House, R.J., Hanges, P.J., Javidan, M., Dorfman, P.W., Gupta, V. & GLOBE associates (2004). *Leadership, culture and organizations: The GLOBE study of 62 nations.* Thousand Oaks, CA: Sage.

Hsu, F.L.K. (1985). The self in cross-cultural perspective. In A.J. Marsella, G. DeVos, & F.L.K. Hsu (Eds), *Culture and self: Asian and Western perspectives* (pp. 24–55). New York: Tavistock.

Huang, C.M., & Park, D. (in press). Cultural influences on facebook photographs. *International Journal of Psychology.* DOI: 10.180/00207594.2011.649285

Huang, L.L., Liu, J.H., & Chang, M. (2004). The 'double identity' of Taiwanese Chinese: A dilemma of politics and culture rooted in history. *Asian Journal of Social Psychology, 7,* 149–189.

Huang, X., & Van de Vliert, E. (2003). Where intrinsic job satisfaction fails to work: National moderators of intrinsic motivation. *Journal of Organizational Behavior, 24,* 159–179.

Huang, X., & Van de Vliert, E. (2004). Job level and national culture as joint roots of job satisfaction. *Applied Psychology: An International Review, 53,* 329–348.

Hui, C.H. (1988). Measurement of individualism-collectivism. *Journal of Research in Personality, 22,* 17–36.

Hui, C.H., Triandis, H.C., & Yee, C. (1991). Cultural differences in reward allocation: Is collectivism the explanation? *British Journal of Social Psychology, 30,* 145–157.

Hui, H.C., & Cheng, I.W.M. (1985). Effects of second language proficiency of speakers and listeners on person perception and behavioral intention: A study of Chinese bilinguals. *International Journal of Psychology, 22,* 421–430.

Hui, K.Y.V., & Bond, M.H. (2009). Target's face loss, motivations, and forgiveness following relational transgression: Comparing Chinese and US cultures. *Journal of Social and Personal Relationships, 26,* 123–140.

Huismans, S. (1994). The impact of differences in religion on the relation between religiosity and values. In A.M. Bouvy, F. van de Vijver, P. Boski, & P. Schmitz (Eds), *Journeys into cross-cultural psychology* (pp. 255–267). Lisse, NL: Swets & Zeitlinger.

Hunt, E. (2012). What makes nations intelligent? *Perspectives on Psychological Science, 7,* 284–306.

Huntington, S.P. (1996). *The clash of civilizations and the remaking of world order.* New York: Simon & Schuster.

Huynh, C.T. (1979). *The concept of endogenous development centered on man.* Paris: UNESCO.

Huynh, Q., Devos, T., & Smalarz, L. (2011). Perpetual foreigner in one's own land: Potential implications for identity and psychological adjustment. *Journal of Social and Clinical Psychology, 30,* 133–162.

Huynh, Q., Nguyen, A.D., & Benet-Martínez, V. (2011). Bicultural identity integration. In S.J. Schwartz, K. Luyckx, & V.L. Vignoles (Eds), *Handbook of identity theory and research* (Vol. 2, pp. 827–843). New York: Springer.

Hwang, A., Francesco, A.M., & Kessler, E. (2003). The relationship between individualism-collectivism, face and feedback and learning processes in Hong Kong, Singapore and the United States. *Journal of Cross-Cultural Psychology, 34,* 72–91.

Hwang, K.K. (2006). Constructive realism and Confucian relationalism: An epistemological strategy for the development of indigenous psychology. In U. Kim, K.S. Yang, & K.K. Hwang (Eds), *Indigenous and cultural psychology: Understanding people in context* (pp. 73–107). New York: Springer.

Ichheiser, G. (1943). Misinterpretations of personality in everyday life and the psychologist's frame of reference. *Character and Personality, 12,* 145–160.

Igarashi, T., Kashima, Y., Kashima, E., et al. (2008). Culture trust and social networks. *Asian Journal of Social Psychology, 11,* 88–101.

Imai, L., & Gelfand, M. (2010). The culturally intelligent negotiator: The impact of cultural intelligence (CQ) on negotiation sequences and outcomes. *Organizational Behavior and Human Decision Processes, 112,* 83–98.

Inglehart, R. (1997). *Modernization and post-modernization: Cultural, economic and political change in 43 nations.* Princeton, NJ: Princeton University Press.

Inglehart, R., & Baker, W.E. (2000). Modernization, cultural change and the persistence of traditional values. *American Sociological Review, 65,* 19–51.

Inglehart, R., Basanez, M., & Moreno, A. (1998). *Human values and beliefs: Political religious, sexual and economic norms in 43 nations: Findings from the 1990—1993 World Values Survey.* Ann Arbor, MI: University of Michigan Press.

Inglehart, R., Foa, R., Peterson, C., & Welzel, C. (2008). Development, freedom and rising happiness: A global perspective (1981–2007). *Perspectives on Psychological Science, 3,* 264–285.

Inglehart, R., & Klingemann, H.D. (2000). Genes, culture, democracy, and happiness. In E. Diener & E.M. Suh (Eds), *Culture and subjective well-being* (pp. 165–183). Cambridge, MA: MIT Press.

Inglehart, R., & Oyserman, D. (2004). Individualism, autonomy and self-expression: The human development syndrome. In H. Vinken, J. Soeters & P. Ester (Eds), *Comparing cultures: Dimensions of culture in a comparative perspective* (pp. 74–96). Leiden, NL: Brill.

Inglehart, R., Welzel, C., & Klingemann, H. (2003). The theory of human development: A cross-cultural analysis. *European Journal of Political Research, 62,* 341–379.

Inkeles, A., & Smith, D.H. (1974). *Becoming modern: Individual change in six developing countries.* Cambridge, MA: Harvard University Press.

Inkson, K., & Khapova, S. (2008). International careers. In P.B. Smith, M.F. Peterson & D.C. Thomas (Eds), *Handbook of cross-cultural management research* (pp. 151–164). Thousand Oaks, CA: Sage.

Irons, W. (2001). Religion as a hard-to-fake sign of commitment. In R. Nesse (Ed.), *Evolution and the capacity for commitment* (pp. 292–309). New York: Russell Sage Foundation.

Ishii, K., Reyes, J.A., & Kitayama, S. (2003). Spontaneous attention to word content versus emotional tone: Differences among three cultures. *Psychological Science, 14*, 39–46.

Jackson, J.S., Brown, K.T., Brown, T.N., & Marks, B. (2001). Contemporary immigration policy orientations among dominant group members in Western Europe. *Journal of Social Issues, 57*, 431–456.

Jahoda, G. (1986). A cross-cultural perspective on developmental psychology. *International Journal of Behavioral Development, 9*, 417–437.

James, W. (1892). *Psychology: Briefer course.* London: Macmillan.

Jasinskaya-Lahti, I., Liebkind, K., Horenczyk, G., & Schmitz, P. (2003). The interactive nature of acculturation: Perceived discrimination, acculturation attitudes and stress among young ethnic repatriates in Finland, Israel and Germany. *International Journal of Intercultural Relations, 27*, 79–97.

Jasperse, M., Ward, C., & Jose, P. (2012). Identity, perceived religious discrimination and psychological well-being in Muslim immigrant women. *Applied Psychology: An International Review, 61*, 250–271.

Javidan, M., House, R.J., Dorfman, P.W., Hanges, P.J., & Sully de Luque, M. (2006). Conceptualizing and measuring cultures and their consequences. A comparative review of GLOBE's and Hofstede's approaches. *Journal of International Business Studies, 37*, 897–914.

Jensen, L.A., Arnett, J.J., & McKenzie, J. (2011). Globalization and cultural identity. In S.J. Schwartz, K. Luyckx & V.L. Vignoles (Eds), *Handbook of identity theory and research* (pp. 285–301). New York: Springer.

Jetten, J., Postmes, T., & McAuliffe, B. (2002). 'We're all individuals': Group norms of individualism and collectivism, levels of identification and identity threat. *European Journal of Social Psychology, 32*, 189–207.

Ji, L.J., Nisbett, R.E., & Su, Y.J. (2001). Culture, change and prediction. *Psychological Science, 12*, 450–456.

Ji, L.J., Peng, K.P., & Nisbett, R.E. (2000). Culture, control and perception of relationships in the environment. *Journal of Personality and Social Psychology, 78*, 943–955.

Jones, E., Gallois, C., Barker, M., & Callan, V. (1994). Evaluations of interactions between students and academic staff: Influence of communication, accommodation, ethnic group and status. *Journal of Language and Social Psychology, 13*, 158–191.

Jose, P., & Bellamy, M. (2012). Relationships of parents' theories of intelligence with children's persistence/learned helplessness: A cross-cultural comparison. *Journal of Cross-Cultural Psychology, 43*, 999–1018.

Jost, J., & Banaji, M. (1994). The role of stereotyping in system justification and the production of false consciousness. *British Journal of Social Psychology, 22*, 1–27.

Jost, J., Kivetz, Y., Rubini, M., et al. (2005). System-justifying functions of complementary regional and ethnic stereotypes: Cross-national evidence. *Social Justice Research, 18*, 305–333.

Jurowski, C., & Gursoy, D. (2004). Distance effects on residents' attitudes towards tourism. *Annals of Tourism Research, 31*, 296–312.

Kağıtçıbaşı, Ç. (1970). Social norms and authoritarianism: A Turkish-American comparison. *Journal of Personality and Social Psychology, 16*, 444–451.

Kağıtçıbaşı, C. (1978). Cross-national encounters: Turkish students in the United States. *International Journal of Intercultural Relations, 2*, 141–160.

Kağıtçıbaşı, Ç. (1982). Old-age security value of children: Cross-national socio-economic evidence. *Journal of Cross-Cultural Psychology, 13*, 29–42.

Kağıtçıbaşı, Ç. (1990). Family and socialization in cross-cultural perspective: A model of change. In J. Berman (Ed.), *Cross-cultural perspectives: Nebraska symposium on motivation*, 1989 (pp. 135–200). Lincoln, NB: Nebraska University Press.

Kağıtçıbaşı, Ç. (1997). Whither multiculturalism? *Applied Psychology: An International Review, 46*, 44–49.

Kağıtçıbaşı, Ç. (2005). Autonomy and relatedness in cultural context: Implications for self and family. *Journal of Cross-Cultural Psychology, 36*, 403–422.

Kağıtçıbaşı, Ç. (2007). *Family, self and human development across cultures: Theory and applications*. Mahwah, NJ: Erlbaum.

Kağıtçıbaşı, Ç., Sunar, D., Bekman, S., et al. (2009). Continuing effects of early enrichment in adult life: The Turkish early enrichment program 22 years later. *Journal of Applied Developmental Psychology, 30,* 764–779.

Kam, C.C.S., & Bond, M.H. (2008). The role of emotions and behavioral responses in mediating the impact of face loss on relationship deterioration: Are Chinese more face-sensitive than Americans? *Asian Journal of Social Psychology, 11,* 175–184.

Kamins, M., & Dweck, C. (1999). Person versus process praise and criticism: Implications for contingent self-worth and coping. *Developmental Psychology, 35,* 835–847.

Kanagawa, C., Cross, S.E., & Markus, H.R. (2001). 'Who am I': The cultural psychology of the conceptual self. *Personality and Social Psychology Bulletin, 27,* 90–103.

Karau, S.J., & Williams, K.D. (1993). Social loafing: A meta-analytic view of social integration. *Journal of Personality and Social Psychology, 65,* 681–706.

Kardiner, A., & Linton, R. (1945). *The individual and his society.* New York: Columbia University Press.

Karlins, M., Coffman, T.L., & Walters, G. (1969). On the finding of social stereotypes: Studies in three generations of college students. *Journal of Personality and Social Psychology, 13,* 1–16.

Kärtner, J., Keller, H., Lamm, B., et al. (2007). Manifestations of autonomy and relatedness in mothers' accounts of their ethnotheories regarding child care across five cultural communities. *Journal of Cross-Cultural Psychology, 38,* 613–628.

Kashima, E.S., & Hardie, E.A. (2000). The development and validation of the relational, individual and collective self-aspects. *Asian Journal of Social Psychology, 3,* 19–48.

Kashima, Y. (2000). Conceptions of person and culture for psychology. *Journal of Cross-Cultural Psychology, 31,* 14–32.

Kashima, Y., & Kashima, E. (1998). Culture and language: The case of cultural dimensions and personal pronoun use. *Journal of Cross-Cultural Psychology, 29,* 461–486.

Kashima, Y., Kashima, E., Kim, Y., & Gelfand, M. (2006). Describing the social world: How is a person, a group and a relationship described in the east and the west? *Journal of Experimental Social Psychology, 42,* 388–396.

Kashima, Y., Yamaguchi, S., Kim, U., et al. (1995). Culture gender and self: A perspective from individualism-collectivism research. *Journal of Personality and Social Psychology, 69,* 236–255.

Katigbak, M.S., Church, A.T., Guanzon-Lapena, M.A., et al. (2002). Are indigenous personality dimensions culture specific? Philippine inventories and the five-factor model. *Journal of Personality and Social Psychology, 82,* 89–101.

Katz, D., & Braly, K.W. (1933). Racial prejudice and social stereotypes. *Journal of Abnormal and Social Psychology, 30,* 175–193.

Keller, H. (2007). *Cultures of infancy.* Mahwah, NJ: Erlbaum.

Keller, H., Borke, J., Lamm, B., et al. (2009). Distal and proximal parenting as alternative parenting strategies during infants' early months of life: A cross-cultural study. *International Journal of Behavioral Development, 33,* 412-420.

Keller, H., Borke, J., Lamm, B., et al. (2011). Developing patterns of parenting in two cultural communities. *International Journal of Behavioral Development, 35,* 233–245.

Keller, H., & Lamm, B. (2005). Parenting as the expression of socio-historical time: The case of German individualization. *International Journal of Behavioral Development, 29,* 238–246.

Keller, H., Lamm, B., Abels, M., et al. (2006). Cultural models, socialization goals and parenting ethnotheories: A multicultural analysis. *Journal of Cross-Cultural Psychology, 37,* 155–172.

Keller, H., Lohaus, A., Völker, M., Cappenberg, S., & Chasiotis, A. (1999). Temporal contingency as an independent component of parenting behavior. *Child Development, 70,* 474–485.

Keller, H., Papaligoura, Z., Kunsemueller, P., Voelker, S., et al. (2003). Concepts of mother-infant interaction in Greece and Germany. *Journal of Cross-Cultural Psychology, 34,* 677–689.

Kelley, H.H. (1952). Two functions of reference groups. In G.E. Swanson, T.M. Newcomb & E.L. Hartley (Eds), *Readings in social psychology* (pp. 410–414). New York: Holt, Rinehart.

Kennedy, J.C., Fu, P.P., & Yukl, G.A. (2003). Influence tactics across twelve cultures. In W.H. Mobley & P.W. Dorfman (Eds), *Advances in global leadership* (Vol. 3, pp. 127–147). Oxford, UK: Elsevier.

Kenrick, D., Griskevicius, V., Neuberg, L., et al. (2010). Renovating the pyramid of needs: Contemporary extensions built upon ancient foundations. *Perspectives on Psychological Science, 5,* 292–314.

Kerr, C., Dunlop, J.T., Harbison, F.H., & Myers, C.A. (1960). *Industrialism and industrial man.* Cambridge, MA: Harvard University Press.

Khaleque, A., & Rohner, R. (2012). Pancultural association between perceived parental acceptance and psychological adjustment of children and adults: A meta-analytic review of worldwide research. *Journal of Cross-Cultural Psychology, 43,* 784–800.

Khan, N., & Smith, P.B. (2003). Profiling the politically violent in Pakistan: Self-construals and values. *Peace and Conflict: Journal of Peace Psychology, 9,* 277–295.

Kim, H., & Markus, H. (1999). Deviance or uniqueness, harmony or conformity? A cultural analysis. *Journal of Personality and Social Psychology, 77,* 785–800.

Kim, M.S. (1994). Cross-cultural comparisons of the perceived importance of interactive constraints. *Human Communication Research, 21,* 128–151.

Kim, M.S., Hunter, J.E., Miyahara, A., Horvath, A.M., Bresnahan, M., & Yoon, H.J. (1996). Individual versus culture-level dimensions of individualism-collectivism: Effects on preferred conversational styles. *Communication Monographs, 63,* 1, 29–49.

Kim, U. (1994). Individualism and collectivism: conceptual clarification and elaboration. In U. Kim, H.C. Triandis, Ç. Kağıtçıbaşı, S.C. Choi & G. Yoon (Eds), *Individualism and collectivism: Theory, method, and applications.* (pp. 19–40). Thousand Oaks, CA: Sage.

Kim, U., Yang, K.S., & Hwang, K.K. (Eds) (2006). *Indigenous and cultural psychology: Understanding people in context.* New York: Springer.

Kirkman, B., Lowe, K., & Gibson, C. (2006). A quarter century of culture's consequences: A review of empirical research incorporating Hofstede's cultural values framework. *Journal of International Business Studies, 37,* 285–320.

Kirkman, B.L., & Shapiro, D.L. (2001). The impact of team members' cultural values on cooperation, productivity and empowerment in self-managing work teams. *Journal of Cross-Cultural Psychology, 32,* 597–617.

Kitayama, S., Duffy, S., Kawamura, T., & Larsen, J.T. (2003). Perceiving an object and its context in three cultures: A cultural look at New Look. *Psychological Science, 14,* 201–206.

Kitayama, S., & Ishii, K. (2002). Word and voice: Spontaneous attention to emotional utterances in two languages. *Cognition and Emotion, 16,* 29–59.

Kitayama, S., Ishii, K., Imada, T., Takemura, K., & Ramaswamy, J. (2006). Voluntary settlement and the spirit of independence: Evidence from Japan's 'northern frontier'. *Journal of Personality and Social Psychology, 91,* 369–384.

Kitayama, S., & Karasawa, M. (1997). Implicit self-esteem in Japan: Name letters and birthday numbers. *Personality and Social Psychology Bulletin, 23,* 736–742.

Kitayama, S., Markus, H.R., & Kurokawa, M. (2000). Culture, emotion and well-being: Good feelings in Japan and the United States. *Cognition and Emotion, 14,* 93–124.

Kitayama, S., Markus, H.R., Matsumoto, H., & Norasakkunkit, V. (1997). Individual and collective processes in the construction of the self: Self-enhancement in the United States and self-criticism in Japan. *Journal of Personality and Social Psychology, 72,* 1245–1267.

Kitayama, S., Park, H., Sevincer, A.T., Karasawa, M., & Uskul, A.K. (2009). A cultural task analysis of implicit independence: Comparing North America, Western Europe and East Asia. *Journal of Personality and Social Psychology, 97,* 236–255.

Kitayama, S., & Uchida, Y. (2003). Explicit self-criticism and implicit self-regard: Evaluating self and friend in two cultures. *Journal of Experimental Social Psychology, 39,* 476–482.

Kitayama, S., & Uskul, A.K. (2011). Culture, mind, and the brain: Current evidence and future directions. *Annual Review of Psychology, 62,* 419–449.

Kleinman, A. (2004). Culture and depression. *New England Journal of Medicine, 351,* 951–953.

Kluckhohn, F., & Strodtbeck, F. (1961). *Variations in value orientations.* Evanston, IL: Row, Peterson.

Knafo, A., & Schwartz, S.H. (2001). Value socialization in families of Israeli-born and Soviet-born adolescents in Israel. *Journal of Cross-Cultural Psychology*, *32*, 213–228.

Knafo, A., Schwartz, S.H., & Levine, R. (2009). Helping strangers is lower in embedded cultures. *Journal of Cross-Cultural Psychology*, 40, 875–879.

Kohn, M.L., Naoi, A., Schoenbach, C., Schooler, C., & Slomczynski, K.M. (1990). Position in the class structure and psychological functioning in the United States, Japan and Poland. *American Journal of Sociology, 95*, 964–1008.

Kosic, A., & Phalet, K. (2006). Ethnic categorization of immigrants: The role of prejudice, perceived acculturation strategies and group size. *International Journal of Intercultural Relations, 30*, 769–782.

Kriss, P., Loewenstein, G., Wang, X., & Weber, R. (2011). Behind the veil of ignorance: Self-serving bias in climate change negotiations. *Judgment and Decision Making, 6*, 602–615.

Kuhn, M.H., & McPartland, R. (1954). An empirical investigation of self attitudes. *American Sociological Review*, *19*, 68–76.

Kühnen, U., & Hannover, B. (2000). Assimilation and contrast in social comparisons as a consequence of self-construal activation. *European Journal of Social Psychology, 30,* 799–811.

Kühnen, U., Hannover, B., Roeder, U., et al. (2001). Cross-cultural variations in identifying embedded figures: Comparisons from the United States, Germany, Russia and Malaysia. *Journal of Cross-Cultural Psychology*, *32*, 365–371.

Kühnen, U., Hannover, B., & Schubert, B. (2001). The semantic-procedural interface model of the self: The role of self-knowledge for context-dependent versus context-independent modes of thinking. *Journal of Personality and Social Psychology, 80,* 397–409.

Kurman, J. (2001). Self-enhancement: Is it restricted to individualistic cultures? *Personality and Social Psychology Bulletin, 27*, 1705–1716.

Kurman, J. (2003). Why is self-enhancement low in certain collectivist cultures? An investigation of two competing explanations. *Journal of Cross-Cultural Psychology*, *34*, 496–510.

Kurman, J., & Ronen-Eilon, C. (2004). Lack of knowledge of a culture's social axioms and adaptation difficulties among immigrants. *Journal of Cross-Cultural Psychology*, *35*, 192–208.

Kurman, J., & Sriram, N. (2002). Interrelationships among vertical and horizontal collectivism, modesty and self-enhancement. *Journal of Cross-Cultural Psychology*, *33*, 71–86.

Kvaloy, B., Finseraas, H., & Listhaug, O. (2012). The public's concern for global warming: A cross-national study of 47 countries. *Journal of Peace Research*, *49*, 11–22.

Kwan, V.S.Y., Bond, M.H., & Singelis, T.M. (1997). Pancultural explanations for life satisfaction: Adding relationship harmony to self-esteem. *Journal of Personality and Social Psychology*, *73*, 1038–1051.

Labov, W. (2010). Unendangered dialect, endangered people: The case of African American Vernacular English. *Transforming Anthropology, 18*, 15–27.

Laland, K., & Galef, B. (2009). *The question of animal culture*. Cambridge, MA: Harvard University Press.

Lalonde, R.N., Hynie, M., Pannu, M., & Tatla, S. (2004). The role of culture in interpersonal relationships: Do second generation South Asian Canadians want a traditional partner? *Journal of Cross-Cultural Psychology*, *35*, 503–524.

Lalwani, A., & Shavitt, S. (2009). The 'me' I claim to be: Cultural self-construal elicits self-presentational goal pursuit. *Journal of Personality and Social Psychology*, *97*, 88–102.

Lam, A., & Zane, N. (2004). Ethnic differences in coping with interpersonal stressors: A test of self-construals as cultural mediators. *Journal of Cross-Cultural Psychology, 35,* 446–459.

Lam, S.F., Lau, I.Y., Chiu, C.Y., Hong, Y.Y., & Peng, S.Q. (1999). Differential emphases on modernity and Confucian values in social categorization: The case of Hong Kong adolescents in political transition. *International Journal of Intercultural Relations, 23*, 237–256.

Lamoreaux, M., & Morling, B. (2012). Outside the head and outside individualism-collectivism: Further meta-analyses of cultural products. *Journal of Cross-Cultural Psychology*, *43*, 299–327.

Landes, D.S. (1998). *The wealth and poverty of nations*. New York: Norton.

Lau, S., Lew, W.J.F., Hau, K.T., Cheung, P.C., & Berndt, T.J. (1990). Relations among perceived parental control, warmth, indulgence, and family harmony of Chinese in mainland China, *Developmental Psychology, 26*, 674–677.

Lawson, S., & Sachdev, I. (2000). Codeswitching in Tunisia: Attitudinal and behavioral dimensions. *Journal of Pragmatics, 32*, 1343–1361.

Lay, C., Fairlie, P., Jackson, S., et al. (1996). Domain specific allocentrism-idiocentrism: A measure of family connectedness. *Journal of Cross-Cultural Psychology, 29*, 434–460.

Lee, A.Y., Aaker, J.L., & Gardner, W.L. (2000). The pleasures and pains of distinct self-construals: The role of interdependence in regulatory focus. *Journal of Personality and Social Psychology, 78*, 1122–1134.

Lee, Y.T., & Duenas, G. (1995). Stereotype accuracy in multicultural business. In Y.T. Lee, L.J. Jussim & C.R. McCauley (Eds), *Stereotype accuracy: Towards appreciating group differences* (pp. 157–186). Washington, DC: American Psychological Association.

Lenneberg, E.H., & Roberts, J.M. (1956). The language of experience: A study in methodology. *International Journal of American Linguistics* (Memoir 13, Supplement 22), 1–33.

Lesch, K., Bengel, D., et al. (1996). Association of anxiety related traits with a polymorphism in the serotonin transporter gene regulatory region. *Science, 274*, 1527–1531.

Leung, A.K.Y., & Cohen, D. (2011). Within- and between-culture variation: Individual differences and the cultural logics of honor, face and dignity cultures. *Journal of Personality and Social Psychology, 100*, 507–526.

Leung, K. (1987). Some determinants of reactions to procedural models for conflict resolution: A cross-national study. *Journal of Personality and Social Psychology, 53*, 898–908.

Leung, K. (1997). Negotiation and reward allocation across cultures. In P.C. Earley & M. Erez (Eds), *New perspectives on international industrial/organizational psychology* (pp. 640–675). San Francisco, CA: New Lexington.

Leung, K., & Bond, M.H. (1984). The impact of cultural collectivism on reward allocation. *Journal of Personality and Social Psychology, 47*, 793–804.

Leung, K., & Bond, M.H. (1989). On the empirical identification of dimensions for cross-cultural comparisons. *Journal of Cross-Cultural Psychology, 20*, 133–152.

Leung, K., & Bond, M.H. (2004). Social axioms: A model of social beliefs in multi-cultural perspective. In M.P. Zanna (Ed.), *Advances in Experimental Social Psychology* (Vol. 36, pp. 119–197). San Diego, CA: Elsevier Academic Press.

Leung, K., & Bond, M.H. (2007). Psycho-logic and eco-logic: Insights from social axiom dimensions. In F. van de Vijver, D. van Hemert & Y.H. Poortinga (Eds), *Multilevel analysis of individuals and cultures* (pp. 199–221). Mahwah, NJ: Erlbaum.

Leung, K., Bond, M.H., de Carrasquel, S.R., et al. (2002). Social axioms: The search for universal dimensions of beliefs about how the world functions. *Journal of Cross-Cultural Psychology, 33*, 286–302.

Leung, K., Lam, B., Bond, M.H., et al. (2012). Developing and evaluating the social axioms survey in eleven countries: Its relationship with the five-factor model of personality. *Journal of Cross-Cultural Psychology, 43*, 833–857.

Leung, K., Smith, P.B., Wang, Z.M., & Sun, H. (1996). Job satisfaction in joint venture hotels in China: An organizational justice analysis. *Journal of International Business Studies, 27*, 947–963.

Leung, K., & Van de Vijver, F. (2008). Strategies for strengthening causal inferences in cross-cultural research: The consilience approach. *International Journal of Cross-Cultural Management, 8*, 145–169.

Leung, K., Wang, Z.M., & Smith, P.B. (2001). Job attitudes and organizational justice in joint venture hotels in China: The role of expatriate managers. *International Journal of Human Resource Management, 12*, 926–945.

Leventhal, G.S. (1976). The distribution of rewards and resources in groups and organizations. In L. Berkowitz & E. Walster (Eds), *Advances in Experimental Social Psychology* (Vol. 9, pp. 91–131). New York: Academic.

Levin, S., Henry, P.J., Pratto, F., & Sidanius, J. (2003). Social dominance and social identity in Lebanon: Implications for support of violence against the West. *Group Processes and Intergroup Relations, 6*, 353–368.

Levin, S., & Sidanius, J. (1999). Social dominance and social identity in the United States and Israel: In-group favoritism or out-group derogation? *Political Psychology, 20*, 99–126.

LeVine, R.A. (1989). Cultural environments in child development. In N. Damon (Ed.), *Child development today and tomorrow* (pp. 349–378). San Francisco, CA: Jossey-Bass.

Levine, R.V., & Bartlett, C. (1984). Pace of life, punctuality and coronary heart disease in six countries. *Journal of Cross-Cultural Psychology, 15*, 233–255.

Levine, R.V., & Norenzayan, A. (1999). The pace of life in 31 countries. *Journal of Cross-Cultural Psychology*, *30*, 178–205.

Levine, R.V., Norenzayan, A., & Philbrick, K. (2001). Cross-cultural differences in helping strangers. *Journal of Cross-Cultural Psychology*, *32*, 543–560.

Levine, R.V., Sato, S., Hashimoto, T., & Verma, J. (1995). Love and marriage in eleven cultures. *Journal of Cross-Cultural Psychology*, *26*, 554–571.

Levine, T.R., Bresnahan, M.J., Park, H.S., Lapinski, M.K., et al. (2003). Self-construal scales lack validity. *Human Communication Research*, *29*, 210–252.

Lewin, K. (1936). Some socio-psychological differences between the United States and Germany. *Character and Personality*, *4*, 265–293.

Lewin, K. (1939). Field theory and experiment in social psychology: Concepts and methods. *American Journal of Sociology*, *44*, 868–896.

Lewin, K., Heider, G., & Heider, F. (1936). *Principles of topological psychology*. New York: McGraw-Hill.

Lewis, R., Goto, S., & Kong, L. (2008). Culture and context: East Asian American and European American differences in P3 event-related potentials and self-construal. *Personality and Social Psychology Bulletin*, *34*, 623–634.

Li, H.Z. (2002). Culture, gender and self-close-others connectedness in Canadian and Chinese samples. *European Journal of Social Psychology*, *32*, 93–104.

Li, H.Z. (2004). Gaze and mutual gaze in inter- and intra-cultural conversation. *International Journal of Language and Communication*, *3*, 20–26.

Li, J. (2004). Learning as a task or as a virtue: US and Chinese preschoolers explain learning. *Developmental Psychology*, *40*, 595–605.

Li, L.M.W., & Bond, M.H. (2010). Value change: Analyzing national change in citizen secularism across four time periods in the World Values Survey. *Social Science Journal*, *47*, 294–306.

Licata, L., Sanchez-Mazas, M., & Green, E.T. (2011). Identity, immigration, and prejudice in Europe: A recognition approach. In S.J. Schwartz, K. Luyckx & V.L. Vignoles (Eds), *Handbook of identity theory and research* (Vol. 2, pp. 895–916). New York: Springer.

Lin, Z., Lin, Y., & Han, S. (2008). Self-construal priming modulates visual activity underlying local/global perception. *Biological Psychology*, *77*, 93–97.

Lind, E.A. (2001). Thinking critically about justice judgments. *Journal of Vocational Behavior*, *58*, 220–226.

Lind, E.A., Tyler, T.R., & Huo, Y.J. (1997). Procedural context and culture: Variation in the antecedents of procedural justice judgments. *Journal of Personality and Social Psychology*, *73*, 767–780.

Lindholm, C. (1997). Does the sociocentric self exist? Reflections on Markus and Kitayama's 'Culture and the Self'. *Journal of Anthropological Research*, *53*, 405–422.

Lindsey, D.T., & Brown, A.M. (2002). Color naming and the phototoxic effects of sunlight on the eye. *Psychological Science*, *13*, 506–512.

Linssen, H., & Hagendoorn, L. (1994). Social and geographic factors in the explanation of the content of European nationality stereotypes. *British Journal of Social Psychology*, *33*, 165–182.

Linville, P., Fischer, G.W., & Yoon, C. (1996). Perceived covariation among the features of in-group and out-group members: The out-group covariation effect. *Journal of Personality and Social Psychology*, *70*, 421–436.

Li-Ripac, D. (1980). Cultural influences on clinical perception: A comparison between Caucasian and Chinese-American therapists. *Journal of Cross-Cultural Psychology*, *11*, 327–342.

Little, T.D., Lopez, D.F., Oettingen, G., & Baltes, P.B. (2001). A comparative-longitudinal study of action-control beliefs and school performance: On the role of context. *International Journal of Behavioral Development*, *25*, 237–245.

Little, T.D., Oettingen, G., Stetsenko, A., & Baltes, P.B. (1995). Children's action-control beliefs about school performance: How do American children compare with German and Russian children? *Journal of Personality and Social Psychology*, *69*, 686–700.

Liu, J. H., Goldstein-Hawes, R., et al. (2005). Social representations of events and people in world history across 12 cultures. *Journal of Cross-Cultural Psychology*, *36*, 171–191.

Liu, J.H., & Hilton, D.J. (2005). How the past weighs on the present: Social representations of history and their role in identity politics. *British Journal of Social Psychology*, *44*, 537–556.

Liu, J.H., Lawrence, B., Ward, C., & Abraham, S. (2003). Social representations of history in Malaysia and Singapore: On the relationship between national and ethnic identity. *Asian Journal of Social Psychology*, *5*, 3–20.

Liu, J.H., Paez, D., Hanke, K., et al. (2012). Cross-cultural dimensions of meaning in the evaluation of world history? Perceptions of historical calamities and progress in cross-cultural data from thirty societies. *Journal of Cross-Cultural Psychology*, *43*, 251–272.

Liu, J.H., Paez, D., Slawuta, P., et al. (2009). Representing world history in the 21st century: The impact of 9/11, the Iraq war and the nation state on dynamics of collective remembering. *Journal of Cross-Cultural Psychology*, *40*, 667–692.

Liu, J.H., Wilson, M., McClure, J., & Higgins, T. (1999). Social identity and the perception of history: Cultural representations of Aotearoa/New Zealand. *European Journal of Social Psychology*, *29*, 1021–1047.

Liu, L., Friedman, R., Barry, B., Gelfand, M., & Zhang, Z. (2012). The dynamics of consensus building in intra-cultural and intercultural negotiations. *Administrative Science Quarterly*, *57*, 269–304.

Lonner, W.J. (1980). The search for psychological universals. In H.C. Triandis & W. Lambert (Eds), *Handbook of cross-cultural psychology* (Vol.1, pp.143–204). Boston, MA: Allyn & Bacon.

Lucas, R., & Diener, E. (2008). Can we learn about national differences in happiness from individual responses? A multilevel approach. In F. van de Vijver, D. van Hemert & Y. Poortinga (Eds), *Multilevel analyses of individuals and cultures* (pp. 223–248). New York: Erlbaum.

Lucas, T., Parkhill, M., Wendorf, C., et al. (2008). Cultural and evolutionary components of marital satisfaction: A multidimensional assessment of measurement invariance. *Journal of Cross-Cultural Psychology*, *39*, 109–123.

Lumsden, C.J., & Wilson, E.O. (1981). *Genes, mind and culture*. Cambridge, MA: Harvard University Press.

Lynn, R. (1990). The role of nutrition in secular increases in intelligence. *Personality and Individual Differences*, *11*, 263–285.

Lynn, R., & Vanhanen, T. (2002). *IQ and the wealth of nations*. Westport, CT: Praeger.

Maass, A., Karasawa, M., Politi, F., & Suga, S. (2006). Do verbs and adjectives play different roles in different cultures? A cross-linguistic analysis of person representation. *Journal of Personality and Social Psychology*, *90*, 734–750.

Mahalingam, R. (2007). Essentialism, power and the representation of social categories: A folk sociology perspective. *Human Development*, *50*, 300–319.

Mak, A.S., & Buckingham, K. (2007). Beyond communication courses: Are there benefits in adding skills-based EXCELL sociocultural training? *International Journal of Intercultural Relations*, *31*, 277–291.

Mak, M.C.K., Bond, M.H., Simpson, J.A., & Rholes, W.S. (2010). Adult attachment, perceived support and depressive symptoms in Chinese and American cultures. *Journal of Social and Clinical Psychology*, *29*, 144–165.

Malinowski, B. (1922). *Argonauts of the western Pacific*. New York: Dutton.

Malinowski, B. (1927). *Sex and repression in savage society*. London: Humanities Press.

Man, D.C., & Lam, S.S.K. (2003). The effects of job complexity and autonomy on cohesiveness in collectivistic and individualistic work groups: A cross-cultural analysis. *Journal of Organizational Behavior*, *24*, 979–1001.

Markus, H.R., & Hamedani, M.G. (2007). Sociocultural psychology: The dynamic interdependence among self systems and social systems. In S. Kitayama & D. Cohen (Eds), *Handbook of cultural psychology* (pp. 3–39). New York: Guilford.

Markus, H.R., & Kitayama, S. (1991). Culture and the self: Implications for cognition, emotion, and motivation. *Psychological Review*, *98*, 224–253.

Markus, H.R., & Kitayama, S. (2003). Culture, self, and the reality of the social. *Psychological Inquiry*, *14*, 277–283.

Markus, H.R., & Kitayama, S. (2010). Cultures and selves. *Perspectives on Psychological Science*, *5*, 420–430.

Marques, J.M., Abrams, D., & Serodio, R. (2001). Being better by being right: Subjective group dynamics and derogation of in-group deviants when generic norms are undermined. *Journal of Personality and Social Psychology*, *81*, 436–447.

Marriott, H. (1993). Spatial arrangements in Japanese-Australian business communication. *Journal of Asia Pacific Communication*, *4*, 107–126.

Marsella, A. (2011). Psychology and globalization: Understanding a complex relationship. *Journal of Social Issues*, *68*, 454–472.

Marsh, A., Elfenbein, H., & Ambady, N. (2003). Non-verbal 'accents': Cultural differences in facial expressions of emotion. *Psychological Science*, *14*, 373–376.

Maslow, A.H. (1943). A theory of human motivation. *Psychological Review*, *50*, 370–396.

Masuda, T., Gonzalez, R., Kwan, L., & Nisbett, R.E. (2008). Culture and aesthetic preference: Comparing the attention to context of East Asians and Americans. *Personality and Social Psychology Bulletin*, *34*, 1260–1275.

Masuda, T., & Nisbett, R.E. (2001). Attending holistically versus analytically: Comparing the context sensitivity of Japanese and Americans. *Journal of Personality and Social Psychology*, *81*, 922–934.

Matsumoto, D. (1999). Culture and self: An empirical assessment of Markus and Kitayama's theory of independent and interdependent self-construal. *Asian Journal of Social Psychology, 2*, 289–310.

Matsumoto, D. (Ed.) (2001). *Handbook of culture and psychology*. New York: Oxford University Press.

Matsumoto, D. (2002). Methodological requirements to test a possible in-group advantage in judging emotions across cultures: Comment on Elfenbein and Ambady (2002) and evidence. *Psychological Bulletin*, *128*, 236–242.

Matsumoto, D., Consolacion, T., Yamada, H., et al. (2002). American-Japanese cultural differences in judgments of emotional expressions of different intensities. *Cognition and Emotion*, *16*, 721–747.

Matsumoto, D., & Hwang, H.S. (2012). Culture and emotion: The integration of biological and cultural contributions. *Journal of Cross-Cultural Psychology*, *43*, 91–118.

Matsumoto, D., & Kudoh, T. (1993). American-Japanese cultural differences in attributions of personality based on smiles. *Journal of Nonverbal Behavior*, *17*, 231–243.

Matsumoto, D., & Kupperbusch, C. (2001). Idiocentric and allocentric differences in emotional expression, experience and the coherence between expression and experience. *Asian Journal of Social Psychology*, *4*, 113–131.

Matsumoto, D., Leroux, J.A., Bernhard, R., & Gray, H. (2004). Unraveling the psychological correlates of intercultural adjustment potential. *International Journal of Intercultural Relations*, *28*, 281–309.

Matsumoto, D., Olida, A., Schug, J., et al. (2009). Cross-cultural judgments of spontaneous facial expressions of emotion. *Journal of Nonverbal Behavior*, *33*, 213–238.

Matsumoto, D., Olida, A., & Willingham, B. (2009). Is there an in-group advantage in recognizing spontaneously expressed emotions? *Journal of Nonverbal Behavior*, *33*, 181–191.

Matsumoto, D., & Van de Vijver, F. (Eds) (2011). *Cross-cultural research methods in psychology*. Cambridge, UK: Cambridge University Press.

Matsumoto, D., & Willingham, B. (2006). The thrill of victory and the agony of defeat: Spontaneous expressions of medal winners at the 2004 Athens Olympic Games. *Journal of Personality and Social Psychology*, *91*, 568–581.

Matsumoto, D., & Willingham, B. (2009). Spontaneous facial expressions of congenitally and non-congenitally blind individuals. *Journal of Personality and Social Psychology*, *96*, 1–10.

Matsumoto, D., & Yoo, S.H. (2006). Towards a new generation of cross-cultural research, *Perspectives on Psychological Science*, *1*, 234–250.

Matsumoto, D., Yoo, S.H., Fontaine, J., et al. (2008). Mapping expressive differences around the world: The relationship between emotional display rules and individualism versus collectivism. *Journal of Cross-Cultural Psychology*, *39*, 55–74.

Mayer, B., Tromsdorff, G., Kağıtçıbaşı, C., & Mishra, R. (2012). Family models of independence/interdependence and their intergenerational similarity in Germany, Turkey and India. *Family Science*, *3*, 64–74.

McAuley, P., Bond, M.H., & Kashima, E. (2002). Towards defining situations objectively: A culture-level analysis of role dyads in Hong Kong and Australia. *Journal of Cross-Cultural Psychology, 33*, 363–380.

McClelland, D.C. (1961). *The achieving society*. Princeton, NJ: Van Nostrand.

McCrae, R.R. (2000). Trait psychology and the revival of personality-and-culture studies. *American Behavioral Scientist*, *44*, 10–31.

McCrae, R.R., Costa, P.T. Jr., Pilar, G.H., Rolland, J.-P., & Parker, W.D. (1998). Cross-cultural assessment of the five-factor model: The Revised NEO Personality Inventory. *Journal of Cross-Cultural Psychology*, *29*, 171–188.

McCrae, R.R., Costa, P.T. Jr., & Yik, M.S.M. (1996). Universal aspects of Chinese personality structure. In M.H. Bond (Ed.), *The handbook of Chinese psychology* (pp. 189–207). Hong Kong: Oxford.

McCrae, R.R., Terracciano, A., et al. (2005a). Universal features of personality traits from the observer's perspective: Data from 50 cultures. *Journal of Personality and Social Psychology, 88,* 547–561.

McCrae, R.R., Terracciano, A., et al. (2005b). Personality profiles of cultures: Aggregate personality traits. *Journal of Personality and Social Psychology, 89,* 407–425.

McCrae, R.R., Terracciano, A., Realo, A., & Allik, J. (2007). Climatic warmth and national wealth: Some culture-level determinants of national character stereotypes. *European Journal of Personality, 21,* 953–976.

McCrae, R.R., Terracciano, A., Realo, A., & Allik, J. (2008). Interpreting GLOBE societal practices scales. *Journal of Cross-Cultural Psychology, 35,* 805–810.

McCrae, R.R., Yik, M.S.M., Trapnell, P.D., Bond, M.H., & Paulhus, D.L. (1998). Interpreting personality profiles across culture: Bilingual, acculturation, and peer rating studies of Chinese undergraduates. *Journal of Personality and Social Psychology, 74,* 1041–1055.

McLaren, L. (2012). The cultural divide in Europe: Migration, multiculturalism and political trust. *World Politics, 64,* 199–241.

McShane, K., Hastings, P., Smylie, K., & Prince, C. (2009). Examining evidence of autonomy and relatedness in urban Inuit parenting. *Culture and Psychology, 15,* 411–431.

Mead, M. (1928). *Coming of age in Samoa: A psychological study of primitive youth for Western civilization.* New York: Morrow Quill.

Meeus, J., Duriez, B., Vanbeselaere, N., & Boen, F. (2010). The role of national identity representation in the relation between in-group identification and out-group derogation: Ethnic versus civic representation. *British Journal of Social Psychology, 49,* 305–320.

Mercer Consulting Group (2008). Companies increase number of expats. www.globalhrnews.com/story.asp =?sid=1149.

Mesoudi, A. (2009). How cultural evolutionary theory can enhance social psychology and vice versa. *Psychological Review, 116,* 929–952.

Mesquita, B., & Leu, J. (2007). The cultural psychology of emotion. In S. Kitayama & D. Cohen (Eds), *Handbook of cultural psychology* (pp. 734–759). New York: Guilford.

Milanovic, B. (2007). Globalization and inequality. In D. Held & A. Kaya (Eds), *Global inequality: Patterns and explanations* (pp. 26–49). Cambridge, UK: Polity Press.

Milgram, S. (1961). *Obedience to authority: An experimental view.* New York: Harper, Row.

Miller, D.E. (1999). *Reinventing American Protestantism: Christianity in the new millennium.* Berkeley, CA: University of California Press.

Miller, J.G. (1984). Culture and the development of everyday social explanation. *Journal of Personality and Social Psychology, 46,* 961–978.

Miller, J.G. (1997). Cultural conception of duty: Implications for motivation and morality. In D. Munro, J.F. Schumaker & A.C. Carr (Eds), *Motivation and culture* (pp. 178–192). New York: Routledge.

Minard, R.D. (1952). Race relationships in the Pocahontas coal field. *Journal of Social Issues, 8*(1), 29–44.

Minkov, M. (2011). *Cultural differences in a globalizing world.* Bingley, UK: Emerald.

Minkov, M. (2012). *Cross-cultural analysis: The science and art of comparing the world's modern societies and their cultures.* Thousand Oaks, CA: Sage.

Minkov, M., & Hofstede, G. (2012). Is national culture a meaningful concept? Cultural values delineate homogeneous national clusters of in-country regions. *Cross-Cultural Research, 46,* 133–159.

Mischel, W. (1968). *Personality and assessment.* New York: Wiley.

Mischel, W. (1977). The interaction of person and situation. In E. Magnusson & N.S. Endler (Eds), *Personality at the crossroads: Current issues in interactional psychology* (pp. 333–352). Hillsdale, NJ: Erlbaum.

Miyamoto, Y., & Kitayama, S. (2002). Cultural variations in correspondence bias: The critical role of attitude diagnosticity of socially constrained behavior. *Journal of Personality and Social Psychology, 83,* 1239–1248.

Moghaddam, F. (2008). *Multiculturalism and intergroup relations.* Washington, DC: APA Books.

Mok, A., Morris, M.W., Benet-Martinez, V., & Karakitapoglu-Aygun, Z. (2007). Embracing American culture: Structures of social identity and social networks among first generation biculturals. *Journal of Cross-Cultural Psychology*, *38*, 629–635.

Molinsky, A. (2007). Cross-cultural code-switching: The psychological challenges of adapting behavior in foreign cultural interactions. *Academy of Management Review*, *32*, 622–640.

Montiel, C.J., & Shah, A.A. (2004). Effects of political labeling and perceiver's dominant group position on trait attributions of terrorist/freedom-fighter. *International Journal of Psychology*, *39*, 11.

Montreuil, A., & Bourhis, R.Y. (2001). Majority acculturation orientations toward 'valued' and 'devalued' immigrants. *Journal of Cross-Cultural Psychology*, *32*, 698–719.

Morelli, G.A., Rogoff, B., & Angelillo, C. (2003). Cultural variation in young children's access to work or involvement in specialized child-focused activities. *International Journal of Behavioral Development*, 27, 264–274.

Morling, B., & Lamoreaux, M. (2008). Measuring culture outside the head: A meta-analysis of individualism-collectivism in cultural products. *Personality and Social Psychology Review*, *12*, 199–221.

Morris, D., Collett, P., Marsh, P., & O'Shaughnessy, M. (1979). *Gestures, their origins and distribution*. Briarcliff Manor, NY: Stein & Day.

Morris, M.W., & Leung, K. (2000). Justice for all? Progress in research in cultural variation in the psychology of distributive and procedural justice. *Applied Psychology: An International Review*, *49*, 100–132.

Morris, M.W., & Peng, K.P. (1994). Culture and cause: American and Chinese attributions for social and physical events. *Journal of Personality and Social Psychology*, *67*, 949–971.

Morris, M.W., Williams, K.Y., Leung, K., Larrick, R., Mendoza, M.T., Bhatnagar, D., et al. (1998). Conflict management style: Accounting for cross-national differences. *Journal of International Business Studies*, *29*, 729–747.

Morrison, E.W., Chen, Y.R., & Salgado, S.R. (2004). Cultural differences in newcomer feedback-seeking: A comparison of the United States and Hong Kong. *Applied Psychology: An International Review*, *53*, 1–22.

Moscardo, G., & Pearce, P.L. (1999). Understanding ethnic tourists. *Annals of Tourism Research*, *26*, 416–434.

Mosquera, P.M.R., Manstead, A.S.R., & Fischer, A.H. (2000). The role of honor-related values in the elicitation, communication and experience of pride, shame and anger: Spain and the Netherlands compared. *Personality and Social Psychology Bulletin*, *26*, 833–844.

Mosquera, P.M.R., Manstead, A.S.R., & Fischer, A.H. (2002). Honor in the Mediterranean and Northern Europe. *Journal of Cross-Cultural Psychology*, *33*, 16–36.

Mõttus, R., Allik, J., & Realo, A. (2010). An attempt to validate national mean scores of conscientiousness: No necessarily paradoxical findings. *Journal of Research in Personality*, *44*, 630–640.

Mõttus, R., Allik, J., Realo, A., Pullman, H., et al. (2012). Comparability of self-reported conscientiousness across 21 countries. *Journal of European Personality*, *23*, 306–317.

Mõttus, R., Allik, J., Realo, A., Rossier, J., et al. (2012). The effect of response style on self-reported conscientiousness across 20 countries. *Personality and Social Psychology Bulletin*, *38*, 1423–1436.

Muensterberger, W. (1969). Orality and dependence: Characteristics of southern Chinese. In W. Muensterberger (Ed.), *Man and his culture: Psychoanalytic anthropology after 'Totem and taboo'* (pp. 295–329). New York: Taplinger.

Muethel, M., & Bond, M.H. (in press). National context and individual employees' trust of the out-group: The role of societal trust. *Journal of International Business Studies*.

Munroe, R.L., Munroe, R.H., & Shimmin, H. (1984). Children's work in four cultures: determinants and consequences. *American Anthropologist, 86*, 342–348.

Munroe, R.L., Munroe, R.H., & Winters, S. (1996). Cross-cultural correlates of the consonant-vowel (cv) syllable. *Cross-Cultural Research*, *30*, 60–83.

Muramoto, Y. (2003). An indirect self-enhancement in relationship among Japanese. *Journal of Cross-Cultural Psychology, 34*, 552–566.

Murdock, G.P. (Ed.) (1967). *Ethnographic atlas*. Pittsburgh, PA: University of Pittsburgh.

Na, J., Grossman, I., Varnum, M., Kitayama, S., Gonzalez, R., & Nisbett, R. (2010). Cultural differences are not always reducible to individual differences. *Proceedings of the National Academy of Sciences of the USA, 107,* 6192–6197.

Na, J., & Kitayama, S. (2011). Spontaneous trait inference is culture-specific: Behavioral and neural evidence. *Psychological Science, 22,* 1025–1032.

Nelson, G.L., al Batal, M., & el Bakary, W. (2002). Directness versus indirectness: Egyptian Arabic and US English communication style. *International Journal of Intercultural Relations, 26,* 39–57.

Nelson, G.L., el Bakary, W., & al Batal, M. (1993). Egyptian and American compliments: A cross-cultural study. *International Journal of Intercultural Relations, 17,* 293–314.

Neuberg, S., Judice, T., & West, S. (1997). What the need for closure scale measures and what it does not: Towards differentiating among related epistemic motives. *Journal of Personality and Social Psychology, 72,* 1396–1412.

Newman, L.S. (1993). How individualists interpret behavior: Idiocentrism and spontaneous trait inference. *Social Cognition, 11,* 243–269.

Ng, S.H. (2001). Influencing through the power of language. In J.P. Forgas & K.D. Williams (Eds), *Social influence: Direct and indirect processes. The Sydney symposium of social psychology* (pp. 185–197). New York: Psychology Press.

Ng, S.H., & He, A.P. (2004). Code-switching in tri-generational family conversations among Chinese immigrants in New Zealand. *Journal of Language and Social Psychology, 23,* 28–48.

Ng, S.H., He, A.P., & Loong, C.S.F. (2004). Tri-generational family conversations: Communication accommodation and brokering. *British Journal of Social Psychology, 43,* 449–464.

Ng, S.H., Hossain, A., Ball, P., Bond, M.H., et al. (1982). Human values in nine countries. In R. Rath, H.S. Asthana, D. Sinha & J.B.P. Sinha (Eds), *Diversity and unity in cross-cultural psychology* (pp. 196–205). Lisse, NL: Swets & Zeitlinger.

Ng, S.H., Loong, C.S.F., He, A.P., Liu, J.H., & Wetherall, A. (2000). Communication correlates of individualism and collectivism: Talk directed at one or more addressees in family conversations. *Journal of Language and Social Psychology, 19,* 26–45.

Niiya, Y., & Ellsworth, P.C. (2012). Acceptability of favor requests in the United States and Japan. *Journal of Cross-Cultural Psychology, 43,* 273–285.

Nisbett, R.E. (2003). *The geography of thought.* New York: Free Press.

Nisbett, R.E., Aronson, J., Blair, C., et al. (2012). Intelligence: New findings and theoretical developments. *American Psychologist, 67,* 130–159.

Nisbett, R.E., & Cohen, D. (1996). *Culture of honor: The psychology of violence in the south.* Boulder, CO: Westview.

Nisbett, R.E., Peng, K.P., Choi, I., & Norenzayan, A. (2000). Culture and systems of thought: Holistic versus analytic cognition. *Psychological Review, 108,* 291–310.

Niu, C.P., Wang, A.C., & Cheng, B.S. (2009). Effectiveness of a moral and benevolent leader: Probing the interactions of the dimensions of paternalistic leadership. *Asian Journal of Social Psychology, 12,* 32–39.

Noels, K., Clément, R., & Gaudet, S. (2004). Language and the situated nature of ethnic identity. In S.H. Ng, C.N. Candlin & C.Y. Chiu (Eds), *Language matters: Communication, culture and identity* (pp. 245–266). Hong Kong: City University of Hong Kong Press.

Noorderhaven, N.G., & Tidjani, B. (2001). Culture, governance and economic performance: An explorative study with a special focus on Africa. *International Journal of Cross-Cultural Management, 1,* 31–52.

Norenzayan, A., Choi, I., & Nisbett, R.E. (2002). Cultural similarities and differences in social inference: Evidence from behavioral predictions and lay theories of behavior. *Personality and Social Psychology Bulletin, 28,* 109–120.

Norenzayan, A., & Shariff, A.F. (2008). The origin and evolution of religious prosociality. *Science, 322,* 58–62.

Norenzayan, A., Smith, E.E., Kim, B.J., & Nisbett, R.E. (2002). Cultural preferences for formal versus intuitive reasoning. *Cognitive Science, 26,* 653–684.

Norman, W.T. (1963). Toward an adequate taxonomy of personality attributes: Replicated factor structure in peer nomination personality ratings. *Journal of Abnormal and Social Psychology, 66,* 574–583.

Nsamenang, A.B. (1992). *Human development in cultural context: A third world perspective.* Newbury Park, CA: Sage.

Oakes, P.J., Turner, J.C., & Haslam, S.A. (1991). Pereceiving people as group members: The role of fit in the salience of social categorisations. *British Journal of Social Psychology, 30,* 125–144.

O'Connor, S., & Fischer, R. (2012). Predicting societal corruption across time: Values, wealth or institutions? *Journal of Cross-Cultural Psychology, 43,* 644–659.

Oettingen, G., Little, T.D., Lindenberger, U., & Baltes, P.B. (1994). Causality, agency and control beliefs in East versus West Berlin children: A natural experiment in the control of context. *Journal of Personality and Social Psychology, 66,* 579–595.

Oetzel, J.G., & Ting-Toomey, S. (2003). Face concerns in interpersonal conflict: A cross-cultural empirical test of the face negotiation theory. *Communication Research, 30,* 599–624.

Oetzel, J.G., Ting-Toomey, S., Masumoto, T., Yochi, Y., Pan, X.H., Takai, J., & Wilcox, R. (2001). Face and face-work in conflict: A cross-cultural comparison of China, Germany, Japan and the United States. *Communication Monographs, 68,* 235–258.

Oguri, M., & Gudykunst, W.B. (2002). The influence of self-construals and communication styles on sojourners' psychological and sociocultural adjustment. *International Journal of Intercultural Relations, 26,* 577–593.

Ohbuchi, K., Fukushima, O., & Tedeschi, J.T. (1999). Cultural values in conflict management: Goal orientation, goal attainment and tactical decision. *Journal of Cross-Cultural Psychology, 30,* 51–71.

Oishi, S., Diener, E., Scollon, C., & Biswas-Diener, R. (2004). Cross-situational consistency of affective experiences across cultures. *Journal of Personality and Social Psychology, 86,* 460–472.

Okazaki, S. (1997). Sources of ethnic differences between Asian American and White American college students on measures of depression and social anxiety. *Journal of Abnormal Psychology, 106,* 52–60.

Osgood, C., May, W., & May, M. (1975). *Cross-cultural universals of affective meaning.* Urbana, IL: University of Illinois Press.

Owe, E., Vignoles, V.L., et al. (2012). Beyond West versus East: Culture and self-construals across 38 nations. Manuscript submitted for publication.

Owe, E., Vignoles, V.L., et al. (2013). Contextualism as an important facet of individualism-collectivism: Personhood beliefs across 37 national groups. *Journal of Cross-Cultural Psychology, 44,* 24-45.

Oyserman, D. (2010). *Culture as situated cognition.* Keynote address to the 29th Congress of the International Association for Cross-Cultural Psychology, Melbourne, Australia.

Oyserman, D. (2011). Culture as situated cognition: Cultural mindsets, cultural fluency and meaning making. *European Review of Social Psychology, 22,* 164–214.

Oyserman, D., Coon, H.M., & Kemmelmeier, M. (2002). Rethinking individualism and collectivism: Evaluation of theoretical assumptions and meta-analyses. *Psychological Bulletin, 128,* 3–72.

Oyserman, D., & Lee, S. (2007). Priming 'culture': Culture as situated cognition. In S. Kitayama & D. Cohen (Eds), *Handbook of cultural psychology* (pp. 255–279). New York: Guilford Press.

Oyserman, D., & Lee, S. (2008). Does culture affect what and how we think? Effects of priming individualism and collectivism. *Psychological Bulletin, 134,* 313–342.

Özgen, E. (2004). Language, learning and color perception. *Current Directions in Psychological Science, 13,* 95–98.

Paez, D., Liu, J., Techio, E., Slawuta, P., Zlobina, A., & Cabecinhas, R. (2008). 'Remembering' World War 2 and willingness to fight: Sociocultural factors in the social representation of historical warfare across 22 societies. *Journal of Cross-Cultural Psychology, 39,* 373–380.

Paris, L., Howell, J., Dorfman, P., & Hanges, P. (2009). Preferred leadership prototypes of male and female leaders in 27 countries. *Journal of International Business Studies, 40,* 1396–1405.

Parkes, L.P., Schneider, S.K., & Bochner, S. (1999). Individualism-collectivism and self-concept: Social or contextual? *Asian Journal of Social Psychology, 2,* 367–383.

Parsons, T., & Shils, E. (Eds) (1951). *Towards a general theory of action.* Cambridge, MA: Harvard University Press.

Patterson, M.L., Iizuka, Y., Tubbs, M., Ansel, J., Tsutsumi, M., & Anson, J. (2007). Passing encounters East and West: Comparing Japanese and American pedestrian interactions. *Journal of Nonverbal Behavior, 31,* 155–166.

Peabody, D. (1985). *National characteristics*. Cambridge, UK: Cambridge University Press.

Peabody, D., & Shmelyov, A.G. (1996). Psychological characteristics of Russians. *European Journal of Social Psychology, 26*, 507–512.

Pearson, V.M.S., & Stephan, W.G. (1998). Preferences for styles of negotiation: A comparison of Brazil and the US. *International Journal of Intercultural Relations, 22*, 67–83.

Pedersen, P., Draguns, J., Lonner, W.J., & Trimble, J. (1996). *Counseling across cultures*. Thousand Oaks, CA: Sage.

Pehrson, S., Brown, R., & Zagefka, H. (2009). When does national identification lead to the rejection of immigrants? Cross-sectional and longitudinal evidence for the role of essentialist in-group definitions. *British Journal of Social Psychology, 48*, 61–76.

Pehrson, S., Vignoles, V.L., & Brown, R. (2009). National identification and anti-immigrant prejudice: Individual and contextual effects of national definitions. *Social Psychology Quarterly, 72*, 24–38.

Pelto, P. (1968). The difference between 'tight' and 'loose' societies. *Transaction, 5*, 37–40.

Peng, K.P., & Nisbett, R. (1999). Culture, dialectics and reasoning about contradiction. *American Psychologist, 54*, 741–754.

Pennebaker, J.W., Rimé, B., & Blankenship, V.E. (1996). Stereotypes of emotional expressiveness of northerners and southerners: A cross-cultural test of Montesquieu's hypotheses. *Journal of Personality and Social Psychology, 70*, 372–380.

Pepitone, A. (1976). Toward a normative and comparative bias cultural social psychology. *Journal of Personality and Social Psychology, 34*, 641–653.

Pe-Pua, R. (2006). From decolonising psychology to the development of a cross-indigenous perspective. In U. Kim, K.S. Yang & K.K. Hwang (Eds), *Indigenous and cultural psychology: Understanding people in context* (pp. 109–137). New York: Springer.

Peristiany, J.G. (Ed.) (1965). *Honor and shame: The values of Mediterranean society*. London: Weidenfeld & Nicholson.

Pettigrew, T.F. (1998). Reactions toward the new minorities of Western Europe. *Annual Review of Sociology, 24*, 77–103.

Pettigrew, T.F., & Meertens, R.W. (1995). Subtle and blatant prejudice in Western Europe. *European Journal of Social Psychology, 25*, 57–75.

Pettigrew, T.F., & Tropp, L.R. (2006). A meta-analytic test of intergroup contact theory. *Journal of Personality and Social Psychology, 90*, 751–783.

Phalet, K., & Claeys, W. (1993). A comparative study of Turkish and Belgian youth. *Journal of Cross-Cultural Psychology, 24*, 319–343.

Phalet, K., & Schönpflug, U. (2001). Intergenerational transmission of collectivism and achievement values in two acculturation contexts: The case of Turkish families in Germany and Turkish and Moroccan families in the Netherlands. *Journal of Cross-Cultural Psychology, 32*, 186–201.

Phinney, J., & Vedder, P. (2006). Family relationship values of adolescents and parents: Intergenerational discrepancies and adjustment. In J. Berry, J. Phinney, D. Sam & P. Vedder (Eds), *Immigrant youth in cultural transition: Acculturation, identity and adaptation across national contexts* (pp. 143–165). Mahwah, NJ: Erlbaum.

Pierson, H.D., & Bond, M.H. (1982). How do Chinese bilinguals respond to variations of interviewer language and ethnicity? *Journal of Language and Social Psychology, 1*, 123–139.

Pike, K. (1967). *Language in relation to a unified theory of the structure of human behavior*. The Hague, NL: Mouton.

Piker, S. (1998). Contributions of psychological anthropology. *Journal of Cross-Cultural Psychology, 29*, 9–31.

Pilati, R., Milfont, T., Ferreira, M.C., et al. (2011). Brazilian *jeitinho*: Understanding and explaining an indigenous psychological construct. *Interamerican Journal of Psychology, 45*, 29–38.

Piontkowski, U., Florack, A., Hoelker, P., & Obdrzalek, P. (2000). Predicting acculturation attitudes of dominant and non-dominant groups. *International Journal of Intercultural Relations, 24*, 1–26.

Piontkowski, U., Rohmann, A., & Florack, A. (2002). Concordance of acculturation attitudes and perceived threat. *Group Processes and Interpersonal Relations, 5*, 221–232.

Pittam, J., Gallois, C., Iwawaki, S., & Kroonenberg, P. (1995). Australian and Japanese concepts of expressive behavior. *Journal of Cross-Cultural Psychology, 25*, 451–473.

Poortinga, Y.H. (2009). Intervention programs for use across societies. In S. Bekman & A. Aksu-Koç (Eds), *Perspectives on human development, family and culture* (pp. 301–313). Cambridge, UK: Cambridge University Press.

Poortinga, Y.H., & Van de Vijver, F. (1987). Explaining cross-cultural differences: Bias analysis and beyond. *Journal of Cross-Cultural Psychology, 18*, 259–282.

Poortinga, Y. H., & Van Hemert, D.A. (2001). Personality and culture: Demarcating between the common and the unique. *Journal of Personality, 69*, 1033–1060.

Poppe, E. (2001). Effects of changes in GNP and perceived group characteristics on national and ethnic stereotypes in central and Eastern Europe. *Journal of Applied Social Psychology, 31*, 1689–1708.

Poppe, E., & Linssen, H. (1999). In-group favoritism and the reflection of realistic dimensions of difference between nation states in Central and East European nationality stereotypes. *British Journal of Social Psychology, 38*, 85–103.

Portes, A., & Zhou, M. (1993). The new second generation: Segmented assimilation and its variants. *Annals of the American Academy of Political and Social Science, 530*, 74–96.

Pratt, D., & Wong, K. (1999). Chinese conceptions of 'effective teaching' in Hong Kong: Towards culturally sensitive evaluation of teaching. *International Journal of Lifelong Education, 18*, 241–258.

Pratto, F., Liu, J.H., Levin, S., Sidanius, J., et al. (2000). Social dominance orientation and the legitimation of inequality across cultures. *Journal of Cross-Cultural Psychology, 31*, 369–409.

Prentice, D., & Miller, D. (2007). Psychological essentialism of human categories. *Current Directions in Psychological Science, 16*, 202–206.

Prentice, D., Miller, D., & Lightdale, J. (1994). Aysmmetries in attachments to groups and to their members: Distinguishing between common-identity and common-bond groups. *Personality and Social Psychology Bulletin, 20*, 484–493.

Price, S., & Brosnan, S. (2012). To each according to his need? Variability in the responses to inequity in non-human primates. *Social Justice Research, 25*, 140–169.

Pruitt, D.G., & Carnevale, P.J. (1993). *Negotiation in social conflict*. Pacific Grove, CA: Brooks-Cole.

Purdie, N., Hattie, J., & Douglas, G. (1996). Students' conceptions of learning and their use of self-regulated learning strategies. *British Journal of Educational Psychology, 88*, 87–100.

Pyszczynski, T., Greenberg, J., Solomon, S., Arndt, J., & Schimel, J. (2004). Why do people need self-esteem? A theoretical and empirical review. *Psychological Bulletin, 130*, 435–468.

Rabbie, J., & Horwitz, M. (1988). Categories versus groups as explanatory concepts in intergroup relations. *European Journal of Social Psychology, 18*, 117–123.

Ramesh, A., & Gelfand, M. (2010). Will they stay or will they go? The role of job embeddedness in predicting turnover in individualistic and collectivistic cultures. *Journal of Applied Psychology, 95*, 807–823.

Ramirez-Esparza, N., Gosling, S., Benet-Martinez, V., & Pennebaker, J. (2006). Do bilinguals have two personalities? A special case of cultural frame-switching. *Journal of Research in Personality, 40*, 99–120.

Rao, A., & Hashimoto, K. (1996). Intercultural influence: A study of Japanese expatriate managers in Canada. *Journal of International Business Studies, 27*, 443–466.

Ralston, D.A., Vollmer, G.R., Srinvasan, N., Nicholson, J.D., Tang, M,, & Wan, P. (2003). Strategies of upward influence: A study of six cultures from Europe, Asia and America. *Journal of Cross-Cultural Psychology, 32*, 728–735.

Ray, R.D., Shelton, A.L., Hollon, N.G., Matsumoto, D., Frankel, C.B., Gross, J.J., & Gabrieli, J. (2010). Interdependent self-construal and neural representations of self and mother. *Social Cognitive and Affective Neuroscience, 5*, 318–323.

Redding, S.G. (1990). *The spirit of Chinese capitalism*. Berlin, Germany: De Gruyter.

Redfield, R., Linton, R., & Herskovits, M.J. (1936). Memorandum on the study of acculturation. *American Anthropologist, 38*, 149–152.

Reicher, S.D., Haslam, S.A., & Hopkins, N. (2005). Social identity and the dynamics of leadership: Leaders and followers as collaborative agents in the transformation of social reality. *Leadership Quarterly, 16*, 547–568.

Reicher, S.D., & Hopkins, N. (1996). Seeking influence through characterising self-categories: An analysis of anti-abortionist rhetoric. *British Journal of Social Psychology*, *35*, 297–311.

Reisinger, Y., & Turner, L.W. (2002). *Cross-cultural behaviour in tourism: Concepts and analysis*. Oxford, UK: Elsevier.

Remland, M.S., Jones, T.S., & Brinkman, H. (1995). Interpersonal distance, body orientation and touch: Effects of culture, gender and age. *Journal of Social Psychology*, *135*, 281–297.

Richards, G. (2010). Loss of innocence in the Torres Straits. *The Psychologist*, *23*, 982–983.

Ricks, D.A. (1993). *Blunders in international business*. Cambridge, MA: Blackwell.

Rimé, B., Kanyangara, P., Yzerbyt, V., & Paez, D. (2011). The impact of Gacaca tribunals in Rwanda: Psychosocial effects of participation in a truth and reconciliation process after a genocide. *European Journal of Social Psychology*, *41*, 695–706.

Risch, N., Burchard, E., Ziv, E., & Tang, H. (2002). Categorization of humans in biomedical research: genes, race and disease. *Genome Biology*, *3*, 2007–2012.

Ripmeester, N. (1997). *Looking for work in the United Kingdom*. www.labourmobility.com

Rivers, W.H.R. (1901). Introduction and vision. In A.C. Haddon (Ed.), *Reports of the Cambridge anthropological expedition to the Torres Straits* (Vol. 2, part 1). Cambridge, UK: Cambridge University Press.

Rockstuhl, T., Dulebohn, J.H., Ang, S., & Shore, L.M. (2012). Leader-member exchange (LMX) and culture: A meta-analysis of LMX across 23 countries. *Journal of Applied Psychology*, *114*, 1097–1130.

Rogoff, B. (1990). *Apprenticeship in thinking: Cognitive development in social context*. New York: Oxford University Press.

Rohmann, A., Florack, A., & Piontkowski, U. (2006). The role of discordant acculturation attitudes in perceived threat: An analysis of host and immigrant attitudes in Germany. *International Journal of Intercultural Relations*, *30*, 683–702.

Rohner, R.P. (1984). Toward a conception of culture for cross-cultural psychology. *Journal of Cross-Cultural Psychology*, *15*, 111–138.

Rohner, R.P., & Pettengill, S.M. (1985). Perceived parental acceptance-rejection and parental control among Korean adolescents, *Child Development*, *56*, 524–528.

Rokeach, M. (1973). *The nature of human values*. New York: Free Press.

Rosenberg, N.A., Pritchard, J.K., Weber, J.L., Cann, H.M., et al. (2002). Genetic structure of human populations. *Science*, *298*, 2381–2385.

Rosenthal, D., & Feldman, S. (1992). The nature and stability of ethnic identity in Chinese youth: Effects of length of residence in two cultural contexts. *Journal of Cross-Cultural Psychology*, *23*, 214–227.

Rossette, A., Brett, J., Barsness, Z., & Lytle, A. (2012). When cultures collide electronically: The impact of e-mail and social norms on negotiation behavior and outcomes. *Journal of Cross-Cultural Psychology*, *43*, 628–643.

Rothbaum, F., Morelli, G., & Rusk, N. (2011). Attachment, learning and coping: The interplay of cultural similarities and differences. In M. Gelfand, C.Y. Chiu & Y.Y. Hong (Eds), *Advances in Culture and Psychology* (Vol. 1, pp. 153–215). New York: Oxford University Press.

Rothbaum, F., & Tsang, B.Y.P. (1998). Love songs in the US and China: On the nature of romantic love. *Journal of Cross-Cultural Psychology*, *29*, 306–319.

Rothbaum, F., Weisz, J., Pott, M., Miyake, K., & Morelli, G. (2000). Attachment and culture: Security in the United States and Japan. *American Psychologist*, *55*, 1093–1104.

Rotter, J.B. (1966). Generalised expectancies for internal versus external control of reinforcement. *Psychological Monographs*, *80*, Whole No. 609.

Rozin, P. (2007). Food and eating. In S. Kitayama & D. Cohen (Eds), *Handbook of cultural psychology* (pp. 391–416). New York: Guilford.

Ruback, R.B., Pandey, J., Begum, H.A., Tariq, N., & Kamal, A. (2004). Motivations for and satisfaction with migration: An analysis of migrants to New Delhi, Dhaka and Islamabad. *Environment and Behavior*, *36*, 814–838.

Ruddiman, W.F. (2003). The anthropogenic greenhouse era began thousands of years ago. *Climatic Change, 61,* 261–293.

Rudmin, F. (2006). Debate in science: The case of acculturation. *AnthroGlobe Journal.* Available at http.www. anthroglobe/info/docs/rudminf_acculturation_061204.pdf.

Rudmin, F. (2009). Concepts, measures and models of acculturative stress. *International Journal of Intercultural Relations, 33,* 106–123.

Rumbaut, R.G. (2008). Reaping what you sow: Immigration, youth, and reactive ethnicity. *Applied Developmental Science, 12*(2), 108–111.

Ryan, R., & Deci, E.L. (2000). Self-determination theory and the facilitation of intrinsic motivation, social development and wellbeing. *American Psychologist, 55,* 68–78.

Ryan, R., & Deci, E.L. (2006). Self-regulation and the problem of human autonomy: Does psychology need choice, self-determination and will? *Journal of Personality, 74,* 1557–1585.

Ryan, R.M., & Deci E.L. (2011). A self-development theory perspective on social, institutional, cultural and economic supports for autonomy and their importance for well being. In V. Chirkov, R. Ryan & K. Sheldon (Eds), Human autonomy in cross-cultural context: Perspectives on the psychology of agency, freedom and well-being, *Cross-Cultural Advancements in Positive Psychology, 1,* 45–64.

Sadri, G., Weber, T., & Gentry, W. (2011). Empathic emotion and leadership performance: An empirical analysis across 38 countries. *Leadership Quarterly, 22,* 818–830.

Salamon, S. (1977). Family bonds and friendship bonds: Japan and West Germany. *Journal of Marriage and the Family, 39,* 807–820.

Salvatore, J., & Prentice, D. (2011). The independence paradox. In J. Jetten & M. Hornsey (Eds), *Rebels in groups: Dissent, deviance, difference and defiance* (pp. 201–218). Chichester, UK: Wiley.

Sam, D.L., & Berry, J.W. (Eds) (2006). *The Cambridge handbook of acculturation psychology.* Cambridge, UK: Cambridge University Press.

Sam, D.L., & Berry, J.W. (2010). Acculturation: When individuals and groups of different cultural backgrounds meet. *Perspectives On Psychological Science, 5,* 472–481.

Sampson, E.E. (1981). Cognitive psychology as ideology. *American Psychologist, 36,* 730–733.

Sanchez-Burks, J., Lee, F., Choi, I., Nisbett, R., et al. (2003). Conversing across cultures: East-west communication styles in work and non-work contexts. *Journal of Personality and Social Psychology, 85,* 363–372.

Sani, F. (Ed.) (2008). *Self-continuity: Individual and collective perspectives.* New York: Psychology Press.

Savitz, J.B., & Ramesar, R.S. (2004). Genetic variants implicated in personality: A review of the more promising candidates. *American Journal of Medical Genetics, Part B: Neuropsychiatric Genetics, 131B,* 20–32.

Schalk-Soekar, R.G.S., Van de Vijver, F.J.R., & Hoogsteder, M. (2004). Attitudes toward multiculturalism of immigrants and majority members in the Netherlands. *International Journal of Intercultural Relations, 28,* 533–550.

Schaller, M., Norenzayan, A., Heine, S., Yamagishi, T., & Kameda, T. (2010). *Evolution, culture and the human mind.* New York: Psychology Press.

Scherer, K.R. (1997). The role of culture in emotion-antecedent appraisal. *Journal of Personality and Social Psychology, 73,* 902–922.

Scherer, K.R. (2009). The dynamic architecture of emotion: Evidence for the component process model. *Cognition and Emotion, 23,* 1307–1351.

Scherer, K.R., Banse, R., & Wallbott, H.G. (2001). Emotion inferences from vocal expression correlate across languages and cultures. *Journal of Cross-Cultural Psychology, 32,* 76–92.

Scherer, K.R., & Brosch, T. (2009). Culture-specific appraisal biases contribute to emotional dispositions. *European Journal of Personality, 23,* 265–288.

Scheu, U.D. (2002). Cultural constraints in bilinguals' code-switching. *International Journal of Intercultural Relations, 24,* 131–150.

Schiefer, D. (2013). Cultural values and group-related attitudes: A comparison of individuals with and without migration background across 24 countries. *Journal of Cross-Cultural Psychology, 44,* 245–262.

Schimmack, U., Oishi, S., & Diener, E. (2005). Individualism: A valid and important dimension of cultural differences between nations. *Personality and Social Psychology Bulletin, 9*, 17–31.

Schmitt, D.P. (2003). Universal sex differences in the desire for sexual variety: Tests from 52 nations, six continents and 13 islands. *Journal of Personality and Social Psychology, 85*, 85–104.

Schmitt, D.P. (2005). Is short-term mating the maladaptive consequence of insecure attachment? A test of competing evolutionary perspectives. *Personality and Social Psychology Bulletin, 31*, 747–768.

Schmitt, D.P. (2008). Evolutionary perspectives on romantic attachment and culture: How ecological stressors influence dismissing orientations across genders and geographies. *Cross-Cultural Research, 42*, 220–247.

Schmitt, D.P., Alcalay, L., et al. (2003). Are men universally more dismissing than women? Gender differences in romantic attachment across 62 cultural regions. *Personal Relationships, 10*, 307–331.

Schmitt, D.P., Alcalay, L., et al. (2004). Patterns and universals of adult romantic attachment across 62 cultural regions: Are models of self and of other pancultural constructs? *Journal of Cross-Cultural Psychology, 35*, 367–402.

Schmitt, D.P., Allik, J., McCrae, R., & Benet-Martinez, V. (2007). The geographic distribution of Big Five personality traits: Patterns and profiles of human self-description across 56 nations. *Journal of Cross-Cultural Psychology, 38*, 173–212.

Schmitt, D.P., Realo, A., Voracek, M., & Allik, J. (2008). Why can't a man be more like a woman? Sex differences in Big Five personality traits across 55 nations. *Journal of Personality and Social Psychology, 94*, 168–192.

Schneider, B., Goldstein, H., & Smith, D. (1995). The ASA framework: An update. *Personnel Psychology, 48*, 747–773.

Schug, J., Yuki, M., & Maddux, W. (2010). Relational mobility explains between- and within-culture differences in self-disclosure to close friends. *Psychological Science, 21*, 1471–1478.

Schwartz, S.H. (1992). Universals in the content and structure of values: Theoretical advances and empirical tests in 20 countries. In M. Zanna (Ed.), *Advances in experimental social psychology* (Vol. 25, pp. 1–65). Orlando, FL: Academic.

Schwartz, S.H. (1994). Beyond individualism and collectivism: New cultural dimensions of values. In U. Kim, H.C. Triandis, C. Kağıtçibasi, S.C. Choi, & G. Yoon (Eds), *Individualism and collectivism: Theory, method and applications* (pp. 85–119). Thousand Oaks, CA: Sage.

Schwartz, S.H. (2004). Mapping and interpreting cultural differences around the world. In H. Vinken, J. Soeters, & P. Ester (Eds), *Comparing cultures: Dimensions of culture in a comparative perspective* (pp. 43–73). Leiden, NL: Brill.

Schwartz, S.H. (2006). A theory of cultural value orientations: Explication and applications. *Comparative Sociology, 5*, 136–182.

Schwartz, S.H. (2009). Culture matters: National value cultures, sources and consequences. In R. Wyer, C.Y. Chiu & Y.Y. Hong (Eds), *Understanding culture: Theory, research and applications* (pp. 127–150). New York: Psychology Press.

Schwartz, S.H. (2011). Values: Individual and cultural. In F. van de Vijver, A. Chasiotis & S. Breugelmans (Eds), *Fundamental questions in cross-cultural psychology* (pp. 463–493). Cambridge, UK: Cambridge University Press.

Schwartz, S.H., & Bardi, A. (1997). Influences of adaptation to communist rule on value priorities in Eastern Europe. *Political Psychology, 18*, 385–410.

Schwartz, S.H., & Bardi, A. (2001). Values hierarchies across cultures: Taking a similarities perspective. *Journal of Cross-Cultural Psychology, 32*, 268–290.

Schwartz, S.H., Bardi, A., & Bianchi, G. (2000). Value adaptation to the imposition and collapse of communist regimes in Eastern Europe. In S.A. Renshon & J. Duckitt (Eds), *Political psychology: Cultural and cross-cultural perspectives* (pp. 217–237). London: Macmillan.

Schwartz, S.H., Cieciuch, J., Vecchione, N., et al. (2012). Refining the theory of basic individual values. *Journal of Personality and Social Psychology, 103*, 663–688.

Schwartz, S.H., Melech, G., Lehmann, A., Burgess, S., Harris, M., & Owens, V. (2001). Extending the cross-cultural validity of the theory of basic human values with a different method of measurement. *Journal of Cross-Cultural Psychology, 32*, 519–542.

Schwartz, S.H., & Sagiv, L. (1995). Identifying culture-specifics in the content and structure of values. *Journal of Cross-Cultural Psychology*, *26*, 92–116.

Schwartz, S.J., Pantin, H., Sullivan, S., Prado, G., & Szapocznik, J. (2006). Nativity and years in the receiving culture as markers of acculturation in ethnic enclaves. *Journal of Cross-Cultural Psychology*, *37*, 345–353.

Schwartz, S.J., Unger, J.B., Zamboanga, B.L., & Szapocznik, J. (2010). Rethinking the concept of acculturation: Implications for theory and research. *American Psychologist*, *65*, 237–251.

Schwartz, S.J., Vignoles, V.L., Brown R., & Zagefka, H. (in press). The identity dynamics of acculturation and multiculturalism: Situating acculturation in context. In V. Benet-Martínez & Y. Hong (Eds.), *Oxford handbook of multicultural identity: Basic and applied psychological perspectives*. New York: Oxford University Press.

Sedikides, C., & Brewer, M.B. (Eds) (2001). *Individual self, relational self, collective self*. Philadelphia, PA: Psychology Press.

Sedikides, C., Gaertner, J., & Toguchi, Y. (2003). Pan-cultural self-enhancement. *Journal of Personality and Social Psychology*, *84*, 60–79.

Sedikides, C., Gaertner, L., & Vevea, J.L. (2005). Pancultural self-enhancement reloaded: A meta-analytic reply to Heine (2005). *Journal of Personality and Social Psychology, 89*, 539–551.

Sedikides, C., Gaertner, L., & Vevea, J.L. (2007a). Inclusion of theory-relevant moderators yields the same conclusions as Sedikides, Gaertner, and Vevea (2005): A meta-analytic reply to Heine, Kitayama, and Hamamura (2007). *Asian Journal of Social Psychology 10*, 59–67.

Sedikides, C., Gaertner, L., & Vevea, J.L. (2007b). Evaluating the evidence for pancultural self-enhancement. *Asian Journal of Social Psychology, 10*, 201–203.

Seeley, E., Gardner, W., et al. (2003). Circle of friends or members of a group? Sex differences in relational and collective attachment to groups. *Group Processes and Interpersonal Relations*, *6*, 251–263.

Segall, M.H. (1999). Why is there still racism if there is no such thing as 'race'? In W.J. Lonner, D.L. Dinnel, D.K. Forgays & S.A. Hayes (Eds), *Merging past, present and future in cross-cultural psychology* (pp. 14–26). Lisse, NL: Swets & Zeitlinger.

Segall, M.H., Dasen, P.R., Berry, J.W. & Poortinga, Y.H. (1999). *Human behavior in global perspective*. Boston, MA: Allyn & Bacon.

Seki, K., Matsumoto, D., & Imahori, T.T. (2002). The conceptualization and expression of intimacy in Japan and the United States. *Journal of Cross-Cultural Psychology*, *33*, 303–319.

Semin, G.R. (2009). Language, culture, cognition: How do they intersect? In R. Wyer, C.Y. Chiu & Y.Y. Hong (Eds), *Understanding culture: Theory, research and application* (pp. 259–270). New York: Psychology Press.

Semin, G.R., Gorts, C.A., Nandram, S., & Semin-Goossens, A. (2002). Cultural perspectives on the linguistic representation of emotion and emotion events. *Cognition and Emotion*, *16*, 11–28.

Semin, G., & Rubini, M. (1990). Unfolding the concept of person by verbal abuse. *European Journal of Social Psychology*, *20*, 463–474.

Serpell, R. (1979). How specific are perceptual skills? A cross-cultural study of pattern reproduction. *British Journal of Psychology*, *70*, 365–380.

Seymour, P.H.K., Aro, M., & Erskine, J.M. (2003). Foundation literacy acquisition in European orthographies. *British Journal of Psychology, 94*, 143–174.

Shackelford, T.K., Schmitt, D.P., & Buss, D.M. (2005). Universal dimensions of human mate preferences. *Personality and Individual Differences*, *39*, 447–458.

Shavitt, S., Torelli, C., & Riemer, H. (2011). Horizontal and vertical individualism and collectivism: Implications for understanding psychological processes. In M. Gelfand, C.Y. Chiu, & Y.Y. Hong (Eds), *Advances in culture and psychology* (Vol. 1, pp. 309–350). New York: Oxford University Press.

Sherif, M. (1966). *Group conflict and cooperation: Their social psychology*. London: Routledge.

Shirts, G. (1995). Beyond ethnocentrism: Promoting cross-cultural understanding with BAFA BAFA. In S.M. Fowler & M.G. Mumford (Eds) *Intercultural sourcebook: Cross-cultural training methods* (Vol. 1, pp. 93–100). Yarmouth, MN: Intercultural Press.

Shrauger, J. (1975). Responses to evaluation as a function of initial self-perceptions. *Psychological Bulletin*, *82*, 581–596.

Shteynberg, G., Gelfand, M. & Kim, K. (2009). Peering into the 'magnum mysterium' of culture: The explanatory power of descriptive norms. *Journal of Cross-Cultural Psychology, 40*, 46–69.

Shuter, R. (1976). Proxemics and tactility in Latin America. *Journal of Communication, 26*, 46–52.

Shweder, R.A. (1991). *Thinking through culture: Expeditions in cultural psychology*. Cambridge MA: Harvard University Press.

Shweder, R.A., & Bourne, E.J. (1982). Does the concept of the person vary cross-culturally? In A.J. Marsella & G.M. White (Eds), *Cultural conceptions of mental health and therapy* (pp. 93–137). Dordrecht, NL: Riedel.

Sibley, C., & Liu, J. (2012). Social representations of history and the legitimation of social inequality: The causes and consequences of historical negation. *Journal of Applied Social Psychology, 42*, 598–623.

Sidanius, J., & Pratto, F. (2001). *Social dominance: An intergroup theory of social hierarchy and oppression*. New York: Cambridge University Press.

Silbereisen, R.K., & Wiesner, M. (2002). Lessons from research on the consequences of German unification: Continuity and discontinuity of self-efficacy and the timing of psychosocial transitions. *Applied Psychology: An International Review, 51*, 291–317.

Simoons, F. (1970). Primary adult lactose intolerance and the milk drinking habit: A problem and biological and cultural interrelations. II. A cultural historical hypothesis. *American Journal of Digestive Diseases, 15*, 695–710.

Singelis, T.M. (1994). The measurement of independent and interdependent self construals. *Personality and Social Psychology Bulletin, 20*, 580–591.

Singelis, T.M., Bond, M.H., Sharkey, W.F., & Lai, S.Y. (1999). Unpackaging culture's influence on self-esteem and embarrassability: The role of self-construals. *Journal of Cross-Cultural Psychology, 30*, 315–341.

Singelis, T.M., & Sharkey, W.F. (1995). Culture, self-construal and embarrassability. *Journal of Cross-Cultural Psychology, 26*, 622–644.

Singelis, T.M., Triandis, H.C., Bhawuk, D., & Gelfand, M. (1995). Horizontal and vertical dimensions of individualism and collectivism: A theoretical and measurement refinement. *Cross-Cultural Research, 29*, 240–275.

Singleton, R., Jr., & Kerber, K.W. (1980). Topics in social psychology: Further classroom demonstrations. *Teaching Sociology, 7*, 439–452.

Sinha, D. (1997). Indigenous psychology. In J.W. Berry, Y.H. Poortinga, & J. Pandey (Eds), *Handbook of cross-cultural psychology* (2nd edn., Vol. 1, pp. 129–169). Needham Heights, MA: Allyn & Bacon.

Smith, P.B. (2004a). Nations, cultures and individuals: New perspectives and old dilemmas. *Journal of Cross-Cultural Psychology, 35*, 6–12.

Smith, P.B. (2004b). Acquiescent response bias as an aspect of cultural communication style. *Journal of Cross-Cultural Psychology, 35*, 50–61.

Smith, P.B. (2006). When elephants fight, the grass gets trampled: The GLOBE and Hofstede projects. *Journal of International Business Studies, 37*, 915–921.

Smith, P.B. (2008). Indigenous aspects of management. In P.B. Smith, M.F. Peterson & D.C. Thomas (Eds), *Handbook of cross-cultural management research* (pp. 313–332). Thousand Oaks, CA: Sage.

Smith, P.B. (2011a). Communication styles as dimensions of national culture. *Journal of Cross-Cultural Psychology, 42*, 216–233.

Smith, P.B. (2011b). Cross-cultural perspectives on identity: Conceptions and measurement. In S.J. Schwartz, K. Luyckx, & V.L. Vignoles (Eds), *Handbook of identity theory and research* (pp. 249–266). New York: Springer.

Smith, P.B., & Bond, M.H. (1998). *Social psychology across cultures*. Hemel Hempstead, UK: Prentice Hall.

Smith, P.B., Dugan, S., & Trompenaars, F. (1996). National culture and managerial values: A dimensional analysis across 43 nations. *Journal of Cross-Cultural Psychology, 27*, 231–264.

Smith, P.B., Giannini, M., Helkama, K., Maczynski, J., & Stumpf, S. (2005). Identification and relational orientation predictors of positive national auto-stereotyping. *International Review of Social Psychology, 18*, 65–90.

Smith, P.B., Huang, H.J., Harb, C., & Torres, C. (2012). How distinctive are indigenous ways of achieving influence? A comparative study of *guanxi, wasta, jeitinho* and 'pulling strings'. *Journal of Cross-Cultural Psychology, 43*, 136–151.

Smith, P.B., & Misumi, J. (1989). Japanese management: A sun rising in the West? *International Review of Industrial and Organizational Psychology, 4,* 329–369.

Smith, P.B., Misumi, J., Tayeb, M., Peterson, M., & Bond, M.H. (1989). On the generality of leadership style measures. *Journal of Occupational Psychology, 62,* 97–109.

Smith, P.B., Peterson, M.F., Leung, K., & Dugan, S. (1998). Individualism-collectivism and the handling of disagreement: A 23 nation study. *International Journal of Intercultural Relations, 22,* 351–367.

Smith, P. B., Peterson, M.F., & Schwartz, S.H. (2002). Cultural values, sources of guidance and their relevance to managerial behavior: A 47 nation study. *Journal of Cross-Cultural Psychology, 33,* 188–208.

Smith, P.B., Peterson, M.F., & Thomason, S. (2011). National culture as a moderator of the relationship between managers' use of guidance sources and how well work events are handled. *Journal of Cross-Cultural Psychology, 42,* 1101–1121.

Smith, P.B., Torres, C., Hecker, J., et al. (2011). Individualism-collectivism and business context as predictors of behaviors in cross-national work settings. *International Journal of Intercultural Relations, 35,* 440–451.

Smith, P.B., Torres, C., Leong, C.H., Budhwar, P., Achoui, M., & Lebedeva, N. (2012). Are indigenous approaches to achieving influence in business organizations distinctive? A comparative study of *guanxi, wasta, jeitinho, svyazi,* and 'pulling strings'. *International Journal of Human Resource Management, 23,* 333–348.

Smith, P.B., Trompenaars, F., & Dugan, S. (1995). The Rotter locus of control scale in 43 countries: A test of cultural relativity. *International Journal of Psychology, 30,* 377–400.

Smith, P.K., Cowie, H., Olafsson, H., et al. (2003). Definitions of bullying: A comparison of terms used, and age and gender differences, in a 14-nation international comparison. *Child Development, 73,* 1119–1133.

Snibbe, A.C., & Markus, H.R. (2005). You can't always get what you want: Educational attainment, agency and choice. *Journal of Personality and Social Psychology, 88,* 703–720.

Snyder, C., & Fromkin, H. (1980). Abnormality as a positive characteristic: Development and validation of a scale measuring need for uniqueness. *Journal of Abnormal Psychology, 86,* 518–527.

Snyder, M. (1987). *Public appearances/private realities: The psychology of self-monitoring.* New York: Freeman.

Sorrentino, R., Otsubo, Y., Yasunagaga, S., Nezlek, J., et al. (2005). Uncertainty orientation and social behavior: Individual differences within and across cultures. In R. Sorrentino, D. Cohen, J. Olson & M. Zanna (Eds), *Cultural and social behavior: The Ontario symposium Volume 10* (pp. 181–206). Mahwah, NJ: Erlbaum.

Spears, R. (2011). Group identities: The social identity perspective. In S.J. Schwartz, K. Luyckx & V.L. Vignoles (Eds), *Handbook of identity theory and research* (Vol. 1, pp. 201–224). New York: Springer.

Spencer-Rodgers, J., Boucher, H.C., Peng, K., et al. (2009). Cultural differences in self-verification: The role of naive self-dialecticism. *Journal of Experimental Social Psychology, 45,* 860–866.

Spiro, M.E. (1993). Is the Western conception of the self 'peculiar' within the context of the world cultures? *Ethos, 21,* 107–153.

Spreitzer, G.M., Perttula, K.H., & Xin, K.R. (2005). Traditionality matters: An examination of the effectiveness of transformational leadership in the United States and Taiwan. *Journal of Organizational Behavior, 26,* 205–227.

Staerkle, C., Sidanius, J., Green, E., & Molina, L. (2010). Ethnic minority-majority asymmetry in national attitudes around the world: A multilevel analysis. *Political Psychology, 31,* 491–519.

Staub, E., Pearlman, L., Gubin, A., & Hagengimana, A. (2005). Healing, reconciliation, forgiving and the prevention of violence after mass genocide or mass killing: An intervention and its experimental evaluation in Rwanda. *Journal of Social and Clinical Psychology, 24,* 297–334.

Stavrova, O., Fetchenhauer, D., & Schlösser, T. (2012). Cohabitation, gender and happiness: A cross-cultural study in 30 countries. *Journal of Cross-Cultural Psychology,* 43, 1063–1081.

Steel, P., & Ones, D. (2002). Personality and happiness: A nation-level analysis. *Journal of Personality and Social Psychology, 83,* 767–781.

Stephan, W.G., Diaz-Loving, R., & Duran, A. (2000). Integrated threat theory and intercultural attitudes: Mexico and the United States. *Journal of Cross-Cultural Psychology, 31,* 240–259.

Stephan, W.G., & Stephan, C.W. (1996). Predicting prejudice. *International Journal of Intercultural Relations, 20,* 1–12.

Stephan, W.G., Stephan, C.W., Abalakina, M., et al. (1996). Distinctiveness effects in intergroup perceptions: An international study. In H. Grad, A. Blanco, & J. Georgas (Eds), *Key issues in cross-cultural psychology* (pp. 298–308). Lisse, NL: Swets & Zeitlinger.

Stephan, W.G., Ybarra, O., & Bachman, G. (1999). Prejudice toward immigrants: An integrated threat theory. *Journal of Applied Social Psychology, 29,* 2221–2237.

Stephan, W.G., Ybarra, O., Martinez, C.M., et al. (1998). Prejudice toward immigrants to Spain and Israel: An integrated threat analysis. *Journal of Cross-Cultural Psychology*, *29*, 559–576.

Stepick, A., Dutton Stepick, C., Eugene, E., Teed, D., & Labissiere, Y. (2001). Shifting identities and intergenerational conflict: Growing up Haitian in Miami. In R.G. Rumbaut & A. Portes (Eds), *Ethnicities: Children of immigrants in America.* (pp. 229–266). Berkeley: University of California Press.

Stern, P.C. (2011). Contributions of psychology to limiting climate change. *American Psychologist*, *66*, 303–314.

Sternberg, R. (2007). Intelligence and culture. In S. Kitayama & D. Cohen (Eds), *Handbook of cultural psychology* (pp. 547–568). New York: Guilford.

Stewart, S.M., Bond, M.H., Kennard, B.D., Ho, L.M., & Zaman, R.M. (2002). Does the Chinese construct of *guan* export to the West? *International Journal of Psychology, 37*, 74–82.

Suh, E.M. (2002). Culture, identity consistency, and subjective well-being. *Journal of Personality and Social Psychology, 83*, 1378–1391.

Suh, E.M., Diener, E., & Updegraff, J. (2008). From culture to priming conditions, Self construal influences on life satisfaction. *Journal of Cross-Cultural Psychology, 39*, 3–15.

Suinn, R.M., Ahuna, C., & Khoo, G. (1992). The Suinn-Lew Asian self-identity acculturation scale: Concurrent and factorial validation. *Educational and Psychological Measurement*, *52*, 1041–1046.

Super, C.M., & Harkness, S. (1986). The developmental niche: A conceptualization at the interface of child and culture. *International Journal of Behavioral Development, 9*, 545–570.

Super, C.M., & Harkness, S. (1997). The cultural structuring of child development. In J.W. Berry, P.R. Dasen & T.S. Saraswathi (Eds), *Handbook of cross-cultural psychology* (2nd edn, Vol. 2, pp. 1–39). Needham Heights, MA: Allyn & Bacon.

Sussman, N. (2002). Testing the cultural identity model of the cultural transition cycle: Sojourners return home. *International Journal of Intercultural Relations, 26*, 391–408.

Sussman, N., & Rosenfeld, H. (1982). Influence of culture, language and sex on conversational distance. *Journal of Personality and Social Psychology, 42*, 66–74.

Swami, V., Frederick, D., et al. (2010). The attractive female body weight and female body dissatisfaction in 26 countries across 10 world regions: Results of the international body project 1. *Personality and Social Psychology Bulletin, 36*, 309–325.

Swart, H., Hewstone, M., Christ, O., & Voci, A. (2011). Affective mediators of intergroup contact: A three-wave longitudinal study in South Africa. *Journal of Personality and Social Psychology, 101*, 1221–1238.

Tafarodi, R.W., Lo, C., Yamaguchi, S., et al. (2004). The inner self in three countries. *Journal of Cross-Cultural Psychology, 35*, 97–117.

Tafarodi, R.W., Marshall, T., & Katsura, H. (2004). Standing out in Canada and Japan. *Journal of Personality, 72*, 785–814.

Tajfel, H. (Ed.) (1981). *Human groups and social categories: Studies in social psychology.* Cambridge, UK: Cambridge University Press.

Tajfel, H., & Turner, J.C. (1979). An integrative theory of intergroup conflict. In W.G. Austin & S. Worchel (Eds), *The social psychology of intergroup relations* (pp. 33–47). Monterey, CA: Brooks-Cole.

Takemura, K., & Yuki, M. (2007). Are Japanese groups more competitive than Japanese individuals? A cross-cultural validation of the interindividual-intergroup discontinuity effect. *International Journal of Psychology, 42*, 27–35.

Takemura, K., Yuki, M., & Ohtsubo, Y. (2010). Attending inside or outside: A Japanese-US comparison of spontaneous memory of group information. *Asian Journal of Social Psychology, 13*, 303–307.

Takeuchi, R., Yun, S., & Tesluk, P.E. (2002). An examination of crossover and spillover effects of spousal and expatriate cross-cultural adjustment on expatriate outcomes. *Journal of Applied Psychology, 87*, 655–666.

Taras, V., Kirkman, B.L., & Steel, P. (2010). Examining the impact of Culture's Consequences: A three-decade, multilevel, meta-analytical review of Hofstede's cultural value dimensions. *Journal of Applied Psychology, 95,* 405–439.

Taras, V., Steel, P., & Kirkman, B. (2012). Improving national-cultural indices using a longitudinal meta-analysis of Hofstede's dimensions. *Journal of World Business, 47,* 329–341.

Tausch, N., Hewstone, M., Schmid, K., Hughes, J., & Cairns, E. (2011). Extended contact effects as a function of closeness of relationship with ingroup contacts. *Group Processes and Interpersonal Relations, 14,* 239–254.

Taylor, S.E., Sherman, D., Kim, H.S., et al. (2004). Culture and social support: Who seeks it and why? *Journal of Personality and Social Psychology, 87,* 354–362.

Terracciano, A., Abdel Halek, A., et al. (2007). National character does not reflect mean personality trait levels in 49 cultures. *Science, 310,* 96–100.

Tetlock, P. (2003). Thinking the unthinkable: Sacred values and taboo cognitions. *Trends in Cognitive Sciences, 7,* 320–324.

Thomas, D.C. (1999). Cultural diversity and work group effectiveness: An experimental study. *Journal of Cross-Cultural Psychology, 30,* 242–263.

Thomas, D.C. (2008). *Cross-cultural management: Essential concepts.* Thousand Oaks, CA: Sage.

Thomas, D.C., & Fitzsimmons, S. (2008). Cross-cultural skills and abilities: From communication competence to cultural intelligence. In P.B. Smith, M.F. Peterson & D.C. Thomas (Eds), *Handbook of cross-cultural management research* (pp. 201–215). Thousand Oaks, CA: Sage.

Thomas, D.C., & Lazarova, M. (2006). Expatriate adjustment and performance: A critical review. In G. Stahl & I. Bjorkman (Eds), *Handbook of research in international human resource management* (pp. 247–264). Cheltenham, UK: Elgar.

Thomas, D.C., & Ravlin, E.C. (1995). Responses of employees to cultural adaptation by a foreign manager. *Journal of Applied Psychology, 80,* 133–146.

Ting-Toomey, S. (1988). A face negotiation theory. In Y.Y. Kim & W.B. Gudykunst (Eds), *Theory in intercultural communication* (pp. 215–235). Newbury Park, CA: Sage.

Tinsley, C.H. (2001). How negotiators get to yes: Predicting the constellation of strategies used across cultures to negotiate conflict. *Journal of Applied Psychology, 86,* 583–593.

Tinsley, C.H., & Brett, J.M. (2001). Managing workplace conflict in the United States and Hong Kong. *Organizational Behavior and Human Decision Processes, 85,* 360–381.

Tinsley, C.H., & Weldon, E. (2003). Responses to a normative conflict among American and Chinese managers. *International Journal of Cross-Cultural Management, 3,* 183–194.

Tomasello, M. (2011). Human culture in evolutionary perspective. In M. Gelfand, C.Y. Chiu, & Y.Y. Hong (Eds), *Advances in culture and psychology* (Vol. 1, pp. 5–51). New York: Oxford University Press.

Tooby, J., & Cosmides, L. (1992). The psychological foundations of culture. In J.H. Barkow, L. Cosmides, & J. Tooby (Eds), *The adapted mind: Evolutionary psychology and the generation of culture* (pp. 19–136). New York: Oxford University Press.

Trafimow, D., Triandis, H.C., & Goto, S.G. (1991). Some tests of the distinction between the private self and the collective self. *Journal of Personality and Social Psychology, 60,* 649–655.

Triandis, H.C. (1972). *The analysis of subjective culture.* New York: Wiley.

Triandis, H.C. (1977). *Interpersonal behavior.* Monterey, CA: Brooks/Cole.

Triandis, H.C. (1993). Collectivism and individualism as cultural syndromes. *Cross-Cultural Research, 27,* 155–180.

Triandis, H.C. (1995). *Individualism and collectivism.* Boulder, CO: Westview.

Triandis, H.C., Chan, D., Bhawuk, D., et al. (1995). Multimethod probes of allocentrism and idiocentrism. *International Journal of Psychology, 30,* 461–480.

Triandis, H.C., Chen, X.P., & Chan, D.K.S. (1998). Scenarios for the measurement of individualism and collectivism. *Journal of Cross-Cultural Psychology, 29,* 275–289.

Triandis, H.C., Leung, K., Villareal, M., & Clack, F.L. (1985). Allocentric versus idiocentric tendencies: Convergent and discriminant validation. *Journal of Research in Personality, 19,* 395–415.

Triandis, H.C., McCusker, C., & Hui, C.H. (1990). Multimethod probes of individualism and collectivism. *Journal of Personality and Social Psychology*, *59*, 1006–1020.

Tripathi, R.C. (1988). Aligning development to values in India. In D. Sinha & H.S.R. Kao (Eds), *Social values and development: Asian perspectives* (pp. 315–33). New Delhi: Sage.

Trommsdorff, G. (1985). Some comparative aspects of socialization in Japan and Germany. In I.R. Lagunes & Y.H. Poortinga (Eds), *From a different perspective: Studies of behavior across cultures* (pp. 231–240). Lisse, NL: Swets & Zeitlinger.

Trommsdorff, G. (2009). Intergenerational relations and cultural transmission. In U. Schönpflug (Ed.), *Cultural transmission: Psychological, developmental, social and methodological* aspects (pp. 126–160). Cambridge, UK: Cambridge University Press.

Trommsdorff, G., & Nauck, B. (Eds) (2005). *The value of children in cross-cultural perspective: Case studies from eight societies.* Lengerich, Germany: Pabst.

Turnbull, C.M. (1972). *The mountain people: The Ik of the mountains in Uganda, the Sudan and Kenya.* New York: Simon & Schuster.

Turner, J.C., Hogg, M.A., Oakes, P.J., Reicher, S., & Wetherell, M.S. (1987). *Rediscovering the social group: A self-categorization theory.* Oxford, UK: Blackwell.

Tweed, R., & Lehman, D. (2002). Learning considered within a cultural context: Confucian and Socratic approaches. *American Psychologist*, *57*, 89–99.

Tyler, T.R. & Lind, E.A. (1992). A relational model of authority in groups. In M.P. Zanna (Ed.), *Advances in Experimental Social Psychology* (Vol. 25, pp. 115–191). San Diego, CA: Academic Press.

Tylor, E.B. (1871). *Primitive cultures.* London: Murray.

Uleman, J.S., Rhee, E., Bardoliwalla, N., Semin, G.R., & Toyama, M. (2000). The relational self: Closeness to in-groups depends on who they are, culture and the type of closeness. *Asian Journal of Social Psychology*, *3*, 1–18.

Umaña-Taylor, A.J., Bhanot, R., & Shin, N. (2006). Ethnic identity formation during adolescence: The critical role of families. *Journal of Family Issues*, *27*, 390–414.

United Nations, Department of Social and Economic Affairs (2006). *World population policies, 2005.* New York: United Nations.

United Nations, Department of Social and Economic Affairs (2007). *The millenium development goals report, 2007.* New York: United Nations.

United Nations Development Program (2004). *Human development report.* New York: Oxford University Press. Available at http://hdr.undp.org/reports/global/2004.

United Nations Development Program (2006). *Human development report.* New York: Oxford University Press. Available at www.//hdr.undp/org/en.

United Nations, Economic and Social Affairs Division (2010). World urbanization prospects: The 2009 revision population database. Available at www.esa.un.org/wup2009/unup/p2k0data.asp

Urry, J. (1990). *The tourist gaze: Leisure and travel in contemporary society.* London: Sage.

Uskul, A., Cross, S., Sunbay, Z., Gercek-Swing, B., & Ataca, B. (2012). Honor-bound: The cultural construction of honor in Turkey and the Northern United States. *Journal of Cross-Cultural Psychology*, *43*, 1131–1151.

Uskul, A., Hynie, M., & Lalonde, R.N. (2004). Interdependence as a mediator between culture and interpersonal closeness for Euro-Canadians and Turks. *Journal of Cross-Cultural Psychology*, *35*, 174–191.

Uskul, A., Kitayama, S., & Nisbett, R. (2008). Ecological basis of cognition: Farmers and fishermen are more holistic than herders. *Proceedings of the National Academy of Sciences*, *105*, 8552–8556.

Van Baaren, R., Maddux, W., Chartrand, T., et al. (2003). It takes two to mimic: Behavioral consequences of self-construals. *Journal of Personality and Social Psychology*, *84*, 1093–1102.

Vandello, J.A., & Cohen, D. (2003). Male honor and female infidelity: Implicit scripts that perpetuate domestic violence. *Journal of Personality and Social Psychology*, *84*, 997–1010.

Vandello, J.A., Cohen, D., Grandon, R., & Franiuk, R. (2009). Stand by your man: Indirect prescriptions for honorable violence and feminine loyalty in Canada, Chile and the United States. *Journal of Cross-Cultural Psychology*, *40*, 81–104.

Van der Zee, K., Atsam, N., & Brodbeck, F. (2004). The influence of social identity and personality on outcomes of cultural diversity in teams. *Journal of Cross-Cultural Psychology*, *35*, 283–303.

Van der Zee, K., & Van Oudenhoven, J.P.L. (2001). The multicultural personality questionnaire: reliability and validity of self and other ratings of multicultural effectiveness. *Journal of Research in Personality*, *35*, 278–288.

Van de Vijver, F.J.R., & Hambleton, R.K. (1996). Translating tests: Some practical guidelines. *European Psychologist*, *1*, 89–99.

Van de Vijver, F.J.R., & Leung, K. (1997). *Methods and data analysis for cross-cultural research*. Thousand Oaks, CA: Sage.

Van de Vijver, F.J.R., & Leung, K. (2000). Methodological issues in psychological research on culture. *Journal of Cross-Cultural Psychology*, *31*, 33–51.

Van de Vliert, E. (2007). Climato-economic roots of survival versus self-expression cultures. *Journal of Cross-Cultural Psychology*, *38*, 156–172.

Van de Vliert, E. (2009). *Climate, affluence and culture*. Cambridge, UK: Cambridge University Press.

Van de Vliert, E. (2011). Climato-economic origins of variation in in-group favoritism. *Journal of Cross-Cultural Psychology*, *42*, 494–515.

Van de Vliert, E. (in press). Climato-economic habitats support patterns of human needs, stresses and freedoms. *Behavioral and Brain Sciences*.

Van de Vliert, E., Huang, X., & Levine, R.V. (2004). National wealth and thermal climate as predictors of motives for volunteer work. *Journal of Cross-Cultural Psychology*, *34*, 62–71.

Van de Vliert, E., Ohbuchi, K., Van Rossum, B., Hayashi, Y., & Van der Vegt, G.S. (2004). Conglomerated contending by Japanese subordinates. *International Journal of Conflict Management.*, *15*, 192–207.

Van de Vliert, E., & Postmes, T. (2012). Climato-economic livability predicts societal collectivism and political autocracy better than parasitic stress does. *Behavioral and Brain Sciences*, *35*, 94–95.

Van de Vliert, E., Shi, K., Sanders, K., Wang, Y., & Huang, X. (2004). Chinese and Dutch interpretations of supervisory feedback. *Journal of Cross-Cultural Psychology*, *35*, 417–435.

Van de Vliert, E., & Smith, P. B. (2004). Leader reliance on subordinates across nations that differ in development and climate. *Leadership Quarterly*, *15*, 381–403.

Van Hemert, D., Van de Vijver, F., & Vingerhoets, A. (2011). Culture and crying: Prevalences and gender differences. *Cross-Cultural Research*, *45*, 399–431.

Van Herk, H., & Poortinga, Y. (2012). Current and historical antecedents of individual value differences across 195 regions in Europe. *Journal of Cross-Cultural Psychology*, *43*, 1229–1248.

Van Ijzendoorn, M., & Sagi-Schwartz, A. (2008). Cross-cultural patterns of attachment: Universal and contextual patterns. In J. Cassidy & P. Shaver (Eds), *Handbook of attachment: Theory, research and clinical applications* (2nd edn, pp. 880–905). New York: Guilford.

Van Oudenhoven, J.P., Askervis-Leherpeux, F., Hannover, B., Jaaersma, R., & Dardenne, B. (2001). Asymmetrical international attitudes. *European Journal of Social Psychology*, *32*, 275–289.

Van Oudenhoven, J.P, De Raad, B., et al. (2008). Terms of abuse as expression and reinforcement of cultures. *International Journal of Intercultural Relations*, *32*, 174–185.

Van Oudenhoven, J.P., Mechelse, L., & De Dreu, C.K.W. (1998). Managerial conflict management in five European countries: The importance of power distance, uncertainty avoidance and masculinity. *Applied Psychology: An International Review*, *47*, 439–456.

Van Oudenhoven, J.P.L., Mol, S., & Van der Zee, K.I. (2003). Study of the adjustment of western expatriates in Taiwan ROC with the multicultural personality questionnaire. *Asian Journal of Social Psychology*, *6*, 159–170.

Van Oudenhoven, J.P.L., Prins, K.S., & Buunk, B.P. (1998). Attitudes of majority and minority members towards adaptation of immigrants. *European Journal of Social Psychology*, *28*, 995–1013.

Van Oudenhoven, J.P.L., & Van der Zee, K.I. (2002). Predicting multicultural effectiveness of international students: The multicultural personality questionnaire. *International Journal of Intercultural Relations*, *26*, 679–674.

Varnum, M., Grossman, I., Kitayama, S., & Nisbett, R. (2010). The origin of cultural differences in cognition: The social orientation hypothesis. *Current Directions in Psychological Science*, *19*, 9–13.

Vauclair, C.M., & Fischer, R. (2011). Do cultural values predict individuals' moral attitudes? A cross-cultural multilevel approach. *European Journal of Social Psychology*, *41*, 645–657.

Vedder, P., Van de Vijver, F., & Liebkind, K. (2006). Predicting immigrant youth's adaptation across countries and ethnocultural groups. In J. Berry, J. Phinney, D. Sam & P. Vedder (Eds), *Immigrant youth in cultural transition: Acculturation, identity and adaptation across national contexts* (pp. 143–165). Mahwah, NJ: Erlbaum.

Veenhoven, R. (2010). Life is getting better: Societal evolution and fit with human nature. *Social Indicators Research*, *97*, 105–122.

Verkuyten, M. (2001). 'Abnormalization' of ethnic minorities in conversation. *British Journal of Social Psychology*, *40*, 257–278.

Verkuyten, M., & Masson, K. (1996). Culture and gender differences in the perception of friendship by adolescents. *International Journal of Psychology*, *31*, 207–217.

Vidal, J., & Watts, J. (2009). Copenhagen: The last ditch drama that saved the deal from collapse. www.guardian.co.uk/environment/2009/de/20/copenhagen-climate-global-warming

Vignoles, V.L. (2009). The motive for distinctiveness: A universal, but flexible human need. In C.R. Snyder & S. Lopez (Eds), *Oxford handbook of positive psychology* (2nd edn, pp. 491–499). New York: Oxford University Press.

Vignoles, V.L. (2011). Identity motives. In S.J. Schwartz, K. Luyckx, & V.L. Vignoles (Eds), *Handbook of identity theory and research* (Vol. 1, pp. 403–432). New York: Springer.

Vignoles, V.L., Chryssochoou, X., & Breakwell, G.M. (2000). The distinctiveness principle: Identity, meaning and the bounds of cultural relativity. *Personality and Social Psychology Review*, *4*, 337–354.

Vignoles, V.L., Regalia, C., Manzi, C., Golledge, J. & Scabini, E. (2006). Beyond self-esteem: Influence of multiple motives on identity construction. *Journal of Personality and Social Psychology*, *90*, 308–333.

Vygotsky, L.S. (1934/1962). *Thought and language*. Cambridge, MA: MIT Press.

Wallbot, H.G., & Scherer, K.R. (1986). How universal and specific is emotional experience? Evidence from 27 nations in five continents. *Social Science Information*, *25*, 763–795.

Wamala, S., Boström, G., & Nyqvist, K. (2007). Perceived discrimination and psychological distress in Sweden. *British Journal of Psychiatry*, *190*, 75–76.

Wan, C., & Chiu, C.Y. (2009). An intersubjective consensus approach to culture: The role of intersubjective norms versus cultural self in cultural processes. In R. Wyer, C.Y. Chiu & Y.Y. Hong (Eds), *Understanding culture: Theory, research and applications* (pp. 79–91). New York: Psychology Press.

Wan, C., Chiu, C.Y., Peng, S., & Tam, K.P. (2007). Measuring cultures through intersubjective norms: Implications for predicting relative identification with two or more cultures. *Journal of Cross-Cultural Psychology, 38*, 213–226.

Wan, C., Chiu, C.Y., Tam, K.P., Lee, S.L., Lau, I.Y.M., & Peng, S.Q. (2007). Perceived cultural importance and actual self-importance of values in cultural identification. *Journal of Personality and Social Psychology*, *92*, 337–354.

Wang, Q., & Ross, M. (2005). What we remember and what we tell: The effects of culture and self-priming on memory representations and narratives. *Memory, 13*, 594–606.

Ward, C. (1984). Thaipusam in Malaysia: A psycho-anthropological analysis of ritual trance, ceremonial possession and self-mortification practices. *Ethos, 12*, 307–334.

Ward, C. (2013). *Beyond culture shock*. Hove, UK: Routledge.

Ward, C., & Berno, T. (2011). Beyond social exchange theory: attitudes toward tourists. *Annals of Tourism Research*, *38*, 1556–1559.

Ward, C., Berno, T., & Main (2002). Can the cross-cultural adaptability inventory predict sojourner adjustment? In P. Boski, F.J.R. van de Vijver & A.M. Chodynicka (Eds), *New directions in cross-cultural psychology* (pp. 409–23). Warsaw: Polish Psychological Association.

Ward, C., Bochner, S., & Furnham, A. (2001). *The psychology of culture shock*. Hove, UK: Routledge.

Ward, C., Fischer, R., Lam, F., & Hall, L. (2009). The convergent, discriminant, and incremental validity of scores on a measure of cultural intelligence. *Educational and Psychological Measurement, 69*, 85–105.

Ward, C., & Kus, L. (in press). Back to and beyond Berry's basics: The conceptualization, operationalization and classification of acculturation. *International Journal of Intercultural Relations*.

Ward, C., Leong, C.H., & Low, M.L. (2004). Personality and sojourner adjustment: An exploration of the big five and the cultural fit proposition. *Journal of Cross-Cultural Psychology, 35*, 137–151.

Ward, C., & Rana-Deuba, A. (1999). Acculturation and adaptation revisited. *Journal of Cross-Cultural Psychology, 30*, 422–442.

Ward, C., & Rana-Deuba, A. (2000). Home and culture influences on sojourner adjustment. *International Journal of Intercultural Relations, 24*, 291–306.

Ward, C., Wilson, J., & Fischer, R. (2011). Assessing the predictive validity of cultural intelligence over time. *Personality and Individual Differences, 51*, 138–142.

Waters, M. (1994). Ethnic and racial identities of second generation immigrants in New York city. *International Migration Review, 28*, 795–820.

Watkins, D., Akande D., Fleming, J., Ismail, M., Lefner, K., Regmi, M., et al. (1998). Cultural dimensions, gender, and the nature of self-concept: A 14 country study. *International Journal of Psychology, 33*, 17–31.

Watson, O. (1970). *Proxemic behavior: A cross-cultural study*. The Hague, NL: Mouton.

Watson, W.E., Johnson, L., & Zgourides, G.D. (2002). The influence of ethnic diversity on leadership, group process and performance: An examination of learning teams. *International Journal of Intercultural Relations, 26*, 11–16.

Watson, W.E., Kumar, K., & Michaelsen, L.K. (1993). Cultural diversity's impact on interaction process and performance: Comparing homogeneous and diverse task groups. *Academy of Management Journal, 36*, 590–602.

Weber, M. (1947). *The theory of social and economic organization* (A.M. Henderson & T. Parsons, Trans.). New York: Free Press.

Wei, L., & Yue, L. (1996). 'My stupid wife and ugly daughter': The use of pejorative references as a politeness strategy by Chinese speakers. *Journal of Asia Pacific Communication, 7*, 129–142.

Weisfeld, C., Dillon, L., Nowak, N., et al. (2011). Sex differences and similarities in married couples: Patterns across and within cultures. *Archives of Sexual Behavior, 40*, 1165–1172.

Weisfeld, G., Nowak, N., Lucas, T., et al. (2011). Do women seek humorousness in men because it signals intelligence? A cross-cultural test. *Humor: International Journal of Humor Research, 24*, 435–462.

Weisz, J., Rothbaum, F., & Blackburn, T. (1984). Standing out and standing in: The psychology of control in America and Japan. *American Psychologist, 39*, 955–969.

Welzel, C. (2010). How selfish are self-expression values? A civicness test. *Journal of Cross-Cultural Psychology, 41*, 152–174.

Welzel, C. (in press). *Human empowerment and the contemporary quest for emancipation*. New York: Cambridge University Press.

Welzel, C., & Inglehart, R. (2010). Agency, values and well-being: A human development model. *Social Indicators Research, 97*, 43–63.

Wheeler, L., Reis, H.T., & Bond, M.H. (1989). Collectivism-individualism in everyday social life: The middle kingdom and the melting pot. *Journal of Personality and Social Psychology, 57*, 79–86.

Whiting, B.B. (1976). The problem of the packaged variable. In K.A. Riegel & J.F. Meacham (Eds), *The developing individual in a changing world* (Vol. 1, pp. 303–309). The Hague, NL: Mouton.

Whiting, B.B., & Whiting, J.W.M. (1975). *Children of six cultures: A psychocultural analysis*. Cambridge, MA: Harvard University Press.

Whorf, B. (1956). *Language, thought, and reality*. Cambridge, MA: Massachusetts Institute of Technology Press.

Wiessner, P., & Pupu, N. (2012). Toward peace: Foreign arms and indigenous institutions in a Papua New Guinea society. *Science, 337*, 1651–1654.

Wikan, U. (1999). Culture: The new concept of race. *Social Anthropology, 7*, 57–64.

Wildschut, T., Pinter, B., Vevea, J., et al. (2003). Beyond the group mind: A quantitative review of the inter-individual-intergroup discontinuity effect. *Psychological Bulletin, 129*, 698–722.

Wilkinson, R.G. (1996). *Unhealthy societies: The afflictions of inequality*. London: Routledge.

Williams, A., Garrett, P., & Tennant, R. (2004). Seeing the difference, feeling the difference: Emergent adults perceptions of 'good' communication with peers and adolescents. In S.H. Ng, C.N. Candlin, & C.Y. Chiu (Eds), *Language matters: Communication, culture and identity* (pp. 111–153). Hong Kong: City University of Hong Kong Press.

Williams, J., & Best, D. (1990). *Sex and psyche: Gender and self viewed cross-culturally*. Newbury Park, CA: Sage.

Williams, J. E., Satterwhite, R.C., & Saiz, J.L. (1998). *The importance of psychological traits: A cross-cultural study*. New York: Plenum.

Witkin, H.A. (1950). Individual differences in the case of perception of embedded figures. *Journal of Personality*, *19*, 1–15.

Witkin, H.A., & Berry, J.W. (1975). Psychological differentiation in cross-cultural perspective. *Journal of Cross-Cultural Psychology*, *6*, 4–87.

Witkin, H.A., Moore, C.A., Goodenough, D.R., & Cox, P.W. (1977). Field-dependent and field-independent cognitive styles and their educational implications. *Review of Educational Research*, *47*, 1–64.

Wohl, M., Branscombe, N., & Reysen, S. (2010). Perceiving your group's future to be in jeopardy: Extinction threat induces collective angst and the desire to strengthen the ingroup. *Personality and Social Psychology Bulletin*, *36*, 898–910.

Wong, S. S. W., Bond, M.H., & Rodriguez Mosquera, P.M. (2005). The influence of cultural value orientations on self-reported emotional expression across cultures. *Journal of Cross-Cultural Psychology*, *39*, 224 229.

World Tourism Organization (2011). *UNWTO tourism highlights*, 2010. Available at www.unwto.org.

Wu, F.H. (2001). *Yellow: Race in America beyond black and white*. New York: Basic.

Wu, M., & Xu, F. (2012). Paternalistic leadership: From here to where? In X. Huang & M.H. Bond (Eds), *Handbook of Chinese organizational behavior* (pp. 449–466). Hong Kong: Oxford University Press.

Wyer, R., & Hong, J. (2010). Chinese consumer behavior: The effects of content, process and language. In M.H. Bond (Ed.), *The Oxford handbook of Chinese psychology* (pp. 623–639). Hong Kong: Oxford University Press.

Xygalatas, D., Mitkidis, P., Fischer, R., Reddish, P., Skewes, J., Geertz, A.W., Roepstorff, A., & Bulbulia, J. (2013). Extreme rituals promote prosociality. *Psychological Science*.

Yagmur, K. (2011). Does ethnolinguistic vitality theory account for the actual vitality of ethnic groups? A critical evaluation. *Journal of Multilinguistic and Multicultural Development*, *32*, 111–120.

Yamagishi, T. (2011). Micro-macro dynamics of the cultural construction of reality: A niche-construction approach to culture. In M.J. Gelfand, C.Y. Chiu & Y.Y. Hong (Eds), *Advances in culture and psychology* (Vol. 1, pp. 251–308). New York: Oxford University Press.

Yamagishi, T., Hashimoto, & Schug, J. (2008). Preferences versus strategies as an explanation for culture-specific behavior. *Psychological Science*, *10*, 579–584.

Yamagishi, T., Mifune, N., Liu, J., & Pauling, J. (2008). Exchanges of group-based favors: In-group bias in the prisoner's dilemma game with minimal groups in Japan and New Zealand. *Asian Journal of Social Psychology*, *11*, 196–207.

Yamagishi, T., & Yamagishi, M. (1994). Trust and commitment in the United States and Japan. *Motivation and Emotion*, *18*, 129–166.

Yamaguchi, S. (2004). Further clarification of the concept of *Amae* in relation to attachment and dependence. *Human Development*, *47*, 28–33.

Yamaguchi, S., Greenwald, A., Banaji. M., et al. (2007). Apparent universality of positive implicit self-esteem. *Psychological Science*, *18*, 498–500.

Yamaguchi, S., Kuhlman, D., & Sugimori, S. (1995). Personality correlates of allocentric tendencies in individualist and collectivist cultures. *Journal of Cross-Cultural Psychology*, *26*, 658–672.

Yang, D., Chiu, C.Y., Chen, X., et al. (2011). Lay psychology of globalization and its social impact. *Journal of Social Issues*, *67*, 677–695.

Yang, K.S. (1986). Chinese personality and its change. In M.H. Bond (Ed.), *The psychology of the Chinese people* (pp. 106–170). Hong Kong: Oxford University Press.

Yang, K.S. (1988). Will societal modernization eventually eliminate cross-cultural psychological differences? In M.H. Bond (Ed.), *The cross-cultural challenge to social psychology* (pp. 67–85). Newbury Park, CA: Sage.

Yang, K. S. (2000). Monocultural and cross-cultural indigenous approaches: The royal road to the development of a balanced global psychology. *Asian Journal of Social Psychology, 3*, 241–263.

Yang, K.S., & Bond, M.H. (1980). Ethnic affirmation by Chinese bilinguals. *Journal of Cross-Cultural Psychology, 11*, 411–425.

Yang, K.S., & Bond, M.H. (1990). Exploring implicit personality theories with indigenous or imported constructs: The Chinese case. *Journal of Personality and Social Psychology, 58*, 1087–1095.

Yeung, L. (2003). Management discourse in Australian banking contexts: In search of an Australian model of participation as compared with that of Hong Kong Chinese. *Journal of Intercultural Studies, 24*(1), 47–63.

Yeung, V., & Kashima, Y. (2012). Culture and stereotype communication: Are people from Eastern cultures more stereotypical in communication? *Journal of Cross-Cultural Psychology, 43*, 446–463.

Ying, Y.W., & Liese, L.H. (1991). Emotional wellbeing of Taiwan students in the US: An examination of pre-arrival to post-arrival differential. *International Journal of Intercultural Relations, 15*, 345–366.

Yu, A.B. (1996). Ultimate life concerns, self and Chinese achievement motivation. In M.H. Bond (Ed.), *The handbook of Chinese psychology* (pp. 227–246). New York: Oxford.

Yuki, M. (2003). Intergroup comparison versus intragroup cooperation: A cross-cultural examination of social identity theory in North American and East Asian cultural contexts. *Social Psychology Quarterly, 66*, 166–183.

Yuki, M. (2011). Intragroup relationships and intergroup comparisons as two sources of group-based collectivism. In R.M. Kramer, G.J. Leonardelli, & R.W. Livingston (Eds), *Social cognition, social identity, and intergroup relations: A Festschrift in honor of Marilynn Brewer* (pp. 247–266). New York: Taylor & Francis.

Yuki, M., Maddux, W., & Brewer, M. (2005). Cross-cultural differences in relationship- and group-based trust. *Personality and Social Psychology Bulletin, 31*, 48–62.

Yukl, G.A., Fu, P.P., & McDonald, R. (2003). Cross-cultural differences in perceived effectiveness of influence tactics for initiating or resisting change. *Applied Psychology: An International Review, 52*, 68–82.

Zagefka, H., Binder, J., & Brown, R.J. (2010). Acculturation attitudes, fit, prejudice: Majority and minority attitudes in a longitudinal three-nation study. Unpublished manuscript, Royal Holloway, University of London.

Zagefka, H., & Brown, R.J. (2002). The relationship between acculturation strategies, cultural fit and intergroup relations: Immigrant-majority relations in Germany. *European Journal of Social Psychology, 32*, 171–188.

Zangwill, I. (1909). *The melting pot.* New York: McMillan.

Zhang, S., & Kline, S. (2009). Can I make my own decision? A cross-cultural study of perceived social network influence in mate selection. *Journal of Cross-Cultural Psychology, 40*, 3–23.

Zhang, Y., Kohnstamm, G., Slotboom, A.M., Elphick, E., & Cheung, P.C. (2002). Chinese and Dutch parents' perceptions of their children's personality. *Journal of Genetic Psychology, 163*, 165–178.

Zhang, Y., Feick, L., & Price, L. (2006). The impact of self-construal on aesthetic preference for angular versus rounded shapes. *Personality and Social Psychology Bulletin, 32*, 794–805.

Zhang, Y., & Mittal, V. (2007). The attractiveness of enriched and impoverished options: Culture, self-construal and regulatory focus. *Personality and Social Psychology Bulletin, 33*, 588–598.

Zhou, X., He, L., Yang, Q., Lao, J., & Baumeister, R.F. (2012). Control deprivation and styles of thinking. *Journal of Personality and Social Psychology, 102*, 460–478.

Zhu, Y., Zhang, L., Fan, J., et al. (2007). Neural basis of cultural influence on self-representation. *Neuroimage, 34*, 1310–1316.

Zou, X., Tam, K., Morris, M., et al. (2009). Culture as commonsense: Perceived consensus versus personal beliefs as mechanisms of cultural influence. *Journal of Personality and Social Psychology, 97*, 579–597.

Author Index

Subject Index